Understanding People and Organisations: An Introduction to Organisational Behaviour

Linda Maund

Stanley Tho[illegible]lishers) Ltd

Dedication

This book is dedicated to my students – past, present and future.

First published in 1999 by
Stanley Thornes Publishers Ltd
Ellenborough House
Wellington Street
Cheltenham
GL50 1YW
UK

A catalogue record for this book is available from The British Library.

99 00 01 02 03 / 10 9 8 7 6 5 4 3 2 1

ISBN 0 7487 2404 4

Typeset by
Northern Phototypesetting Co Ltd, Bolton
Printed and bound in Great Britain by
T.J. International Ltd, Padstow, Cornwall

Contents

List of figures

List of tables

Acknowledgements

The author and publishers wish to thank the following for permission to use copyright material:

Anat Arkin for material from 'Hold the production line', *People Management*, 6.2.97, pp. 22–27; Butterworth Heinemann, a division of Reed Educational & Professional Publishing Ltd, for Figs. 7.1 and 7.2 from M Belbin, *Team Roles at Work* (1993) pp. 78, 23; S Caulkin, for adapted material from 'The knowledge within', *Management Today*, August (1997) pp. 28–32; Copyright Clearance Center, Inc on behalf of Academy of Management for adapted material from D K Hurst, 'Cautionary tales from the Kalahari: How hunters become herders and may have trouble changing back again', *Academy of Management Executive*, 3:5 (1991) pp. 74–86; The Economist for material from 'Togetherness has its perils', *The Economist*, 14.1.95; 'Keeping them happy', *The Economist*, 25.11.95, p. 32; and 'Instant coffee as management theory', *The Economist*, 25.1.97, p. 83. Copyright © The Economist, London 1995, 1995, 1997; Financial Times for adapted material from Lucy Kellaway, 'The many layers of business hostility', *Financial Times*, 6.10.97, p. 14; Diane Summers, 'Get the best out of staff', *Financial Times*, 9.7.97, p. 8; Tim Brown, 'Nurturing a culture of innovation', *Financial Times*, 17.11.97, p. 12; A Cohen, 'The price of honesty', *Financial Times*, 2.9.96, p. 16; 'Women who make a difference', *Financial Times*, 18.2.97, p. 13; R Goffee and J W Hunt, 'The end of management? Classroom versus the boardroom' *Financial Times*, 22.3.96, Mastering Management insert, No. 20, p. 4; Richard Donkin, 'A moral stance', *Financial Times*, 8.9.97, p. 16; Richard Donkin, 'Shoe factory provides an offshore spur', *Financial Times*, 26.11.97, p. 19; J Mahoney, 'Discrimination and privacy: Summary', *Financial Times*, 26.1.96, Mastering Management insert, No. 12, p. 9; M Matthews, 'In praise of maturity', *Financial Times*, 27.2.97, p. 11; Fig. 1.3 from 'Culture is not enough' in 'Managing across cultures', *Financial Times*, 9.12.95, Mastering Management insert, p. 4; and Table 1.3 from 'The personality factor', *Financial Times*, 16.12.95, Mastering Management insert, No. 8, pp. 2–3; Financial Times Management for Fig. 10.8 adapted from T Hannagan, *Management Concepts and Practices* (1995) p. 40; and Figs. 9.7, 9.9 adapted from D Keuning, *Management: A Contemporary Approach* (1998) pp. 352, 353; Gulf Publishing Company for Fig. 7.9 from Robert R Blake and Anne Adams McCanse, *Leadership Dilemmas – Grid Solutions* (1991) p. 29. Copyright © 1991 by Robert R Blake and the Estate of Jane S Mouton; Haymarket Management Publications Ltd for adapted material from 'Time to trust the worker', *Management Today*, September (1996) p. 20; M Brown, 'Design for working', *Management Today*, March (1997) pp. 77–84; D Lewis, 'When in Rome...', *Management Today*, August (1996) pp. 77–78; and 'The protection of reputation becomes a core concern', *Management Today*, October (1997) p. 6; Hodder & Stoughton Ltd for Fig. 1.6 adapted from R Gross, *Psychology: The Science of Mind and Behaviour* (1996), p. 745; IPD Enterprises Ltd for adapted material from 'Empowering Employees...Maverick Style', Master Class, Seminar B7, IPD National Conference, 23–25 Oct. (1996); Kluwer Academic Publishers for adapted material from R R Sims, 'Linking Groupthink to Unethical Behavior in Organizations', *Journal of Business Ethics*, 11 (1992) pp. 651–62; Leadership & Organizational Development Journal for Fig. 7.19 from J R Nicholls, 'A New Approach to Situational Leadership', *Leadership and Organizational Development Journal*, 6:4 (1985); McGraw-Hill Publishing Company for Fig. 10.6 adapted from M Pedlar et al, *A Manager's Guide to Self-Development*, 3/e (1994) p. 24; Nuala Moran for material from 'Look to the corporate federations', Outsourcing supplement, *Daily Telegraph*, 28.5.97; New Scientist for 'Don't be so moody', *New Scientist*, 23.11.96; Personnel Publications Ltd for material from Paul Watson, 'Diversity challenge', *People Management*, 1.5.97, pp. 30–31; Neil Merrick, 'The Lion's share', *People Management*, 12.6.97, pp. 34–5, 37; Jilly Welch, 'Creature comforts', *People Management*, 19.12.96, pp. 20–23; D Barton,

'Changing the job mix to encourage latent talent', *People Management*, 11.7.96, p. 23; H Rowland and L Harris, 'Doctor know', *People Management*, 5.3.98, pp. 50–52; Mark Thatcher, 'A victim of 'flame culture', *People Management*, 26.6.97, p. 29; O Black, 'Addressing the issue of take on new tactics to score', *People Management*, 12.6.97, p. 16; and Fig. 8.21 adapted from 'Mayo and Lank's Complete Learning Organisation Benchmark' included in 'Changing the soil spurs new growth', *People Management*, 16.11.95, p. 28; Plenum Publishing Corporation for Fig. 10.11 from T Cummings and C L Cooper, 'A cybernetic framework for the study of occupational stress', *Human Relations*, 32 (1979) pp. 395–419; Professional Manager for Fig. 4.11 adapted from M Tampoe, 'Knowledge workers – the new management challenge', *Professional Manager*, November (1994) p. 13; and adapted material from M Rawson, 'Whose side are you on?', *Professional Manager*, November (1997) p. 3; Reed Business Information for adapted material from P McCurry, 'Levi's links offices to Brussels HQ', *Personnel Today*, 3.7.97, p. 22; N Daly, 'Staff consultation seen as business necessity', *Personnel Today*, 19.6.97, p. 15; N Daly, 'Firm gears teams to career development', *Personnel Today*, 2.10.97, p. 2; and 'Study casts doubt on honesty tests', *Personnel Today*, 16.1.97, p. 1; Roehampton Institute London for their Mission Statement; C Sharman, for adapted material from 'Looking for tomorrow's leaders', *Management Today*, August (1997) p. 5; Times Higher Education Supplement for material from 'Women losing out in science', *THES*, 5.9.97, p. 5. Copyright © Times Supplements Ltd, 1997; Times Newspapers Ltd for material from Matthew Lymns and Rufus Olins, 'The brain teasers', *The Sunday Times*, 28.7.96, p. 3. Copyright © Times Newspapers Limited, 1996; Gordon H Walker for material from his letter, 'Squaring up to problem of quality circle', to the *Financial Times*, 22.8.97, p. 14;

Every effort has been made to trace the copyright holders but if any have been inadvertently overlooked the publishers will be pleased to make the necessary arrangement at the first opportunity.

Preface

Understanding People and Organisations: An Introduction to Organisational Behaviour aims to address the key issues related to how individuals live their lives in the workplace. The text aims to take a scientific and scholarly look at the underpinnings of organisational behaviour as a discipline in a framework of contemporary practice which includes both applications and misapplications of the available knowledge of human behaviour.

Organisational behaviour is the study of individuals and groups within an organisation and is made even more complex because of the changes which are taking place. Changes in the economy have resulted in a wide range of mergers, acquisitions, delayering, and downsizing during the 1980s and early 1990s. Such changes have affected countless members of the workforce, resulting in individuals leaving their places of employment while others stayed on. Changes in the global economy have brought about changes in the workplace as well. The early 1990s brought about new markets in Russia, eastern Europe and the People's Republic of China. For the United Kingdom, there was a dramatic change with the unification of a European market system. Such changes have brought about significant consequences for all individuals – not just those in paid employment.

The overarching theme of this book is the provision of quality within a stakeholder society which concerns the behaviour of individuals as much as it does statistics and efficiency. The provision of quality is still a driving force as the new millennium approaches. This key theme is supported by various sub-themes such as globalisation, work diversity, cultural diversity, technology, and ethics. Such are the themes which challenge managers and which demand that individuals develop and adjust to an ever-changing environment. All individuals need to understand and come to terms with such concepts in order to maintain the health of both themselves and the organisations for which they work. This text can help to equip students with the knowledge and skills needed to achieve such goals.

A further distinguishing feature of *Understanding People and Organisations: An Introduction to Organisational Behaviour* is the pedagogical belief that effective learning requires the acquisition of objective knowledge and the development of skills in an interactive way. Thus the theory and practice embedded in the subject of Organisational Behaviour needs to be translated into application. As a result, this text is based on the conviction that organisational behaviour includes *knowing* concepts, ideas, and theories as well as *practising* skills, abilities, and behaviours to enhance the behaviour and management of people in the workplace.

Understanding People and Organisations: An Introduction to Organisational Behaviour is fashioned to fit modularised courses which are taught within semesters. It is designed either to be read as a single text or each chapter can be read as a self-sufficient section which the reader can use for a specific topic of interest, for example, for a topic or assignment, or chapters can be read in relation to each other. Each chapter contains learning objectives, exercises, cases, discussion questions, and references and further reading.

Part 1, Understanding Individuals, looks at the concepts which need to be understood when trying to understand how individuals work. Chapter 1, Personality, and Chapter 2, Perception, describe different aspects of personality theory and how their perceptual sets work. Chapter 3, Communication and learning, includes sections on how individuals communicate and how they learn within the organisation. Chapter 4, Motivation, looks at the development of motivational theories, while Chapter 5, Job design, considers various approaches to the design of work.

The individual theme is developed in Part 2, Understanding groups, which looks at the role of groups and teams within an organisation, with Chapter 6, Introducing groups and group behaviour, concentrating on the role of groups and Chapter 7, Group dynamics and affectiveness, developing the theme by concentrating on the dynamics of groups and their effectiveness within the organisation.

Part 3, Understanding organisations, takes the role of the individual and the workings of groups into an organisational perspective by, in Chapter 8, Organisational structure and design, taking a macro-level look at how organisations are designed and structured. In Chapter 9, Dynamics of organisations, the key issues of the management of change, organisational conflict, and organisational culture are developed. In Chapter 10, The role of management, there is an evaluation of the ever-changing role of management as it relates to *Understanding People and Organisations: An Introduction to Organisational Behaviour*.

Each of the three parts of the text is followed by a consideration of the ethics involved for individuals, groups, and organisations respectively.

Introduction

This section is in two parts:

A Introduction to understanding people and organisations;
B Explaining and predicting behaviour in the workplace.

A. Introduction to understanding people and organisations

Learning objectives

After studying this section you should be able to:

- understand some of the key issues in studying organisational behaviour;
- analyse the relationship of organisations to stakeholders;
- describe differing approaches to the study of organisational behaviour;
- understand some of the key research issues in the field.

What is organisational behaviour?

The very concept of organisational behaviour may seem like a contradiction. How can an artificial construct – an organisation – 'behave' in the way we might expect of a person? To understand the nature of the subject, it is important to begin with some definitions. One commonly accepted definition is put forward by Pettinger (1996): '[Organisational behaviour is] concerned with the study of the behaviour and interaction of people in restricted or organised settings' (p. 1).

This definition isolates a number of elements which go together to make up the study of organisational behaviour: organisations, groups, and individuals.

Organisations

The first element to be considered is that of the organisation which Buchanan and Huczynski (1997) define as: '... social arrangements for the controlled performance of collective goals' (p. 9).

Organisations can be seen as collections of people who come or are brought together to carry out a common purpose. To this extent a family might be seen as an organisation since it is a group of individuals with a number of possible common goals such as mutual protection and support. However, most commentators would define organisations as more formal structures, consciously created and designed and usually on a more elaborate scale than a basic family unit. Indeed, Pettinger's (1996) description of organisational behaviour focuses on structure and function within organisations. In particular, the above definition given by Buchanan and Huczynski (1996) lays emphasis on '... the controlled performance of collective goals'; that is, the creation of an explicit set of objectives. This emphasis on goals is also highlighted in other descriptions of organisations, for example, according to Hannagan (1997):

> Organisations of one type or another are essential for productive work because they bring people together with raw materials and equipment in order to achieve a variety of goals. (p. 4)

It is these objectives which bring the organisation into existence, and then determine how it is designed, constructed and run. One of the most important themes in the study of organisational behaviour is how organisations can best be designed so as to achieve their goals.

Pettinger's (1996) definition helps to answer the paradox outlined at the beginning. Organisations provide a framework within which people's behaviour is directed towards certain ends. Organisations are designed to give each individual a particular set of responsibilities, motivations, sanctions and rewards which ensure that each individual contributes their share to those goals. As a result, an organisation has a profound influence on the way an individual within that organisation behaves. Its success will be measured in part by its ability to change individual behaviour and channel it to meet particular goals.

However, people are not machines that can be programmed to meet organisational objectives unquestioningly. When individuals come together in an organisation, they bring their own needs, aspirations and skills, and they interact in often unexpected and unplanned ways. These types of behaviour may be quite independent of, or even conflict with, the structure and objectives of the organisation. To this extent it is legitimate to talk about *organisational behaviour*, whether it is the particular types of behaviour expected of individuals within organisations or the way they behave in organisations in practice.

Groups and individuals

Pettinger's (1996) definition also suggests that an essential ingredient in organisations and organisational behaviour is the 'group'. It is necessary to understand the differences between groups and organisations. The definition of a group can be very broad, involving any body of people or things with some shared attribute, from university graduates (sharing a common qualification) to people queuing in a building society (sharing a common predicament!). A commonly accepted definition of a group within organisational behaviour is that of Schein (1988):

> ... group is any number of people who (1) interact with each other, (2) are psychologically aware of each other, and (3) perceive themselves to be a group. (p. 145)

Here the emphasis is on psychological groups, where the members of the group share some consciousness that they are a group and act together to achieve shared objectives. Within this definition of groups, they are defined internally by the members of the group articulating a group identity rather than by an external observer imposing his/her own classification.

In many respects, organisations can be seen as groups. However, this group definition suggests relatively small numbers of people who can interact and communicate directly. Most organisations will be too large to allow this to occur, and will, in fact, consist of a number of groups which combine to form the organisation as a whole. Organisations can be seen as artificial constructs: structures in which individuals and groups operate. Groups in the psychological sense used here are more organic entities, their structure and dynamics determined by the personal interactions of their individual members.

In seeming to achieve their objectives, organisations may well create formal groups, for example those working together on a production line, with a clearly defined identity, roles and objectives. However, the experience of being in a group may well generate a duty, separate identity, meaning and function for its members than those planned or intended by the organisation. Indeed, the organisation may well generate new, unplanned, informal groups as individuals discover and articulate a quite separate identity within an organisation as a result of joining it. As the original definition of organisational behaviour suggests, a key theme in the subject is the often complex relationships and interactions between organisations and groups, both formal and informal, within them.

Those relationships are complex because organisations consist of individuals with a diverse mix of characteristics, needs and goals which will be influenced by, and will influence, the groups they belong to and the organisations within which they, and the groups they belong to, act. The study of organisational behaviour can be seen as that of the interactions between organisations, groups and individuals and, particularly, how those interactions can be managed to fulfil the organisation's objectives.

Management

This emphasis introduces a fourth ingredient into this introductory discussion of organisational behaviour: management. In achieving its objectives through groups and individuals, an organisation will depend on its managers. This is reflected in the way management and its role within organisations are defined. Pettinger (1996) defines management in the sense of being a role – managerial:

> ... the ability to plan, organise, co-ordinate and control activities in the pursuit of effective performance. (p. 7)

As this definition suggests, management seeks to fulfil the goals of the organisation by the effective use of its resources, particularly the individuals and groups within the organisation for which the manager is responsible. Managers do so both by the design and implementation of organisational systems and procedures and by the way they influence and lead individuals and groups within the organisation.

The dynamics of organisational behaviour, in the interaction between organisations, their objectives and structures, the dynamics of groups and individuals and the integrating function of management, is shown in Figure 1 below.

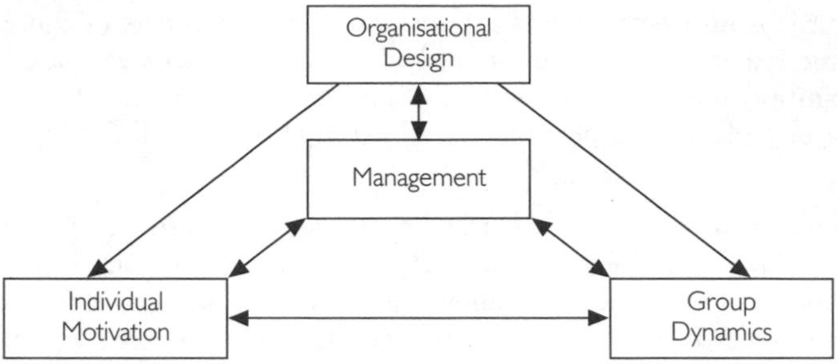

Figure 1 The dynamics of organisational behaviour

Organisational goals

The definition of organisations given earlier in this section emphasises their *raison d'être* as the achievement of goals. The definition of organisational behaviour focused on assesses the interactions of individuals, groups and organisations in the context of their impact on organisational performance. It is necessary to start, therefore, with an initial discussion of organisational objectives. This is the benchmark for assessing organisational, group and individual effectiveness. In order to understand organisational objectives, it is pertinent to consider the concept of stakeholders.

Satisfying stakeholders

A stakeholder is anyone who has a legitimate interest in the activities of an organisation. As Figure 2 shows, businesses need to deal with a wide range of stakeholders.

Such stakeholders can be divided into three basic groups:

- internal stakeholders
- connected stakeholders
- external stakeholders.

Internal stakeholders

The internal stakeholders of a business are its managers and employees. In many companies, the managers will themselves be employees of the business, responsible to its owner. If the company is a public or private limited company, the management team will be responsible to the shareholders. A company's managers will act on behalf of its owners in managing the workforce to meet the objectives set by the owners. Their interests will, therefore, overlap but will be distinct from those of the rest of the workforce. Employees will have a number of interests in the business. These include two obvious concerns: job security and reward.

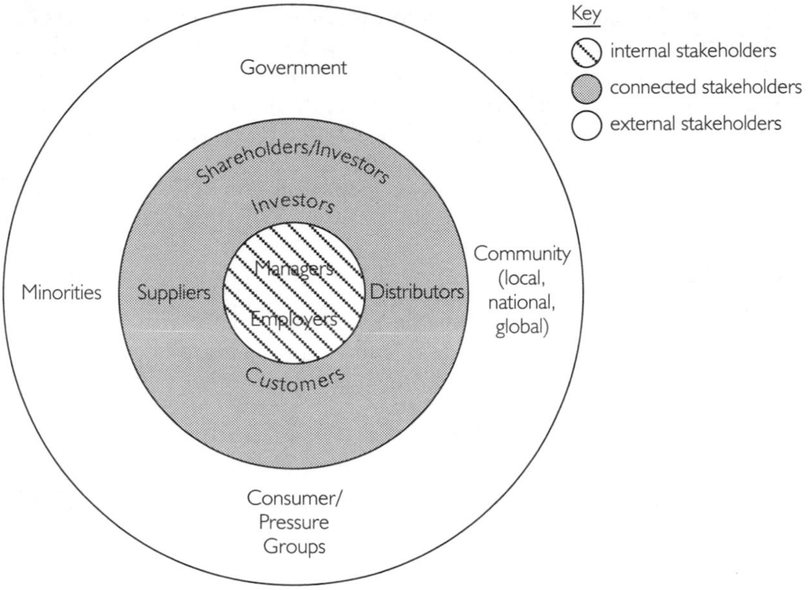

Figure 2 Types of stakeholders

Employees will want to ensure that their jobs are secure. This concern will include securing continuity of employment for individuals, sustaining the overall number of jobs in the business and protection from arbitrary or unfair dismissal. It will also include protecting the content of jobs from changes which might make them more insecure or difficult.

All people who work in a business will want a reward for their efforts in the form of, for example, the best pay and conditions that they can achieve. They will also want rewards which they feel reflect the value of their work and the market rate for the job compared to other workers in comparable jobs – they will search for equity.

However, a workforce may well have a number of wider interests which managers also need to take account of – recognition and fulfilment are two of the key ones.

Employees will want to be respected and treated fairly by management and thus gain recognition for their efforts. Individual workers need to feel that they are valued, their status and contribution recognised, and that managers consult them.

Most employees prefer jobs which give them some degree of responsibility, challenge and creativity leading to a sense of fulfilment. Many employees find the social side of work particularly important, and prefer to work in teams and to have the time to socialise. Others may want opportunities for training and career progression to exploit their talents more fully and secure greater recognition, rewards, and security.

As employees, most managers share these aspirations with their subordinates and their superiors. They will have an interest in ensuring their own security, levels of reward, appropriate recognition and job satisfaction. However, as managers with overall responsibility for the business, they will also have an interest in meeting the needs of other stakeholders. They will be directly responsible to the investors in the business for its success and profitability. They will, therefore, have a strong interest in meeting the investors' goals. The same responsibility for the business also means that they need to look to the interests of customers, since it is the customers and, ultimately, the profits made from them which keep the business going. As discussed in later stages of the book, one of the key roles of management is to try to reconcile the competing interests of these three groups of stakeholders: customers, investors, and employees.

Connected stakeholders

Beyond the immediate boundaries of the firm are other parties with a direct connection to the business and amongst these the three most important are:

- customers
- investors
- shareholders.

Customers have a number of interests in the activities of a business which are broadly concerned with:

- price
- fitting the needs of the customer
- quality and reliability
- availability
- service.

In general, customers will look for the best price when they shop for a product or service. The need to be competitive on price puts an obvious pressure on profits, creating a potential area of conflict with investors. Investors in turn will expect managers to keep a tight control on costs. Since a major element of the costs of a business is the cost of labour, pressure from customers and investors may impact on employees' productivity: how efficiently they can work with the available resources. Pressures on prices, profits and costs may mean lower wage increases and workers having to work harder to improve productivity.

However, customers may not judge a product or service solely on price. They will choose one which best suits their needs. In some cases, bread for instance, competing products or services from differing firms may be identical, in which case price becomes the deciding issue. In others, customers may want something tailored to their specific requirements. In this case they may be prepared to pay a higher price for the customised product. If so, businesses will need to be particularly sensitive to customer needs. Managers and employees may need to show extra flexibility, perhaps in developing a wide range of product types or in researching customer likes and dislikes. They will need to balance producing customised products with the higher costs involved in such operations, and their resulting pressure on prices. In doing so they will need to get the right balance of price and fit to give the customer value for money, whilst providing investors with the returns they expect.

Increasingly, customers are also looking for high levels of quality and reliability in the goods and services they buy. Quality has been one of the major weapons in the success of Japanese firms in gaining access to western markets in the post-war period. This emphasis on quality puts pressure on costs and necessitates higher levels of commitment and skill from both management and staff to improve production methods and eradicate errors.

There is, of course, little point in having a good product to sell if it is not available when and where the customer needs it. As markets have become more competitive and customer expectations have increased, consumers have become less tolerant of shortages or delays in availability. In the past, businesses overcame any problems in supply by holding large levels of stock, despite the costs of storage and depreciation and pressure on working capital. The need to reduce costs, together with competition from Japanese companies in particular, has pushed more and more firms into keeping stocks low and developing just-in-time (JIT) delivery and production systems. These systems, which need to react quickly to changes in demand, require flexibility and skill from both management and workforce.

Just as customers have come to expect more in such areas as price, quality and availability, so they increasingly expect higher standards of service, whether it be when they first seek information about a product or service, when they buy it, or in the support they receive after purchasing the product. They expect businesses to adapt to their needs rather than the other way round. High standards of service require motivated and well-trained staff with the authority to deal effectively with customer queries and needs.

Businesses can call on a wide range of sources of finance – from government grants to ploughing back part of their own profits into the business. Such *investors* are sourced from two main areas related to public limited companies:

- shares bought by shareholders
- loans provided by banks.

Private limited companies also depend on shares as a main source of finance, although these shares cannot be sold on the Stock Exchange. Both these and small businesses are often also reliant on banks for finance.

Shareholders are individuals or groups who have bought 'shares' in the company. There are two main financial benefits to the holding of shares. Firstly, depending on the amount of profit earned in a particular year, a business will set aside a proportion of its profit to pay out as an annual 'dividend' to shareholders. Secondly, shares can be bought and sold on the stock market. If a business is doing well, the value of its shares will tend to increase beyond the price originally paid by shareholders, giving them the opportunity to sell shares to other investors at a profit.

In return for providing the business with finance through the purchase of shares, most shareholders are able to elect the firm's board of directors at annual meetings of shareholders (some classes of share do not give their owners voting rights). Shareholders would not usually be involved in the day-to-day running of the business, which is left to management.

The managers of a business need to keep shareholders satisfied for two reasons. Firstly, shareholders can vote to remove the board of directors if they are unhappy with the company's performance. Secondly, if they are concerned about the business's poor performance, they may sell their shares to avoid any fall in the share price. Selling shares in such circumstances would be seen by the stock market as a danger signal, accelerating the fall in the value of shares. A serious collapse in the share price of a company would undermine its ability to raise further finance, and worry remaining shareholders and any other investors (for instance, banks) and creditors (for instance, suppliers) to whom it owed money. If sufficiently concerned, a business's creditors (the people to whom it owed money) could force a business into bankruptcy by demanding the immediate repayment of outstanding debts and forcing the sale of the business's assets to achieve this.

Most companies have two types of shareholder:

- individual investors
- institutional investors.

Whilst most businesses will have some individual shareholders, most shares are owned by institutions such as pension funds which invest money to get the best return for themselves and their clients. The immediate concern of both individual and institutional shareholders will usually be the size of annual dividend they receive. In the longer term, they will be concerned with those factors which may increase the share price. These factors include, firstly, a business's improving financial performance, which will increase its valuation by the stock market and the value of its shares. Secondly, the possible acquisition by others, for instance rival firms. Such acquisition would involve the potential purchaser offering shareholders an attractive price for their shares to get their vote for a takeover.

The loyalty of investors to a company is, therefore, conditional on its being able to perform well enough to provide an attractive annual dividend and a steadily increasing share price. It may also be conditional on the business avoiding any takeover bids which might attract shareholders to sell their shares. Whilst some takeovers might only be a threat to management, if the new owners installed a new leadership to run the businesses their way but left the rest of the firm intact, others might be a threat to the whole workforce. Some takeovers are made to amalgamate businesses to produce a larger and more efficient whole.

This might involve removing overlapping jobs and making people redundant as the two firms are made one. A third reason for a takeover might be because those concerned see an opportunity for profit in breaking up and selling individual parts of the business. They might calculate that this might generate a better return than if the business remained intact. Breaking up the business in this way would threaten the security of managers and employees.

The final groups of connected stakeholders are *distributors and suppliers*. Like customers, both suppliers and distributors will look for the best price they can get from a business. The supplier will want to charge the highest price for supplying, for example, raw materials or components to a business. Suppliers may also want to produce as cheaply as possible to get the maximum return from the prices they charge. Distributors will want to buy as cheaply as they can so that they have the greatest scope for marking up the final price they charge to the end user. Complex distribution arrangements can lead to high prices for consumers since they bear the brunt of attempts by individuals in the distribution chain to mark up the price successively so that each person gets their 'cut'.

Both suppliers and distributors will want to control the flow of materials and goods in a way that suits them. A supplier will want a secure and stable pattern of demand, so will look to develop long-term relationships with the business. Suppliers may sometimes be resistant to just-in-time (JIT) systems. These have been developed by businesses to allow them to order raw materials and components only when they need them, rather than stockpile materials. JIT systems reduce the costs and risks of holding large amounts of raw materials and components. However, because they depend on supplying small amounts at frequent intervals, they require more time and expertise to operate well, and will tend to leave the supplier holding on to the stock and, therefore, taking more of a risk if demand drops. JIT systems may also lead to less certainty and predictability for suppliers as supply rises and falls in direct relation to production levels, which in turn change with each fluctuation in market demand.

Distributors, on the other hand, might well welcome a JIT system since it means that they may not need to hold much stock themselves. They will want supply to fit their needs, and push for the right to return what is not sold, keeping any risk with the producer and not with them. Both suppliers and distributors will also bargain with a business for the best credit terms, delaying payment for as long as possible to help their cash flow. Powerful suppliers charging high prices for raw materials and powerful distributors forcing manufacturers to sell at a low price can significantly reduce a company's profitability. This can be seen from the case study below.

CASE STUDY
Exporting: the case of Flymo

Flymo is a medium-sized British company employing 450 people which makes lawnmowers. In the late 1980s Flymo believed it would be difficult to establish itself in the European marketplace owing to a perceived lack of demand for 'hover' mowers with which the company had made its name in the UK. As a consequence, it developed a wheel rotary mower especially for continental markets, which it launched in 1989. However, the performance of the new product was disappointing, but, surprisingly for the company, after improving the design of its hover mowers, sales of these began to accelerate, particularly in France, Denmark and Norway. Such was the turnaround in export fortune that management predicted a quadrupling of export sales in the next four years.

Underpinning these sales projections was a major change in distribution strategy. The company's products were previously distributed and sold by a number of continental sales companies belonging to Flymo's parent group, Electrolux. These companies tended to sell direct to wholesalers, with disastrous results. The mark-up from sales company to wholesaler to retailer effectively doubled the equivalent UK price. In Scandinavia, for example, the final selling price was more than four times the factory cost compared with less than two and a half times the factory cost in Britain.

Flymo first persuaded the companies to sell directly to retailers, cutting overheads and thus selling prices. They also argued for adding mass distribution outlets (for example, hypermarkets) to the network of specialist retailers. To reinforce this shift, Flymo proposed a fundamental two-stage change in control. Firstly, staff from the sales companies would cease to report to Electrolux: they would instead be integrated into Flymo itself via a central organisation run from the UK. Its managing director would be responsible for all Flymo sales, including export sales. Key managers would be appointed in major markets and staff there made directly accountable.

The second stage would be to replace the current structure of four European regions with a pan-European distribution structure serviced by a single UK warehouse guaranteeing three-day delivery. From Autumn 1993, local sales staff in France were brought into Flymo and linked directly to the UK computer network with shipping, though not invoicing, undertaken directly from the UK. The intention was to transfer this structure eventually to other European markets.

Source: unknown

External stakeholders

There is a wide range of external stakeholders which includes the local community, minority groups, pressure groups and the global community. However, the key external stakeholder is government – national and regional.

The government has a range of interests in a business, which are partly economic and partly political. Economic interests include the maximising of income, employment and efficiency, which must be balanced with the political interest of protecting customers, employees, and the community.

Governments have an obvious interest in maximising tax revenue from businesses, whether directly through corporation tax or indirectly through the payment of value added tax (VAT), for example. They will want to keep a close eye on businesses to ensure that they are paying all they should. This need will be balanced against the concern to encourage a thriving and profitable manufacturing and service sector as the key means of reducing unemployment. The level of unemployment will have an obvious impact on the government's overall popularity. It will also have a major impact on government finance. High levels of unemployment will increase government levels of spending on social security payments to the unemployed. At the same time, unemployment reduces income from personal taxation, as less people earn enough to pay tax, and also reduces income from indirect taxation on consumer spending such as VAT. Significant levels of unemployment will also have an indirect influence on consumer confidence and spending, thus, again, reducing government income. Governments are then faced with having to reduce their own expenditure, which may itself increase unemployment, or borrow money to cover the deficit.

An efficient business sector will also be essential to international competitiveness. If governments are to maintain a healthy balance of payments, they need businesses strong enough to compete in export markets and fight off competition from imports at home.

The wider role and its relationship to this text

Organisations need to differentiate themselves from their competitors because they must make the way they meet customer needs distinctive from and better than that of their competitors. In the currently highly competitive conditions this response needs to be constantly reviewed and developed. Markets are increasingly volatile and therefore difficult to predict and interpret. Organisations run the risk of failing to recognise and adapt to customer needs.

Such demands place huge pressure on organisations, and on the groups and individuals who work in them. Increasingly competitive conditions have forced organisations to become leaner, leaving a smaller workforce with increased workloads and levels of responsibility leading to consequent pressures and stresses. With more demanding customers and more volatile markets has come an increased need for more creative, responsive and flexible staff.

The issues of balancing stakeholder interests run right through the book, which is divided into four parts as explained in the Preface. The Introduction gives an overview of understanding people and organisations as well as ideas on explaining and predicting behaviour in the workplace. Part 1 is an introduction to the discipline of organisational behaviour and to the themes of the text as it relates to current and projected trends. Part 1, Understanding individuals, addresses specific aspects of individual behaviour within organisational settings. Chapter 1 describes the constituent parts of personality. Chapter 2 describes perceptual processes and offers an introduction to stereotyping. Chapter 3 develops the individual theme by discussing the key aspects of effective communication and identifying the communication characteristics of the best managers; it discusses techniques for reflective listening and an approach to various forms of non-verbal communication, besides giving an overview of the importance of learning within a learning organisational setting. Chapter 4 presents evolving and contemporary theories of motivation and discusses how to motivate people in the workplace. In Chapter 5 the purpose of and approaches to job design are discussed together with current models for understanding work in an increasingly technological age. Part 1 concludes with a consideration of how individuals and ethics interact.

Part 2, Understanding groups, examines the key areas of working in groups and teams – a significant part of current organisational practice. Chapter 6 introduces groups and teams and discusses the importance of teams within organisations. Chapter 7 develops this theme with an analysis of the group as a decision-making and social entity; it discusses group conflict and the effectiveness of groups in relation to leadership. There is then a consideration of groups and ethical issues.

In Part 3, Understanding organisations, the themes of individuals and groups are moved forward by a shift of focus from individuals and groups to the organisation. Chapter 8 provides a macro-level perspective of how organisations are designed and describes alternative structural configurations. Chapter 9 takes up the issues of organisational culture, conflict and change, and Chapter 10 brings the issues together with an assessment of the role of management and managers in relation to decision-making, leadership, frustration and stress and managing effectively. This section also concludes with a discussion of ethical problems relating to management.

Approaches to the study of organisational behaviour

The study of organisational behaviour has evolved over time with a number of key figures and events in its development. Such events can be presented in chronological order.

Table 1 below gives some key figures who have significantly contributed to the development of the field.

Table 1 Some chronological events and key figures in the development of the field of organisational behaviour

Period	Key figures and their work
1911	**FREDERICK W TAYLOR** Developed the principles for the maximisation of job efficiency (see Chapter 5).
1927–1932	**ELTON MAYO** Led a research team at the Western Electric Company which established the importance of social and environmental factors in job performance (see Chapter 5).
1947	**MAX WEBER** Concentrated his efforts on bureaucracies which led to a further study of the formal structural characteristics of organisations (see Chapter 8).
1951	**RALPH STODGILL** Established the Ohio State research team which distinguished the major characteristics of leadership (see Chapter 7).
1958	**FREDERICK FIEDLER** Propounded the situational theory of leadership in that different styles of leadership were appropriate for different situations.
1959	**FREDERICK HERZBERG** With his associates he described the various factors which contribute to job satisfaction and dissatisfaction (see Chapter 4).
1962	**JOHN FRENCH and BERTRAM RAVEN** Established the bases of social power which are used by individuals in organisations.
1964	**ROBERT BLAKE and JANE MOUTON** Researched into organisational development and developed the grid training technique (see Chapter 8).
1964	**VICTOR VROOM** Developed the expectancy theory of motivation (see Chapter 4).
1966	**DANIEL KATZ and ROBERT KAHN** Studied the processes of organisations and developed the open systems approach to the study of organisations (see Chapter 5).
1968	**EDWIN LOCKE** With his fellow researchers he put forward the idea of the goal-setting motivational process (see Chapter 4).
1972	**IRVING JANIS** Propounded the idea of *groupthink* being a barrier to effective decision-making in groups and teams (see Chapter 7).
1975	**RICHARD HACKMAN and GREGORY OLDHAM** Developed the job characteristics model of motivation through job design (see Chapter 5).
1978	**JEFFREY PFEFFER and GERALD SALANCIK** Developed the concept that power lies in the hands of those who control the required resources (see Chapter 7).
1985	**EDGAR SCHEIN** Provided the theoretical basis for the further development of organisational culture (see Chapter 9).

Table 2 below gives an overview of the approaches to the study of organisational behaviour.

Table 2 Approaches to the study of organisational behaviour

Context	**Approach**	**Key assumptions**	
1900–1918	Classical/'organisers'	Human relations/'behaviourists'	
Era of mass-production; expansion of state bureacracy	**Characteristics:** analysis of work tasks; rules for improved division of labour; organisations seen as machines	**Characteristics:** recognition of pyschological and social needs of people at work	
	Taylor scientific management; Fayol – analysis of man. functions	Mayo and Hawthorne experiments	
1918–1945			
1945–1980	Systems	Contingency	Modernist
'Long boom'; increasing affluence; consumerism	**Characteristics:** integration of classical and human relations schools; organisation as a system/organism; socio-technical approach	**Characteristics:** effective job/organ. design dependent on circumstances	**Assumptions:** positivist; scientific
1980–2000		Symbolic-interp.	Post-modern
More unstable econ. conditions; globalisation; increasing competition; impact of IT; 'post-industrial' society		**Characteristics:** importance of culture; conflict in organisations	**Assumptions:** social construction of reality; multiple perspectives

Current issues				
	IT and org design e.g. re-engineering; 'virtual' organisations; 'lean' operations	team-working; empowerment	org. culture; conflict and change	gender; cross-cultural, management, ethical issues

Whilst it is important to understand how people behave and organisations work, it is essential that you understand how to explain and predict behaviour in the workplace.

B. Explaining and predicting behaviour in the workplace

Learning objectives

By the end of this section you should be able to:

- describe the purpose of research into the behaviour of people;
- summarise the principal criteria which can be used to evaluate research;
- identify the main research designs used by researchers in Organisational Behaviour;
- distinguish between the advantages of laboratory experimentation and fieldwork;
- appreciate the ethical issues related to research in the behavioural sciences.

Overview

In order to understand existing research and/or to carry out personal research, an individual has to understand what research is. In his text Jankowicz (1995) stated that research was the systematic gathering of information. It is about helping in the search for truth, and whilst an individual may never find the ultimate truth – with regard to understanding the individual and organisations that would be in the context of how any person would behave in an organisation – ongoing research would add to the body of knowledge within Organisational Behaviour by supporting some theories, opposing others, and adding new ones.

Purposes of research

A researcher in organisational behaviour tries to approach problems and questions of behaviour in the workplace as scientifically as possible. By doing so, he or she will make a systematic investigation of hypotheses about the relationships among natural phenomena and, as a consequence of this, be able to predict various phenomena. Whatever the project being undertaken, there are two types of research:

- basic
- applied.

Basic research

This type of research is aimed at adding new knowledge to an existing body of information. It does not tend to be designed to solve problems. Such knowledge may not apply directly to organisations – at least in the first instance – but it can mature into relevant information. In the field of Organisational Behaviour, this sort of work is usually carried out by research scientists and university readers and professors.

Applied research

The purpose of applied research is to attempt to solve particular problems or answer a specific question or questions. The research is carried out within an organisation or organisations and the information gained is relevant for use by managers in the workplace. University readers and professors carry out this sort of research, as do consultants and managers themselves.

Research terminology

In order to understand a piece of research and/or to carry out personal research, it is necessary for the researcher to understand the terminology used. There are a number of books to help research in business and management – some are given at the end of this section.

The key terminology includes:

- variable: dependent, independent, and moderating (contingency)
- hypothesis
- causality
- correlation co-efficient
- theory.

Variable

A **variable** is any general characteristic that can be measured and that changes either in amplitude, intensity, or both. Some examples of variable in Organisational Behaviour are stress, personality, norms, and job satisfaction.

A **dependent variable** is a response that is affected by an independent variable. It is the dependent which the researcher is interested in investigating. In organisational research the most popular dependent variables being researched are culture, conflict, stress, and job satisfaction.

An **independent variable** is the presumed cause of some change in the dependent variable. Examples of these being researched in the organisational context are motivation, emotional intelligence, rewards, and organisational design.

It is necessary to note that a variable can be used in a dependent or independent way – it will depend upon the hypothesis (see below) attributed by the researcher.

Example: Downsizing

Downsizing can be used as a dependent or an independent variable. This reflects the fact that the label given to a particular variable depends on its place in the hypothesis. To take the statement 'Increases in downsizing can lead to an increase in job satisfaction' is to use the term 'downsizing' as an independent variable.

However, in the statement 'Increases in job satisfaction lead to a decrease in downsizing', *downsizing* becomes a dependent variable.

A researcher also needs to consider the issue of a moderating variable (contingency variable), which diminishes the effect of the independent variable on the dependent variable.

Example: Moderating or contingency variable

Let A be the independent variable.
Let B be the dependent variable.
Let C be the moderating or contingency variable.

If A happens then the result will be B but only under conditions C.

For example, if there is an increase in the amount of learning in the workplace (A), then there will be a change in the individual's productivity (B), but this effect will be moderated by the environment (C).

Hypothesis

According to Saunders *et al.* (1997) a hypothesis is: 'a testable proposition about the relationship between two or more events or concepts …' (p. 71).

It relates strongly to variables (see above) in that a hypothesis is really a tentative explanation about the relationship between two or more variables.

Example: Downsizing

In the example given above, the statement that 'Increases in downsizing can lead to an increase in job satisfaction' is an example of a hypothesis.

Causality

As can be seen from the above example, a hypothesis implies a relationship, e.g. there is a relationship between *downsizing* and *job satisfaction*. This cause and effect is known as causality: changes in the independent variable are assumed to cause changes in the dependent variable. However, a researcher working in a behavioural context must remember that even if a relationship is found, it is possible to make an incorrect assumption of causality.

Correlation co-efficient

Whilst the researcher may believe that there is a relationship between two or more variables, it is important that he or she knows the strength of that relationship. The term correlation co-efficient refers to the indication of that strength and is expressed as a number from –1.00 (a perfect negative relationship) to +1.00 (a perfect positive correlation). When two variables vary directly with one another, the correlation will be expressed as a positive number. When they are inversely related (i.e. one increases as the other decreases) the correlation is expressed as a negative number. Should the two variables vary independently of each other, it is said that the correlation between the two is zero.

Example: Downsizing and job satisfaction

A researcher has been investigating the relationship between downsizing and job satisfaction to see whether downsizing of the workforce had an effect on the job satisfaction of the remaining members of the workforce within the organisation. By using the statistics on downsizing provided by the organisation and the attendance and punctuality records of the others, the researcher might be able to see whether there is a relationship between the two variables.

Question
Imagine that the researcher found a correlation coefficient between downsizing and job satisfaction of +50.

Is this a strong association? Or a weak one?

Answer
There is no precise numerical cut-off separating strong and weak relationship. The researcher would need to apply a standard statistical test to determine whether or not the relationship was a significant one.

Theory

A theory helps researchers to decide on the way they design their research. Gill and Johnson (1991) define a theory as: 'a formulation regarding the cause and effect relationships between two or more variables, which may or may not have been tested' (p. 166).

A theory is a systematic description of interrelated concepts or hypotheses that tries to explain and predict events. Within Organisational Behaviour, theories are also often referred to as *models*.

Because it deals with issues related to people within the workplace, Organisational Behaviour is full of such theories/models. There are theories on what motivates individuals to work, what is the best way to lead a group, the ideal design of an organisation, and how to turn dysfunctional conflict into functional conflict. Such theories/models tend to have the common thread that they reflect science at work. Researchers are testing existing theories and applying models upon which they suggest new theories. This results in Organisational Behaviour being a proactive discipline which is continually evolving.

Evaluating research

In evaluating research, the onus is on the reader to take note of three key issues:

- validity
- reliability
- generalisability.

Validity

The validity of a piece of research is the extent to which the completed research actually measures what it set out to measure.

Reliability

The reliability of a measure is the extent to which it is consistent over a period of time. If such measures lack reliability, then little confidence can be placed in the results they provide.

Example: Measurement of a team's performance

Suppose that the researcher measures a team's performance today using a questionnaire, with a view to measuring the same thing in three months' time. If one assumes that nothing has changed, the responses from individuals should be very similar to the first enquiry. If they are, then the measure can be assessed as having a high level of reliability.

Some researchers make two questions the same, e.g. Q2 and Q9, and if the responses to these two questions are the same, then the other responses could be said to be reliable.

Downsizing

Suppose that a researcher wants to measure the effect of downsizing on the job satisfaction of the remaining workforce. He or she may ask questions of that workforce about their pay, rewards, managerial supervision and holiday allowance. The researcher may then calculate the mean of the answers received and use such a figure to represent job satisfaction.

It could be argued that this is not a valid measurement because, for example, pay, rewards and holiday allowance may be unrelated to the task itself. This means that the researcher has obtained data that do not mean what he or she thinks they mean – they are not valid.

Therefore, researchers must ensure that they use measures that are valid as well as reliable.

Generalisability

The reader must consider whether the research is generalisable. That is, to what degree are the results of the research applicable to groups of individuals other than those who participated in the original study?

Types of research design

A research design can be said to be the set of procedures which are used to test the predicted relationships among the phenomena being investigated. The design will address a number of issues, including:

- the definition of the relevant variables;
- the means of measuring such variables;
- how the variables are related to each other.

The choice of research design will depend upon the strengths and weaknesses of each design option and a researcher will choose that method which is most appropriate for the work being carried out. There are four types of research design frequently used by researchers within Organisational Behaviour, although these are not mutually exclusive:

- case study
- field survey
- laboratory experiment
- field experiment.

Case Study

Robson (1993) defined case study as: '... the development of detailed, intensive knowledge about a single "case", or a small number of related "cases" ' (p. 40).

It is an in-depth analysis of a single setting. The design of a case study is used when little is known about the events being investigated and the researcher wants to look at relevant concepts within a particular setting in an intensive way. Within this type of research, the researcher can use a variety of different methods of gathering information, including semi-structured interviews, questionnaires and participant observation. The case study method can be an effective and useful research tool so long as the researcher appreciates its limitations and takes them into account when he or she formulates the conclusions.

Advantages	Disadvantages
in-depth probing yields rich variety of data	data cannot be readily generalised
facilitates discovery of unexpected relationships	data may be biased because researcher is close to situation
global observation may raise data beyond that originally expected	time consuming

Field survey

A field survey typically relies on a questionnaire distributed to a sample of people selected from a wider population. It can focus on a variety of topics relevant to Organisational Behaviour, including workers' attitudes towards their jobs (e.g. job satisfaction, rewards) and/or on the wider perceptions of the workforce regarding, for example, the design of the organisation, and attitudes to quality provision of goods/services that the organisation provides to its customers.

The field survey can be a very useful means of gathering large quantities of data and assessing general patterns of relationships amongst variables. However, like any research method, the researcher must be aware of the advantages and disadvantages of such a method:

Advantages	Disadvantages
can survey a large population	may reveal only shallow information
provides abundance of data in quantifiable form	may neglect attitudes and feelings
statistical analysis easy to facilitate	design requires expertise and is time consuming
possible to compile normative data for comparative purposes	relationships amongst variables tend to be accentuated in responses, i.e. people tend to respond to all questions in the same way
	gives researcher little or no control
	many inherent sources of potential error

Laboratory experiment

A laboratory experiment takes place in an artificial environment where the researcher has most control over the variables being investigated. The latter can be manipulated and examined within a controlled environment.

Advantages	Disadvantages
high degree of control over variables	lack of realism – rarely duplicates real-life situations
ability to measure variables precisely	difficult to generalise findings to organisational settings
	some issues cannot be investigated in a laboratory setting, e.g. downsizing

Field experiment

The field experiment to some extent counteracts the disadvantages of the laboratory setting in that the former is conducted in an actual organisation. In the organisation (i.e. in the field) the researcher makes an attempt to control some variables and manipulate others in order to gauge the effects of the manipulated variables on the outcome variables.

Example: Downsizing and job satisfaction

The researcher might wish to assess the effects of a downsizing policy on job satisfaction. He or she might design a field experiment in which one organisation adopts a particular pattern in dealing with downsizing and a different organisation, as similar as possible to the initial organisation, serves as a control organisation. Issues such as attendance and punctuality are monitored at both organisations. If attendance increases and punctuality increases in the experimental organisation and there is no change in the control organisation, the researcher will probably conclude that the policy in the experimental organisation was successful.

Like all research methods, the field experiment has certain pros and cons. However, these are best shown in comparison with its closely linked method, the laboratory experiment:

Advantages	Disadvantages
organisational setting provides greater realism	lack of control over events which may occur in the experimental organisation
generalisation to other organisations more valid	contamination of results if participants find out their respective roles in the research
	thus they behave differently from the norm (the Hawthorne effect)
	such changes may cause potential difficulties for the host organisation

Ethical issues

A key issue related to research with people is that of ethics. Such issues have been rehearsed elsewhere in this text and can be related to the area of research. However, there are two key areas related to research:

- the provision of protection for participants;
- reporting of the results.

Provision of protection for participants

All participants in any study must be protected and not have their privacy violated – this is related to the issue of care for another human being.

For consideration

Suppose that a researcher is studying conflict behaviour in a working environment. A good way to increase people's willingness to participate is to promise that their identities will not be revealed.

Should participation be voluntary?

Having made a guarantee of confidentiality, should the researcher keep to it?

How can the researcher avoid difficulties related to participation?

The answer to the first two issues should be 'Yes'. Having made a guarantee of confidentiality, the researcher is obliged to adhere to it. Participation should be voluntary and prospective participants should have the ongoing right to withdraw from the research at any time without having to give a reason. The researcher can avoid difficulties by good communication, and ensuring that each participator is given a thorough explanation of the purpose of the research and the nature of the research conditions. The researcher should not expose participants to any physical or psychological harm. Most researchers work within codes of ethical practice developed by their employers.

Reporting of results

The researcher should report the results accurately – particularly when reporting research procedures and methods. Such reporting should also be candid. It is up to others to assess the validity of the research project and allow them, using the same methods, to carry out a similar piece of work with a different population thus letting them, in turn, learn about how the original findings generalise.

It can be seen, therefore, that understanding people in organisations requires thorough and methodical study with the marrying of theory and practice using reliable and valid methods of investigation.

Questions for discussion

1 Why should students of Organisational Behaviour have an understanding of research methodology?
2 Upon what does the best research design depend?
3 Why must a researcher consider the ethical codes of research before planning a research investigation?

References and further reading

Buchanan, D. and Huczynski, A., 1997 (3rd edn), *Organizational Behaviour: An Introductory Text* (London: Prentice Hall)

Gill, J. and Johnson, P., 1991, *Research Methods for Managers* (London: Paul Chapman)

Hannagan, T., 1997, *Management: Concepts and Practices* (London: Pitman)

Jankowicz, A.D., 1997 (2nd edn), *Business Research Projects for Students* (London: Chapman & Hall)

Pettinger, R., 1996, *Introduction to Organisational Behaviour* (Basingstoke: Macmillan)

Robson, C., 1993, *Real World Research* (Oxford: Blackwell)

Saunders, M., Lewis, P. and Thornhill, A., 1997, *Research Methods for Business Students* (London: Pitman Publishing)

Schein, E.H., 1988 (3rd edn), *Organizational Psychology* (London: Prentice Hall)

Part 1: Understanding individuals

1 Personality

Learning objectives

After studying this chapter you should be able to:

- define what is meant by 'personality';
- understand the relationship between personality, attitudes, and behaviour;
- assess the impact of national cultures on personality traits;
- categorise the differing approaches to studying personality;
- assess and evaluate the nomothetic and idiographic approaches;
- judge the pros and cons of personality testing.

CASE STUDY

Diversity challenge

The Amoco Corporation conducted a worldwide survey of its workforce in 1988, analysing the views of 29,000 people. At that time, senior managers were under the impression that they headed a healthy organisation providing valued and satisfying employment. But the results turned out to be both surprising and disappointing.

When asked whether they felt it was safe to express their views, 57 per cent of respondents said 'No'. More than half of the employees (55 per cent) felt that individuals could not challenge the company's traditional business practices. Half of the workforce agreed that Amoco made little effort to listen to their opinions, while 38 per cent felt that they would be penalised for making a mistake when trying to find an innovative solution that, by its nature, included an element of risk.

The research also revealed that most of Amoco's middle and senior managers were white men who had spent their entire careers with the firm. The oil industry has always had difficulty attracting women into engineering positions, and the survey confirmed that this was a deep-seated problem. Eighteen months later, as a direct result of the findings, Amoco launched the Renewal Programme, designed to correct organisational weaknesses and to improve the company's approach to diversity management. The programme was based on a range of core values, one of which stated: 'Our individual and collective actions and talents create our competitive advantage.'

Adopting diversity as a corporate philosophy was one thing; actually implementing it and changing the company's culture was quite another. In 1991, Amoco took the first step towards cultural change, providing communication to and meeting skills training for all of its staff. At the same time, it tried to ensure that every employee was part of a 'natural work team'. Basic diversity training was included to encourage them to listen to and respect their colleagues' views.

In 1993 a global diversity advisory council was started which was responsible for exploring all diversity issues, advising the board of directors, determining gaps in the strategic management of diversity and identifying targets for the composition of the workforce. Several local diversity advisory councils (Dacs) were set up at lower levels of the organisation to address local issues; they were made up of local volunteers with a responsibility to advise senior regional managers – there are now 40 Dacs throughout the world, working in locations such as Trinidad, Egypt and the UK.

The Dacs promote the view that teams of individuals from different cultural and ethnic backgrounds, and with varying personalities and experiences, will consider issues from different perspectives. Amoco has taken a broad definition of diversity. It is primarily about ensuring that all individuals are valued; that their opinions are both considered and respected; and that they have an equal voice in the decision-making process. This should happen regardless of not just their race, creed, colour of skin and sex, but also their personality, career background and grade.

When asked what factors might put employees at a disadvantage, 49 per cent of respondents stated that personality traits had restricted their career prospects – a higher percentage than for the more traditional areas of race and sex.

Employees felt that, to be successful, they needed to be extrovert, outspoken, open to change or, as one individual put it, 'hell-bent on new initiatives'. On the other hand, they though that being introverted, quiet and not a 'change agent' reduced an employee's career opportunities.

Amoco is clearly still failing to make full use of the skills and energy of individuals who feel this way. The UK Dac is currently implementing plans that it hopes will address these concerns. It is hoped that through training there will be an emphasis on the fact that diversity goes beyond issues of race, colour and sex, and that it includes more subtle issues such as personality traits.

Adapted from P. Watson, 'Diversity challenge' in *Personnel Management*, 1 May 1997, pp. 30–32

Introduction

Managers need to be able to address certain questions related to the personality of individual members of the workforce. For example, whether personality influences attitudes and behaviour; whether personality can be measured and, therefore, behaviour predicted; whether an individual's personality can be changed and whether there are best ways of recruiting and selecting staff.

This chapter investigates the ways of defining what is meant by personality and how it can influence behaviour through the mediating influence of attitudes. The contrasting approaches to the study of personality represented by the trait and situational, the nomothetic and idiographic traditions are discussed. The work of nomothetic writers such as Jung (1923, 1949), Freud (1949), Eysenck (1965, 1995) and Cattell (1973) is considered and compared with the idiographic work of writers such as Allport (1961), Kelly (1955) and Rogers (1942, 1951, 1970). There is a consideration of whether national cultures have any impact on the question of personality traits. The chapter introduces ways of assessing the relative merits of these two traditions before considering how this assessment impacts on the value of personality testing.

Individual differences and organisational behaviour

Individuals are unique because of their skills, abilities, personalities, perceptions, attitudes, values, and personal sense of morality. By assessing these, individuals can be seen to be similar to or different from one another and it is the individual differences which represent the core of what challenges management, since no two individuals are alike. For managers this is a particular problem because they work with people who have numerous individual characteristics; therefore the more that a manager is aware that such differences exist, the more he or she can work with other people. Figure 1.1 shows some of the variables which influence the behaviour of individuals.

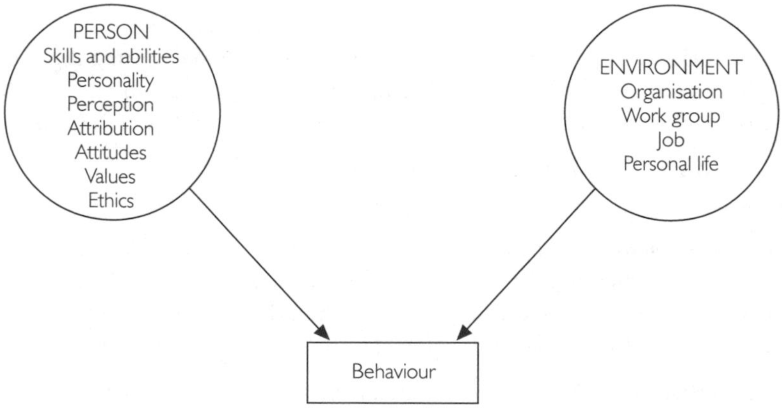

Figure 1.1 Variables which influence individual behaviour, after Nelson and Quick (1994, p. 78)

Lewin's (1951) work formed the basis for contemporary understanding of how individuals differ when he posited that behaviour is a function of both the person and the environment. He did this in the form of an equation:

$$B = f\ (P, E)$$

where B = Behaviour, P = Person, and E = Environment. This view was advocated by the interactional psychology approach which, according to Nelson and Quick (1994), 'emphasizes that in order to understand human behavior, we must know something about the person and about the situation' (p. 78).

The above emphasises the need to study both people and the situation: people consist of individual differences which are discussed within this chapter and the situation consists of the environment the individual operates in and includes such things as teams, social situations, and other environmental factors. One of these key individual differences is that of personality.

Personality

No single definition of personality is universally accepted but a common component of definitions given for personality is contained in several key theoretical approaches which can be taken in the study of personality.

Bennett (1997) defines personality as: 'the totality of all the individual's dispositions and motives to behave in a certain way' (p. 55); and Nelson and Quick (1994) consider it to be: 'a relatively stable set of characteristics that influence an individual's behaviour' (p. 79).

Gross (1996) defines personality as: 'those relatively stable and enduring aspects of individuals which distinguish them from other people, making them unique, but which at the same time allow people to be compared with each other' (p.8 and p.744).

A definition posited by Maddi (1989) contains some significant ideas which are relevant to individuals studying behaviour in organisations:

> Personality is a stable set of characteristics and tendencies that determine those commonalities and differences in the psychological behavior (thoughts, feelings, and actions) of people that have continuity in time and that may not be easily understood as the sole result of the social and biological pressures of the moment. (p. 10)

He considers personality theory to be a general theory of behaviour which is an attempt to describe and understand behaviour all of the time. This is a difficult task – some say impossible – because in endeavouring to define personality an attempt is being made to try to explain the very essence of human beings. As will be seen later in this chapter, personality theorists tend to describe what individuals have in common and what they have that is different from other individuals. This is the uniqueness of each individual and as a consequence no two people can be expected to respond to others in a particular way in the workplace – regardless of the situation. The very complexity of individual personality makes the management of people extremely challenging and interesting. Maddi (1989) also brings out a key feature of personality, believing that it is stable and that it has continuity over time. Whilst individuals do change over time, there is rarely a radical change in personality; however, it may be affected over time as an influence of formative development and, at a slower pace, as a result of the experiences of life itself.

Determining individual personality

There is no one answer to the question of what determines an individual's personality because of the number of variables involved in the development of an individual's personality. Figure 1.2 below shows that there are, however, three key personality determinants:

- heredity
- environment
- situation.

The relationship between heredity and environment influences on personality is sometimes known as the 'nature/nurture' debate. Some studies have supported the heredity/nature viewpoint. For example, identical twins who have been separated at birth and raised apart in different situations were found later to share similar personality traits and career preferences.

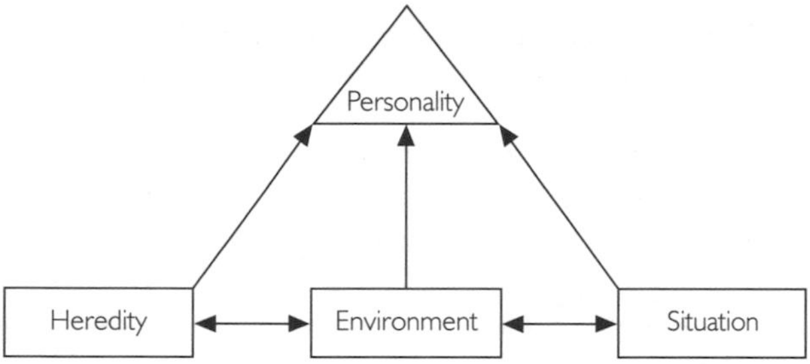

Figure 1.2 Sources of personality differences

Heredity

This refers to those factors that were determined at conception – the genes. Such constituents as physical stature, gender, temperament, and energy levels are characteristics which are usually considered to be either completely, or predominantly, influenced by our genes. If this were so, then all personality factors would be fixed at birth and no amount of experience could alter them. If you were calm, quiet and easy-going at birth it would be said, under the heredity view, that it would not be possible to change such attributes. This is not an adequate explanation of personality.

Environment

The view that personality is affected by the environment (environment/nurture) considers that the important influences of environmental factors such as family, social group membership, life experiences, education and culture are a shaper of personality. The latter is a key influence in the workplace where organisations are increasingly facing global competition and the workforce is diverse in nature.

According to Hellriegel *et al.* (1995) culture refers to: 'the distinctive ways that different human populations or societies organize their lives' (p. 43).

Individuals who are born into a particular culture are exposed to the norms (acceptable standards) of that culture and thus culture has a significant effect on the personality of an individual. It is through culture that different roles in society – and thus in the workplace – are enacted. For example, in the Western European workplace individuals who are independent and competitive are rewarded for such behaviour whilst the Japanese generally reward individuals for being co-operative and group-oriented. There are exceptions to this, which only goes to show that culture helps to determine only broad patterns of behaviour similarity among people. It is the differences which tend to be extreme – most cultures are not homogeneous.

There are no personality types specific to any particular country or nation. Whilst it might be possible to find highly assertive and non-assertive individuals in almost any country, it is not possible to do this on the basis of a specific country. However, it is a common belief that any one nation's culture influences the dominant personality characteristic of the members of its population. It may well be possible to support such a view by looking at one of the key attributes of personality – authoritarianism.

Authoritarianism (discussed later in this chapter) is closely related to the concept of power and distance. For example, in countries which have a high power-distance (e.g. Brazil, Mexico, Cuba) there ought to be a large number of people amongst the ruling/political leaders with authoritarian personalities. This can perhaps be contrasted with the UK which actually rates below average on the power-distance scale; it therefore follows that there would be fewer authoritarian personalities in the UK than in the high power-distance countries.

Wood (1995) believes that the differences between individuals from different cultures may be fewer than those between individuals from the same culture: 'ideology [a systematic set of beliefs and values] and personality cuts "across" national boundaries and tends to form important dimensions along which individuals from different backgrounds coalesce' (p. 4).

He also believes that personality is similar to character: 'the result of both innate predispositions and experiences when growing up' (p. 4).

Taking the Jungian extroversion–introversion continuum, Wood states (1995) that it can be applied to a number of organisational behaviour concepts such as individual differences, team work, and the function of operations. It is also his view that introverts and extroverts are easy to recognise by someone from the same culture, but not quite so easily by someone from a different culture. Figure 1.3 opposite shows Wood's (1995) hypothesised relationship between culture, ideology and personality.

The organisation is a reflection of the society's culture as a whole, and even though culture has an impact on the development of employees' personalities, not all individuals will respond to cultural influences at an equal pace and in a similar way. Managers still make the error of assuming that their subordinates are like themselves.

Situation

Situational factors will further influence the effects of heredity and environment (including national culture) on personality. Whilst an individual's personality will remain stable over time, it is changeable depending upon the situation individuals find themselves in. Every situation demands different things of an individual and therefore that individual will draw upon the different aspects of their personality to deal with the event they are faced with. However, personality attributes are more stable if taken in a cluster rather than as individual traits – if this is done then they might be more meaningful. This is a logical view, yet there is no classification to advise what set situations will call on what specific aspect of personality and so managers have no set guide to help them. However, what is known is that certain situations are more relevant than others in influencing personality. For example, behaviour in the workplace is likely to be different from that exhibited at a nightclub.

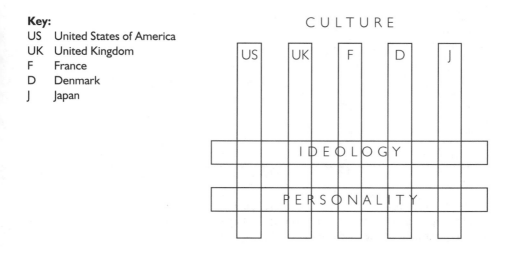

Key:
US United States of America
UK United Kingdom
F France
D Denmark
J Japan

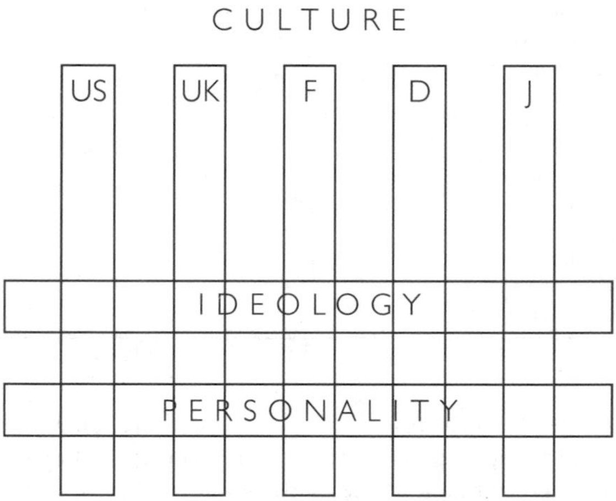

Figure 1.3 A culture matrix after Wood (1995, p. 4)

The general consensus view is that heredity, environment and situational factors shape personality, thus giving a balanced view to the determining of individual personality.

Theories of personality

Within the generally accepted definitions of behaviour, given above, there are several different approaches to the study of personality and its key theoretical components which are shown in Table 1.1 below.

Table 1.1 Approaches to the study of personality

THEORY TYPE / APPROACH	Trait/type/factor-analytic/ psychometric. Personality seen as consisting of enduring peronality traits. Heredity is a major influence. Limited managerial influence over behaviour – selecting staff through psychometric testing is critical.	Situational. Behaviour and even personality can change as a result of situational influences. Greater scope for management to influence behaviour.
Nomethetic Identifying personality factors applying to people in general.	Freud (1949) Jung (1923, 1949) Eysenck (1965, 1995) Cattell (1973)	
Idiographic Identifying the unique personality characteristics of individuals.	Allport (1961)	Kelly (1955) Rogers (1942, 1951)

As can be seen from Table 1.1 above there are a number of ways of modelling the principal viewpoints on personality. However, the key ones which have, individually and collectively, influenced the study of personality in organisations are:

- trait or type
- psychodynamic
- humanistic
- integrative.

Trait or type

These theories come nearest to describing the structure of personality in a way which helps match the everyday use of the word. Such theories use words such as happy, sad, outgoing, cheerful, aggressive. These are known as traits and are the basic elements which predispose individuals to behave in a particular way. In doing this there is an assumption that everyone possesses a number of personality traits yet each one draws upon such traits to a different extent. According to the trait theory an individual who exhibits some strong traits is highly likely to possess certain others. It follows, then, that personality comprises some 'trait clusters' with other traits in evidence which are similar to those within the cluster.

Allport and Odbert (1936) found that there were more than 18,000 terms in use for describing the personal characteristics of individuals. After having removed from this list those words which were evaluative rather than descriptive and others which were in temporary use, they were left with around 5,000 terms. Allport (1961) went on to further reduce this number to two basic kinds:

- *Common traits*
  These are the subject matter of the nomothetic approach and they are basic and applicable to all members of a particular cultural, ethnic or linguistic origin. For example, with increased globalisation and international competition has come the need for individuals to be assertive, and Allport (1961) would consider that this trait would be on a continuum from, say, weak to strong.

- *Individual traits*
  These are the subject matter of the idiographic approach and constitute a unique cluster of personal dispositions (to use Allport's (1961) word) based on the individual's unique:

  - experiences in life; and
  - ways of organising their own world.

  However, Allport (1961) went on to say that individual traits are just that and cannot be generalised to all people, so such traits could not, therefore, be open to measurement by tests (see Measuring personality, below) and could only be discovered by a very careful, systematic and detailed study of individual people.

According to trait theorists, traits have the same psychological meaning for all individuals and people only differ in the extent to which particular traits are present. For example, they would believe that all individuals are assertive, but that assertiveness varies in intensity from individual to individual. Allport (1961) further believed that any comparisons which were made between individuals could only be carried out in terms of those traits which were common to them. At the very best, such a view can only provide a very rough approximation to any specific personality. For example, there are numerous kinds of assertiveness. If two managers are labelled 'assertive', it does not mean that their assertiveness is identical in kind but that they are different in their intensity of assertiveness.

This nomothetic approach (studying personality 'generally') is precise in that it compares people in terms of a stated number of traits (dimensions) so that the individual differences can be discovered. However, this is based on the assumption that it is possible to compare one individual with another on stated dimensions and this is the weakness which Kelly (1955) discussed when he adopted an idiographic approach by stressing the unique individualness of personality.

Allport (1961) was the researcher who most strongly posited the trait approach to personality, but Cattell (1973) was another important advocate of trait theory who identified sixteen traits which formed the basis for individual differences related to behaviour. He used adjective-based bi-polar continua such as warmhearted/cool, assertive/submissive, unconventional/conformist. There has been more recent work on the role of traits in personality with McCrae (1989) proposing that it is possible to reduce traits to five basic factors. He called this 'the big five' and they comprised introversion, agreeableness, the will to achieve, emotional stability, and openness to experience. Research is still continuing to find out whether this view can be supported and, particularly, to find out whether 'the big five' can be used to predict individual behaviour. Nicholson (1995) believes that personality is a key factor in work performance and that 'the big five' dimensions are key and can be assessed in the workplace setting. He believes that personality can be defined as 'those characteristics that account for consistent patterns of behaviour shaped by age, culture, gender, education, professional experience and social class – but there is a crucial genetic base' (p. 4).

Although Nicholson (1995) believes that differences in personality can be seen as varieties of 'the big five' he emphasises that: 'Although personality colours all behaviour it does not necessarily predict how we act – ability and circumstances are often influential' (p. 4).

Closely allied to the work of Cattell (1973) was that of Eysenck (1965) who used the term *type*, which was previously used to describe individuals who belonged to one or other group or category. That is, an individual could only be assigned to one type and not to several. In his later investigations Eysenck (1995) stated that the descriptor 'type' is not popular today and when it is used it is only to describe combinations of traits that are found to correlate.

The identified traits are not, according to Eysenck (1995), independent of each other but are correlated in certain patterns. This suggests that there is a more complicated map and that there is more complexity in the theory than was first thought. Eysenck (1995) now refers to types as *dimensions* which represent continua along which everyone can be positioned.

Personality traits tend to be most valuable only concerning those individuals who hold the extreme poles on the continuum of the type, for example on the introvert–extrovert continuum. It might be possible to predict some common behaviours among extreme extroverts or individuals who are highly anxious. Robbins (1991) depicted this as in Figure 1.4 below.

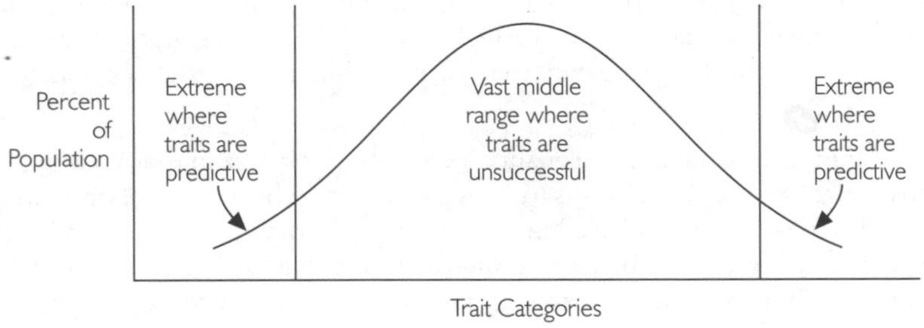

Figure 1.4 Predictive validity of personality traits after Robbins (1991, p. 94)

It follows, therefore, that it is possible to attempt to group traits in an effort to identify individual personality traits. That is, instead of searching for specific individual characteristics, certain qualities can be grouped together into a single category. For example, ambition and aggression tend to be highly correlated and could, therefore, be placed in a cluster with, say, assertiveness. All efforts to reduce the number of individual personality traits to common clusters seem to isolate extroversion–introversion and something approximating high anxiety–low anxiety. As can be seen in Figure 1.5, Robbins (1991) attempted this.

	High anxiety	Low anxiety
Extrovert	Tense, excitable, unstable, warm, sociable and dependent	Composed, confident, trustful, adaptable, warm, sociable and dependent
Introvert	Tense, excitable, unstable, cold and shy	Composed, confident, trustful, adaptable, calm, cold and shy

Figure 1.5 Four type theories after Robbins (1991, p. 95)

There has been considerable criticism of the trait approach to personality. Some people believe that by identifying traits alone one is limited and that it is necessary to remember that personality is dynamic and unstable. It is also argued that those who support the trait approach ignore the situational issues and the view that personality is inconsistent and varies as a function of such situational factors.

Psychodynamic

These theories have developed from the views of Carl Gustav Jung (1875–1961), a former pupil of Sigmund Freud (1856–1939) whose theories of the mind were based on years of investigation and illumined the way individuals think about themselves; his theories have had immense influence upon modern thought. Freud (1949) constantly revised and modified his views throughout his life but he posited his psychoanalytical theory during the years 1900 to 1930. He was also of the opinion that human nature was flawed in that individuals were inherently destructive and irrational – his view of human nature was very pessimistic.

Freud (1949) was interested in the unconscious determinants of behaviour; he perceived personality as being the interaction between three parts of a personality: the id, the ego and the superego. The id was that part of the personality which was the most primitive and which was the drive source for an individual's most basic, uncensored behaviour. According to Freud (1949) the superego was that part of the personality which acted as the individual's conscience, and contained the social responsibility and moral judgement aspects of the personality. Freud (1947) believed that an individual experienced a continual conflict between the id and the superego and it was only through the services of the ego that the individual could use defence mechanisms and come to some sort of sense of reality. This psychodynamic theory of personality helps people to understand that the focus is on the unconscious and hidden aspects that influence an individual's behaviour.

Jung (1923) was also a psychodynamic theorist but he disagreed fundamentally with Freud's (1949) view that the unconscious mind dictated the behaviour of individuals; Jung (1923) preferred to distinguish between the personal and the collective unconscious. That is, he believed that an individual's consciousness can be changed because of the individual's personal experiences which are inherited and common to all individuals. Jung (1923) therefore based his view on the notion that although people were basically different, they were also basically similar and his classic work put forward the idea that the population is composed of two basic types of people: extroverts and introverts. Following on from this basic premise, he then identified two types of perception (sensing and intuiting) and two types of judgement (thinking and feeling).

Gross (1996) cites the example of extroversion being a 'type concept based on the observed correlations of sociability, liveliness, activity and so on' (p. 752). Perception is about how individuals gather information and is dealt with in detail in the next chapter, whilst judgement is about how individuals make decisions. Together they represent the key mental functions that all individuals use. Taking these basic premises, Jung (1949) believed that the similarities and differences between humans could be understood only by combining their preferences. For example, when faced with having to do something, an individual chooses one way over another way and so shows that we have preferences. Jung (1949) believed that an individual has a preference towards introversion or extroversion – just as we have a preference for catching a ball with the right or left hand. We may be able to catch a ball in either hand but when taken by surprise we will have a tendency to use a preferred hand in order not to drop the ball. Jung's (1949) theory suggests that not only do individuals have such preferences, but also that no one preference is better than another. For example, preferring to catch a ball with the left hand is not better than catching it with the right hand – so long as it is caught (if that is the desire). Such differences as there are, according to Jung (1949), should be honoured and recognised, thus becoming understood and appreciated for what they are.

There are four basic preferences in trait type theory and two possible choices of each of the four preferences as adapted from Kroeger and Thuesen (1981) and shown in Table 1.2 below.

Table 1.2 Type theory and descriptors

Extroversion	**Introversion**
Outgoing	Quiet
Publicly expressive	Reserved
Interacting	Concentrating
Speaks, then thinks	Thinks, then speaks
Gregarious	Reflective
Sensing	**Intuiting**
Practical	General
Specific	Abstract
Feet on the ground	Head in the clouds
Details	Possibilities
Concrete	Theoretical
Thinking	**Feeling**
Analytical	Subjective
Clarity	Harmony
Head	Heart
Justice	Mercy
Rules	Circumstances
Judging	**Perceiving**
Structured	Flexible
Time oriented	Open ended
Decisive	Exploring
Makes lists/uses them	Makes lists/loses them
Organised	Spontaneous

These key dimensions can be placed on paired continua as below:

Extroversion (E) ←——→ Introversion (I)

This continuum represents where an individual finds their energy. The extrovert (E) finds it from the interaction with others whilst the introvert (I) finds it from being alone. Extroverts, therefore, have wide social networks whilst introverts tend to have a narrower range of relationships. Jung (1923) believed that this was not because introverts lacked social skills but because they preferred the internal environment of ideas, thoughts and concepts. These two classifications can be found in the workplace, with extroverts preferring task variety and wishing to be interrupted by visits from colleagues. Communication for these people is very free but sometimes, later, they regret what they have said. On the other hand, introverts like to think things out on their own and concentrate for long periods of time. Also, they like to work in isolation on projects over time and concentrate on the minutiae of work. They also dislike telephone interruptions and sometimes find it difficult to recall names and faces.

Sensing (S) ←——→ Intuiting (N)

This represents the perceptual ability of the individual and is dealt with in detail in the next chapter. It has to do with how individuals collect information because what is collected reflects the interests of the individual. The sensor (S) pays attention to all the information gathered through all the senses whereas the intuitor (N) uses intuition, or 'gut feeling' rather than paying attention to what actually exists. In the workplace, sensors tend to require specific answers to their direct questions and prefer exact and well-defined instructions. Because of this, such people err towards jobs that have visible, tangible, and measurable results so that they can fine-tune their existing skills rather than learn fresh ones. On the other hand, an intuitor enjoys learning and becomes annoyed with repetitive detail, finding it easier to be multi-tasking.

Thinking (T) ←——→ Feeling (F)

This continuum is about how individuals make their decisions. The thinker (T) tends to consider all the options very carefully, prefers to be as objective as possible, and analyses situations, whilst the feeler (F) makes decisions based on a more personal, value-oriented basis and is thus more sympathetic. In the workplace it is the thinkers who do not exhibit high levels of emotion and who are often at odds with people who do. Their strongest relationships are with other people's thoughts rather than their behaviour. Being analytically biased they want to put things in logical frameworks whilst feelers are more comfortable with emotion and enjoy wanting to please others; they respond well to praise and reward.

Judging (J) ←——→ Perceiving (P)

It is through this continuum that the individual takes a view of their environment. A judger (J) prefers to plan and organise their life and enjoys decision-making, whilst the perceiver (P), in contrast, is happier in a more flexible situation and enjoys spontaneity and being open rather than being a closed judger. For example, if J asks P to choose a place for a meeting, J will just decide and get on with it whilst P will offer a choice of a dozen possible venues. In the workplace, judgers tend to see things as 'right' or 'wrong' and enjoy task achievement, so they tend to keep lists and tick off items when they have been dealt with. Perceivers tend to be more laid back in their attitude, preferring to see what happens as a matter of course, and in the meantime they collect new information rather than make hasty decisions. They tend to be curious and tend to be data collectors but often start projects without completing them – they have many balls up in the air.

As can be seen from Table 1.2 above the preferences combine to form sixteen types as shown in Table 1.3 opposite.

From Table 1.3 it is possible to examine the combinations in detail. Macdaid *et al.* (1987) used as an example ESTJs who are extroverted, sensing, thinking, and judging. Such people see the world as it is (S); make their decisions objectively (T); and enjoy structure, schedules and considerable order (J). An amalgam of these qualities, with the individual's preference for interaction, makes them natural managers. They are perceived as being dependable, practical and job-completing, are conscious of the hierarchical chain of command, and see work as goal oriented and reachable through rules and regulations. They tend not to tolerate disorganisation and always need to be in control. What comes out from this work is that there are not good or bad types, but that each type has its strengths and weaknesses.

Walck (1991) carried out work on the relationship between type and specific managerial behaviour. For example, the introvert (I) and the feeler (F) have been shown to be more effective at participative management than their counterparts: the extrovert (E) and the thinker (T). Continued work shows that type theory is valued by managers because it is simple in its design and because of its accuracy in depicting personalities – although it needs to be remembered that it is a matter of perception and situation.

Humanistic

This approach to personality emphasises individual growth and improvement and represents a school of thought which dismisses scientific attempts to study human beings, seeing such attempts as inaccurate and inappropriate. The key work here is that of Carl Rogers (1970) who believed that everyone has a basic drive towards self-actualisation – the quest to be all that an individual can be. The humanistic approach concentrates on individual growth and self-improvement and because it is specifically people-centred it centres on an individual's perception of the world. The humanistic view contributes to an understanding of self and its importance in personality theory with the approach that the perception an individual has of self is the most important part of personality. It was this view that led Rogers (1970) to his form of psychotherapy known as *client-centred therapy*. The central tenet of Rogers' (1970) work – the concept of self (the organised and consistent set of perceptions and beliefs which an individual holds about himself or herself) – includes the idea of self-awareness of what the individual believes they are and what they are capable of doing. This in turn then influences the perception of their world and their behaviour in that world. For example, a manager may be perceived by her colleagues and superiors to be highly successful and is therefore respected by them, yet she herself perceives herself as a failure. Rogers (1970) calls this *incongruence*.

Table 1.3 Characteristics frequently associated with each type

ISTJ	ISFJ	INFJ	INTJ
"Doing what should be done" Organizer, compulsive, private, trustworthy, rules and regulations, practical	"A high sense of duty" Amiable, works behind the scenes, ready to sacrifice, accountable, prefers "doing"	"An inspiration to others" Reflective/introspective, quietly caring, creative, linguistically gifted, psychic	"Everything has room for improvement" Theory based, skeptical, "my way," high need for competency, sees world as a chessboard
Most responsible	Most loyal	Most contemplative	Most independent
ISTP	**ISFP**	**INFP**	**INTP**
"Ready to try anything once" Very observant, cool and aloof, hands-on practicality, unpretentious, ready for what happens	"Sees much but shares little" Warm and sensitive, unassuming, short-range planner, good team member, in touch with self and nature	"Performing noble service to aid society" Strict personal values, seeks inner order/peace, creative, nondirective, reserved	"A love of problem solving" Challenges others to think, absentminded professor, competency needs, socially cautious
Most pragmatic	Most artistic	Most idealistic	Most conceptual
ESTP	**ESFP**	**ENFP**	**ENTP**
"The ultimate realist" Unconventional approach, fun, gregarious, lives for here and now, good at problem solving	"You only go around once in life" Sociable, spontaneous, loves surprises, cuts red tape, juggles multiple projects/ events, quip master	"Giving life an extra squeeze" People oriented, creative, seeks harmony, life of party, more starts than finishes	"One exciting challenge after another" Argues both sides of a point to learn, brinksmanship, tests the limits, enthusiastic, new ideas
Most spontaneous	Most generous	Most optimistic	Most inventive
ESTJ	**ESFJ**	**ENFJ**	**ENTJ**
"Life's administrators" Order and structure, sociable, opinionated, results driven, producer, traditional	"Hosts and hostesses of the world" Gracious, good interpersonal skills, thoughtful, appropriate, eager to please	"Smooth-talking persuaders" Charismatic, compassionate, possibilities for people, ignores the unpleasant, idealistic	"Life's natural leaders" Visionary, gregarious, argumentative, systems planner, takes charge, low tolerance for incompetence
Most hard charging	Most harmonizing	Most persuasive	Most commanding

NOTE: I = introvert; E = extravert; S = sensor; N = intuitor; T = thinker; F= feeler; J = judger; and P = perceiver.

Source: Reproduced by special permission of the publisher, Consulting Psychologists Press, Inc., Palo Alto, CA 94303, from *Report Form for the Myers-Briggs Type Indicator* by Isabel Briggs Myers. Myers-Briggs Type Indicator and MBTI are registered trademarks of Consulting Psychologists Press, Inc. Further reproduction is prohibited without the publisher's written consent.

A second key researcher in this field was George Kelly (1955). He took a personal construct approach which has at its centre the individual and how he views his world; it is defined by Gross (1996) as a theory which 'attempts to understand the person in terms of his/her experience and perception of the world, a view of the world through the person's own eyes and not an observer's interpretation or analysis which is imposed on the person' (p. 761).

It is a very complex theory but is consistent in its detail and is believed by its disciples to be essential to the application of everything individuals do. Personal Construct Theory (PCT) is a formal and rather unusual theory of personality because it acts as a basic structure from which the clinical and other theoretical parts of the approach can be derived. It is an idiographic approach and a total psychology because it incorporates concepts which traditionally have their individual areas; for example, learning theory and emotion. The basis of PCT is the 'fundamental postulate' which, according to Dalton and Dunnett (1992), states that: 'A person's processes are psychologically channelized by the ways in which he anticipates events' (p. 1).

Since it is stated as a 'fundamental postulate' it has to be taken as true and is not open to question. Kelly (1953) focuses his theory on the individual as a whole, rather than any part of him/her, any group, or any particular behaviour. This holistic approach sees the individual as a complete entity. The PCT approach is *phenomenological* because it tries to understand the individual in the light of their experiences and their perception of their own world rather than through the eyes and perception of others. Kelly (1955) was unhappy with the views of Freud (1949) and the behaviourist theories, so his model was radical. He propounded the metaphor of *man the scientist* (now known as 'person the scientist') and believed that all people engaged in what is often considered to be the personal field of traditional scientists – making their own theories about the real world out there – instead of confining it to scientists *per se*.

It can be seen from this that Kelly's (1955) PCT is a philosophy rather than a theory of personality. Since he stated that it was necessary for individuals to have some understanding of the world they operate in psychologically, any assumptions made would be inaccurate: he was more explicit than other theorists about this, calling it *constructive alternativism*. Simply, this means that the individual's world is constantly changing and on the move and, therefore, the individual is constantly trying to get hold of that world but can only, at best, construct their own version of it. It is this huge range of alternative ways of construing (making sense of the same event) which makes Kelly's (1955) theory so fruitful.

Integrative

This approach takes a much broader and more integrative approach to the study of personality. Nelson and Quick (1994) define such an approach as 'a broad theory that describes personality as a composite of an individual's psychological processes' (p. 80).

In their work Byrne and Schulte (1990) believed that some of these characteristics include emotions, cognitions, attitudes, values and the tendency for an individual to respond to different situations in a similar way – *dispositions*. There are influences, such as genetics and experiences, on such dispositions which can, as a result of such influences, be modified. The integrative approach concentrates on the person (dispositions) and the situational variables and uses this summation to predict the behaviour of an individual.

As can be seen from the above discussion, personality theories differ from each other depending upon whether they are attempting to compare individuals in terms of a specified number of traits or dimensions which are common to everyone (nomothetic) or whether they are attempting to identify individuals' unique characteristics and qualities (idiographic). Gross (1996) classifies personality theories in this manner as can be seen from Figure 1.6 below.

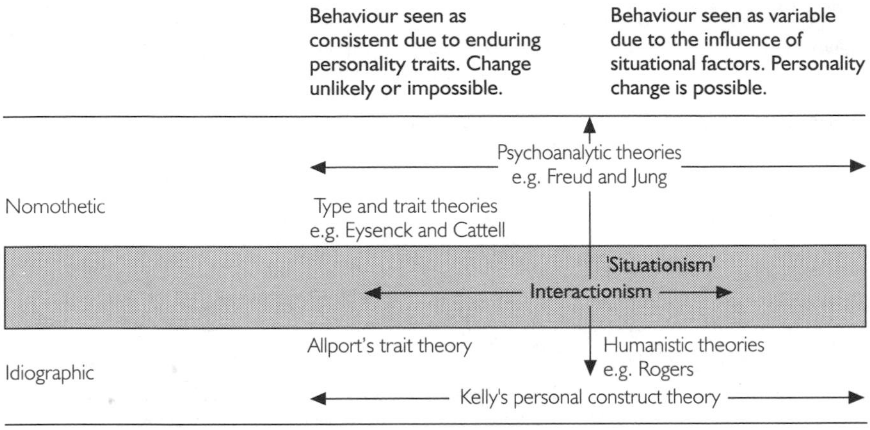

Figure 1.6 A classification of personality theories after Gross (1996, p. 745)

Personality and attitudes

It is very difficult to define attitudes because they embrace a complex amalgam of beliefs and feelings that an individual has about, for example, ideas, situations, and other people. Attitudes are yet another part of the way an individual is made up and although they are conceptually similar to personality attributes, they are quite different from them. As has been seen in our discussion above, personality attributes are shaped early in an individual's life and whilst there may be some attitudes which are also so shaped, there are others which can be formed and/or changed very quickly. It is through attitudes that individuals express how they actually feel. For example, when a manager says that she appreciates the way that her subordinates have worked in their teams, she is actually expressing an attitude about the way the organisation has tackled its structure and design.

Major personality attributes

In order that the goals of an organisation may be met, managers must learn as much as they can about personality, and as can be seen from the discussion of personality above there are numerous personality characteristics. However, there are a number (as indicated in Table 1.4 below, with a following discussion on each) which have a significant influence on how individuals behave in organisations.

Table 1.4 Major personality attributes

Personality attribute	Descriptor
Locus of control	The degree to which an individual believes that his or her behaviour impacts on the consequences of that behaviour.
Self-esteem	The level to which an individual feels that he or she is capable of doing a task or job.
Self-efficacy	An individual's beliefs and expectations about his or her ability to accomplish a specific task or job effectively.
Self-monitoring	The extent to which an individual compares his or her behaviour with clues given by other people and other situations.
Machiavellianism	An attribute of personality where an individual behaves in a way which is aimed at gaining power and controlling the behaviour of others.
Positive/Negative affect	*Positive affect*: where an individual emphasises the positive aspects of self, others, and the environment.
	Negative affect: where an individual emphasises the negative aspects of self, others, and the environment.
Risk propensity	The degree to which an individual is prepared to take chances and make risky decisions.
Authoritarianism	An individual who feels that differences in power and status are appropriate when linked to hierarchical systems such as organisations.
Dogmatism	Reflects the openness of an individual and the level to which he or she will take on board others' views and beliefs.

Locus of control is, according to Nelson and Quick (1994): 'An individual's generalized belief about internal control (self-control) versus external control (control by the situation or others)' (p. 80).

The key research in this area is that of Rotter (1966) who believed that individuals who perceive that they do have control of what happens to them have an internal locus of control, whereas those who think that circumstances or other people dictate their fate have an external locus of control.

Application of locus of control

You are a member of a team of four students who are producing a joint report on an Organisational Behaviour concept. Two members exhibit distinct behaviours as described below. How does their behaviour relate to their locus of control?

Marcia did not meet the agreed deadline for her contribution to the report and said that it was because the relevant information was not in the library and that she could not find the librarian to do the search for her.

Jack met his deadline and said it was because he worked hard at finding the information he wanted by seeking alternative sources of information.

You could say that because Marcia attributed the blame for not meeting her deadline to others, rather than to her lack of skill or to her poor performance, she exhibited an external locus of control.

However, Jack felt that he had met his deadline because he had control of his life and, unlike Marcia, did not lack ability or motivation and thus he exhibited an internal locus of control.

Johnson *et al.* (1984) believe that individuals who show an external locus of control should be encouraged to view their efforts as a determinant of outcomes as they relate to the task or job. That is, they should attempt to control it. Individuals with an external locus of control, according to Luthans (1988), will be reluctant to take the credit for a job well done and will often attribute success to another person's contribution or support.

Self-esteem

This is the degree to which individuals feel that they are worthy and deserving. If they have a high level of self-esteem they are more likely to aim for higher status tasks and jobs showing a high level of confidence in their ability. Their rewards are likely to be intrinsic to their performance and accomplishments. Individuals with a low level of self-esteem will exhibit the polar behaviours and will be content to remain at the bottom of the ladder and repeatedly question their own ability, with any rewards likely to be extrinsic rather than intrinsic. Self-esteem is very situational and so managers should do all they can to ensure that members of the workforce are in a position to raise their own level of self-esteem.

Self-efficacy

This is related to how individuals believe that they will effectively complete a task. Individuals who show a high level of self-efficacy believe that they not only have the ability and motivation to get things done but can also overcome any hurdles in their path to achievement. Such individuals draw on one or more of four sources of self-efficacy:

- prior experiences;
- modelling themselves on others who are perceived as successful;
- persuasion from others;
- assessment of personal competencies (physical and emotional).

The fact that an individual has a belief in self is a significant factor in achievement and can thus lead to a high level of performance. Managers can use empowerment and power-sharing to help an individual to increase his or her level of self-efficacy.

Self-monitoring

This is becoming a powerful personality characteristic in modern organisations as individuals attempt to base their behaviour on clues given to them by other people. An individual who operates a high self-monitoring policy is in tune with behaviours that are situationally appropriate, whereas those with a lower self-monitoring policy tend to act on their internal states rather than by monitoring the external environment. Research in this area is in its infancy but it is expected that individuals who have a high self-monitoring approach will tend to work well in high performance work teams and be enthusiastic contributors to situations which require individuals to be flexible.

Machiavellianism

This term in modern use describes any individual behaviour which is directed towards gaining power and controlling the behaviour of others. Christie and Geis (1970) cite research which suggests that such a trait varies from individual to individual. Individuals who are high in this trait tend to exhibit behaviours which are rational and unemotional, have a willingness to lie in order to attain their personal goals, and place little weight on loyalty and friendship. Some such individuals enjoy manipulating the behaviour of others. On the other hand, individuals with a low level of Machiavellianism tend to exhibit the opposite pole of descriptors.

Positive/negative effects

Positive/negative effects are a recently described personality characteristic and concentrate on the effects of persistent mood dispositions in the workplace. Individuals who have a positive effect tend to concentrate on the positive aspects of themselves, others, and the environment. Those who accentuate the negative are said to see the negative side of self, others, and the environment. In the workplace, both the positive and negative affect individuals but in totally opposing ways. Managers need to be able to turn the negative into the positive through, for example, participative decision-making.

Risk-propensity

Risk-propensity is the degree to which an individual is prepared to take chances and risks. A manager who tries out new ideas and gambles on new services or products would be in this category. Such an individual is useful for organisations in the ever-changing environment of the late 1990s and forthcoming millennium because he or she is a catalyst for innovation. A manager with a low propensity to take risks may keep the organisation stagnant, although by maintaining the status quo such a person might be useful in bringing calm to a troubled sea – a useful skill.

Authoritarianism

A person who behaves in an authoritarian way believes that power and status differences are appropriate within organisations which tend to be hierarchical. A manager who tends towards authoritarianism will take orders from a superior because of that person's role rather than accepting the orders while probably questioning them, which a non-authoritarian would do. Authoritarians tend not to sit comfortably in the flatter, delayered, team-working organisation because they are incapable of using the structure to empower individuals to take more responsibility for their work and behaviour.

Dogmatism

This is a personality characteristic which refers to the rigidity of an individual's beliefs and to the level of openness he or she has for the opinions and beliefs of others. In modern organisations these are referred to as *close-minded* and *open-minded*. A manager may be responsible for a certain activity within the organisation and would carry this out in a set manner. Being dogmatic, he or she will not be open to new ideas or amendments to procedures – even if such amendments would improve efficiency. Conversely, a less dogmatic manager would be open-minded and would listen to ideas from others, activating those which would enhance efficiency. As with authoritarianism, individuals who exhibit dogmatism find it difficult to be useful in the changing nature of organisations where open-mindedness is more important than closed-mindedness.

Measuring personality

CASE STUDY

The brain teasers

When Bill Castell, chief executive of Amersham International, the health sciences group, was looking for a new finance director, he turned, as usual, to a psychologist for advice. Before Andrew Allner was offered the job, the Guiness executive had to do more than demonstrate his competence with a spreadsheet and calculator.

Along with the other leading candidates, Allner had to face a panoply of assessments devised by Psycom International, one of the growing number of organisational psychologists working with Britain's top companies.

Allner, 42, like potential managers at companies such as Mars, United Biscuits, and Thorn EMI, faced a series of psychometric exercises that attempted to establish not only his intellectual capacity but his behaviour patterns and values, including his politics and spiritual beliefs. All of these ingredients were thrown into the melting pot before any conclusions were reached about the candidate's fitness for the job at Amersham.

Castell says: 'When I am trying to recruit, especially externally, I am trying to assess an individual on several different levels. I look at his or her integrity, morality and body language. I am also trying to sell my company and myself. So there is an awful lot going on, and I find it immensely helpful to get an analysis. It plays back to me, for example, whether the individual will ultimately stand up to a strong character such as myself, and be able to make a contribution.'

Allner performed well, not just on the psychological tests, but also on live case studies and a series of one-to-one interviews with Castell's fellow directors, as well as a consultant from Psycom. If Allner's psychological profile had raised too many concerns, he would not have landed the promotion he was seeking.

'I have discarded people because of that test,' says Castell.

Adapted from *The Sunday Times*, 'The brain teasers', Business Focus, 28 July 1996, p. 3.

The above case only touches the tip of the iceberg in the potency of psychometric testing as it particularly affects recruitment and selection. The term *psychometric testing* is often interchanged with the terms *occupational testing* and *psychological testing*. As the case shows, they are all sophisticated tools which can be used as tests to measure an individual's differences in a variety of areas which include intelligence and ability. The use of psychometric tests is not new, having been in existence for over fifty years, but their use has increased as the job selection process has become more and more sophisticated. This process has come about through the changing nature of work and its tasks and the rapid adoption of electronic information processing (EIP). As a consequence, psychometric testing has taken a higher profile within a large number of organisations such as National Westminster Bank, Halifax and Ford/Jaguar.

Fowler (1997) states that: 'Psychometric tests are often categorised as assessing either ability (cognitive tests) or personality' (p. 45); he goes on to state that they are divided into three principal types which test:

- *specific abilities* such as numeracy skills, verbal reasoning, and spatial perceptions;
- *general mental abilities or general intelligence* such as analytical reasoning and the ability to think critically;
- *psychometric questionnaires* such as general personality tests which are used to test, for example, specific personality traits (values, attitudes), interest preferences, learning styles, and whether the individual is a team player or not.

Psychometric tests are utilised in the workforce for a variety of purposes in a number of circumstances including:

- recruitment and selection
- high performance team building
- career counselling.

By means of psychometric tests carried out by qualified and trained facilitators, organisations can do a better job of selecting, developing and counselling members of the workforce. Such testers have banks of validated tests which can be used for all types of workers, such as salespersons, apprentices, computer programmers, technicians, graduates, and managerial staff. Currently, over 85 per cent of UK organisations use psychometric testing in an attempt to make the best use of their principal asset – the workforce. Organisations such as Barclays, ICL, ICI, Guardian Royal Exchange and Lloyds Bank all use psychometric testing in relation to the following issues:

- provision of a cost-effective solution to selection and promotion decisions including the monitoring of the quality, standards, and practices of such selection;
- provision of quality internal staff selection and promotion;
- improvement in the utilisation of current workforce members;
- identification of strengths and weaknesses which will help:
  (a) to bring about effective performance in a specific and relevant job
  (b) identify development training needs
  (c) improve promotion decisions
- operation of fair and positive assessment practices in line with Equal Opportunities legislation;
- comparing the abilities of applicants and the workforce with those of comparable organisations;
- potential for improvement in the profitability of the organisation by ensuring it has the right person in the right job.

Tests are designed mostly by occupational psychologists who provide them and the supporting documentation to evaluate the results, but only to those individuals who are trained and licensed to the competence level recommended by the British Psychological Society. It is more usual for organisations to use the services of agencies such as consultant occupational psychologists to facilitate the organisation's testing procedures. This is where the difficulties in the use of psychometric tests have arisen. According to Pickard (1996): 'The popularity of psychometrics has boomed over the past decade, but several tribunal cases over alleged discrimination have led to confusion' (p. 20).

Wood (1997) also takes up the key points raised by Pickard (1996) by stating that: 'Publishers of psychometric tests need to improve the twin pillars of validity and reliability if they are to be of help in [Human Resources]' (p. 32).

The theme of reliability and validity was also taken up by McHenry (1997) when he gave a speech at the British Psychological Society's occupational psychology conference; he stated that American psychometric tests are being used without modifying them for British consumption and that such a practice is 'at best risky, at worst discriminatory' (p. 32).

This banner was taken up by Kent (1997 (a) and (b)) who also reported the fact that most psychometric tests in the UK were designed for the USA and might not be suitable for use with UK staff. Both McHenry (1997) and Kent (1997 (a) and (b)) cite the same example when the statement, 'I very much like hunting', was answered 'True' by 70 per cent of American men, but by only 10 per cent of British men in a psychometric test adopted by a UK organisation.

During the 1940s a mother–daughter team became interested in the work of Carl Jung (1875–1961) and linked this with individual differences and similarities amongst individuals so as to produce the eponymous Myers–Briggs Type Indicator (MBTI) – discussed fully earlier in this chapter – which was a way of putting theory into practice. The MBTI is used extensively within organisations in an attempt to understand individual differences and has been used in career counselling, building high-performance work teams, management and the resolution of conflict.

The MBTI test labels people as extroverted (E) or introverted (I), sensing (S) or intuitive (N), thinking (T) or feeling (F), and perceiving (P) or judging (J). The use of the MBTI test can help to improve employee self-awareness and help managers to understand how they come across to others who may perceive them differently.

Understanding the MBTI test

What characteristics would you expect an INTJ to have?

Such persons would be 'visionary', being full of original thoughts and having a considerable intrinsic drive to carry out their own ideas and purposes. They would be sceptical, critical and independent with a determined and stubborn streak and they would tend to be practical and realistic, taking a matter-of-fact approach to things. Such persons would have a natural head for business because they enjoy organising and running everything.

How about the ENTP type?

This is a person who likes to conceptualise and who is very quick and ingenious, and has the ability to be good at all things. Such persons are resourceful and can solve challenging problems but they might overlook routine activities.

While the results of an MBTI test might well help to explain the behaviour of members of the workforce, however, the results might be due to the fact that behaviour is changed because someone is observing that behaviour (the 'Hawthorne effect'). The reasons for or against using such a test may well be irrelevant since its use does tend to improve employee productivity.

The MBTI test is increasingly being used in organisations and there is supporting evidence from research to show that the test has good reliability and validity as a measuring instrument for identifying type (Carlson (1985) and Murray (1990)). The types have been found to be related to other factors such as learning style, teaching style, choice of career, style of decision-making, and style of management. It is also increasingly being used to build high-performance teams and to build on members' strengths and to help individual members appreciate the differences between members.

There are a number of personality instruments which are in common use within organisations today and these are identified in Table 1.5 below.

Table 1.5 Major personality instruments in current use after Nicholson (1995, p. 4)

Measure	**Origins and use**	**Content**
16 PF	One of the first instruments designed by factorial statistical methods by Cattell in the 1950s. Still widely used in business.	16 Factors, encompassing the main dimensions of personality
MYERS-BRIGGS TYPE INDICATOR (MBTI)	Developed from a Jungian theoretical framework, it is unusual in placing respondents into an array of types rather than on continuous dimensions. Widely used in vocational applications.	16 types derived from 4 scales. Excludes "emotionality" but measures "Extraversion" and other factors.
EYSENCK PERSONALITY INVENTORY (EPI)	Pioneering measure with strong and varied research credential. More used in clinical than occupational settings.	Three dimensions assessed: Neuroticism (emotionality), Extraversion and Psychoticism.
OCCUPATIONAL PERSONALITY QUESTIONNAIRE (OPQ)	UK commercially developed suite of measures, with extensive business database norms. Unusual for focus on work relevant factors.	Varying numbers of factors measured by different scoring methods. Encompasses the main dimensions of personality plus some occupational variants.
THE CALIFORNIA PERSONALITY INVENTORY (CPI)	A classic US originating measure. Used in various management studies, but relatively little applied in the UK.	18 scales covering the main dimensions of personality and some less commonly measured factors.
THE NEO-PI	One of the most recently developed instruments, comprehensive in design with strong theoretical base and extensive research support.	Designed to represent the "Big Five" structure, with 6 subscales for each dimension, yielding 30 in all.

Integrity tests

There has been a development in the use of tests to recruit and select staff – especially honesty or integrity tests. This development is considered by some people to be pernicious. Such tests are designed to predict whether or not a member of the workforce is likely to engage in behaviour which is dishonest, or counter-productive to the interests of the organisation for which he or she works. The tests are designed to attempt to predict the chance of an individual carrying out, for example, one or more of the following activities:

- cheating
- low productive performance
- industrial sabotage
- stealing.

There are two types of integrity test: overt and personality. The former assesses an individual's attitudes and prior behaviour whilst the latter assesses personality characteristics that have been found to predict negative behaviour.

CASE STUDY

Study casts doubt on honesty tests

Integrity tests used by major firms have been accused of blocking the recruitment of some honest candidates. Many trustworthy people fail tests designed to screen out potential thieves or fraudsters during selection interviews, the annual Occupational Psychology conference heard last week.

Researcher Chris Moon told the conference that, in a recent study, nearly 60 per cent of honest people hired by a US supermarket failed an honesty test compared with 83 per cent of known thieves.

'These tests are not properly constructed and validated', said Moon. 'A street-wise person could fake an integrity questionnaire and honest employees have been known to fail integrity tests.'

He alleged that the tests either assume that risk-taking, free-thinkers will steal from their employer or rely on thieves being open about their dishonesty.

In the UK, retailer Peacocks, Shell-subsidiary City Petroleum, and Peugeot's logistics arm Gefco all use written honesty tests supplied by Permetrics at a cost of £25 per job candidate.

ATH-1 [Attitudes To Honesty] is based on a comparison of convicted prisoners' attitudes to theft or dishonesty and of those from a sample of the general public. Permetrics claims the test can predict poor timekeeping, disobedience, absenteeism, fraud and sabotage.

'Psychologists are sceptical about anything they think offers an easy solution to a difficult problem', said Permetrics director Victor McDonald. 'Not everyone can afford the money occupational psychologists charge.'

Source: 'Study casts doubt on honesty tests' in *Personnel Today*, 16 January 1997, p. 1

The above case highlights some of the difficulties faced by smaller organisations and the issues of reliability and validity discussed earlier in this chapter. However, it is a growing aspect of psychometric testing and, according to Kent (1997), tests to reveal a job applicant's criminal tendencies can exclude bad influences. He reports that experts are sceptical about such tests, and honest recruits, as documented in the case above, can lose out. Chris Moon, who reported as above, is researching into the use of integrity tests and his claim that tests actually block the recruitment of honest candidates has fuelled the scientific and ethical debate sparked off by such exercises. Kent (1997) believes that: 'To some extent, integrity testing is no different from any other form of psychometric testing. It requires the same sensitivity to each applicant's privacy and ensuring the information gathered contributes to an overview of an individual' (p. 32).

Yeung (1996) reported on the desire of individuals to attempt to achieve a stable level of existence; he highlighted the issue of mood-swings as shown in the case below.

CASE STUDY

Don't Be So Moody

Sweating is one of the physical correlates of being hot. But unlike body temperature, mood doesn't have a direct physical correlate, so if psychologists want to know how someone feels they need only ask.

To make it possible to get an objective snapshot of people's moods in different situations, psychologists have created tools such as the Profile of Mood States (often referred to as the POMS) and the State Anxiety Inventory. POMS and the State Anxiety Inventory are actually lists of adjectives such as 'resentful', 'cheerful', and 'peeved' that the people being studied are asked to rate according to how they feel at that particular moment. For example, 1 = 'very much', 2 = 'a bit', 3 = 'not at all'.

The mood questionnaires that are most widely used today are geared towards negative moods because they were originally designed to help pick up anxiety disorders and depression. Now, psychologists are coming up with a new breed of questionnaires – for example the Subjective Exercise Experiences Scale – that are designed to pick up positive mood swings.

Source: R. Yeung, 'Don't Be So Moody' in 'Racing to Euphoria', *New Scientist*, 23 November 1996, p. 29.

Nicholson (1995) states that:

> Personality measures tend to ... be overused in business as a selection tool on the naive assumption that they predict performance; they are under-used as an aid to self assessment and team building. Some measures are simply poor quality and badly administered. Well made tests, though, are hard to 'fake' because of the line of questioning with the underlying model difficult to discern and manipulate. (p. 4)

The way forward

Writing in 1995, Nicholson stated: 'In recent decades there has grown up a huge industry of personality measurement, bewildering in variety and usage, and increasingly used by business' (p. 2).

Things have escalated since Nicholson (1995) wrote his article yet his basic premise still stands: 'We need to understand how and why we differ in personality: to what ends can personality be measured and how can we use this knowledge in business?' (p. 2).

This means that it is necessary to understand the process of interpreting information about other people in the workplace – perception.

Questions for discussion

1 You have a student in your team who is a hard worker and comes from a disadvantaged background. Do you think it is fair to give her a higher than borderline grade because of this?

2 Which has the strongest impact on personality: heredity or environment? What about the situational issues?

3 How can potential employers attempt to assess the personality variables of applicants for a specific post?

References and further reading

Allport, G., 1961, *Pattern and Growth in Personality* (New York: Holt)

Allport, G. and Odbert, H.S., 1936, 'Trait names: A psycho-lexical study' in *Psychological Monographs: General and Applied* No 47 (Whole of No 211)

Bennett, R., 1997, *Introduction to Organisational Behaviour* (London: Pitman)

Buss, D.M. and Cantor, N. (eds), 'Neo-pi with Other Instruments' in *Personality Psychology: Recent Trends and Emerging Directions* (New York: Springer-Verlag) pp. 237–345

Byrne, D. and Schulte, L.J., 'Personality Dimensions as Predictors of Sexual Behavior' in J. Bancroft (ed.), *Annual Review of Sexual Research*, Vol. 1 (Philadelphia: Society for the Scientific Study of Sex, 1990)

Carlson, J.G., 'Recent Assessment of the Myers–Briggs Type Indicator' in *Journal of Personality Assessment* No 49, 1985, pp. 356–365

Cattell, R.B., 1973, *Personality and Mood by Questionnaire* (San Francisco: Jossey-Bass)

Christie, R. and Geis, F.J. (eds), 1970, *Studies in Machiavellianism* (New York: Academic Press)

Cramp, L., 'A test of character' in *People Management*, 5 December 1996, p. 21

Dalton, P. and Dunnett, G., 1992, *A Psychology for Living: Personal Construct Theory for Professionals and Clients* (Chichester: John Wiley)

Eysenck, H.J., 1965, *Fact and Fiction in Psychology* (Harmondsworth: Penguin)

Eysenck, M.W. and Keane, M.J., 1995, *Cognitive Psychology: A Student's Handbook* (Hove: Lawrence Erlbaum Associates)

Fowler, A., 'How to select and use psychometric tests' in *People Management*, 25 September 1997

Freud, S., 1949, *An Outline of Psychoanalysis* (New York: Norton)

Gross, R., 1996 (3rd edn), *Psychology: The Science of Mind and Behaviour* (London: Hodder & Stoughton)

Hellriegel, D., Slocum, J.W. and Woodman, R.W., 1995 (7th edn), *Organizational Behavior* (St Paul, MN: West Publishing)

Institute of Personnel and Development, 'Psychological Testing', in *Key Facts* (insert in *People Management*, 28 August 1997

Johnson, F., Luthans, F. and Hennessey, H.W., 'The Role of Locus of Control in Leader Influence Behavior' in *Personnel Psychology*, 1984, pp. 61–75

Jung, C.G., 1923, *Psychological Types* (New York: Harcourt & Brace)

Kelly, G.A., 1953, *The Psychology of Personal Constructs*, Vols 1 and 2 (USA, New York: Morton)

Kent, S., 'Mettle fatigue' in *Personnel Today*, 16 January 1997(a), pp. 24–25, 27

Kent, S., 'Criminal element' in *Personnel Today*, 16 February 1997(b), pp. 31–32

Kroeger, O. and Thuesen, J., 1981, *Typewatching Training Workshop* (Fairfax, VA: Otto Kroeger Associates)

Lewin, K., 1951, 'Formalization and Progress in Psychology' in D. Cartwright (ed.), *Field Theory in Social Science* (NewYork: Harper)

Luthans, F., 'Successful vs Effective Real Managers' in *Academy of Management Executive*, May, 1988, pp. 127–132

Luthans, F., Hodgetts, R.M. and Rosenkranz, S.A., 1988, *Real Managers* (Cambridge, MA: Ballinger)

McCrae, M., 1989, 'Why I Advocate the Five Factor Model: Joint Factor Analysis' in D.M. Buss and N. Cantor (eds), Personality Psychology: *Recent Trends and Emerging Directions* (New York: Springer Verlag), pp. 237–345.

Macdaid, G.P., McCaulley, H. and Kainz, R.I., 1987, *Myers-Brigg Type Indicator: Atlas of Type Tables* (Gainsville, Florida: Center for the Applications of Psychological Type)

McHenry, R., 'Tried and Tested' in *People Management*, 23 January 1997, pp. 32–34, 35, 37

Maddi, S.R., 1989 (5th edn), *Personality Theories: A Comparative Analysis* (Homewood, Ill: Dorsey)

Murray, J.B., 'Review of Research on the Myers–Briggs Type Indicator' in *Perceptual and Motor Skills*, No 70, 1990, pp. 1187–1202

Nelson, D.L. and Quick, J.-C., 1994, *Organizational Behavior: Foundations, Realities, and Challenges* (St Paul, MN: West Publishing)

Nicholson, N., 'The personality factor' in 'Mastering Management' insert No 8 in *Financial Times*, 16 December 1995, pp. 2–3

Pickard, J., 'The wrong turns to avoid with tests' in *People Management*, 8 August 1996, pp. 20–23, 25

Robbins, S.P., 1991 (5th edn), *Organizational Behavior: Concepts, Controversies, and Applications* (London: Prentice Hall International)

Rogers, C., 1970 (2nd edn), *On Becoming a Person: A Therapist's View of Psychotherapy* (Boston: Houghton Mifflin)

Rotter, J.B., 'Generalized Expectancies for Internal vs. External Control of Reinforcement' in *Psychological Monographs*, Part 80 in No 609, 1966

'Study casts doubt on honesty tests' in *Personnel Today*, 16 January 1997, p. 1

The Sunday Times, 'The brain teasers', Business Focus, 28 July 1996, p. 3

Walck, C., 'Training for Participative Management: Implications for Psychological Type' in *Journal of Psychological Type*, No 21, 1991, pp. 3–12

Watson, P., 'Diversity challenge' in *Personnel Management*, 1 May 1997, pp. 30–32

Wood, J.D., 'Culture is not enough' in 'Managing Across Cultures' in *Financial Times*, Mastering Management insert, 9 December 1995, pp. 2–4

Wood, R., 'Credibility, a tricky test for publishers' in *Personnel Today*, 13 February 1997, p. 19

Yeung, R., 'Don't Be So Moody' in 'Racing to Euphoria', *New Scientist*, No 2057, 23 November 1996, pp. 28–31

2 Perception

Learning objectives

After studying this chapter you should be able to:

- define what is meant by perception;
- understand the processes underlying perception;
- specify two underlying reasons why individuals may be biased in their perception of others;
- describe how an individual might unintentionally reinforce their first impressions of another individual;
- explain what is meant by impression management;
- analyse the key features of the attribution theory;
- assess the impact of perceptual processes on the way individuals see others;
- analyse the particular cases of gender and cross-cultural stereotyping.

Introduction

CASE STUDY

'Female lads' take on male tactics to score

Women under 30 are as assertive and as confident of their own abilities as men, a UK-wide study into leadership has discovered.

The gap between the sexes in the attributes traditionally needed to push people through to top management jobs has closed dramatically in just one generation, according to research by Oxford Psychologists Press. Compared with their grandmothers, or even their mothers, today's intake of female staff is more likely to boast, take risks and break rules to achieve their goals.

OPP's chairman, Robert McHenry, who has spent the past year analysing the responses of thousands of 'average' British workers to the CPI personality test, has come to the conclusion that the 'female lad' really does exist.

'These women are presenting themselves very much as their fathers – not their mothers – do', he said. 'To all intents and purposes, they view themselves as lads would.'

Equal opportunities groups are concerned about how the results have affected the careers of women over 30. The fact that the test measures self-perception, rather than skills, and that traditional leadership abilities such as independence and aggression are increasingly seen as outmoded, both point to the need for a radical overhaul.

All the questions are about women's perception of themselves, which is very complex. The only way some women have made it is to see themselves as one thing, and then present a different picture. Chris Burgess, policy development manager at the Equal Opportunities Commission, said the EOC would look into the findings of the research carefully. 'Basing selection purely on one's perception of self is dangerous – I would like to see colleagues or mentors also scoring candidates to get a true picture. And it is time social responsibility and caring started to score highly on management scales.'

Adapted from J. Welch, ' "Female lads" take on male tactics to score' in *People Management*, 12 June 1997, p. 16.

As can be seen from the above case, perception plays a significant part in understanding how people make sense of their own behaviour and that of others. In today's more dynamic and unpredictable environment, people working in organisations need to be able to absorb increasing amounts of information and make increasingly difficult and ever more responsible decisions. They need to be more proactive – reacting flexibly and creatively to new situations. How individuals perceive the complex world around them has never been so important as it is in today's ever-changing work environment. Similarly, in the modern world of team working and closer customer contact, how employees perceive others, whether within or outside the organisations, and are themselves perceived, has become ever more significant. This chapter investigates the various processes of perception and provides the necessary context for understanding communication and theories of learning which are considered in Chapter 3.

Understanding perception

According to Keuning (1998) perception can be defined as: 'the process in which individuals interpret sensory impressions, so that they can assign meaning to the environment' (p. 369).

Perception is an active psychological process through which an individual chooses stimuli and then organises them in a way which is meaningful to that same individual. Consequently it is a social process – it involves the way that individuals view the world around them using their five senses (taste, smell, hearing, touch, and vision); some would also argue that the sixth sense (intuition) is also part of the social perception process. Perception is made up of a number of different processes because individuals receive information in many different forms from the senses – spoken word, visual images or movement and shapes. Therefore, it is through the perceptual processes that the individual assimilates the varied types of incoming information for the purpose of interpreting it. It is through social perception that individuals start to understand themselves and their surroundings.

However, there is a distinction between perception and sensation. An individual's senses continually receive information from the outside world and in order to make sense of such sensory information it needs to be sifted, ordered and interpreted. Perception is this active process of interpretation and without such a process, sensation would be overwhelming, chaotic and meaningless. Perception is, therefore, both a barrier and a gateway to the rich but bewildering world of sensory experience. It blocks, orders and processes into patterns which an individual can cope with and understand.

The process of perception

Perception comprises two key features:

- reception and selection
- organising and interpreting information

which are shown *in situ* in Figure 2.1 below.

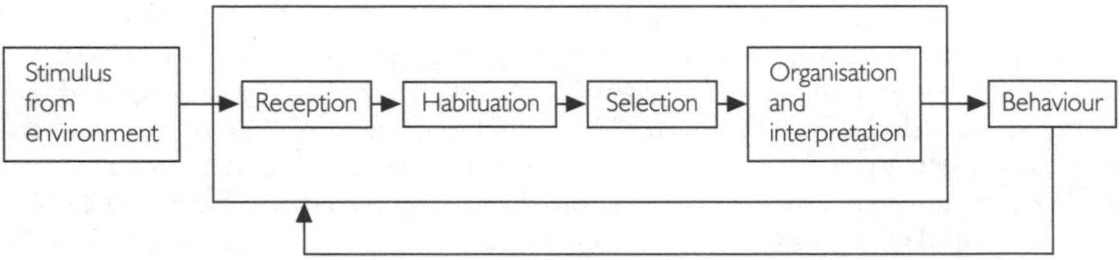

Figure 2.1 The process of perception

Reception and selection

In the first stage of perception, an individual receives external sensory information. Even at this early stage there is a process of selection determined, for example, by the physical limits or thresholds of the individual's senses and their capacity to respond to them. Noises that are too high or too low in pitch or volume to be heard, for example, will not be registered.

The second stage sees the individual only able to focus for any length of time on a small range of the vast array of surrounding sensory information. A member of the workforce automatically filters out much of the background noise around her, for example. If a sound is familiar, constant and unobtrusive, such as the droning of a computer systems box, she will fail to register it unless, for example, it stops, in which case she may react to the change. This familiarisation process is known as *habituation* and is the decrease in response to familiar stimuli. Through habituation an individual raises her perceptual threshold to exclude a potential overload of stimuli so that she can concentrate on what she considers to be more important at the time and thus disregard what is familiar to her. It can be seen as one form of *selective attention*.

Selective attention is the ability – which is often unconscious – to select and concentrate on certain sensory data whilst screening out other data. Such a process of reception and selection will be influenced by both internal and external factors as shown in Figure 2.2 on page 33.

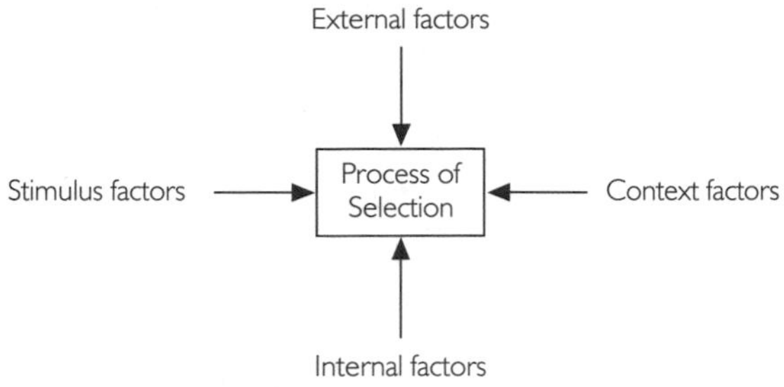

Figure 2.2 The process of selection

If other stimulus factors are all considered, attention is drawn to data which are presented more vividly than others. Individuals tend to notice, for example, things that are:

moving	rather than	static
large	rather than	small
bright	rather than	dull
loud	rather than	quiet
repeated	rather than	one-off
unfamiliar	rather than	familiar
interrupted	rather than	regular
contrasted	with their	background.

What an individual selects will also be influenced by its context. For example, she may not consciously notice a dog in a street under normal conditions. Yet, if she has been told a rabid dog is on the loose, she is much more likely to perceive any dog that comes into view!

Any selection will also be influenced by internal factors. As an example, if a member of the workforce is hungry, he is more likely to be aware of appetising smells emanating from the organisation's restaurant than when he is not hungry. If an individual has a deadline to meet, he may be more aware of a ticking clock. All individuals will pick up on the importance of such internal psychological factors in what is perceived and this is discussed in detail in this chapter.

Organising and interpreting information

Habituation is only one of the processes by which individuals not only select but begin to organise and interpret information internally, screening out what is regarded as significant from the mass of sensory data around them. A number of others have been identified by the Gestalt School of psychology led by Max Wertheimer (1880–1943). *Gestalt* is a German word meaning 'shape', 'form' or 'organised whole'. The word is used to describe an object of perception – a pattern or form – where the properties of the whole cannot adequately be deduced from an understanding of the sum of the properties of the individual elements that constitute that object. In other words, a 'factory' is more than just a collection of bricks, cement and doors. Gestalt theory has six key principles of organisation:

- figure-ground
- grouping/proximity
- closure
- similarity
- continuity and symmetry
- part–whole relationship.

Figure-ground

The figure-ground principle focuses on the way in which individuals distinguish objects by contrasting them with the background in which they are placed. A classic example is that of the Rubin vase (circa 1915) which is shown in Figure 2.3 below.

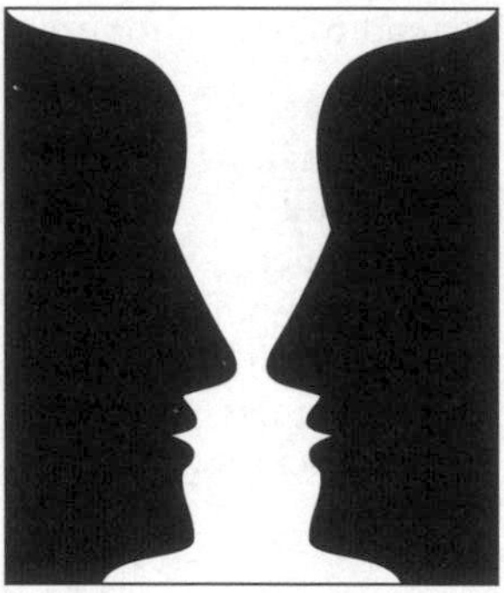

Figure 2.3 The Rubin vase

Depending on whether a person interprets the white or black as background, the image shows either a white vase or the silhouettes of two people facing each other – it is reversible. When the vase is the focus of attention, the black profiles constitute the ground and when attention is given to the profiles, the vase becomes the ground.

Grouping/proximity

The grouping or proximity principle focuses on an individual's inherent tendency to understand and organise sensory information through patterns based on his or her proximity in space or time. Any parts of a picture or a figure which are seen to be close together (either in space or in time) are generally perceived by an individual as being 'together'. Looking at the lines in Figure 2.4(a), an individual is likely to perceive it as four pairs of parallel lines. Similarly, Figure 2.4(b) would be seen as a group of four dots, followed by a group of three dots, then a pair of dots and, finally, a single dot.

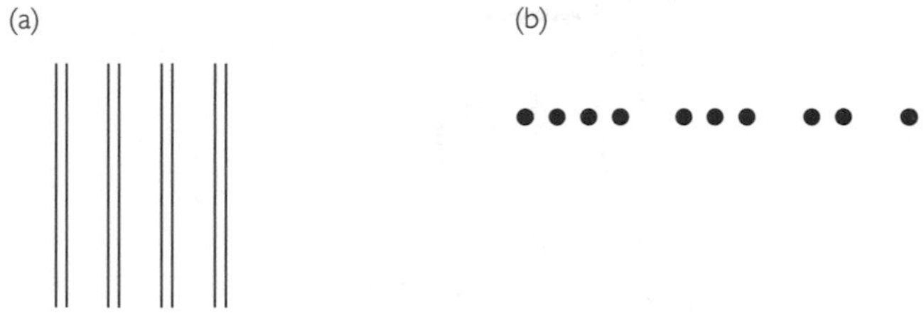

Figure 2.4 Example of grouping/proximity

Closure

The closure principle demonstrates another way in which individuals seek to impose order and meaning in their life. If they see something incomplete or apparently arbitrary, there is an inherent tendency to impose a meaning or order by mentally filling in the gaps. Some examples are given in Figure 2.5 below.

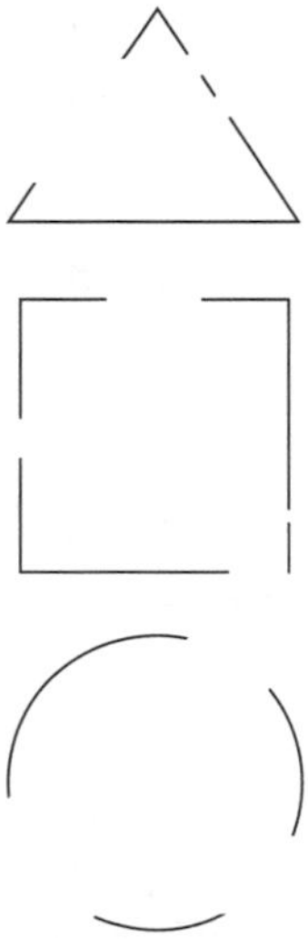

Figure 2.5 Examples of closure

Here an individual will tend to identify any signs of a pattern suggested by the lines and complete them, in this case identifying a triangle, a square, and a circle. Individuals will usually close any incomplete figures in order to make sense of what they actually see. Closed figures are much easier to perceive than partial or incomplete ones. Another example of this was posited by Morgan and King (1966), as shown in Figure 2.6 below, where an individual will be likely to complete the pattern to see a number thirteen or the letter B.

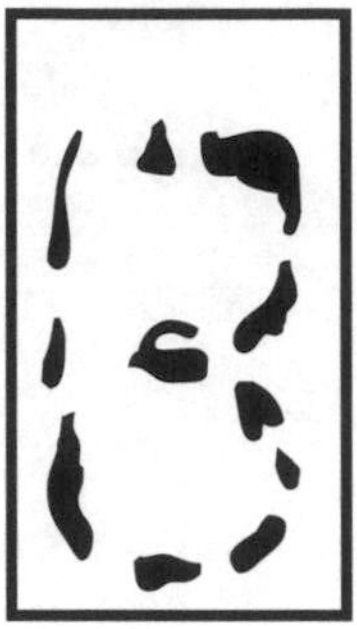

Figure 2.6 Closure after Morgan and King (1966)

Similarity

Individuals tend to perceive similar parts together as forming a familiar group. Gross (1996, p. 220) gives an example using patterned dots and crosses, as can be seen in Figure 2.7 below.

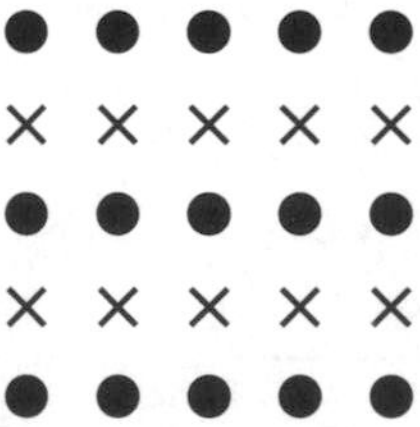

Figure 2.7 Example of similarity

By looking at the pattern above, an individual will probably see alternating rows of dots and crosses (rather than columns of dots and crosses intermingled).

By rotating the diagram on to its side, it is more likely that an individual will see columns of dots alternating with columns of crosses.

Continuity and symmetry

People tend to see similar parts of a figure which looks as though it is in straight or curved lines but only when, in total, their shapes are recognisable to the perceiver. As can be seen in Figure 2.8(a) on page 37, the crosses are seen as making up a square rather than as twelve individual crosses. Again, as in Figure 2.8(b), a circle rather than twelve crosses is usually seen.

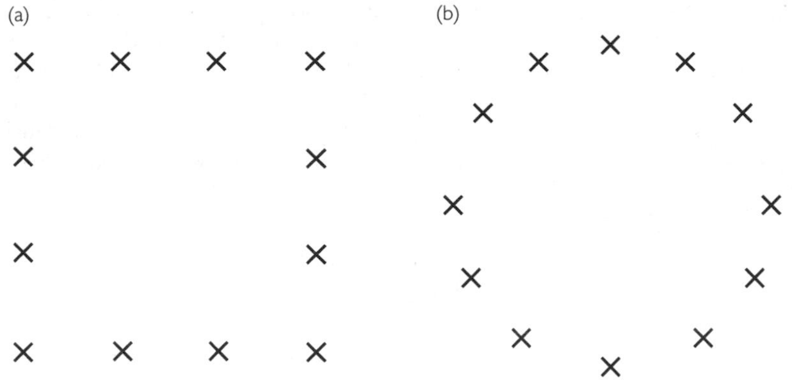

Figure 2.8 Examples of continuity and symmetry

Part–whole relationship

This is the principle of the Gestalt view that the whole is greater than the sum of its parts; it is illustrated in Figure 2.8(a) and Figure 2.8(b) above in that each pattern comprises twelve crosses but the gestalts are different even though the parts are similar. The latter are determined principally through proximity, and continuity and symmetry.

Perception and reality

The work of the Gestalt School and others, such as Vernon (1955), has shown that the process of perception consists of a complex and continuous dialogue between the sensory data received and the tools brought to bear in interpreting it. Much of the process is unconscious and it means that any view of the world will always be a selective one, mediated by the interpretative framework people use to make sense of it. In many ways, people do not perceive reality but only a selected interpretation of it.

PARIS IN THE THE SPRING

This interpretative framework can prevent individuals from perceiving what is really there and can be illustrated by a simple example. As you were reading this text you will have glanced at the phrase in the box above. Most people do not consciously spot the fact that the word 'the' is repeated. They will automatically have corrected the error to create a meaningful sequence of words. Their performance of reality will have been distorted, in this case constructively, by the unconscious application of an internalised set of rules, in this example those of grammar, to create a meaningful pattern.

This example also shows that the way individuals perceive is also something which is learned – it is a social construct. In this case, the perception of the phrase with the extra 'the' will be determined by our understanding of the rules of grammar. If these have not been learnt, then individuals may well not spot the repeated pattern of letters though they will be able to read the phrase itself. Similarly, individuals tend to learn to use certain inherited categories to order and interpret their perceptions. People tend to use the term 'male' in the same way to identify a person with a commonly accepted set of physical characteristics, in contrast to 'female' for example, or the term 'car' to identify a particular category of machine. If all people came from a society without 'cars', no one would understand the term – and would therefore have to learn this way of categorising this aspect of a particular experience.

In most of the above examples, the ways that reality is perceived are common to the majority of people, all of whom tend to use figure-ground distinctions, group, closure, proximity, similarity or continuity and symmetry principles. However, as can be seen, in the example of the term 'male', differences in the way the world is perceived have begun to arise among individuals. Whilst all might agree on the physical attributes which distinguish male from female, individuals might have very different views on what being 'male' or 'female' is – depending on, for example, the cultural background, and on individual attitudes and experience.

Perceptual interpretation

There are three key parts to the successful perceptual interpretation of information:

- characteristics of the perceiver (P)
- characteristics of the target (T)
- characteristics of the situation (S).

Characteristics of the perceiver (P)

Virtually all management activities rely on perception and there are several characteristics of the perceiver which may well affect such social perception:

- familiarity
- attitudes
- mood
- self-concept
- cognitive structure.

Familiarity

Familiarity is about relationships with the individual being perceived – the target. When individuals are familiar with another person, they have multiple observations upon which to base their impressions of that other person. If accurate information is gathered it is likely that the perception of the target is also accurate. However, familiarity is not always equated with accuracy because, on occasions, when the perceiver and the target know each other well, an individual will be likely to filter out any information that is inconsistent with what they perceive that the person is like. An example in the workplace would be appraisal when the appraiser and the appraisee are familiar with each other.

Attitudes

Attitudes affect a perceiver's perceptions of another person. For example, if an individual is interviewing internal candidates for a promotion and if the job specification of the new appointment requires the individual to, say, collect outstanding debts from customers, the interviewer may perceive that 'male' characteristics such as being aggressive, decisive and competitive are important and this may affect the interviewer's attitude to the female candidates being interviewed.

Mood

Forgas and Bower (1987) believe that mood plays an important part in the way individuals are perceived by others. Individuals who are in a happy mood think differently about others than when they happen to be miserable. There is a further input by mood into the process of perception when an individual receives information which is consistent with their mood state. For example, if a manager is in a happy and positive mood she will form more positive impressions of those around her. Conversely, when she is in a negative and unhappy frame of mind, the manager will tend to evaluate others unfavourably.

Self-concept

An individual's self-concept forms a key part of the social perception process because, for example, when an individual has a positive self-concept he will perceive the same in others. Conversely, if the same manager has a negative self-concept, he will perceive these negative traits in others. Therefore, a manager who has a deep understanding of himself will be able to perceive others more accurately.

Cognitive structure

Cognitive structure refers to an individual's pattern of thinking. Some individuals concentrate their perceptions of others on physical attributes such as physical appearance, height and weight, whilst others tend to focus on the more central personality dispositions. The more complex the cognitive structure of an individual, the greater the ability of that individual to perceive the multiple characteristics of another person rather than attending to just a few narrow personality traits.

Characteristics of the target (T)

In all situations, including the workplace, the characteristics of the person being perceived – the target – influence social perception. The key characteristics are:

- physical appearance
- communication skills
- intentions of the target.

The first thing an individual sees of another person is their *physical appearance*: what they are wearing. Clothing is a key indicator about an individual; colours, for example, affect the entire perception of another individual. For example, in an interview, a candidate dressed conservatively and smartly is more likely to be taken more seriously than an individual dressed in torn jeans and a dirty T-shirt. However, there are other criteria to be taken into account here; for example, the situation may demand that the candidate has to show their expertise in a task which is, by its very nature, dirty, thus requiring suitable attire.

Individuals who are perceived as physically attractive also face such stereotypical attitudes (discussed in detail later in this chapter). For example, often a petite, visually attractive, blonde female is labelled a 'bimbo' and an overweight person as inherently 'idle'.

The *communication skills* (verbal and non-verbal) of the target will affect the perceiver's view of them. For example, such factors as tone, dialect, accent and the very topics they speak about, will allow the perceiver to make judgements about the target. Also, the body language of the target sends cues to the perceiver – how the target is sitting, moving their arms, for example. Such issues are discussed in more detail in the next chapter.

The *intentions of the target* are important because the target's behaviour is observed by the perceiver. For example, a member of a project team may, when she sees the project team leader, think 'Here comes more work for me' or 'Here comes Jim to thank us for the work we have done'. Whatever the perceiver's interpretation of the target it will always affect the way that the perceiver views the target.

Characteristics of the situation (S)

This is a key factor in the perception process because the *situation* influences the perceiver's view of the target. The social context of the situation has a major influence on the social perception process. For example, a subordinate may be used to seeing his manager only in the workplace which generates certain behaviour characteristics, yet when this same manager is seen at a nightclub – with its associated behaviour characteristics – the subordinate as the perceiver gains a different impression of the manager. Additionally, there is a consideration of the strength of the situational cues. Some situations give very strong cues as to what is appropriate behaviour. In the previous example, it can be assumed that the manager's behaviour in the workplace is accounted for by the situation – the fact that he is *at work* and, the behaviour of the same person in the nightclub is because he is *at the nightclub*. The perceiver, therefore, assumes that the behaviour of the individual can be explained by the situation rather than the personality of the person being perceived.

Heider (1958) called this latter concept the *discounting principle*. An example in the workplace might be when the team leader asks a member of the team about his interests and hobbies in a way that seems to show genuine interest. Actually, the team leader treats all members of her team in the same way and is probably trying to get something from the target.

Individual perceptual set

The role of individual experience introduces another dimension into the nature of perception and lies at the very heart of perception being an active rather than a passive process. Added to the basic process of perception which all people tend to share are layers of internal influences which make individuals perceive the world in their own unique way. This is known as a *perceptual set*.

Allport (1995) believed that a perceptual set was a tendency by individuals to perceive only certain aspects of what they see and to ignore all others. It is composed of an individual's personal image or map of the physical and social world around them. Through their perceptual set an individual tends to receive, select, order and interpret the world according to their own unique background, experiences and assumptions. Figure 2.9 shows the influences at work in an individual's perceptual set.

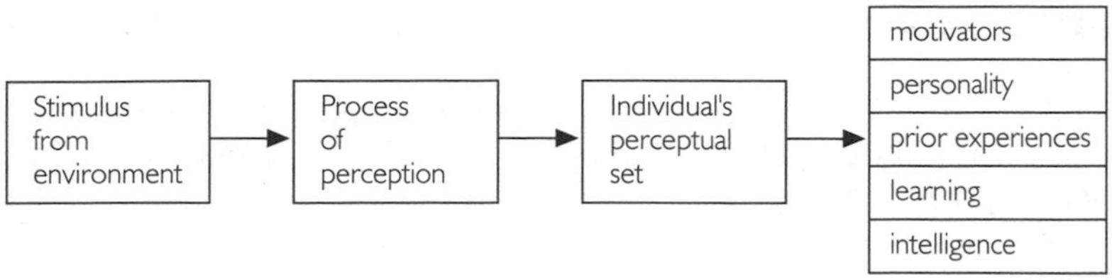

Figure 2.9 The individual's perceptual set

On a surface level are the particular needs and motives with which a person encounters a particular stimulus. If angry or upset, for example, they may interpret the behaviour of another very differently than if they were feeling happy and confident. If the former, they may interpret someone's question as threatening, intrusive or obstructive; if the latter, they might see it as supportive and constructive.

On a deeper level, a person's personality and past experience will shape how they perceive the world. Someone educated to dislike foreigners, and with little experience of people from other countries, will perceive someone from another country very differently than would another person with a different background and education. Similarly, as has been previously seen, individuals from and indeed within different societies or cultures may have quite different notions of what being 'male' or 'female' entails.

Individuals' intelligence, and the degree to which they may reflect on and analyse what they perceive, will also determine how they understand and react to a particular stimulus. Particularly, it will influence how far they may question their initial assumptions. A simple example of that process of questioning has already been encountered in the figure-ground example. Whilst a person may start by seeing only one of the images, most people quickly learn how to see both, demonstrating a dynamic response to perception. Similarly, the ability to reflect on a broadening range of experience may well lead someone to question the role models for males and females that they had initially been taught.

Perceptual set works, according to Vernon (1955), in two ways. Firstly, it is a *selector*, where the individual has expectations which helps them to focus their attention on specific sensory stimulation being inputted. Secondly, it is an *interpreter*, where the individual knows what to do with the input received and goes on to process the data, classifying it, understanding it and drawing inferences from it.

Whilst all people share similar ways of perceiving the world in many areas, perceptions of self, the world and others may differ very significantly from those of colleagues. Therefore, communication becomes a more complex and difficult process.

Individual perceptual sets mean that individuals tend to select only information that fits the existing patterns and expectations brought to bear in making sense of the world, and so information that does not seem to fit is filtered out. The result is that a person's understanding of the world will always be partial and may even, in some circumstances, be profoundly inadequate.

Since much of the process is unconscious, and because individual perceptual sets are so deeply embedded, it can be very difficult to detect and resolve the limitations in the perception of the world – the process of learning thus becomes more complex.

Perceptual paradox

These implications have given rise to the concept of the *perceptual paradox* which stems from the fact that individuals bring a host of prior assumptions and expectations to the process of perception. Individual perceptual sets provide a necessary framework for selecting, organising and interpreting experience, and without them there would be no benchmarks against which to measure and understand perceptions. However, they may also serve to distort and limit what is perceived and how it is interpreted. Perceptual sets may set up strong barriers against experience which challenges key values and the strength of these barriers is dependent on the degree to which those perceptual sets sustain the fundamental sense of identity and meaning. Experience which threatens this fundamental sense of self is more likely to be ignored or rejected.

Perception in action: how individuals see others

The process of perception in action is in the different ways individuals perceive people. The process of perceiving others is very complex. Such a process is shown in Figure 2.10 below.

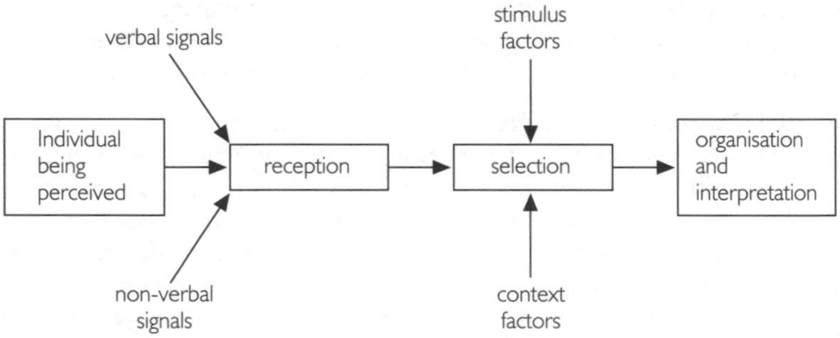

Figure 2.10 The process of perceiving others

In the reception phase, individuals are influenced by a wide range of verbal and non-verbal signals. Whilst what is said is important, how it is said can be even more so. Messages about our feelings and attitudes are usually communicated in the following way:

- 7% from the words individuals use (verbal)
- 38% from the accent, tone, etc of voice used (paralanguage)
- 55% from body language (kinesics).

This range of verbal and non-verbal information can be further divided into two types:

- static (information which generally remains constant in any encounter)
- dynamic (information which may change during the encounter).

Static information includes such things as:

- gender
- age
- height

- ethnicity
- accent.

All of this data, much of it unconsciously absorbed, provides a pattern of clues from which individuals then select, order and interpret. However, before even that process begins, stimulus and context factors will influence what is perceived and how selection is activated.

Once individuals have selected the range of data that arises from an encounter with another person, they unconsciously sift through and order it into a set of assumptions about that individual which immediately colours how they react to them and interpret their words and actions. This entire process is dynamic. Perception of another colours an individual's response to that person. They will go through the same process of perception and response, providing a completely new set of data to deal with, confirming the original response. Gurcham (1995) illustrates this as shown in Figure 2.11 below:

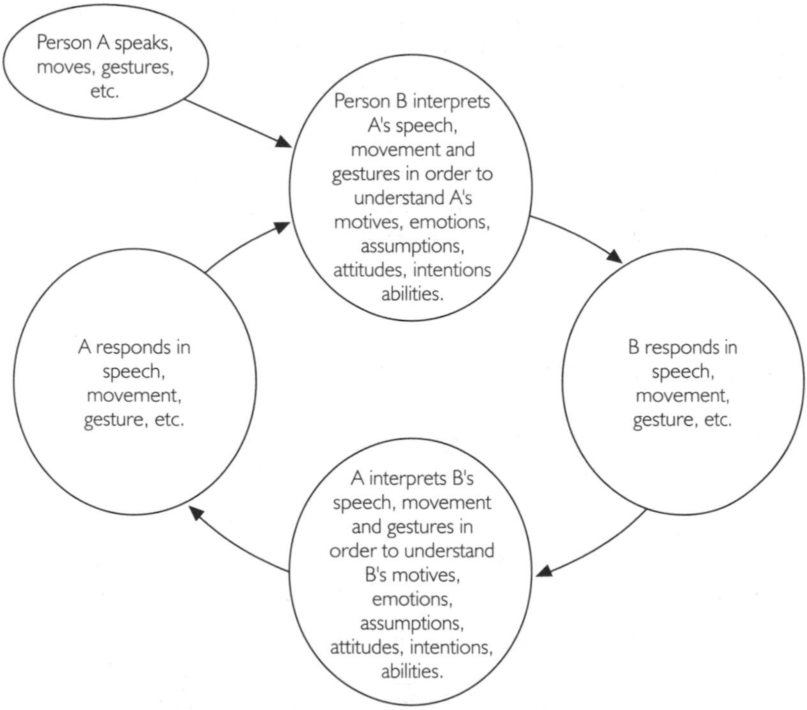

Figure 2.11 The process of perception and response after Gurcham (1995)

However, first impressions may be decisive in what is subsequently selected and how it is interpreted: how the relationship with another person then develops and the longer-term assumptions about them. These first impressions are usually described through the concept of the *primacy effect*. As an example, studies suggest that information heard first is less likely to be contradicted by information received later. It has also been shown that a negative first impression is more difficult to change than a positive one. The complex range of signals perceived and the importance of the primacy effect has given rise to the study of *impression management*.

Impression management

This is the process of managing people's images of another person and it emerged in the late 1950s. It seeks to improve awareness of the range of unconscious as well as conscious, non-verbal as well as verbal, signals given to others and how they might be consciously managed to create the right impression. Through impression management individuals will attempt to control the impression which others have of them. It is normal for an individual to want to make a favourable impression on others. This is particularly so in the workplace where a positive work environment depends on competition for jobs, positive task performance and performance-related pay or salary increases. Giacolone and Rosenfeld (1990) reported that individuals use several techniques in order to control the impressions which others have of them.

One of these key techniques is that of *self-enhancing* where the individual focuses attention on enhancing others' impressions of the person using the technique. Examples here would be name dropping, managing one's appearance, and descriptions of self. As to whether such techniques are effective, it has been found that those who use such techniques tend to perform better and are more likely to gain higher ratings related to their work performance. Rafaeli and Pratt (1993) reported that the attributes of dress such as colour, style, and material do influence the image that others have of the organisation for which the person being perceived works. Therefore, impression management has potential advantages for both the individual member of the workforce and the organisation itself.

Ordering perceptions of others

A previous section investigated ways people receive and select information about others. As has been seen, individuals then bring their own attitudes, experiences and assumptions – their individual perceptual sets – to bear on how they then organise and interpret this information. How this process works, the way it relates to defending a person's core values and hence sense of self, and how this can limit what we perceive and how we can be seen, are what is known as *projection* – or what is more correctly called *assumed similarity*.

Projection/assumed similarity is the process of projecting an individual's feelings and attitudes onto another person. It occurs, for example, when individuals view others favourably because they seem to reflect their own individual attitudes and characteristics. For example, someone with a strong sense of regional identity may favour others with the same regional accent, and will assume that they have all the favourable characteristics that he associates with that regional identity and with himself. He will tend to highlight those characteristics that fit his expectations while screening out others that do not. It can also spring from individuals exaggerating traits in others which they repress in themselves. A repressed homosexual, for example, may be the first to look for, and stigmatise, apparent signs of homosexuality in others. A failing manager may regard her subordinates as incompetent as a way of coping with her own inadequacy. Freud (1949), for example, identified projection as a defence mechanism – which is an unconscious response; in the case of the poor manager, displacing feelings of inadequacy onto others.

Attribution theory

Moorhead and Griffin (1995) state that the attribution theory 'suggests that we observe behavior and then attribute causes to it' (p. 68). It is thus the process of interpreting the world through an individual's perceptions of causality.

Attribution theory was developed separately in the 1950s and 1960s by Heider (1958) and Kelley (1971). They argued that individuals attempt to structure their experiences of the world by looking at the causes behind events; that is, people try to explain why others behave as they do. In doing so, they suggested that individuals tend to discriminate between internal causality (the power of individuals to influence events) and external causality (the power of environmental factors to determine events). In doing so, individuals thus tend to attribute causes in a way which supports a sense of self. As a result there is a tendency to attribute personal success to internal factors and failure to external causes, whilst making the opposite diagnosis of the success or failure of others – as discussed under *self-serving bias* later in the chapter.

In making these attributions, Kelley (1971) argued that individuals tend to use three basic criteria:

- *Distinctiveness*. How different is the behaviour in question from the usual pattern for the individual in question? Moorhead and Griffin (1995) described this as 'the extent to which the same person behaves in the same way at different times' (p. 68). Put another way, whether the problem in performance is unique to a particular task or person or whether it is apparent in other aspects of the whole job.
- *Consensus*. How similar is that behaviour to the behaviour displayed by most other individuals in these circumstances? Moorhead and Griffin (1995) state this as being 'the extent to which the other people in the same situation behave in the same way' (p. 68). It is about how widespread a behaviour is within an organisation.
- *Consistency*. Is the behaviour typical of the individual or an exceptional act? Moorhead and Griffin (1995) believed this to be 'the degree to which the same person believes in the same way at the same time' (p. 68). That is, the frequency of the performance.

Kelley (1971) suggested that individuals typically attribute behaviour to internal forces when they perceive low distinctiveness, low consensus and high consistency, and to external forces when behaviour is seen as having high distinctiveness, high consensus and low consistency. These links are shown in Figure 2.12 below:

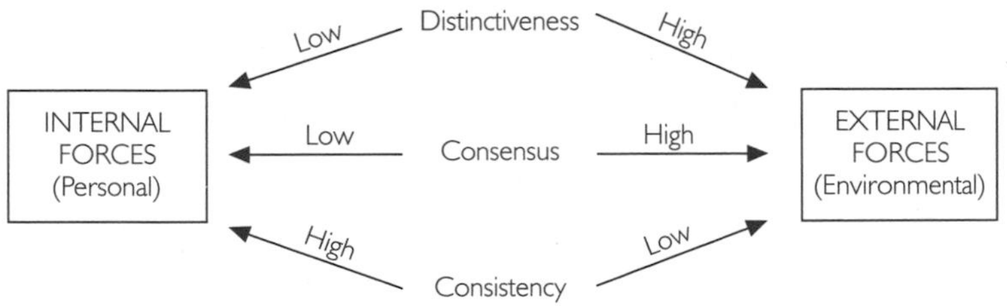

Figure 2.12 The attribution theory

An additional consideration in assessing performance is whether the behaviour was due to 'stable' or 'unstable' factors:

- stable factors such as ability, complexity of the task;
- unstable factors such as degree of effort needed, or luck.

Combining stable/unstable with internal/external attributions provides a model for explaining performance as shown in Table 2.1 below.

Table 2.1 Attributes of stable and unstable factors

Factors	**Internal attributions**	**External attributions**
Stable factors	Ability	Task difficulty
Unstable factors	Effort	Luck

Individuals form attributions based on whether the cues (consensus, distinctiveness, and consistency) are either low or high. Figure 2.13(a) and (b) below examples how the combination of such cues can help managers to form decisions on internal or external attributions.

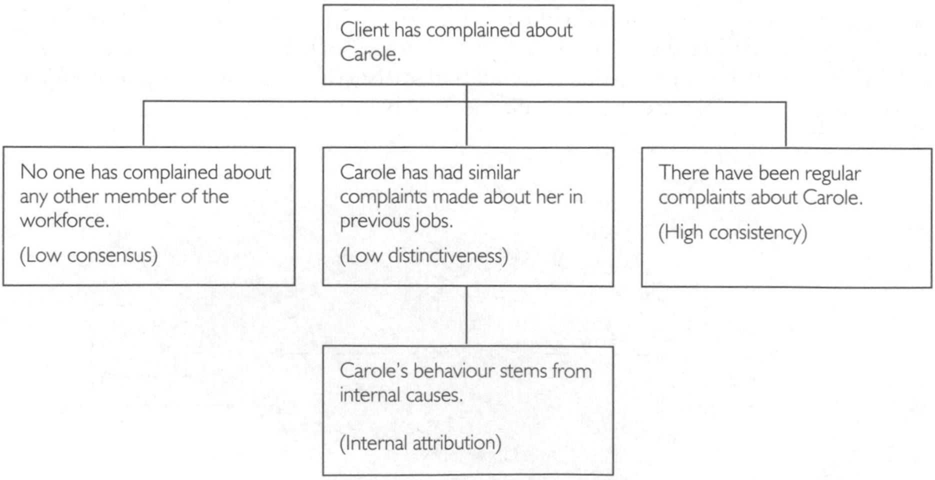

Figure 2.13 (a) Example of internal attribution

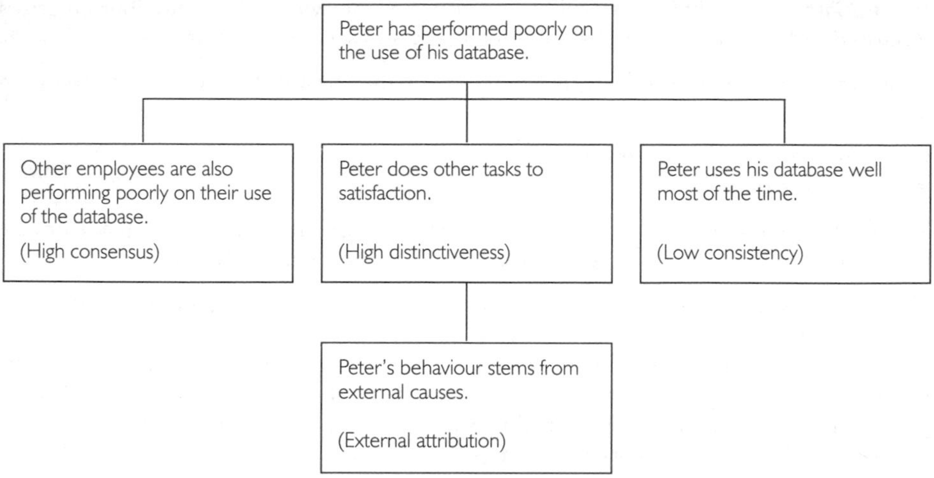

Figure 2.13 (b) Example of external attribution

Using the example given in Figure 2.13(a) above, suppose a complaint has been received from a client about Carole. She is the only person clients have complained about (low consensus). When looking at Carole's personnel records, it is noted that she was the subject of similar complaints in her previous job (low distinctiveness). The complaints have been coming in steadily and regularly for six months (high consistency). In the case of Carole, a manager would be likely to make an internal attribution and come to the conclusion that the complaints must come from the way that Carole is behaving. This combination of low consensus, low distinctiveness and high consistency leads to internal attributions.

However, as is shown in Figure 2.13(b) above, other cue combinations produce external attributions. For example, high consensus, high distinctiveness, and low consistency produce external attributions. For example, Peter is not using his database accurately. Upon investigation, the team leader finds that such poor performance is universal within the team (high consensus), and that for most of the time Peter carries out his database functions well (low consistency). The team leader will decide that something about the work situation itself caused the poor performance – perhaps all members of the team have too much work to do (work overload), too little to do (work underload) or the deadlines are too tight and impossible to achieve.

On the basis of the above information, a manager will make either an internal (personal) attribution or an external (situational) attribution. Internal attributions might include such behaviour as low effort, lack of commitment, and lack of ability. The external attributions are outside the control of the subordinate and could well include such items as failure of equipment or goals which are unrealistic.

The manager must then decide on the source of the responsibility for the lack of performance and try to correct the problem. In doing so, he can choose from a wide range of responses including an expression of personal concern, subordinate reprimand or the provision of training. Those managers who attribute the cause of poor performance to a person (an internal cause) will respond more harshly than managers who attribute the cause to the work situation (an external cause).

It is important that managers avoid using either of the two common attribution errors discussed earlier – fundamental attribution error, and self-serving bias.

When an individual uses the attribution theory he may be affected by two very common errors:

- fundamental attribution error
- self-serving bias.

The *fundamental attribution error* operates when the individual has a tendency to make attributions to internal causes when focusing on another person's behaviour.

The tendency to attribute one's own successes to internal causes and one's failures to external causes is labelled as the *self-serving bias*. For example, when a student finds she has received grade E with the feedback from the tutor on an essay, she is likely to say 'The tutor gave me an E'. However, if she receives grade A, the same student will say 'I have earned an A'. That is, when an individual succeeds she tends to take credit for it but if she fails, she blames the situation on others.

A manager needs to take into account cultural differences in both the fundamental attribution error and the self-serving bias. Such errors tend to apply only to the Western world because in other cultures, for example, India, individuals tend to believe in fate, and think it is responsible for most of what happens in life – such cultures tend to emphasise the external causes of behaviour.

The behaviour of an individual is strongly influenced by the way that individuals interpret the events around them. By understanding the causes of behaviour individuals make an attempt to explain, predict and control future behaviour. A manager will use attributions throughout her work responsibilities, particularly in her relationships with subordinates who rely on the manager to reward their performance. The manager has to determine the causes of an individual's behaviour and she will then perceive this to be her responsibility.

Attribution and performance management

Attribution theory has important significance for managers because they use attribution theory to infer things about their subordinates' behaviour and performance. As has been seen, such attributions may not always be accurate. For example, if a manager has a positive relationship with his own superior then it is not likely that he will be held responsible for most problems within his area of responsibility – the superior will attribute the problem to the external environment.

Where a manager and his subordinates share similar perceptions and attitudes, they will tend to evaluate each other highly. Conversely, if they do not perceive each other positively, they are likely to blame each other for any problems in performance or production. Nelson and Quick (1994) present an attribution model which specifically addresses how supervisors respond to poor performance and which can be seen in Figure 2.14.

Attribution theory can help to explain how managers reward performance in a differential way. For example, a manager who attributes a subordinate's behaviour to internal causes may reward that person better than when she attributes good performance to

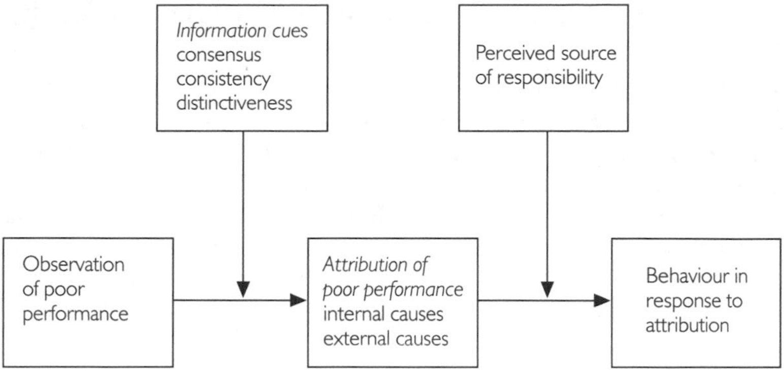

Figure 2.14 The attribution model after Nelson and Quick (1994)

external causes, such as assistance from other subordinates or good training. Managers are also accountable to their superiors for their behaviour and they are often asked to explain such behaviour and actions. Individuals who make external attributions actually behave in a way which blames factors external to the individual for any problems. For example, a student may say that a piece of coursework is too difficult, or that the time allowed to do it is too short to write an adequate answer, or the computer facilities available are inadequate. In doing this, he also makes attributions about the causes of his own behaviour – it is closely related to the theory of locus of control.

Locus of control

Locus of control is a major personality attribute which has been dealt with in detail in Chapter 1. However, it is a key aspect of social perception. Moorhead and Griffin (1995) define locus of control as a concept which 'relates to the extent to which an individual believes that her behavior has a direct impact on the consequences of that behavior' (p. 57).

Members of the workforce who favour an internal attribution perspective are more likely to believe that they can influence their work performance through their own abilities and efforts. Those with an external locus of control are more likely to believe that their performance is determined by circumstances outside their control. The former group may therefore attribute poor performance in others to inability or lack of effort rather than task difficulty, for example. In contrast, the latter would tend to ascribe such performance to issues of luck and task complexity. In both cases, the result could mean a misreading of the real causes of poor behaviour and the wrong kind of response to colleagues or subordinates.

Halo effect

Another kind of impact which projection or attribution has on the way individuals perceive others is the *halo effect*. Gross (1996) defines it as: 'A kind of implicit personality theory, in which one positive (or negative) trait is used to infer other positive (or negative) traits' (p. 378).

It is a process in which perception of an individual is influenced by a single, striking characteristic.

The term 'halo effect' was coined by the psychologist Edward Thorndyke (1874–1949) in the early 1920s. He observed that people tended to give particular emphasis to one trait or characteristic they perceived in an individual, which could then effectively block out others in determining their assumptions about them. In doing so they could give an individual either a positive or negative halo. In the latter case, this is something known as the 'rusty halo effect'. An example might be someone arriving late for an interview. Even if this were for good reasons, this lateness might dominate perceptions of the individual, creating a poor impression (negative halo) which effectively counteracted all the other signals he might give to the contrary.

In contrast, punctuality or a smart appearance might be singled out as evidence of an individual's worth irrespective of other traits or the actual quality of her work, and would thus create a positive halo. It is not difficult to see the way the halo effect arises from projection and attribution. Someone who attributes her success and status to her own qualities of smartness and punctuality may well project those assumptions onto those she meets, focusing exclusively on those traits, or the lack of them, in her assessment of their character and worth.

Thus individuals tend to let their assessment of an individual on one trait influence their evaluation of that person on other specific traits. That is, if a manager believes that a subordinate is outstandingly good in one area of work, say interpersonal communication skills, he will be likely to rate that individual highly in all areas of work performance, regardless of the subordinate's actual performance.

Bernardin and Pence (1980) coined the phrase 'halo and horns effect'. Whilst this refers to the halo effect it is particularly related to characteristics which are undesirable in an individual's behaviour – the negative aspects. It is clear that the halo and horns effect is a constituent part of a personality theory, yet it can have undesirable effects. If an individual spends too much time avoiding the halo and horns effect he might well have his attention distracted from trying to accurately perceive the behaviour of others.

Barriers to social perception

The characteristics of the perceiver (P), target (T), and situation (S) discussed earlier all affect social perception. It is a complex process and it is not, therefore, possible for every member of the workforce to have accurate social perceptual skills. Regardless of the level of competence in the social perception of others, there are barriers which will prevent any individual from accurately perceiving a target. Such barriers may be in the form of:

- selective attention
- first impression error
- implicit personality theories
- self-fulfilling prophecies
- stereotyping.

Selective attention and *stereotyping* are key concepts in social perception and have been dealt with elsewhere in the chapter.

The tendency to formulate long-lasting opinions about another individual that are based on initial perceptions and are usually inaccurate, is called the *first impression error*. The perceiver forms a swift opinion of an individual immediately they are encountered and therefore neglects what that individual is all about. Such initial perceptions can have negative effects in the workplace. For example, in a job interview the panel may make a faulty decision on their first impressions of the candidates; for example the fact that one candidate is conservatively dressed implies to the panel that she will therefore work smartly. Such reliance on first impressions does not bode well for long-term work relationships.

As was seen in the last chapter, individuals tend to form views of other people based on how those people behave. Such theories are often 'mini-theories' and are called *implicit personality theories* and all individuals have them. Such theories often lead to misconceptions about other people and they allow individuals to take short cuts instead of attempting to integrate all new inputs of information. In doing this an individual clusters traits and makes patterns with those which are similar.

Any situation whereby the expectations of an individual about others she perceives can affect any interaction with them in such a way that the expectations of the perceiver are fulfilled is called a *self-fulfilling prophecy*. The *pygmalion effect* is the popularised term for the self-fulfilling prophecy. This theory is based on a story in Greek mythology about the King of Cyprus, Pygmalion, who made a statue of a woman and fell in love with it. He then prayed to the goddess of love, Aphrodite, for a wife like it, and she endowed the statue with life. Hence the use of the title *Pygmalion* by George Bernard Shaw for his play about Henry Higgins who turned a flower girl (Eliza Doolittle) into a society lady through the development of her linguistic skills: this play formed the basis of a musical called *My Fair Lady*. A manager's expectations of a subordinate will affect both the manager's behaviour towards the individual and the individual's response.

Through projection and attribution individuals can deploy their perceptual sets to order and interpret their experiences of others. However, one of the most important of all is through the use of *stereotypes*. Gross (1995) defines stereotypes as 'a kind of implicit personality theory which relates to the characteristics of an entire social group' (p. 378).

Moorhead and Griffin (1995) define stereotyping as 'the process of categorizing or labeling people on the basis of a single attribute or characteristic' (p. 66).

The term stereotyping was first developed by Walter Lippmann (1889–1974) in the early 1920s. He noticed that, in seeking to understand people, individuals tend to create stereotypes into which those individuals can be placed, classified and more easily understood. Stereotyping involves creating mental sets of personality types. People look for clusters of characteristics and behaviour which seem to link individuals into distinct groups. For example, an individual may identify what he thinks are common characteristics amongst accountants: that they are hard-working, practical, thorough and a little dull. In other words he has developed a stereotype for accountants. Stereotypes of this kind may not only link a set of common characteristics but provide some sort of explanatory framework for them. Underpinning the exampled stereotype for accountants may be a set of assumptions that the technical nature of accountancy training and the motives for a career in accountancy will tend to attract people with these characteristics. When an individual encounters an accountant he will seek to relate that person to his own stereotype for accountants, and will classify and explain his behaviour according to the model he has established.

Stereotypes have a number of functions:

- they help people to give a structure to their experience of others, allowing them to classify that experience and give it a meaning;
- they provide models which allow people to explain, predict and analyse individual behaviour;
- they provide a means of reinforcing an individual's own sense of identity and values.

Stereotyping has both an empirical value – a way of ordering experience – and a psychological value. An individual's sense of identity, as will be shown in later chapters, is often tied up with membership of, and loyalty to, one or more groups. Group identity is defined both by identifying a common set of characteristics of group membership, and by distinguishing that identity from other groups. The creation of stereotypes is a way of defining these key differences between groups. The stronger the sense of identity with a group, and the greater the importance individuals ascribe to that sense of group identity, the stronger will be the stereotypes of other groups against which group identity is defined and articulated.

The norms and standards of conduct of a group of which an individual is a member will inform both the kinds of stereotypes used and the identity which recognises an individual's right to make such judgements.

Stereotypes are, therefore, a necessary tool for analysing people but they may lead to oversimplification and distortion if the stereotypes are themselves crude and not interpreted dynamically. However, their psychological function often means that this is precisely what happens. As has been seen more generally, the process of perception is deeply influenced by the assumptions brought to bear and is all too open to a highly selective and partial interpretation of individuals and experience in defiance of self. These two processes can act to reduce a person's dynamic use of stereotyping. Stereotypes thus become mere prejudice because they become rigid and unchanging, and are often interpreted pejoratively. For example, accountants are, by definition, dull; and thus all accountants are automatically assumed to fit the stereotype, irrespective of their actual behaviour.

Stereotyping of this type often clusters around key areas as shown in Table 2.2 below.

Table 2.2 Stereotyping around clusters

Cluster	Example
gender	women are the 'weaker' sex
age	older people are inflexible young people are unreliable
class	all working-class people are loud and vulgar
religion	all members of the Church of England are middle-class
politics	all Conservative voters are upper-class, live in the country, and support fox hunting
nationality	all Germans are orderly, hard-working, and right-wing
race	Asian people are all 'inscrutable'

Stereotyping is not confined to the classification of individuals but can also occur within organisations, and particularly in relation to gender and nationality.

Stereotyping and gender

Attitudes to women in business are a classic example of stereotyping. Traditionally, notions of masculinity and femininity have been defined as contrasting and mutually reinforcing stereotypes, as can be seen in Table 2.3 below.

Table 2.3 Masculinity/femininity reinforcing stereotypes

Male	Female
the 'bread-winner'	the 'homemaker'
active	passive
aggressive/decisive	peaceful/consensual
competitive	co-operative
analytical	intuitive

Viewed this way by male managers, women were seen as insufficiently forceful and analytical to survive the tough masculine world of business. Their role and skills lay in being wives and mothers, to which traditional (and natural) roles they would always be drawn. Recruiting and promoting women were therefore seen as inherently risky. Even if their abilities did not quite fit the stereotype, young single women were regarded as likely to marry and retreat to their traditional 'home-making' role, thus wasting the investment in their training. At best, they might be allowed into those support functions, such as human resources, where their cooperative approach and intuitive communication skills could have a role to play.

Those women who did try to access the male world of management were stigmatised for threatening the boundaries between male and female stereotypes. For example, they were further stereotyped by male colleagues as frustrated spinsters over-compensating for their failure to accept or succeed in the female sphere from which they had come and to which they properly belonged. They risked being caricatured as aberrations, trying too hard to be imitations of men. They also risked being excluded from the masculine culture of management with its male camaraderie focused around, for example, the gentlemen's club, pub or sports-field. Indeed, their presence was seen as a threat to that culture.

This process of stereotyping has been shown to be self-reinforcing. Reinforcement of women into more responsible managerial positions has been slow, their presence has been seen as threatening by male colleagues and they have been excluded from the kind of networks that support effective managerial activity and influence recruitment. The pressures of surviving this environment have acted as a disincentive to women trying to make their way up the managerial ladder, leaving senior management still male-dominated in many areas of business and public life.

The undermentioned case is an example of how women are missing out in perceived 'male' environments.

CASE STUDY

Women losing out in science

More than one third of female science graduates are employed in jobs for which they are overqualified, according to research published this week, writes Julia Hinde.

Thirty-two per cent of employed female science graduates aged between 21 and 65 are in non-professional jobs for which a degree is not normally required, according to Judith Glover, of the Roehampton Institute London, and Jane Fielding, of Surrey University, who have analysed results from annual labour force surveys. The figure for male science graduates is just 19 per cent.

Twenty years ago, the figures for female science, engineering and technology (SET) graduates were 19 per cent, and 16 per cent for males.

The research also indicates that one in three employed female SET graduates are teachers, but just one in ten male SET graduates choose a teaching career.

A longitudinal analysis of work histories of male and female SET graduates using the National Child Development Study, which includes all those born in Britain in a certain week in 1958, also reveals that women are significantly less likely to stay in scientific professional jobs than men.

The results show women are more likely to be in temporary short-term jobs and female employment in professional science jobs decreases over time, especially over the age of 29, which coincides with an apparent peak in childbirth. But employment as teachers increases correspondingly.

The report finds a lack of parity between female graduates without children and male SET graduates. At the age of 33, 56 per cent of men are in SET professional or managerial jobs, compared with 34 per cent of childless women.

Seven per cent of men are working in teaching at the age of 33, compared with 24 per cent of women without children and 40 per cent of women with children.

Dr Glover said: 'We have always suspected that women with science degrees become teachers and do less well economically. This has now been confirmed.'

Source: J. Hinde, *Times Higher Education Supplement*, 5 September 1997, p. 5.

Stereotyping and culture

Individuals will perceive things depending upon their individual culture. Try the following example:

Try this

Read the following sentence counting the number of times the letter 'f' appears.

Finished files are the result of years of scientific study combined with the experience of years.

Students with English as a second language see all six whereas those who are native English speakers will probably see only three.

Adler (1991) used this as an example of cultural conditioning and stated that native English speakers believe that *of* is an unimportant word and tend to ignore it.

Goffee (1997) discusses the importance of cultural diversity, stating that it is a 'hot issue' (p. 240) because of the 'growing diversity of societies, growth of cultural awareness among ethnic groups and the rise of the global corporation' (p. 240).

Although an understanding of the process of perception raises the level of awareness in individuals, humans do not necessarily perceive reality – especially in a manner which is detached and unemotional. Medcof and Roth (1979) posited the view that the barriers between an individual and the world outside him or her operate at very basic levels: 'Despite the impression that we are in direct and immediate contact with the world, our perception is, in fact, separated from reality by a long chain of processing' (p. 4).

Perception is a complex process which involves filters through which individuals view the world. As discussed in the previous chapter Kelly (1955) calls these our *personal constructs* through which individuals channel the way they conceptualise and anticipate events. One of the key ways of dealing with such constructs is through effective communication and the process of learning. As Thompson and McHugh (1995) stated: 'the process of learning is itself dependent on the development of the perceptual process which shapes our world' (p. 227).

Questions for discussion

1. How can managers improve their perceptual skills?
2. How can the self-serving bias and the fundamental attribution error be avoided?
3. Suppose that a manager makes an incorrect attribution for a subordinate's poor performance (for example, the manager cites equipment failure), and peers know that the employee is actually at fault. Should they whistleblow on their colleague?

References and further reading

Adler, N., 1991, *International dimensions of Organizational Behavior* (Boston: PWS-Kent)

Allport, G.W., 1995, *Becoming – basic considerations for a psychology of personality* (New Haven, Connecticut: Yale University Press)

Bernardin, H.J. and Pence, E.C., 1980, 'Effects of rate training: creating new responsibility and decreasing accuracy' in *Journal of Applied Psychology* No 65, pp. 60–66

Forgas, J.P. and Bower, G.H., 'Mood Effects in Person–Perception Judgments' in *Journal of Personality and Social Psychology* 1987, No 53, pp. 53–60

Freud, S., 1949, *An Outline of Psychoanalysis* (New York: Norton)

Giacolone, R.A. and Rosenfeld, P. (eds), 1990, *Impression Management in Organizations* (Hillsdale, NJ: Erlbaum)

Goffee, R., 'Cultural Diversity' in *Mastering Management* (London: Financial Times/Pitman, 1997), pp. 240–246

Gross, R., 1996 (3rd edn), *Psychology: The Science of Mind and Behaviour* (London: Hodder & Stoughton)

Gurcham, M., 1995 (2nd edn), *Interpersonal Skills at Work* (London: Prentice-Hall)

Heider, F., 1958, *The Psychology of Interpersonal Relations* (New York: Wiley)

Hinde, J., 'Women losing out in science' in *Times Higher Education Supplement*, 5 September 1997, p. 5.

Kelly, G.A., 1955, *The Psychology of Personal Constructs* (Vols 1 and 2) (New York: Morton)

Kelley, H.H., 1971, *Attribution in Social Interaction* (Morristown, NJ: General Learning Press)

Keuning, D., 1998, *Management: A Contemporary Approach* (London: Pitman Publishing)

Medcof, J. and Roth, J. (eds), 1979, *Approaches to Psychology* (Milton Keynes: Open University Press)

Moorhead, G. and Griffin, R.W., 1995 (4th edn), *Organizational Behavior: Managing People and Organizations* (Boston, Mass: Houghton Mifflin)

Morgan, C.T. and King, R.A., 1996 (3rd edn), *Introduction to Psychology* (Maidenhead: McGraw-Hill)

Nelson, D.L. and Quick, J.C., 1994, *Organizational Behavior: Foundations, realities, and challenges* (St Paul, MN: West Publishing)

Rafaeli, A. and Pratt, M.G., 'Tailored Meanings: On the Meaning and Impact of Organizational Dress' in *Academy of Management Review*, January 1993, pp. 32–55

Salancik, G.R. and Pfeffer, J., 'A Social Information Processing Approach to Job Attitudes and Design' in *Administrative Science Quarterly*, 1978, No 23, pp. 224–253

Thompson, P. and McHugh, H., 1995 (2nd edn), *Work Organisations: A Critical Introduction* (Basingstoke: Macmillan)

Times Higher Educational Supplement, 'Women losing out in science', 5 September 1997, p. 5

Vernon, M.D., 'The functions of schemata in perceiving' in *Psychological Review*, 1955, No 62, pp. 180–192

Welch, J., ' "Female lads" take on male tactics to score' in *People Management*, 12 June 1997, p. 16

3 Communication and learning

Learning objectives

After studying this chapter you should be able to:

- appreciate the importance of effective communication in the workplace;
- assess the various methods of communication available;
- describe contemporary information technologies used by the workforce;
- practise good reflective listening skills;
- select the most appropriate methods of communication for any situation;
- define *learning*, *reinforcement*, *punishment*, *extinction*, and *goal setting*;
- distinguish between classical conditioning, operant conditioning, and social learning theory;
- identify the links between personality and successful learning.

Introduction

CASE STUDY

Addressing the issue of good communication

In July 1996 *People Management* carried an article written by an experienced business communicator, Octavius Black, wherein he looked at how different definitions of communication competency affected managerial effectiveness. He wrote:

'What is a communication competency? Definitions vary widely and the line between "competency" and "skill" is often blurred.

Knowing how to use e-mail is a communication competency in one major public-sector organisation [see below]. This is a stage ahead of organisations that simply have a competency labelled "communication". Others merely include communication as a vital element within other competencies, such as team-building, influencing, and coaching.'

The definitions should be clear. Black describes communication competency as 'the ability to understand the choices involved in communication and to choose appropriately [in order] to influence outcomes and achieve desired objectives'. He sees communication skills as 'the ability to execute the communication in the chosen way'.

The Electricity Supply Board (ESB) in the Republic of Ireland has developed a new approach. Its definition of communication competencies for its managers is closely aligned with leadership competencies. Separate categories reflect three different roles: as a manager of the organisation, as the manager for a district or department, and as a team leader.

Competencies in the first category include 'communicating national messages in an effective way by taking collective responsibility and ownership for the content, ensuring recipients' understanding of the messages and knowing the organisation's position on difficult issues and rationale for decisions'. Managers can no longer pass on company messages while distancing themselves from unpopular decisions. To be competent, managers need to create the right impact on their audience.

Adapted from: Octavius Black, in *People Management*, 25 July 1996, p. 44

In the above case Black (1996) makes a strong case for organisational members to be effective communicators if the objectives of the organisation are to be met. Managers must promote collaboration, enlist support, and provide clear expectations to mobilise the commitment, intelligence and creativity of employees by being effective communicators. They also need to be able to improve the skills of their colleagues, through training and appraisal, in the workplace. It is through the process of communication that individuals interact and human and physical resources are amalgamated to produce outputs and to attain individual and organisational objectives. However, the concept of communication is complex and not always fully understood.

In the provision of quality, organisational members must fight against ineffective communication. When organisations grow profitable, they often become complacent and lose the ability to respond quickly to changes in the market place. Effective communication increases understanding about the need to reduce such complacency, thus allowing the members of the organisation to be more proficient communicators so that, as a result, the organisation can become a leader in its field. The way to prevent ineffective communication is to make positive changes and improvements whilst the organisation is still financially strong and to encourage organisational members to become effective communicators in order that the goals of the organisation may be met.

Communication can be said to be the process by which two or more people exchange information and share meaning. Interpersonal communication involves communication between two people. Successful interpersonal communication in the workplace involves reading, listening, managing and interpreting information and interacting with all stakeholders of the organisation. Effective communication is brought about only when it is understood fully by all members of the workforce that individuals can choose an appropriate medium of communication.

Effective communication is vital to the survival of the organisation and acts as a co-ordinator of all activities within the organisation. Communication is a medium by which information can be shared because it is through communication that individuals express and share their individual emotions. It can be seen, therefore, that communication is not just about facts and figures but more about being a catalyst for the expression of individual emotions such as fear, displeasure, confidence, and happiness.

The communication process

No single model of communication takes into account all the elements that may be involved in a specific situation – regardless of the chosen communication medium. Communication models are simplified attempts to show how the complex concept of communication is carried out. All models have three common components:

- the *source*, which can be an individual or a group
- the *message*, which may be written, a gesture, or electronically processed
- the *receiver*, which could be an individual or a group.

The model in Figure 3.1 below gives the key elements in a communication process.

Figure 3.1 Basic communication model

In any communication process there are four key factors:

- message transmission
- encoding and decoding
- communication channels
- feedback.

Message transmission

The individual sender has some sort of concept concerning the message which is to be shared with others and such information has to be *encoded*, that is, put in some form that makes transmission possible. Such an idea can be in the form of words, symbols, sounds, or expressions that can be transmitted through an appropriate medium. Such transmission may involve face-to-face interaction, written messages, drawings, digital formats or any other method of getting the information to the receiver.

The message is received through the human senses, and the receiver *decodes* the message and interprets the decoded message by assigning meaning to its symbols. However, the receiver may interpret the message in a different way from that which the sender wished. This would result in ineffective communication: i.e. the message has not been interpreted by the receiver as the sender wanted.

Therefore, for the communication to be effective, both the *source* and the *receiver* must understand the code system being used. The source can encode and the receiver can only decode according to the experience each one has had. That is, they must have had similar experiences for the communication to be effective. If the sender uses information related to the receiver's past experience, then it is likely that the message will be encoded accurately.

However, such shared experience does not guarantee that the message will produce the desired response: the message is more than the code system. For example:

- if the source does not have adequate or accurate information, the message generated has little chance of producing desired responses;
- it is the receiver, not the sender/source, who determines that the message is encoded efficiently;
- the attitudes, experiences, and motivations of the receiver determine whether the message is decoded in a way that corresponds to the intentions of the sender/source.

Encoding and decoding

Both parties to the communication *encode* and *decode*. Encoding is the process by which the sender's ideas are turned into symbols that constitute the message – putting ideas into words. Decoding is the process by which the receiver interprets the symbols contained in the message by determining what such symbols refer to.

Inputs always affect outputs because individuals are constantly encoding information from the environment, interpreting it, and decoding it. As information passes *through* an individual, it is changed by the interpretation which, in turn, changes the individual.

Communication channels

The channel is a vital part of the communication process in that the choice of an inappropriate channel may mean that the message is not acted upon in the manner the sender would wish. For example, in face-to-face communication it is considered by some that the non-verbal cues are as important as the verbal message itself. That is, facial expressions, gestures and intonation give the verbal message more meaning – this is discussed later on in this chapter.

Channels of communication gain importance because of two issues:

- the increased experience of a particular individual; and
- the increased sensitivity of non-verbal communication.

Single-channel communications are seldom used. In a speech communication, sound may well be the primary channel but non-verbal communication adds other channels as do environmental factors such as ventilation, lighting, chair placement and the nature of the audience.

Feedback

The receiver's response to the message constitutes the feedback loop of the communication as portrayed in Figure 3.1 above. The receiver verifies the message through *feedback* to the sender which indicates that the message has been understood – usually by carrying out the action requested.

Methods of communication

There are three primary methods of communication used in the workplace:

- written
- oral
- non-verbal.

Frequently, these methods are combined to provide reinforcement of the message and the choice of method depends on the:

- audience
- nature of the message

- urgency (or confidentiality)
- costs of transmission.

Written communication

There are many kinds of written communication used within business organisations:

- the *letter* is a formal communication with an individual outside the organisation;
- the *memorandum* (memo) is usually addressed to one person within the organisation and normally addresses a single issue;
- the *report* generally summarises the progress/results of a project and often provides information which supports decision-making;
- *manuals* tell staff how to operate machines and give information about organisational processes and procedures;
- *forms* are standardised documents on which information is reported;
- *electronic transmission* through digital methods.

Oral communication

This is the most common form of communication and is pervasive within most organisations. Conversations can be formal or informal and take place in, for example:

- informal situations
- the process of carrying out tasks
- formal speeches and presentations.

Oral communication is a powerful medium of communication because it includes not only the speaker's words but also the changes in pitch, volume, tone, and speed. These are the cues to the listener so that they can interpret the message. The receiver also interprets oral messages in context, taking into account any previous communications and, maybe, the reactions of other receivers of the oral transmission. Frequently it is the top echelons of management who set the tone for oral communication throughout the organisation.

Non-verbal communication

Most forms of communication are accompanied by some sort of non-verbal communication which includes all the elements associated with human communication that are not expressed orally or in writing. These are key issues and are dealt with in detail later on in this chapter.

Electronic information processing

Kanter (1997) confirms that the use of technology has brought about changes in communication methods in the world of work (see Chapter 5); she states that by: '... linking everyone up by computer, you encourage the flow of ideas from the margin. In opening up the lines of communication, the centre is saying "Hey, we want to hear from you" ' (p. 20).

She believes that although times have changed the core of her message has not, stating: 'I think we already know a lot about what should be done. Now managers just have to go to it' (p. 20).

However, changes in the workplace are happening so rapidly that it is often difficult for the workforce to keep abreast of innovations – particularly those based on new technologies such as computerised information-processing systems, new types of telecommunication systems, and combinations of these. Individuals now send and receive communications on their computer terminals. Additionally, a whole new industry is developing in the long-distance transmission of data between computers.

The 'office of the future' is now here. Most offices have a facsimile (fax) machine, a copier, and personal computers linked into a single integrated system with access to numerous databases and electronic mail (e-mail) systems. There is now in existence what is known as the 'intelligent office' incorporating into ever-changing patterns of job design (see Chapter 5) such concepts as hot-desking, hotelling and open plan. According to Brown (1996) workers are being weaned from the territorial need to have a desk of their own whilst managers are making economic savings through such systems. With the rise of electronic communication systems, people have much less need to be together in a central location.

The electronic office links managers, clerical employees, professional workers, and sales personnel in a communication network that uses a combination of computerised data storage, retrieval, and transmission systems. New information processing and transmission technologies have created new media, symbols, message transmission methods, and networks for organisational communication. Such methods of communication have made a radical change to work and personal relationships and have disrupted the familiar ways of accomplishing tasks. There are the potential hazards of information overload, loss of records in a 'paperless' office, and the dehumanising effects of electronic equipment.

This fully integrated communication information office system (the electronic office) links people in a communication network through a combination of computers and electronic transmission systems. The effects of such systems have not yet been fully realised, and developments are still continuing to bring about different systems of electronic communication. Such changes have had an even more considerable impact on organisational behaviour, and managers should appreciate that there are individuals who have a specific viewpoint on the matter which may affect effective communication. These views are likely to fall into one of two camps. Firstly, there are the *technophiles* who are totally convinced that all new technology must be an asset to management. The view here is that everyone will benefit because information and communication technology (ICT) has the potential to:

- enhance the speed and quality of organisational decision-making;
- increase transparency, thus making information available to more people;
- facilitate the free flow of information;
- increase the accuracy of information.

Secondly, there are the *technosceptics* who identify any number of organisational problems each time a new technology is introduced into the workplace. Such people believe that ICT can:

- increasingly formalise the organisation's culture;
- bring about a reduction in face-to-face communication;
- increase the centralisation of power and control.

The most commonly used ICT is e-mail which, at its inception, was considered to be the answer to all ills related to communication in the workplace. Reasons given include that it:

- permits the free flow of communication;
- makes information available at the press of a key;
- provides easy and quick contact with individuals and groups.

E-mail lacks the intimacy and powerfulness of face-to-face communication but users have developed compensatory activities for this by using jargon and abbreviations (*smilies*) which are used to express emotion on the computer screen. There did actually grow an industry in such *emoticons* including, for example, :–) to represent happiness, :–(for unhappiness, and :–O for shock. Nowadays, these are only used by new users of e-mail.

It is e-mail's lack of intimacy which has brought about difficulties for managers. This psychological distancing has evolved into distrust by users in the information received because individuals tend to seek verbal verification of information, reply to e-mails less promptly than to messages received over voice mail, and senior managers tend to disseminate bad news, such as dismissal notices, rather than good/positive news through e-mail. Whilst there are these two views on the role of ICTs, most users *do* consider that e-mail is not suitable for any communication which relates to coaching, mentoring, appraisal, or discipline.

Corbett (1997) reports that e-mail has brought about an increase in gossip in the workplace. Verbal gossip might have a positive role within the workplace, for example, in providing new members of the organisation with an induction into organisational culture as well as acting as a means of allowing team members to stay together by providing a means for the alleviation of stress. It follows, therefore, that e-mail gossip has increased in popularity as e-mail itself has become more popular. The advantage to managers of e-mail gossip over the conventional grapevine is that it can be technically monitored.

Communication networks

Communication is about the satisfaction of the individual's felt needs, and it uses the available tools to affect the behaviour of others and also to achieve objectives. It is used to inform, interpret, and motivate. Regardless of the behaviour required from a receiver, the individual is attempting to gain a behavioural response in order to satisfy his or her felt needs. Consequently, effective communication will only be brought about if the receiver knows what the sender means and thus reacts (behaves) in the way the sender requires.

Therefore, communication is a social system. What were once simple communication systems – for example, individuals used to be given the information they needed to work with others within the same system – have now developed into more complicated social systems composed of small-group communication networks within a larger organisational network. Such systems allow for the structural flow and content of communication and also support the organisational structure itself. Communication also supports the organisational culture, beliefs, attitudes, and value systems that enable the organisation to operate.

Managing communication

Messages are not always understood because the feedback from the receiver was not as the sender desired. The degree of correspondence between the message intended by the sender and the message understood by the receiver is called *communication fidelity*. Fidelity can be diminished anywhere in the communication process, from source to feedback. Additionally, organisations may have characteristics that impede the flow of information.

Such barriers to communication block or significantly distort successful communication. Effective managerial communication skills help to overcome some, but not all, barriers to communication in organisations; such barriers may only be temporary and can be overcome. The first step is to be aware and recognise this fact. Five significant barriers to effective communication are:

- physical separation
- status difference
- gender differences
- cultural diversity
- language and meaning.

Physical separation

The physical separation of people in the workplace poses a significant barrier to effective communication. The rise of the technological capability of allowing an ever-increasing percentage of the workforce to carry out its responsibilities away from the workplace is not in itself a barrier to effective communication; but the resistance to such a change is. Such technology is not as information-rich as face-to-face communication. Periodic face-to-face interactions can help physical separation problems because interactions such as these give more cues in the form of non-verbal cues. The richer the communication, the more the chance that the message will be correctly understood.

Status differences

Status differences are related to power and thus affect the effectiveness of communication. Effective interpersonal communication skills make supervisors and their subordinates more approachable and reduce the risks of problems related to status differences. The move towards flatter, leaner organisations may indicate fewer hierarchical differences but new information technologies and the rise of teamwork and cell structures provide another way of overcoming status difference barriers because they encourage the formation of non-hierarchical working relationships.

Gender differences

Communication barriers can be explained in part by differences in conversation styles. Some believe that women benefit from approaches and techniques for communication different from those used by their male colleagues. For example, women tend to prefer to converse face to face, whereas men are comfortable sitting alongside and concentrating on some focal point in front of them, for example, a report or visual display unit (VDU).

Hence, conversation style differences *may* result in a failure of communication between men and women. Male–female conversation is really cross-cultural communication. It is important for all to appreciate that an understanding of gender-specific differences in conversational style is a key to effective communication. The latter can be improved further if each seeks clarification of the other's meaning rather than freely interpreting meaning from one's own frame of reference.

Cultural diversity

Cultural diversity and international patterns of behaviour can confuse effective communication. There are important international differences in work-related values which have implications for motivation, leadership, and team work in organisations. People work to habitual patterns of behaviour within organisations and outsiders working to a different cultural pattern of behaviour are outside effective communication. Such differences can be overcome by increasing awareness and sensitivity. This is dealt with later on in this chapter.

Language and meaning

Meanings are in the minds of individuals. Language is central to effective communication and can pose a barrier if its use obscures meaning and distorts intent – it is a highly developed and complex system. Most of the desirable and undesirable qualities of language result from that characteristic. No necessary connection exists between the language symbol and what it symbolises – for example, it might be said that something is beautiful when the opposite is what is actually what is believed. The use of jargon and technical language can convey precise meaning only if all parties to the communication are familiar with the meanings of such techniques. Physical things have both a functional value and a symbolic value. The latter is often what leads the individual to accept or reject a specific object. For example, when choosing a new car the decision is not always based on economic and/or functional grounds – one also needs to take into account the symbolic value of a 'prestigious image' car.

Towards effective communication

In today's flatter organisations with their increased use of groups, teams and cell structures (see Chapters 6 and 7), there are now more people in supervisory roles, and with such roles comes an increased need to be effective in the communication process. Effective communicators tend to have expertise in common skills and tend to be:

- expressive speakers
- empathetic listeners
- persuasive leaders
- sensitive to the feelings of others
- managers of information.

Expressive speakers tend to speak accurately and clearly and are not afraid to express their thoughts, ideas, and feelings in public. They tend towards extroversion and their subordinates know exactly where they stand with such people.

Expressive speakers tend to be *empathetic listeners* because they use reflective listening skills (see later section) to the limit and are thus responsive to all. Apart from hearing the words of others, they tend to be able to hear the feelings and emotions of the actual message being transmitted and not just the content and ideas of that message. Such people are very approachable and listen to suggestions – and complaints.

The most effective managers and supervisors are *persuasive leaders* because they can exercise power and influence over others in order to achieve the organisation's objectives. They encourage others to do their best and achieve results; they avoid autocratic styles and instead favour allowing their team members to decide for themselves. There is a situational exception to this – when there is an emergency (for example, a life-threatening event) such people are directive and assertive – all followers obey without question because it is not their normal style of leadership.

Effective supervisors are *sensitive to the feelings of others*, avoiding any situation which might reduce the self-esteem of their team. They give criticism and feedback in a positive and supportive manner and with confidence. There are no public reprimands and they work to enhance the self-esteem of all.

The more efficient communicator is also an efficient *information manager*; such people ensure that they are disseminators of information through the widest possible range of communication media. They are also effective managers of gossip, which is, according to Waddington and Fletcher (1997), 'an important feature of organisational communication' (p. 33).

Effective listening

Communication is a key activity within the workplace and in order for it to be effective, all employees need to be able to be active reflective listeners. This is a skill, which can be learned and practised, and by use of it the transmitter/sender and the receiver can fully understand the message sent. The key emphasis is on the receiver, who through effective reflective listening can clarify the meaning within the message. It is characterised in three ways:

- an emphasis on the personal elements of the communication process – that the sender is animate;
- a concentration on the feelings communicated within the message – the thoughts and ideas of the sender;
- an understanding that the concentration is on the sender of the message and not on the person receiving it.

Are you an effective reflective listener?

You might think that you are a good listener – after all, don't your friends ask you to 'Listen to this . . .'? However, how much do you hear of what they say to you? It is possible to become an active listener through practice – here are ten tips to help people to be better listeners. How many of these do you adhere to?

1 **Stop talking**
If your mouth is moving you cannot possibly be listening.

2 **Put the speaker at ease**
Be friendly – put the speaker at ease. Smile – but don't use a fixed, inane grin.

3 **Show the speaker you want to listen**
Move your papers away from you. Put anything you have in your hands aside. Keep your eyes off your watch and on those of the speaker.

4 **Remove distractions**
Close your door and turn off the telephone.

5 **Empathise with the speaker**
Try to put yourself in the speaker's position and consider how he or she must be feeling.

6 **Be patient**
No two people deliver a message at an identical pace – give the speaker time to get the message across to you – don't anticipate the contents of the message.

7 **Keep control of your temper**
Be patient and do not lose your cool.

8 **Keep the criticism at bay**
Do not criticise too much – even if you think it is constructive in nature. Any form of criticism can stifle the discourse.

9 **Ask questions**
Paraphrase the speaker's message as a means of clarification.

10 **Stop talking**
Do not talk until the speaker has finished – even though it will be a temptation to do so.

Adapted from: C. Hamilton and B.M. Kleiner, 'Steps to Better Listening' in *Personnel Journal*, February 1987

Cross-cultural communication

Cross-cultural communication is a topical issue in management development, and according to Blum (1997): 'Employees in culturally diverse organisations are increasingly demanding appropriate management and communication' (p. 4).

According to Blum (1997) in order to ensure that communication is effective across national cultures, it is essential that a manager understands the importance of culture (discussed further in Chapter 9). By understanding different national behavioural norms managers can better manage across national cultures and it is through the manner of their communication that understanding is expressed. Blum (1997) defines cross-cultural communication as: 'the ability to interact verbally and non-verbally by sending, receiving and decoding messages appropriately' (p. 5).

As was seen in Chapter 2, all aspects of communication are dominated by an individual's perception of the situation: it is about how the communicators *feel* about each other. An individual's perception is dominated by his interpretation of the behavioural signals according to his own national identity and, therefore, its cultural norms. Blum (1997) suggests that the use of translators is dangerous because: 'nationally biased reference points can obscure what is actually being said, either verbally or non-verbally' (p. 5).

She goes on to say that when an individual communicates across national culture boundaries, there are certain issues which must be taken into account, such as the:

- different reference points;
- sensitive nature of such issues;
- need to adapt communication style and strategy accordingly.

Taking these three issues into account, the individual must then consider what is involved in any cross-cultural communication. Blum (1997) suggests the following:

- understanding the expectations of the audience;
- selection of appropriate channels of communication;
- identification of appropriate communication styles;
- the articulation of messages in a sensitive way;
- recognition of the values within which the communication is taking place.

It could well be argued that communication across national boundaries does not differ from that within local boundaries. However, effective cross-cultural communication requires: '... a deeper awareness of what is important to your audience and what additional factors you need to consider when planning your communication approach' (Blum, 1997, p. 5).

Are any of your fellow students from other countries?

Check your classes to see whether there are any fellow students who are from other countries. Within what framework do you operate when communicating with them? Upon what factors did you base your communication technique? Try answering the following questions to help you in the future:

What is the reference point/cultural 'dimension' of those students?
How is this reflected in your behaviour, style and values and those of your fellow students?
What impact do you want your communication to have?
Is the communication appropriate, given the culture within which you are working?
Are your communication objectives relevant, realistic and culturally appropriate?
What are the appropriate communication channels for the culture within which you are working?
How will you measure your success?

Adapted from: S. Blum, 'Preventing Culture Shock' in *Review* (Smythe Dorward Lambert, London), Winter/Spring 1997, pp. 4–5.

Non-verbal communication

Non-verbal communication includes all elements of communication that do not involve words or language. The six basic kinds of non-verbal communication are:

- proxemics
- kinesics
- facial and eye contact
- paralanguage
- chronemics
- object language/artefacts.

Proxemics

The study of an individual's perception and use of space, including territorial space, is called proxemics. As shown in Figure 3.2 below, the bands of space extending outward from the individual are called *territorial space/s*. Each band constitutes comfort zones within which different cultures prefer different types of interaction with others. Territorial space varies greatly across cultures. Individuals often become uncomfortable when operating in territorial spaces different from those in which they are familiar. Relationships shape the use of territorial space – the more familiar individuals are, the nearer they will invade the territory of others.

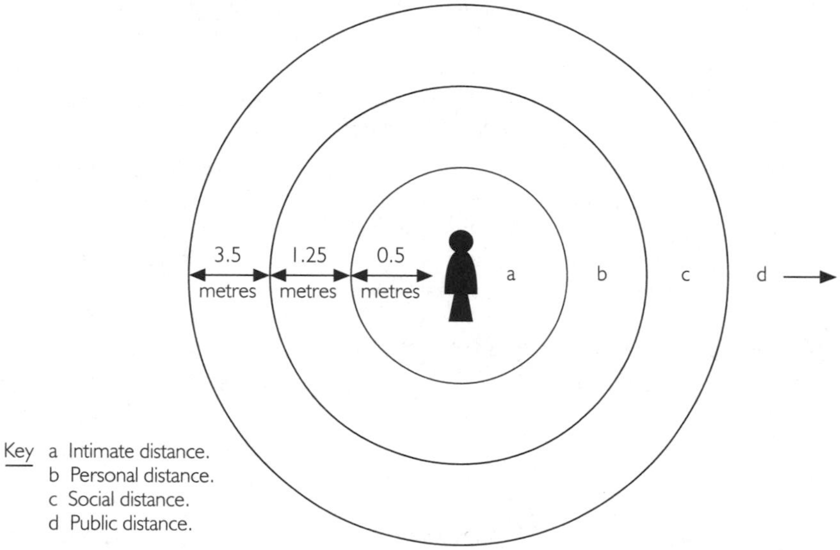

Figure 3.2 Zones of territorial space in United Kingdom culture

Seating dynamics is an aspect of proxemics and is the art of seating people in certain positions according to the person's purpose in communications. Figure 3.3 below shows some common seating dynamics.

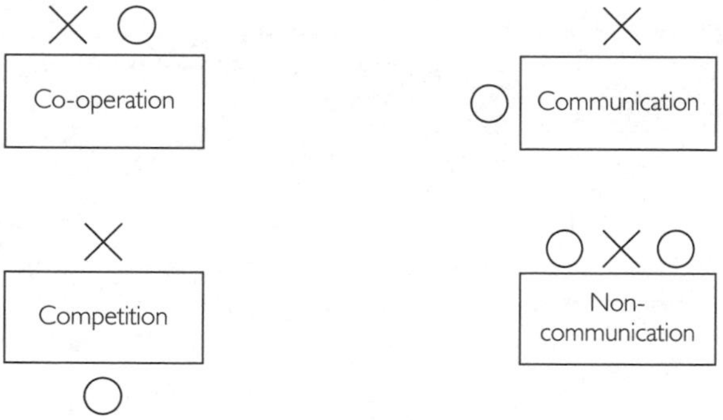

Figure 3.3 Seating dynamics

Kinesics

The study of body movements, including posture, is called kinesics. Like proxemics, it is culturally bound and there is no single universal gesture.

CASE STUDY
When in Rome …

The Italians are charming, intelligent people to whom Europe owes a great cultural debt. They are excellent communicators and combine ultra-keen perception with ever-present flexibility. Their continual exuberance and loquacious persuasiveness often produce an adverse reaction with reserved Britons, factual Germans and taciturn Scandinavians. Yet such northerners have everything to gain by adapting to the Italians' outgoing nature, meeting them halfway in their idea for dialogue. There is plenty of business to be done with the Italians, who export vigorously in order to survive.

Italians may appear to be disorganised, but don't forget Italy is the fifth-largest industrial nation in the world and has outperformed even the Germans and Americans in such areas as domestic appliances and some categories such as cars. On top of that they have an enormous hidden or black economy, synonymous with shady dealings. Whilst Italian business dealings may feel dishonest – businesses frequently get round rules – remember that this is the way they do business and you may well be able to benefit from this flexibility. They will regard your rather rigid, law-abiding approach as short-sighted or even blind. They do not consider their own approach to be in any way corrupt.

Italian negotiators often seem to proceed in a roundabout manner and will discuss things from a personal or semi-emotional angle, while a northerner tries to concentrate on the benefit for his company and stick to the facts of the particular deal. Italians will also jump ahead to later points on the agenda or will re-discuss points that you think have already been settled. If you are in the chair, you have to create some kind of order, but you can only do this by establishing firm rules in advance. One German … used yellow, red and green cards to discipline people at meetings. This humorous but firm approach achieved the desired result.

A lack of self-discipline is also demonstrated by poor time-keeping. Italians have a different concept of time from that of northerners and Americans. They do not arrive for appointments on time. Punctuality in Milan means they are twenty minutes late and in Rome half an hour. It is not possible to change them, so you have to adapt and be prepared to wait 15–45 minutes before an Italian counterpart arrives. Alternatively, you can deliberately turn up half an hour late.

Italian wordiness versus north European succinctness is a constant pain in internal company communication. Both sides wish to achieve clarity but one is doing so through many words and the other through short messages and memos. A compromise must be reached. The northerner must teach himself to be more explicit and explanatory, but also encourage his Italian colleague to be more concise and economical with words and ideas, and, when practical, to put them in writing.

Overall then, a northerner should approach business deals with Italians with adequate time for the exercise and a store of patience. He must be prepared to discuss at length and maintain calm. An Italian may get overheated on some point, but changes a moment later. Italians also quarrel among themselves at the table, but are solid colleagues thereafter. In the course of doing business, you may speak much more freely with Italians than with most other Europeans, but do not exaggerate directness or bluntness. Remember that their communication style is eloquent, wordy, demonstrative and apparently emotional. This is normal for them, over-dramatic for you. Do not be led into the belief that waving arms and talking with the hands denotes instability. They think you, by contrast, are rather wooden and distant.

Source: D. Lewis, 'When in Rome …', in *Management Today*, August 1996, pp. 77–78

Facial and eye behaviour

The face is the richest source of non-verbal communication and, together with eye behaviour, gives cues to the receiver. The face often gives unintended clues to emotions that the sender is trying to hide. Eye contact can enhance reflective listening and it varies by culture – a direct gaze indicates honesty and forthrightness in the United Kingdom but this may not be true in other cultures. For example, in some Asian cultures it is considered good behaviour to bow the head in deference to a superior rather than to look the manager in the eye.

Paralanguage

Paralanguage consists of variations in speech, such as pitch, loudness, tempo, tone, duration, laughing and crying. People make attributions about the sender by deciphering paralanguage cues.

Can you use paralanguage effectively?

Read the following five sentences aloud, making a strong verbal emphasis on the word which is highlighted in bold type.

How did she do that?
How **did** she do that?
How did **she** do that?
How did she **do** that?
How did she do **that?**

By shifting the emphasis, the sentence can convey different meanings. The way the voice is used is an important element in understanding messages.

Try the sentences again in the same way.

Chronemics

Chronemics is the use of time and is often overlooked as an element of non-verbal communication. Time is often viewed as a commodity that can be spent, saved, earned, or wasted. European society is very time consuming, as reflected in our dependence on clocks and time schedules. It is expressed everywhere in the workplace through completion dates for projects, specific pay periods and working hours.

Object language

This is sometimes known as *artifacts* and refers to the communication that results from the display of material things. Some of the objects that frequently influence communication are clothes, furniture, methods of transport, and architectural arrangements. Individuals attempt to enhance their personal object language by purchasing items such as clothes and trinkets. Office furniture and its arrangement can affect communication patterns, and physical settings convey information about the kind of activities that are to take place and the kind of behaviours that are acceptable.

Non-verbal communication is important for managers because of its impact on the meaning of the message. However, the manager must consider the total message and each medium of communication. People's confidence in their ability to decode non-verbal communication is greater than their accuracy in doing so.

Knowledge of communication will always be important to anyone who wishes to function more effectively within the workplace. It is a vital link between people that makes it possible for organisations to function – a skill which is imperative to success and which, if deficient within any worker, will result in a non-profitable organisation. It is a skill which can be learned.

Introducing learning

All managers, and human resource managers in particular, need to understand how an individual learns and develops if they are to achieve the goals and objectives of the organisation. Morgan (1988) stated that managers must:

> ... find ways of developing and mobilizing the intelligence, knowledge, and creative potential of human beings at every level of organization ... become increasingly skilled in placing quality people in key places and developing their full potential. It will become increasingly important to recruit people who enjoy learning and relish change and to motivate employees to be intelligent, flexible, and adaptive. (p. 7)

And things have not changed today. Kanter (1992) believes that it is essential that employees are developed as key components within the organisation because they are the only thing which will enable the organisation to survive – they are the lynchpin. They will require, according to Barrow and Loughlin (1993), a number of abilities and skills such as:

- *a high level of education* – up to first degree level so that they can use the technology and understand their own contribution to the decisions required in their jobs;
- *the ability to learn new skills and adapt to changing circumstances* – through continuous development individuals must take responsibility for their own learning and ensure that all their skills are current and that they have the ability to learn new skills;
- *the ability to work in organisations with flatter structures and few levels of management* – which requires the setting of personal objectives, working in self-managed teams and making decisions;

- *the ability to interface with people at all levels* – including customers, superiors and team members;
- *the ability to problem-solve* – through creative thinking.

Defining learning

Like a number of concepts met within the field of organisational behaviour, learning is difficult to define and can be ambiguous in its conceptual use. However, an appreciation of learning in context is important to the understanding of learning in action within the organisation. Most writers – particularly those who take a psychological approach to learning – tend to agree that learning brings about a permanent change in behaviour. This aspect of a change in behaviour is important because it distinguishes two different aspects which are pertinent to the workplace. Firstly, *practice*, which tends to be related to events that are deliberately planned, and, secondly *experience*, which may have been intentionally arranged – remembering that it is possible to learn unintentionally – or may have occurred spontaneously in the natural course of events.

A central theme of today's learning organisations (discussed in Chapter 8) is 'learning to learn' and self-development through active learning. Maund (1994) believes that workers cannot be brought together without spontaneous learning taking place and that as a result they will change their behaviour to fit in a variety of ways. For example, at the simplest level, team members will learn each other's names, technical jargon, and the availability of information and resources; at a more sophisticated level they will learn about the behaviour of their colleagues and supervisor and thus develop attitudes which can have complex effects on their behaviour which, in turn, will confirm or alter the manager's attitudes towards them.

Pettinger (1996) incorporates the fundamental aspects of learning in his definition: 'the process by which skills, knowledge, attitudes and behaviour are formed and developed' (p. 82).

There are a number of factors which enable learning and development to take place:

- education
- training
- socialisation
- experience.

According to Pettinger (1996) learning and development are also a result of conditioning and restriction which he states are: '... whereby the individual is persuaded to adopt, and ultimately accept, guidance, regulation, conformity and compliance in particular situations' (p. 82).

Views of learning

When accepting the view that learning is a permanent change in behaviour which has come about as a result of experience, it is possible to appreciate that it is not just a cognitive activity – that is, it is not merely thinking and collecting knowledge about a subject. For example, learning the text of this book parrot-fashion does not mean that you have learned. This is the *behaviourist approach* – an assumption that observable behaviour is a function of its consequences. All learning is based upon two key theories: classical and operant conditioning.

Classical conditioning

This is the modifying of an individual's behaviour so that a conditioned stimulus is matched with an unconditioned stimulus and elicits an unconditioned response. The theory is based on the work of a Russian physiologist, Ivan Pavlov, who worked with dogs to support his views. His dogs secreted saliva (*unconditioned response*) when they were given food (*unconditioned stimulus*). When he presented the dogs with a *conditioned stimulus* (Pavlov used a bell) at the same time as the unconditioned stimulus (the food), he caused the dogs to salivate (*conditioned response*).

Workers are not dogs, yet they may behave in the same way if classical conditioning methods are used by managers. For example, a peripatetic consultant may well get lower back pain (unconditioned response) as a result of poor posture (unconditioned stimulus) in the car seat. However, if the consultant becomes aware of the pain in the back only when the mobile telephone in the car rings (conditioned response), then she might very well develop a conditioned response (lower back pain) as soon as the telephone rings.

Do any of your lecturers use classical conditioning?

In medieval times the students of the universities, such as Oxford and Cambridge, were considered to have learned if they could recite large passages verbatim during classes: an example of classical conditioning.

Reflect on your university classes – are there any aspects of classical conditioning taking place?

Your answer will depend upon your own experiences. You might well feel that classical conditioning is a logical approach to learning but that it has its limitations. Did you consider the following?

- As a human you are more complex than a dog and are less amenable to cause-and-effect conditioning.
- Your environment is also complex and not amenable to stimulus–response manipulations.
- When making decisions you would consider a high degree of complexity and this would override any simple conditioning.

Operant conditioning

Operant conditioning happens when behaviour is modified by means of positive or negative consequences following specific behaviours. It is based on the belief that behaviour is a function of its consequences, which could be positive or negative. It is through this resultant behaviour that an individual influences or shapes future behaviour. There are three distinct strategies which help this process:

- reinforcement
- punishment
- extinction.

A number of organisations use the ideas within this theory in an effort to get members of the workforce to behave in a required way – this is called *organisational behaviour modification*.

Through *reinforcement* acceptable behaviour is enhanced and through *punishment* and *extinction* undesirable behaviours are extinguished. All organisations have a standard of behaviour which is acceptable and some behaviours which are not. Such behaviours are usually emphasised through the culture (reviewed in Chapter 9) of the organisation. However, a specific behaviour in one context might not be acceptable within another. For example, a worker might well be a member of the Reserve Forces, and be trained to use sophisticated weapons designed to kill. However, if he used these skills in the workplace in an attempt to downsize the staff, his behaviour would not be construed as contextually acceptable. Such a situation also raises ethical issues about what is desirable and undesirable behaviour.

It is management which uses reinforcement and punishment in an attempt to encourage acceptable behaviours. Positive consequences are brought about as a result of any behaviour which is found to be attractive or pleasurable, for example, performance related pay or promotion. Negative consequences are the result of behaviour which an individual finds unattractive or aversive. Examples here might be a forced transfer, or disciplinary action. The important thing to remember here is that the consequences of an individual's behaviour – be they positive or negative – are defined for the individual receiving them: they are person-specific. It follows, then, that individual, gender and cultural differences may be very important when considering positive or negative consequences of behaviour.

The use of positive or negative consequences follows a specific behaviour and therefore reinforces or punishes that particular behaviour. Research shows that when an individual's behaviour is followed by a positive consequence, then the original behaviour is reinforced and is likely to continue. Conversely, any behaviour which is followed by a negative consequence is likely to reoccur. Figure 3.4 below shows how positive and negative consequences can be applied or withheld in the strategies of reinforcement and punishment.

	REINFORCEMENT (Desirable behaviour)	PUNISHMENT (Undesirable behaviour)
POSITIVE CONSEQUENCES	Apply	Withhold
NEGATIVE CONSEQUENCES	Withhold	Apply

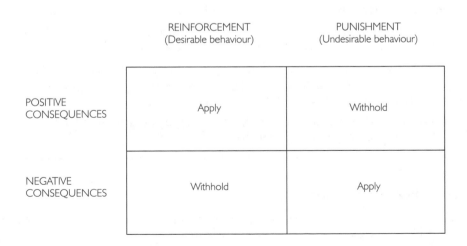

Figure 3.4 Reinforcement and punishment strategies

Extinction is an alternative to punishment and is any behaviour which is used in an attempt to weaken a behaviour in others by attaching some sort of consequence (positive or negative) to it. The basic philosophy behind this technique is that by ignoring the behaviour it will disappear, but it does take patience and time. An example here would be when an individual ignores (no consequence) the bigoted comments (behaviour) of a colleague. It is more effectively used in tandem with positive reinforcement of behaviour which is deemed desirable. In the above example, this would mean complimenting the bigoted colleague for any constructive comments (reinforcing desirable behaviour) whilst ignoring the bigoted comments (extinguishing undesirable behaviour). However, it is sometimes necessary to give a swift punishment and extinction procedures would not be suitable. Examples here would be in the case of theft from the organisation or unethical behaviour. In learning, it is important that there is a concentrated effort to manage the consequences of behaviour.

Social learning theory

Bandura (1977) offered an alternative to classical and operant conditioning in his social learning theory, which considered that learning happens because individuals observe the behaviour of others and model themselves upon them. Examples here would be a worker who models herself on the leadership style of a manager she admires. It is through the behaviour of superiors that individuals learn to pattern their own responses. Bandura's (1977) theory has its central idea in the notion of *self-efficacy* – individuals' beliefs and expectancies of their ability to accomplish a task efficiently – which is part of the perception process (previously discussed in Chapter 2). People who have a high level of self-efficacy tend to be effective learners – at least, more effective than those at the other end of the continuum. According to Bandura (1977) it is possible to enhance low levels of self-efficacy through any of four methods:

- *performance accomplishments* – which means: just get on with it;
- *vicarious experiences* – model behaviour on someone else: watch someone else doing it;
- *verbal persuasion* – become convinced by someone else to get on with it;
- *emotional arousal* – get excited by it.

Can you recall a skill that you have mastered?

Remember a skill that you have mastered; for example, driving a car. Do you think that you were a skilled driver when you passed your test? Are you one now?

We know from our experience that to integrate any skill into a behaviour takes considerable practice and yet most of us approach our learning from the traditional lecture approach rather than by using forms that mirror behaviour.

Is your organisational behaviour tutor facilitating learning or using the traditional lecture approach? What effect has this on your learning?

Personality and learning

In Chapter 1 there was a discussion on Jung's (1923) theory of personality differences and two particular elements of this theory relate closely to learning.

- *Introverted and extroverted distinctions*. If you believe that there is a continuum of the above, then introverts need quiet time to study, concentrate, and reflect on what they are learning; whereas the extrovert needs to interact with others and share the process.

- *Personality functions*. Particular functions such as feeling, thinking, and sensitiveness have implications for learning. Table 3.1 shows the relationship between personality functions and learning.

Table 3.1 Personality functions and learning

Personality preference	**Implications for learning by individuals**
Information gathering	
Intuitors	Prefer theoretical frameworks. Look for some sort of meaning in all materials. Try to make sense of the whole scheme of work. Attempt to find possibilities and interrelationships.
Sensors	Prefer facts and empirical information. Want to apply the theory. Attempt to master the details. Use what is realistic and possible.
Decision-making	
Thinkers	Analyse data and information. Are fairminded and even-handed. Seek logicality rather than direct conclusions. Like to remain at a distance from the work.
Feelers	Interpersonally involved. Usually fairminded and happy to keep the peace. Look for subjective and fair results. Dislike factual, objective analysis.

Adapted from: O. Kroeger and J.M. Thuesen, 1988, *Type Talk: The 16 Personality Types That Determine How We Live, Love, and Work* (New York: Dell Publishing)

Each worker has a preferred model of gathering information, evaluation, and decision-making. For example, feelers will want to find out what other people think about a report and look for a fair result, whereas intuitive thinkers are likely to want to look at a report and use their hunches about implementation.

Individuals and learning

No individual learns in the same way as any other since all individuals learn at different paces and at different times and life stages. There are some who can acquire knowledge and skills easily whilst others find it more difficult. Investigations into learning theory suggest that learning is based on any, some, or all of the following:

1 **Intrinsic motivation.** The higher the level of intrinsic motivation individuals have the more likely they are to learn and thus bring about a permanent change in their behaviour. If, for example, they believe that learning something has a reward in a form they want, say increased esteem, they will learn.
2 **Facilitating quality.** If the learning environment and teaching quality are perceived by the learners to be good, they are more likely to learn.
3 **Pressure.** External pressure from others desiring the individual to learn will include the intrinsic desire to learn the norms of fellow workers and the culture of the organisation.
4 **Specific drives.** Intrinsic desires to keep abreast of expertise in their specific area through continuous professional development will drive individuals to learn.
5 **Personality factors.** If individuals have the attitude and disposition to acquire new skills and competencies then they will improve their knowledge and qualities.

Pettinger (1996) believes that the result of successful learning is to:

> ... increase the range, depth and interactions of thoughts, ideas and concepts, as well as skills, knowledge, attitude, behaviour and experience; to increase the ability to organise and reorganise these; and to order them in productive and effective activities (whatever that may mean in the particular set of circumstances). (p. 84)

Each learning event has its own learning curve showing the relationship between behaviour, action and experience. Such cycles highlight the importance of testing and experience and the need for the learner to be able to distinguish between abstract learning through practice and performance. Figure 3.5 shows the various learning curves which are dependent upon the matter to be learned.

Learning cycles

Even though there appears to be no universally accepted *theory* of learning, the concept of learning *styles* is an important development for members of the workforce within an organisation because it might help to illuminate how people learn from experience. When planning specific learning activities, it would be prudent that the training method allow for the fact that some people learn better by one style than another, and some may indeed reject certain styles altogether (Honey and Mumford, 1986). It is beneficial, therefore, if programmes are planned with a knowledge of learners' own preferences regarding learning styles, although it is not necessarily advisable that *only* the preferred style is adhered to by individuals.

Kolb (1974) suggested that there were four stages in influencing learning: the experience; observation and reflection; theorising and conceptualisation; testing and experimentation. To be effective, the learner correspondingly needs four different but complementary kinds of abilities which Kolb (1974) illustrated using the model represented in Figure 3.6 on page 80.

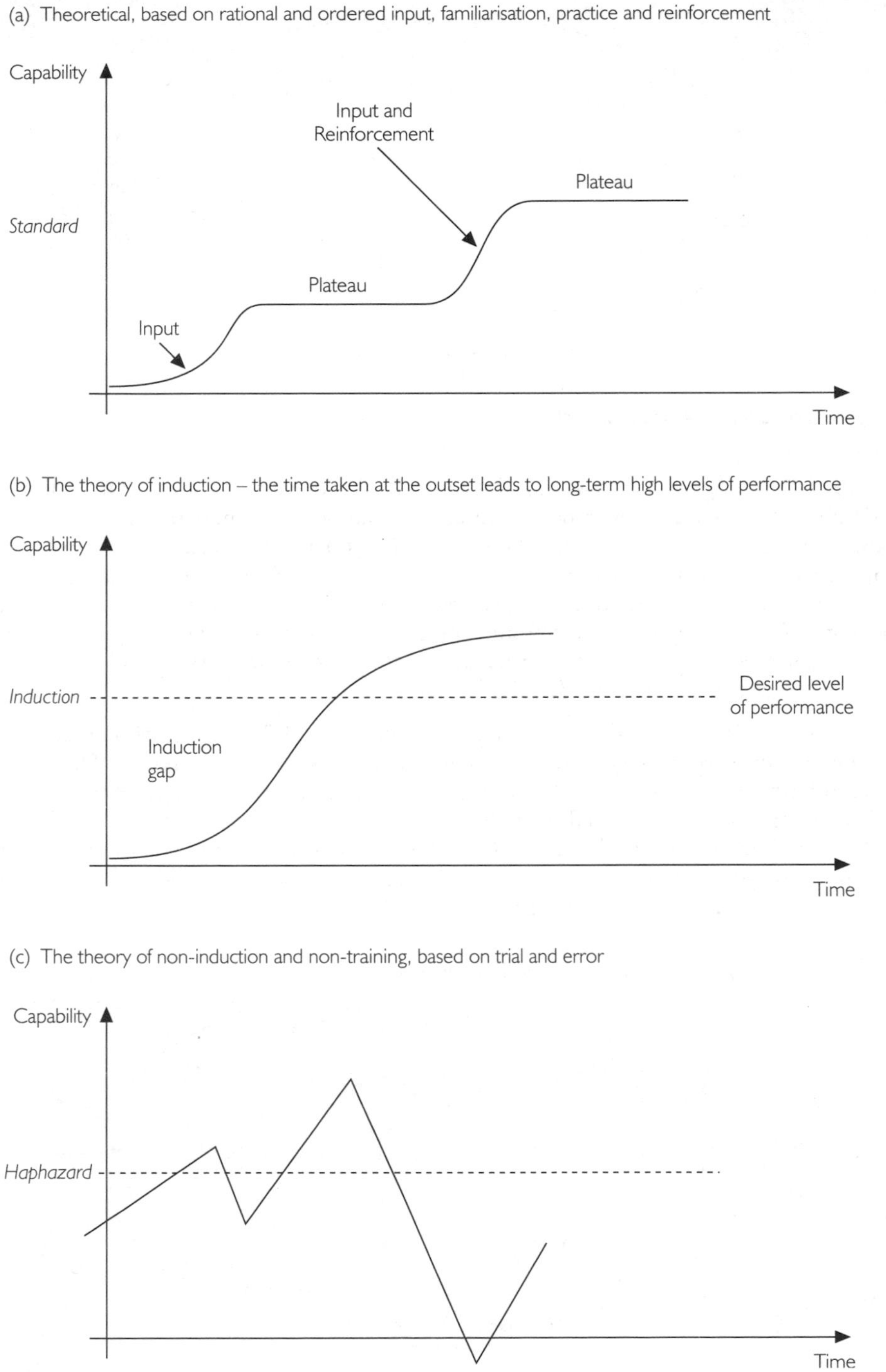
(a) Theoretical, based on rational and ordered input, familiarisation, practice and reinforcement
Capability
Input and
Reinforcement
Plateau
Standard
Plateau
Input
Time
(b) The theory of induction – the time taken at the outset leads to long-term high levels of performance
Capability
Induction
Desired level
of performance
Induction
gap
Time
(c) The theory of non-induction and non-training, based on trial and error
Capability
Haphazard
Time

Figure 3.5 Learning curves

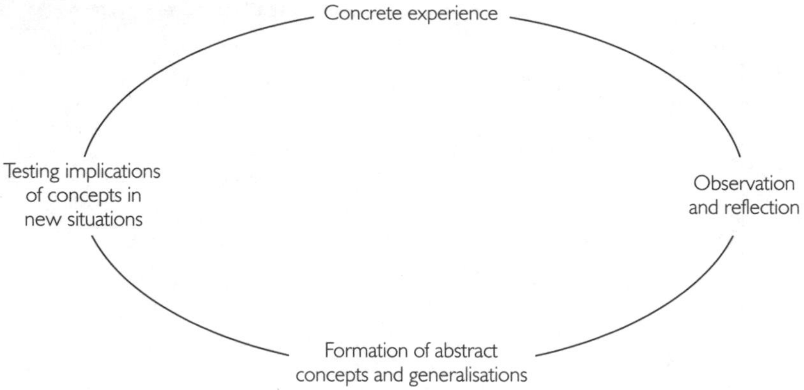

Figure 3.6 Kolb (1974) learning cycle

Kolb (1974) suggested that this ideal is difficult to achieve and argued that, in fact, the required abilities might even be in conflict. He claimed that most people are better at, and prefer, some of the four stages rather than others. For instance, an actuary might give preference to abstract conceptualisations and active experimentation whilst a manager may have greater concern for concrete experience and the active application of ideas. The essence of the theory is learning from experience, the nature of which is described as a continuous cycle or process. However, his *abstract conceptualisation stage* could well be more correctly described as *academic learning*.

Building on his theoretical base, Honey and Mumford (1986, 1992) defined four major categories of learning styles: activist, reflector, theorist, and pragmatist. These correspond with the four stages in the Kolb (1974) cycle, i.e. concrete experience (activist), observation and reflection (reflector), formation of abstract concepts and generalisations (theorist), and testing implications of concepts in new situations (pragmatist). Hence, Maund (1994) suggests that Kolb's (1974) model can be integrated with Honey and Mumford's (1986, 1992) theory as indicated in Figure 3.7 below.

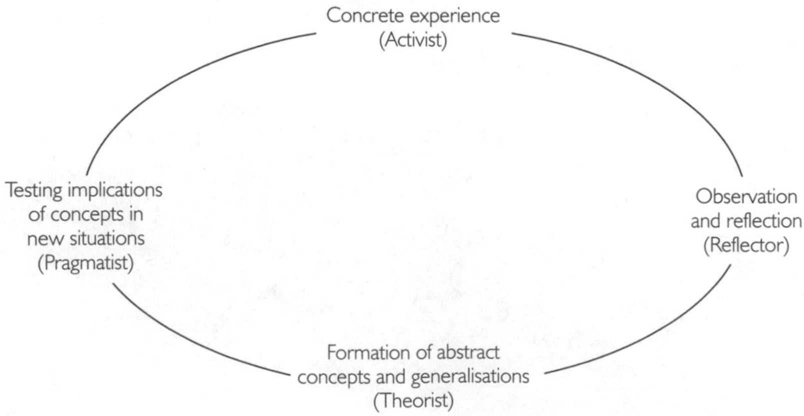

Figure 3.7 Merging the Kolb (1974) learning cycle with the Honey and Mumford (1986, 1992) learning cycles

Honey and Mumford's (1986, 1992) adaptation of the Kolb (1974) cycle is helpful to managers who assist their employees in their learning because of its potential utility for learning styles (activists, reflectors, theorists, pragmatists), which could well be seen as more relevant to the world of work and as significant aids for trainers and learners who want to develop an interest in learning.

Both models have a cyclical appreciation of learning strategies – learners may move around the cycle – and yet neither model indicates an appreciation of the fact that it is not a staged cycle; therefore individuals may ignore or utilise one or more of the learning styles.

During the course of their continuing research and applications, Honey and Mumford (1986, 1993) developed a Learning Styles Questionnaire (LSQ) on self-description, employing established norms for different types of people such as those engaged in research and development, production or finance. Such a questionnaire is a useful measuring instrument for the manager and for the individual learner and could ultimately yield data which would constitute a valuable guide for, for instance, determining an optimum composition of groups within which individual members of a team can learn. Whilst membership of project teams is selected by managers using criteria other than group dynamics and composition, the LSQ has an advantage in defining composition of smaller groups within the workplace.

For the individual worker it provides a self-diagnostic tool as a guide to building on strengths (best learning styles) and overcoming weaknesses (least favoured learning styles), leading to the adoption of a richer variety of methods. Thus, the worker is more adaptable and flexible and is more likely to assist in meeting the organisation's goals. To this end, Honey and Mumford (1986, 1993) gave advice on how to make the best use of individual learning strengths and how to improve and practise each of the four styles. Their work has been developed within organisations and is now a key measure of individual learning styles.

Individuals will differ in the ways they prefer to learn, partly in reaction to the instructional modes provided in the organisation, but more generally in terms of a distinction between holistic and serialistic styles of learning. Individual workers who adopt a *holistic* learning strategy want to see the 'whole picture' and how their present learning fits into the organisation's goals as a whole, and what its purpose is. In learning, such workers thrive on everyday examples, illustrations, diagrams and anecdotes, they look for links with similar ideas and they also build up more idiosyncratic forms of understanding which are personally satisfying. In other words, they want relevance to their work. In contrast, employees preferring *serialist* learning strategies tend to focus narrowly on the particular task or topic, and for them learning needs to be step by step, concentrating first on the details and on the connected logic, progressively building up their own skills and developing their understanding.

If workers are to own their learning and bring about a permanent change in behaviour they must use holistic strategies (relating ideas and developing a personal organisation) and serialist strategies (examining both the evidence and the logic); indeed some members of the workforce will have such strong learning styles that their learning will be ineffectively incomplete, being dominated either by overgeneralisation or too narrow a vision. Through training and development workers can be encouraged to carry out the more complete forms of learning which lead to conceptual understanding and, thus, a higher level of competency.

Barriers to learning

There are a number of barriers to learning which a worker might face. For example, fear of failure, or the inability (or unwillingness) to expend time and effort. In the rapidly changing work environment it is not sufficient to *acquire* the standard knowledge and skills; the ability to *transfer* such knowledge and skills is paramount to the continuous learning process required of workers in today's world. The successful learning environment is one in which attention is paid to minimising demotivating factors by creating a supportive climate and by developing workers' confidence in their ability to tackle and overcome barriers to learning; in other words, an environment which fosters and encourages the natural self-generating learning process. This is an important aim because employees who have grown as learners will continue to be competent at *learning* and will thus take the lead in managing change and developing themselves in the process. It is the role of the learning organisation (discussed in Chapter 8) to ensure that the workforce appreciates the importance of learning because it takes place in a complex, interacting system. The outcomes of learning depend on the combined effects of the whole learning environment provided by the organisation and its design as well as on the training and development provided.

Goal setting

Within the workplace goal setting is closely linked to learning. Goal setting is the process of deciding on the required objectives of an organisation which will ultimately guide and direct the behaviour of individuals within the organisation. It originally surfaced in the work of the scientific management school, members of which believed that performance standards would lead to higher work performance.

It is not easy to identify work goals since they tend to be an umbrella term and workers tend to 'just do it', and different organisations will define their goals in their own way. Some organisations use the SMART system to communicate their approach to effective goals. SMART is an acronym for the five most commonly used characteristics used to specify goals:

Specific

Measurable

Attainable

Realistic

Time-bound.

If the goals are specific and challenging then an individual will concentrate on them and is, therefore, likely to be effective in learning what is required to achieve the goals – this can be seen in Figure 3.8.

Through these measurable and achievable goals comes feedback concerning goal progress. Not all goals are quantifiable, and qualitative goals are extremely valuable. The latter could include the desire to improve team-member relationships; indeed, qualitative goals may be sufficient in themselves.

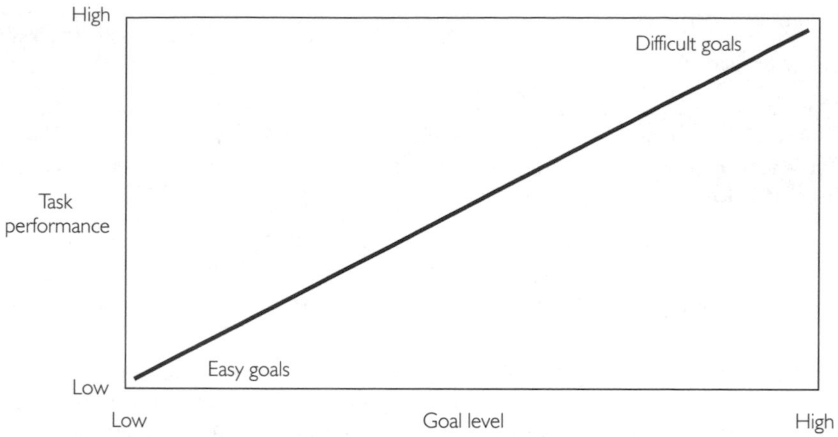

Figure 3.8 Goal level and task performance

Time-bound goals help with measurability, whether the time be implicit or explicit. For example, without a time limit a salesperson will not be able to compare her goals with those of previous time periods. However, there is not always a finely tuned limit concerning the achievement of personal goals.

Overall, goal setting serves one or more of several functions, each of which is related to the way individuals learn, by:

- increasing work motivation and thus the performance of tasks;
- reducing stress by reducing dysfunctional conflict;
- improving the validity and reliability of performance evaluation.

People in organisations learn from the consequences of what they do and, therefore, it is vital that managers and supervisors take care when they apply any form of positive or negative reinforcement. It is through these experiences that individuals are intrinsically motivated – a concept which is reviewed in the next chapter. However, before you move on, try your skills in identifying the issues related to effective communication and learning which are reflected in the following case.

CASE STUDY

A victim of 'flame culture'

For a five-month period in 1995, Jack Philips had no face-to-face communication with his line manager, despite the fact that she worked in the office next door to his. Instead, he received a stream of e-mails that became increasingly critical and derogatory.

Philips (not his real name), an inspection and registration officer for a local authority, would dread returning to the office. On one occasion after a weekend away he logged on to the authority's e-mail system to find 53 messages waiting for him.

'The language she used on the e-mails was intimidating. It was short, it was curt and it was rude,' he says. 'She would say: "I tried to contact you the other day. I couldn't get hold of you. Why is this? Where is that? Why haven't you done this? I'm fed up with chasing you." '

The bullying began to escalate, and Philips found he was criticised in meetings and deprived of the resources to do his job properly. Following an office move, he found he was the only member of staff not to have a table and chair and was forced to sit on boxes and work on a table housing the printer.

Philips says that the line manager was using the distancing effect of e-mails to cover up her own lack of interpersonal skills. E-mails could be dispatched quickly and effortlessly, with no thought for the consequences. They offered power without responsibility, but had a profound effect on his self-esteem and employee morale generally.

'The office was like a morgue. The use of e-mail stifled conversation. People were frightened to talk about ordinary things. When you came back from a holiday, for instance, nobody would inquire whether you had a good time. The normal interaction with colleagues was blocked, because there was a whole feeling of distrust.'

Eventually, Philips complained to a senior manager, but the result was a charge of gross misconduct against him. The charges were never substantiated and now he is in limbo: suspended from his job, but unable to seek redress while he is still receiving a salary. To suggest that he is disheartened is an understatement.

'I used to be a confident person, but I am not anymore,' he says. 'I am stuck at home feeling worthless and useless.'

Source: Mark Thatcher, 'A victim of "flame culture" ' in *People Management*, 26 June 1997, p. 29.

Questions for discussion

1 What non-verbal behaviours do you find most helpful in others when you are attempting to talk with them? When you attempt to listen to them?

2 What methods have you found to be the most helpful in overcoming barriers to communication that are physical? Status based? Cultural? Linguistic?

3 If there were a conflict between your self-evaluation of your work and that given to you by your evaluator or peers, how would you specifically respond? How does this relate to the theory of learning?

References and further reading

Bandura, A., 1977, *Social Learning Theory* (Englewood Cliffs, NJ: Prentice-Hall)

Barrow, M.H. and Loughlin, H.M., 1993, 'Towards a Learning Organization in Great Metropolitan Foods Europe' in G. Willis (ed.) *Your Enterprise School of Management* (Bradford: MCB University Press), pp. 195–208

Beardwell, I. and Holden, L., 1997 (2nd edn), *Human Resource Management: A Contemporary Perspective* (London: Pitman)

Black, O., 'Addressing the issue of good communication', in *People Management*, 26 June 1997, p. 29.

Blum, S., 'Preventing Culture Shock' in *Review* (Smythe Dorward Lambert, London), Winter/Spring 1997, pp. 4–5

Brown, M., 1996, 'Space shuttle' in *Management Today*, January 1996, pp. 66–74

Corbett, M., 'Wired and Emotional' in *People Management*, 26 June 1997, p. 26

Hamilton, C. and Kleiner, B.M., 'Steps to Better Listening' in *Personnel Journal*, February 1987

Honey, P. and Mumford, A., 1986 and 1992, *The Manual of Learning Styles* (UK, Maidenhead: Honey)

Jung, C.G., 1923, *Psychological Types* (New York: Harcourt & Brace)

Kanter, R.M., 'It's a people thing' in *Financial Times* (in 'The Management Interview' by V. Griffith), 24 July 1997, p. 20

Kanter, R.M., 'Creating a habitat for the migrant manager' in *Personnel Management*, October 1992, pp. 38–40

Kolb, A., 'On Management and the Learning Process' in D.A. Kolb, I.N. Rubin and J.M. McIntyre (eds), 1974, *Organisational Psychology: A Book of Readings* (Englewood Cliffs, NJ: Prentice Hall)

Kroeger, O. and Thuesen, J.M., 1988, *Type Talk: The 16 Personality Types that Determine How We Live, Love, and Work* (New York: Dell Publishing)

Lewis D., 'When in Rome …', in *Management Today*, August 1996, pp. 77–78

Locke, E.A., 'The Ideas of Frederick W. Taylor: An Evaluation' in *Academy of Management Review*, No 7, 1982, pp. 14–24

Maund, L.C., 1994, *The role of conflict in the teaching and learning of undergraduates: A Case Study* (unpublished PhD thesis, Guildford: The University of Surrey)

Morgan G., 1988, *Riding the Waves of Change: Developing Managerial Competencies for a Turbulent World* (San Francisco: Jossey Bass)

Pettinger, R., 1996, *Introduction to Organisational Behaviour* (Basingstoke: Macmillan)

Thatcher, M., 'A victim of flame culture', in *People Management*, 26 June 1997, p. 29

Waddington, K. and Fletcher C., 'Oh I heard it on the grapevine' in *Professional Manager*, July 1997, p. 33

4 Motivation

Learning objectives

By the end of this chapter, you should be able to:

- define what is meant by motivation;
- understand the differing approaches to the study of motivation;
- compare the work of Maslow (1943, 1954, 1971) with that of his successors;
- contrast the range of process theories of motivation;
- understand the relationship of motivation to work performance;
- assess motivation across cultures;
- understand the special needs of knowledge workers;
- describe strategies for motivating staff.

Introduction

CASE STUDY

Shoe factory provides an offshore spur

High winds, stormy seas and harsh working conditions are part of the job for those who work on oil-drilling platforms in the North Sea. Workers are not there for the love of it, but for good wages and the two-week breaks back on land that alternate with the two weeks of 12-hour shifts.

It is difficult to get workers to take responsibility in such conditions, but an experimental programme on two platforms run by Shell UK Exploration and Production does seem to have improved the involvement of employees and resulted in increased productivity.

The experiment began two years ago when Tom Brown, manager of the Dunlin Alpha and Cormorant Alpha platforms, was working out how to manage costs over the remaining twenty years or so of likely production by the platforms. Instead of cutting jobs he believed he could improve productivity by giving employees more responsibility for their work.

In search of ideas, he visited the K-Shoes factory in Kendal which had been running an empowerment programme for two years. 'I saw an enthusiasm in their workforce that I didn't see in my own workforce,' he says.

As part of the investigation the human resource consultancy which had been involved in the K-Shoes project surveyed the workers on the offshore platform. Upward appraisal for managers was introduced with employees filling in questionnaires about their bosses, and the managers were then given feedback on their strengths and weaknesses. Workers were given a questionnaire designed to measure their attitudes to their job and the extent of their practical knowledge. Over a period of time individuals began to generate ideas to improve production and the people who have the ideas are put in touch with people who can give them an answer. Responsibility has been given for allocating work to self-managed teams.

As a result of being given more responsibility the workers on the oil-drilling platforms have become more motivated.

Adapted from R. Donkin, 'Shoe factory provides an offshore spur' in *Financial Times*, 26 November 1997, p. 19.

As the above case shows, individuals within contemporary organisations face a number of challenges which include:

- increasing pressure and stress
- greater responsibility and initiative
- the need for flexible and creative thinking.

In a more globalised and competitive environment, organisations are having to exercise ever tighter control on costs. Many organisations have downsized, and increasing numbers are going through the process of removing layers of management, at both the top and the middle of their organisation structure.

In responding to a more demanding and volatile environment, organisations are having to become quicker and more responsive to their markets, with many devolving decision-making further down the organisation's hierarchy. Pressures on costs and the need to improve levels of service have also led many organisations to introduce more flexible, efficient work practices.

Such a mercurial environment – with the accompanying devolution of responsibility – has put pressure on individuals to be more creative in response to how they discover and satisfy the needs of the customer. In turn, these pressures require individuals to be highly motivated and to work together as proactive partners, with more freedom to take decisions and handle information. The case study above illustrates this factor and highlights the fact that performance at work is the product of the interaction between capability and motivation.

The nature of work motivation

As was seen in the discussion on personality (see Chapter 1), individuals have a number of different outlooks on the world. Such views result in differing kinds of motivation, which can be said to be the process by which an individual wants and chooses to engage in certain specified behaviours.

Mullins (1996) suggests that the underlying concept of motivation is: 'some driving force within individuals by which they attempt to achieve some goal in order to fulfil some need or expectation' (p. 480).

Moorhead and Griffin (1995) believe that motivation is: 'a set of forces that lead people to behave in particular ways' (p. 78).

From definitions such as these it can be seen that motivation is the driving force which makes an individual act to meet a need, which will result in either fulfilment or frustration. If individuals' motivational driving forces are blocked before they achieve their desired goal there are two possible outcomes:

- frustration
- constructive behaviour

as shown in Figure 4.1 below.

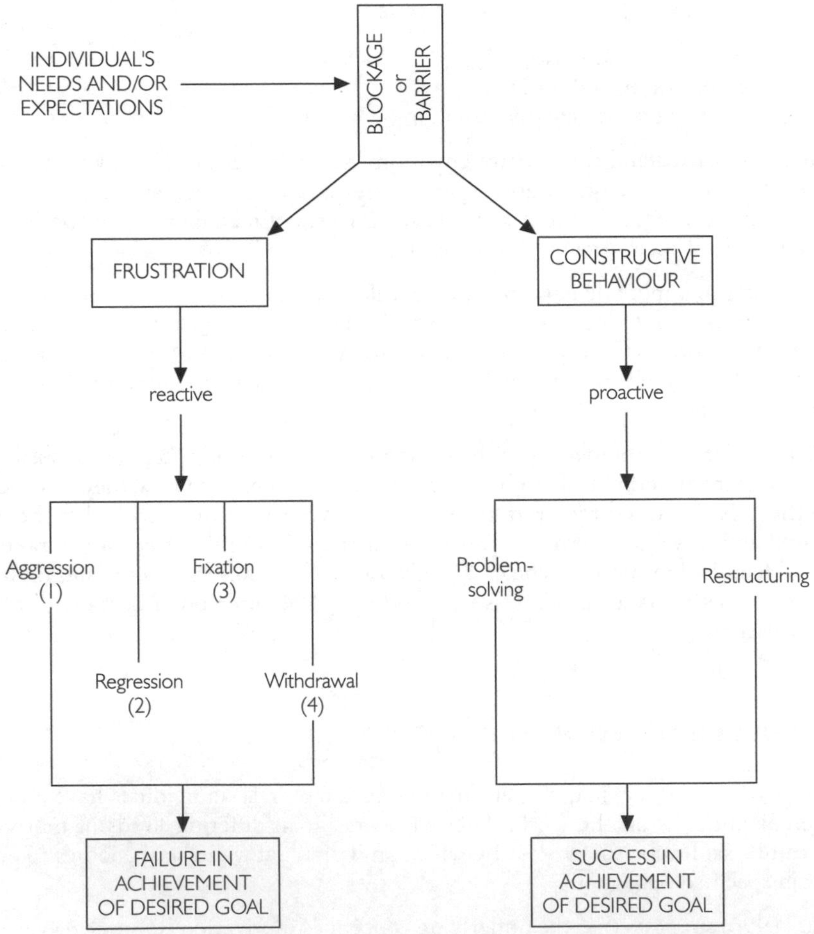

Figure 4.1 Basic model of frustration

For example, in the drive to achieve promotion at work individuals, when reaching some blockage or barrier (say, no promotion being offered by the organisation in a particular financial year), might activate their frustration by being reactive using any, or all, of the following behaviours:

1 by being *aggressive*, for example acting in a hostile and offensive manner;
2 *regressing* in their job, for example by lapsing into poor work habits or by backsliding;
3 *fixation* on the issue, for example becoming preoccupied by the fact that there are no promotions available, and they thus become set in their way of thinking;
4 *withdrawing* from the situation and disengaging from the workplace and its activities.

All, or any, of the above behaviours are likely to result in failure to achieve the desired goal (promotion) even when a post does become available.

More constructive and proactive behaviour, however, is likely to bring about the achievement of the desired goal (e.g. promotion):

5 *problem-solving*, i.e. finding ways forward to improve their chances when the time comes; this can include:
6 *restructuring*, whereby the individual finds an alternative goal, for example taking on additional responsibility in a different area of work.

The activities of an organisation can only be carried out through the combined efforts of the individual members of the workforce and such a relationship is determined by two key factors:

- what motivates the individual to work;
- the personal fulfilment gained from it.

It is in the best interest of a manager to ensure that subordinates are motivated to behave in ways which are directed towards the achievement of the organisation's goals. Since all members of an organisation's workforce need to behave in a way that helps that organisation achieve its objectives, it is essential that all individuals are motivated to perform at peak levels. Such a performance would include behaviours such as working to their full potential, high levels of attendance and punctuality, and fulfilling the organisation's mission. However, just because individuals are motivated, it does not necessarily mean that their performance level is high: other factors such as individual capability, and the situation, need to be taken into account. Therefore, motivation is related to other key factors and can be stated as below:

$$P = f\,(M + C + S)$$

where P = performance, M = motivation, C = capability, and S = situation (*f* means 'function of').

Using the example of individuals striving for promotion which itself requires a high level of performance – they must want to do their current job (motivation), be able to do the job (capability), and be in the environment with the resources (situation) to do the job. If there is a deficiency in any of these three areas an individual's performance will not be of a high level. It is the manager's responsibility to ensure that all three criteria are met.

Essential components in the motivational process

The essential components in the motivational processes are shown in Figure 4.2 below.

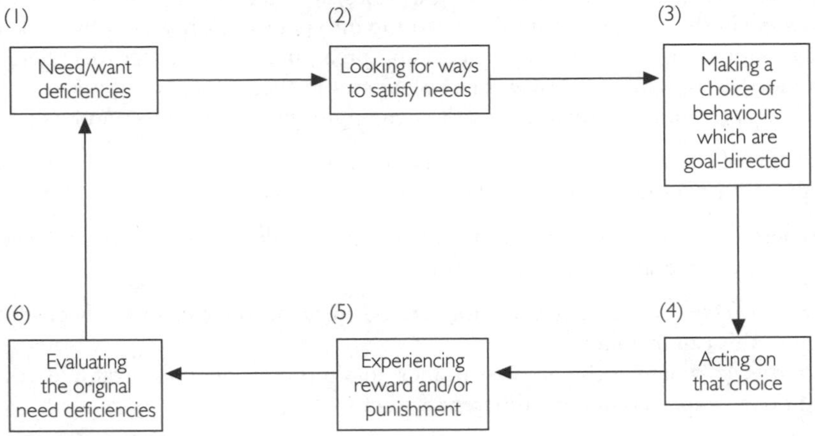

Figure 4.2 Essential components of the motivational process

The starting point in the motivational process is the identification of a need (anything a person perceives he or she wants). There is, however, a distinction between a *need* and a *want*. A need is usually something an individual must have in order to survive and is therefore usually physiological in nature (for example, water and food). A *want* tends to be non-essential for physical survival (for example, a television set). However, discussions on motivation tend to use the word 'need' to encompass both needs and wants.

As can be seen in Figure 4.2 above, an individual firstly (1) experiences deficiencies in a need and when these are of a strong enough nature, he or she will seek to find ways to satisfy these needs (2). For example, individuals who want promotion may well institute ways of acquiring the skills they need to meet that wish. They will then choose the best behaviour that will satisfy their goal (3). However, whilst they may be directed in all their behaviour to seek promotion, they are faced with more than one option at the same time to achieve their desired end. For example, they may elect to attend training courses, and/or work harder, and/or network outside the organisation in the hope of gaining their promotion in a different organisation. Whatever the decision, they will act on their choice/s (4) which will result in their experiencing rewards and/or punishments (5). They may find that their new schedule of training means long hours of study at the expense of their social life. Alternatively, they may find that it results in higher levels of performance and, then, the promotion they desired in the first place. Finally, they will assess the extent to which they have achieved their original need deficiency (6). If they have received their promotion, they will have satisfied that particular need.

Needs can be better divided into two types of needs as shown in Table 4.1 below:

Table 4.1 Needs and motives

Needs	Example	Type
Primary: required for survival and sustenance	Water, food, shelter	Physiological: instinctive
Secondary: usually exhibited in the workplace	Achievement, power affiliation, social intercourse	Psychological: learned from environment and culture

An individual's secondary needs tend to be exhibited within the workplace and are therefore important when considering the motivation of workers. It is part of an individual's psychological contract. 'Performance' is an opaque word – difficult to define and difficult to measure. Motivation and performance are parts of an employment relationship and through the concepts of a psychological function a manager can better understand such a relationship. Sims (1994) defines this psychological contract as: 'the set of expectations held by the individual employee that specify what the individual and the organization expect to give and to receive from each other in the course of their work relationship' (p. 375).

A similar view is posited by Guzzo and Norman (1994) more succinctly: 'a part of the glue that binds employees to organisations' (p. 448).

The psychological contract asks that individuals take more risks and deal with ambiguity and uncertainty – all of which used to be the responsibility of the organisation. This displacement of risk has very much affected the motivation of members of the workforce, and such psychological contracts offered by the organisation must align with the individual's unique needs. No two individuals will be motivated by the same thing: age, gender and culture are key components – as is time: what motivates an individual at the start of their career may not do so a few years later.

Motivated behaviour is goal directed, purposeful behaviour – it is very hard to find any behaviour which is not motivated. How exactly the underlying motives are conceptualised depends very much on the perceptions of the individual. The word *motive* derives from the Latin word for 'move' (*movere*) and it can vary in its length and intensity. For example, the decision to have a drink of water to satisfy the need to slake a thirst can be made quickly; however, a career move needs to be considered over time. As such, it is the individual's reason for acting in one way rather than in any other way or ways. An individual's choice will depend upon their particular motive. Hence, there is a connection between needs, motives, and behaviour:

- a *need* is a stimulus for action;
- *motives* are the channels through which the individual thinks the need can best be satisfied and thus reflect the specific behavioural choices enacted by the person;
- manifestation of motives is actual *behaviour*: they are learned needs which influence behaviour by leading individuals to pursue particular goals because they are socially valued.

Therefore, motivation can also be considered to be cognitive, because through the process of knowledge acquisition and decision-making individuals can choose their desired outcomes, and thus set in motion the actions appropriate to achieving them.

For example, where individuals decide they want promotion it might be because they want more money and more recognition (needs). They therefore decide to work longer hours and make all their hours more productive in order to attract the attention of their superiors (benefits). They then actually put in longer, more productive hours and work towards perfection (behaviours). Such is the goal-oriented aspect of motivation where an internal psychological process of initiating, energising, directing and maintaining goal-directed behaviour is brought about.

Development of motivational theories

The various theories put forward by writers in the field are not conclusive. However, as shown in the framework in Figure 4.3 below it is possible to give a basic overview.

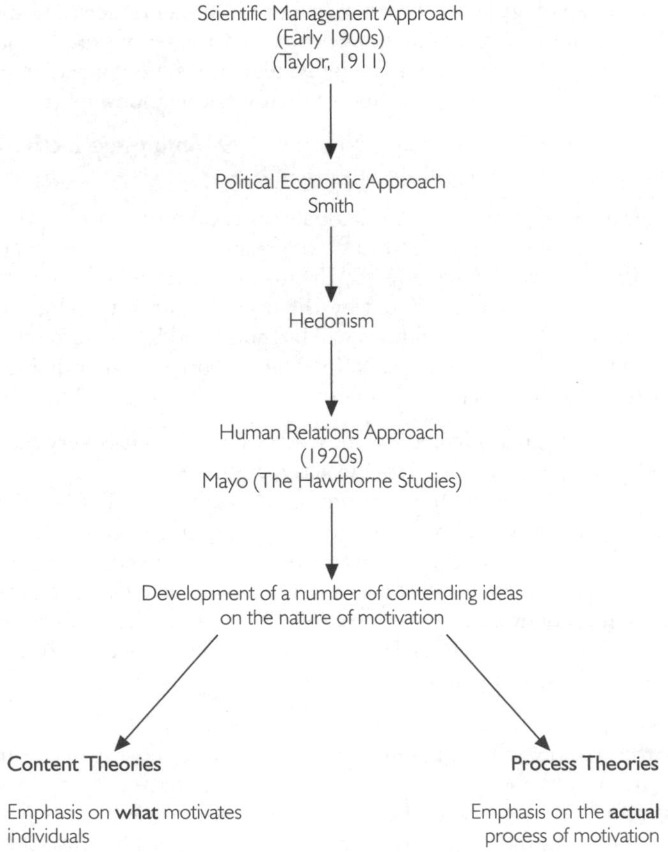

Figure 4.3 An overview of approaches to workplace motivation

There are many competing theories of motivation, all of which try to explain the nature of motivation itself. They are all partially true and have in common some explanations of behaviour in the workplace. To identify a generalised theory of motivation would appear to be futile. However, an investigation of the key theories of motivation indicates a division into two contrasting approaches:

- *content approaches* which place the emphasis on *what* motivates;
- *process approaches* which emphasise the *actual process* (or method) of motivation.

Because of the complexity of motivation there can be no single answer to what motivates individuals to work productively. Different theories provide a convenient framework within which attention can be directed to the issue of how to motivate individuals to work willingly and effectively towards the goals of the organisation. Since the complex and various theories are not conclusive, each having their own critics (particularly the content theories of motivation), or have been subjected to alternative findings which claim to contradict original ideas, it is necessary for managers to understand the different theories available with their accompanying implications for both manager and subordinate. Thus, evaluation of available theories is critical.

Evaluation of motivational theories

Investigation into motivational theories shows that current views do not always have the significance that some writers have subsequently placed upon them. Whilst it is easy to contradict any generalised observation on any aspect of human behaviour, what motivates an individual to work well seems to have attracted considerable study. When evaluating any motivational theory (or any theory) a manager must carefully consider two key facets:

- the underlying concepts and key points of the original theory: its message;
- what the *original* author(s) actually claimed (or did not claim) for the theory.

An example here would be Maslow (1943) and his hierarchy of needs model (discussed further below) when he made it clear that his theory:

- should only be considered to be a framework for future research with limitations stated;
- actually stated that the hierarchy of needs was in no fixed order and that there were certain to be exceptions to that order with some individuals also motivated by a reversal of the need hierarchy;
- does not suggest that a need must be satisfied before a subsequent need arises.

The importance of the evaluation of motivational theory is at the centre of managers' responsibility towards subordinates. It is also vital that they bear in mind the relevance and applications of available theories.

As has been seen above, a major determinant of motivation is the particular situation in which individual members of the workforce find themselves [$P = f(M + C + S)$]. Motivation is also time specific. Different theories of motivation should not be considered to be self-contained 'techniques' or 'motivational tips for managers' to be used in any given situation. A manager needs to balance the advantages and disadvantages of each theory and be able to draw upon different theories and adapt: use a 'pick-and-mix' approach as appropriate. Such a contingency approach will permit the manager to apply motivational techniques appropriately in particular workplace situations.

Early theories of motivation

It is important to appreciate the early theories of motivation because:

- they provide a foundation for contemporary and evolving views;
- they generally contain common sense and intuition;
- appreciation of them can give managers insights into motivation in the workplace.

Taylor (1911) and the Scientific Management Approach

The work of the founding father of scientific management, Frederick Taylor (1911), was based on a relatively simple model of motivation, that of 'rational economic man'. This model looked at goals and extrinsic factors as the key to motivation. If individuals were given a precisely defined set of tasks, a clear set of objectives, and the extrinsic driver of increasing economic rewards related to performance, then they would calculate the benefits of improving their output and their productivity would rise. The only barriers would be the limitations imposed by the processes and the resources available, and the capability of the worker to do the job. Conversely, the threat of removing such economic rewards would serve as a way of punishing and correcting low productivity.

As Taylor (1911) discovered, workers did not, in practice, respond in the way this motivational model predicted because it was shown that the driver of economic reward was not sufficient to improve performance. Taylor (1911) did, however, identify the key ingredients in motivation, which were clearly defined tasks and objectives backed by some sort of reward structure (which provides a foundation for effective motivation).

Adam Smith (1723–1790) and the Political–Economic Approach

Smith (1723–1790) believed that an individual's self-interest was God's providence and not that of any government. That is, an individual was motivated by self-interest for economic gain in order to buy the necessities of life. By implication, this meant that financial and economic incentives to work were the most important considerations in understanding the behaviour of individuals. He further believed that members of the workforce would be more productive when motivated by their own self-interest. Nelson and Quick (1994) defined self-interest as: 'What is in the best interest and benefit of an individual' (p. 144).

Smith's (1776) political–economic notions were similar to the motivational assumptions within Taylor's (1911) theory – that individuals are always motivated by self-interest and economic gain.

Hedonism

Hedonism is based on an ethical theory: the doctrine that the pursuit of pleasure is the highest good. In general usage, hedonism is the indulgence in sensual pleasures, with individuals adopting a tendency to opt for comfort and pleasure and the avoidance of anything that brings with it pain or discomfort. This doctrine, that pleasure is the chief good, cannot explain what motivates the behaviour of some individuals. For example, an amateur swimmer exerts herself regularly, and willingly, whilst a hedonist prefers to sit and relax; some people participate in unpaid, voluntary work for long hours. The limit of the principle of hedonism to motivation led to the Human Relations approach to processes of motivation.

Human Relations Approach/(Mayo (1920s) Hawthorne Studies

This view of motivation was based on the Hawthorne Studies carried out in the 1920s which suggested that favourable attitudes in employees result in motivation to work even harder. Such a viewpoint posited that individuals are motivated by other things than money – probably by social interaction. It was assumed that if an individual was satisfied with his job, production and performance would rise. Like the hedonistic principle, the human relations approach proved not to have answers for the many questions that it raised.

Such theories helped to develop more sophisticated models of motivation as shown in Table 4.2 below.

Table 4.2 The development of motivational theories

Approach	Reason	Type	Key Researchers
Content	Looks at nature of needs	Understanding the nature of needs usually related to the workplace	Maslow (1943, 1954, 1971) McClelland (1953) McGregor (1960) Herzberg (1966) Alderfer (1972)
Process	How people set about fulfilling their needs	How to motivate people to achieve the organisation's objectives	Tolman (1932) Lewin (1938) Vroom (1964. 1970) Adams (1965) Porter and Lawler (1968) Tampoe (1994)
Contingency	Appreciation of situation and the environment	Different ways of motivating people are required for different individuals and circumstances	
Empowerment	Organisational arrangements which allow employees autonomy	Team work to allow discretion and un-supervised decision-making responsibility	

Needs theories

Motivation is a complex subject and is influenced by many variables. Individuals have a variety of changing (and of conflicting) needs and expectations which they will attempt to satisfy in a number of different ways. Such needs and expectations within the workplace overlap as can be seen in Figure 4.4 below.

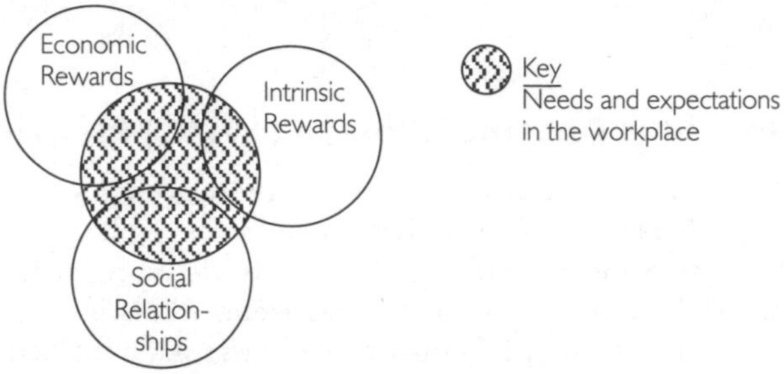

Figure 4.4 The overlap of needs and expectations

Maslow's (1943, 1954, 1971) hierarchy of needs

A more elaborate model of motivation was provided by Maslow (1943, 1954, 1971) who incorporated Taylor's (1911) emphasis on individuals' economic motivation within an overall hierarchy of needs as shown in Figure 4.5 below.

Figure 4.5 Maslow's (1943) theory of human motivation

As can be seen from Figure 4.5 above, Maslow's (1943) hierarchy is often depicted as a pyramid, suggesting a progression from basic, universal needs to more advanced, individualised needs. Each step can be seen as a stepping stone to those above, the individual focusing on a higher type of need as the preceding need is fulfilled. Maslow (1943) argued that, when a lower need was satisfied, the individual's aspirations would move on. Motivation would no longer focus on the satisfied need. In his view, a need which has been satisfied no longer acts as a motivator. In 1954 Maslow updated his hierarchy of needs into several levels as shown in Table 4.3 below where each need is described together with its potential implications in the workplace.

Table 4.3 Maslow's (1954) needs with workplace implications

Need	Description	Workplace Implications
Self-actualisation	The need for fulfilment of an individual's potential; the need for physical and intellectual challenge; creativity; the freedom to take initiatives	Challenging jobs Varied tasks Assuming responsibility Opportunities for job progression
Esteem	The desire for respect and status; the need to feel competent, confident and valued	Level of seniority within the organisation Symbols of status within the organisation Challenging but achievable goals Positive feedback from managers and colleagues
Social (Love)	The desire for affection; the need to give and receive love; the need to belong to a group	Friendly working relationships within individuals Opportunities to socialise (formal and informal) Working in groups
Safety and Security	The need for protection from danger, pain, or the deprivation of physiological needs; to feel secure from these threats; the desire for order and predictability	Job security Arrangements for dealing with healthcare, sickness, retirement or redundancy Clear objectives and role definition Predictable routine
Physiological	Satisfaction of basic needs for survival: air, water, food, light, warmth, sleep, sex	Wage sufficient for subsistence Adequate work environment Provision for food and drink breaks Reasonable working hours and rest breaks

Maslow (1971) explained that he did not mean the hierarchy of needs to be regarded as a rigid description of the development of human needs, but as a model to help people to understand the complexity of needs within any one individual with some of the ways they can interrelate. Most people in extreme conditions of physical want and insecurity would concentrate on basic physiological and safety needs before anything else. Maslow (1971) recognised that their needs would begin to vary in a more stable environment. Individuals would put differing emphases on the relative importance and precedence of higher needs, depending on their outlook. They might also pursue a number of needs simultaneously, seeking both esteem and self-actualisation in, for example, carrying out a particular job.

As has been seen in the analysis of personality in Chapter 1, individuals may tend to be extrovert or introvert in character. Extroverts might, for example, emphasise the fulfilment of esteem needs more than the need for safety. They might also equate them with self-actualisation needs, regarding the achievement of status as the principal definition of fulfilment. If sufficiently confident, they might feel little need to attract the love of others and devote little energy to trying to meet this need.

Introverts, on the other hand, might concentrate on the satisfaction of safety needs and regard them as more important than the need for self-actualisation, preferring routine and predictability to challenge and initiative. Indeed, needs might even conflict within individuals, with, for example, introverts reluctant to pursue esteem and self-actualisation needs because they might create risks which conflicted with safety needs.

A further complication is an individual's perception of needs and their relative importance. One example might be the person who emphasises esteem needs and seeks to achieve status, authority and respect, because they consciously (or unconsciously) see that as a way to meet more fundamental security and love needs; such people use status to give them greater security and attract the attention and friendship of others. Individuals may well have widely differing perceptions of what gives them esteem: some may emphasise salary, others the number of subordinates reporting to them.

Early critics of Maslow (1943, 1954, 1971) have pointed out these problems in the ways individuals perceive and rank needs, and their implications for his model as a predictor of a particular individual's motivation. Two studies, first by Hall and Nougaim (1968) and then by Lawler and Suttle (1972), attempted to map changing strengths of need within Maslow's (1943, 1954, 1971) hierarchy compared to need satisfaction. Their results, whilst showing some correlations between levels of individual need strength and satisfaction, concluded that there was a limited statistical significance in the relationship between kinds of need. Hall and Nougaim (1968), using a sample of managers, in particular emphasised how the perception of needs and their importance changed over time in their sample of managers as their circumstances changed, varying between the need for esteem and self-actualisation for example, depending on where they were in their career path.

Maslow's (1943, 1954, 1971) main contribution has been to isolate the range of needs that individuals have and his work may be compared with a number of other motivational models. In various ways these have attempted to redress some of the criticisms made of Maslow's (1943) seminal work.

McClelland (1965): avoidance, achievement, power and affiliation

McClelland (1965) identified three distinct needs which he called 'manifest needs':

- the need for achievement (n-Ach)
- the need for power (n-Pow)
- the need for affiliation (n-Aff).

The achievement, power and affiliative motives, which broadly correspond to Maslow's (1943, 1954, 1971), lay emphasis on self-actualisation, esteem and belonging needs.

McClelland (1965) also said that there were *avoidance motives* which were primarily concerned with protecting the individual from danger and he linked them to Maslow's (1943, 1954, 1971) lower-order needs. Individuals have different levels of these needs, which are also affected by national culture. For example, some individuals have a high need for power whereas others have only a moderate or low need for power.

McClelland (1965) has concentrated particularly on the achievement need as a key motivational force for successful managers in organisations. For such managers, the need for power, a sense of belonging or even for economic reward may be less important than the right kind of challenge. Such achievers are characterised by a number of traits:

- they prefer moderate task difficulty – those tasks which provide sufficient challenge but which are realistically achievable;
- they tend to be innovative, preferring the challenge of new ideas and ways of working to established methods;
- they prefer personal responsibility: the freedom to take risks and make their own decisions rather than relying on close supervision from above or the reassurance of group responsibility and decision-making;
- they need clear feedback: an objective appraisal of their performance to recognise their achievements and focus on remaining challenges; for such managers, economic reward will be seen less as an end in itself than as a recognition of achievement;
- they expect to have power in the organisation to which they belong: however, as with economic reward, they desire power less for itself than as a means to give them the freedom and authority to achieve organisational goals.

McClelland (1953, 1965) is the key psychologist associated with the n-Ach research. During his research he found out that individuals who scored high tended to perform better on a number of tasks, including numerical tests and literacy tests (anagrams), and that they preferred to work with someone who was known as an 'expert' at the job rather than one who was 'less expert' yet 'friendly'. Such people also tended to have a high internal locus of control whilst low scorers had a high external locus of control (see Chapter 2), blaming their external environment for low achievement.

McGregor (1960) and his Theory X and Theory Y

It is important to appreciate the usefulness of need hierarchy when trying to manage a workforce. McGregor (1960) grouped Maslow's (1943, 1954, 1971) hierarchical needs into 'lower order needs' (physiological, safety and security needs) and 'higher order needs' (social (love), esteem, and self-actualisation) needs. Based on this, McGregor (1960) propounded two alternatives concerning members of the workforce which he identified as Theory X and Theory Y.

McGregor (1960) felt that it did not matter what initiated an individual's motivation since it was still the manager's responsibility to organise the production elements – such as finance, materials, machinery, and individuals – to meet economic ends. However, he did believe that individual members of the workforce should be treated differently by managers, depending upon whether the individual was motivated by lower order or higher order needs.

According to McGregor (1960) individuals who were motivated by lower order needs were likely to be aligned to Theory X assumptions whilst those motivated by higher order needs would generally fall within Theory Y. The suppositions of Theory X and Theory Y are based upon a bipolar assumption of how individuals work and are described in Table 4.4 below.

Table 4.4 Theory X and Theory Y after McGregor (1960)

Theory X	**Theory Y**
negative	*positive*
directive, with individuals who: are lazy dislike work need coercion and control are threatened with punishment avoid responsibility lack ambition value security	facilitative, with individuals who: treat work as normally as leisure are self-directed are committed to objectives are committed to organisational rewards seek responsibility are autonomous yet accountable are creative are knowledge workers
Such individuls are controlled by a centralised bureaucratic system and the use of authority and hierarchical power.	Such individuals are internally directed where organisational goals are inter-related.

Herzberg's (1966) Hygiene and Growth factors

Statistical research on Maslow's (1943, 1954, 1971) work suggested to Herzberg (1966) the importance of satisfying existence factors as a prerequisite to other, higher forms of motivation and this lies at the heart of the third model of motivation. Herzberg (1966) distinguished between:

- *Hygiene factors* which broadly correspond to Maslow's (1943, 1954, 1971) lower-level needs. These have a negative function and their absence will produce dissatisfaction, hence Herzberg's (1966) description of them as 'dissatisfiers'. However, their presence will not produce motivation, only a neutral state. Meeting these needs is a prerequisite to tackling what will influence motivation.
- *Growth factors* (or *motivators*): corresponding to Maslow's (1943, 1954, 1971) higher-level needs, these have a positive function, hence Herzberg's (1966) use of the term 'satisfiers'. Whilst meeting the needs of hygiene factors simply removes potential causes of dissatisfaction, attending to growth factors tends to motivate or satisfy individuals.

Herzberg's (1966) distinction between hygiene and growth factors has parallels with McClelland's (1965) work on motivation.

Alderfer (1972) and the ERG theory

Alderfer (1972) recognised the importance of Maslow's (1943, 1954, 1971) views; he believed they contributed to a body of knowledge on motivation yet was of the opinion that Maslow's original need hierarchy (see Figure 4.5) was not sufficiently precise in its identification and categorisation of human needs. Alderfer (1972) has suggested three basic categories of need which overlap with the five put forward by Maslow (1943, 1954, 1971):

- *Existence needs* which are concerned with the basic requirements for sustaining life, and which broadly correspond to Maslow's (1943, 1954, 1971) physiological and safety needs.
- *Relatedness needs* which cover relationships to the social environment, including relationships with other people, and which correspond to Maslow's emphasis on belonging needs and to the need for esteem from others.
- *Growth needs* which concentrate on individual potential for development, and correspond, in part, to achieving self-esteem and, in particular, to Maslow's emphasis on self-actualisation.

This overlap can be seen in Figure 4.6 below.

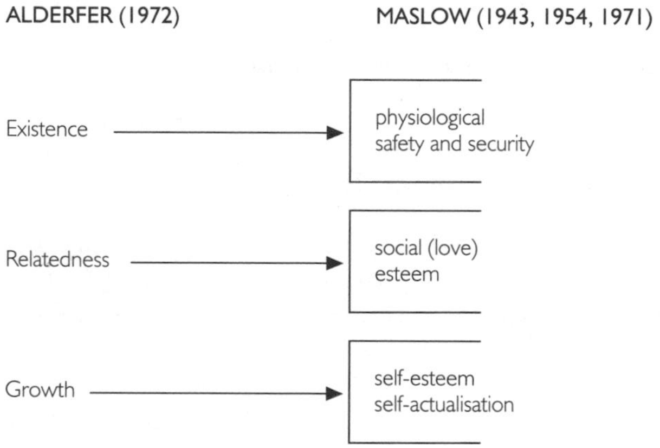

Figure 4.6 Alderfer's (1972) ERG model related to Maslow's (1943, 1954, 1971) hierarchy of needs

Alderfer's (1972) model recognises some of the problems in Maslow's (1943, 1954, 1971) hierarchy by suggesting a more dynamic relationship between levels. As an example, Alderfer identified a frustration–regression process in which, if an individual is continually frustrated in achieving growth needs, for example, she may focus even more strongly on fulfilling relatedness needs to compensate. Alderfer's work suggests that a potential strategy for managers, when faced with a subordinate unable to make the job progression she would like in order to meet her growth needs, might be to help her achieve her relatedness needs more fully.

All the above theorists worked on the aspect of a need hierarchy, which is a belief that an individual's behaviour is determined by a progression of physical, social and psychological needs which, like motivations, change over time. Figure 4.7 below shows a comparison of such key theorists.

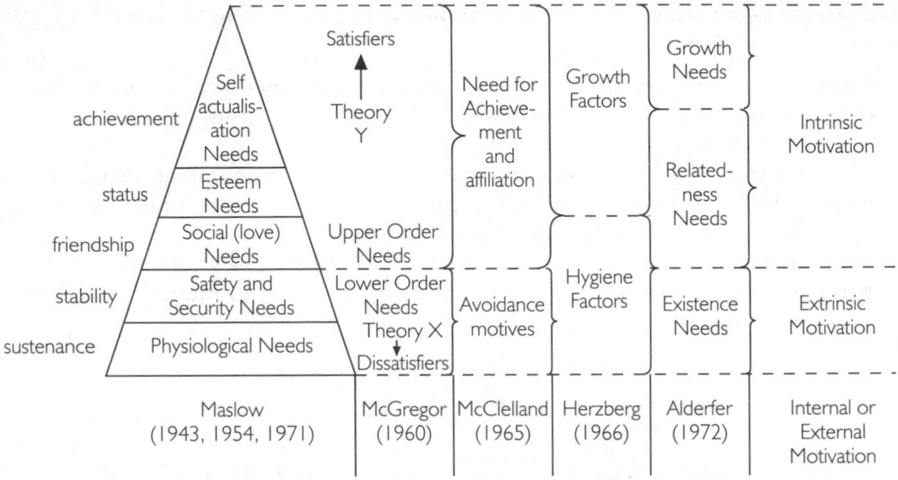

Figure 4.7 A comparison of the views of key needs theorists

Justice theories of motivation

Justice theories concentrate on the cognitive process: they assume that individuals are conscious and active in how they learn, using past experiences as a basis for current behaviour, because those individuals will make a decision about whether the effort is worth it. Such theories are process theories which suggest that an individual is motivated to gain what he feels is a fair return for his efforts in the workplace. This does not mean that the individual strives to get as much as he can – a difficult concept for some people to understand.

According to researchers such as Greenberg (1987) the development has broadened into theories: distributive justice and procedural justice. Such terms reflect the increasing level of awareness of ethics and social responsibility.

- *Distributive justice*: This is related to an individual's belief that he has actually received a fair reward or anticipates that he will receive a fair reward.
- *Procedural justice*: This term describes a situation where an individual believes that the procedures for the allocation of rewards used within the organisation are fair. Folger and Konovsky (1989) started work in this area and their research showed that this area was of increasing importance to individuals.

If individuals believe that their pay is much lower relative to others doing the same job in another organisation, they might well perceive distributive injustice. However, if they perceive that their own organisation is rewarding as much as is possible and the system for distributing such rewards is transparent and fair, they will probably perceive a situation of procedural justice. According to McFarlin and Sweeney (1992) such persons would be likely to have a low satisfaction related to pay but their commitment to their employer is likely to be high. However, what is not clear is how the perceptions affect an individual's behaviour in the workplace.

Equity theory of motivation (Adams, 1965)

This is a justice theory expounded by Adams (1965) who gave the name *equity theory* to a simple assertion that members of any workforce wish to be treated fairly. The theory centres on an individual's desire to be treated equitably in relation to others and to avoid inequality – the belief that one is being treated unfairly when compared to another person. It is only one of many facets of the social comparison processes (Goodman, 1977) – an individual evaluates their own situation in the context of the situation of another (comparison-other). It is the most highly researched concept within the social comparison process, besides being the one which is more plainly concerned with motivation in the workplace.

Individuals tend to use a four-stage course in the formation of perceptions related to equity. For example, a worker will follow the following procedures:

1 evaluate how they are being treated by the organisation;

2 evaluate how a comparison-other/s (for example, someone in the same project team) is/are being treated by the organisation;

3 compare the results of (1) and (2) above;

4 experience either equity or inequity.

Huseman, Hatfield and Miles (1989) supported the above process, believing that individuals thus balance their contributions to, and the rewards for, a task by comparing their perceptions with those of others. Such an equity comparison is expressed in terms of input–outcome ratios.

Inputs are what the individuals bring with them, such as education, past experience, knowledge, loyalty, and effort. *Outcomes* are what they receive in return, such as salary, social recognition, intrinsic rewards. Therefore, equity processes contain a considerable aspect of an individual's psychological contract because any assessment of input–outcome relationships will depend upon:

- objective information such as salary, holiday requirement;
- perceptive information such as level of effort.

Such a comparison can be formulated as a psychological equation:

$$\frac{\text{Outcome (self)}}{\text{Input (self)}} \quad \text{compared with} \quad \frac{\text{Outcome (other)}}{\text{Input (other)}}$$

If both sides balance, the individual will then have experienced a sensation of equity. However, if there is an imbalance, they will feel inequity. Adams (1965) makes the specific point that it does not matter if the perceived outcomes and incomes are unequal – what is important is that the ratios are the same. For example, a member of the workforce may believe that the other person deserves a higher salary because she works harder – in this case, the individual has rationalised her view that the other person has an acceptable higher outcome–input ratio. If, however, she feels that her comparison-other has outcomes which are disproportionate to her inputs she will then perceive a level of inequality. This can be see in Figure 4.8:

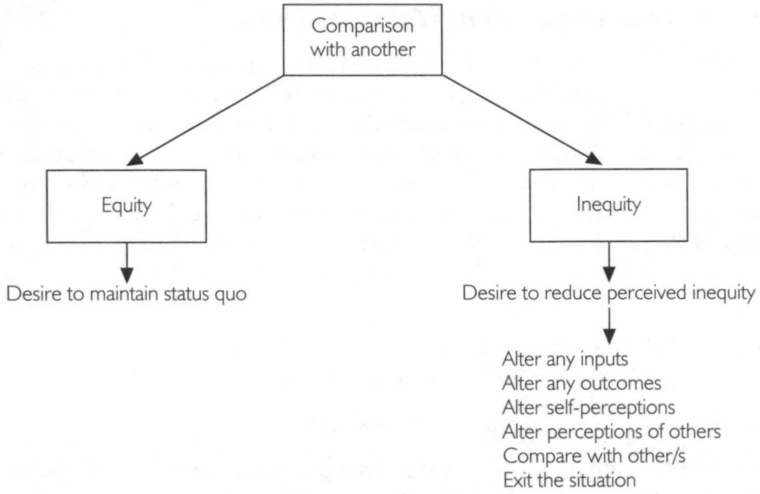

Figure 4.8 An individual's response to perceived equity and inequity

If an individual perceives that there is an equity situation she will attempt to maintain that situation – to keep the status quo. Her input level will remain the same only so long as she perceives that her outcomes do not change and the inputs–outcomes of the comparison-others also remain constant. Should she perceive an initial inequality, or a situation of inequality occurs, she will be motivated to do something to bring about a state of equity by carrying out any of the following behaviours:

1 **Alter any input**. She could change any of her own inputs, for example, by reducing her efforts. In this way she alters her own ratio. If she feels that she is not being rewarded enough, she may also decide to decrease her efforts.

2 **Alter any outcomes**. The individual may well alter her perception of the current value of her outcomes. As a result she might make a request for more money, or seek other areas whereby she can increase her income. Some individuals even resort to activities such as theft and fraud.

3 **Alter self-perceptions**. This is a much more complicated response than (1) and (2) above because when an individual has perceived the inequity she may well decide to alter the original assessment of her own input. In this way, it might be assessed that she is actually contributing less but receiving more outcome than was originally thought.

4 **Alter perceptions of others**. She may well decide to amend her perception of the comparison-other's inputs and outcomes. For example, if she feels unrewarded for her own hard work and efforts, she may well come to the view that her comparison-other is actually putting in more hours and achieving more tasks than she herself originally thought.

5 **Compare with other/s.** The individual can change her comparison-other. It might be that she perceives that her original comparison-other has specific skills and talents and is not a fair person to compare herself with. She will thus select another member of the workforce who might give her a more valid basis for comparison.

6 **Exit the situation**. This is the last resort. An individual may feel that the level of inequity she perceives cannot be resolved and so the only way to regain equity is to

leave the situation, for example by moving to another area of work within the organisation or leaving the organisation altogether.

According to Pinder (1984) most of the research carried out in the field of equity theory has concentrated on a narrow band of concepts centred on pay compared with the quantity/quality of outcomes. His work reinforced the view that people tend to resort to the practical usage of equity theory when they perceive that they are underpaid.

Huseman *et al.* (1987) found that some individuals were more likely than others to be sensitive to perceptions of inequality. Their research stated that some workers paid more attention to their relative value in an organisation than did their colleagues through the equity-based comparison process. Such others tended to be more personally focused on their own situation without regard to that of others.

Motivating individuals and rewards

Equity theory has implications for managers when it comes to organisational rewards. A previous section looked at content theories and at the nature of needs and their potential importance to different individuals. These needs provide a force which pushes people into contemplating actions which may fulfil their needs. On the other side of the coin are the potential rewards which are promised to an individual to fulfil his needs if he performs a given task. These act as a force to pull people into meeting the organisation's objectives.

In between are a number of variables which determine how people respond to rewards. A key issue is the tension between an individual's ability and his perception of the effort-needed to achieve the reward. If the required effort is seen as too great in relation to the individual's ability, he will be discouraged, especially, though not exclusively, if his need is not sufficiently strong. Such a perception may counterbalance both the need and the attractiveness of the reward which will now seem unattainable.

All organisations have easily identifiable rewards in the formal sense: pay, and the assignment of tasks. They also have more informal rewards (such as an intrinsic satisfaction, self-worth, achievement) which are very difficult to identify – let alone measure. The difficulty is that it is the latter which are frequently at the core of an individual's perceptions when he comes to assessing his perception of equity. Such social comparisons are increasingly becoming a powerful feature of the workplace.

Moorhead and Griffin (1995) identify three clear messages for managers:

- The basis of the reward system must be transparent in that it needs to be understood by everyone. If quantity is going to be rewarded rather than quality, that needs to be clearly communicated to all.
- Rewards are perceived as being multifaceted because individuals get different rewards: some tangible (pay), some intangible (achievement).
- People have differing understandings of what reality is – which is based on their perception (see Chapter 2). For example, a team leader may know that his team members are being fairly rewarded but the members themselves may not agree.

As can be seen, theories are often complicated when applied in the workplace. Dornstein (1988) reinforced this view by stating that individuals in the workplace have a wide choice of strategies by which to establish their equity and their comparison-other choice and although individuals often choose similar workers as a comparison, they do not always do so.

The equity theory proposed by Adams (1965) developed over time as the workplace became more complex. Organisations are now competing in a complex world with globalisation, work diversity and social responsibility being key considerations.

Vroom (1964, 1970), Expectancy Theory/VIE Theory

Another key process theory is expectancy theory wherein there are two principal researchers:

- Vroom (1964, 1970) Expectancy Theory/VIE Theory
- Porter and Lawler (1968) Expectancy Theory.

The basic model was propounded by both Tolman (1932) and Lewin (1938). However, Vroom (1964, 1976) identified two key variables under the umbrella term *expectancy theory*, which is generally used for applying the theory to the workplace. Two key variables are:

- *Valence*, which is the anticipated reward from an outcome – the value or importance that an individual gives to a reward. It is concerned with what an individual expects from an outcome as opposed to the actual content and value of the outcome. The valence of an outcome may be directly related to the outcome desired – some individuals may desire higher wages because they like to accumulate money – or it may concentrate on the social standing that this outcome might confer; higher wages might bring an improved lifestyle and status.
- *Expectancy*, which is the perceived probability of performing sufficiently well to achieve the outcome and thus the reward – the belief of an individual that the more effort he puts in the higher his level of performance will be. Expectancy measures an individual's perception of the likelihood that his actions will be successful and lead, ultimately, to the rewards which meet his needs.

In measuring valence, Vroom (1964, 1970) also introduced a third variable:

- *Instrumentality*, which is the calculation of the number and degree of rewards resulting from achieving an outcome – that is, the individual's performance is related to the rewards. It measures the degree to which performance of a task leads to the rewards which then fulfil the needs that first motivated the performance of the task. This measurement is determined by the relationship between first- and second-level outcomes.

  First-level outcomes are those related directly to the carrying out of the task itself, for instance its successful completion or an improved level of performance or productivity. Such outcomes must be related to organisational goals and be performance related, and can be contrasted with second-level outcomes which are related to the benefits conferred by performance of the task, for example higher wages, promotion, and recognition from superiors and colleagues. Such outcomes are individual and needs-related, describing the rewards conferred as a result of successful first level outcomes. The distinction Vroom (1964, 1970) makes between these outcomes is important. An individual would tend to be demotivated if either good performance (first-level outcome) does not lead to appropriate rewards (second-level outcomes), or such second-level outcomes do not seem to be related to quality of performance.

The overall calculation of motivational force needs to take account of the range of outcomes from a particular action, for instance the possible isolation and unpopularity an individual might experience from colleagues as a result of being singled out for, say, promotion. Clearly, valence is dependent on instrumentality. If a person believes that good performance will not lead to the desired second-level outcomes, valence will be low.

The degree to which an individual is motivated to act is determined by a number of variables. In the first place, the reward must be seen as appropriate and attractive in meeting a need. At the level of the individual, motivation is then determined by the ability to carry out the task required to achieve the reward, and the perception of the effort needed to achieve that reward. If the effort required is seen as too great in relation to the ability to carry out the task and the attractiveness of the reward, the individual will not be motivated to act. Motivation, then, is based on the expectation that an individual has of the most favourable outcome.

Vroom (1964, 1970) distinguished between performance of a task (first-level outcome) and the rewards successful performance of that task might bring (second-level outcomes). Expectancy is focused on the achievement of first-level outcomes; instrumentality on the range of available second-level outcomes. He calculated the strength of individual motivation, the motivational force, as the sum of the products of the valences of all outcomes (V) times the strength of expectancies that action will result in achieving these outcomes (E). He expressed this mathematically as:

$$M = (E + V)$$

where M = motivation to behave, E = subjective probability or expectation that the behaviour will lend to a particular outcome, and V = valence, or strength of preference for the outcome.

Vroom (1970) later argued that whilst the strength or 'force' of an individual's motivation to act in a particular way can be expressed as a result of the above formula it did not take account of all the values involved. That is because in most situations there will be a number of different outcomes as a result of particular behaviours. For example, in the quest for promotion an individual may work harder and as a result this can affect, say, an individual's:

- financial reward
- workplace friendships
- status in the organisation
- levels of personal fitness/fatigue
- social and family life.

Therefore, the equation needs to be summed across all of these possible outcomes. Vroom (1970) amended his formula to read:

$$M = \underset{\Sigma}{n} (E + V)$$

where Σ (Greek sigma) means 'summation – add up all the values (n) of the calculation in the brackets'.

It therefore takes into account all values: positive, neutral, and negative.

Try this exercise

If behaviour depends on the outcomes that an individual personally values, and the expectations that a particular type of behaviour will lead to those outcomes, then it is possible to use expectancy theory to predict the answer to the question:

'Will you pass your Organisational Behaviour course?'

Porter and Lawler (1968), Expectancy Model

Vroom's (1964) pioneering work was further developed by Porter and Lawler (1968) in their expectancy model which differs significantly from that of Vroom (1964) in that it considers the contribution of roles, perceptions, abilities, and traits. At the start of the cycle of motivation, effort is one function of the value of the employee's potential reward (valence) and the perceived reward for that effort (expectancy). The individual combines this effort with his or her abilities, personality traits, and role perceptions in order to determine actual performance. An individual's performance results in two kinds of rewards:

- *Extrinsic rewards* which are tangible outcomes. These are rewards which derive from the organisation itself and then act on individuals within the workforce. For example, the issue whether there should be parity of pay or individual bonuses based on performance, or changes in the content and responsibility of duties, or the nature of management supervision.
- *Intrinsic rewards* which are intangible. They derive from the experience of work itself for each individual. Examples here might be a sense of challenge and achievement, recognition and responsibility.

An individual judges the value of his or her performance to the organisation and then uses social comparison processes to form an impression of the equity of the rewards received. There is an effect on subsequent behaviour by the individual because actual performance following effort influences future perceived effort–reward probabilities.

Porter and Lawler (1968) argue that it is important to have both types of reward for effective motivation, but that intrinsic rewards are more likely to produce job satisfaction than extrinsic rewards. Their distinction has parallels with Herzberg's (1966) hygiene factors (corresponding to extrinsic rewards) and motivators (corresponding to intrinsic rewards). However, they recognise that the relative importance of these two types of reward is contingent on the job itself – if the nature of the work is varied and challenging, it provides the potential for strong intrinsic rewards. If not, extrinsic rewards will be a more important factor in motivation, though Porter and Lawler (1968) argue that, if this is the case, overall motivation may be weaker. They also suggest that extrinsic rewards do not often provide a direct link to performance.

A final key variable in the Porter and Lawler (1968) model is *perceived equitable rewards*; this is an individual's perception of the level of reward he or she feels to be fair in relation to the demands of the job and the effort he or she has expended.

Porter and Lawler (1968) pointed out that, in awarding what they consider to be appropriate rewards, managers need to be aware of not just what they consider to be equitable but also how such rewards relate to individual and collective perceptions of fair treatment:

if actual rewards fall short of perceived equitable rewards, individuals will be demotivated. Failure here could, therefore, invalidate the whole process of motivation.

Implications of the expectancy theory

The result of the intrinsic and extrinsic rewards measured against performance and mediated by a framework of individual and collective perceived equitable rewards, is a given level of satisfaction. Satisfaction is not the same as motivation – it is the outcome of the process of motivation and only affects performance if it informs the individual's sense of the value of the reward that results from effort to achieve a given objective. If it does so, an individual will be encouraged to sustain or improve that effort. The continued value of the reward, driven by sustained levels of satisfaction, must remain high compared to effort and perceived equitable rewards.

Porter and Lawler's (1968) model of the motivational process differs from Vroom's (1964) in a number of important respects:

- It introduces ability and role perception as influencing the quality of performance alongside the degree of effort applied.
- It distinguishes between kinds of what Vroom (1964) would term second-level outcomes.
- Perhaps, most fundamentally, the model questions the distinction in Vroom's (1964) model between first- and second-level outcomes and its assumption that individuals see work purely as a means to other ends – such as pay. Instead it identifies the experience of work itself as a potential force of satisfaction. Satisfaction is seen not as the cause but the effect of good performance.
- The model adds assessment of the fairness of rewards as an important element in individual motivation.

Expectancy theory is very complicated in its entirety and is thus difficult to test: measuring is very difficult and can thus invalidate the theory – especially if viewed as a scientific paradigm. Also, it assumes that individuals are rational and objective whereas they are more likely to be irrational and lack objectivity. The very fact that expectancy theory is complex makes it hard to apply to the workforce and so implications and applications are complex to assess. A manager would need to:

- be aware of what rewards are wanted by each employee as an individual;
- be aware of how valuable the rewards are to that individual;
- adjust the relationships in order to create motivation.

Regardless of these criticisms the theory is valid, according to researchers on work motivation such as Pinder (1984). Nadler and Lawler (1983) state that some of the fundamental guidelines for managers include:

- determining the primary outcomes each employee wants;
- deciding what levels and kinds of performance are needed to meet organisational goals;
- making sure the desired levels of performance are possible;
- linking desired outcomes and desired performance;
- analysing the situation for conflicting expectancies;

- making sure the rewards are large enough;
- making sure the overall system acknowledges performance (pp. 67–78).

The model begins with the individual's perception of the value of the reward balanced against the perceived effort in achieving the reward, corresponding broadly to Vroom's (1964, 1970) valence and expectancy. These two determine the level of effort committed by the individual to achieving the reward. Actual performance is then determined by a combination of degree of effort with the level of ability of the individual to perform the task and his perception of the best way of performing it (role perception). If performance is successful, it results in two types of reward: intrinsic, relating to the personal satisfaction achieved in completing the task successfully; and extrinsic, relating to the external rewards given by the company. A final ingredient is the perception of how equitable the final reward is compared to those given to others. Receiving rewards which are seen as equitable helps to maximise the level of satisfaction felt.

Need theories concentrate on the content of motivation whilst expectancy theory (as does equity theory) concentrates on the process of motivation. Such theories attempt to explain and determine how individuals choose from a range of behaviour available. That is, how individuals choose between the several or many courses of action available to them. It is perceived as a cognitive and calculating approach, with an individual calculating the three elements: expectancy (if an individual made an effort would she be able to perform the task?), instrumentality (if she completed the task satisfactorily, would it lead to outcomes which could be identified?), and valence (how much does she value the outcomes?)

Vroom (1964, 1970) stated that when considering expectancy and instrumentality, they could both be expressed as probabilities whilst valence was subjective in its value. Such an interpretation would mean that if an individual had a zero view of any one of the three elements, her overall motivation to pursue that particular course of action would also be nil.

If managers accept the views of the expectancy theory, the implications are important for motivating members of the workforce. Such managers would need to ensure that for every individual each of the conditions (expectancy, instrumentality and valence) was satisfied. For example, to motivate a university lecturer, a line manager would need to ensure that the individual perceives that he possesses the required skills to carry out his tasks to at least a satisfactory level (expectancy). The lecturer would need to perceive that a satisfactory to excellence performance must be rewarded (instrumentality), and he would need to perceive that the rewards which are offered for a satisfactory to excellent performance are attractive and desirable (valence).

However, expectancy theory does not consider any explanations as to *why* an individual values (or does not value) particular outcomes. Such an issue does not consider needs: it proposes that individuals should be asked how much they value something, but not *why* they value it. Again, an example of process rather than content.

Since Vroom (1964, 1970) presented his expectancy theory it has been modified by numerous researchers and practitioners, each concentrating on attempting to identify and measure outcomes and expectancies. However, Porter and Lawler (1968) refined the expectancy theory in an attempt to develop an expectancy theory that supported their view that when individuals are adequately rewarded, high levels of performance could lead to satisfaction. The Porter and Lawler (1968) model is shown in Figure 4.9.

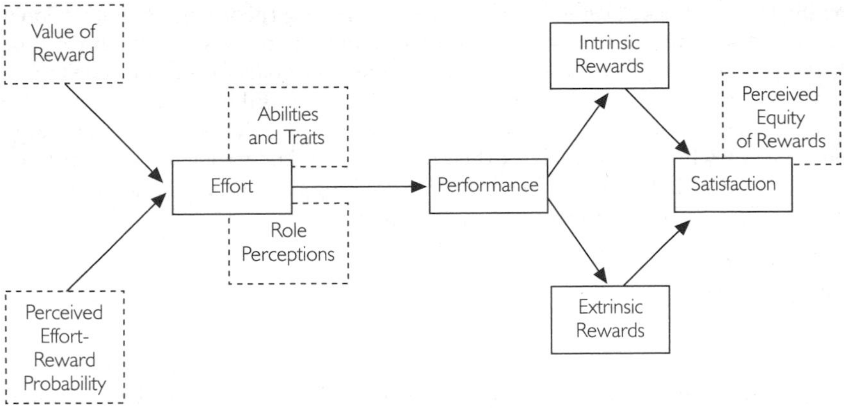

Figure 4.9 The Porter and Lawler (1968) model of motivation

Subsequent attention has focused on two key expectancies: the first expectancy measuring an individual's perception that a given amount of effort will result in achieving necessary performance; and the second expectancy measuring the individual's perception of how far a given level of performance will achieve a desired outcome.

The goal setting theory of motivation (Locke, 1968)

Whilst the expectancy theory of motivation is seen as being the most complex (and most complete) theory of motivation, there have been others developed which can help in the understanding of motivation in the workplace. The goal setting theory has proved to be particularly useful to managers in an effort to augment their existing knowledge of how to motivate their subordinates. A goal can be defined as 'a desirable objective to aim for and achieve'.

The word 'goal' has two meanings in organisational terms. It is used, firstly, as a framework for managing the motivation of individuals by setting themselves goals and aiming their activities towards achieving them. Secondly, goals are often used by organisations as a means of control for monitoring and measuring how the organisation is meeting its objectives. For example, if a university has decided to increase its student intake by, say, five per cent, a lecturer can use individual goals to help the organisation to meet the overall goal. It is necessary for an organisation to review its long-term effectiveness and it can do this through comparing an individual's short-term performances with their goals.

The previous chapter (Chapter 3) investigated the role of social learning theory and communication. According to Bandura (1977) social learning theory is one of the better ways of describing the role and importance of goal setting in organisations. The theory suggests that individuals who achieve their goals have an accompanying feeling of personal pride (or shame and disappointment if they do not achieve the goals). The level of pride or shame will depend upon whether the individual feels that they can actually achieve that goal within the organisation. Such a belief is called *self-efficacy* – the belief that an individual can still accomplish their goals even if failure has been experienced in the past. When individuals take pride in their work and strive to do the best possible job, they are committed to the goals they have set out to reach.

It was the work of Locke (1968) which sealed goal setting theory into a motivational setting with the assumption that individuals behave in certain ways as a result of conscious goals and purpose. It follows, then, that if managers set goals for subordinates they will, therefore, be able to influence the behaviour of those subordinates. If this hypothesis is accepted, managers then have the challenge of developing a detailed understanding of all the processes by which individuals set their objectives and how they work towards achieving them. Locke's (1968) original version of goal setting theory contained two key characteristics which were said to shape the performance of an individual:

- goal difficulty
- goal specificity.

Goal difficulty is measured by the extent to which the goal is challenging and requires effort. If an individual is working towards the achievement of a goal it may be assumed that she will work harder to achieve more difficult goals. However, if the individual sees the goal as being unobtainable, she may well find it not worth striving for. For example, if a manager asks a subordinate to increase her productivity by 200 per cent she will become disillusioned, whereas given a more realistic objective (although still difficult) of, say a 25 per cent increase, she may find this an incentive.

The more difficult the goal the more essential it is that the manager reinforces the behaviour which leads to the achievement of that goal. The more difficult the goal and the more positive the reinforcement, the more likely it is that the individual will strive towards even more difficult goals.

Goal specificity refers to the clarity and degree of preciseness of the stated goal. It is necessary for goals to be stated in specific terms if they are to be achieved. For example, if a student aims to 'increase effort' such a goal is non-specific and would be better expressed as 'increase my grade by ten per cent by the end of the academic year'. However, some goals are difficult to state in such definite terms. For example, in the workplace it is difficult to state goals if an individual is working in areas such as organisational reputation or job satisfaction.

The basics of goal setting theory have become very popular with organisations and researchers alike and because of this Locke and Latham (1979) developed Locke's (1968) original theory into what is known as the 'expanded goal setting theory of motivation' as shown in Figure 4.10 below.

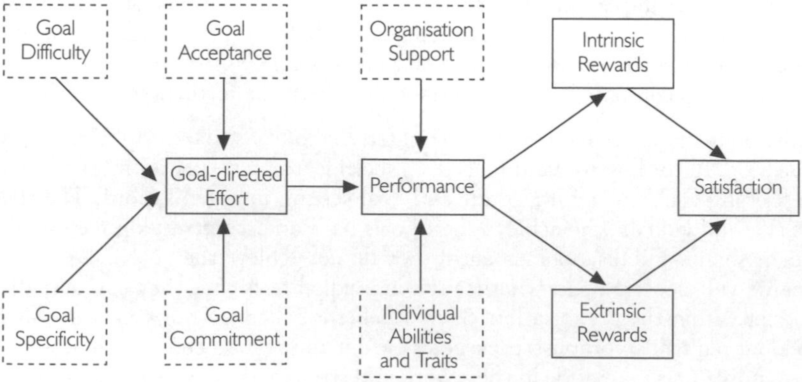

Figure 4.10 The expanded goal setting theory of motivation after Locke and Latham (1979)

The expanded theory added two other key characteristics:

- goal acceptance
- goal commitment.

'*Goal acceptance* relates to the extent to which an individual accepts the goal as his own whilst *goal commitment* is the extent to which an individual is intrinsically interested in achieving the goal. The more that an individual internalises the goal the more likely he is to achieve it, and therefore actual performance is determined by the interaction of:

- goal directed effort
- organisational support
- individual abilities
- personality traits.

The expanded version put forward by Locke and Latham (1979) is similar to the view of Porter and Lawler (1968).

Evolving theories of motivation: participation and empowerment

Two key motivational processes have come to be important in contemporary organisations:

- participative management
- empowerment.

Participative management is the process of giving individuals a say in decisions relating to their work whereas *empowerment* is related to the organisational arrangements that allow employees more autonomy, discretion and unsupervised decision-making responsibility. Empowerment encompasses the principle of participation and is relevant to all aspects of an individual's existence. Both terms are bandied about in organisations today but, in essence, are not new. Hence, an understanding of the historical perspective is important in understanding both participation and empowerment as they relate to motivation.

Attribution theory and motivation

In Chapter 2 the role of attribution in perception was discussed and this can now be extended to the motivational implications. The work of Kelley (1971) was key to this view and he believed that individuals observe their behaviour through the process of self-perception. Such perceptions allow individuals to decide whether their behaviour is a response to external or internal factors. This is called the 'attribution of causes' because individuals will decide whether they are basically extrinsically or intrinsically motivated and as a result will develop a preferred pattern of incentives. If they believe that they are extrinsically motivated, workers will value external rewards such as pay or status awards but if they value intrinsic motivation they will look for intrinsic incentives such as additional autonomy and increased personal decision-making.

Deci (1971) carried out research in the application of attribution theory to motivation and reasoned that if an intrinsically motivated individual was paid on an incentive basis (that is, the provision of extrinsic rewards) it would make her become more extrinsically motivated and less intrinsically motivated. His research showed that if an individual is paid to do something she already liked doing (intrinsically motivated), her level of 'liking' diminishes. As a result, attributional processes appear to play a meaningful role in employee motivation in the workplace – especially with the rise of complexity within organisations.

Motivation and alienation

Motivation is also about avoiding alienation, especially as a result of technical and status changes. Organisations and their managers need to be aware that organisations are by no means the only (or even the most important) focus for individuals' needs and the ways they set about fulfilling them. Many employees may view the organisation within which they work as a means for meeting only basic physiological and safety needs, looking for belonging, esteem and self-actualisation needs elsewhere – perhaps in the family or in their social life outside work. Their commitment to the organisation may, therefore, be limited, with a primary concern to protect safety needs which might well conflict with the organisation's need to change to meet new requirements or to secure greater involvement from individuals in improving performance.

This approach to motivation may be especially characteristic of those workers with the most routine and undemanding jobs where the apparent opportunities for the satisfaction of higher-level needs are least. Studies by Goldthorpe (1968) of manual workers working in factories and Weaver (1988) of workers in the hotel and catering industry suggested that they had an *instrumental orientation* to their work. Even in the Goldthorpe (1968) study, where the workers' pay was above average, their principal concern remained with physiological and security needs: with pay and job security. Work was seen only as a means to an end through which to satisfy other needs and interests outside work.

One of the challenges that face organisations which need greater commitment from their staff is to overcome this perception and to raise the organisation's importance as a focus for need fulfilment and, therefore, for the commitment and creativity of employees. A study by Blackburn and Mann (1979) of workers in low-skilled jobs found a range of types of work motivation, ranging from the purely instrumental to an enjoyment of other aspects of work such as working with colleagues, the experience of autonomy and opportunities for promotion. Such research illustrates the potential of motivating such workers, a theme which is returned to in Chapter 5 when discussing job design.

Motivation and knowledge workers

CASE STUDY
Key features of a knowledge-based health service organisation

General management features

- Routine monitoring of the external environment.
- Participative management style.
- Routine monitoring of performance using measures meaningful to the organisation.
- Recognition of the contribution of all staff to decision-making.
- Effective systems such as information management, and training and development.

- Working across hierarchies and functions.

Best practice in management applied to research and development

- Top management and board commitment to research and development.
- Clear roles and accountabilities.
- Evidence of leadership from the chief executive.
- Powerful champions and role-models promoting research and development.
- Training and development addressing research and development issues.

Features specific to health service

- Links between clinical audit, education and quality.
- Clear links with universities.
- The availability of a library.
- A climate of assessment and evaluation.
- Evidence of analytical and research skills.
- Supporting information technology and staff skilled in using information technology.

Source: H. Rowland and L. Harris, 'Doctor know' in *People Management*, 5 March 1998, pp. 50–52

In carrying out work within the National Health Service, Rowland and Harris (1998) stated that their research showed that:

> many of the foundations of effective knowledge management are already present: a focus on quality and performance, business drivers and IT [information technology] systems. HR's [Human Resources] contribution can be the managing of potentially disparate strands into a change process that makes sense for the people. (p. 52)

As can be seen from the case study above, it is possible to have a framework for motivating knowledge workers, but there must be a catalyst within each organisation – in the case of the National Health sector investigated above, it was the research and development strategy.

Knowledge management is now seen as one of the keys to a competitive economy, and therefore knowledge workers have to be motivated to be innovative and creative.

Infield (1998) states:

> As in all new management theories, there is a great deal of confusion surrounding the concept of knowledge management. Even pinning down an agreed definition for 'knowledge' causes problems. (p. 1)

Lyon (1998) agrees with Infield (1998) and defines the central concept of knowledge management as:

> ... [residing] within people: a distinction is drawn between explicit knowledge and tacit knowledge, and knowledge management systems are about trying to bring the two together. (p. 1)

She defines tacit knowledge as what resides in an individual's head while explicit knowledge consists of those things an individual can write down and record.

Contemporary organisations work in a globalised market with the increased use of technology. With this has come a need to motivate the expanding number of knowledge workers who have to deal with an increasingly scientific and industrialised workplace. Tampoe (1994) defines such workers as those who need to use their information to produce the outcomes required by the organisation, the community, and the individual worker. Such individuals can be difficult to motivate and their performance needs to be judged on both the astuteness of the idea and the efficacy of that knowledge as it is applied to the organisational goals. Knowledge workers have a considerable amount of creativity which needs to be harvested and realistically converted into organisational outcomes. Such a focus has brought about a new challenge for managers – how to motivate the increasing number of knowledge workers within the organisation. Since such knowledge and creativity are personal to the individual member of the workforce, blanket motivational theories are not satisfactory in the motivation of such workers. Tampoe (1994) believes that the value of such knowledge workers is based on the values which such individuals place on the rewards for their efforts. Managers also need to understand that the performance of such workers is dependent upon four key characteristics:

- task competence
- task and role clarity
- peer and manager support
- corporate awareness

which are key components of motivational theory and entail individuals having to concentrate on the effectiveness of these variables, and the recognition that knowledge workers need to be to self-managing. Tampoe (1994) designed this as shown in Figure 4.11 below.

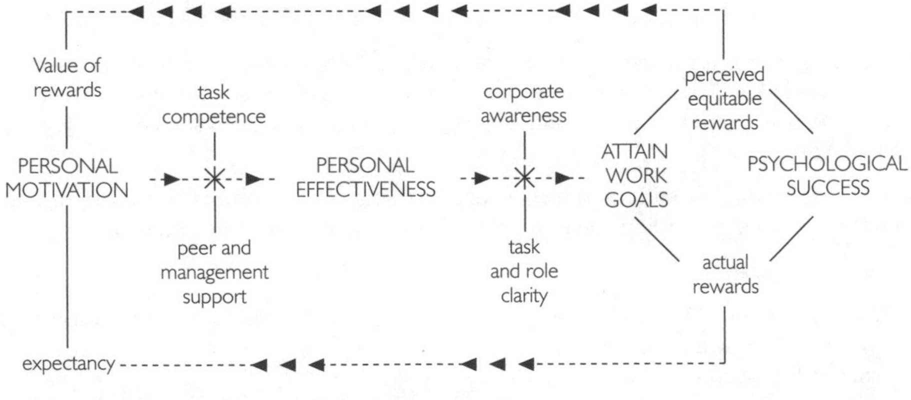

Figure 4.11 Motivating knowledge workers after Tampoe (1994, p. 13)

Source: M. Tampoe, 'Knowledge Workers – The New Management Challenge' in *Professional Manager*, November 1994, p. 13.

Holder (1997) believes that effective knowledge management depends on harnessing expertise, and says that no organisation can afford to neglect the expertise which they have within them: 'Managing knowledge is expensive but the cost of not managing knowledge is enormous' (p. 10).

Knowledge workers are creative and it is necessary for organisations to nurture a culture of innovation: as can be seen from the case study below.

CASE STUDY

Nurturing a culture of innovation

Innovation requires, above all else, a willingness to embrace chaos. It means giving free rein to people who are opinionated, wilful and delight in challenging the rules. It demands a loose management structure that does not isolate people in departments or on the rungs of a ladder. It needs flexible work space that encourages a cross-fertilisation of ideas. And it requires risk-taking.

Yet if innovation has become an over-used buzzword, it is only because we all recognise innovation as a competitive weapon, a necessary component for future success.

Innovation is not something prescriptive. You can't legislate for it. Rather, it is something organic, something that grows and is nurtured, usually from the bottom of the organisation up. Innovative cultures usually begin with a tangible project the success of which gives birth to another and another. Such projects or definable goals are also the elements which keep the fun and freedom from degenerating into non-productive anarchy. Moreover, if you want the combined workforce behind you, but take away their desks, their titles and their personal power bases, you must give them something in return. Job satisfaction is a great motivator.

In a culture of innovation, enlightened trial and error beats careful planning, and risk becomes an essential part of the process. Rapid prototyping means that you can evaluate a concept before you have invested too much in it. It also gives the participants the stimulation of seeing their ideas put into practice and sustains their enthusiasm when more concrete rewards are less evident.

Source: T. Brown, 'Nurturing a culture of innovation' in *Financial Times*, 17 November 1997, p. 12

Perspectives on participation and empowerment

The Human Relations School (1930s to mid-1950s) made the assumption that if employees were happy and satisfied they would naturally work harder and thus increase their productivity. Because of this premise, the movement encouraged a wider appreciation of the importance of worker participation within the organisation. The premise was that when given an opportunity to take part in organisational decision-making employees would be satisfied and this, in turn, would result in improved performance. Managers who adopted this view made the supposition that the participation of the employee would result in an increase in satisfaction and they paid less regard to the derival of satisfaction from other input which could be valuable in meeting the organisation's goals. As time went on, managers began to realise that the input of an employee was a valuable entity in itself apart from the presumed effect on satisfaction.

The role of participation and empowerment in motivation can be expressed in terms of both the content- and the process-based motivational theories – particularly the expectancy theory. When individuals are permitted to participate in the decision-making process they then 'own' such decisions and are, consequently, committed to executing such decisions correctly. In seeing decision-making through all its processes (need for achievement, provision of recognition and responsibility, enhancement of self-esteem) individuals satisfy their own needs and are helped to self-actualise.

Realms of participation

When employees are permitted to make their own decisions based on individual expertise and experiences they generally improve their own productivity and go on to make decisions related to the job in general: for example, deciding the most appropriate work methods and use of equipment. However, decision-making is not confined only to decisions relating to an employee's own job but also entails decisions relating to management and associated administrative tasks: for example, when to take a break. If the employee is a member of a work team he might well be able to schedule variations and days off for all members of the team. What has started off as individual employee participation is increasingly being extended to broader issues such as quality – by making decisions in the process and procedures of the workplace individuals can help to maintain the quality of the organisational product/service.

CASE STUDY

It's good to talk? Call centres and motivation

Hold the production line

Call centres are one of the fastest-growing sectors of business in the 1990s. Currently one in 250 of the European working population works full- or part-time in a call centre (1.1% in the UK). This figure is set to rise to one in a hundred by 2001 (2.2% in the UK). Pioneered in this country in motor insurance by Direct Line, and in banking by First Direct, there are now few types of goods or services which cannot be obtained over the telephone. For customers they offer the promise of flexibility and immediate access, for businesses the opportunity of huge cost savings by replacing the traditional functions of high-street shops or banks with leaner, centralised operations. Amongst the biggest sectors for call centre activity currently in Europe are consumer products (25%), financial services (19%), travel and tourism (14%) and remote shopping (13%).

Whilst 40% of call centre staff are involved in telemarketing and sales, over half are concerned with the care of existing customers. Staff answering calls from customers use computer screens to access information and often have standardised procedures to follow, even down to prepared scripts. There is considerable pressure to keep up with the pace of incoming calls whilst responding effectively to customer enquiries. As an example, the Co-operative Bank has two call centres which employ over 1,200 staff. The centres operate 24 hours a day and fielded an estimated seven million calls from customers in 1996.

Managers are able to monitor activity with unpredicted accuracy. Automated call distribution systems (ACDs) not only eliminate the need for a central switchboard, putting calls directly through to staff, but also monitor the length of calls, completion times and whether they lead to sales. This information can be used to determine individual pay. As a 1996 report by the Financial Services union, Bifu, concluded: 'Performance-related pay is made easier by ACD systems, because all work can be monitored in detail electronically and customer calls can be taped. Employees can be easily subjected to arbitrary quantitative, as well as qualitative, performance criteria.'

First Direct use a range of methods to assess staff. These range from managers sitting next to staff receiving calls to remote monitoring which measures, for example, average call duration. The company argues that call monitoring plays a key role in enabling First Direct to deliver a first-class service and argues that it does not have a demotivating effect on employees.

Stress levels, motivation problems and staff turnover are thought to be greater in call centres than in more conventional office environments. According to unpublished research by the Decisions Group, which operates centres for such clients as American Express, Microsoft and Sony, satisfaction levels amongst staff drop dramatically after six months. 'What we have found', says Kevin Hook, principal consultant at the Decisions Group, 'is that there is a hugely significant relationship between levels of perceived control over the pace of work and people's job satisfaction and stress. As you would expect, if people have low control over their jobs, they experience high levels of stress and low levels of job satisfaction.' The problem is worse in particularly controlled environments where staff follow some sort of scripting system and where staff breaks are scheduled. In the longer term, career opportunities for the mainly female staff within call centres are often very limited. As a result, disaffected staff find a number of ways of subverting the monitoring system, for example by taking a call and saying nothing so that the caller hangs up, or letting the caller hang up whilst remaining on the line so the other calls can't get through.

A number of solutions have been developed to deal with these problems. The Automobile Association (AA), for example, has recently retrained its staff to take more than one type of call. Insurance staff can now deal with membership enquiries, for example, whilst those who usually provide traffic and weather information can also handle emergency breakdown calls. The AA has found this new system both gives it greater flexibility and means that staff find it more motivating and rewarding. As well as multi-skilling, the AA has changed the role of its call centre team managers. They now concentrate on developing and coaching their staff by sitting and guiding them through calls. The AA believe this 'coaching culture' motivates staff through the attention they receive whilst motivating team managers through their new responsibilities.

As one of the pioneers in the field, First Direct have gone even further, experimenting in doing without team managers or supervisors. Chris Hancock, who heads the bank's call-centre operations, sees self-managed teams as a possible option for employees who want to pursue a career in the call centre rather than moving on to other parts of the business. The company has also looked at team-based assessment of staff, where staff listen to and give feedback to and on each other. As a result, Hancock says that staff turnover is not a problem, not least because staff are recruited more for communication skills than previous experience on financial services. First Direct is also able to offer many opportunities for career progression to those who want it.

Source: A. Arkin, 'Hold the production line' in *People Management*, 6 February 1997, pp. 22–27.

Motivation and management

The work of the writers on motivation provides an important resource for managers. It highlights the range of needs which underpin the process of motivation and emphasises the significance of belonging-needs and points, for example, to team-working both as a source of satisfaction and as a powerful potential motivating force. If team work can be aligned with organisational objectives, it can provide a strong motivator for team members who want to support team goals and values. This identification of esteem needs suggests the importance of praise and recognition by managers to staff performance. Research from the Hawthorne Experiments (1920s) has suggested how motivation and performance can be improved in this way.

As has already been discussed, motivation is also about avoiding alienation, especially as a result of process approaches, technology and status. Organisations and their managers need also to be aware that organisations may be by no means the only, or even the most important, focus for individuals' needs and the ways they set about fulfilling them. Many employees may view the organisation within which they work as a means for meeting only basic physiological and safety needs; and they may look for belonging, esteem and self-actualisation needs elsewhere, perhaps in the family or in their social life outside work. Their commitment to the organisation may, therefore, be limited, with a primary concern to protect safety needs which may well conflict with the organisation's need to change to meet new requirements or to secure greater involvement from individuals in improving performance.

The identification of the central importance of self-esteem needs also suggests the need, where it can be achieved, for creative, challenging and varied work, which points to the importance of good work design. This is supported by Porter and Lawler's (1968) emphasis on the role of intrinsic rewards as a major source of job satisfaction and a powerful source of motivation and commitment. As they point out, the experience of work itself can be the important ingredient in the cycle of satisfaction and motivation, with extrinsic rewards performing more a hygienic function.

Vroom's (1964, 1971) work highlights the importance of valence, instrumentality and expectancy as key issues in effective motivation. If performance and rewards are not strongly correlated, and the balance of effort to level of performance required is seen as excessive or unrealistic, the process of motivation will be compromised. Porter and Lawler (1968) also emphasise that rewards need to be generally accepted as fair if they are to be effective. Goals in work need, therefore, to be generally accepted amongst staff as reputable, clear and realistic, and measures of performance as objective, transparent and consistent. Rewards must also exceed the benchmarks laid down by perceived basic rewards. Some of the research discussed in this chapter suggests that a high degree of valence and instrumentality can be a significant motivator.

However, research on motivation and the significance of job satisfaction also reveals the incompleteness of the subject. It suggests a complex relationship between job satisfaction and performance indicating that, unless there are clear targets, benchmarks and, ultimately, rewards laid down for performance, increasing job satisfaction may not, of itself, improve the level of performance. Their complexity was reflected, for example, in the practice of downshifting by some companies in the 1990s towards competitive performance and related pay schemes. In highlighting instrumentality and expectancy, research within the field of motivation would seem to support the concept of performance-related pay.

However, other aspects of that research highlight the problems often associated with it. If performance-related pay is introduced as a substitute for more conventional pay arrangements it infringes perceived equitable rewards and might also be seen to undermine the safety needs identified by Maslow (1943) and others. Employees would see such schemes as exploitative: they (employees) would have to give greater levels of performance for the same level of reward. It may be especially difficult to establish equitable and transparent means of measuring levels of performance among differing individuals in a wide range of circumstances and markets. It also draws attention to extrinsic rewards when, as Porter and Lawler (1968) suggest, intrinsic satisfaction from the experience of work itself may be more significant. Indeed such intrinsic satisfaction may even be undermined by a process of being manipulated and confined by a framework of financial targets. Such schemes may also be seen as dysfunctional, pitching individuals against one another, undermining not only safety but also societal and esteem needs. Such schemes have also been interpreted by staff as lacking in understanding rather than being supportive and encouraging individuals to improve their performance.

Motivation and cultural differences

Most of the research in the theory and practice of motivation has been carried out by researchers in the United States of America with people who see themselves as members of that culture. Consequently, motivational theories need to be considered for their potential universality and there are, without doubt, some cultural differences – especially with regard to the needs theories advanced by Maslow (1943, 1954, 1971), McClelland (1953), Herzberg (1966) and the process theory advanced by Vroom (1964, 1970). Whilst self-actualisation may well be the objective of people in the United States of America, security may be the most important need in cultures such as Greece and Japan where, according to work carried out by Hofstede (1980), they have a high need to avoid uncertainty. It seems that whilst some Western cultures find the need for achievement to be high, others do not value it so much. Hines (1981) was one of the researchers who tested this theory in other countries. Hofstede's (1980) findings about the United States of America were not replicated in New Zealand where it was found that supervisory styles and interpersonal relationships were of key importance to workers. It is the expectancy theory which may offer a solution within cultures that value individualism; and it may help to make more co-operative those people who work within a collectivist culture where rewards are more closely tied to team efforts and thus reduce the utility of the expectancy theory.

Such issues as highlighted in this chapter do not invalidate the principle of performance-related pay as an important element in motivation, but they do suggest that it is a further option in a range of options and theories that managers can combine in providing effective motivation for staff. In this way, a manager takes existing theories of motivation and using the contingency approach enables individuals to become empowered to meet the goals of the organisation through the way that their jobs are designed.

Questions for discussion

1 What do you think are the most important motivational needs for the majority of people at work? Do you think that your individual needs differ from those of most people?

2 If you perceived inequity in your job, what strategy do you think would be the most helpful to you in resolving that inequity? What tactics would you consider to be the most effective in achieving the perceived equity?

3 At what level of Maslow's (1943) hierarchy of needs are you currently living? Are you basically satisfied at this level?

References and further reading

Adams, J.S., 'Towards an Understanding of Inequity' in *Journal of Abnormal and Social Psychology*, November 1963, pp. 422–436

Adams, J.S., 'Inequity in Social Exchange' in L. Berkowitz (ed.), 1965, *Advances in Experimental Social Psychology* (New York: Academic Press), Vol. 2, pp. 267–299

Alderfer, C.P., 1972, *Human Needs in Organizational Settings* (New York: Free Press)

Arkin, A., 'Hold the production line' in *People Management*, 6 February 1997, pp. 22–27

Arnold, J., Cooper, C.L. and Robertson, I.T., 1995 (2nd edn), *Work Psychology: Understanding Human Behaviour in the Workplace* (London: Pitman)

Bandura, A., 1977, *Social Learning Theory* (Englewood Cliffs, NJ: Prentice-Hall)

Beardwell, I. and Holden, L. (eds), 1997 (2nd edn), *Human Resource Management: A Contemporary Perspective* (London: Pitman)

Blackburn, R.M. and Mann, M., 1979, *The Working Class in the Labour Market* (London: Macmillan)

Brown, T., 'Nurturing a culture of innovation' in *Financial Times*, 17 November 1997, p. 12

Deci, E.L., 1971, 'Effects of Externally Mediated Rewards on Intrinsic Motivation' in *Journal of Applied Psychology*, Vol. 18, pp. 105–115

Donkin, R., 'Shoe factory provides an offshore spur' in *Financial Times*, 26 November 1997, p. 19

Dornstein, M., 1988, 'Wage reference groups and their determinants: a study of blue-collar and white-collar employees in Israel' in *Journal of Occupational Psychology*, Vol. 61, pp. 221–235

Folger, R. and Konovsky, M.A., 1989, 'Effects of procedural and distributive justice on reactions to pay rise decisions' in *Academy of Management Journal*, No 32, pp. 115–130

Freud, S., 1949, *An Outline of Psychoanalysis* (New York: Norton)

Goldthorpe, J. *et al.*, 1968, *The Affluent Worker* (Cambridge: Cambridge University Press)

Goodman, P.S., 1977, 'Social Comparison Processes in Organizations' in B.M. Staw and G.R. Salancik (eds), *New Directions in Organizational Behavior* (Chicago: St Clair), pp. 97–131

Greenberg, J., 1987, 'A taxonomy of organizational justice theories' in *Academy of Management Review*, Vol. 12, pp. 9–22

Guzzo, R. and Norman, K.A., 1994, 'Human resource practices as communications and the psychological contract' in *Human Resource Management*, Fall, Vol. 38, No 3

Hall, D.T. and Nougaim, K.E., 'An Examination of Maslow's Need Hierarchy in an Organizational Setting' in *Organizational Behavior and Human Performance*, February 1968, Vol. 3, pp. 12–35

Herzberg, F., 1966, *Work and the Nature of Man* (Cleveland: World)

Hines, G.H., 1981, 'Cross-Cultural Differences in Two-Factor Theory' in *Journal of Applied Psychology*, Vol. 58, pp. 313–317

Hofstede, G., 1980, 'Motivation, Leadership, and Organization: Do American Theories Apply Abroad?' in *Organization Dynamics*, Vol. 9, pp. 42–63

Hollenbeck, J.R., Williams, C.R. and Klein, J.H., 1989, 'An empirical examination of the antecedents of commitment to difficult goals' in *Journal of Applied Psychology*, Vol. 74, pp. 18–23

Holder, V., 'The high price of know how' in *Financial Times*, 14 July 1997, p. 10

Huseman, R.C., Hatfield, J.D. and Miles, E.W., 1987, 'An empirical examination of the antecedents of commitment to difficult goals' in *Journal of Applied Psychology*, Vol. 74, pp. 18–23

Huseman, R.C., Hatfield, J.D. and Miles, E.W., 'The Equity Sensitivity Construct: Potential Implications for Worker Performance' in *Journal of Management*, December 1989, pp. 581–588

Infield, N., 'Recuperating Knowledge' on Internet: http:www.knowledge-management.co.uk, 21 January 1998

Kelley, H.H., 1971, *Attribution to Social Intervention* (Morristown, NJ: General Learning Press)

Landy, F.J., 1985 (3rd edn), *Psychology of Work Behaviour* (Homewood, Ill: Dorsey Press)

Lawler, E.E. and Suttle, J.L., 1972, 'A Causal Correlational Test of the Need Hierarchy Concept' in *Organizational Behaviour and Human Performance*, Vol. 7, pp. 265–287

Lewin, K., 1938, *The Conceptual Representation and the Measurement of Psychological Forces* (Durham, NC: Duke University Press)

Locke, E.A., 'Toward a Theory of Task Motivation and Incentives' in *Organizational Behaviour and Human Performance*, May 1968, pp. 157–189.

Locke, E.A. and Latham, L., 1979, *Organized Dynamics* (New York: American Management Association)

Lyon, J., 'Understanding knowledge' on Internet: http:www.knowledge-management.co.uk, 21 January 1998

McClelland D.C., 1965, 'Achievement Motivation Can Be Learned', in *Harvard Business Review* 43, pp. 6–24

McClelland, D.C., Atkinson, J., Clark, R. and Lowell, E., 1953, *The Achievement Motive* (New York: Appleton-Century-Crofts)

McFarlin, D.B. and Sweeney, P.D., 1992, 'Distributive and procedural justice as predictors of satisfaction with personal and organizational outcomes' in *Academy of Management Journal*, No 35, pp. 626–637

McGregor, D.M., 1960, *The Human Side of Enterprise* (New York: McGraw-Hill)

Maslow, A., 1943, 'A Theory of Human Motivation' in *Psychological Review*, Vol. 50, No 4, pp. 370–396

Maslow, A., 1954, *Motivation and Personality* (New York: Harper & Row)

Maslow, A., 1971, *The Farther Reaches of Human Nature* (Harmondsworth: Penguin Books)

Moorhead, G. and Griffin, R.W., 1995 (4th edn), *Organizational Behavior: Managing People and Organizations* (Boston: Houghton Mifflin)

Mullins, L. 1996 (4th edn), *Management and Organisational Behaviour* (London: Pitman)

Nadler, D.A. and Lawler, E.E., 1983 (2nd edn), 'Motivation: A Diagnostic Approach' in J.R. Hackman, E.E. Lawler and I.W. Porter (eds), *Perspectives on Behaviour in Organizations* (Homewood, Ill: Dorsey Press)

Nelson, D.L. and Quick, J.C., 1994, *Organizational Behavior – Foundations, Realities and Challenges* (St Paul, MN: West Publishing)

Pinder, C., 1984, *Work Motivation* (Glenview, Ill: Scott, Foresman)

Porter, I.W. and Lawler, E.E., 1968, *Managerial Attitudes and Performance* (Homewood, Ill: Dorsey Press)

Roethlisberger, F.J., Dickson, W.J. and Wright, H.A., 1950, in *Management and the Worker: An Account of a Research program Conducted by the Western Electric Company, Hawthorne Works, Chicago* (Cambridge, Mass.: Harvard University press), pp. 270–290

Rowland, H. and Harris, L., 'Doctor know' in *People Management*, 5 March 1998, pp. 50–52

Sims, R.R., 1994, 'Human resource management's role in clarifying the new psychological contract' in *Human Resource Management*, Fall, Vol. 33

Smith, A., *An Inquiry into the Nature and Causes of the Wealth of Nations*, (C.J. Bullock, ed.) Vol. 10 of the Harvard Classics (New York: Collier)

Tampoe, M., 'Knowledge Workers – The New Management Challenge' in *Professional Manager*, November 1994, pp. 12–13

Taylor, F.W., 1911, *Principles of Scientific Management* (New York: Harper & Row)

Tolman, E.C., 1932, *Purposive Behavior in Animals* (New York: Appleton-Century-Crofts)

Vroom, V.H., 1964/1970, *Work and Motivation* (New York: Wiley)

Weaver, T., 'Theory M: Motivating with Money' in *Cornell HRA Quarterly*, November 1988, Vol. 29, No 3, pp. 40–45

5 Job design

Learning objectives

After studying this chapter you should be able to:

- discuss traditional approaches to job design;
- describe the job characteristics model and the motivating potential score;
- explain the interdisciplinary approach to job design;
- explain the relationship between technology and job design;
- compare Japanese, German, and Scandinavian approaches to work;
- discuss the key components of work design from traditional and contemporary perspectives.

Introduction

CASE STUDY

Changing the job mix to encourage latent talent

Skill development ... depends upon job design. However, job design depends on organisational design: jobs can only have the essential characteristics if overall organisational structure is designed to allow it. Isn't this where we should focus any attempt on 're-engineering' a business? If we are to align businesses to processes we could start by aligning jobs to processes.

The ideal is that each job in an organisation spans the complete process of the organisation's business: the job starts with the basic 'input' to the organisation and ends with the final product or service. The boundaries of the job and the boundaries of the organisation match. This also cuts out the squabbling and blaming that occurs so often when there are internal job boundaries. The organisation is designed to create jobs that motivate, encourage reponsibility, build self-esteem and make skill development happen almost automatically. People focus on the job instead of on internal politics and this allows the organisation to respond more rapidly than one that has its work processes broken into little empires.

Many industries and professions are designing jobs more narrowly than is necessary and so are creating problems for their businesses. The software industry is just one example. If more projects were designed to align jobs with the software development process, employeres would be more flexible. In turn, this could mean that the industry would become more attractive to young people, leading to a boost in the overall numbers as well. If this style of job design brings so many benefits, why isn't it happening everywhere? There are three main obstacles:

1 We have a tradition of poor job design. Few managers have ever formally studied

the subject and therefore few question the traditional way of designing organisations.

2 Breaking a work process into many small stages gives an illusion of control that appeals to those who need to feel in control. Of course, it is only an illusion.

3 Skill is a political commodity. Some aspects of a work process may be of higher status or bring higher rewards than others, so people strive to achieve skill monopolies over these parts of the process.

Jobs aligned to the work process means multi-skilling, with everyone taking a share of all skills and a responsibility for all stages.

Adapted from D. Barton, 'Changing the job mix to encourage latent talent' in *People Management*, 11 July 1996, p. 23

The above case illustrates many of the difficulties faced by organisations as they attempt to redesign jobs in order to keep abreast of the evolving changes in organisational design. Which job design offers the best intrinsic motivation for the workforce? What effect do evolving ideas on management such as ergonomics, team working, business process re-engineering (BPR) and empowerment have on job design? How does technology affect job design? This chapter discusses how aspects of job design have shifted from scientific management through ergonomics to the modern notions of empowerment and autonomous team-working with their flexible methods of job design and how such designs affect the motivation and workplace stress of members of the workforce.

The purpose of job design

Job design is about the way that tasks are combined to form complete jobs in the workplace, whilst *job redesign* has its focus on how existing jobs are changed: for example, by redesigning jobs management may be able to increase motivation around, say, the introduction of autonomous work teams. The umbrella term *job design* encompasses a specification of tasks that are to be performed by employees in the organisation and it includes any anticipated interpersonal and task relationships. This occurs all the time in the workplace as people communicate and is increasingly so in the flat, lean organisation structures. For example, a project leader may consciously or unconsciously change the job-related tasks of her team members in order to meet the evolving needs of the customer. Because tasks change, as do the means of performing them, it is essential that all members of the workforce have an understanding of how to design and redesign jobs so that the needs and goals of individuals and the organisation are met. It would be ideal if all employees' competencies were utilised so that a quality product/service could be provided. At best, there are always ways of attaining substantial improvements in job design which will benefit the customer and, on the way, intrinsically motivate the employee. For example, improvements in the design of production workers' jobs in the motor car industry have improved the quality of the cars and, on the way, the changes have benefited the workforce. Such a framework for job design can be seen in Figure 5.1.

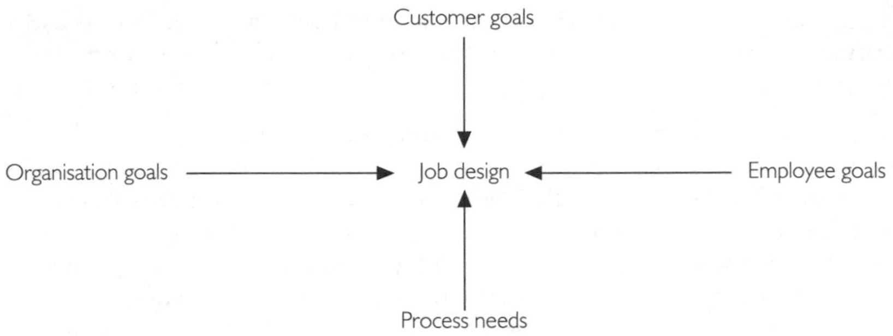

Figure 5.1 Framework for job design

Organisations are involved in a transformation process in that they turn inputs into outputs. In an open system which requires constant interaction with the organisation's environment, the workforce needs to be able to provide inputs and energy to ensure that the system is able to operate. For example, an organisation working in an open system would have external inputs such as knowledge, components, resources and expectations which they would process through technology, expertise and synergy, into the outputs of products, services and waste. A successful conversion process requires the co-operation of all within the organisation and to achieve this objective it is necessary to constantly review job design and redesign.

All organisations – be they profit or non-profit making – are primarily concerned with maximising value: providing 'added value' through the conversion process. They do this through five key areas: costs, productivity, economy, reliability, and control.

Traditionally, *cost* includes the price of production or supply and correlates the expense of materials and labour to prices and wages with the additional apportionment of overhead expenses. However, cost also includes elements of job design such as the expense involved in correcting errors and maintaining a quality product/service; the speed of workforce response in that they have the required competencies to hand; the dependability of the supply of the goods/services required by the customer; and the flexibility of the workforce in that they are multi-skilling.

Productivity is a performance measure and is one of the most important aspects of operations management. It has received increasing attention over the past few years. If the transformation process is to be improved there have to be methods available for measuring current effectiveness and the added value the organisation provides. Productivity, however, is not a single measure but is used in conjunction with others to evaluate operations management. Such criteria are: the cost of the transformation process; the quality of the product/service; the delivery to customers (sometimes segregated into delivery speed and delivery dependability); and flexibility of the process.

The *economy* is concerned with the transformation process which has, at the basic level, two agents: the consumer and the producer. The consumer attempts to maximise its utility or satisfaction by purchasing goods/services which give it the greatest value related to the price charged for them. The producer, on the other hand, attempts to increase its profits either by producing goods/services which deliver better value than those of the competition or by reducing its costs. Managers need to understand their customers in order to meet customer needs at a lower cost, at maximum customer satisfaction and with a competitive advantage. Such a customer strategy has an influence on work design and redesign since workers have to provide the organisation with an economical service.

Reliability features at all stages of the transformation process since workers have to rely on their co-workers, supervisors on subordinates, team leaders on team members, customers on suppliers, and so on. Reliability implies honesty and trustworthiness and dependability at all stages of production and provision. Dependency exhibits itself as relationships between the organisation and its employees and also between particular groups. In the economic framework, it is the ability to persuade people to work because of their need to earn money to satisfy their physiological and psychological needs. Reliability and dependency are therefore key factors in the design and redesign of jobs.

The work of organisations has to be organised and *controlled* and it is the same with job design and job redesign because both relate to the transformational process. Control is a co-ordinating function which ensures that stability is maintained with a realisation that remedial action may need to be made where high points and low points start to become obvious. It is also necessary for the organisation to ensure the maximisation and optimisation of resources at each stage of their cycle which includes the workforce and their way of working.

Customers now expect value as a matter of course and they tend to relate it to cost, quality, speed of delivery, and flexibility. These factors are best dealt with under the umbrella term of Total Quality Management (TQM), which is not a system but an organisational philosophy. It is a long-term strategy adopted by organisations which makes continuous improvement a responsibility of *all* employees – hence it is closely linked with job design and redesign. TQM requires of all the workforce (including the Chief Executive Officer (CEO) and his or her executive team) a dedication to meeting customers' needs and expectations. This will include a range of areas but specifically:

1 designing quality into products and services;

2 preventing defects but correcting those that do appear immediately and without cost to the customer;

3 constantly improving the quality of goods/services to the extent that it is economically and competitively feasible to do so.

In the current business climate most firms are committed to the quality philosophy and strive to improve both productivity and quality. Firms such as Ford, The Royal Mail, British Telecom and IBM have all used the concepts of TQM (or some variation of them) to improve the quality of service for customers. Hence, such a philosophy has affected work design and redesign in ways such as the use of autonomous work teams and works councils.

However, organisations make choices and some are more explicit than others. Such choices are not free and unbounded because they need to be placed within the constraints of the organisation's environment: for example, legislation, the level of available technology, or the state of the labour market. There is also a relationship with work organisation and job design or redesign because the organisation has to decide whether jobs will be broadly or narrowly defined. Whether the workforce will be organised into teams or will individuals have their own roles? If autonomous teams are initiated, will they comprise specialists or generalists? Are the jobs to be enriched or enhanced? What are the jobs designed to do: exercise skill and autonomy so that individuals use their discretion and self-develop, or are they to be restricted and controlled so that the worker will find discretion and self-development limited?

Whilst job design and redesign is about providing quality it has entrenched within it the need to fulfil the needs of the employees. In the modern world of work this is related to what is known as the *psychological contract*. According to Warr (1996), the latter in employment:

> ... denotes the informal and largely unwritten expectations of employees and employers about their mutual rights and obligations, and about expected inducements and contributions. (p. 177)

Job design and redesign has a close link with the motivation of the workforce. If carried out effectively, motivation and commitment can be generated in any worker or work team – whatever the situation – provided that the behavioural satisfaction aspect of the job is also addressed. However, the opposite is also true: where jobs and occupations are not perceived by the workforce to be effective, productive or satisfying, then demotivation and demoralisation will occur. The subject of motivation is dealt with in detail in Chapter 4; however, in relation to job design and redesign, motivation as related to individual needs is central. If one is to establish realistic concepts of the changing work environment it is necessary to establish new frames of reference. For example, to review the critical work of Maslow (1960, 1980) on the theory of a hierarchy of needs as it relates to job design and redesign is necessary because the latter balances needs and goals. Slack *et al.* (1995) believe that there are 'performance objectives ... relevant in job-design decisions' (p. 343), as shown in Figure 5.2 below.

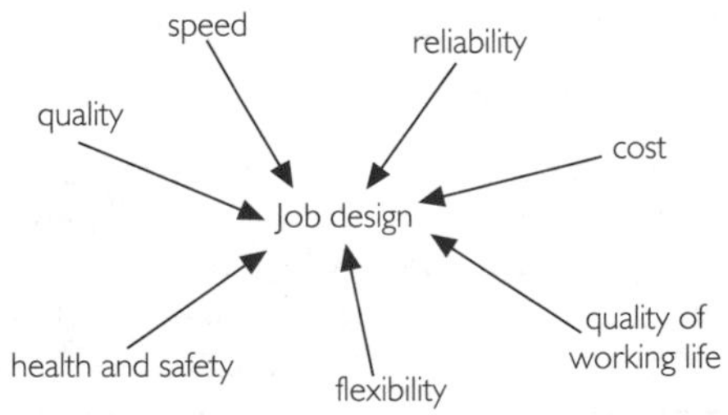

Figure 5.2 Factors which can affect job satisfaction

It is necessary for organisations to find ways in which the higher-order needs (self-actualisation and esteem) can be satisfied without necessarily meeting the lower-order requirements (physiological, safety, and social) in the traditional way. The concept of the psychological contract can provide a valuable frame of reference to stimulate fresh thinking and to blow away much of the empty rhetoric about new management ideas; for example, empowerment.

Several of these factors have been previously discussed; however, there are other considerations which need to be taken into account, such as:

1 *Health and safety*. Any job design or redesign must consider the health and safety of the individual worker, the work team or the user of the product/service.

2 *Flexibility*. Job design and redesign attempts to develop a fully flexible workforce by ensuring that all the workers as individuals or as members of work teams are capable of carrying out each of the tasks required. Flexibility is basic to the transformation process of changing inputs into outputs. It is the responsibility of the organisation to provide staff development so that individuals can be both competent and flexible.

3 *Quality of working life (QOWL)*. The workforce is now better educated, less unionised and more used to dealing with changing values and aspirations. Although these will not lessen the motivation to work, they are altering the rewards that people seek from work and the balance they seek between work and other aspects of life. Increasingly members of the workforce are considering *downshifting*, which is the reduction of time spent at work and the increasing of time spent on leisure activities and time with the family. Such attention to 'quality time' is a holistic approach to the quality of life. The quality of work life (QOWL) represents the degree to which people are able to satisfy their important personal needs through their work and it is an important goal for many in the workforce. Thus, job design and redesign must take such factors into consideration by ensuring that jobs have task variety, there are opportunities for continuous development and stress levels are kept only at the positive tension level.

Approaches to job design

Approaches to job design have concentrated on two variables in achieving the balance between meeting needs and goals:

Processes ◄————► People

There is an interaction between job design/redesign and *process* because accomplishing anything in an organisation more often than not requires a knowledge of whom to see and how to present an idea to that person. Process refers to how tasks of the organisation are carried out and, regardless of how the job is designed or redesigned, all workers participate in such processes as decision-making, leadership, communication, motivation, and conflict-resolution, and process is closely related to decision-making. It may be necessary to make changes in design and process in order to meet individual and organisational needs. Process determination depends on ways of working and the individual personalities and teams involved. There are key groups who may need to be consulted, e.g. team leaders, and customers; not to do so is likely to minimise or nullify an effective process.

A key factor in process determination is time and there is a trade-off between the quality and volume of information that can be gathered and the time available to do this. Whilst time may allow for the gathering of pertinent information with a view to careful examination and evaluation, costs could be offset by a quick decision.

Since the consideration of process helps to achieve efficiency in the best way possible, it is important to recognise that account must be taken of the *people* who do the job as it relates to such factors as quality, productivity and flexibility considered earlier in this chapter.

Collectively, process and people need to be balanced and the search for this stabilisation leads to the consideration of alternative methods of job design. To concentrate on either one at the expense of the other will produce an imbalance. Gaining such a balance is often related to the areas of job satisfaction and job performance.

Since job design/redesign is the planning and specification of job tasks within the workplace this encompasses both the specification of task attributes and the creation of the work environment for these attributes. It is the manager's responsibility to design/redesign jobs that will be motivational for the individual worker as shown in Figure 5.3 below.

Individual needs + task attributes + work setting —lead to→ satisfaction and performance

Figure 5.3 Job design and motivation

However, there is no firm relationship between job satisfaction and other outcomes in the workplace. By addressing the issues of motivation – especially intrinsic motivation – a manager may be able to improve an individual's job satisfaction. However, it is a tenuous and unsupported link because job satisfaction is an attitude which incorporates an individual's cognitive, affective and evaluative reactions towards his or her job.

Attitudes are real but they are intangible and not directly visible and hence measuring job satisfaction is a difficult task. Several techniques for assessing aspects of work environments do exist; they include rating scales, questionnaires, critical incidents, and interviews. In the current organisational climate managers discuss the success or failure of specific issues in relation to *employee morale*. Practising managers suggest that successful organisations are ones in which morale is high whilst those that cannot compete are low in morale. In other words, it is the opinion of managers that job satisfaction exerts strong effects on important aspects of organisational behaviour such as task performance, staff turnover and absenteeism. However, such a relationship is difficult to confirm. As can be seen in Chapter 4, several key studies have attempted to come to a definitive conclusion on this. The difficulty lies in the appreciation of attitudes which do affect behaviour in many instances, but not always. Attitudes can be blocked by external factors or conditions. Since attitudes are most likely to shape overt actions when they are specific and strong, they are less likely to produce effects when they are general or weak. Consequently, the impact of job satisfaction cannot be readily visible in all situations and contexts. However, there are some indications that work-related attitudes do often influence job satisfaction.

For consideration

Jane and Lisa work for the same organisation. Both have to get up early in the morning in order to arrive at work on time and both also dislike commuting into and out of the city.

Question

Which of them is more likely to telephone in sick or take a day off for other reasons?

Answer

The answer appears to be obvious: the one who dislikes her job within the organisation.

That job satisfaction does affect absence from the workplace as described above is indicated by the findings of many different studies. Argyle (1989) investigated the association between job satisfaction, absenteeism and labour, and came to the conclusion that both absenteeism and turnover were affected by factors other than job satisfaction but stated that where there is a high level of job satisfaction there was less likely to be absenteeism and resignations from the workplace.

However, this relationship is very modest rather than strong because job satisfaction is just one of many different factors influencing an individual's decision to turn up, or not, for work. Work carried out by Mowday *et al.* (1984) concentrated on voluntary turnover of staff. They found that the lower the individuals' level of satisfaction with their jobs, the more likely they were to resign and seek further job opportunities. Similarly, this relationship is modest and for similar reasons as given above. Many factors which relate to individuals, their jobs and economic situation condition their decision to leave one job for another. When the unemployment rates rise, there tends to be a lower correlation between job satisfaction and turnover. However, there are factors affecting job satisfaction which also affect voluntary turnover. Oldham and Fried (1987) measured turnover among their study participants and found that poor environmental conditions – such as poor lighting, open-plan offices – were related to increased voluntary turnover.

The findings of such key studies seem to suggest that factors that reduce job satisfaction often increase turnover as well. However, there is no proof that it is a causal effect, i.e. that low job satisfaction is a direct cause of turnover – but it is consistent with other evidence suggesting that this is the case.

It is a commonsense notion that job satisfaction leads directly to effective task performance but it is still an area where there is no consensus of opinion. There is some evidence that suggests that job satisfaction is directly linked to task performance or productivity.

Vroom (1964) in his study on work and motivation found that there was no simple relationship (low median correlation –0.14) between job satisfaction and job performance. In a later work Miller and Monge (1986) found evidence for the view that the opportunity to participate in decision-making increases job satisfaction and that such positive attitudes, in turn, facilitate productivity. However, the overall picture is more complex since some studies (Luthans, 1992) suggest that job satisfaction has little, if any, effect on task performance and productivity. This might be for a number of reasons.

Firstly, in some workplaces there is minimal room for significant changes in performance because the jobs are structured in such a way that the individuals holding them *must* maintain at least some level of performance. Secondly, there is often little leeway for *exceeding* such minimum standards. This is related to the input–output situation discussed earlier in this chapter – if a worker increases his own output, this may have no impact because needed output from other workers, who have not increased their own output or effort, is lacking. This can have a demotivational impact on the individual because he may have high job satisfaction and thus increase his output, but may find he has little to do. Thus even very high levels of job satisfaction can have little overall effect on productivity. Thirdly, it may be a truism that job satisfaction and productivity are not directly linked. It may appear that any apparent relationship between them might stem from the fact that both are related to another factor – reward.

This is a key issue in today's organisations – particularly in relation to the change in organisation design to flat structures and the related introduction of teams. Porter and Lawler (1968) worked on this area and came to the conclusion that past levels of performance lead to the receipt of both extrinsic rewards (pay, promotion, company car) and intrinsic rewards (self-esteem, accomplishment). They found that if workers judged these rewards to be fair, they came to perceive a link between their performance and such outcomes. This had ongoing effects: it could encourage high levels of effort and, therefore, good performance. Also it might well lead to high levels of job satisfaction. That is, high productivity and high job satisfaction may both stem from the same conditions but the two factors may themselves not be linked.

Therefore, job satisfaction may not be directly related to performance in many respects. This might well be true when related to 'standard' measures of performance: job satisfaction does not, by itself, strongly affect the quantity or quality of an individual's output. However, it may well influence other aspects of an individual's on-the-job behaviour, for example, actions in their social life that enhance social relationships and co-operation within an organisation such as offering to help co-workers, being cheerful in disposition, co-operating, loyalty to the organisation, etc. It is likely that the higher an individual's level of job satisfaction the more likely they are to engage in such social behaviours in the workplace.

A more recent study by Bassett (1994) supports this point of view, since whilst reviewing key studies in the relationship between job satisfaction and productivity, he concludes that there is no universal solution to the issue. However, he does make the point that by investigating job design/redesign managers may be able to raise the job satisfaction of their workforce.

Formal theories on job design are a fairly recent development; the earliest work ignored the balance required and concentrated on processes at the expense of people. This can be seen particularly when looking at the evolution of job design/redesign from the scientific management school.

Scientific management and job design

Taylor (1911) argued that jobs should be studied in a scientific way and broken down into their smallest component tasks. Such tasks would then be standardised so that individual workers could carry out a specific task. Such a view followed from that of Adam Smith (1776) who suggested that jobs should be specialised so that output could be increased. Such specialisation paved the way for the assembly line system used by such industries as car manufacturing.

Taylor (1911) stated that his philosophy of scientific management rested on a few foundational principles:

1 use of scientific determination to identify each element of a job;

2 the scientific selection and training of the workforce;

3 the co-operation of management and labour to meet the work objectives in accordance with scientific method;

4 a more equal division of responsibility between managers and the workforce with managers doing the planning and supervising, and the workers carrying out the tasks.

This could be carried out by monitoring the best workers through studying and timing them at their individual tasks and then training other workers to that same standard. Then changes could be introduced such as differential pay rates in order to increase productivity. This is, in today's parlance, 'performance-related pay'.

Organisations still have a wide range of tasks to complete and integrate in order to meet their objectives and they achieve this by allocating tasks and responsibilities to individuals or teams through job design/redesign. Since the latter specifies the nature of those tasks and responsibilities, how they are grouped together, and especially the degree of discretion afforded to employees over their execution, managers have to consider the variants related to the allocation of work and how it is carried out.

Work can be defined as mental or physical activity that has productive results. Organisational psychologists have studied the concept of work as it relates to the principles of scientific management. The umbrella term used is *work study*, which is the application of techniques to investigate method study and work measurement. Such methods are used to examine all aspects of the human task which affect how efficiently the job is carried out in relation to costs and projected improvements. By using *method study* managers can systematically record and critically examine tasks as they are currently being carried out and propose easier and more effective methods to reduce costs. *Work measurement* requires the manager to apply techniques that are specifically designed with a view to a trained operative carrying out a specific task at a defined level of performance and quality.

Advantages of scientific management

The beginning of scientific management was concerned with maximising efficiency and getting as much work as possible out of the workforce. Hence, scientific management emphasised the importance of effective job design/redesign – the effort to plan work tasks in a systematic manner. In retrospect, it can be recognised that the grandfather of scientific management, Taylor (1911), offered a limited focus on organisations since he was only addressing work at the lowest level of the organisation – appropriate to the managerial task of a supervisor.

In today's working world Taylor (1911) still has an influence since he created the foundation for the study of industrial engineering or production management. Even though he focused on a very limited segment of organisational activity, Taylor (1911) did revolutionise the manager's task and there were certain advantages to the approach including:

1 explicit demonstration that managers should carefully assess the best way for each job to be done to maximise efficiency;

2 leading to the manager's responsibility to explicitly:

(a) recruit/select
(b) train
(c) motivate

workers to ensure the best way was followed;

3 management having greater control over process and people.

Scientific management principles also have advantages which are related to the workforce:

1 work simplification can allow workers of diverse ethnic and skill backgrounds to work together in a systematic way;

2 work simplification can lead to production efficiency in the organisation and thus to higher profits at lower costs;

3 people often seek many goals through their work – from enhanced status to personal fulfilment;

4 some attention was directed to the importance of human behaviour at work;

5 efficiency is increased because by increasing the output per worker, reducing worker control and reducing underemployment all workers gain a standard similar to that of an effective worker;

6 standardisation is across the board and reduces every activity to a simple set of tasks;

7 the deskilling of workers at every stage of production;

8 the need for decision-making is reduced;

9 the simplification of tasks can result in increased learning;

10 standardisation of tasks can facilitate learning and greater specialisation and expertise;

11 simple tasks may be better open to automation.

However, there is always another viewpoint to do with the identification of problems associated with the use of scientific management:

1 the fundamental limitation is that it undervalues the human capacity for thought and ingenuity;

2 the economic argument for work simplification tends to treat the workforce as a means of production and thus dehumanises it;

3 other factors which affected performance, such as the quality of leadership, were not considered;

4 an oversimplified approach was taken to what was a complex concept requiring the appreciation of the social nature of work and work settings and the attention of practising managers;

5 all workers are reduced to a mean;

6 workers are deskilled, thereby removing the role of judgement, responsibility, and autonomy;

7 it introduces overt supervisory discipline to ensure tasks are carried out to the measured standard;

8 it reduces decision-making at grass roots level.

The problems associated with scientific management in today's workplace can be divided into three key areas: the impact on employees, ethical implications, and the resulting impact on performance, quality, and flexibility.

Impact on employees

The key theme underlying all the problems associated with the utilisation of scientific management in organisations concentrates on the concept of alienation. Like attitudes, alienation is more a descriptive word than an easily defined concept. Blauner (1964) considers it in terms of four dimensions: powerlessness, meaningless, isolation, and self-estrangement. However, these terms are not mutually exclusive and other feelings can be taken into account.

Alienation is a key cause of dysfunctional conflict within the workplace and has to be taken into account when designing/redesigning jobs in order to eliminate it – or at the very least, minimise its effects. Alienation can be exhibited through any of the following ways:

- *Powerlessness.* The inability to influence any aspect of working conditions including the amount of work, the quality, speed, and direction.
- *Meaninglessness.* The inability to recognise the contribution which individuals make to the total work output.
- *Isolation*. This could be either physical or psychological. Physical isolation is when individuals are allocated workstations away from their colleagues and their tasks are designed to keep human interaction to a minimum. Physical isolation results in psychological deprivation which entails being distanced from supervisors, managers and others in the organisation.
- *Lack of self-esteem.* Individuals have a self-perception of their self-worth and apprehend that they lack value in the eyes of the management.
- *Identity crisis.* Following on from a lack of self-worth is a lack of identity with the host organisation so that the commitment of the individual does not bring rewards.
- *Lack of a future.* When there is no chance of promotion, change of direction or advancement.
- *Environmental factors.* General rejection based on a number of factors such as management styles, lack of positive communication, participation, responsibility and involvement. Physical factors can increase such alienation, e.g. poor working conditions and an unsatisfactory work environment.
- *Lack of equality.* Alienation can result when the worker perceives inequality in rewards between workers at the same grade.

Ethical implications

There are a number of ethical considerations concerned with scientific management. Whilst it was popular during the early twentieth century and was one of the first approaches to management it concentrated on the efficiency of individual workers as systems rather than as people. The system did not balance process and people in the transformation process, and brought about some consideration of the ethics of management. Scientific management showed that whilst the workers appeared to be satisfied with their remuneration, they expressed a high level of dissatisfaction with the actual work that they did. According to Walker and Guest (1952) reporting on their study of Detroit car workers, the workforce complained about six specific aspects of their jobs:

- rigid pacing of the assembly line
- repetitiveness
- low skill requirement
- narrowness of job task
- limited social intercourse
- no control over related tools and techniques.

There evolved a view amongst managers utilising job specialisation techniques in their organisations that although such techniques might increase efficiency, a continuation of such techniques would result in a number of negative consequences. Some of these had specific ethical implications as follows:

- they were perceived as a sweating system to use workers as indentured slaves;
- they placed workers into a life of repetitive monotony;
- management were more concerned with process than with people;
- they treated individuals as machines working to the lowest common denominator and eliminated from them the capacity to be responsible and accountable;
- they put workers into a system where they were subject to managerial discipline and dictatorial approaches to control;
- they encouraged the practice of *soldiering* where the worker works more slowly than he or she actually can.

Impact on performance, quality and flexibility

Accompanying scientific management there came associated individual related aspects of low morale, high absenteeism, low quality production, sabotage of targets and system inflexibility. However, it was not until the 1930s that notable changes occurred in management's perception of the relationship between the individual and the workplace and this perception took on board such considerations neglected by scientific management. It was at this time that serious and now classic research studies led to the emergence of organisational behaviour as a field of study, which included the negative aspects of scientific management.

Some of the greatest organisational researchers in the United States of America contributed to the Hawthorne Studies which took place between 1927 and 1932 and which led to some of the first discoveries of the importance of human behaviour in organisations. The studies were conducted primarily by researchers from Harvard University led by Elton Mayo, and incorporated four developments:

1 **Experiments in illumination**. The Hawthorne studies are best remembered for the experiments related to illumination and gave rise to the phrase *the Hawthorne effect*. The research tested the effects of illumination on worker productivity of females in the Western Electric factory. As the intensity of illumination in the experimental group was reduced, productivity increased. The Hawthorne effect demonstrated that people

behave differently from they way they might otherwise behave when they are being observed.

As a result of this first study when the issue of interest in the workforce appeared to have an effect on morale and productivity, the researchers extended their study to a second stage.

2 **Relay assembly test room**. Five women were observed in detail in an attempt to ascertain whether changes in environment and working conditions affected productivity. The results validated the first study and the researchers concluded that employee attitudes and sentiments that had not been previously considered were critically important in organisations. There was less absenteeism and quality of work improved.

The researchers found the results of their two studies baffling and decided to extend their studies to a larger population to see whether their findings were valid and reliable.

3 **Experiments in interviewing workers**. In 1928 some 300 interviewers wandered through the factory interviewing the workforce. From this study the researchers developed guidelines for interviews and the concept of guaranteed confidentiality led to revealing openness from employees. This contradicted the views of scientific management which supported control from the hierarchy and which did not allow accountability for employees.

The researchers then went on to the final part of their longitudinal study.

4 **The bank wiring room**. A group at the factory was put on a piece rate plan for seven months in order to find out whether the group output would increase to correspond with an increase in pay. The outcome was unexpected. The sample group actually paced their work throughout the experiment according to group norms. Thus the power of the peer group and the importance of group influence and dynamics on individual behaviour and productivity were confirmed.

The Hawthorne Studies put the principle of scientific management to bed and identified the concept of *social surface*. That is, there appeared to be formal and informal elements (see Figure 5.4) within organisations which scientific management principles had overlooked and which had a key impact on performance, quality, and flexibility.

Many theorists refer to the Hawthorne Studies as the root of organisational behaviour and the studies provided the foundations for the human relations movement. Human relationists believe that employee satisfaction is a major determinant of performance. One prominent human relationist writer, Douglas McGregor (1960), developed the concepts of Theory X and Theory Y. Theory X takes a negative and pessimistic view of workers, whereas Theory Y takes a more positive and optimistic approach. McGregor advocated the Theory Y style of management. Maslow (1943) was another pioneer in the human relations movement, developing the hierarchy of needs theory mentioned earlier. Organisational behaviour began to merge as a mature field of study in the late 1950s and early 1960s.

Contemporary viewpoints on scientific management have shifted the responsibility for the use of its principles from the hands of managers to those of the workers so as to make the latter more accountable for their own job design/redesign. Whilst the philosophy of scientific management is now difficult to adopt, some of its methods and techniques can be adapted when designing/redesigning jobs.

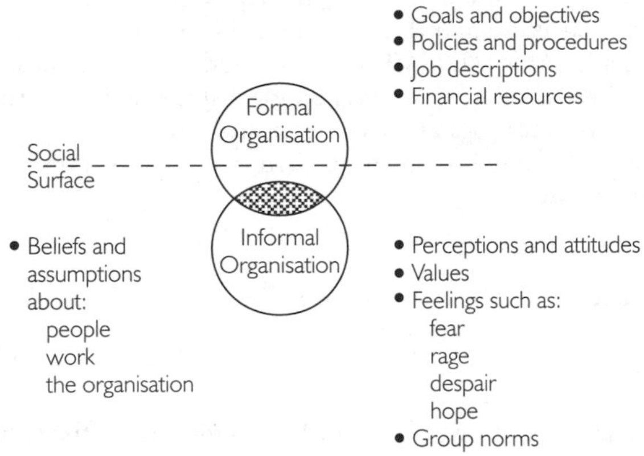

Figure 5.4 Concept of social surface, after Nelson and Quick (1994, p. 8)

Adapted from D.L. Nelson and J.C. Quick, *Organizational Behavior: Foundations, Realities, and Challenges*, 1994, St Paul, MN: West Publishing, p. 8

Ways of understanding work motivation

The Job Characteristic Model (JCM) developed by Hackman and Oldham (1976) provided a model (see figure 5.5 below) for analysing the motivational attributes of jobs. In essence, it was a framework for understanding how a person fitted a job by the interaction of core job dimensions with critical psychological states within a person.

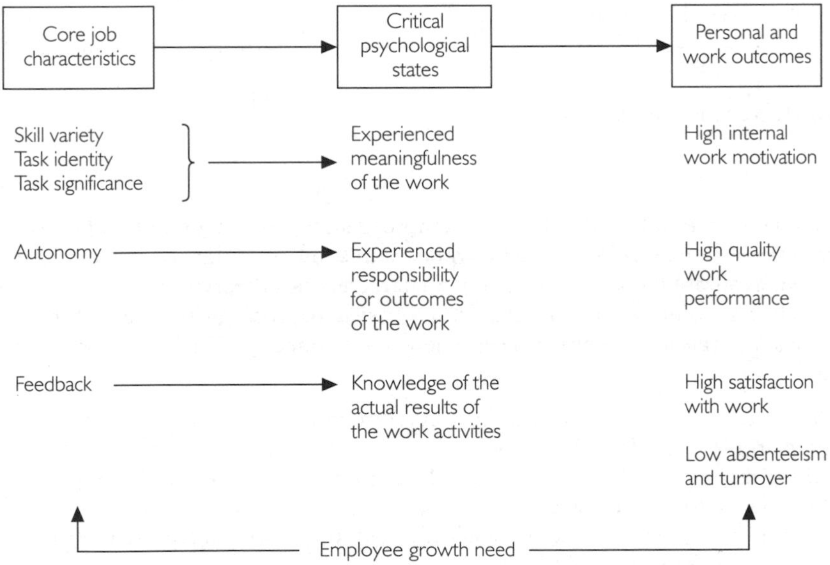

Figure 5.5 The job characteristics model, after Hackman and Oldham (1976)

Hackman and Oldham (1976) also developed, in conjunction with the JCM model, a tool which could be used to measure and thus diagnose the elements in the JCM. This they called the Job Diagnostic Survey (JDS). The latter could be used to measure the five core job characteristics and the three critical psychological states shown in the model in Figure 5.5. The core job characteristics are said to stimulate the critical psychological states in the manner shown in Figure 5.5 which, in turn, results in varying the personal and work outcomes of an individual.

The five core job characteristics are:

- *Skill variety.* The degree to which the worker uses a multiplicity of skills and talents with a number of different activities.
- *Task identity.* The degree to which the task requires completion, i.e. from start to finish with an identifiable outcome.
- *Task significance.* The degree to which the task is significant to the worker, be it in the organisation or the external environment.
- *Autonomy.* The degree to which the job provides ultimate freedom and independence related to work planning and procedures.
- *Feedback.* The degree to which the worker receives feedback on the process and results of the task.

Hackman and Oldham (1976) believed that the five core characteristics interacted to determine an overall Motivating Potential Score (MPS) for a named task. The MPS indicates a job's potential for motivating the holders of that job. An individual worker's MPS can be determined by using the undermentioned equation in Figure 5.6.
The JCM includes the two factors of *growth and strength* (the desire to self-actualise) which

$$\text{MPS} = \frac{\left[\begin{matrix}\text{Skill}\\ \text{variety}\end{matrix}\right] + \left[\begin{matrix}\text{Task}\\ \text{identity}\end{matrix}\right] + \left[\begin{matrix}\text{Task}\\ \text{significance}\end{matrix}\right]}{3} \times \left[\text{Autonomy}\right] \times \left[\text{Feedback}\right]$$

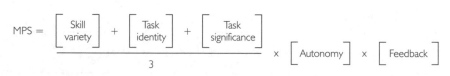

Figure 5.6 The Motivating Potential Score

act as a moderator. People with a high growth need strength usually respond more positively to tasks with high MPSs, whilst workers with a low growth need strength tend to respond less favourably to such jobs. The job characteristics theory tends also to suggest that core job dimensions could stimulate three critical psychological states according to the relationships specified in the model. These are defined by Hackman and Oldham (1976) as:

- *Experienced meaningfulness of the job.* The degree to which the worker feels the job has meaning and is valuable and worthwhile.
- *Experienced responsibility for work outcomes.* The degree to which the worker is personally accountable for the results of his or her work.
- *Knowledge of results.* The degree to which the employee receives feedback on the performance and effectiveness of his or her work.

Whilst this model may be useful in understanding and determining job-fit, its application must be carefully considered in view of the increasing diversity of the workforce and the implicit cultural differences which accompany such a diversity discussed later in this chapter.

However, the JCM has limitations because it focuses only on a limited range of variables. Kelly (1993) has taken the JCM model forward by stating that the model does not give consideration to developments in motivation, job satisfaction, and performance. He does criticise the underlying research methodology, stating that this might account for the JCM being limited in its application. Kelly found that there were rises in job performance after there had been a pay rise and/or losses in jobs which had occurred simultaneously with job design/redesign. As a result of his own research, Kelly propounded his own twin-track model of job redesign as shown in Figure 5.7 below.

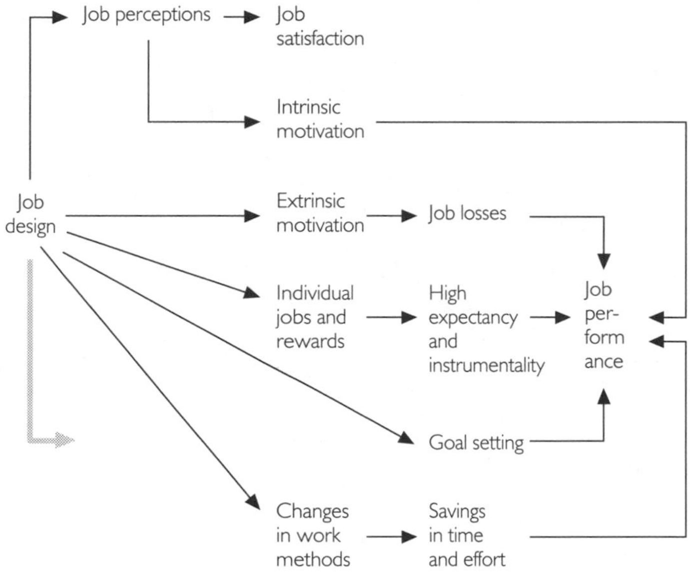

Figure 5.7 Twin-track model of job design, after Kelly (1993)

Kelly (1993) proposes that there are two key pathways related to job design/redesign: satisfaction/motivation, and job performance. The thesis is that any change in work methods, pay rates, job security, and individual rewards can come about because of job design/redesign *as well as or instead of* changes in job characteristics. In turn, any change in job characteristics will affect satisfaction and motivation. However, the other changes have a more direct impact on job performance.

Redesigning work to increase levels of motivation

It is possible to contrast approaches in terms of impact and complexity. *Impact* is the extent to which a particular approach is likely to be linked to factors unrelated to the job-in-hand – for example, performance, reward systems, appraisal methods (top down, bottom up, or 360°), organisational structure, leadership and participation styles, empowerment, working conditions, team composition and norms; in addition, the effects these are likely to have on both productivity and quality. *Complexity* means the extent to which the job design approach is likely to require:

- changes in multiple factors;
- involvement of individuals with diverse skills at various organisational levels;
- high levels of decision-making skills for successful implementation.

The relationship between impact and complexity can be seen in Figure 5.8 below.

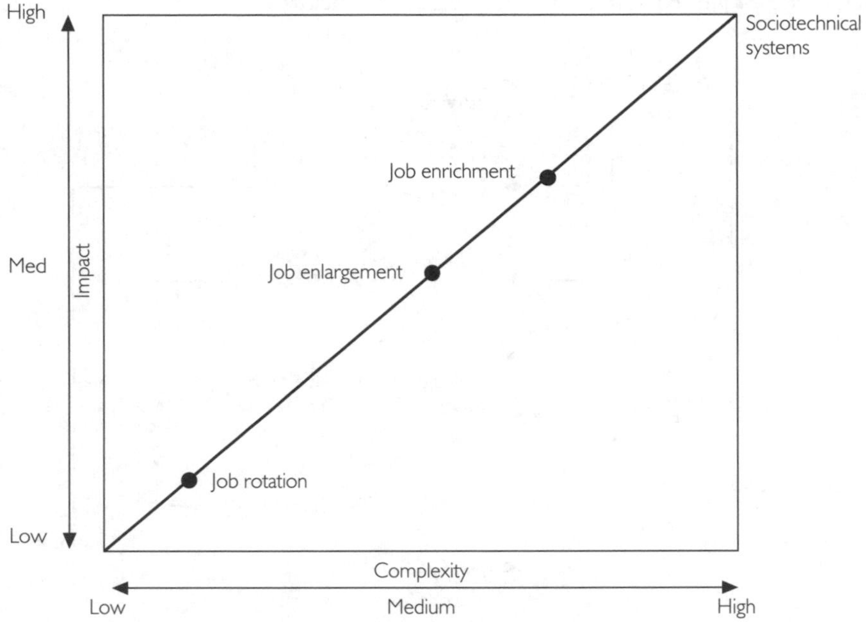

Figure 5.8 The five common approaches to job design contrasted in terms of impact and complexity

Three key approaches to job design have been developed and can be summarised as:

- job rotation
- job enlargement
- job enrichment.

Job rotation

Job rotation involves the moving of individual workers from one task to another in an effort to minimise boredom and monotony. When job rotation is introduced the tasks themselves do not change, it is the rotation of the workers that changes. Consequently, it is the worker who rotates round the tasks. It was this narrow definition of routine tasks which stopped job rotation from achieving the results expected of it. The workers experienced several boring routine jobs rather than just one, and although each rotation might have initiated an interest it was very short-lived. Rotation can also decrease efficiency because it sacrifices proficiency and expertise. However, it can be an effective technique for training to allow individuals to become versed in different skills, and in management development it gives the trainee a holistic view of the organisation and its workings.

Job enlargement

This is sometimes referred to as *horizontal job loading*; it simply involves giving the worker more tasks which other workers might have performed. This was an effort to give the worker a variety of tasks so as to alleviate the monotony of narrowly defined tasks. However, like job rotation, it usually fails to have the required effect. Doing more meaningless tasks does not intrinsically motivate the worker or change the nature of the job – the monotony still remains.

Job enrichment

Job rotation and job enlargement can be seen as extensions of specialisation; they were limited in their approach. In the 1950s there emerged the idea of job enrichment which was based on the idea of giving the individual more tasks to perform but with the additional element of control over how to perform them. This moved the practice away from horizontal loading (adding more tasks) to vertical loading (giving the individual control over the tasks). According to Herzberg (1968) it was expected that as a result of the implementation of vertical loading a worker's job would be enriched in all or any of six ways:

- they would be held *accountable* for their performance;
- there would be a sense of *achievement* because there would be a belief that they were doing something which was beneficial and constructive;
- they would benefit from *feedback* about their performance;
- they would be able, as far as possible, to complete their jobs at their own *work pace*;
- wherever possible, they would have *control* over their own job components/resources;
- they would experience *personal growth and development* through the learning of new skills.

In recent times job enrichment has not been a favoured management tool, principally because the practice has met with varying degrees of success and it did not, in general, produce the expected outcomes. However, there are some positive aspects of job enrichment – significantly in the efforts of managers and organisational theorists who have developed the theory into more contemporary, complex and sophisticated approaches such as autonomous work teams and empowerment discussed later in this chapter.

Human factor approach (ergonomics)

The approaches to job design became more sophisticated as organisations endeavoured to strive for quality and excellence in a globalised market with an ever increasing diversity of workers. There developed a perspective known as the *human factor approach* which focuses on minimising the physical demands and biological risks in the workplace. This approach is sometimes referred to as *ergonomics* and is particularly related to equipment design, being: 'the analysis and design of work equipment and environments to fit human physical and cognitive capabilities' (Arnold *et al.*, p. 38).

Ergonomics is usually associated with job design and new technology. Social scientists and psychologists in particular have researched into a variety of concerns related to new technology. Particularly, ergonomists have worked to improve the compatibility of new technology with the information-processing capabilities of human beings.

The aim of this approach is to make sure that when jobs are designed the expectations do not exceed the individual's physical capabilities to perform them. Such considerations led to an appreciation of workers as people rather than completers of tasks.

Ergonomics, as the study of the physical environment of work, is an element of the biological approach to job design/redesign which itself has a number of positive outcomes including:

- less physical effort
- less physical fatigue
- fewer health complications
- fewer medical concerns
- lower absenteeism
- higher job satisfaction.

However, there are negative outcomes in the form of higher financial costs because of changes in equipment or in the job environment.

The biological approach to job design/redesign emphasises the individual's interactions with the physical aspects of the work environment and is principally concerned with the amount of physical exertion, such as muscular effort, required by a body activity such as lifting. Additionally, ergonomics is related to poor design of systems, for example that at Three Mile Island when nuclear materials contaminated the surrounding area and threatened disaster. Investigations found that poor design of the control room operator's job caused the disaster.

Ergonomics is also about the design of the working environment. With the concentration on spatial design and the introduction of new working practices such as 'hotelling' and 'hot desking' has come the increasing need for ergonomists.

Models for understanding work

CASE STUDY

Creature comforts

According to the new generation of office designers and ergonomists, our feelings towards work can be altered and even manipulated by the introduction of, say, natural light, plants and sweeping staircases – as much as they can by improvements in pay or promotional prospects. As a result, a proliferation of sofas, fish tanks and pastel-hued boardrooms is starting to invade even the most conservative companies. The role that office design can play in getting the most out of the workforce provides a compelling reason for personnel practitioners to become more strategically involved in environmental planning. The need for more flexible spaces to keep up with the changes in work practices necessitates a fresh look at how those spaces are put together.

Downsizing has left companies with neither structure nor 'heart' and they are creating offices that house fewer permanent staff but with the need to service greater numbers of workers: does everyone have a desk and if not, what do you give them?

Morgan Lovell had incorporated cordless technology and created a workspace for employees armed only with laptop PCs and mobile phones. Its designs encourage workers to move around and make more creative use of space, fostering, it believes, greater communication, creativity and flexibility. Pathways through the office are curved and coloured to lead people through areas devoted to meeting spaces, teamwork and individual work areas, while creating a softer, more pleasing environment. An important benefit of this greater movement is the extra contact that staff have with each other.

Adapted from J. Welch, 'Creature comforts' in *People Management*, 19 December 1996, pp. 20–23

To understand more recent theories of job design, there is a need to look more closely at the nature of work and the way it has changed, together with the requirement for the analysis of the nature of work.

The first model considers three key concepts:

- work-flow uncertainty
- task uncertainty
- task interdependence.

Interconnected with these three components is the concept of *groupware* which means that teams and individual employees are able to work faster, share information, make positive decisions, and achieve personal and organisational goals.

Work-flow uncertainty

Work-flow uncertainty is the amount of knowledge that a worker has concerning when the inputs are due to be received and when they will require processing. If there is little work-flow uncertainty, the employee will, as a consequence, have little autonomy to decide which, when, or where tasks will be performed – there is minimum discretion available for the worker.

Task uncertainty

Task uncertainty relates to the amount of knowledge that a worker has about how to perform the task when the time comes for it to be carried out. If there is little task uncertainty, the employee has a considerable amount of knowledge about how to produce the required results. However, high task uncertainty is accompanied by very few pre-specified ways for dealing with some or all of the tasks related to the job. As a result, in order to complete the task to a required level, the employee must have experience, accurate judgement, intuition and problem-solving skills of the highest standard. See Figure 5.9 below.

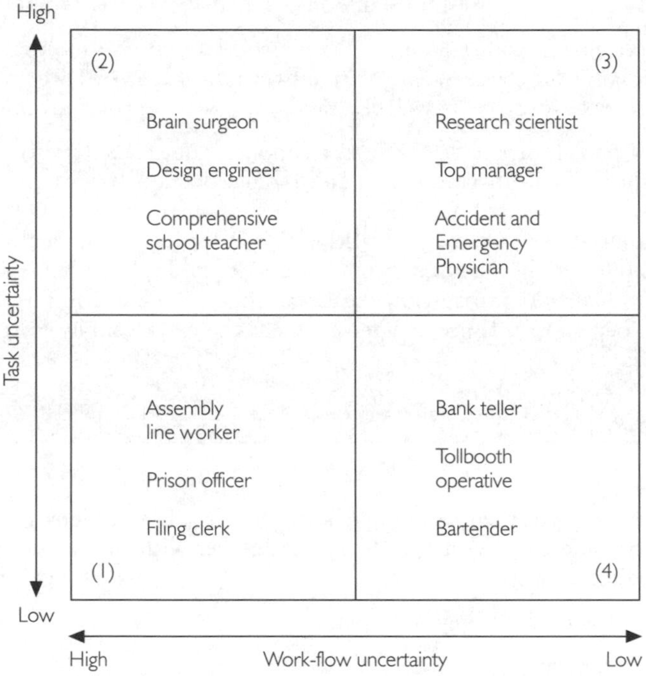

Figure 5.9 Possible combinations of work-flow uncertainty and task uncertainty

Each of the four cells contains examples of jobs which fall mainly into each descriptor. It is important that jobs are not stereotyped by applying them *only* to one single position on the grid. Job redesign often modifies jobs and changes their levels of task and work-flow uncertainty. For example, managerial jobs (including some top-management jobs) could range from the extreme upper right corner in cell 3 to closer to the centre of the grid. Additionally, some jobs do not fit neatly into a single cell. For example, an auditor's job at an accounting firm might generally be plotted somewhere in the centre of the grid.

If a job enrichment programme is introduced it generally has the result of increasing task uncertainty and/or work-flow uncertainty. Figure 5.9 also suggests that some people who occupy cell-3 type jobs may experience stress from too much work-flow and task uncertainty.

The second model related to understanding work is task interdependence.

Task interdependence

Task interdependence is the degree to which decision-making and co-operation between two or more workers are needed for them to perform their jobs effectively. There are three basic types of interdependent tasks relations:

- pooled
- sequential
- reciprocal.

Pooled interdependence happens when employees can carry out their jobs without communicating much with others in the organisation.

Sequential interdependence is the result of when one worker has to complete certain tasks before another worker can perform his or her specific tasks. That is, the outputs of one employee are the inputs for another employee or other employees. Such interdependencies could be part of a long chain, e.g. the aircraft manufacturing industry.

Reciprocal interdependence occurs when outputs from one individual (or team) become the inputs for others and vice versa. Such interdependence is a common factor in everyday life and particularly relates to team-working, e.g. a soccer team, a family, a decision-making team, and a class project assigned to a group of students. Reciprocal interdependence usually requires sophisticated interpersonal skills such as collaboration, communication, and team decision-making.

Interdependence is a key factor when redesigning jobs. Increasing pooled interdependency would decrease the amount of required co-operation between tasks. That is, less co-ordination between jobs means less sequential and/or work-flow uncertainty for the workers involved. With the introduction of new work technologies has come a possible change in task interdependence and a reduction in work-flow uncertainty. The introduction of groupware may well enhance the reciprocal interdependence between two work functions, e.g. sales and production. However, it needs to be remembered that these aids may also reduce both task and work-flow uncertainty for others, e.g. sales representatives.

The changing nature of work: the rise of technology

Technology is very difficult to define because like other organisational behaviour concepts, for example, culture, it is different things to different people depending upon their individual perceptions. A number of writers have attempted a definition but each one has concentrated on a different approach which will tend to mirror their own life experiences and the year of writing. For example, those writing in the pre-1980s would tend to have a broad approach whilst later writers would lean towards the more narrow. The definitions they have provided tend to sit on a 'broad' to 'narrow' continuum with the former concentrating on the traditional, mechanistic approach; such an approach takes the view that it refers to machinery and equipment which is used to carry out the transformational process within production. For example, Perrow (1967) stated that:

> Technology is … the actions that an individual performs on an object, with or without the assistance of mechanical devices, in order to make some change in that object. (p. 194)

Others tend to take the narrower and more concise view that technology applies to the members of the workforce and therefore they take a more organic approach to the appreciation of technology.

For the purpose of this discussion an all-encompassing definition is proposed:

> Technology can be said to be the intellectual and mechanical processes used by an organisation to transform the inputs into outputs such as products and/or services in order to meet the objectives of the organisation.

Technological changes in the workforce have been continuous for generations – they are nothing new! Throughout history peoples have been developing mechanistic methods of improving the ways of doing things. It is the term 'new technology' which has evolved from the early 1980s. There are two forms of new technology which have had an effect on job design/redesign in the workplace: *advanced manufacturing technology* (AMT) which incudes a wide range of equipment which adds to the manufacturing process; and what is commonly termed *office technology* which concentrates on storage, retrieval, presentation, and the manipulation of information.

During the latter part of the twentieth century social scientists have researched the key issues concerned with this new technology. For example, some ergonomists (people who study the relationship between workers and their environment) have attempted to improve the compatibility between humans and technology.

Jobs are frequently designed/redesigned to minimise the requirements for specific skills, reduce the need for decision-making from operatives and to reduce labour costs. Along with such a scientific view comes a potential for human dissatisfaction and a lack of continuous development. The introduction of new technology has meant that there has been the potential for deskilling even further. However, this is not always the case because when incorporated into job design/redesign with the balance of process and people in mind, new technology can maintain and even enhance existing skills. It is the *nature* of the skills which tends to change. Unfortunately, new technology is often introduced piecemeal without a holistic investigation and this brings about the need to rely on technical experts. When introduced with the wider organisational implications in mind, new technology can enhance the nature of work.

Whilst technological change has been more an evolution than a revolution, there have been considerable innovations over the past few years which particularly affect how individuals work. As can be seen in Chapter 10, managers face increasing challenges related to rapidly changing technology with the responsibility of putting that technology to good use within the organisation. The slower they are at doing this, the more slowly the economic advantages will accrue to the organisations for which they work.

New technologies are being designed but organisations tend to be slow in adopting such innovations – they need to be flexible and adaptable in their design, structure, and managing skills.

Technological changes

Any change that affects the way people work is a technological change – it is not purely related to information technology. Some of the more familiar relate to:

- telecommuting
- expert systems
- automation and robotics.

Telecommuting is transmitting work from a home computer to the office by the use of a modem. One of the first companies to experiment with this idea was IBM who installed computer terminals at key workers' homes. However, there are advantages and disadvantages to telecommuting – see Table 5.1 below for some of them.

Table 5.1 Advantages and disadvantages of telecommuting

Advantages	Disadvantages
Flexibility	Distractions
Time saved not commuting to and from work	Lack of socialisation with colleagues
Enjoy comforts of home	Lack of communication with supervisors/subordinates

Another technological change is the use of *expert systems* which are computer-based applications which use a computer representation of the expertise attributed to humans in a specialised field of knowledge in order to solve problems. Thomas and Ballard (1995) define them as: 'computer packages designed to mimic the decision-making processes of experts in a given field' (p. 155).

By using such expert systems a non-expert in a specified field can perform as expertly as an expert in that same field because the system has within it the required knowledge, framework, rules and regulations of the stated topic and it is also able to adapt to new rules as the programme is being used. As the user works through the programme, the latter will adapt its knowledge as a result of that interaction and thus make inferences which will then allow it to make the most appropriate decision and offer alternatives on the information given to it. There are limitless applications of this use of expert power from investment analysis, human resource decisions as they relate to anti-discrimination laws to the preparation of an academic paper.

Automation and robotics are also changing the way jobs are designed but are particularly concerned with how existing jobs can be redesigned. There is a growing reliance on automation and robotics with their accompanying advantages and disadvantages as suggested in Table 5.2 below.

Table 5.2 Advantages and disadvantages of automation and robotics

Advantages	Disadvantages
Eliminates boring, routine and hazardous jobs	Dehumanises jobs
	The worker has less to do
Workers can be moved to more interesting and challenging jobs	The worker becomes an adjunct to the technology
Speed of process	
Accuracy in completion of the task	
No illness requiring time off	

Automation and robotics – an example

You might well have, at some time, worked as a check-out operator in a large supermarket. If you haven't, you will have been a customer at one.

Think about the components of the job – how much of it is automated and how much does this affect the check-out operator?

Your answer would depend upon your personal experiences. However, you probably considered that automation had dehumanised the job because optiscan technology reads the prices from the barcodes attached to the products as the operator passes them over a flat screen. Whilst the check-out operator might well have become more efficient because of this, he or she has much less to do. More recent check-out units are able to call out the prices, the total bill, and the customer's change – they can even be programmed to give an oral message to the customer; for example, 'Thank you for your custom – have a nice day'. The operator is merely an adjunct to the technology.

Technological advances have given organisations the opportunity to alter the structure of organisations and jobs within them. There has been a development in the way that people communicate at work. Through total quality management programmes managers have sought to alter the traditional communications systems to complement the newer approaches to work design – for example, teamwork. Such a perspective brings with it the question of power and the sharing of information which has been discussed in other chapters. Through some technological systems it is possible to disseminate power and information to everyone within the organisation and, especially, downwards. Increasingly, organisations are sharing with the entire membership of the organisation information which once used to be secured at the organisational apex.

The three technologies discussed above (telecommuting, expert systems, and automation and robotics) are standard practices in organisations today. The challenges which face managers today and which are also related to work design concern the more advanced technologies and the practices which have come about as a result of such innovations. They all continue to reshape job design – some will be passing fashions but others will remain part of the work environment and the way jobs are designed. Some of the key developments are:

- information storage and processing
- communications
- advanced materials
- biotechnologies
- superconductivity.

Improvements in information processing and storage continue to increase. Currently desktop computers' capability is measured in gigabytes (billion words) and some computers have a capacity measured in terabytes (trillion words). Megabyte capacity (million words) is obsolescent. There continue to be improvements in the price:performance ratios of equipment which means that it will soon be very inexpensive to apply machine intelligence to jobs currently being performed by human beings.

The UK has a digital telephone communications network which uses fibre optics technology which uses laser beams to send data along minute fibre tubes. Such a system is smaller, cheaper and more reliable than a wire cable and because it uses lights to send data the resultant transmission is highly accurate. Since the data is in digital form, modems can turn analogue to digital (and vice versa) extremely quickly.

Smaller quantities of raw materials are now required in the processing industries and this has meant a significant decline in jobs within the extractive industries – for example, coal mining. There have also been considerable developments in new materials such as ceramics and reinforced plastics which has meant that manufactured products now last longer. Thus the skills required of workers have changed, as has the design of their jobs.

The development of *superconductive materials* is having a rapid effect on industry. Such materials are able to carry electrical currents without any loss of energy and thus the efficiency of electric motors is improved.

It is not only in the manufacturing industries that developing technology has changed the design of work. By the year 2000 both agriculture and health services will continue to change dramatically because of the considerable advances in *biotechnology*, especially in the ability to manipulate life forms at the cellular and sub-cellular levels.

Technological developments and the changing nature of managerial work

Technological innovation affects the nature of most jobs within an organisation but has had a specific impact on those members of the workforce who process information. With the increased use of self-managed teams (see Chapters 6 and 7) has come the ability to access information at all levels of the organisation through all sorts of technological systems.

In the traditional design of work, individuals often tended to extend their breaks whereas nowadays it is more likely that managers will have to encourage their workers to take more frequent breaks. Working with a computer having a keyboard input can encourage repetitive strain injury (RSI) and there is the chance that, without careful monitoring, individuals will suffer eye strain, neck and back strain, and headaches as a result of sitting at a computer terminal for too long. Individuals are also now so used to technology giving them a response very quickly that they are becoming very short with co-workers who, because they are human, may take longer to reply and may not be as accurate as the computer.

Managers can now use *computerised monitoring* to check up on employee performance but with this has come the potential for misuse.

Examples of computerised monitoring

It is now possible for an employer to listen in to any telephone conversation which is made by an employee. Do you think that they should have this right and also use it?

Your opinion will differ from that of some of your fellow students – perhaps you could share your views with them.

In a recent survey of human resource managers, 64 per cent said 'Yes' but only if the employer was investigating a financial loss. If the purpose of monitoring was for updating the quality of services then the response was 'No' for 66 per cent of the respondents. Most of the human resource managers surveyed (94 per cent) stated that if the employees were advised in advance that their conversations *could* be monitored, then it was in order to do so.

Source: *Human Resource Magazine*, September 1992, p. 21

There are a number of industries which routinely monitor employees' telephone calls. For example, the airline industry, telecommunications, and mail-order organisations. Employers like the ability to monitor the telephone calls of their employees on the grounds that they believe it improves performance and customer service. However, the employees are not so convinced because under such scrutiny they tend to react with high levels of negative stress (see Chapter 10) and become anxious and exhausted from the strain.

Technology and the working environment

Many of the predictions concerning the influence of technology have proved to be correct – for example, the use of the microchip and how it revolutionised job design. However, there have been others which have not lived up to expectations and a principal one here concerns the so-called 'office of the future'. Brown (1997) reflects on such predictions which came to the fore in the early 1990s, stating that for a significant section of the working population:

> ... the traditional office would soon become a thing of the past. Wage slaves would become teleworkers, beavering away at home, attached to their offices by an electronic umbilical cord (telephone and personal computer) but otherwise free to organise and carry out their work as they chose. (p. 77)

He went on to state that it was estimated that by the mid-1990s there would be more than two-and-a-half million teleworkers using modern technology to do their jobs – regardless of where they were geographically situated. Brown (1997) sourced statistics which showed that in the UK just 5 per cent of the total number expected were actually teleworking and that the situation was the same in other countries and there was no evidence that the proportion of teleworkers to the working population was on the increase.

Colin Jackson, as managing director of the business consultancy Organisation and Technology Research (OTR), did warn people in the early 1990s that the estimation of the demand for teleworking was grossly exaggerated – indeed, he himself overestimated the market by a factor of ten, according to Brown (1997). Jackson stated that there were three factors which had to be met if teleworking was to become as important as was anticipated:

- the jobs had to be suitable for teleworking;
- the individuals had to be suited to teleworking;
- organisations had to have staff who were capable of managing such teleworkers.

Organisations found it difficult to meet just one of the above criteria and to secure all three turned out to be impossible for most organisations except for those which were small-scale like journalism and the writing of computer software. Jackson stated that to secure all three key premises was: 'a bit like the chances of finding a one-legged accordion player who was a fighter pilot in the Second World War' (Brown, 1997, p. 79).

It is important to understand that teleworking was overestimated as a means of designing jobs because there are now some further developments based on that premise which can be given the overall term 'the virtual office'.

The *virtual office* is already with us and affects the way individuals' jobs are designed – many workers work in this environment without fully realising that it is a virtual office. As Brown (1997) says: '... a grand-sounding term simply denotes an ordinary office complemented by fairly everyday equipment like mobile phones and laptop computers which mean that office workers don't need to be in the office itself to get on with their job' (p. 79).

As Colin Jackson of OTR believes, the virtual office is for those workers whose jobs are designed such that they normally work in an office but are in and out of the office either to the outside environment (customers) or to other offices, or branches of the same organisation – that is, they are away from their desks. Such workers require support and, to put this in economic terminology, demand and supply is there for the virtual office but it was not present for teleworking. The evolution in digital technology (see above) has meant a growth in speedy and accurate communication which allows individuals to work away from their desk.

Architect Francis Duffy (former president of the Royal Institute of British Architects (RIBA)) has stated that the key to office design, and thus the design of individuals' jobs, is in 'understanding the relative importance of interaction and autonomy in job functions' (Brown, 1997, p. 84) and he has proposed an office design which is divided into four models as shown in Figure 5.10 below.

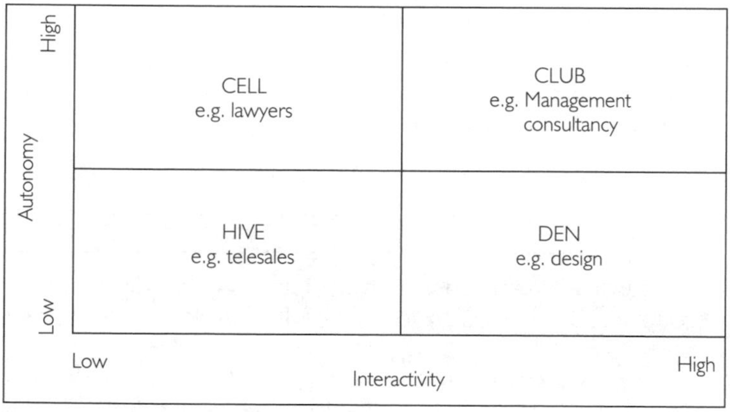

Figure 5.10 Four model design of the office, after Brown (1997)

- *The hive.* In this design the workers have a low level of autonomy and low interaction and the hive works best for repetitive tasks which need little consultation with others. Examples here would be data entry or call centres. Hives are open-plan with standard workstations containing a personal computer (which may be networked) and a telephone.

- *The cell.* Individuals here have a high level of autonomy and a low interaction and the cell is for those who have a limited need to talk to colleagues and who operate mostly at an independent level. Examples here would be lawyers and accountants. A cell is usually heavily partitioned and may well be a separate office.
- *The den.* Employees here have low autonomy and high interaction where jobs are designed to have an element of decision-making which often involves group activity and which draws on a range of skills. Dens are best suited for creative activities such as the production of a magazine. They tend to be open-plan rooms separated from other groups.
- *The club.* This is for those whose jobs require high autonomy and high interaction. Examples would be university lecturer and management consultant both of which involve considerable communication with colleagues and a high degree of independence. Clubs can incorporate desk-sharing and many modern elements of office design such as sofa areas with coffee tables and the use of mobile furniture, e.g. trolleys.

The virtual office is the ultimate minimalist office and is now beginning to become popular. However, there are intermediate practices which are common in organisations and which affect the design of jobs. Two of these are ***hot-desking*** and ***hotelling*** where the point of the systems is to wean workers away from their territory – the instinctive need to have and to hold space which is their own. Through hot-desking and hotelling, staff who are not permanently based at the office cease to possess their own desk. Through effective organisational planning and job design, such people are able to commandeer a workstation/desk whenever they need to come into the host organisation. Through hotelling or hot-desking the right to have one's nameplate on a door or desk is taken away – the retention of such a culture is very expensive since an office building is typically unoccupied for 15 hours out of 24 and is occupied only for a fraction of time, if at all, at the weekends. Hotelling is depersonalising the workstation – that is, removing all the personal bits and pieces which people tend to use to territorise their work area.

Thus a smaller space can produce the same or a better output than what preceded it. Some organisations are changing work design by introducing shift-working to offices and the only thing fighting this is convention.

CASE STUDY

How the creative use of office space can avoid relocation costs

When management consultants Andersen Consulting realised three years ago that continued expansion would mean it might soon outgrow its headquarters in Arundel Street it hit on a radical solution. Instead of searching for another building it looked around for another way to organise the present one that would allow for growth.

The solution, partially implemented already [now fully] was to turn the HQ into a sort of hotel, only in this case the guests booked in to work rather than to sleep the night. Since a lot of its fee-earning consultants were by the nature of their jobs peripatetic, spending more time in the offices of clients than in Andersen's office, the organisation decided that they didn't need offices and desks of their own. They could simply book in, just as they would in an hotel, when they needed an office. 'We realised there were many days when a lot of the space was unoccupied even though people had names on the desks', says Tim Arnold, Andersen's director of property and facilities management. 'We took the view that by being a bit more creative we could move forward into a much more efficient way of working and at the same time brighten the offices up to a much higher standard with a much better standard of service.'

The offices now have several different types of workstation, designed for anything from a transitory touchdown to a stay of a day or more. The booking system is PC-based. Consultants who want a workstation can either book in person, by phone or by voice-mail or e-mail. The request is acknowledged and fed into the system; then each morning the floor administrator gets a read-out with the day's booking. Andersen's Paris organisation has gone further than the London one. In early January all 1000 staff will move [have moved] from Andersen's existing building at La Défense to an office right at the centre of Paris where the Champs Elysées meets the Avenue George V. Everyone, up to and including the partners, will have to use a workplace booking system, says François Jacquenoud, the partner in charge of the move, who calls it a just-in-time office. As well as bookable work spaces the new Paris office will have a complete floor designed to look rather like an executive lounge at an airport.

Instead of booking in, people who are coming to the offices for a very short period will use this club lounge. They might be meeting people, collecting their mail, or just touching base at the office to get a sense of belonging, says Jacquenoud. 'They will be able to sit and rest, read the papers, discuss things with their peers. There will also be compact workstations in the lounge that they'll be able to use without the necessity of booking before they come.' Persuading the partners to join the scheme was a big breakthrough. The partners accept that there is a trade-off between privacy and comfort. They are losing their proprietary rights to space, says Jacquenoud, but getting instead one of the most magnificent and best equipped offices in the centre of Paris. Another thing which appeals to the partners is that the building makes a statement about Andersen. 'We're saying that even our senior partners spend most of their time at clients' offices, not at HQ. We're also saying to clients that our mission is to help them become more successful and the George V set-up is a living demonstration of what we can do for them. We're saying "We've been able to make our people change – even our senior partners – in order to achieve a strategic goal in our business." '

Adapted from M. Brown, 'Design for working' in *Management Today*, March 1997, pp. 77–84

Whilst there are economic arguments in favour of new technology and new designs for making the work environment and work more technologically efficient, it is essential that the feelings of the workforce are considered. Since work is an important part of the organisational member's life, it needs to be borne in mind that individuals need a psychologically secure base. Technology is continuing to dissolve distance and location is becoming irrelevant to the conduct of work, thus affecting how the jobs of individuals are designed and, particularly, redesigned to cope with technological innovation.

Technology and economic considerations

The nature of work can also be affected by economic factors which have been dealt with earlier in this chapter. The key economic factors which can change the nature of work are to:

- reduce costs
- increase productivity
- increase performance
- maintain quality
- reduce the reliance on skilled labour
- introduce new technology to maintain competitiveness.

The introduction of new technology and the consideration of economic factors have had an impact on a number of issues such as bringing about:

- an increase in white collar and service jobs
- more individuals with higher-level skills
- increased uncertainty in the workplace
- more flexibility in task ability
- more responsibility in the handling of difficult issues such as downsizing
- a more prominent focus on customer needs
- a concentration on continuous improvement.

Modern theories of work design: sociotechnical systems

The consideration of the fact that organisations are made up of people (the social system) using tools, techniques and knowledge (the technical system) to produce goods and services for consumers brought into being the sociotechnical system. Both the social and the technical systems had to be redesigned in relationship to one another and to the demands of those in the external environment. It emphasises the demands of stakeholders (customers, suppliers, etc) and the internal implications needed to respond to those demands. There is a need, therefore, to modify job design in the light of the increasing diversity of the workforce.

CASE STUDY

In praise of maturity

When the Nationwide Building Society wants to recruit employees, it makes a point of ignoring dates of birth: its system of telephone shortlisting precludes any mention of age. Denise Walker, employee relations manager, says the result is that by 'selecting people for interview solely on the basis of their ability, we get a genuine mix of people coming forward, including a lot more older people'.

Far from discriminating against older employees, Nationwide is encouraging them. It recently ran a newspaper recruitment campaign aimed at more mature applicants.

The building society says that some of its older financial advisers not only achieve better sales figures than their younger counterparts, but also stay in the job longer. It is happy to employ 65-year-olds on fixed-term contracts and its oldest employee is 72.

Nationwide is not the only organisation to see commercial benefits in employing older workers and is part of the Employers Forum on age. Other members include the Bank of England, British Telecommunications, Marks & Spencer and the Confederation of British Industry.

Skills shortages facing many UK employers – particularly in health, engineering and information technology – can only be addressed if industry rethinks its attitude to age. It adds that a mixed-age workforce brings benefits such as reduced absenteeism and staff turnover.

The forum warns that the 'youth cult' operated by many employers, particularly in top-flight financial companies, has led to spiralling recruitment costs. With demographic changes leading to an ageing population, the number of young people available for recruitment is in sharp decline.

Adapted from M. Matthews, 'In praise of maturity' in *Financial Times*, 27 February 1997, p. 11

Such a diverse workforce will affect the effectiveness of the organisation and the redesigning of jobs within it. Whilst it could be argued that every organisation is a sociotechnical system, it may not necessarily be based on the principles which are part of such an approach, i.e. it may be by accident rather than design.

The ultimate aim of a sociotechnical system is to provide a best-fit approach between the available technology, people, and the needs of the organisation. Such an approach is about the interdependence of tasks and this, therefore, becomes the basis of the formation of workplace teams. Such a design can be seen to be aligned to the principles of job enrichment discussed earlier.

Modern approaches to work design

Modern approaches to work design which build on the sociotechnical approach are:

- participation and empowerment
- team working
- flexible working
- business process re-engineering

all of which have major implications for management style and organisational culture.

Participation and empowerment

Job enrichment processes seek to make jobs more meaningful and challenging by means of handing responsibility to work-teams through participation and empowerment. Participation is brought about by giving individual workers a voice in making decisions about their own work whereas empowerment goes one stage further by allowing workers to set their own work goals, make their own decisions, and solve problems within their sphere of responsibility and authority. It is aligned closely to team working.

Empowerment is a broader concept which incorporates participation in a wide variety of areas such as work itself, the context of work, and work environment. In its initial stages of recognition (1930s through to 1950s) employers considered that participation was simply a means of increasing satisfaction. As is indicated in the case study below, managers neglected to see that it had potential as a valuable input.

CASE STUDY

Time to trust the worker: How can you empower employees while they still clock on?

Will the time-honoured procedure of clocking on and off for work have any place in the new millennium? Or have such systems had their day? The old-fashioned punch-card device is irrelevant to this question, incidentally. Technology is replacing punch-card systems with more modern methods using swipe cards, but that doesn't affect the principle. And it's clear the principle is still widely applied: organisations which state that they empower their workers still expect them to clock on for work. If one is trying to empower employees, making them clock on implies that organisations are not confident that the employees can keep an accurate tally on their time.

Far from dying out, the practice is on the increase here and there, particularly where employers are adopting flexible working practices. There is scepticism about flexible working as a justification for clocking on. Some firms are becoming more controlling and their control is far more rigid than necessary. Angela Baron of the Institute of Personnel and Development agrees with this viewpoint. Many companies claim to be empowering their workforces although in reality they are not. If an organisation is trying to build a culture of trust, it doesn't seem appropriate to have a clocking-in system.

Tate & Lyle introduced a card-operated access control system covering its 1,000 employees eight years ago. Such a card system provides information used for a variety of purposes including security, pay, job-costing, time and attendance. Since the site is open 24 hours a day there was concern from a safety point of view. Now the system has been reviewed and the employees have become empowered, although time and attendance is overviewed by line managers. However, Lucas Industries have phased out any clocking-in for all its 24,000 employees.

Adapted from *Management Today*, September 1996, p. 20

Empowerment is about sharing power within an organisation: individuals cannot be empowered, but organisations can use their job designs and structures to empower people. Modern organisations have grown flatter and leaner (some say meaner) through such concepts as downsizing, which, in turn, has eliminated layers of management and has increased the use of team-working. As a consequence, empowerment has become more and more important. Empowerment involves the sharing of power in such a way that individuals learn to believe in their ability to do the job. Empowerment is driven by the idea that the individuals closest to the work and to the customers should make the decisions and that this, in turn, makes the best use of employees' skills and talents. Linked to this is *open-book management* which means giving employees all the information any owner receives if the latter wants employees to act like owners and care for the organisation. Empowerment is a concept which is easy to champion but very difficult to practise.

CASE STUDY

Harvester

Harvester, the UK restaurant chain, took steps to empower its restaurant and kitchen staff. The chefs decided what the menus for each week were to be and how often these were to be changed. They then became responsible for ordering the necessary levels and quality of stock, for ensuring that supplies were delivered, for ensuring their storage complied with legal and best professional standards and for chasing up any quality defects. They were responsible for setting ordering patterns, purchasing new kitchen equipment and ensuring that the place was clean. They dealt with the food and premises, inspections and inspectors, and implemented any changes necessary as a result.

The restaurant staff (that is, waiters and waitresses) became responsible for all aspects of the eating area. They were required to clean and polish the tables, put flowers and candles out, and see that the restaurant was clean, tidy and welcoming to customers. They would greet customers, show them to their seats, and take and process orders. At the end of the work period, they were to clean the restaurant area, check for security and close it down and lock up.

Both chefs and restaurant staff would handle any customer complaints directly, according to the nature of the complaint; rather than putting this through sophisticated managerial processes, these would be dealt with at the front line.

The company was therefore able to remove the differentiated, non-productive (or largely non-productive) jobs of head waiter, restaurant manager, work supervisor and general manager. Chefs and waiting staff were given large initial pay increases in return for accepting these ways of working.

The organisation adopted methods of supervision and control based on a roving and mobile area manager system (area managers would visit each of their sites at least once a week), a flexible but agreed budgeting system that enabled the staff to make a large range of decisions, and an emergency/problem-solving 24-hour hotline to the area management.

Source: R. Pettinger, *Introduction to Organisational Behaviour*, 1996 (Basingstoke: Macmillan), pp. 231–232

There are four key guidelines on how managers can empower others:

- by expressing positive confidence in their staff
- by creating positive opportunities for employees to participate in decision-making
- by removing bureaucratic restraints
- by setting inspirational, yet achievable, goals.

There is also a risk of failure in attempts to empower employees: particularly, when delegating responsibility the empowering authority must be prepared for the possibility of failure, which is something that managers do not tolerate well. To avoid failure or to learn from the experienced failure, it is vital that empowerment is accompanied by positive feedback through counselling and/or coaching.

Team working

A key evolution which has taken place in job design/redesign – particularly related to job enrichment – is that of the use of autonomous work groups and team working (see Chapters 6 and 7). Such methods are based on the sociotechnical approach to work organisation with the addition of technological process production methods. Additional to this is the way work is managed through an integration of the culture of the organisation which includes the structure and dynamics of the group/team. As can be seen in the chapters on groups, whilst the effectiveness of team work may not always be positive, it does appear to give individuals a higher level of job satisfaction which is related to the higher degrees of responsibility, autonomy, and accountability.

When jobs are designed/redesigned to utilise autonomous work groups they need to have key components:

- the overall goals are set for the group but members decide the most appropriate means by which the objectives are to be achieved;
- team members have wider discretion over the planning, execution, and control of their own task;
- collectively the group has the range of skills to undertake the task it has been set;
- the level of external control is reduced and the supervisory role is more supportive in the provision of advice and support;
- feedback and evaluation are related to the group as a whole and not to individuals within the group.

Advantages of team working

One of the areas which has developed as an aspect of job enrichment is allowing employees to be in contact with users of their output. Establishing customer relationships is often a logical outcome of natural work teams. Far too often workers end up working directly for their supervisors rather than for the customers/clients. For example, in a word processing centre, certain operators can be assigned to specific clients or to teams of, say, salespersons or engineers. This increases the quality of service and should any enquiries arise the customer can work directly with the employee to resolve the issue.

Ownership of product/service

Employees who work at all stages of the unit production or service tend to identify more with the finished products than do those workers who perform only part of the same job. In allowing workers to build a complete product or task cycle it is likely that there will be a sense of pride and achievement in the working effort.

Direct feedback

Modern job design techniques stress feedback to the employee directly from the performance of the task. For example, reports or computer output may go to the employee directly rather than to their supervisors. Linked to this is the technique that allows the worker to check his or her own work before others do thus also increasing the accuracy of feedback.

Quality circles

Spector (1996) defines a quality circle as 'a group intervention that gives employees the opportunity to have greater input into issues at work' (p. 317).

It is, therefore, an organisational system introduced in an attempt to empower individuals. Such groups of people meet periodically to discuss any concerns that they have and to assess solutions to meet the problem. The groups normally are composed of individuals with similar jobs, and discussions tend to resolve around issues of product quality and the efficiency of production. Quality circles are common in a variety of organisations and work the same way as autonomous work groups and they are popular because they are easy to implement and consume minimal resources.

The advantages of quality circles for the individual worker are:

- individuals are able to participate more;
- participation can result in stimulation and enjoyment for the individual;
- more interpersonal communication can take place, thus providing a welcome break from routine;
- problems can be discussed with fellow workers.

The principal advantage for the organisation is that quality circles can result in improved production procedures because the people who actually carry out the work are usually in a better position to know – and have more knowledge about – what the problems are and how they can be solved. However, as can be seen in the following case study, the success of quality circles depends upon the environment within which they are used.

CASE STUDY

Squaring up to the problem of the quality circle

Sir, The rise and fall of quality circles does ... make an interesting study of the life-cycle of management techniques ... Their apparent loss of popularity may be due to the fact that many businesses saw quality circles as offering instant solutions to quality problems without the need for more fundamental changes, whereas these problems were often systemic and not capable of resolution at workforce level. It took time and harsh reality for this to show.

There is nothing wrong with the quality circle concept itself. Some Western businesses still use it successfully and have notched up some excellent and measurable results. However, it works only where it can be gradually absorbed into the culture of an organisation, taking care over the training required and the workings of the concept.

There are many management techniques available to help the development of a business. These are tools, and like any tools they must be used in the right way, by people who have been taught their existence and how to use them, and kept sharpened and maintained for use.

Above all, they must be appropriately selected for the particular job they have to do. After all, there is no point in criticising a scalpel because it has failed to do the job of a hammer.

> The 'current management practices' ... often mean flying by the seat of the pants, with all the consequent management fire-fighting and waste of resources. If more of the improvement techniques available were put to more frequent use in a more structured and determined way by better-trained managers, we should hear less talk of fads – and perhaps have less need for downsizing.
>
> Source: Letter to the Editor of the *Financial Times*, 22 August 1997, p. 14

Worker flexibility

A perspective on job design/redesign which is emerging and becoming increasingly popular is the concept of flexible workers. Worker flexibility is becoming a popular method of designing jobs. In some ways, worker flexibility is simply an evolution of the job rotation model discussed earlier. It helps organisations to enhance their effectiveness by training workers to perform a variety of tasks. Linked to this is the concept of performance rewards because employees usually receive a pay increase as they master each task. The organisation can then transfer employees to different jobs as needed.

There are differences between simple job rotation and flexible worker approaches. In the flexible worker approach:

- workers get transferred across completely different jobs rather than across narrow tasks within the same job;
- workers receive a financial incentive for becoming more flexible;
- the rotation itself is usually spontaneous and exciting whereas in simple rotation the changes are mechanical and a matter of routine.

Business Process Re-engineering (BPR)

Job design is one of the key areas of organisational re-engineering efforts. BPR is a way of thinking about organisations which includes breaking away from the outdated rules and assumptions that underlie how tasks have been performed in the past. A key principle of BPR is the elimination or prevention of barriers which could themselves create a distance between employees and their customers. With BPR, organisational design needs to be based on the collection of those tasks which create additional value known as *processes*. Processes are those activities and tasks which add value to the product or service. For example, product development, customer acquisition, customer service, and the fulfilment of orders.

Michael Hammer (a professor at the Massachusetts Institute of Technology) first coined the term *re-engineering* in a 1990 article entitled 'Reengineering Work: Don't Automate, Obliterate'. More recently, he stated that re-engineering is the cornerstone of job design:

> Reengineering means radically changing how we do our work. That's a very important word – work. People often ask me questions about managing, but for me the issue is work. Work is the way in which we create value for customers, how we design, invent and make products, how we sell them, how we serve customers. Reengineering means radically rethinking and redesigning those processes by which we create

value and do work. (R. Kaarlgaard, ASAP interview, Mike Hammer, *Forbes ASAP*, 25 February 1994, pp. 69–75)

The re-engineering process is more comprehensive than the design approaches previously discussed in this chapter – it is more a blend of various features such as:

- utilising some of the principles of scientific management;
- focusing on added value through making the customer the centre of attention at all stages;
- redesigning the organisation into a flatter structure in order for it to become lean;
- using the principles of empowerment;
- changing working systems to fit in with the leaner organisation design, e.g. autonomous work teams.

Re-engineering is, therefore, about the redesign of organisational processes (including job design) in order to achieve major gains in cost, time, and the provision of services. It is a proactive way of making organisations start from the beginning and redesign themselves around their most important processes and people rather than take their current form and make incremental changes. New organisations have an advantage: they have no impediments such as an existing structure or established ways of doing things. They can start the process by establishing what the customer actually wants from the organisation and then developing a strategy to provide it. Whether it is organisational redesign or starting from afresh, strong leadership from the top down is essential in order to achieve success. There is a certain parallel between current job designs (autonomous work teams) and the design of organisations using re-engineering: neither necessarily results in a certain organisational form.

There are, however, critics of BPR. Gabriel (1996) reports that a director of one of the top forty UK companies stated that:

> Any consultant who mentions process re-engineering to me just once will be out the door. We have to look beyond the internal now and the consultants who earn their fees will be the ones with the most interesting, perhaps the weirdest, ideas for business change.

Whilst BPR is still in evidence, there have been post-BPR activities. Gertz and Baptista (1996) reflected on the concern of chief executives about downsizing when their best people leave their organisations. The chief concern is 'growth' and how to achieve it after re-engineering and becoming a leaner and, perhaps, meaner organisation. Whilst such techniques may have left organisations in a situation where they can survive the onslaught of recession and competition, they did not make them any richer.

Research carried out by Gertz and Baptista (1996) indicated that a growing organisation is a fun organisation to work in and that a happy staff tended to work more hours and more productively. The researchers noted that firms tended to erect their own barriers after BPR and were unable to move into creative areas of growth, including: customer franchise management (choosing customers selectively and discovering their needs), developing a rapid products/services strategy; and channel management, where they find more effective ways to link customer groups with services.

Job design across cultures

Job design clearly varies across cultures: culture is discussed in detail in Chapter 10. It was Volvo in Scandinavia who pioneered the use of autonomous work teams as a basis for job design. In Germany also (firstly in West Germany) innovations in job design have been progressive. In Japan, participative management systems and quality circle programmes are now so widespread that they are the norm. There have been discussions of job design related to countries yet job design itself has not systematically been researched across cultural boundaries.

Successful organisations of the future will have replaced patriarchy with partnerships, and managers will have a crucial role in helping their surbordinates achieve a positive cultural environment through empowerment.

Nixon (1995) developed an empowerment model (see Figure 5.11) related to training people to bring about cultural change and thus make the most of increasing workforce diversity.

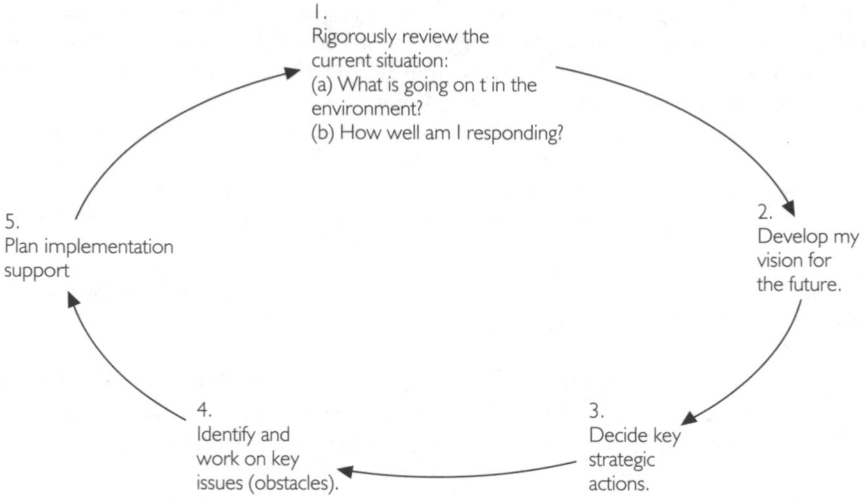

Figure 5.11 Cultural change – an empowerment model

Japanese, German, and Scandinavian perspectives

The Japanese, Germans, and Scandinavians have unique perspectives towards the designing of jobs and the organisation of work. The Japanese started working on job design and culture in the early 1950s as a result of the work of Deming (1986) (Deming worked as a management consultant into his mid 90s!) which concentrated on product quality. Central government also became actively involved in the economic resurgence of Japan and encouraged organisations to conquer industries rather than concentrating on the maximisation of profits. The political theory at the time was that of collectivism which can be defined as: 'A cultural orientation in which individuals belong to tightly knit social frameworks, and they depend strongly on large extended families or class'; and this also had implications in Japan for how work was – and still is – done. The Japanese system differed from the Western model of Taylorism where the emphasis was on the individual worker; the Japanese work system emphasised the strategy of encouraging collective and co-operative working arrangements. Figure 5.12 below shows the concepts and practices which the Japanese emphasise: performance, accountability, and other- or self-directedness in defining work; whereas the Western work culture emphasises the positive affect, personal identity, and social benefits of work.

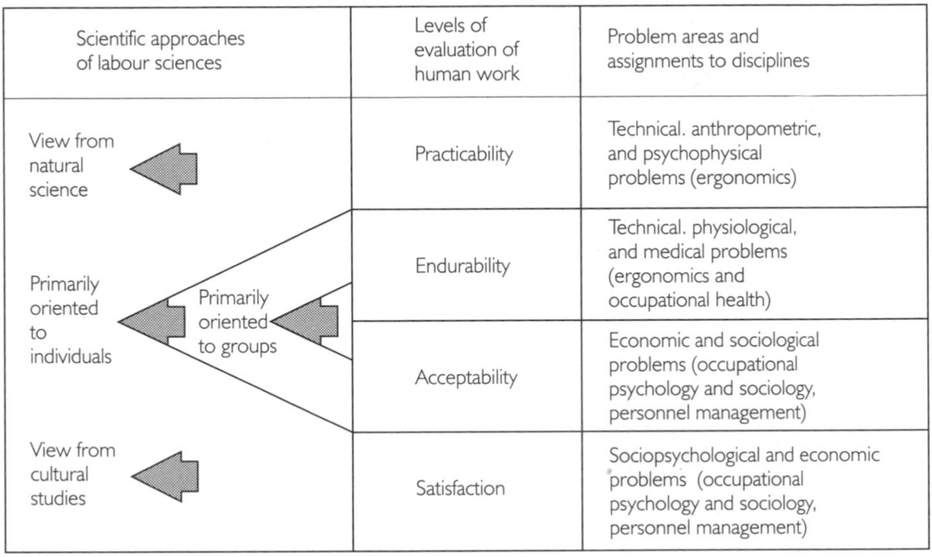

Scientific approaches of labour sciences
Levels of evaluation of human work
Problem areas and assignments to disciplines
View from natural science
Practicability
Technical. anthropometric, and psychophysical problems (ergonomics)
Endurability
Technical. physiological, and medical problems (ergonomics and occupational health)
Primarily oriented to individuals
Primarily oriented to groups
Acceptability
Economic and sociological problems (occupational psychology and sociology, personnel management)
View from cultural studies
Satisfaction
Sociopsychological and economic problems (occupational psychology and sociology, personnel management)

Figure 5.12 Hierarchical model of criteria for the evaluation of human work

As can be seen from the case study below, there is no right way to design or redesign jobs – it is a matter of using the best way to get tasks done, which, nowadays, means working in groups and teams.

CASE STUDY
Empowering Employees … Maverick Style

Ricardo Semler, president of Semco S/A, the Brazilian marine and food-processing machine manufacturer, is internationally famous for creating the world's most unusual workplace. Semler's management philosophy of empowering employees and looking at corporate structures in new ways, is a serious challenge to the ingrained model of the corporate pyramid.

At Semco, workers choose their bosses. Financial information is shared with everyone. Thirty per cent of its employees determine their own salaries. And self-managed teams replace hierarchy and procedure.

Source: Institute of Personnel and Development, 'Empowering Employees … Maverick Style', Master Class, Seminar B7, IPD, National Conference, 23–25 October 1996; Wimbledon: IPD

Questions for discussion

1 What should managers learn from the traditional approaches to the design of work used in Europe?

2 What are the most important emerging issues in the design of work?

3 How do Japanese, USA, German, and Scandinavian approaches to work differ from one another?

References and further reading

Argyle, M., 1989 (2nd edn), *The Social Psychology of Work* (London: Penguin)

Arnold, J., Cooper, C.L. and Robertson, I.T., 1995 (2nd edn), *Work Psychology: Understanding Human Behaviour in the Workplace* (London: Pitman)

Barton, D., 'Changing the job mix to encourage latent talent' in *People Management*, 11 July 1996, p. 23

Bassett, G., 'The Case Against Job Satisfaction' in *Business Horizons* Vol. 37, No 3, May–June 1994, pp. 61–68

Blauner, R., 1964, *Alienation and Freedom* (Chicago: University of Chicago Press)

Brown, M., 'Space shuttle' in *Management Today,* January 1996, pp. 66–74

Brown, M., 'Design for working' in *Management Today,* March 1997, pp. 77–84

Deming, W.E., 1986, *Out of the Crisis* (Cambridge, Mass: Massachusetts Institute of Technology Press)

Financial Times, 'Squaring up to the quality circle', Letter to the Editor, 22 August 1997, p. 14

Gabriel, C., 'Forget BPR, think digital' in *Consultancy,* September 1996, p. 44

Gertz, D.L. and Baptista, P.A., 1996, *Grow to be Great: Breaking the Downsizing Cycle* (USA: Free Press: Simon and Schuster)

Hackman, J.R. and Oldham, G., 'Motivation Through the Design of Work: Test of a Theory' in *Organizational Behavior and Human Performance*, Vol. 16, 1976, pp. 250–279

Hammer, M., 'Reengineering Work: Don't Automate, Obliterate' in *Harvard Business Review*, July–August 1990, pp. 104–112

Herzberg, F., 1966, *Work and the Nature of Man* (Cleveland: World)

Human Resource Magazine, September 1992, p. 21

Institute of Personnel and Development, 'Empowering Employees ... Maverick Style', Master Class, Seminar B7, IPD, National Conference, 23–25 October 1996 (Wimbledon: IPD)

Kaarlgard, R., ASAP interview, Mike Hammer: *Forbes ASAP*, 25 February 1994, pp. 69–75

Kelly, J.E., 1993, 'Does job redesign theory explain job redesign outcomes? in *Human Relations*, No 45, pp. 753–754

Luczak, H., ' "Good Work" Design: An Ergonomic, Industrial Engineering Perspective' in J.C. Quick, L.R. Murphy and J.J. Hurrell (eds), 1992, *Stress and Well-being at Work* (Washington DC: American Psychological Association), pp. 96–112

Luthans, F., 1992 (6th edn), *Organizational Behavior* (Maidenhead: McGraw-Hill)

McGregor, D., 1960, *The Human Side of Enterprise* (New York: McGraw-Hill)

Management Today, September 1996, p. 20

Maslow, A., 1960 and 1980, *Motivation and Personality* (London: Harper & Row)

Matthews, M., 'In praise of maturity' in *Financial Times*, 27 February 1997, p. 11

Miller, K.I. and Monge, P.R., 1986, 'Participation, Satisfaction, and Productivity: A Meta-analytic Review' in *Academy of Management Journal*, No 29, pp. 727–753

Mowday, R.T., Koberg, C.S. and McArthur, A.W., 1984, 'The psychology of the withdrawal process: A cross-validational test of Mobley's intermediate linkages model of turnover in two samples' in *Academy of Management Journal*, No 27, pp. 79–94

Nelson, D.L. and Quick, J.C., 1994, *Organizational Behavior: Foundations, Realities, and Challenges* (St Paul, MN: West Publishing)

Nixon, B., 'Training's role in empowerment' in *People Management*, 9 February 1996, pp. 35–38

Oldham, G.R. and Fried, Y., 1987, 'Employee reactions to workspace characteristics' in *Journal of Applied Psychology*, No 72, pp. 75–80

Perrow, C., 1967, 'A framework for the comparative analysis of organizations' in *American Sociological Review*, Vol. 32, No 2, pp. 194–208

Pettinger, R., 1996, *Introduction to Organisational Behaviour* (Basingstoke: Macmillan)

Porter, I.W. and Lawler, E.E., 1968, Management Attitudes and Performance (Homewood, Ill: Dorsey Press)

Slack, N., Chambers, S., Harland, C., Harrison, A. and Johnston, R., 1995, *Operations Management* (London: Pitman)

Smith, A., 1937 (originally published in 1776), *An Inquiry into the Nature and Causes of the Wealth of Nations* (New York: Modern Library)

Spector, P.E., 1996, *Industrial and Organizational Psychology: Research and Practice* (Toronto: Canada)

Taylor, F.W., 1911, *The Principles of Scientific Management* (New York: Harper & Row)

Thomas, R. and Ballard, M., 1995, *Business Information: Technologies and Strengths* (Cheltenham: Stanley Thornes)

Vroom, V., 1964, *Work and Motivation* (London: Wiley)

Walker, C.R. and Guest, R., 1952, *The Man on the Assembly Line*, (Cambridge, Massachusetts: Harvard University Press)

Warr, P., 1996 (2nd edn), *Psychology at Work* (London: Penguin Books)

Welch, J., 'Creature comforts' in *People Management*, 19 December 1996, pp. 20–23

Ethical issues

Learning objectives

After studying this section you should be able to:

- appreciate the development of ethical reasoning;
- discuss the principal stages of moral development;
- identify the connection between ethical behaviour and work diversity.

Introduction

One of the difficulties in defining ethics and morals lies in the ways that they are learned. Most people learn expected standards of behaviour from their parents/guardians, religious affiliation, reading, school environment, and peers. During a normal lifetime such ethics and morals are learned and changed as societal values change.

The forces of childhood experiences are particularly important in the shaping of an individual's ethical decision-making. So very important, in fact, that many people believe that an individual would have no value system at all unless he or she had experienced very strong inputs from parents/guardians and other closely affiliated adults. It is known today that people who react in an 'instinctive' manner are those who have not examined the values which they gained in their formative years. To be effective members of any society individuals have to build into their lives what they have learned in childhood related to the position of what is perceived by them to be right and wrong. It is in this way that individuals develop their own value systems and attitudes to their environment and situation. The judgement of peers and superiors about their actions will have a major effect on their future behaviour.

Finally, as individuals progress into early adulthood and on to positions of responsibility, the reactions from others will further work to modify their ideas of right and wrong and, consequently, their behaviour. These forces are very strong and often in conflict with each other – such is the situation that human beings find themselves in. Every decision made by an individual will produce an intrinsic force.

Individual differences and ethical behaviour

The issue of ethics and social responsibility is one of the key concepts for organisational behaviour in the closing century and part of this attention focuses on the influence that individual differences might have on moral behaviour and individual social responsibility. A study carried out by Trevino and Youngblood (1990) suggested that locus of control and cognitive moral development (an individual's level of moral judgement) are important in helping to explain whether an individual will behave ethically or unethically. People appear to pass through stages of moral reasoning and judgement as they mature and judgement with regard to right and wrong becomes less dependent on outside influences (such as peers and colleagues). It also becomes less self-centred. At the higher levels of cognitive moral development, an individual develops a deeper understanding of the principles of justice, ethical behaviour, and balancing individual and social rights.

Kohlberg (1981) believes that individual moral reasoning is developmental and that individuals move from the more basic, primary stages to higher levels. However, not everyone reaches the higher levels because some people do not develop the capacity to involve themselves in the more difficult moral reasoning of the advanced stage. His three levels of development translate into six stages of progression, with individual need being preeminent.

Stages One and Two

In these stages, individuals see only their own needs in a conflict situation. These are the levels children are at when they think they must have whatever they want whenever they want it. Some adults are stuck at this level throughout their lives and are seen by others as self-centred (although sometimes what others think is self-centredness may only be a healthy awareness of one's own needs – it is a matter of balance).

Stages Three and Four

This is when the individual has developed sufficiently to appreciate the idea of fairness based on society's idea of the same. Here an individual will be looking at how the collective group of people (society) has determined what is right and good. Moral judgements are based on such things as 'That's the way I was brought up'.

Stages Five and Six

This is a principled understanding of fairness based on the individual's conception of equality and reciprocity. In this final level, which many individuals never achieve (some question whether an individual can ever get to Level Six), moral judgements are based on a thoughtful and analytical process which the individual has cultivated over a long period of time.

Maturity helps to bring about moral development and Kohlberg (1981) believes that involving people in discussion of ethical issues helps them to develop better moral reasoning skills and thus aid their moral development.

Individuals with a mature attitude and with high internal locus of control appear to exhibit more ethical behaviour when making decisions within the workplace than do those with a high external locus of control. Further, a person with higher levels of cognitive moral development is more likely to behave ethically than others are. Individuals in the workplace need to appreciate the differences between values, integrity, morals and responsibility while also addressing ethics in the organisation and the responsibility of that organisation to its stakeholders.

According to Mahoney (1996): '... individuals who invest a large part or a major proportion of their lives in a particular company are morally entitled to have some expectations about how they are treated by, and in, that company' (p. 9).

Ethics and work diversity

Today an understanding of individual ethical values is particularly important – more so than in the past – and they will continue to be so. One significant reason for this is increasing globalisation and its accompanying concept of work diversity.

CASE STUDY

Individual ethics and work diversity

Everyone has different expectations of a company – particularly those who work for it. Many aspects of employment are covered by legislation, others depend on the observance of ethical values and norms.

Discrimination against someone is wrong where it is not job-related – it is *individual* when practised unchecked by prejudiced members of an organisation, *structural* when it relates to job or promotion conditions, and *occupational* when it reflects a common presumption that certain classes of people are only capable of performing certain tasks.

Positive discrimination has been a popular remedy in the past. But the effect can be disproportionate and carries the risk of creating new victims, low self-esteem and low workforce morale.

Affirmative action – planning and executing deliberate, institutional and ethical steps to remove imbalances – does not go so far and can involve actions in the recruitment, interviewing and training fields.

The dividing line between working life and private life is another delicate area. Information should be restricted to those who 'need to know' but a company is entitled to know the reason for adverse performance.

Source: J. Mahoney, 'Discrimination and privacy: Summary' in *Mastering Management*, No 12, p. 9, insert in *Financial Times*, 26 January 1996

Diversity is reflected by differences in gender, age, disabilities, ethnicity, sexual orientation, values, and education. According to Jamieson and O'Mara (1991) the better educated will require a work environment that is stimulating, informative, and challenging.

Questions for discussion

1 Using the case 'Individual ethics and work diversity', what actions could a specific organisation take to encourage ethical behaviour in the area of diversity at work?

2 What type of ethical dilemmas have you faced in your life?

3 Discuss your view of the implementation of tests to identify the brightest students and thus provide them with a university education.

References and further reading

Jamieson, D. and O'Mara, J., 1991, *Managing Workforce 2000* (USA, San Francisco: Jossey-Bass)

Kleiner, K., 'Testing the gender gap' in *New Scientist*, 23 November 1998, No 2057, p. 49

Kohlberg, L., 1981, *The Philosophy of Moral Development* (USA: San Francisco: Harper & Row)

Mahoney, J., 'Discrimination and privacy: Summary' in *Mastering Management*, No 12, p. 9, insert in *Financial Times*, 26 January 1996

Trevino, L.K. and Youngblood, S.A., 'Bad apples in bad barrels: A causal analysis of ethical decision making behaviour' in *Journal of Applied Psychology*, 1990, No 75, pp. 378–385

Part 2: Understanding groups

6 Introducing groups and group behaviour

Learning objectives

After studying this chapter you should be able to:

- understand the concepts of *groups*, *roles* and *teams*;
- understand the difference between formal and informal groups;
- discuss the influence of groups on the individual;
- explain the process of decision-making within groups;
- apply the techniques of brainstorming, sociograms, interaction process analysis, and behaviour analysis;
- assess the relationship between group cohesiveness, goals, and productivity;
- appreciate how groups develop and proceed;
- identify the key variables of group dynamics;
- appreciate the various types of power within groups;
- discuss the key aspects of leadership within groups;
- explain the developments related to empowerment and high performance work teams.

Introduction

CASE STUDY

Hawthorne Studies – The Bank Wiring Room

In Chapter 5 there is a discussion of the importance of the Hawthorne Studies which spanned the years 1927 to 1932. The final stage of these studies took place in the bank wiring room wherein a group was put on a piece-rate plan for seven months in order to find out whether the group output would increase to correspond with an increase in pay.

The outcome was unexpected. The sample group actually paced their work throughout the experiment according to group norms. Thus the power of the peer group and the importance of group influence and dynamics on individual behaviour and productivity were highlighted.

It was these studies by Elton Mayo and his team which emphasised the importance of group dynamics within the workplace.

The nature of a group

This chapter introduces groups and is critical to the understanding of how people behave in the workplace because working in groups has become a major aspect of the working environment and is thus an important component in the understanding of organisational behaviour. Two key factors need to be taken into account at this stage:

- the behaviour of individuals within a group is more than the sum total of each person acting on their own since each individual working in a group behaves differently from the way they do when they are alone; this is called *synergy* and can be best formulated as $1 + 1 = 3$;
- work groups are fundamental to all organisations, particularly those in today's climate where organisational design tends towards being flat and lean.

There are a number of ways of defining a group, each depending upon the situation, contingency and criteria used. Such a definition of a group can be very broad, involving any body of people or things with some shared attribute such as shown below:

- committees
- boards of directors
- quality circles
- production teams
- surgical teams in hospitals
- flight crews
- sales teams
- repair crews
- university graduates
- queues in building societies.

University graduates share a common qualification whilst people queuing in a building society share a common predicament!

A generally accepted definition of a group within the study of organisational behaviour is that by Schein (1988): 'any number of people who (1) interact with one another; (2) are psychologically aware of one another; and (3) perceive themselves to be in a group' (p. 145).

Spector's (1996) definition supports Schein's (1988): 'A work group is a collection of two or more people who interact with one another and share some interrelated task goals' (p. 302).

Both describe psychological groups where members of the group share some consciousness that they are a group and act together to achieve a shared objective or objectives. Within this definition, they are defined internally by the members of the group articulating a group identity rather than by an observer imposing an external classification. Such group definitions suggest a relatively small number of people who can interact and communicate directly.

Organisations can be seen as artificial constructs: structures in which individuals and groups operate. Groups in the psychological sense used here are more organic entities and their group dynamics are determined by the personal interactions of their individual members.

Characteristics of psychological groups

There are some identifiable characteristics of a psychological group identified by Adair (1985):

- a socially definable membership
- a group consciousness
- a sense of shared purpose or a common set of goals
- interdependence
- interaction
- the ability to act in a unitary manner.

Study observations of groups identify characteristics of a well-functioning, effective psychological group as including:

- an atmosphere which tends to be comfortable, informal, and relaxed;
- all members of the group understanding and accepting the group task;
- all members are actively listening to each other and discussion is mostly task based;
- members who express their feelings as well as their ideas;
- functional conflict being centred around ideas and methods which are related to the task and not to the individuals within the group;
- the ownership of an operational and functional identity;
- consensus-driven decisions rather than majority vote decisions;
- actions which are decided, allocated, and accepted by all members of the group.

This need for all members to interact has led to the suggestion that, in practice, a psychological group is unlikely to exceed twelve members. Beyond that number the opportunity for frequent interaction between members, and hence group awareness, is considerably reduced.

The nature of a team

Some writers use the terms 'group' and 'team' synonymously. However, there *is* a difference. A team is a task-oriented work group and can be formally designated or informally evolved. Whether formal or informal, all work teams make important and valuable contributions to the organisation and are important to the individual member need satisfaction. Teams differ from groups primarily because they are specifically work oriented and task centred.

Formal and informal groups

Comparing groups and teams introduces the distinction between formal and informal groups.

Formal groups

A formal group is a designated group which has been defined by the organisation's structure and has thus been purposefully created and stipulated to help accomplish the organisation's collective purpose. Thus the individual's purpose is to relate his or her behaviour to the goals of the organisation. Organisations may consciously create formal groups to carry out a particular task or function. Such groups may serve a wide range of purposes, from permanent groups of workers collaborating on a particular stage in the production process to those brought together for a limited period to carry out a specific project. In both cases, individuals are nominated for membership, group roles (such as foreman, supervisor, chairman, or secretary) are allotted, and the group is given specific objectives, appropriate resources, and timescales for meeting those objectives. An example here would be the crew on a long-haul commercial aeroplane.

Thus, formal groups have certain common characteristics:

- they are consciously created by an organisation;
- they have a formal structure;
- they are task oriented;
- their activities contribute directly to the organisation's goals.

Similarly, organisations may also generate unplanned and spontaneous informal groups.

Informal groups

There are two types of informal group. The first occurs where the experience of belonging to a formal group generates a quite separate identity, meaning and function for its members than what is planned or intended by the organisation. Even formal groups will generate their own dynamics and norms and their structure and purpose may evolve over time. A formal group will develop its own informal identity.

The second happens when entirely new informal groups emerge in response to the experience of working within the organisation and cut across formal group boundaries. These groups emerge spontaneously when, as a result of the experience of working within the organisation, individuals discover and articulate a distinct identity. Informal groups are founded on interpersonal relationships and accord between individuals rather than on any role relationships. Their purpose is to serve the psychological and social needs of the members of the group (*relation oriented*) and not wholly to concentrate on the task with which the formal group may be concerned (*task oriented*).

Thus there is an overlap between formal and informal groups because the membership of each can cross the other. For example, informal groups may have members who come from different sections of the organisation: vertically, diagonally and horizontally. Membership is further complicated by the fact that an informal group could well be the same as a formal group, or it might comprise only a section of a formal group.

Members of informal groups choose their own leader who represents the full group membership, whereas in formal groups the leader is appointed by the organisation or by role, e.g. Head of Department. Leadership of an informal group is by various criteria which reflect the values and attitudes of the group members. The principal role of the leader is to turn dysfunctional conflict into functional conflict, lead the membership into goal achievement, and liaise with the management if that role is appropriate. There is more discussion on leadership later on in this book.

The formation of informal groups

There is no single reason why anyone joins an informal group. Most individuals belong to a number of groups both at and away from the workplace, so it is evident that different groups will give different satisfactions to their members. The most common reasons for joining a group are related to the individual's higher order needs of:

- security
- status
- self-esteem
- affiliation
- power
- goal achievement/self-actualisation.

Security

A coalition provides strength and so individuals will experience less self-doubt within an informal group. They will feel safe and therefore more resistant to threats than they might as an individual. New employees or those changing roles are particularly vulnerable in this area and tend to turn to an informal group for guidance and support. Few individuals like to stand alone because they need companionship and mutual understanding to help solve personal and work-related problems. Membership of an informal group can protect an individual from harassment as well as act as a tension-buster thus avoiding dysfunctional stress.

Status

Membership of an informal group can provide recognition and status for its members. For example, winning an archery competition in leisure time and reporting this to an informal group can provide prestige for the individual which might not otherwise be available in a formal group. Membership provides a sense of belonging and identity alongside the opportunity to have role recognition and status.

Self-esteem

An individual can gain a feeling of self-worth by belonging to an informal group. Self-esteem is bolstered if a person feels they are a member of a highly valued informal group.

Affiliation

Most people enjoy the interaction which accompanies group membership, and informal groups tend to be the primary means of providing individuals with their means of fulfilling their needs for affiliation, friendship and social interaction. They also allow members to modify their more formal roles within work groups.

Power

This is an appealing function of an informal group in that it may be the only provider of power for an individual within the workplace. By using the principles of coalition individuals may well get things done that they couldn't do on their own. Additionally, informal groups provide opportunities for individuals to exercise power over others, e.g. as the group leader they may be able to influence others. For individuals with a high need for power, informal groups can be a means of personal fulfilment. The role of power in a group is considered later on in this chapter.

Goal achievement

Informal groups can often achieve an objective which an individual might find daunting. Informal groups provide an opportunity for an individual to pool knowledge, talents, interests or power in order to gain satisfaction or achieve a personal goal.

Groups and organisations

The organisation can only meet a small proportion of an individual's needs – the balance is met by life outside the workplace. Formal groups are in place to meet the objectives of the organisation, whereas it is through informal groups that an individual will attempt to meet some of the higher order level needs. The operation of both formal and informal groups within an organisation will depend upon the design of the organisation, because it is the organisation itself which gives formal groups and, to a lesser extent, informal groups their nature and identity. However, both types of group work within the context of the organisation and there are differences between formal and informal organisations which will affect the nature of groups within the organisation, as shown in Table 6.1 below.

Table 6.1 Informal and formal groups within the organisation

Key concept	Informal groups	Formal groups
Personality and behaviour	spontaneous	conceptual
	outgoing	situational
	emotional	contingency
	imaginative	externally imposed
	dynamic	creative
	unfamiliar	patterned
	bold	stable
	intuitive	group tied
	groupthink	practical
	personal goals	organisation goals
	tender-minded	tough-minded
	self sufficient	other reliant
	relaxed	tense
Perception	emotive	information processing
	social identity	stereotypical
	individual	consensual
	self development	clearly defined
	continuous development	reinforcement
	social theory	
Motivation	physiological needs	work ethic
	self actualisation	pursuit of excellence
	intrinsic	competitiveness
	spontaneous	extrinsic

	safety belongingness status acceptance	acquisitiveness mastery
Job design	sociogram teams groups	organisational charts scientific management top down
Organisational dynamics and control	spontaneous personal cohesive loyalty attached member satisfaction controlled by norms	prescribed by job specification positional functional unattached controlled by threat power based

The importance of groups to individuals

Most people spend their whole lives as a member of several groups – be it, for example, family, social group, workplace group, or leisure activity group. For the majority of people their success as an individual will depend upon their ability to synergise effectively within and with such groups. This individual behaviour carried out within the group (intra) allows the individual to work with other groups (inter) and is highly complex. Individuals may well behave one way when on their own, a different way when in one group (e.g. the family unit) and differently again when in another group (e.g. a university martial arts team). It is usual for an individual to underestimate the degree to which his or her behaviour is affected by the membership of groups – be they formal or informal.

Group identity and territory

Many organisations have an organisational structure which is defined according to their social structures – for example, by assigning the School of Business, School of Sociology and Social Policy, and Human Resources within a university each to a special area. Another way by which activities can be separated is by project teams (see Chapter 5) which arrangement is increasingly a part of modern organisations. Whilst organisations may not deliberately create territories, groups may perceive themselves as linked because of their common locations – for example, the School of Business and the School of Sociology and Social Policy being housed in the same building.

There has not been significant empirical research on territorial boundaries; however, there is evidence that the physical marking of group boundaries (displays of personal belongings, signs, and slogans) is associated with strong group identity within organisations.

However, it is not known whether such boundaries give groups their strong identities or whether groups that are in the process of forming strong identity concentrate on the construction of their own visible boundaries – possibly both forces are working.

A key factor is that a strong group identity has the potential to interfere with inter-group co-operation. If the School of Business and the School of Sociology and Social Policy both have a separate strong identity it is difficult for them to work together. The strength of group identity is situational and a contingency factor, and sometimes needs, therefore, to be weaker – or stronger. Simply, the link with physical structure gives a way of examining existing group identities and could well provide a source of inspiration of what to do if change is required.

How groups influence individuals

The study of groups and teams is highly complex and they have an overriding influence on a number of organisational factors. It is this fact which makes any study of the influence of groups in the workplace dependent upon other key concepts. A principal consideration concerns how the interaction of individuals within a workgroup can affect their individual attitudes and behaviour. Key issues here are related to group norms where individuals learn to socialise within the group, and to cope with group sanctions by the use of judicious judgements and actions in perceived incidents.

Norms

Norms are the rules and sets of behaviour that are expected and accepted by all members of a group or team. Generally, norms define the kind of behaviours which all members of the group feel are essential if the group is to achieve its goals. When individuals join existing groups, they find that norms have often already been established and so, therefore, have to accept such norms if they want to be a member of that particular group.

Norms and organisational regulations

Organisations publish their rules and regulations in the form of manuals and memoranda which the workforce are meant to abide by: employees sometimes ignore such rules. Norms are usually unwritten and are enforced by members of the group. If a group member consistently flouts the norms of the group, the other members of that group sanction her in some way in order to bring her back into line. For example, sanctions could range from physical abuse to threats of expulsion from the group. Conversely, there are often rewards for compliance with the group norms in the form of praise, recognition, and acceptance of the individual by other group members.

Since norms are generally unwritten and often in place when an individual becomes a member, members may be only vaguely aware of what the norms are that operate within that particular group. This is a recipe for disaster, since in order to be functional the group members need to be aware of the group norms because such an awareness will:

- increase individual potential for group freedom and maturity;
- positively or negatively influence the effectiveness of individuals, teams, and the organisation.

Relation to goals

It is the normal practice for teams to adopt norms in order that they may achieve their objectives.

CASE STUDY

Unfair to Lisa?

Paula had been working at Peter's Pet Products for twenty years and was so efficient at her job on the assembly line that she did not really need to give one hundred per cent of her attention to her task. As a result, Paula was often able to socialise and watch the life of the organisation as it evolved around her.

This morning Paula is training a new worker:

'No, that's not right, Lisa. Take it like this, twist your elbow and then your wrist and that will make it much easier.'

'But I was told by the supervisor to do it this way', replied Lisa.

'Don't take any notice of him – he doesn't have to do the job – I've done it for years so there isn't anything I can't show you to make it easier. If you're worried about what the supervisor will say, do it his way when he's around and my way when he isn't – he won't bother to come back after the first few days anyway. You won't be expected to complete even 50 packs per day for the first few weeks.'

'But the supervisor said I have to do 60', came the reply from Lisa.

'Of course he did – then let him do it then! Pace yourself like I do. Hum the national anthem to yourself whilst you pack, use the method I showed you, and you'll be doing 50 packages next week.'

'But what if the supervisor makes me do 60?' Lisa asked.

'Well, he can't do that. You'll start making mistakes if you go too fast. Fifty is about right – a fair day's work for a fair day's pay!' came the retort from Paula.

The above situation serves to illustrate a number of key issues about the norms of a group:

- norms (and goals) set by management may differ from those of the group members;
- co-members may have as much influence as or more influence than managers in pressuring workers to accept stated norms and goals;
- employees are concerned with both task- and relations-oriented behaviours whilst managers are concerned with the former;
- attempts by managers to change group norms are likely to lead to group resistance;
- when group members rationalise their goals and norms, they do so stating they are that way in order to achieve the organisation's objectives;
- members may claim that to increase production will cause workplace stress, increased absenteeism and, thus, decreased performance and production.

The above case shows particularly that when group goals include minimising the influence of managers and increasing the opportunity for members to interact socially, members could perceive the norms as being a desirable restriction on output.

Enforcing norms

Groups form and enforce their norms with respect to the behaviours that they consider to be important. According to Kolesar (1993) group members are most likely to enforce norms under one or more of the following conditions:

- **Norms help the group to survive and provide it with benefits.** The team may well not discuss holiday entitlement with other members of the team to avoid drawing attention to inequalities within the team.
- **Norms simplify or predict expected behaviours of group members.** When members of the team collect money for, say, a birthday gift for one of the other members, a group may decide on a norm to cover such an eventuality. For example, all members donate the same amount, or one person buys the gift within agreed financial limits and the cost is then equally divided amongst the other members, or they buy individual gifts.
- **Norms help to avoid intimate problems.** For example, there might be norms about where the group meets socially (out of people's homes so that comparisons are not made) or about not discussing family issues (so that different ethical issues do not form barriers to the group meeting its goals).

By the use of norms, a group is expressing its values and clarifying its individual identity. Hence people who, say, work in the fashion industry will wear designer, trend-setting outfits because they see it as necessary since it conveys a message to their fellow workers, their customers, and the general public.

Conforming to norms

There are numerous ways in which individuals conform to organisational norms, such as:

- always look busy and do not worry about the results;
- keep your mouth shut;
- keep your opinions to yourself.

The above examples could well relate to organisational norms but there is little research in the field upon which to base the validity of organisational norms, i.e. it is not known whether they do *actually* exist.

However, individuals attempt to conform to perceived organisational norms and, particularly, to the norms of the groups of which they are a member. There are two principal types of conformity – compliance, and personal acceptance.

- *Compliance conformity* is behaviour which reflects the group's desired behaviour because of perceived pressure. Some individuals conform to group norms even if they do not personally agree with them; for example, they might want to be liked by the others in the group and non-conformance may not achieve this.
- *Personal acceptance conformity* is based on positive personal support of the norms of the group and by this the individual's behaviour and attitudes are consistent with the group's norms and goals. It is much stronger than compliance conformity because the individual has internalised the group's norms and goals and thus owns them.

When individuals conform to norms, they may also change their behaviour. In the case 'Unfair to Lisa?' given above, Lisa might well change her behaviour from that required by the supervisor to that proposed by Paula. It might well be that because the group of which Paula is a member is a highly conforming group, Lisa may be obliged to change her behaviour (compliance type of conformity). However, Lisa might want to oppose the change and find it highly stressful (personal acceptance type of conformity). Without norms and reasonable conformity to them, the group of which Lisa is now a member would be working chaotically and would not accomplish its tasks. However, Lisa has to consider that excessive and blind conformity may threaten her individuality and the group's collective ability to change and learn.

The importance of groups in organisations

Groups and work teams are important to organisations in three key areas:

- for the completion of complex and co-operative tasks
- in decision-making
- in improving the levels of productivity.

Completion of complex and co-operative tasks

Bowey and Connelly (1977) suggest types of tasks which are most suitable for group working, that is when:

- co-operation brings about synergy in terms of, say, speed, quality, required criteria, which is not there when an individual works alone;
- joining sub-tasks into one task or area of accountability makes the task more meaningful to the individuals within the group;
- different skills and talents are required to complete the task or achieve the objective;
- the task requires frequent adjustment in activities and in the co-ordination of such activities;
- competition can be channelled into effective achievement of the task;
- stress levels are beyond the normal tension level and individuals need protection.

There are two types of tasks which groups are, typically, given:

- additive
- compensatory.

Additive tasks

These are types of group tasks to which the co-ordinated efforts of individual members of the group are added together to form the group's product. An example of this would be a group of students working together to produce a business report. In the additive process, the individual contributions of the group members are added together to form the final group product. This type of working can encourage a phenomenon known as *social loafing* which is based on the principle that when people know that their work is to be combined with that of others, they reduce the level of their contribution.

Compensatory tasks

This is when the product of the group's efforts is the average of all the individual contributions and encapsulates the benefits of differing points of view and compromise. By sharing judgements, it is likely that a more accurate decision will be made.

Decision-making

An increasing number of decisions in today's organisations are being taken by groups such as Boards of Directors, shareholders, project teams and quality circles. However, whilst there are advantages in group decision-making there are some difficulties involved in the process.

Advantages of group decision-making

- More people bring more information and there is, therefore, a pooling of resources.
- With more people to share the work load it is possible to specialise and thus improve the quality of decisions.
- A homogeneous group brings a diversity of views and increases creativity thus allowing for more alternatives to be taken into account.
- Since individuals in the group have participated in the decision-making process, they are more likely to accept the decision of the group and participate in the implementation.
- A decision made by a group is likely to have more legitimacy than one made by an individual.

Disadvantages of group decision-making

- They can take and waste time through socialising activities and this can reduce management's ability to act quickly when necessary.
- Individuals within groups might be coerced into conforming with the majority view.
- Potential disagreement amongst members may encourage dysfunctional conflict; particularly when the group leader intimidates the other members.
- The decision could be dominated by a few members who form a coalition in order to get the decision made. This is particularly damaging to the decision-making process if such a coalition comprises low- to medium-ability members.
- Group members will share responsibility for the decision made but there is no actual person accountable for the final outcome.

Problems with group decision-making

All organisations will rely upon interdependency in order to solve the differing problems which they face over time. Such decisions are made as individuals or by group consensus. However, there are disadvantages in consensual group decision-making of which group members and managers should be aware:

- the time a team takes to make a decision might better be used on other tasks;
- it can create boredom and a feeling that time is being wasted;
- it can reduce intrinsic motivation for the individual.

However, whether a decision is made on an individual or group basis, there is a key technique which can be used to aid the quality of creative decision-making – brainstorming.

Brainstorming

Brainstorming is not a decision-making technique *per se* but a way of eliciting ideas which could then be used to make an effective decision: it is a creative technique carried out traditionally or by electronic means. Whichever means is used, the facilitator has to be non-judgemental and all ideas noted – however bizarre and 'off the issue under consideration' they might appear to be.

Traditional brainstorming

This is usually done with a group of 5–12 individuals and is a process by which the individuals in the group state as many ideas as possible during a defined period of time (usually 10 to 60 minutes depending on the complexity of the issue). Procedural guidelines include:

- the broader and more creative the ideas the better;
- judgement must be totally suspended;
- there must be no criticism of any ideas put forward;
- any previously mentioned ideas must be clustered, i.e. written in related groups.

Brainstorming within a group is more beneficial than by an individual working alone because it allows for more ideas than an individual might have. However, as a technique it is not as effective as is often thought because:

- individuals may not offer ideas immediately because someone else is talking or the facilitator is writing other people's ideas – the result is that the process becomes overloaded;
- group members may be afraid to offer ideas because of what other group members might think of them;
- ideas may not be forthcoming if there is a possibility of them appearing to be critical of existing practices;
- individuals might be put off if supervisors are present.

Electronic brainstorming

The use of electronic brainstorming can offset some of the above concerns and works as follows:

- each member is networked with others in the group;
- software allows each individual to enter ideas as they occur;
- when an individual enters an idea, a random set of the group's ideas is presented on each individual's screen;
- each individual can continue to see new random sets of ideas at will by pressing the appropriate key.

Research on electronic brainstorming carried out by Olaniran (1994) shows a positive view of the process in that it seems to produce more ideas than traditional brainstorming. Electronic brainstorming appears to have considerable potential in idea creativity leading towards effective decision-making because:

- group members cannot identify the source of the idea;
- it is anonymous;
- individual members can contribute freely;
- there is no fear of 'being seen to be foolish' to other members of the workforce and to supervisors/managers;
- ideas are created more spontaneously;
- the advantages are greater the larger the number of networkers.

In general, group decisions tend to be more accurate than those of an individual but this does not necessarily mean that all groups will outperform the decision-making process of an individual. Though individuals are faster at making decisions, for acceptability of the decision the group decision is likely to be more successful. However, it is more efficient for individuals to make decisions because it consumes less time yet, when there is a need to refer to data, a group has the efficiency advantage.

Whilst groups do provide a positive vehicle for performing many of the steps in the decision-making process integrating both breadth and depth, whether decisions made by groups are more effective than those made by an individual, or vice versa, depends upon the situation and managers need to take a contingency view.

There are other ways of decision-making (Nominal Group Technique, Delphic Technique) which are dealt with more fully in Chapter 7.

Improving levels of productivity

When investigating group productivity, one of the key factors which needs to be taken into account is *group cohesiveness*.

Group cohesiveness

Cohesiveness could be defined as the strength of the individual's desire to become a member of the group with its accompanying individual commitment to the group. An influencing factor is the degree of compatibility between the goals and norms of the group and those of the individual who aspires to become a member. If all individuals accept such norms and goals, and have an intrinsic desire to remain in the group, the group will remain cohesive.

Research studies into the relationship between cohesiveness and conformity have shown that the issue is very complex. If the cohesiveness of a group is low, it is usual to find that conformity is also low. However, high cohesiveness does not only exhibit itself in the presence of high conformity. For example, a team which is performing to a high level of productivity may have a high member commitment level and a wish to stay together, whilst they may simultaneously be respecting – and encouraging – individual differentiation in both behaviour and ideas. It is more likely, however, that such behaviour will be exhibited when cohesion is based on a common commitment to the performance goals. It is usual for cohesive groups who have to confront complex problems to encourage and accept non-conformity.

There are factors which affect the cohesiveness of any group and each has a consequence for group cohesiveness which are given in Table 6.2 below.

Table 6.2 Factors affecting group cohesiveness

Factors that increase group cohesiveness	**Consequences of high group cohesiveness**
homogeneous membership mature development small membership frequent interactions clear objectives identification of external threats identification of competition success	goal accomplishment personal member satisfaction increased quality transactions increased quantity transactions groupthink
Factors that decrease group cohesiveness	**Consequences of low group cohesiveness**
heterogeneous membership newly formed large membership geographically dispersed ambiguous objectives fear of failure	difficulty in achieving goals unstable life term few interactions individual centred

Research on group performance has concentrated on the relationship between cohesiveness and group productivity. It appears that the higher the cohesiveness within a group the more effective the members are at achieving the goals of the group. Where groups are low in cohesiveness, the goals are less likely to be achieved and, *if* they are, usually at a lower quality of production. However, highly cohesive groups will not necessarily be more productive in an organisational sense than groups who exhibit the characteristics of a low cohesive group. Figure 6.1 on page 187 shows that when a group's goals are compatible with those of the organisation, a cohesive group is more likely to be productive than one that is not cohesive. This means that if a highly cohesive group has as its principal goal the same goal as that of the organisation within which it works, it is more likely to contribute to the good of that organisation and be more productive in organisational terms. However, even though it is a highly cohesive group, if its goals do not match the organisation's goals, it might well achieve the goal of the group but not that of the organisation; thus it will not achieve a high level of organisational productivity.

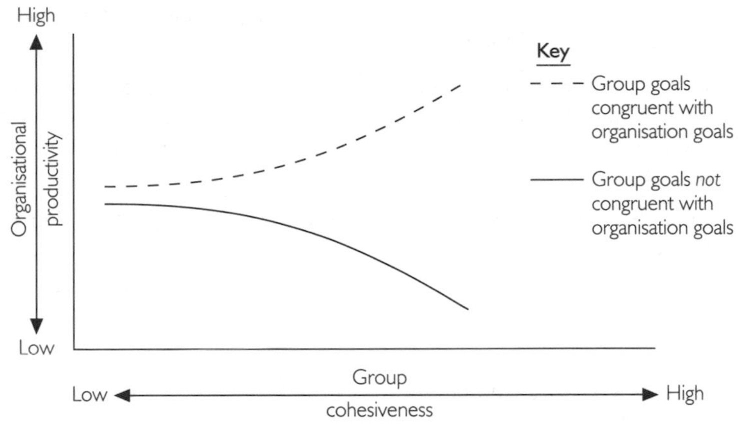

Figure 6.1 The relationship between group cohesiveness, goals and productivity

The effects of groups on performance are a key aspect of organisational behaviour. All individuals within an organisation have to complete tasks with the ultimate aim of achieving the organisation's objectives. The productivity of an individual is influenced by the presence of other people – especially those who are members of the same group. On some occasions an individual's performance is increased by the presence of others – especially when they are competent at the task. However, if, for example, the task is new to the individual and competency has not been achieved, the presence of others in the group can inhibit productivity as shown in the case 'Unfair to Lisa?'. This concept is called *social facilitation* and can be a factor which encourages dysfunctional conflict because the individual faces the dilemma of whether to pay attention to the others in the group or to the task he or she has to do. Organisational researchers call this *evaluation apprehension*. Such a fear of being evaluated or judged by another person accounts for the arousing effect of others' presence.

How groups form

As has been seen from previous sections, groups are formed to satisfy organisational (formal groups) and individual (informal groups) needs. Managers organise formal groups, such as project teams, within organisations because they expect that the groups will collectively achieve the organisation's objectives. Individuals join groups in order to satisfy a personal need.

Understanding why a group forms is an important concept within the study of organisational behaviour.

Example of group formation

Imagine that Jerry has joined a chess club primarily for social contact. Carl joins the club on a temporary basis but is more competitive: then Carl has a different goal to Jerry's. Carl may become irritated when he perceives that the competition has slowed down or stops altogether because the other players are absorbed in social discourse.

Conversely, the regular members may be annoyed when Carl chastises them for poor playing technique or lack of concentration.

Someone who wants to turn such dysfunctional conflict into functional conflict needs to understand why each person joined the chess group. Such inconsistencies arise because each individual had a different reason for becoming a member of the chess club – each joined to satisfy different personal needs.

Settlement of the dispute could well be temporary with the visitor being excluded from the group in the future.

Understanding how groups form helps an individual to work out why people appear to be acting inconsistently. Every group develops its own identity and structure.

Group formation

The key study in the formation of groups was carried out during the Hawthorne Studies (1927–1932) by one of the key researchers in Elton Mayo's team – George Homans (1950). The knowledge gained during this seminal study continues to aid in the understanding of the formation of groups as we head towards the millennium. Homans was a sociologist by nature and training, and whilst working as a member of Mayo's team he turned to the area of how groups actually form. He believed that any social system – of which a group is an example – worked within a three-part environment which itself comprised:

- *physical environment* such as the terrain, climate, and design of the workplace within which the group functions;
- *cultural environment* – the norms, values, attitudes and goals of the group;
- *technological environment* – the level of knowledge which the group collectively has.

The environment is a key factor in group formation because not all forces in the general environment affect organisations or groups in the same way. Environmental uncertainty exists when groups have little information about environmental events and their effect on the group members. If the organisational environment is complex and dynamic, then the group may have little information about evolving issues and have considerable difficulty in predicting them. Such uncertainty results in individuals experiencing high levels of change in mood towards each other within the group and the group's external environment. Such contextual issues concerned Homans (1950) in his work and he called the environment the *external system*. He did this because the environment is anything that is outside the boundaries of the group and is, therefore, by definition beyond the control of the group members. Homans believed that the tasks, emotions and interactions of the group were mutually dependent on one another.

Example of mutual dependency

Charlie and Ben are life-long friends and have both been working for Clarkson Engineering plc for most of their ten-year working life. They have recently been placed in the same project team – Charlie for her expertise in electronic information processing and Ben for his skills in project management.

Question

Since Charlie and Ben interact frequently, how positive or negative are their shared sentiments likely to be?

Answer

You have probably answered in the positive. However, it is important to remember that the more positive the shared emotions the higher the rate of interaction, so encouraging interaction amongst new members of a group can bring about a shared perception.

The links between the contextual variables of Homans' (1950) work are shown in Figure 6.2 below.

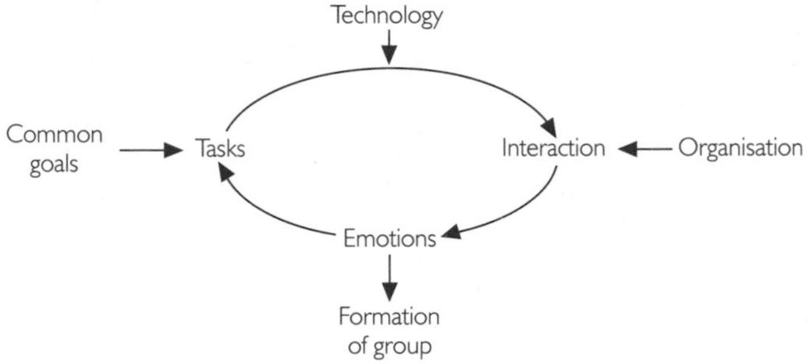

Figure 6.2 The contextual variables after Homans' work

Homans (1950) developed the theory that the external system did not work in isolation but as the individuals within the groups increased their interaction, the group developed its own norms. From this emerged different activities to those specified by the external environment. Groups began to personalise themselves and adopt patterns of behaviour which were not anticipated by the management of the organisation. Thus Homans distinguished between two distinct systems within an organisation:

- *internal system* – the informal system that groups utilised: the norms and values of the group;
- *external system* – the formal system which evolved because of the existing beliefs of how organisations should be managed, e.g. by scientific management techniques.

Homans found that the internal system had been overlooked, and specifically its powerful effect on job design, productivity and quality control.

As his work progressed, Homans (1950) identified that the internal and external systems with the environment worked independently. He found that changes in the environment resulted in changes in both the internal and external systems in operation within the workplace groups. Along with this, any changes in the tasks and norms of the internal systems brought about changes in the three key environmental contexts: the physical, cultural, and technological environments.

For example, a group may come up with a working practice which improves quality and this might generate similar working practices in other groups, thus reaching beyond the

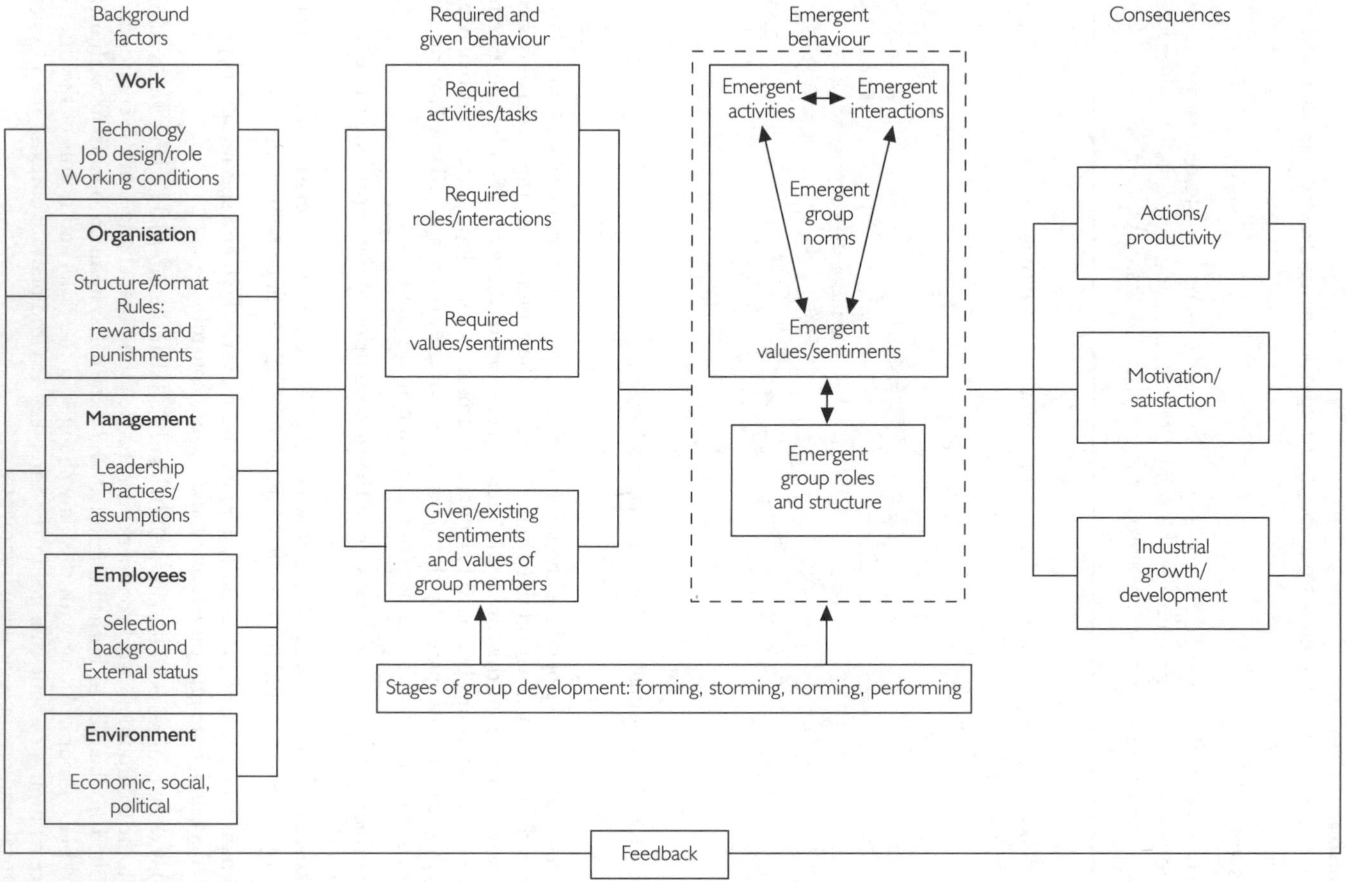

Figure 6.3 How groups form, after Homans, (1950)

organisation's original quality goals. Such changes have brought about an increase in the use of cell structures where the group is responsible for all aspects of the work cycle from idea conception to dealings with the customer on their specific needs. This was the key issue stemming from Homans' work: the explicit recognition that the contextual elements of the environment were dependent upon each other.

Being sociologically based, Homans' work rested principally on how the individuals within the workplace actually *behaved*. Since he carried out this work during a time when scientific management principles were the key guiding light for organisational management, it was not surprising that his approach was ground-breaking. Taking the context from the management viewpoint, Homans distinguished two types of individual behaviour in the workplace:

- *required behaviour* – this was the behaviour expected from individuals by the management in order for the task to be successfully accomplished;
- *emergent behaviour* – this was other behaviour which came about as a result of interpersonal communication between group members and the emotions and sentiments which emerged – such behaviours were often not required by the management.

Tuckman and Jensen (1977) and, separately, Bass and Ryterband (1979) carried out key research on the formation and development of groups; their findings were similar. Both identified a number of key stages in the way that groups develop as summarised in Figure 6.4 below.

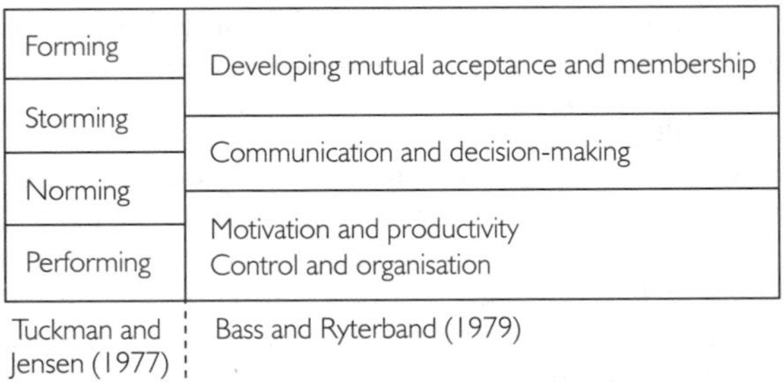

Forming
Storming
Norming
Performing
Developing mutual acceptance and membership
Communication and decision-making
Motivation and productivity
Control and organisation
Tuckman and Jensen (1977)
Bass and Ryterband (1979)

Figure 6.4 A comparison of Tuckman and Jensen's (1977) and Bass and Ryterband's (1979) views on group formation and development

Stage One – Forming

This is the initial stage of the process as members of the group first come together and negotiate the group's composition and terms of reference. At this point group members may well be wary of their potential co-members, and Bass and Ryterband's (1979) model lays particular emphasis on the process of getting to know one another. Group members may well act relatively formally and defensively at first until they have established mutual interests and agreed group membership. Once a certain level of trust has been identified, Tuckman and Jensen's (1977) model emphasises the subsequent process of agreeing group roles and responsibilities, including the question of leadership. They also identified the importance of establishing codes of conduct which group members agree to adhere to in their subsequent dealings with each other. This is particularly important if the group is to survive the storming stage which is discussed below.

Whilst formal groups may have a structure and group roles already set out, the process of forming is still important. Group members will still need to establish trust, accommodate differing personalities and agree a method of working. At this point informal roles and working methods may begin to emerge as stronger personalities begin to exert themselves. Alliances emerge with group members negotiating the rules of conduct.

Stage Two – Storming

Once the group has established a level of trust and provisional ground rules on roles and conduct, it must then negotiate and agree its purpose and agenda. It is at this point that members will feel both the confidence and need to express their views more openly and strongly. Disagreements about the group's role and plan of action may then emerge, thus leading to dysfunctional conflict and hostility. Group members must accommodate this conflict as a necessary prerequisite to establishing a consensus which will allow the group to proceed. This makes the forming stage crucial to group success: if sufficient trust and liking has been built up, and appropriate rules of conduct agreed to allow group members to discuss issues freely and constructively, then the group will have the resilience and means to survive the tensions of storming. If not, the group may break down under the strain of storming.

The storming stage is crucial to the group's future. If the group is to function effectively and secure the commitment of its members, differences of opinion must be aired and resolved to establish a consensus. Individual group members must be allowed to express and discuss views freely if they are to feel commitment to and ownership of the position the group eventually agrees, and thus become fully committed and active members of the group. If storming is either unsuccessful or is avoided, the group will either break down completely or its effectiveness will become compromised by unresolved tensions and divisions.

Stage Four – Norming

Once the issues raised in the storming stage start to be resolved, the group begins to establish norms: agreed principles which govern the group's purpose, agenda and method of working. Bass and Ryterband (1979) associate this stage with the storming process in Tuckman and Jensen's (1977) work in their description of the communication and decision-making stage of group formation: the point at which they see groups as ready to discuss issues and make key decisions about the group's future. As discussed earlier in this chapter, norms provide the framework within which groups can operate smoothly for carrying out individual tasks.

Stage Four – Performing

If the group has progressed successfully through each of the previous stages, it will have the cohesion, structure, and sense of purpose to fulfil its tasks and to maintain momentum until its objectives are fulfilled. Bass and Ryterband's (1979) model divides this stage into two. In the first, the achievement of group consensus gives group members the means and motivation to carry out group goals: their commitment is strong and motivation will derive in part from the intrinsic satisfaction of group membership, loyalty and co-operation. In the second, work is allocated according to an agreed division of labour and mechanisms for reviewing progress and problem-solving are established.

Because organisations now tend to be flat and lean with group lifetime and membership often being short term, two other stages not considered in the above research are adjourning/dying, and mourning.

Adjourning/dying

When the group has completed its task, it will no longer have an objective and so the members will go their separate ways and the group has 'died'. An example of this is when a group of undergraduates have carried out a team project together, presented it for assessment, and received feedback on that project – there is no longer a need for that group to convene, the members go their separate ways and the group 'dies'.

Mourning

As has been seen in earlier discussions, individuals often satisfy their personal needs as a member of a group. Once the group has 'died', individuals might mourn its passing because there is no longer a place for them to satisfy such needs. Fortunately, organisations are now based on groups and so such needs may be satisfied by the individual being a member of another group.

Introducing group dynamics

This section is concerned with understanding how and why groups behave as they do. Group behaviour may seem, on the one hand, fluid and changing, making it difficult to analyse. On the other, the interactions between group members tend to settle into a certain pattern over time. Groups tend to develop common characteristics: in other words, they develop a structure.

Group structure is the relatively stable pattern of relationships between the differentiated elements of a group. Whilst there are a number of ways of investigating group structure, it is best to understand it by looking at groups from two perspectives: as a set of relationships and as a decision-making unit.

A set of relationships

The pattern of social relationships within a group is determined by a number of factors which are shown in Figure 6.5 below.

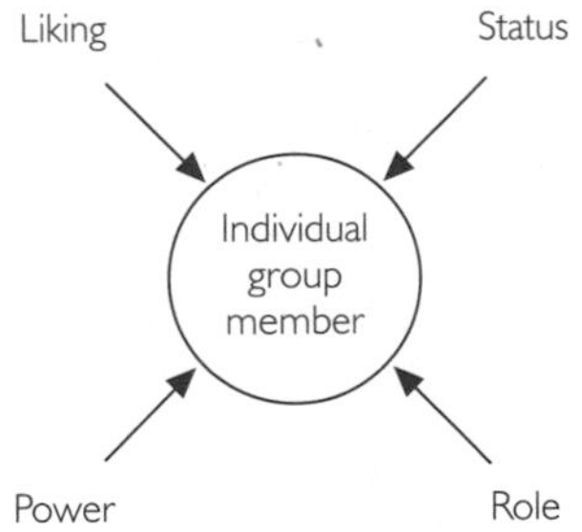

Figure 6.5 Influences on relationships within groups

These contextual factors are interconnected in determining the expected and actual behaviour of individual group members.

Liking

One way of looking at intra-relationships is through a technique known as *sociometry* devised by Moreno (1934). By using this technique investigators can show patterns of human relationships between members of a group. Such relationships depend upon the personal choices made by individuals (for example, selection and rejection) and may be represented diagrammatically in a sociogram using a number of conventional symbols which are clarified in the example given below.

A sociometric test shows the positive and/or negative feelings which individuals have towards others within their group.

Example of a sociogram

A workgroup of ten individuals has decided to form a sub-group in order to complete a whole group task. In order to ensure that the members of the sub-group can work together, the whole group has decided to use sociometric techniques to choose the most effective sub-group.

Each member has been asked to vote on their preferences in answer to the question 'With whom would you like to work?'.

In answer to this question, each member gives three choices.

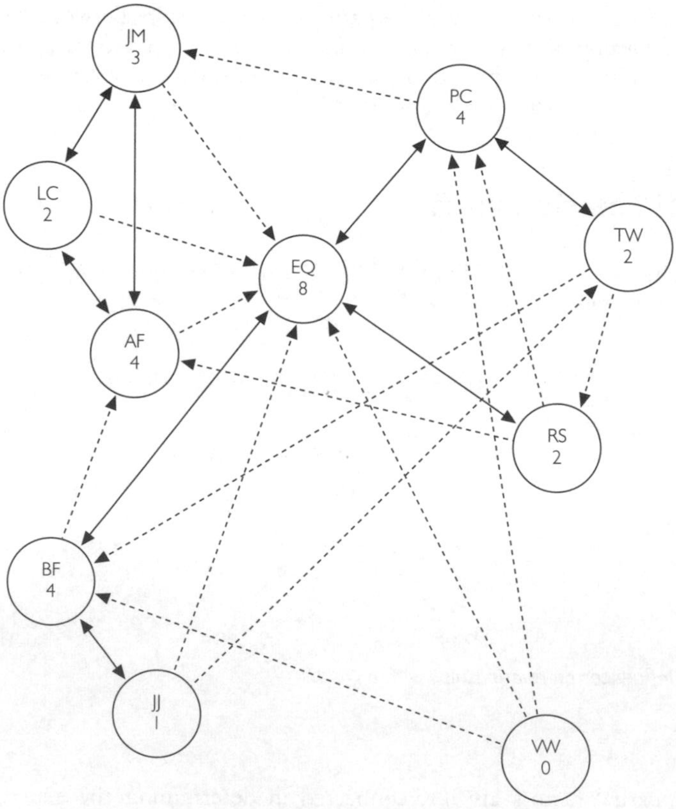

Figure 6.6 A possible outcome of a sociometric analysis for the above scenario

An analysis of the responses can reveal:

(a) those who received the largest number of votes (stars);
(b) those who receive few or no votes (isolates);
(c) those who vote for one another (mutual pairs).

Thus the sociogram efficiently shows the existence of any sub-groupings within the main group – the aim of the exercise.

Key
Letters within the circles (e.g. LC) represent individuals within the group.

Choices of individuals are represented by lines connecting the circles showing the direction of the choice.

Solid lines (————————) show mutual choices.

Dotted lines (– – – –) show one-way choices.

The number of votes received by each individual is shown inside the circle.

Reviewing the sociogram

1 Identify the star.

2 Who is the isolate?

3 There are three individuals which represent a mutual trio – who are they?

You should have identified EQ, VW, and LC-JM-AF, respectively.

Using sociograms in the workplace

The use of sociograms requires participant observation techniques. However, observation alone is inefficient. As with a number of diagnostic tools, it can be dangerous to use the technique without the required training. For example, if the test is used to highlight students who have not adjusted to the class, the highlighting of an isolate could well make that individual feel even less valuable. However, with professionally trained facilitators, sociograms can be used in a number of ways, for example:

- for highlighting required modification to group composition;
- for selecting and training potential leaders;
- for turning dysfunctional conflict into functional conflict.

The utilisation of sociometric testing must be comprehensive and represent a pattern of choice at any stated point in time and in relation to a stated aspect of the group's function (as in the scenario above), such as selection, rejection, repulsion or indifference.

As with all behaviour, the interactions will be situational and contingent.

Status

Status is the prestige ranking of an individual within a group and can be achieved in a number of ways. It can most obviously be conferred by the formal authority and responsibility associated with a particular job. An individual may be able to achieve status within a group through his existing position within the organisation's hierarchy, for instance because he is a manager. Alternatively he may gain status because of the official role he is given when a formal group is set up, for example as its chairman. In these circumstances, that individual has a formal status within the group.

Formal status is the prestige associated with a position, as distinct from the person who may occupy that position. However, status can be achieved in other ways – a group may confer its own status on group members irrespective of their formal status. This is known as *social status* – the relative prestige an individual has as measured by a group.

Such social status may be achieved in a variety of ways. It may be linked, for example, to the liking structure of the group. A charismatic individual able to form strong social bonds with other group members may achieve a higher social status within the group than another group member of equivalent, or even superior, formal status. The ability to identify with and articulate group norms may also confer status. Likewise, conflict with the norms established by the rest of the group can diminish the esteem in which a group member is held by the group as a whole.

The conferring, or withholding, of social status within a group can be a powerful weapon in controlling the behaviour of individual group members. Status is important to people's belonging and self-esteem needs, encouraging them to conform to group norms as a condition of achieving status within the group.

The preservation of status within a group can be a source of dysfunctional conflict.

Power

Power is the ability to influence the behaviour of another individual. An individual's position within a group will also be affected by the power she is able to wield within the group. French and Raven (1962) carried out research to determine the sources of power which a manager (the agent) uses to influence another individual (the target) – their work has become very influential in the field of organisational behaviour. In this study they identified five forms of interpersonal power that managers use:

- reward
- coercive
- legitimate
- referent
- expert.

Reward power

This is power based on the agent's ability to control the rewards that a target wants. Some examples of reward power are:

- salary increases
- bonuses
- performance related pay
- promotions.

Effective use of reward power may result in increased performance but only if the target perceives a correlation between performance and rewards. Therefore, the manager needs to be explicit about the required behaviours of targets that will be rewarded and then make the relationship between that behaviour and the reward very clear.

Coercive power

This is the power that is based on an agent's ability to cause an unpleasant experience for a target and can be exampled as:

- force
- threats of punishment
- verbal abuse
- withdrawal of support.

Legitimate power

This is similar to authority; it is power that is based on position and mutual agreement. The agent and the target agree that the agent has the right to influence the target. It is irrelevant that the manager believes she has the right to influence her workforce. For legitimate power to be effective, the target must believe that the manager has the *right* to tell him what to do.

Referent power

This is an elusive power that is based on charisma – interpersonal attraction. The agent has power over the target because the latter identifies with the agent or wants to model himself on that agent. Transformational (charismatic) leaders tend to have this sort of power. With referent power the agent need not be superior to the target but they are generally most usually individualistic and respected by the target.

Expert power

This is similar to referent power and one individual can have both. Expert power is the power that exists when an agent has information or knowledge that the target wants and needs. Expert power may well work in situations when:

- the target trusts that the information given is correct;
- information is relevant to the target;
- information is of use to the target;
- the target's perception of the agent as an expert is understood to be crucial.

Power: a summary

French and Raven (1962) concluded that if managers use the whole range of power sources on a situational basis, they will be more powerful and will exert greater power.

Power can be aligned with formal status, or it can be exercised through other channels. A charismatic individual who has strong social bonds with other team members, who is able to articulate group norms, and who has a strong grasp of how to achieve group goals, can exercise power within a group out of proportion to his or her formal status and authority.

Since the work of French and Raven most of the research on power has been concentrated upon trying to find out which type of interpersonal power is the most effective within groups. Podsakoff and Schriesheim (1985) reanalysed French and Raven's (1962) work with some surprising outcomes: specifically related to compliance, organisational effectiveness, and the power of the future.

Reward power and coercive power lead to compliance: employees do what their managers tell them – at least temporarily – if that manager threatens them with punishment or offers a reward. However, this is a dangerous use of available power because it might well require the agent to be physically present and/or constantly watchful of the behaviour of individuals within the workforce in order to apply the punishment or reward. The result of this constant surveillance is uncomfortable for both the target and the agent and could result in mutual dependency: the employee will not work unless supervised.

Legitimate power can also lead to compliance. If ordered to do something because the manager says 'I am telling you to do it because I'm the boss', then the subordinate will comply. However, work carried out by Rahim (1989) showed that the use of legitimate power has not been linked to effectiveness within the organisation. It follows, therefore, that in organisations where agents use legitimate power, the organisational goals are not always achieved.

However, referent power does appear to be related to organisational effectiveness. The problem is that such power is the most dangerous because it is potentially extensive and intensive in altering the behaviour of others. Such transformational (charismatic) people are leaders with followers and to avoid the dangers such people must have an accompanying sense of responsibility for others.

According to Naisbitt and Aburdene (1990), of the five sources of power identified by French and Raven (1962), expert power has been referred to as 'the power of the future'. It is through expert power that vital skills, abilities and knowledge are disseminated within the organisation. Workers will internalise everything which they observe and learn from people they perceive to be experts.

Whilst French and Raven (1962) identified the sources or forms of power within organisation, McClelland (1975) took a stronger stance on power as it worked in groups: the 'right' versus the 'wrong' kind of power to use in the workplace.

Positive	P	Negative
social power	O	personal power
contemporary		traditional
evolving	W	used for personal gain
used to create intrinsic		win-lose power
motivation	E	agent treats target as object
used to accomplish		agent wants to get ahead
individual goals	R	power is domination over others

Figure 6.7 The two sides of power according to McClelland (1975)

McClelland (1975) favoured the use of social power by managers. His work indicated that effective managers or group leaders were those who had a high intrinsic need for social power together with a relatively low need for affiliation. He additionally found from his research that agents who used power successfully – regardless of its source – tended to exhibit four key power-oriented characteristics as outlined in Table 6.3.

Table 6.3 McClelland's (1975) key power-oriented characteristics

Power-oriented characteristics	Components
Belief in the authority system.	1 Believes organisation is important. 2 Believes organisation system is valid. 3 Comfortable when influencing. 4 Happy being influenced. 5 Source of power is authority system of which they are a part.
Preference for work and discipline.	1 Enjoy their work. 2 Very orderly in all they do. 3 Committed to the work ethic.
Altruism.	1 Publicly put the organisation and its needs before their own needs. 2 Believe people should have what they are entitled to. 3 Believe people should have what they have earned.

McClelland (1975) was particularly strong on discussing how power should be properly used. When power is utilised for the good of the group, rather than for individual gain, such power is positive.

Intergroup sources of power

Dobbs (1993) reported that in traditional organisations managers tended to make the decision as to who receives what kind of information and also in what detail. In the emerging lean organisations where employees are empowered and work in autonomous teams, all members of the organisation receive the information they require in order to achieve the team goals. Groups or teams within an organisation may use power from several sources of which two are key and give the team control power:

- resource dependency
- strategic contingencies.

A key source of inter-group power is the control of critical resources. If one group holds and controls resources which are required by another group, the first group holds the power and can thus influence the action of the less powerful group. Such is the *resource dependency* model – where one source of group power is the control of valuable resources.

Groups/teams also have power in that they control *strategic contingencies* – that is, the activities that other groups depend on in order to meet their objectives. There are three factors which give a group control over strategic contingency:

- the ability to cope with uncertainty (i.e. reduce uncertainty in others)
- a high degree of centrality (i.e. function is central to the organisation's success)
- non-substitutability (i.e. when the group's activities are difficult to replace).

Role

Many of the factors discussed above converge into determining an individual's role within a group. A role is the expected pattern of behaviour associated with an individual occupying a particular position within a group or an organisation – it is the part an individual plays within the work group and is, by definition, a social factor.

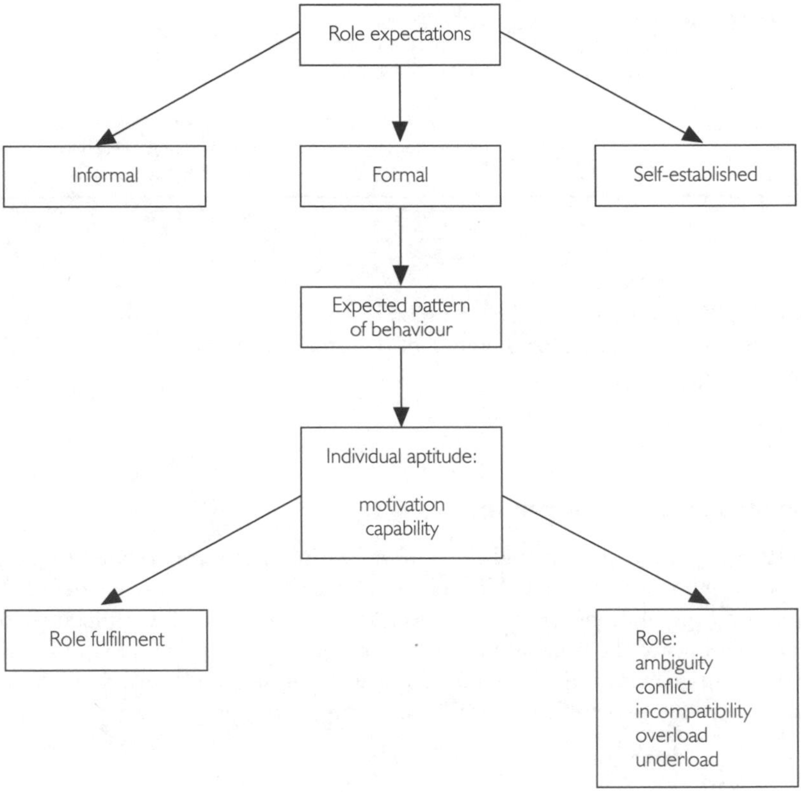

Figure 6.8 The components of role

There are two ways in which one can view the concept of role. One school of thought considers it to be what is known as a *perceived role*, which is when the individual believes that he has to behave in an expected way. The second is known as the *enacted role* which is the behaviour which the individual actually engages in. These are *role demands* which relate to the role or part an individual plays in the organisation or work group. A role demands formal (job related and explicit) requirements as well as informal (social and implicit) requirements. People within the organisation or work group expect another person in a particular role to act in a certain way and they transmit these expectations formally and informally. The individual then perceives the role expectations with varying levels of accuracy and then enacts her role.

However, there can be a misperception which results in either *role ambiguity* or *role conflict*. Role ambiguity occurs when an individual is uncertain about the exact nature of a particular role and role conflict arises when demands of or messages about roles are essentially clear but also somewhat contradictory.

Role incompatibility occurs when the role of the incumbent contains incompatible elements. The cause of this is usually the individual perceiving his role in one way whilst others perceive it in a different way.

Example of role incompatibility

A new manager has joined a company and she feels that in order to keep her subordinates in order it is necessary for her to engage in an autocratic style of leadership. However, the subordinates are used to a consultative style of management where they had responsibility and autonomy for the job and were expecting the new manager to continue with that style of management.

Role overload and underload are connected. *Role overload* is the result of an individual not being able to cope with several roles simultaneously. This may well be the case even when all the roles are required for that individual's tasks. When the organisation does not utilise the individual's skills in a way that that individual could manage, this is called *role underload*.

The key issue is that when a group is observed it can be seen that people are behaving in different ways and doing certain activities. A leading tool for describing and analysing the interactions of group members is one invented by Bales (1950), which he called Interaction Process Analysis (IPA). Using the latter a record is made on a schedule of the number of times a particular category of behaviour occurs, by whom and to whom, within a specific time. Table 6.4 gives the key areas and categories of behaviour related to the observation of intra-group behaviour.

Bales (1950) felt that his classification system was comprehensive enough to cover all actions within groups and used it himself to put forward a thesis of group functioning. He argued that group behaviour could be explained and managed by using such areas of classification given in the analysis above. However, he concentrated on how individuals expressed themselves whilst problem-solving but neglected to look at the aspect of non-verbal communication and ignored the powerful messages of kinesics, proxemics and chronemics. This system also makes the assumption that the observer perceives the interaction taking place the same way as do those who are actually behaving in that manner.

Table 6.4 Bales' (1950) Interaction Process Analysis

Area		Categories of behaviour
SOCIAL-EMOTIONAL AREA	1	**Shows solidarity**, raises others' status, gives help, reward.
	2	**Shows tension release**, jokes, laughs, shows satisfaction.
POSITIVE REACTIONS	3	**Agrees**, shows passive acceptance, understands, concurs, complies.
TASK AREA	4	**Gives suggestion**, direction, implying autonomy for other.
ATTEMPTED ANSWERS	5	**Gives opinon**, evaluation, analysis, expresses feeling, wish.
	6	**Gives orientation**, information repeats, clarifies, confirms.
TASK AREA	7	**Asks for orientation**, information, repetition, confirmation.
QUESTIONS	8	**Asks for opinion**, evaluation analysis, expression of feeling.
	9	**Asks for suggestion**, direction, possible ways of action.
SOCIAL-EMOTIONAL AREA	10	**Disagrees**, shows passive rejection, formality, withholds help.
NEGATIVE REACTIONS	11	**Shows tension**, asks for help, withdraws out of field.
	12	**Shows antagonism**, deflates others' status, defends or asserts self.

Group processes

Group process is the order of interaction between members of a group and includes the verbal and non-verbal interactions of all members of the group. Therefore, group process is closely related to group structure, being the contribution that all members bring to the group.

Example of group processes in action

Imagine that you are a member of a tutorial group considering some aspect of organisational behaviour.

If you observe your fellow members, you may see that some individuals behave consistently with preferred behaviours, e.g. using a sense of humour, chattering rather more than others do, or being serious and quiet.

Such a set of behaviours can be perceived by others to be the adoption of a particular role within the group. As Bales (1950) showed, people do adopt specific roles when working in groups. There is more about this aspect of group behaviour in Chapter 7 where group effectiveness is discussed.

Rackham (1971) used a Behaviour Analysis (BA) system where categories of behaviour were observed, each accompanied by a specific description. This was a development of Bales (1950) and was more detailed in its approach because it considered the non-verbal aspects of interpersonal relationships.

Table 6.5 Behaviour Analysis, after Rackham (1971)

Category	**Description**
Proposing	A behaviour which offers a new concept, suggestion or course of action (and is actionable).
Building*	A behaviour which extends or develops a proposal which has been made by another (and is actionable).
Supporting*	A behaviour which involves a conscious or direct declaration of support or agreement with another person or her concepts.
Disagreeing	A behaviour which involves a conscious or direct declaration of difference of opinion or criticism of another's concepts.
Defending/Attacking**	A behaviour which attacks another person or defensively strengthens an individual's own position. Attacking behaviour usually involves overt value judgements and often contains emotional overtones.
Blocking/Difficulty Stating	A behaviour which places a block or difficulty in the path of a proposal or concept without offering a reasoned statement of disagreement. Blocking/Difficulty Stating behaviour therefore tends to be rather bald, e.g. 'It won't work' or 'We couldn't possibly accept that.'
Open	A behaviour which exposes the individual who performs it to risk of ridicule or loss of status. This behaviour may be considered as the opposite of Defending/Attacking, including within this category admissions of mistakes or inadequacies provided that these are made in a non-defensive manner.
Testing Understanding*	A behaviour which seeks to establish whether or not an earlier contribution has been understood.
Summarising	A behaviour which summarises, or restates in compact form, the content of previous discussions or considerations.
Seeking Information	A behaviour which seeks facts, opinions or clarification from another individual or individuals.
Giving Information	A behaviour which offers facts, opinions or clarification from another individual or individuals.
Bringing in**	A behaviour which excludes, or attempts to exclude, another member.

Key * What 'successful' groups do.
** What 'successful' groups do not do.

It can be seen, therefore, that group processes are very important in the workplace. To use the example of social loafing mentioned earlier and that of synergy ($1 + 1 = 3$), sometimes the sum of the formula is not always 3! In group tasks where each member's contribution is not clearly visible, there is a tendency for individuals to decrease their effort. That is, social loafing illustrates a process loss as a result of using groups. However, group processes can also produce positive results and impact on a group's actual effectiveness, as shown in Figure 6.9.

Potential group effectiveness	+	Process gains	–	Process losses	=	Actual group effectiveness

Figure 6.9 Effects of group processes

Leadership structure

Work groups are not disorganised gangs – they all have a structure which shapes the behaviour of individual members and makes it possible to explain and predict a large portion of individual behaviour within the group. Additionally, the structure affects the performance of the group itself. Another key variable is that of leadership.

Studies into the interaction between individuals in small groups have concentrated on the importance of the emergent (informal) leadership in accomplishing the goals of the group. An *informal leader* is an individual whose influence within the group develops over a period of time and it is based on the individual's unique ability to help the group achieve its goals. There are three key types of leaders related to groups:

- multiple leaders
- effective team leaders
- formal leaders.

Multiple leaders

Conventional wisdom states that any group will have one individual who emerges as the leader of that group. However, a group has at any one time a number of goals which could, for example, be either relations oriented or task oriented. For example, one leader may be more inclined to lead by using interpersonal relationships whilst another may be concerned with concentrating on the task rather than the needs of the individuals who are working towards achieving the task. One individual may not have all the personal characteristics required to achieve the group's objectives. Informal leaders of work groups are not likely to emerge unless the formal leader (e.g. the designated project team leader) ignores the task related goals or lacks the required interpersonal skills to effect their success. Relations oriented leaders of work groups generally emerge informally.

Effective team leaders

The leader of the group or team will influence all the key aspects of that group. Variables such as the size, composition of members, roles, norms, and goals are all within the influence of the leader. Therefore, the latter will assume a key role in both the intra- and inter-relationships of the group. For example, he or she may screen potential new members, and moderate dysfunctional communication between group members.

Formal leadership

Most work groups have a formal leader who is identified by a role title such as 'Project Leader', 'Cell Leader', or 'Task Force Leader'. In the current context, there are some key issues which relate to leadership and the performance of a group.

The studies which have concentrated on the effects of leader traits on group performance have generally provided inconclusive results. Far more promising results have been obtained when situational variables (e.g. the task structure, characteristics of followers) have been used as moderating variables. If it is a goal of the group to achieve high group satisfaction, participative leadership appears to be more effective than autocratic leadership. But in some situations, the group can be guided by a directive, autocratic leader who will encourage the group to outperform its participative counterpart.

The bulk of contemporary research studies has focused on trying to identify the contingency variables associated with leader success: that is, when should a leader be democratic, when should a leader be autocratic, and when genuinely laissez-faire?

CASE STUDY

Team working

Team leaders at Leyland Trucks earn extra career development opportunities instead of higher pay than other team members.

After introducing a flatter structure the organisation axed traditional shopfloor supervisors. The incentive for team leaders to take on more responsibility would be the chance to acquire skills rather than cash. The use of a flatter structure created more opportunities for shopfloor staff to move on and act as skilled floaters, slotting in where they were needed.

Fellow team members pick the person to lead them, although they also have to pass a battery of tests before their role is confirmed. Such leaders can also be deselected by team members – this has only happened once at Leyland Trucks as a result of a mutual decision.

Leyland Trucks admit that they did not always have such a strong tradition of employee involvement. They mismanaged the introduction of technology by not involving the staff. As a result, a financial crisis occurred and a new approach which emphasised the importance of team working, motivating and listening to staff's concerns followed.

Adapted from N. Daly, 'Firm gears teams to career development' in *Personnel Today*, 2 October 1997, p. 2

Strengths and weaknesses of teamwork

Teamwork has become a key feature in modern management theory and practice with a belief that by grouping employees into problem-solving task teams, organisations will be able to:

- empower workers
- create cross-departmental fertilisation
- level ineffective hierarchies.

However, there are limitations to the application of teamwork methods in the workplace and, according to Griffiths (1997), these have been investigated by various managers and academics. Some of the concerns are as follows.

Overemphasis on harmony

Conflict is discouraged yet turning dysfunctional conflict into functional conflict (see Chapter 9) is a creative process and teams often provide their best work when disagreements are put to positive use. Some team leaders positively try to discourage discord because of a fear that it might split up the team's cohesiveness although it could discourage groupthink.

Too much discord

Whilst a level of tension can be functional it is possible that excessive tension may also destroy team effectiveness. Team members tend to disagree less and become more productive when they have equal access to up-to-date information. Where there are instances of lack of information, dysfunctional conflict arises and this, in turn, escalates into interpersonal resentment and time wasting on politicking.

Emphasis on individualism

In the 1980s teamworking did not help Apple Computers because of the emphasis the organisation placed early in its existence on individualism. As Griffiths (1997) reported: 'While individual creativity served the company well in its initial phase, growth heightened the need for communication between employees' (p. 12).

At Apple Computers the conflict which arose from lack of information tended to escalate into resentment between individuals. As a result the workforce was individually assigned to cross-functional teams which had the authority to set corporate objectives and goals. However, such a strategy failed because the units within the organisation did not interact: marketing, research and development, and manufacturing, worked in isolation and thus undermined the whole organisation.

As will be seen in Chapter 9, culture is a key organisational concept and when the dominant culture of an organisation stresses the value of individual achievement, responsibility and accountability, rather than collectivism, teamworking will be ineffective.

Even when an organisation does value the collective efforts of work-based teams, these are often undermined by salaries, promotion, and performance-related pay being individually based. Employees need to perceive that working as a member of a team is important to their individual careers because if this is not so, they will behave as individuals rather than collectively.

Feeling of powerlessness

In order to be effective, teams must be able to influence organisational decisions. If teams do not have this capacity they are likely to expend their energies on meaningless tasks which will, cumulatively, result in workers believing that teamwork is not worthwhile.

The relationship between empowerment and teamwork

It is through the concept of empowerment that workers can be persuaded of the importance of teamwork. According to Goldratt (1996): 'empowerment is recognised as one of the necessary conditions for an effective organisation' (p. 9).

Empowerment is an aspect of organisational design (see Chapter 8) which allows individual workers more autonomy, discretion, responsibility, and decision-making powers. It can be a motivational technique (see Chapter 4) and has led to unsupervised work teams becoming very important. It is through empowerment that high-performance work teams come into operation and reluctant members of a team can come to understand the importance of a project.

Failure of senior management to work well together

If senior managers do not work well together there are problems created because team members will attend different meetings which have different priorities. This is linked to problem-solving – if senior management creates problems the employees cannot be expected to be loyal to their superiors: with different priorities comes little common ground.

Meeting-itis

Teams should not do all things together but should prepare their thoughts and contributions independently thus encouraging proactive discussion and creativity with increased choices.

Seeing teams as a solution for all problems

Some people perceive the introduction of teams as a solution to all problems within an organisation. Although teams are suitable for many activities they are not suitable for others, and they should be formed with care being given to the rationale for their use.

The effectiveness of technology has offset the concern that teams cannot be formed if the members are scattered. However, *virtual teams* are now common, which means that team members can work together even though they may be thousands of miles apart. Team members communicate through video conferencing, electronic mail (e-mail), and shared software programmes. It is through such computer networks that the world is becoming a global village. However, the use of virtual techniques has advantages and disadvantages as shown in Table 6.6.

Table 6.6 Advantages and disadvantages of virtual teams

Advantages	**Disadvantages**
no timewasting around the vending machine	isolation from colleagues
	training required so that individuals can cope
members can work in different locations and time zones	cultural differences when teams span several countries
reduction in travel costs	individuals must meet personally before team is set up
faster decision-making	
team members can meet in relationships 'real time'	individuals need physical contact occasionally to build and team culture
	reduction in richness of 'face to face' interaction
	individual is overlooked because technology has priority

One organisation which has adopted virtual teams is Levi Strauss.

CASE STUDY

Levi's links offices to Brussels HQ

Virtual teams have been created in Levi Strauss's merchandising area in Europe, following a departmental reorganisation. Responsibility for developing new clothing lines has shifted from autonomous teams in separate countries to virtual teams reporting to Brussels. This has meant that some staff from national affiliates have moved to Brussels while others have stayed behind and joined virtual teams of eight to twelve people scattered throughout Europe and working on specific projects, such as choosing fabrics and selecting styles. This has resulted in staff having two bosses – their local merchandising manager and their team which will only meet a few times each year.

Teams use e-mail, internal mail and telephone but not video conferencing because it is not suited to fabrics, which staff need to see and feel. However, the organisation has plans to introduce video conferencing soon.

The challenges in building teams have improved team members' English, particularly in southern Europe and France, and encouraged new ways of thinking. The team members now think beyond their own affiliate and see things in a European perspective.

Adapted from P. McCurry, 'Levi's links offices to Brussels HQ' in *Personnel Today*, 3 July 1997, p. 22

From the human resources standpoint, the organisation sees it as essential that the team members are brought together on teambuilding workshops because individuals must feel that they are part of a network and that they belong together.

The organisation feels that it can build a virtual structure, but can only do so on the foundation of an existing human network. Team members are also coached in project work which includes how to structure a project, defining roles and tasks, and measuring progress.

As the above case shows, the disadvantages of virtual teams can be overcome with virtual teams being a proactive empowerment concept. Levi Strauss now looks to Europe as a single market rather than as containing many different markets and so it uses virtual teams which are also high performance work teams.

High performance work teams

These are not new. Vaill (1982) first worked in this area, stating that such teams exhibited certain characteristics in that they:

- measure their excellence against a known external standard;
- perform beyond what is believed to be their personal best;
- improve in terms of excellence on previous performance;
- are judged by informed observers to be substantially better than what was required;
- use fewer resources than were thought to be necessary;
- are viewed as positive examples of sources of ideas and inspiration;
- are perceived to meet the cultural ideals;
- are the only ones who can do that particular task.

High performance work teams and empowerment are closely intertwined because the latter is brought about by the former. An increasing number of United Kingdom organisations have begun to empower their workers – mostly at the bottom end of the organisation. Such organisations include The Body Shop, Virgin Atlantic, and Unipart.

The Japanese approach to teamwork

Current developments in teamworking have their basis in the rise of the economic power of Japan. This power was attributed to Japan's reliance on teamworking within its organisations whereas the West concentrated on individualism rather than on collectivist ideas. Pascale and Athos (1982) stated:

> Because performance is valued less for its own sake than for the sake of the group, it is easier for each member to accede to the will of the majority. Even Japanese industrialists, while possibly as strongly motivated by profit and self-interest as any others, pursue self-interest in the name of the collective interest. Japanese organizational charts show only collective units, not individual positions or titles or names. (p. 127)

Having investigated the principles related to groups and teams together with how they behave, since the goals of the organisation have to be met it is now necessary to move on to the effectiveness of groups and teams.

Questions for discussion

1 Name an organisation that has successfully used high performance groups and empowerment and identify the factors that have made the organisation successful in these areas. Discuss whether the team approach has made a difference to performance and in what ways.

2 Think of a person who you believe is a particularly good team member and identify the reasons why you consider this to be so. Now name a person who is a problem team member and identify the factors which makes this person a problem.

3 Identify the most effective group (or team) of which you are/were a member and identify the reasons why that group (or team) was so effective.

References and further reading

Adair, J.H., 1985, *Effective Team Building* (London: Gower)

Bales, R.F., 1950, *Interaction Process Analysis* (Reading, MA: Addison-Wesley)

Bass, B.M. and Ryterband, E.C., 1979 (2nd edn), *Organizational Psychology* (London: Allyn and Bacon)

Bowey, A.M. and Connelly, R., 'Application of the Concept of Group Working' (unpublished workpaper, Glasgow: University of Strathclyde)

Daly, N., 'Firm gears teams to career development' in *Personnel Today*, 2 October 1997

Dobbs, J.H., 'How to Build Self-Esteem' in *Training and Development*, February 1993, p. 56

French, J.R.P. and Raven, B., 1962, 'The Bases of Power' in D. Cartwright (ed.), *Group Dynamics: Research and Theory* (Evanston, Ill: Row & Peterson)

Goldratt, E.M., 1996, *Empowerment misalignments between responsibility and authority* (Maidenhead: The Goldratt Institute)

Griffiths, V., 'Teamworker's own goals' in *Financial Times*, 18 July 1997

Hatch, M.J., 1997, *Organization Theory: Modern Symbolic and Postmodern Perspectives* (Oxford: Oxford University Press)

Homans, G., 1950, *The Human Group* (New York: Harcourt Brace & World)

Kolesar, P.J., 'Visions, values, milestones: Paul O'Neill starts total quality at Alcoa' in *California Management Review*, Spring 1993, p. 146

Mayo, E., 1933, *Human Problems of an Industrial Civilization* (New York: Macmillan)

McClelland, D.E., 1975, *Power: The Inner Experience* (New York: Irvington)

McCurry, P., 'Levi's links offices to Brussels HQ' in *Personnel Today*, 3 July 1997, p. 22

Moreno, J.L., 1934 *Who Shall Survive?* (Washington DC: Nervous and Mental Diseases Publishing Company)

Naisbitt, J. and Aburdene, P., 1990, *Megatrends 2000* (New York: Morrow)

Olaniran, B.A., 'Group performance in computer-mediated and Face-to-Face communication media', in *Management Communication Quarterly*, 1994, Vol. 7, pp. 256–281

Pascale, R.T. and Athos, A.G., 1982, *The Art of Japanese Management* (Harmondsworth: Penguin Books)

Podsakoff, P.M. and Schriesheim, C., 1985, 'Field Studies of French and Raven's Bases of Power: Critique, Reanalysis, and Suggestions for Future Research' in *Psychological Bulletin*, Vol. 97, pp. 387–411

Rackham, N. (ed.), 1971, *Developing Interactive Skills* (Northampton: Wellens)

Rahim, M.A., 'Relationships of Leader Power to Compliance and Satisfaction with Supervision: Evidence from a National Sample of Managers' in *Journal of Management*, December 1989, pp. 545–546.

Schein, E.H., 1988 (3rd edn), *Organizational Psychology* (London: Prentice-Hall)

Spector, P.E., 1996, *Industrial and Organizational Psychology: Research and Practice* (Toronto: Wiley)

Tuckman, B. and Jensen, N., 1977, 'Stages of Small Group Development Revisited' in *Group and Organisational Studies*, Vol. 2, pp. 419–427

Vaill, P., 'The purposing of high-performing systems' in *Organizational Dynamics*, Autumn 1982, pp. 23–39

7 Group dynamics and effectiveness

Learning objectives

After studying this chapter you should be able to:

- evaluate the group as a decision-making unit;
- identify the advantages and disadvantages of group decision-making;
- compare various teambuilding models;
- assess the various ways members of teams communicate;
- understand the conflicts and pressures experienced by groups;
- discuss the characteristics of effective teams;
- analyse the role of leadership and group effectiveness;
- distinguish between various approaches to leadership;
- understand the role of culture in group dynamics.

CASE STUDY

The Lions share

Before they left for their tour of South Africa, every member of the British Lions rugby touring team participated in an intensive team-building and leadership programme. As they departed they carried with them small plastic cards reminding them of the code of conduct that would govern the way they should behave on the eight-week tour.

But the so-called Lions' laws were not imposed by the tour managers to prevent bad publicity at a time when the public's interest in rugby union is booming. Instead, the code was drawn up by the players themselves on a five-day leadership and team-development programme.

The pre-tour training did not only consist of physical training – as was the case in the past – but also enabled players to get to know the people they would be working with closely over the coming two months. The course interspersed rugby training with classroom-based activities, retaining the players' interest while stressing team development both on and off the field. The task was to bring together a squad of 47 people which included everyone from the baggage carrier to the secretary – as well as the players.

The initial task was to break the ice because many of the participants had never met each other – let alone worked together. The team-building exercises required small groups to carry out various activities which required that they support one another and work as a team. One person had to trust others in the same way as they have to on the pitch. The players welcomed a change from playing rugby and most considered that the team development activities were also important in themselves. Ian McGeehan, the head coach, believes that rugby is the ultimate support game and whatever a player does as part of a team will affect someone else 15 seconds later and although talent was important, players needed the right attitude.

As a result of the team development training the Lions have gelled together so that each member understands what it takes to behave as a team and what is required in terms of planning and decision-making. The non-playing staff agreed with this view, stating that it was invaluable in getting to know everybody's personalities so that they could all work together as a team.

Adapted from N. Merrick, 'The Lions share' in *People Management*, 12 June 1997, pp. 34–35, 37

Introduction

As the above case and the previous chapter illustrate, the concept of groups and teams is complex. The purpose of this chapter is to continue to investigate some other issues which help to make a group effective in achieving its goals: thus the activity of a group as a decision-making body will be further investigated. Effective communication is a key concept, as is the role of conflict and the consideration of the fact that groups may fail to meet their aims. These latter concepts form the basis of group effectiveness with its associated considerations of leadership, inter-group relations and groups across cultures.

The group as a decision-making unit

Some of the factors which influence a group as a structure of social relationships were considered in Chapter 6 and such factors exercise an important influence on the status, role and behaviour of individual group members, and on the dynamics of the group.

This social structure, therefore, has an important impact on the nature and quality of decision-making within a group. Most groups, whether formal or informal, exist to carry out certain tasks. This will be the case whether a group is a formal project team completing its task within the official parameters it has been given, or an informal group such as the bank wiring room team investigated in Elton Mayo's Hawthorne Studies previously discussed, where the team established and enforced its own pace of work against the perceived management pressure to increase its workload.

To understand the interaction of a group's social structure with its decision-making role, it is necessary to first look at the nature of group decision-making in more detail than in Chapter 6. When organisation theorists discuss decision-making they tend to refer to it happening at all levels of the organisation, with top management concentrating on the strategic decisions and the lower levels on day-to-day issues.

The decision-making process can be broken down into detailed steps as shown in Table 7.1 below.

Table 7.1 Breakdown of the key stages of the decision-making model

Decision-making	Description	Typical skills needed
Initiation	proposing tasks or goals defining a group problem providing ideas to start discussion	courage imagination leadership analytical
Information-seeking and gathering	requesting facts seeking information and evidence to enable group to explore relevant issues	inquisitiveness detachment research
Criticism	pointing out weaknesses in evidence and ideas	critical willingness to face conflict
Variation	suggesting alternative approaches or solutions to problems	imagination flexibility detachment
Evaluation	deciding between alternatives to find the best solution	objectivity balance mediation patience analysis
Clarifying and summarising	pulling together ideas clarifying choices	clarity detachment
Choice	deciding final plan of action	decisiveness concern for each solution leadership
Affirmation	gaining consensus for final action plan	conciliation
Planning	deciding how to implement plan	meticulousness
Implementation	carrying out the plan	persistence

As Table 7.1 shows, each of these stages in the decision-making process required different skills and characteristics. The first stage, for example, requires leadership and imagination to institute the process. The second requires critical skills in unpicking ideas and isolating their weaknesses. Later stages involve meticulousness in deciding how to implement the plan and persistence in its implementation. These can be characterised as task function being concerned with problem-solving.

A key issue for groups is that these skills are rarely contained within just one team member. They will be distributed amongst members of the group. Successful groups contain a range of personalities suited to differing stages in the decision-making process. The challenge in creating successful groups is to pick a balanced team and then to ensure that team members maximise their contribution to effective decision-making according to their task strengths.

CASE STUDY
Staff consultation seen as business necessity

Research backed by the European Commission has found clear benefits from involving staff in the decision-making process as employee consultation comes to the fore. The research covered 5,800 European employees and concluded that the more staff are involved in making decisions, the greater the benefits for the company. During the investigations, managers reported that there were significant rises in both quality and output when staff participated in the decision-making process and there were complementary reductions in throughput time and sickness absence. The biggest impact, however, was on quality where 92–95 per cent of managers contacted reported a positive improvement as a result of staff involvement. But nearly one in five employers do not use any form of staff participation.

Advocates of employee involvement point to the success of Japanese firms who have a long tradition in liaising with staff in decisions over immediate work issues. The European Commission has been spurred into action because of the public outcry over car maker Renault's decision to close its factory in Volvoorde, Belgium, without consulting the workers. This was a similar situation to Hoover's decision to shut its Dijon, France, factory. Hoover's move to switch production to Glasgow was the political trigger that led to the adoption of the European Works Council Directive.

However, although staff involvement is positive it is thought by some that the introduction of legislation is a good idea. Employees in many businesses account for a significant part of the cost of a product – some 50 per cent or even more. No company can ignore that fact since output must be maximised – the involvement of staff in work activities leads to higher productivity. Even so, macro solutions rarely work. The Renault situation should have been resolved at the micro level, just as improved performance in companies should come through initiatives rather than by imposition from European legislation.

The British government is as reluctant to introduce legislation, with the Foreign Secretary, Robin Cook, believing that the proposals of the European Commission would affect too many organisations – he stresses that the document is purely consultative and is not even a directive proposal. United Kingdom employers' groups are implacably opposed to the idea of national works councils because they believe it is just 'flavour of the month' and anti-competitive. They feel that if companies consider that consultation is the right approach then it is up to them, but it is not the responsibility of Brussels since management is there to ensure the long-term prosperity of a business.

However, some believe that, in the present political climate in the UK, with an increased emphasis on social dialogue the concerns of the employers could be realistically dealt with at local level. For example, where there is strong leadership – whether firms are committed to involving and consulting staff or are vehemently opposed to it – employers will obtain a successful outcome. Employers who believe that they should be able to base their decisions purely on business logic seem to be losing the argument because such decisions cannot be taken without reference to the larger figure. Economies are interdependent and members need to learn from each other. Europe has a social aspect and system of social provision that people do not wish to lose. It seems that political Europe is now convinced that it must address public opinion and give it something to show that Europe is more than monetary union and that people's needs should be taken into consideration.

Adapted from N. Daly, 'Staff consultation seen as business necessity' in *Personnel Today*, 19 June 1997, p. 15

Whatever the view of management, there is little doubt that the percentage of works councils will increase in the coming years. At mid-year 1997 the percentage of works councils in European firms, that is, the workforce representation in companies within Member States, stood at:

- Spain 59%
- Germany 58%
- Italy 46%
- Netherlands 33%
- France 25%
- Denmark 20%
- United Kingdom 13%
- Sweden 10%
- Ireland 9%
- Portugal 4%

With this development into workteams it is necessary that managers understand the factors which underlie the concept of teamworking.

Belbin (1981) and teambuilding

Research by Belbin (1981) into management teams was for a long time considered to be the principal guide for those wishing to build teams.

Table 7.2 Belbin's (1981) team roles

Type	Symbol	Typical features	Positive qualities	Allowable weaknesses
Company worker	CW	Conservative, dutiful, predictable.	Organising ability, practical common sense, hard-working, self-discipline.	Lack of flexibility, unresponsiveness to unproven ideas.
Chairman	CH	Calm, self-confident, controlled.	A capacity for treating and welcoming all potential contributors on their merits and without prejudice. A strong sense of objectives.	No more than ordinary in terms of intellect or creative ability.

Shaper	SH	Highly-strung, outgoing, dynamic.	Drive and a readiness to challenge inertia, ineffectiveness, complacency or self-deception.	Proneness to provocation, irritation and impatience.
Plant	PL	Individualistic, serious-minded, unorthodox.	Genius, imagination, intellect, knowledge.	Up in the clouds, inclined to disregard practical details or protocol.
Resource Investigator	RI	Extroverted, enthusiastic, curious, communicative.	A capacity for contacting people and exploring anything new. An ability to respond to challenge.	Liable to lose interest once the initial fascination has passed.
Monitor-Evaluator	ME	Sober, unemotional, prudent.	Judgement, discretion, hard-headedness.	Lacks inspiration or the ability to motivate others.
Team Worker	TW	Socially orientated, rather mild, sensitive.	An ability to respond to people and to situations, and to promote team spirit.	Indecisiveness at moments of crisis.
Completer-Finisher	CF	Painstaking, orderly, conscientious, anxious	A capacity for follow-through. Perfectionism.	A tendency to worry about small things. A reluctance to 'let go'.

If members of a team fulfil too few of the above roles, the danger is that the task will not get completed. In an age when change is rapid, it is important that each team has the full set of roles *in situ*. However, it is only a guide and should not act as an exact model for delineation of roles. Belbin (1993) developed the roles and renamed two of the roles because they were more in line with the terminology of today. He replaced 'Chairman' by 'Co-Ordinator', and 'Company Worker' was replaced with 'Implementer'. This may have been a move towards political correctness; however, he did add a further role: that of 'Specialist'. Figure 7.1 below shows the revised team roles.

Belbin's (1993) typology of team roles is an ideal, and can at best be utilised when a team is being conceived rather than when it is already in existence. However, in the workplace, membership of a group, for example a project team, is usually by function rather than by personal qualities. If a team is not communicating well or not achieving the task, the Belbin (1993) model can be used to diagnose any problems. Also, work groups tend to be small and the number of roles identified by Belbin (1993) (nine) may be more than the number of members within the group. Problem-solving teams tend to be smaller than those involved in information-collection and analysis, and so would not, by size, lend themselves to an adoption of the Belbin (1993) principles. The Belbin (1981 and 1993) typology is not the only approach to the selection of group members. There are a large number of consultants who offer their own typologies and people from outside the organisation might well be better able to view the membership of teams less emotively than

Roles and descriptions – team-role contribution			*Allowable weaknesses*
Plant:		Creative, imaginative, unorthodox. Solves difficult problems.	Ignores details. Too preoccupied to communicate effectively.
Resource Investigator:		Extrovert, enthusiastic, communicative. Explores opportunities. Develops contacts.	Overoptimistic. Loses interest once initial enthusiasm has passed.
Co-ordinator:		Mature, confident, a good chairperson. Clarifies goals, promotes decision-making. Delegates well.	Can be seen as manipulative. Delegates personal work.
Shaper:		Challenging, dynamic, thrives on pressure. Has the drive and courage to overcome obstacles.	Can provoke others. Hurts people's feelings.
Monitor Evaluator:	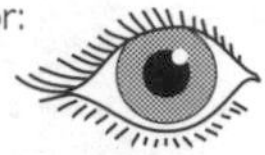	Sober, strategic and discerning. Sees all options. Judges accurately.	Lacks drive and ability to inspire others. Overly critical.
Team Worker:		Co-operative, mild, perceptive and diplomatic. Listens, builds, averts friction, calms the waters.	Indecisive in crunch situations. Can be easily influenced.
Implementer:		Disciplined, reliable, conservative and efficient. Turns ideas into practical actions.	Somewhat inflexible. Slow to respond to new possibilities.
Completer:		Painstaking, conscientious, anxious. Searches out errors and omissions. Delivers on time.	Inclined to worry unduly. Reluctant to delegate. Can be a nit-picker.
Specialist:		Single-minded, self-sharing dedicated. Provides knowledge and skills in rare supply.	Contributes on only a narrow front. Dwells on technicalities. Overlooks the 'big picture'.

Figure 7.1 Team roles as attributed to Belbin (1993)

internal consultants. Belbin's typology (1981 and 1993) has prominence simply because of the extent to which it is based on published research and because it is widely accepted as having focused attention on the importance of different member roles. However, organisations should research other sources and decide for themselves which approach best meets their needs. This contingency approach is often the most satisfactory way of putting together a framework on group work.

Balancing social and decision-making roles

As Belbin (1981 and 1993) emphasises, the potential weaknesses of differing kinds of team player indicate that keeping members of the group motivated, united and focused on overall group objectives, is essential to successful decision-making. However, the process of decision-making itself creates pressures on the group which require a second set of social skills, for example the ability to mediate when disagreement threatens to result in dysfunctional conflict. Work carried out in the USA around the same time as that of Bales (1950) identified skills which can be characterised as *task functions* (see Table 7.3) and *maintenance functions* (see Table 7.4), the latter being concerned with the emotional life and health of the group. However, Bales (1950) did additionally consider self-oriented behaviour through his classification system which encompassed all actions of individuals within a group – this is covered in detail in Chapter 6.

Table 7.3 Task functions

Initiating
Proposing tasks or goals. Defining a group problem, suggesting procedures or ideas for solving a problem.

Information or opinion seeking
Requesting facts, seeking relevant information about a group concern, asking for suggestions and ideas.

Information or opinion giving
Offering facts, providing relevant information about group concerns, stating beliefs, giving suggestions or ideas.

Clarifying or elaborating
Interpreting or reflecting ideas and suggestions, clearing up confusions, indicating alternatives and issues.

Summarising
Pulling together related ideas, restating suggestions after the group has discussed them, offering a decision or conclusion for the group to accept or reject.

Consensus testing
Sending up 'trial balloons' to see if a group is nearing a conclusion, checking with group to see how much agreement has been reached.

Table 7.4 Group building and maintenance factors

Encouraging
Friendly, warm and responsive to others, accepting others, utilising others' contributions, giving others opportunities for recognition.

Expressing group feelings
Sensing feelings, mood, relationships within group, sharing one's own feelings with other members.

Harmonising
Attempting to reconcile disagreements, reducing tension through 'pouring oil on troubled waters', getting people to explore their differences.

Compromising
When own idea or status involved in a dysfunctional conflict, offering to compromise own position, admitting error, disciplining oneself to maintain group cohesion.

Gatekeeping
Keeping communication channels open, facilitating participation of others, suggesting procedure for sharing opportunity to discuss group problems.

Setting standards
Expressing standards for group to achieve, applying standards in evaluating group functioning and production.

Both Bales (1950) and the USA National Training Laboratory Studies (1952) were based on the work of Benne and Sheats (1948) which is still used by behaviourists who continue to study group behaviour. They divided the potential roles of members within a group into three categories:

- group task roles
- group maintenance roles
- individual roles.

Group task roles could only be defined if it was assumed that the task of a group was to select, define, and solve problems. Such roles could be carried out by the group leader or any one of the other members of the group. Benne and Sheats (1948) described the group task roles as:

- initiator-contributor
- information seeker
- opinion seeker
- information giver
- opinion giver
- elaborator
- co-ordinator
- orienter
- energiser
- critic of procedures
- energiser
- procedural technician
- recorder.

The *group maintenance roles* are those activities which are directed towards any behaviour which helps to build a group attitude or which aids in the maintenance of the group norms. These are often multi-roled and the leader or members may perform any of these roles:

- encourager
- harmoniser
- compromiser
- gatekeeper and expediter
- standard getter or ego ideal
- group observer and commentator
- follower.

The *individual roles* are those roles which aid the individuals within the group to meet their personal needs. As such they are not connected to the completion of the group tasks or to how the group functions:

- aggressor
- blocker
- recognition-seeker
- self-confessor
- dominator
- help-seeker
- special interest pleader.

Whichever analysis is used to form the basis of group roles and teambuilding, it is necessary to appreciate the considerations of situational issues and a contingency framework. With leaner, delayered organisations comes the need for individuals to be multi-roled and, as Belbin (1981 and 1993) indicated, individuals will be better able to function within a group if they are willing to develop roles which may not come naturally to them. Thus, training in team-building skills is a growing area of organisational effectiveness.

Communicating within groups

As was discussed in Chapter 3, communication is the process by which two or more people exchange information and share meaning. Effective communication within a group requires careful and experienced communication networks. A work-based team is a small-group network and it is possible to observe the patterns that emerge as the work of the group proceeds and information flows from some people in the group to others. There are four key patterns of communication as shown in Figure 7.2 below.

Key
The lines show the communication links most frequently used in workplace groups.

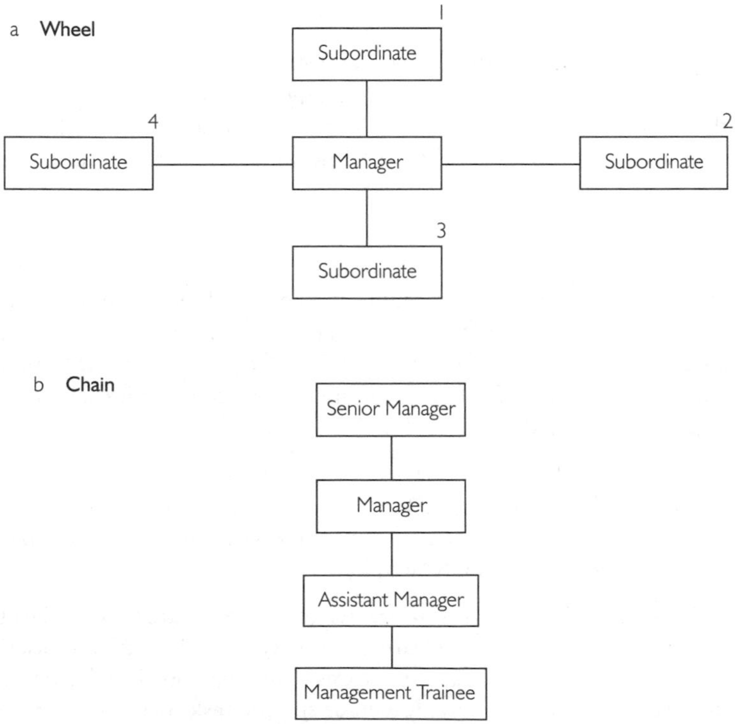

c **Circle**

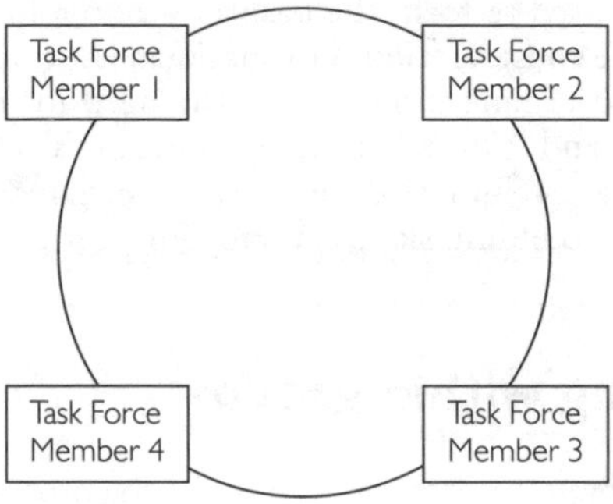

d **All-channel**

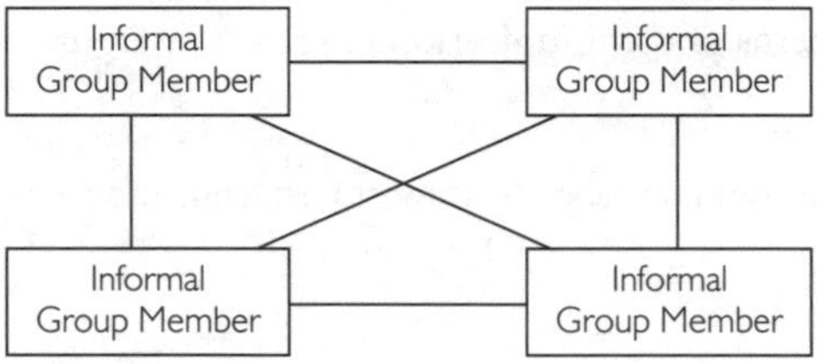

Figure 7.2 Small-group communication networks

In the *wheel network* the information flows between the person at the end of each spoke (subordinate) and the person in the middle (manager). There is no direct communication between those individuals at the end of each spoke; for example Subordinate 1 will not communicate with Subordinate 3. This wheel network is a feature of a traditional work group where the primary communication occurs between the members and the group manager.

In the *chain network* each individual can communicate with the person above and/or the person below. The individuals at each end of the chain will only communicate with one person – below in the case of the Senior Manager and above in the case of the Management Trainee. This is a typical communication network where the organisation is designed hierarchically from the top down and where communication travels up and down the chain of command.

Within the *circle network* each individual can communicate with the people on both sides but not with anyone else. For example, Task Force Member 1 can communicate with Task Force Member 2 and Task Force Member 4 but not with Task Force Member 3. Such a communication method is commonly used by committees.

All the members of an *all-channel network* are free to communicate with all the other members of the group. Such a network is a feature of the leaner, delayered organisations where work is frequently within matrix project teams. This network is a feature of informal groups that have no formal structure, leader, or specific task to accomplish.

Baron and Greenberg (1990) suggested models for relating communication networks to group effectiveness as shown in Table 7.5 below.

Table 7.5 Communication networks and group effectiveness (Baron and Greenberg, 1990)

	Types of Communications Networks			
	Wheel	**Chain**	**Circle**	**All-Channel**
Degree of centralisation	Very high	Moderate	Low	Very low
Leadership predictability	Very High	Moderate	Low	Very low
Average group satisfaction	Low	Moderate	Moderate	High
Range in individual member satisfaction	High	Moderate	Low	Very low

Communication networks form spontaneously and naturally as the interpersonal interaction between workers continues. Networks are rarely permanent because, like other organisational behaviour concepts, they are subject to the task in hand, the situation and the changing membership. As such, communication networks tend to be contingency ones, i.e. the most suitable for the present occasion. Such patterns and characteristics of small-group communication networks are determined by the factors summarised in Table 7.6 below.

Table 7.6 Factors which can influence the development of small-group communication networks

FACTOR	**EXAMPLE**
Task	Decision-making Sequential production
Environment	Type of room Placement of furniture Member dispersal Temperature Light
Personal characteristics	Expertise Openness Speaking ability Group member familiarity Intonation
Group performance factors	Composition Size Roles Age of members Gender of members Norms Cohesiveness

The *task* is a key element in the determination of the group's communication network pattern. If the primary task of the group is the task of decision-making, the all-channel network may evolve in order to provide the information which is needed for the group members to evaluate all the possible alternatives and to use a creative method of decision-making. However, if the group's principal task is just to divide tasks out among themselves sequentially, the chain or wheel network will develop since communication among the members of the group may not be as important for the completion of the task, i.e. it may not require creativity or decision-making skills.

The types of interactions and the frequency of them can be affected by the *environment* within which the group is working. For example, if members of a group are geographically dispersed, then those who are isolated may be considered outsiders and thus weaker communication channels will result. As a result of the latter, separate communication channels may even appear.

The development of a communication network is also influenced by the *personal characteristics* of the members of the group. Elements such as technical expertise, honesty, speaking ability, and the degree to which members know each other are key here. For example, an individual with expert power (see Chapter 6) is more likely to dominate the communication flow during a meeting than those without the knowledge expertise.

Group performance factors also influence the choice or evolution of communication networks. For example, in a flat, leaner organisation where groups have autonomy and work in an environment where information is shared vertically and horizontally, the all-channel network will be used. Also, the smaller the group the more likely it is that the all-channel method will be in operation.

The communication network will strongly influence group effectiveness because the outcome of a group's efforts depends on the co-ordinated actions of all its members. In order to develop an effective working relationship within groups, the managers need to ensure that the groups have all the relevant information to make a considered decision. This can be done by ensuring that members of the groups are in contact with each other by siting them in the same geographical area, or by encouraging access to communication devices such as faxes, e-mail, video-conferencing, hot-desking, and hotelling (see Chapter 5). The use of electronic group mail is now common where group members network by computer. However, they do not benefit from the positive side of face-to-face communication as discussed in Chapter 3.

Participation can also be encouraged by the use of direct questioning of individuals by the manager; for example, 'How would your clients accept this change, Carol?', or by the use of the Nominal Group Technique or the Delphi Technique. Although the latter techniques are about decision-making in groups they are strongly influenced by the communication networks prevalent within a group.

Nominal Group Technique (NGT)

The Nominal Group Technique actually restricts discussion or any other form of interpersonal communication within a group – hence the use of the word 'nominal'. Whilst all members of the group are physically present they operate independently. Specifically, they address a specific issue or problem and carry out the following steps in a logical way:

1 Before any discussion takes place, each member works silently, and independently writes down his or her ideas related to the case in point.

2 Each member verbally presents a single idea in turn with the other members until all ideas have been presented and recorded (flip chart or whiteboard). No discussion is permitted.

3 The group discusses and evaluates the ideas for their validity.

4 Each member individually and silently ranks the ideas formulated in (3) above.

5 The final decision is determined by the ideas with the highest aggregate rank.

The principal advantage of the NGT is that the group meets formally but the method does not restrict independent thinking as does a group which is interacting and communicating at all stages of the process.

Delphi Technique (DT)

The Delphi Technique is more time consuming and much more complex but it is a technique which is suitable for some groups and in some situations. Although it is similar to the NGT, it differs in that it does not require the physical presence of the group's members. In fact, the DT never allows the group members to meet face to face. Because of this, it is a technique which is suitable for the modern electronic age. The following steps characterise the DT:

1 Problem is identified and members asked to provide potential solutions through a series of carefully designed questionnaires/computer based questions.

2 Each member anonymously and independently completes the first questionnaire.

3 Results of the first questionnaire are compiled at a central location/by computer, transcribed, and reproduced.

4 Each member receives a copy of the results.

5 After viewing the results, members are again asked for their opinion/solutions. The results typically trigger new solutions or cause changes in the original position.

6 Steps 4 and 5 are repeated as often as necessary until consensus is reached.

Like the NGT the DT insulates group members from the undue influence of others. It also ignores the value of interpersonal, non-verbal communication and the creativity of shared ideas. The Delphi Technique is particularly useful where groups are scattered throughout the world. For instance, Microsoft can use the computer networked Delphi Technique to query its managers in Cambridge, Salt Lake City and Los Angeles and thus avoid the expense of bringing people physically together. The Delphi Technique is time consuming but is ideal where a speedy discourse and decision is not necessary and where creativity is essential.

Evaluating group effectiveness

Each technique which has been presented in this text – brainstorming (see Chapter 6), the

NGT, or the DT – has its own advantages and disadvantages. However, it is necessary to have an appreciation of how each of these techniques compares with the others so that managers can select the most appropriate means of bringing about group effectiveness. An important study was carried out by Murnighan (1981) which is summarised in Table 7.7.

Table 7.7 Evaluating group effectiveness (Murnighan 1981)

Effectiveness Criteria	**Type of Group**			
	Interacting	**Brainstorming**	**Nominal**	**Delphi**
Number of ideas	Low	Moderate	High	High
Quality of ideas	Low	Moderate	High	High
Social pressure	High	Low	Moderate	Low
Time/money costs	Moderate	Low	Low	High
Task orientation	Low	High	High	High
Potential for interpersonal conflict	High	Low	Moderate	Low
Feelings of accomplishment	High to low	High	High	Moderate
Commitment to solution	High	Not applicable	Moderate	Low
Builds group cohesiveness	High	High	Moderate	Low

The choice of the technique will depend upon which of the criteria is required to be emphasised – the 'best' technique will be defined by the criterion which is used to evaluate the group. For example, using Table 7.7 above:

- the interacting group is good for building team cohesiveness;
- brainstorming will keep social pressures to a minimum;
- the Delphi Technique will help to minimise dysfunctional conflict.

Conflict and failure in groups

Example

There are four people named: Everybody, Somebody, Anybody, and Nobody. There was an important job to be done and Everybody was asked to do it. Everybody was sure Somebody would do it. Anybody could have done it, but Nobody did it. Somebody got angry about that, because it was Everybody's job. Everybody thought Anybody could do it but Nobody realised that Everybody wouldn't do it. It ended up that Everybody blamed Somebody when Nobody did what Anybody could have done.

Source: Anonymous

Groups face conflicting pressures which can, in turn, influence their effectiveness.

Table 7.8 Pressures faced by groups

rational	irrational
informed	ill-informed
considered	ill-considered
decisive	indecisive
focused	unfocused
reflective	egoistic
sensible division of responsibilities	unsuitable division of responsibiities
EFFECTIVE GROUP	INEFFECTIVE, FAILED GROUP
cohesive	diverse
empowering	telling
participative	isolated
sharing	selfish
creative conflict	dysfunctional conflict
dynamic	inertia

It is possible to see how groups fail by looking at the range of responses of an individual to group participation:

Social loafing ▸ Inertia ▸ Group think ▸ Polarisation/risky shift ▸ Alienation/antagonism

PASSIVE ——————————————————————► ACTIVE

As was seen in Chapter 6, *social loafing* is a phenomenon where individuals do not put as much effort into a group as they might if they were working alone. The larger the group, the less effort each individual exerts. Such loafing can be diminished if each individual's contribution to the combined group task is being separately assessed.

When an individual begins to play a role within the group but does so passively and reacts only to others' ideas and suggestions, i.e. does not act pro-actively, then *inertia* is in operation. This is a particular problem if the group activity is conjunctive in nature (see Chapter 6). If inertia is present then the group is slowed down by its weakest link and, therefore, the group's performance and effectiveness is limited to the performance of the least productive member. For example, a group of fell walkers can only move as fast as the speed of the slowest-moving member of the group.

Groupthink

Janis (1982) defined *groupthink* as: 'the psychological drive for consensus at any cost that suppresses dissent and appraisal of alternatives in cohesive decision-making groups' (p. 8).

One reason why groups may not be effective, i.e. by making inefficient or ineffective decisions, could be because of groupthink. Decision-making is a process through which a problem is identified, solution objectives are well defined, a predecision is made, and alternatives are generated and evaluated, with an alternative being chosen, implemented, and followed up. At all stages of this process, groupthink can work to undermine the quality of the decision and thus the effectiveness of the group. Its presence is a serious impediment to group decision-making and it occurs when there is a tendency for the members of a highly cohesive group to so strongly conform to group pressures regarding a certain decision that they fail to think critically, and reject the potentially correcting influences of people outside the group. Thus the result could be poor decisions because of the lack of critical evaluation of ideas and actions.

It was a concept attributed to Janis (1982) and it has a powerful role within group working. It was believed that members of very cohesive groups may have more confidence in their group's decisions than they have doubts about such actions. This view is usually accompanied by such comments as 'We know what we are doing'. Critical thinking is often suspended in favour of conforming to the group, and as a result members become extremely loyal to each other and ignore potentially useful information from other sources which might challenge their group decision. Such behaviour can result in decisions which are uninformed, irrational and, sometimes, immoral.

Such groupthink behaviour can be caused by either or both of two processes:

- social comparison
- persuasive information.

The *social comparison* view suggests that group members may want to make a positive impression on their fellow group members, and do so by strongly endorsing predominant cultural values. People wanting to impress their fellow group members (or at least not embarrass themselves in front of them) will embrace the predominant cultural value – wanting to appear to do the right thing in front of others – and therefore go to the extreme with respect to whatever perspective seems right. It should be borne in mind that this behaviour might well produce either excessive conformity to group norms (groupthink) or excessive contrast to group norms (polarisation).

During the interactions of the members of the group *persuasive information* is exchanged and as discussions progress some group members are exposed to arguments that they had not previously considered. Some of these views will support the individual's predominant viewpoint whilst others may provide information which makes the individual shift towards a different view from that which he or she originally held.

However, by being aware of the symptoms of groupthink (e.g. refusing to accept contradictory data, believing it is above criticism from outsiders, and viewing opposition as weak) members of a group can avoid the process of groupthink. The members should always evaluate ideas and courses of action by, for example, discussing issues and concerns with outsiders, use sub-groups to work on the opposing view, and test the consensus opinion.

The concept of groupthink has a connecting variable which groups utilise when working towards effectiveness; this is known as *group cohesion*, which is the interpersonal attraction binding groups together. Through group cohesion groups can exercise effective control over the group members in relationship to the norms and standards of that group. Groups can fail because of:

- goal conflict
- unpleasant experiences
- domination of a sub-group

and each of these also breaks down the potential of group cohesion. Groups who have a low level of cohesion will find it difficult to exercise any sort of control over the members and each will enforce their own standards of behaviour rather than those of the group combined. Studies show that cohesion within a group can have a calming effect by reducing dysfunctional tension and conflict. Member satisfaction, commitment and interpersonal communication are better in highly cohesive groups. However, groupthink may become a problem within highly cohesive groups.

Janis (1982) in his key work on groupthink identified some symptoms of group cohesion and offered steps which could be used to prevent such behaviours. This is summarised in Table 7.9 below.

Table 7.9 Groupthink and cohesiveness: some symptoms and their prevention

The group has the illusion that it is invulnerable.
The leader can encourage open expression of doubt and/or accept criticism of his or her opinions.

The group rationalises away data that contradicts or does not support their assumptions and beliefs.
Lower status members could offer their opinions before members with higher status.

The group has some self-appointed 'mind guards' who protect the whole group from any data which does not conform to the group's opinions.
The group could develop scenarios which consider the actions of possible competitors or other groups working in the same area.

There is an unquestioned belief in the group's inherent morality.
Opinions can be sought from other groups who might have experience in the same area under discussion.

The group might stereotype other groups or individuals working in the same area as evil, stupid, etc.
The group could be divided into sub-groups at times.

Group members form a coalition to pressurise the minority to conform.
The members of the group could 'import' others to join the discussion on an *ad hoc* basis.

Synergy

Synergy has been discussed in Chapter 6 but suffice it to say that it is a positive force which occurs when group members stimulate new solutions to problems through the process of mutual influence and encouragement within the group. It can provide the ideal response of the individual to the experience of group membership. His or her contribution is active, distinctive, and creative but directed towards achieving the goals established for the group. It is sensitive to, and takes account of, the views and feelings of the other group members.

Polarisation

Polarisation refers to the tendency of group members to shift their views about a given issue to ones that veer more in the direction of the views that they held previously. For example, an individual who is initially in favour of a certain action will feel *more favourably* towards it following a group discussion, and someone who is initially opposed to a certain decision will be *more opposed* to it following a group discussion. Thus, group interaction tends to make individuals more extremely disposed to their initially held beliefs.

Alienation

The concept of alienation has been discussed in Chapter 6. However, it is accompanied with the variable of *risky shift* which does affect the effectiveness of groups. Such a phenomenon has interested organisational behaviour researchers for some time. It is best explained in the form of a scenario.

The risky shift phenomenon

Example

The organisation your brother works for has given him the opportunity to increase his investment portfolio through offering him more shares in the organisation.

- His current portfolio comprises some shares in the organisation together with other investments which are safe and not likely to produce any considerable gains.
- The company for which he works has an uncertain future. However, if the company succeeds, the financial gains will be enormous.
- But he does not know how well it is likely to do.

Would you recommend to your brother that he invest in his company's shares? Explain the reasons for your answer.

It is necessary to consider at what odds the company's success would have to be before one would decide to invest in it. For example, if there was a 90 per cent chance of the company succeeding before your brother had to decide to make the investment, it would be safe to say that your opinion would be unlikely to be cautious. However, if your brother was willing to make the investment when there was only a 10 per cent chance of success, you would tell your brother that he would be taking a high risk if he did invest.

So, what would happen if a group of investors were asked whether they wanted to invest in the same package? Would the group make a riskier or a more conservative decision on the investment than your brother might as an individual?

When working in groups there tends to be give-and-take between the members and one could surmise from this that they would be more likely to make conservative, neutral, middle-of-the-road decisions when it comes to the scenario given. However, a considerable amount of research seriously challenges this received wisdom. In his work, Pruitt (1971) reported that systematic studies showed that groups tended to make riskier decisions than individuals did.

So, in our example, if four individuals recommended that your brother took the riskier course of action if the odds of success were 40 per cent, a group composed of those same individuals might recommend that the riskier course of action be taken if the odds of success were lower: say, 20 per cent. Such a shift in the direction of riskiness by groups compared to individuals is called 'risky shift'.

Since research studies indicate that there is a tendency for groups to make riskier decisions than individuals would, it is necessary for managers to understand the reason why this is the case. It might be because:

- when a group decision is made, no one individual is held accountable for it, and therefore more risky decisions are taken by groups (the diffusion of responsibility hypothesis);
- individuals who have a high need to achieve and take risks may well be more influential in the group discussions (the social comparison hypothesis);
- groups are social entities which encourage interaction, and risk-taking is considered to be a desirable cultural characteristic – particularly in capitalist systems (the cultural value hypothesis).

As has been seen in this chapter and the previous one, groups do work well when the task in hand requires creative thinking and problem-solving based upon expert knowledge and experience. Shaw (1976) reviewed research in the field and suggested that there is support for the opinion that groups do produce more and better solutions to problems than individuals do.

Conflict within groups

Interpersonal conflict is conflict which occurs between two or more individuals, whereas intrapersonal conflict concerns itself with conflict within an individual which is related to social roles. When individuals work in a group, both forms of conflict can come into play and both need to be managed if the group is to be effective in achieving its objectives. Members of a group need to understand that not all conflict is bad: conflict which leads to group failure is dysfunctional and is not to be encouraged. However, some conflict situations can be turned into positive conflict and can thus help to achieve the aims of the group. The concept of conflict is complex and is beyond the scope of this section. However, it is important that individuals understand the key forms of conflict which will affect them when they work in groups.

Intergroup conflict

When dysfunctional conflict occurs between different groups and teams, it is called 'intergroup conflict' and has predictable effects within each group, such as increased:

- group cohesiveness
- concentration of tasks
- group loyalty.

Where there is dysfunctional intergroup conflict there does tend to be a prevailing attitude of 'them and us', where each perceives the other as an enemy and thus each tends to then:

- treat the other group as an enemy
- become more hostile
- decrease intergroup communication.

Whilst competition between groups could well be functional it does need to be carefully managed so that it does not escalate into dysfunctional conflict. If several groups are attempting to achieve the same goal, they tend to exhibit certain common forms of behaviour:

- setting territorial boundaries
- aggressiveness
- prejudice against members of other groups.

Interpersonal conflict

This is conflict which occurs between two or more people. Sources of such conflict are many and include differences such as those related to:

- personality
- attitudes
- values
- perceptual set.

Intrapersonal conflict

When conflict occurs within an individual it is called intrapersonal conflict, of which there are several types.

- interrole
- intrarole
- person-role conflicts.

For a group to be effective individual members need to be able to work in a conflict-positive environment: the group is a small world within the larger organisation. Tjosvold (1991) argued that if conflict is well managed it can add to innovation and productivity. He offered procedures for turning dysfunctional conflict into functional conflict, stating that too many organisations tend to take a win-lose, competitive approach to conflict or – at worst – avoid conflict altogether. Such a negative view of conflict can ensure that a group is ineffective and the activities within it will become destructive. However, a positive view of conflict can lead to a win-win solution.

Within a group the members can take any one of three views of conflict as identified in Figure 7.3.

Categorising group failure

Not all groups achieve their objectives and each has a potential for failure. Allcorn (1989) has provided a model for understanding some of the sources and results of group failure. He categorised four key types of workplace group, broadly characterised by the distribution of power and decision-making within the group as shown in Table 7.10 on page 234.

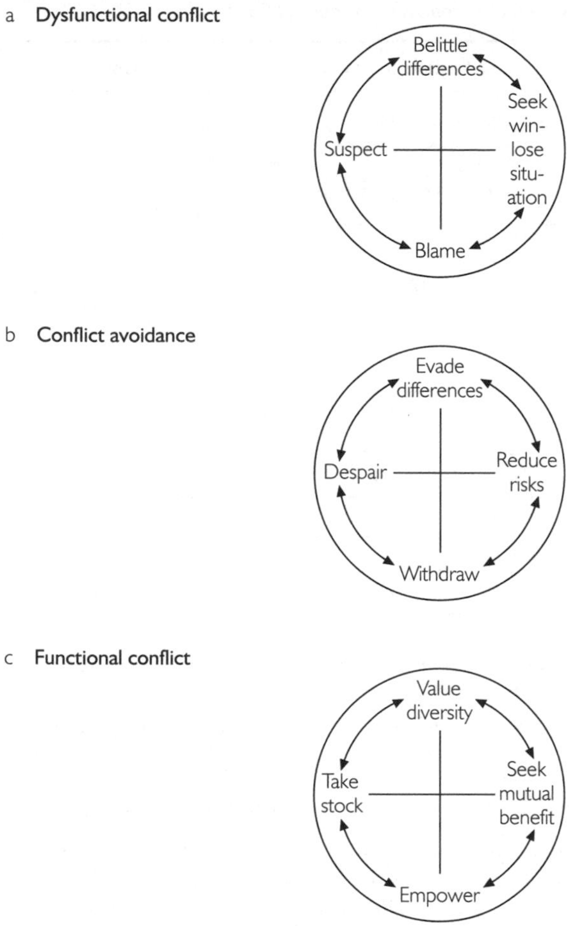

Figure 7.3 Three views of conflict (Tjosvold, 1991)

Allcorn (1989) then went into the importance of culture (see Chapter 9) and the working of groups; he concentrated on the key issues of group characteristics and the impact on individual group members which are outlined in Table 7.11 on pages 236–237.

Table 7.10 Key types of workplace group after Allcorn (1989)

Group type	**Distribution of power**	**Characteristics**
Homogenised	Power lies in group norms which inhibit individual commitment and initiative.	
Institutionalised	Power lies in organisation prescribing group roles and actions.	Defensive groups, providing collective and individual defences against anxiety resulting from group membership
Autocratic	Power lies in a strong group leader.	
Intentional	Power is distributed evenly between organisation, group leader and members, allowing full individual participation.	Non-defensive groups encouraging group membership and partnership, without anxiety.

Success in groups, according to Allcorn (1989), is measured on two criteria:

- strength in decision-making
- strength in maximising the participation and fulfilment of group members.

Homogeneous groups fail on both counts whereas institutionalised groups may well achieve their tasks, but the group's decision-making strength is limited and dependent upon the organisation – the group fails to reach its potential and does not give added value.

Autocratic groups may well achieve their target with the most speed, but their decision-making strength is circumscribed by the abilities of the leader, and they fail to tap the abilities of group members or fully motivate or involve them.

The only group which meets both the criteria – strength in decision-making and in the maximisation of participation and fulfilment of all group members – is the intentional group.

Group effectiveness

Taking up Allcorn's (1989) view, it is possible to consider a definition for the effectiveness of groups. He considered that groups were working satisfactorily if they:

- were effective in decision-making and problem-solving; and
- were effective in involving and motivating group members.

As has been discussed elsewhere, improved job satisfaction does not necessarily lead to improved productivity. However, motivated, proactive teams are ever more important in dynamic, competitive conditions, so achieving both is important. A model for understanding what influences group effectiveness is provided by Kretch *et al.* (1962) and is given in Figure 7.4 below.

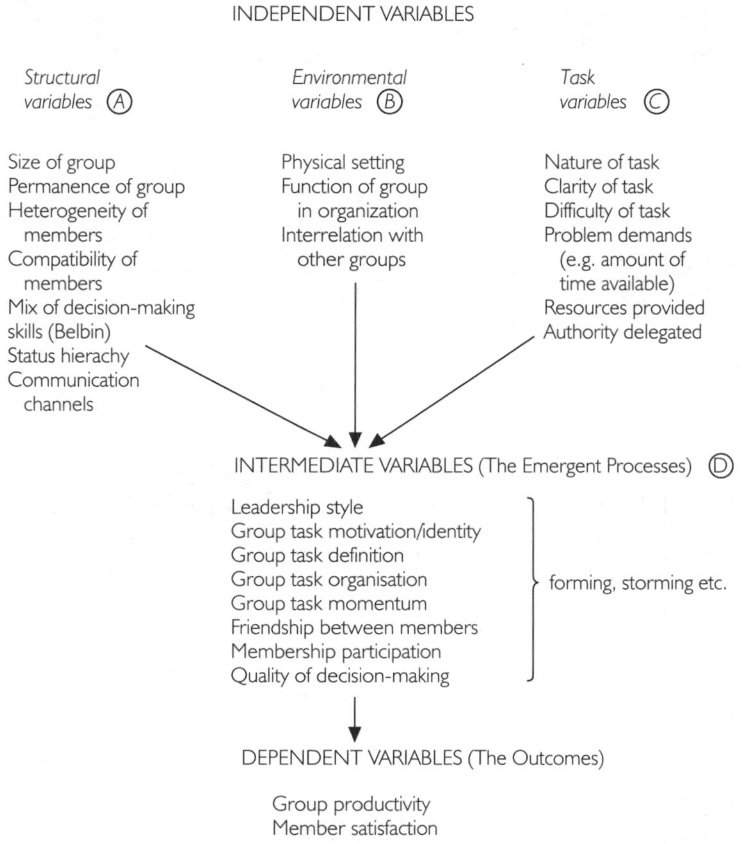

Figure 7.4 Influences on group effectiveness, after Kretch et al.. *(1962)*

The relative importance of these factors is dependent on independent variables. As an example, a simple, clearly defined 'closed' task with well-defined roles will require less success in structural or intermediate variables. However, complex, ambiguous and 'open' tasks may put particular pressure on structural and intermediate variables. Such variables are themselves related to strategic, tactical and operational decision-making dealt with earlier in both the previous chapter and this one.

The importance of the contingency approach can be seen in two areas:

- communication
- leadership.

Table 7.11 Culture of four workplace groups after Allcorn (1989)

		The cultures of the four workplace groups			
Characteristics		**Homogenised Group**	**Institutionalised Group**	**Autocratic Group**	**International Group**
Group characteristics	Leadership	No leader is acknowledged to exist or permitted to arise.	Leadership is designated by the group's operating structure.	The leader is viewed as omnipotent and is clearly in control of the group	A permanent leader may be found among the members or leadership may be passed among members based on each person's unique ability to lead the group at the time.
	Individual roles and status	All members have equal status, with no clear individual roles.	Each member is assigned a particular role and status, and given guidelines for changing the role and status	All members are assigned roles with status, but no clear guidelines are provided.	All members assume and accept roles and status based on the needs of the group and the leader.
	Direction and purpose	Members are unable to find a direction for the group.	The direction of the group is limited by the organisation structure.	All skills for directing the group are held by the leader.	Members actively participate in offering direction to the group.
		Members feel that they and the group have lost their purpose.	Members feel that they have lost their individual purpose in the face of the predominance of the group's goals.	Individuals lose their sense of personal purpose in the face of the all-powerful leader.	Members experience a sense of purpose because they and their contributions are acknowledged by the group.
	Allocation of tasks/ sense of responsibility	Little work on the group's task is accomplished and no plans are made to do any work.	Work on the group's task is accomplished as specified by the organisational work process.	Work on the group's task as specified by the leader is accomplished according to the leader's instructions.	Work on the group's task becomes the responsibility of all the members with no one individual (including the leader) assuming complete responsibility for the work.
		The group acts as though time and the environment have been temporarily suspended, and as if there were nothing more than the group's experience.	The group acts as though the organisation were in control of events and the process, and as if work were to be accomplished as planned.	The group acts as though the leader will take care of everything if he or she is permitted to do so.	The group acts as though all members were responsible for the group's work and leadership.

Characteristics		Homogenised Group	Institutionalised Group	Autocratic Group	International Group
Group characteristics (contd)	Group attitudes to individual members	Some group members may be singled out and stigmatised for their willingness to express their feelings and thoughts. They may be coaxed into increasing emotionalism until they are rendered incompetent and discarded.	Some group members may be singled out and praised for participating in the group as expected, or they may be publicly punished for deviating.	Some members may be singled out for rewards for actions the leader finds supportive, or punished for deviations from the leader's expectations.	Contributions of members are acknowledged by the group as a whole.
		Autonomous behaviour such as the offering of ideas is either attacked or not supported by others.	Autonomous behaviour such as the offering of ideas is controlled by procedures.	Autonomous behaviour such as the offering of ideas may be rewarded or punished by the leader. who may offer no reasons for his or her decision.	Autonomous behaviour is acknowledged as valuable as long as it contributes to the group's purpose.
Impact on individual group members	Fear	Members fear the consequences of speaking out and taking action.	Members fear the consequences of speaking out in other than the prescribed manner, and of taking independent action without prior approval.	Members fear the consequences of speaking out without some idea of the leader's likely response, and of taking independent action without the leader's consent.	Members are eager to offer their points of view regarding the group's work.
	Helplessness	Helplessness is experienced, as others are attacked by group members.	Helplessness is experienced, as those who deviate are attacked.	Helplessness is experienced because little can be done to change the leader's mind or to influence events.	Helplessness is not an element of group membership experience.
	Security	Members feel security in being unnoticed.	Members feel that safety lies in following the rules.	Members feel unsafe and insecure because the leader may become dissatisfied with them unexpectedly.	The group offers a sense of safety and security to its members.
	Frustration	Frustration is evident, in that members feel as if nothing can be done to help the situation. No ideas are generated to improve the group's performance.	Frustration occurs, as members feel that nothing can be done to change the organisation.	Frustration develops because group members cannot solve problems that stem from the leader's direction and style.	Frustrations over the group's progress and direction are openly discussed.

Communication is discussed in Chapter 3 and leadership in Chapter 6.

Designing effective work teams

Apart from the ideas of Belbin (1981, 1993) discussed earlier, there are other ways of deciding how to put individuals into teams with a view to the group being effective. The three key ideas are those of McGregor (1960), Hackman (1987) and Mullins (1996).

McGregor (1960)

McGregor's (1960) seminal work formed the foundation of current work into the composition of effective work teams. Whilst working at the Massachusetts Institute of Technology (MIT) he carried out research in the workplace in an attempt to identify the characteristics of effective work groups in contrast to those of ineffective ones. His key findings were that effective groups exhibit the following characteristics:

- The atmosphere is relaxed and informal and the members appear to be involved and interested in the events taking place.
- Discussion is task-oriented, with all members participating to the full.
- The objective of the group is internalised by all members.
- Individuals listen rather than just hear and are not inhibited in making creative suggestions.
- Conflict is functional because, for example, disagreements are discussed and resolved or accepted.
- Decision is by consensus.
- Whilst criticism is frank it is not personalised.
- Relations are positive, with individuals expressing feelings about the task and about interpersonal relations associated with achieving that task.
- Activities are assigned to individuals and carried out by them.
- Leadership moves according to expert knowledge rather than status.

Hackman (1987)

Hackman (1987) also stated that it was not sensible to put people together at random in the hope that they would form an effective team; he thought managers should take steps towards increasing the likelihood of effective team performance.

Step 1 (Pre-work). It is the manager who identifies the task which needs to be completed. He or she then considers whether it would be best achieved by an individual or a team, taking into account such variables as speed of decision-making, or creativity required to solve the problem. If the answer is that a group would be the better prospect, the manager will then decide on the level of authority that the group should be given and, therefore, the amount of information it has available.

Step 2 (Reducing performance conditions). The manager is responsible for providing the required environment for the team so that it can perform effectively in working towards the set task. This also includes ensuring that the team has the required resources (e.g. human, financial, information) to do the job.

Step 3 (Forming and building a team). Having built the foundations, the principal areas in forming the team are related to *making boundaries* by clarifying the group membership; getting the individual members to *commit* themselves to the tasks, and *clarifying the expected behaviours*: the manager has to clarify which team members will be responsible for which sub-task.

Step 4 (Providing on-going help). It is at this stage that the manager gets involved if the group requires help to overcome any difficulties it has. This may mean dealing with, for example, social loafers and/or providing additional resources.

As has been seen earlier, groups do follow development phases (forming, storming, norming, and performing) and this knowledge can help the manager decide on appropriate interventions. However, the ability to decide on whom to put into a team is something which does not come automatically in the role of manager – it is possible to train people to learn how to use work teams, to improve individual performance, and to ensure each member satisfies their personal needs as a member of that team.

Mullins (1996)

In his discussion of the nature of groups in the workplace, Mullins (1996) stated that harmonious and relation-supported teams exhibit certain characteristics, which he listed as:

- a belief in shared aims and objectives
- a sense of commitment to the group
- acceptance of group values and norms
- a feeling of mutual trust and dependency
- full participation by all members and decision-making by consensus
- a free flow of information and communications
- the open expression of feelings and disagreements
- the resolution of conflict by the members themselves
- a lower level of staff turnover, absenteeism, accidents, errors and complaints.

An analysis of these three pieces of work would highlight some common variables and thus an informed manager should be able to place people in teams so that they would be likely to be effective and meet the tasks set for them.

Leadership and group effectiveness

CASE STUDY

Looking for tomorrow's leaders

Writing in *Management Today* in August 1997, Colin Sharman (UK Senior Partner, KPMG Peat Marwick and a Companion of the Institute of Management) stated that within organisations structures are flatter, staff more mobile, and power and authority vested in the individual and not in the position, and the concept of leadership has changed.

He believes that it is the job of leaders to navigate the inevitable turbulence and change in a world where business is driven by knowledge, networks and relationships.

In the modern environment of internal and external change a new set of leadership skills has come to the fore and Sharman believes that there are three skills and attributes in particular which are now critical: learning, openness, and teamwork.

Leaders must be learners. Gaining qualifications is just the start: the pace of change means that learning has to be a lifelong activity. Those who learn effectively actively seek out development opportunities and experience. Learning gives breadth of perspective and understanding, and this ability to see the bigger picture and the opportunities it presents is the prerequisite for leadership vision.

Closely related to learning is the attribute of openness which is a challenge in itself and, indeed, open to challenge because it is essential to learning, progress and change. Asking for feedback at a corporate, team and individual level is essential to maintaining and improving performance.

By definition, leaders have followers, and great leadership has always been dependent on great teamwork. A new type of team is emerging that is more fluid and flexible than in the past. The composition of this team is less likely to be permanent. It is more likely to be a multi-disciplinary group, drawn together for a period to achieve a particular goal. It might also include outsiders: advisers, customers or suppliers. The best person to lead the team might not always be the most senior. The success of the team will depend on the contribution of each member, and it is the task of the leader to ensure that the output of the group is greater than the sum of its parts. This means much more than carving up a set of tasks: it means real, effective, proactive teamwork, which enables every member of the team to contribute to their full potential. It also means reviewing the way the team is working, and addressing the difficult issues rather than putting the lid on them.

For Sharman, leadership is encapsulated in an anonymous quotation: 'The goal of many leaders is to get people to think more highly of the leader. The goal of a great leader is to get people to think more highly of themselves.'

Adapted from C. Sharman, 'Looking for tomorrow's leaders' in *Management Today*, August 1997,

As can be seen from the above case, the concept of leadership is very complex and constantly changing. However, it is based on well-reported research from which modern leadership views have developed. Leadership as a variable within organisations is discussed in detail in Chapter 10, which covers aspects of management. In this chapter leadership is considered as it affects the workings of groups and teams and their effectiveness.

There are as many definitions of leadership as there are people who have researched into it – there is no universal definition of the concept. All definitions have a number of key elements:

- getting things done through individuals and groups;
- creating effective communication networks;
- resolving dysfunctional conflicts;
- providing direction for individuals, groups, and departments within the organisation;
- providing and organising resources;

- effective decision-making;
- managing change.

Leadership is, therefore, the process of guiding and directing the behaviour of people in the work environment.

Leaders, particularly of formal groups, have a number of functions which have been summarised above in an attempt to come to an agreed definition. However, Kretch *et al.* (1962) identified a comprehensive number of functions which group leaders carry out which help to show how extensive and variable are the attributes and behaviours expected of leaders; these are indicated in Table 7.12 below.

Table 7.12 The functions of a formal group leader (Kretch et al.*, 1962)*

Executive
The top co-ordinator of the group activities and overseer of the execution of decided policies.

Planner
Short- and long-term planning so that the group achieves its objectives.

Policy-maker
Establishes the goals and policies.

Expert
Whilst the leader may not have all the knowledge and expertise at his fingertips, the group will rely upon him to be a fount of information.

External group representative
The link with other groups and the organisation in general acting as the hub of the communication network.

Controller of internal relations
Determines the structure of the group.

Purveyor of rewards and punishment
This is coercive power because the leader controls threats and rewards.

Arbitrator and mediator
Acts as the moderator of interpersonal communications within the group.

Exemplar
An extension of the previous function in that the leader is expected to act as a role model.

Symbol of the group
Establishes the group cognitive focus and ensures that the group is recognised as a distinct entity.

Substitute for individual responsibility
Relieves the individual of responsibility for decision-making, ensuring that the individual is not worried about her individual decisions.

Ideologist
The source of values, beliefs and philosophical foundation for the group.

Father figure
A person with whom individuals can identify and towards whom they can direct their positive emotions.

Scapegoat
Is the target for animosity and aggression, taking on the hostility from individual members and other groups.

As was seen in Chapter 6, groups have a structure which shapes the behaviour of the individuals within them and thus makes it possible to explain and predict a large portion of individual behaviour within groups as well as group performance and productivity. Structural variables such as roles, norms, group size and composition were considered in the previous sections. Another significant factor is a more detailed investigation into formal leadership introduced above.

Groups and leadership

The demands made upon members of the workforce are constantly increasing, tasks are becoming more complex, and timing and co-ordination have become increasingly important. The only way to be really successful is through collaboration – through successful team efforts. Sometimes it is possible to freely choose the members of a group, but, as we have seen, this is not usually the case within an organisation. People are selected for the group based on their expertise and availability, from the same, relatively small, pool of workers. Therefore they usually bring with them their preconceived opinions about each other as well as their personal agendas. Often within an organisation a group and its members are busier minimising their exposure than achieving the task. It is often difficult to form a team that is dedicated to striving for more – a team with each member inspired to contribute to the objectives of the organisation. There are two significant aspects to leadership related to groups:

- formal
- informal.

Formal group leadership

Almost every group within the workplace has a formal leader. Identification is by title or role, for example 'Project Team Leader', 'Supervisor', 'Foreman', 'Committee Chairman'. Such a leadership role contributes to the group's performance, effectiveness, and success. Research which has concentrated on the effects of leadership traits has been inconclusive. However, when situational variables have been taken into account it seems that the task structure of jobs and the characteristics of the followers have been used as moderating variables. In terms of achieving high group satisfaction, participative leadership seems to be more effective than an autocratic style. However, participation does not always lead to higher productivity. For example, if the group is directed by an autocratic leader it will more than likely outperform its participative counterparts. Most research now concentrates on contingency approaches, i.e. *when* should a leader be democratic and *when* should a leader be autocratic.

Informal group leadership

Managers should build positive relationships with leaders of informal groups because it is through such relationships that they can understand the norms and goals of the organisation. Although some managers believe that informal groups are troublesome and potentially disruptive, they should respect the position of such leaders of informal groups.

Whether an individual is a leader of a formal or an informal group, they have common characteristics. It is very important that all managers take every opportunity to illustrate how groups fit into the organisation and how they contribute to the success of the organisation. It is one of their tasks to reinforce individual pride in group membership and the achievements of the group. They need to be able to convert a group into a motivated, close-knit assemblage operating with a coherent strategy as well as on synchronised tactics. A group leader must understand that the concerns of the members of the team need to be addressed and the team targets met – often they achieve a higher level of attainment than was originally imagined because of the creative nature of working in teams. The group leader needs to be able to convert concerns into intermediate objectives in order that the group may meet its goals and, in turn, the organisation its objectives.

The membership of small groups focuses on staff diversity rather than adversity, and empowering group members is extremely important with managers coaching and counselling rather than imposing a role hierarchy. As was stated at the beginning of the discussion of groups, the level at which organisations use small groups and teams depends upon the type of organisation they are and the roles within them.

Action-centred leadership

This range of roles can be categorised from the perspective of groups by looking at the work of Adair (1975) on action-centred leadership. John Adair carried out his studies during the late 1960s and the 1970s whilst he was working at the University of Surrey. His work has formed the foundation of other studies on leadership. His work recognised that there were certain traits, qualities, capabilities and aptitudes that must be present in effective leaders. However, he moved forward from this point and stated that such variables must be translated into action, and he emphasised that the task and the group were the main features of this style of leadership. His work has formed the basis of numerous training courses which are based around the concept of leadership functions; this concept is called 'action-centred leadership'.

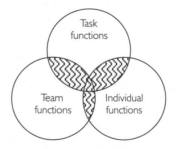

Figure 7.5 Leadership functions model, after Adair (1975)

As can be seen from the above model the three components are interconnected because activity in one area will affect the other two – this is why Adair's (1975) model is a contingency approach. In further analysing Adair's (1975) action-centred leadership theory it is possible to identify the key functions of the principal inter-related components as shown in Table 7.13 on the next page.

Table 7.13 Components of the key interrelated functions, after Adair (1975)

TASK FUNCTIONS
Achieving the objectives of the work group
Defining group tasks
Planning the work
Allocation of resources
Organisation of duties and responsibilities
Controlling quality and checking performance
Reviewing progress

TEAM FUNCTIONS
Maintaining morale and building team spirit
The cohesiveness of the group as a working unit
Setting standards and maintaining discipline
Systems of communication within the group
Training the group
Appointment of sub-leaders

INDIVIDUAL FUNCTIONS
Meeting the needs of the individual members of the group
Attending to personal problems
Giving praise and status
Reconciling conflicts between group needs and needs of the individual
Training the individual

The roles identified by Adair (1975) correlate with those found in the most comprehensive and replicated of the behavioural theories that resulted from research which began at Ohio State University in the late 1940s. These studies attempted to identify independent dimensions of leader behaviour. Having started out with over one thousand such dimensions, the researchers finally categorised them into two categories that substantially accounted for most of the leader behaviour described by their subordinates within the work study. These two dimensions were labelled *initiating structure* and *consideration*.

Initiating structure

This is the extent to which a leader is likely to define and structure their own role and the role of subordinates in the search for goal attainment. It includes all behaviour which tries to organise work, relationships at work, and objectives. A leader who utilises initiating structure tends to:

- assign individual members of the group to defined group tasks;
- expect individuals to reach previously defined performance levels;
- stress the importance of meeting deadlines.

Consideration

This is the extent to which a leader is likely to have job relationships characterised by mutual respect for subordinates' ideas and regard for their feelings. Such a leader will:

- show concern for the comfort of followers;
- concentrate on the function of the group in satisfying the individual's personal needs, e.g. physiological, status, and safety.

Leaders who are considerate can be identified because they usually:

- help their subordinates deal with their personal concerns;

- are friendly and approachable;
- treat all people as equal.

Both 'initiating structure' and 'consideration' as leadership styles will be dependent upon the relative importance of two dimensions: structure and consideration, which are shown in Figure 7.6 below:

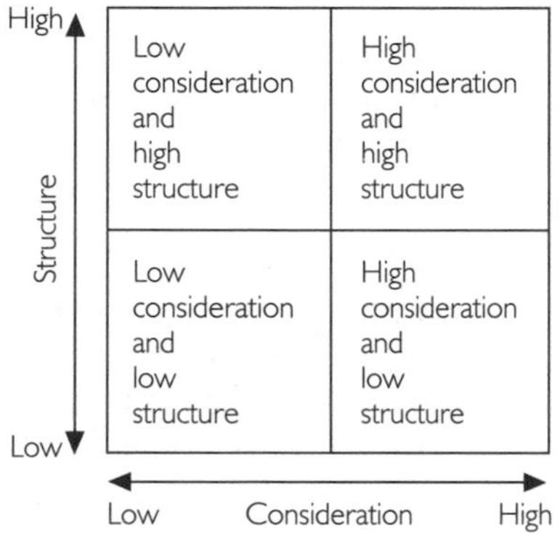

Figure 7.6 The relationship between consideration and structure

Example

Drill instructors in the army tend to be individuals who are high in initiating structure. In initial training camp, such people give orders all the time and structure recruits' activities from dawn to dusk. There is an emphasis on the completion of tasks which takes precedence over the recruit's personal needs. This is probably because considerable learning has to take place in a very short period of time and emphasis is placed upon the acceptance of authority, which is also a component of the socialisation process.

As has been found in other behavioural concepts, individuals do not tend to exhibit only one type of leadership behaviour. Individuals who exhibit high initiating structure and high consideration ('high-high' leaders) tend to achieve high subordinate performance and satisfaction more frequently than those who are low on either initiating structure or consideration, or both. However, the 'high-high' leadership behaviour does not always have positive results. For example, research has shown that individuals who used a high initiating structure to lead their groups, had groups which had:

- more complaints from the team members
- higher absenteeism
- higher turnover

and lower levels of job satisfaction from those people whose tasks were repetitive and mundane. Other research has indicated that high consideration was negatively correlated to performance ratings of the leader by that person's superior.

However, the Ohio State studies did suggest that the 'high-high' style generally resulted in positive outcomes, but there were enough exceptions in the trials to indicate that situational factors needed to be incorporated into the basic theory.

Styles of leadership

The Ohio State studies' identification of the differing dimensions of leadership led to the investigation of differing styles of leadership proposed by Tannenbaum and Schmidt (1958) who believed that there were two types of leader:

- *autocratic* – a leader who dictates decisions down to subordinates;
- *democratic* – a leader who shares decision-making with subordinates;

but that they were on a continuum with autocratic at one end and democratic at the other. As shown in Figure 7.7 below, there is a relationship between the degree of authority and the amount of freedom available to subordinates in reaching decisions. However, most of the research carried out in this area has been concentrated on the two ends of the continuum – the extreme positions.

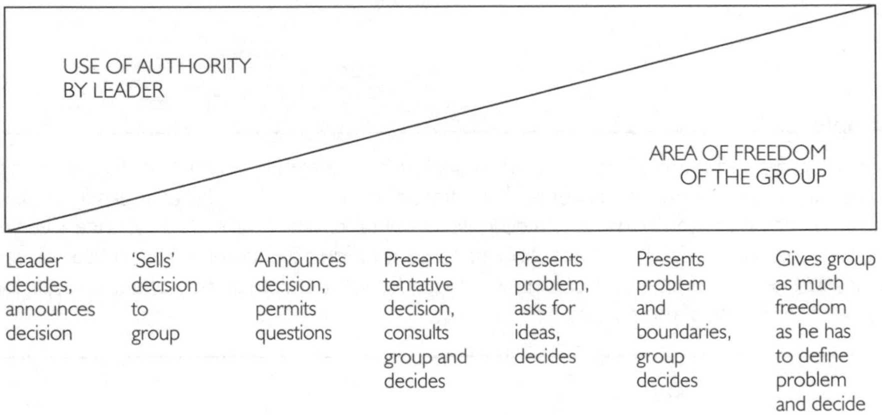

Figure 7.7 Continuum of leader behaviour, after Tannenbaum and Schmidt (1958)

These differing dimensions lead to differing styles of leadership which were mapped out by Tannenbaum and Schmidt (1958) as shown in Figure 7.8.

Other models of leadership within groups look at the aspect of the balance between *initiating structure* and *consideration* and the kind of leadership styles which it suggests. The key models related specifically to leadership in groups are those formulated by Blake and Mouton (1991), House (1987), and Belbin (1993).

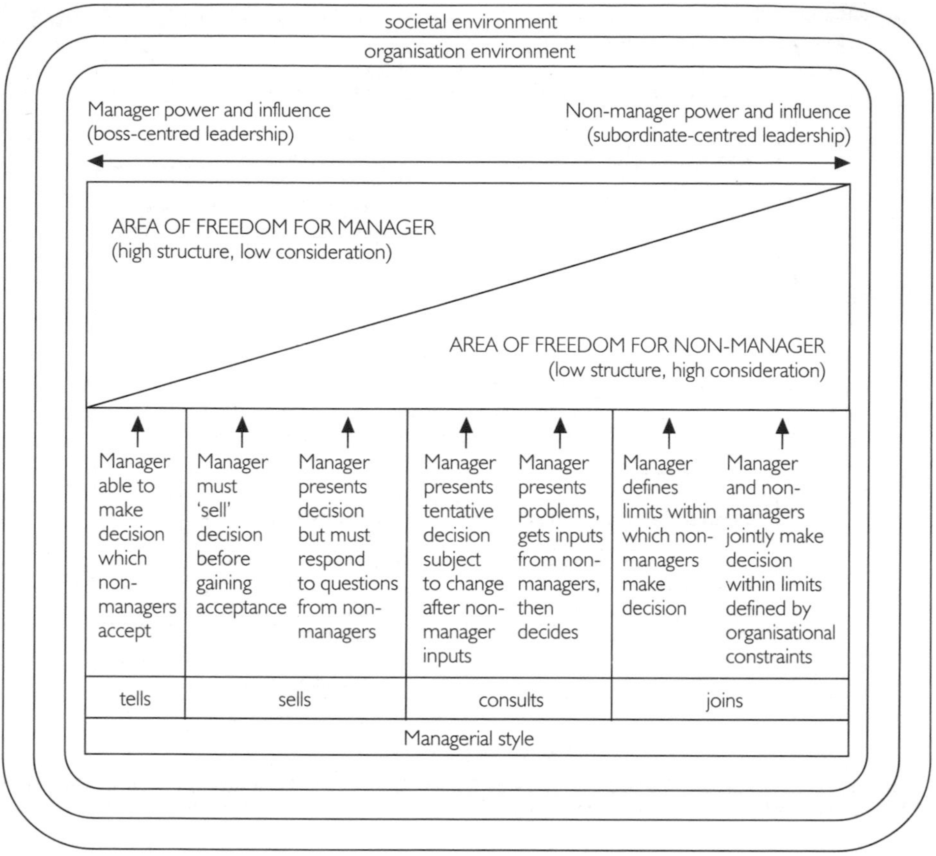

Figure 7.8 Differing styles of leadership related to the environment, after Tannenbaum and Schmidt (1958)

Blake and Mouton (1991) – The Leadership Grid©

Blake *et al.* (1964) developed further the two-dimensional view of leadership by building on the Ohio State dimensions of initiating structure and consideration; they registered their development as the Managerial Grid which was based on the styles of 'concern for people' and 'concern for production'. The Managerial Grid was first published in 1964 and was revised in both 1978 and 1985. In 1991 it was reworked and renamed The Leadership Grid© although it retained the same two categories (concern for production and concern for people) for comparing management styles.

Concern for production (the horizontal axis on the grid) is identified as the level of emphasis which a manager gives to the accomplishment of tasks through achieving a high level of production and gaining positive results or a profit. *Concern for people* (the vertical axis on the grid) relates to the level of emphasis given by the manager to subordinates and peers as individuals and to their needs and desires.

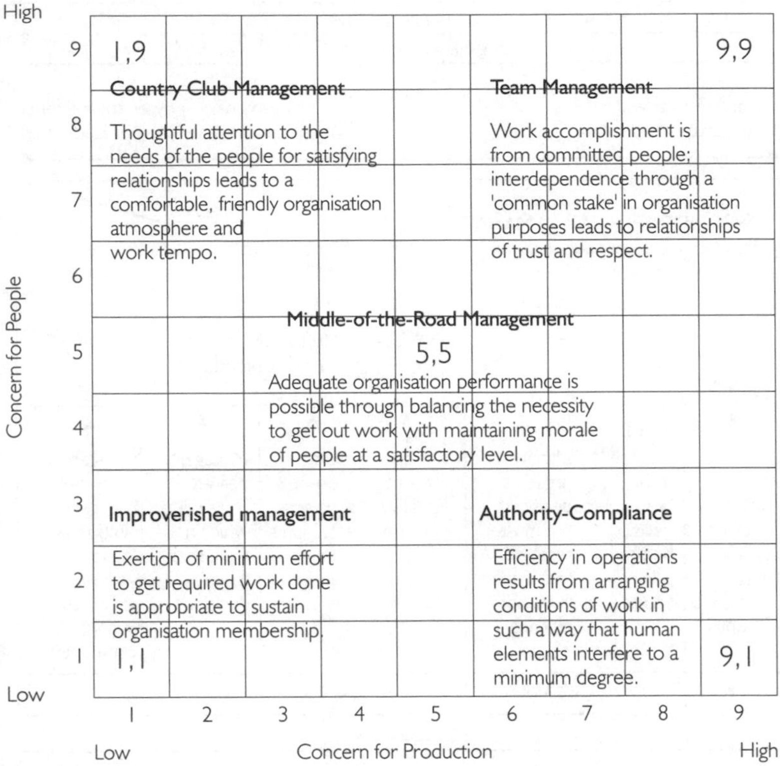

From *Leadership Dilemmas – Grid Solutions*, p. 29 by Robert R. Blake and Anne Adams McCanse. Copyright 1991 © by Robert R. Blake and the estate of Jane S. Mouton. Used with permission. All rights reserved.

Figure 7.9 The Leadership Grid©

Each axis on the grid is on a scale of 1 to 9 which indicates the varying degrees of concern that a manager has for production or people. However, the way that these two concerns are related will depend upon other factors such as the hierarchy within the organisation, assumptions that the manager makes about production and people and the manager's use of power.

Individual managers may have a level of concern for both production and people but the level will depend on the basic attitudes, beliefs and values they hold – as well as the style of management they favour. What is important is how they actually express their concerns.

The corners of the grid give five basic combinations of the depth of concern for production as well as the degree of concern for people:

- an **impoverished manager** (1,1) will tend to have a low level of concern for both production and people and will tend to remain remote from their subordinates and not to welcome change;
- an **authority-compliance manager** (9,1) will exhibit a high level of concern for both production and people and will usually rely on the use of authority to support a centralised system of work;
- the **country club manager** (1,9) shows a low level of concern for production and a high

level of concern for people and believes that if the workforce is contented they will do what is asked of them and achieve what is considered to be an acceptable output level;
- the **middle-of-the-road manager** (5,5) shows a moderate concern for both production and people and tends to accept a policy which leaves the workforce to get on with their tasks and thus avoids any real issues which appear;
- the **team manager** (9,9) has a high concern for both production and people.

The 1991 grid developed two further styles:

- the **paternalistic manager** (9+9) uses punishment and reward in return for disloyalty and obedience;
- the **opportunistic manager** sees management as an exchange of systems where effort is exchanged for effort at the same level and such a manager believes that people will adapt to any situation and gain maximum advantage from it.

House (1987) – Path-Goal Theory

This is a contingency theory of leadership which has arisen out of the findings of the Ohio State leadership studies on initiating structure and consideration discussed earlier. House (1987) believed that it was the leader's job to help followers in such a way that they were able to achieve their individual goals, and ensure that in doing this, they were working towards the objectives of the organisation. He derived the term 'path-goal' from the premise that effective leaders tended to clarify the path that helps followers get from where they are to where they want to be, i.e. to goal achievement, and on the way such leaders reduced the hurdles that lay in the path.

The basis of the theory is that the followers *accept* such behaviour by their leaders and see it as a source of their own immediate or projected need satisfaction. The path-goal theory is a highly motivational theory because the leader's behaviour:

- makes subordinate need satisfaction contingent on effective performance; and
- provides the mentoring, guidance, support and rewards that are necessary for effective performance from the individual.

House (1987) identified four distinctive leadership behaviours:

1 **Directive leader**. This sort of leader liaises with followers and:
   - lets them know what is expected of them;
   - timetables their work;
   - gives specific help for task accomplishment.

There is a distinct match here with the Ohio State dimension of *initiating structure*.

2 **Supportive leader**. Such a leader shows concern for followers and is always supportive. By behaving in such a way, this type of leader mirrors the Ohio State *consideration* variable.

3 **Participative leader**. The key dimension here is of consultation when the leader asks followers for their opinion and acts upon it.

4 **Achievement-oriented leader**. This type of leader sets challenging objectives and expects the very best from all subordinates at all times.

Overall, House (1987) believes that leaders should be flexible because his path-goal theory suggests that the same person in the role of leader is able to display any combination or, indeed, all, of the behaviours in a situational manner. However, as can be seen in Figure 7.10, there are some moderating variables in this viewpoint.

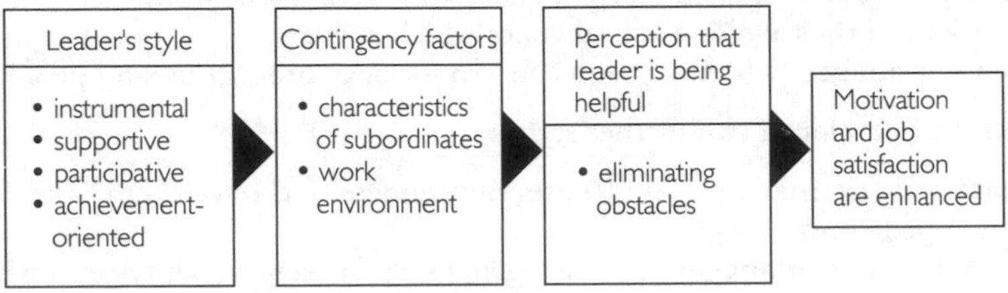

Figure 7.10 Moderating principles in path-goal theory

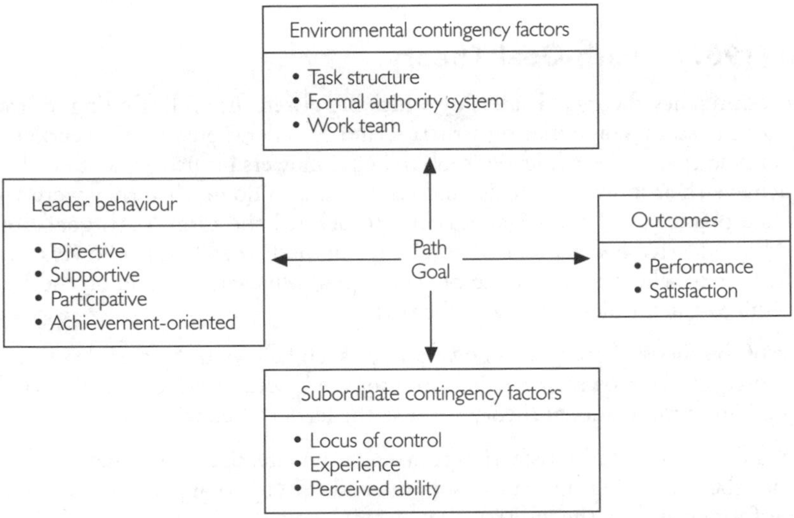

Figure 7.11 The path-goal theory (House, 1987)

As can be seen from Figure 7.11, the path-goal theory suggests that there are two classes of situational or contingency variables that attempt to moderate any leadership behaviour – outcome relationship: those in the environment that are outside the control of the subordinate (task structure, formal authority system, work team) and those which are a part of the personal characteristics of the *subordinate* (locus of control, experience, perceived ability). It is the environmental factors which determine the type of leader behaviour that is required if such subordinate outcomes are to be made the best of. The personal characteristics determine how the environment and the leader behaviour are interpreted.

Briefly, the theory suggests that ineffective leadership will be apparent if it is redundant with the sources of environmental structure or if it is incongruent with the subordinate characteristics. The performance of individuals within the work team is likely to be positively influenced when the leader compensates for anything which is lacking in either the employee as an individual or in the workplace environment. However, a leader should not explain tasks and how to go about them when the team member obviously knows what he or she is doing because such direction will be perceived by the employee as redundant and insulting.

Belbin (1993) – Solo leader and team leader

Belbin (1993) further developed his roles within teams but also distinguished between two types of leader:

- solo
- team.

A *solo leader* can be identified by certain behaviour characteristics:

- rules absolutely without any limits;
- takes risks with other people;
- takes a directive approach;
- identifies stated tasks and objectives;
- by using coercive power, expects people to comply;
- considers themself a role model.

Such leaders are successful in times of crisis when barriers need to be overcome and when decisions have to be made and implemented quickly. Such leaders, according to Belbin (1993), are familiar to all people since most people like to be followers and want to have faith in their leader. However, if the situation is one where followers' faith in the leader is not apparent, solo leaders are discarded.

The *team leader* is the other side of the coin and exhibits characteristics such as:

- sharing the leadership role;
- limiting their role deliberately;
- expressing vision and mission;
- respecting others' skills and talents;
- delegating tasks and responsibilities.

Since the workplace – and, indeed, society – now works in an ever-changing and uncertain environment with the sharing of power being paramount, team leadership is becoming more evident.

As has already been said, there are many theories within the field of leadership and a key issue to be addressed is what should be the most appropriate manner and where should a manager strike a balance in leadership style. To be effective in the leadership role, an individual needs to take on board the contingency approach to leadership.

A number of variables have been identified which it is possible to group, as in Table 7.14 below.

Table 7.14 Contingency factors related to leadership

1	attitudes of the individual manager
	authority of the individual manager
2	attitudes of the subordinates/followers
	potential of the subordinates/followers
	nature of the manager–subordinate relationship
3	nature of the task
	environmental factors

Such variables have been explored by a number of researchers who have each emphasised a different aspect of the above variables.

Tannenbaum and Schmidt (1958) suggested three key variables which affected the contingency approach to leadership in Figure 7.12 below.

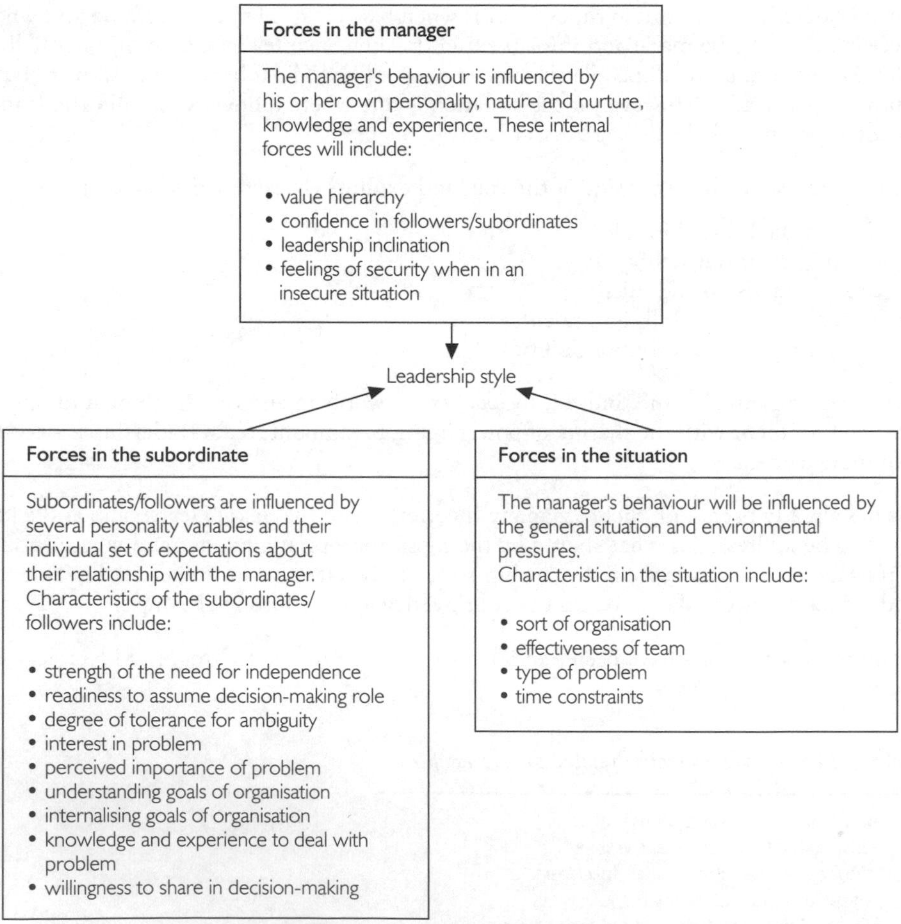

Forces in the manager
The manager's behaviour is influenced by his or her own personality, nature and nurture, knowledge and experience. These internal forces will include:
• value hierarchy
• confidence in followers/subordinates
• leadership inclination
• feelings of security when in an insecure situation
Leadership style
Forces in the subordinate
Subordinates/followers are influenced by several personality variables and their individual set of expectations about their relationship with the manager. Characteristics of the subordinates/ followers include:
• strength of the need for independence
• readiness to assume decision-making role
• degree of tolerance for ambiguity
• interest in problem
• perceived importance of problem
• understanding goals of organisation
• internalising goals of organisation
• knowledge and experience to deal with problem
• willingness to share in decision-making
Forces in the situation
The manager's behaviour will be influenced by the general situation and environmental pressures.
Characteristics in the situation include:
• sort of organisation
• effectiveness of team
• type of problem
• time constraints

Figure 7.12 Contingency factors affecting leadership style, after Tannenbaum and Schmidt (1958)

How individual managers will behave will depend upon:

- their own inclinations
- the readiness of subordinates/followers to assist
- the pressures of the situation.

If all three are positive, the manager will adopt a more consultative style of leadership; if they are negative the manager would be more likely to adopt an authoritative style.

Fiedler (1964) took a slightly different perspective as outlined in Figure 7.13 below.

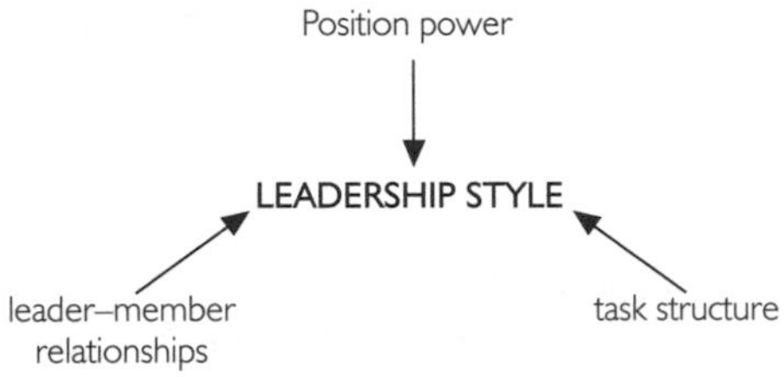

Figure 7.13 Fiedler's (1964) leadership perspectives

It is very important that research work is valid and reliable if researchers are to expect other people to use what they have found out. Fiedler's (1964) contingency theory has been tested frequently for over thirty years, and the data suggest that it works very well and is predictable. His contingency theory suggests that the fit between the leader's need-structure and the favourableness of the leader's situation determines the team's effectiveness in accomplishing their goals. However, the theory does assume that all leaders are either task-oriented or relationship-oriented – which one would depend upon how the individual leader satisfies his or her individual need gratification.

Task-oriented leaders concentrate their efforts on getting the task done whilst relationship-oriented leaders are gratified principally by developing healthy relationships with their followers. Therefore, the effectiveness of both styles will depend upon the favourableness of the situation. This theory, therefore, classifies the favourableness of a leader's situation according to the leader's position power, the structure of the team's task, and the leader–follower relationships.

Least-preferred co-worker

Fielder (1970) developed his earlier theory by classifying leaders using the Least Preferred Co-Worker (LPC) scale. The least preferred co-worker (LPC) is the person a leader has least preferred to work with in the course of their career. It is measured by the use of a projective technique through which the leader is asked to consider a person with whom they have worked and whom they could least work with. This does not necessarily mean that the person chosen is disliked by the leader – such a person is identified only because the leader would not want to work with them because they had difficulty achieving the objectives.

Those who describe their LPC in positive terms – cheerful, considerate, courteous – are classified as having a high LPC and are, as such, relationship-oriented leaders. Those who describe their LPC in negative terms – miserable, inefficient, idle – are classified as low

LPC, or task-oriented, leaders. However, the LPC determination of an individual does not mean that person is unproductive. It only means that the LPC's perception of tasks and/or relationships does not match that of the individual being tested.

This measuring technique is controversial in the field of contingency theory. It has been criticised on both conceptual and methodological grounds because it is a projective technique which is situational and, at best, invalid and unreliable. That is, leadership is a contingency factor which is also situational.

In his overall contingency theory, Fiedler (1964, 1970) is suggesting that when the situation changes so will the leadership style: if the situation is favourable so will the leadership style be (for example, consultative); and if the situation becomes unfavourable so the leadership style will follow suit (e.g. become, possibly, autocratic).

Vroom and Yetton (1973)

Vroom and Yetton's (1973) work was related more to decision-making, within which there was a core of situational variables embedded within the theory which related to leadership style. These variables are outlined in Figure 7.14 below.

Figure 7.14 Vroom and Yetton's (1973) leadership variables

The principal situational variables appropriate to leadership behaviour in the above model are the quality of the decision to be made, the acceptance of that decision by the subordinates/followers, and the environmental factors (for example, available time, available information). Vroom and Yetton (1973) suggested a set of rules which could point to a more autocratic or more consultative leadership style:

1 Is it likely that one decision will be of better quality than any other?

2 Is there enough information available to make a quality decision?

3 Has the problem been organised?

Points 1 to 3 above refer to the quality of the decision whilst the remaining four (4 to 7) below concern the acceptance of those decisions:

4 Is it vital that the decision made is accepted by the subordinates/followers?

5 If the leader made a solo decision, how likely would it be that the subordinates/followers would accept it?

6 Do the subordinates internalise the objectives of the organisation and thus own them?

7 Is functional conflict amongst subordinates/followers likely in preferred solutions?

The points above were suggested as a set of rules which, in turn, direct the leader towards styles that he or she should avoid in a given situation and adopt in yet another, i.e. they are situational. The researchers suggested that the use of a decision-tree (flow chart) might assist the leaders in the adoption of an appropriate leadership style.

Vroom and Jago (1988) subsequently revised this model to include a broader set of variables which could be used, via decision-trees, to isolate a particular type of problem which could then suggest one of their five proposed management styles as shown in Figure 7.15 below.

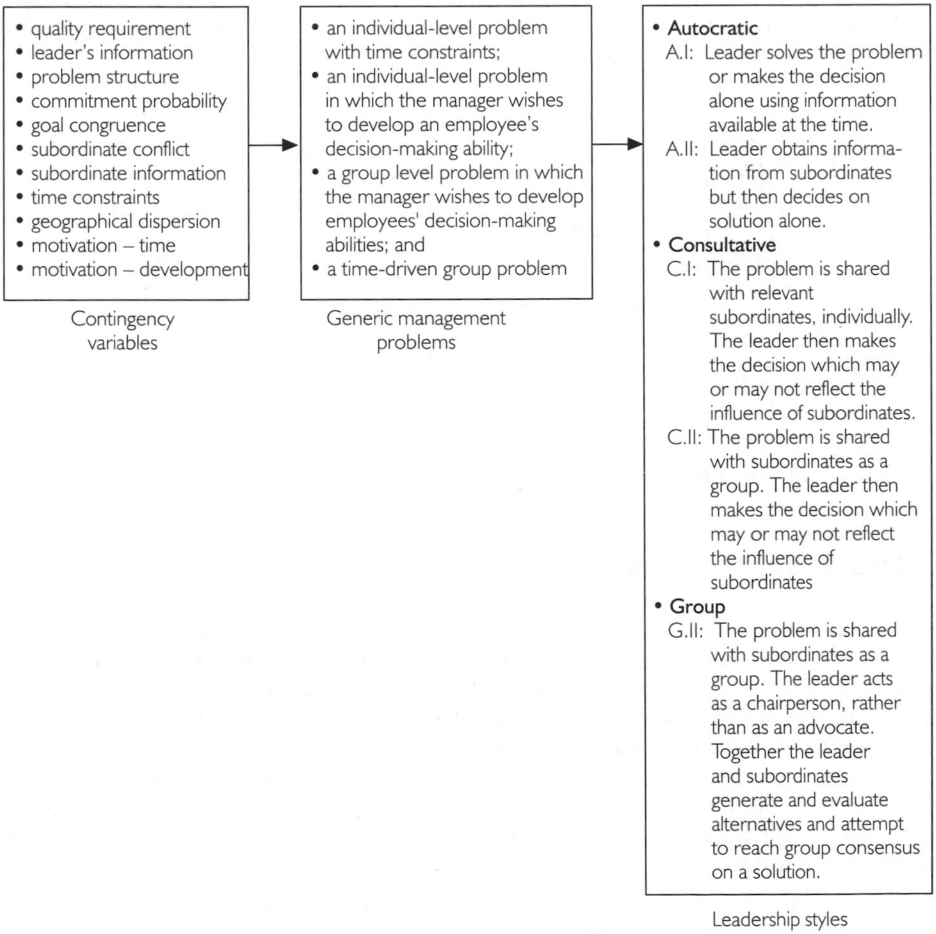
• quality requirement
• leader's information
• problem structure
• commitment probability
• goal congruence
• subordinate conflict
• subordinate information
• time constraints
• geographical dispersion
• motivation – time
• motivation – development
Contingency variables
• an individual-level problem with time constraints;
• an individual-level problem in which the manager wishes to develop an employee's decision-making ability;
• a group level problem in which the manager wishes to develop employees' decision-making abilities; and
• a time-driven group problem
Generic management problems
• Autocratic
A.I: Leader solves the problem or makes the decision alone using information available at the time.
A.II: Leader obtains information from subordinates but then decides on solution alone.
• Consultative
C.I: The problem is shared with relevant subordinates, individually. The leader then makes the decision which may or may not reflect the influence of subordinates.
C.II: The problem is shared with subordinates as a group. The leader then makes the decision which may or may not reflect the influence of subordinates
• Group
G.II: The problem is shared with subordinates as a group. The leader acts as a chairperson, rather than as an advocate. Together the leader and subordinates generate and evaluate alternatives and attempt to reach group consensus on a solution.
Leadership styles

Figure 7.15 Vroom and Jago's (1988) model of management styles

Leadership style: a summary

From the theories discussed so far, it can be seen that leadership is usually determined by two main situational variables:

- personal characteristics of the subordinates/followers
- nature of the task.

If the objectives can be clearly seen by the workers and the objective is transparent and acceptable to all, then any attempt to give further instructions by the leader will result in the subordinates/followers behaving negatively. Conversely, the team members will require a directive style of leadership if the task is unclear and the objectives difficult to accept.

Therefore effective leadership is only possible if both the leader and the followers wish to help each other, and such leadership depends also upon the willingness of the leader to help and the followers to accept help. Furthermore, leadership behaviour is motivational in that it does drive and guide individuals to meet their needs and attain their goals; this can be seen in Figure 7.16 below:

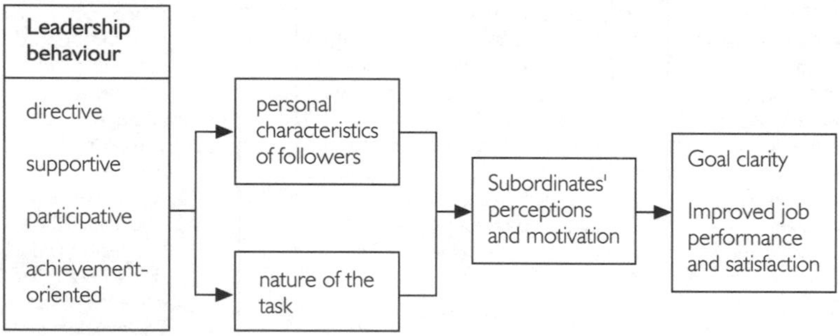

Figure 7.16 The two-way needs of situational leadership

Situational leadership

Situational leadership is a contingency theory which has its focus on the behaviour of followers. If a leader is to be successful it is vital that he or she chooses the right style of leadership. Hersey and Blanchard (1974, 1984) argue that leadership is contingent on the level of the followers' maturity. They emphasised the followers rather than the leader because effective leadership reflects the reality of whether to accept or reject the leader. It does not matter how the leader behaves; the effectiveness of his or her actions will totally depend upon the actions of the followers. Most leadership theories overlook this key variable, which is now even more important in the modern flat, leaner, and delayered organisations where teamwork is the norm.

Hersey and Blanchard (1974, 1988) further developed this view by concentrating on the variable which was neglected by most other leadership researchers – that of maturity: as shown in Figure 7.17.

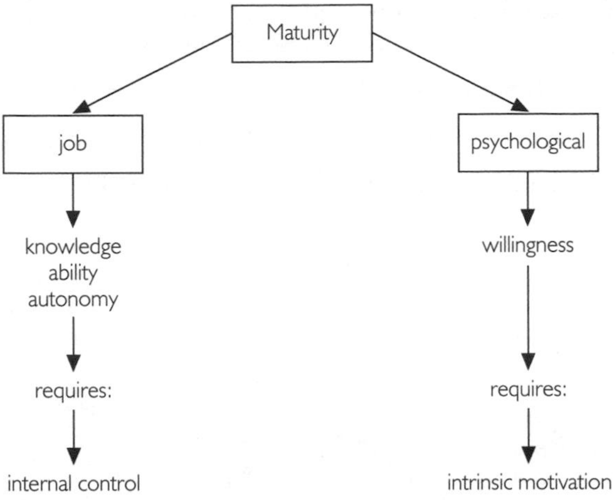

Figure 7.17 Maturity as perceived by Hersey and Blanchard (1974, 1988)

Situational leadership utilises the two dimensions previously attributed to Fiedler (1970) – task and relationship behaviours. However, Hersey and Blanchard (1974, 1988) developed their thesis beyond their predecessor's by:

- considering each as either 'high' or 'low'
- then combining them into four specific leadership styles:
  - telling
  - selling
  - participating
  - delegating

which are described as follows.

Telling (high task/low relationship). Here the leader will provide the role framework and tell people how to behave, and when and where in order to achieve the task. The emphasis here is on directive behaviour.

Selling (high task/high relationship). The leader will balance both directive and supportive behaviour.

Participating (low task/high relationship). The leaders and the followers here share in all decision-making. The principal role for the leader is acting as a facilitator and aiding effective communication.

Delegating (low task/low relationship). This is genuine *laissez faire* where the leader is providing little direction or support.

Hersey and Blanchard (1974, 1988) then went on to define their four stages of maturity.

Key

M1 People are neither competent nor confident and are unwilling to take responsibility or be accountable for their actions.

M2 People are willing to do the tasks but are not able to do them. Although motivated they do not have the required skills to complete the task.

M3 People have the skills but are unwilling to do what the leader asks.

M4 People are willing and also have the skills to do what the leader asks.

Figure 7.18 below integrates the various components into the situational leadership model.

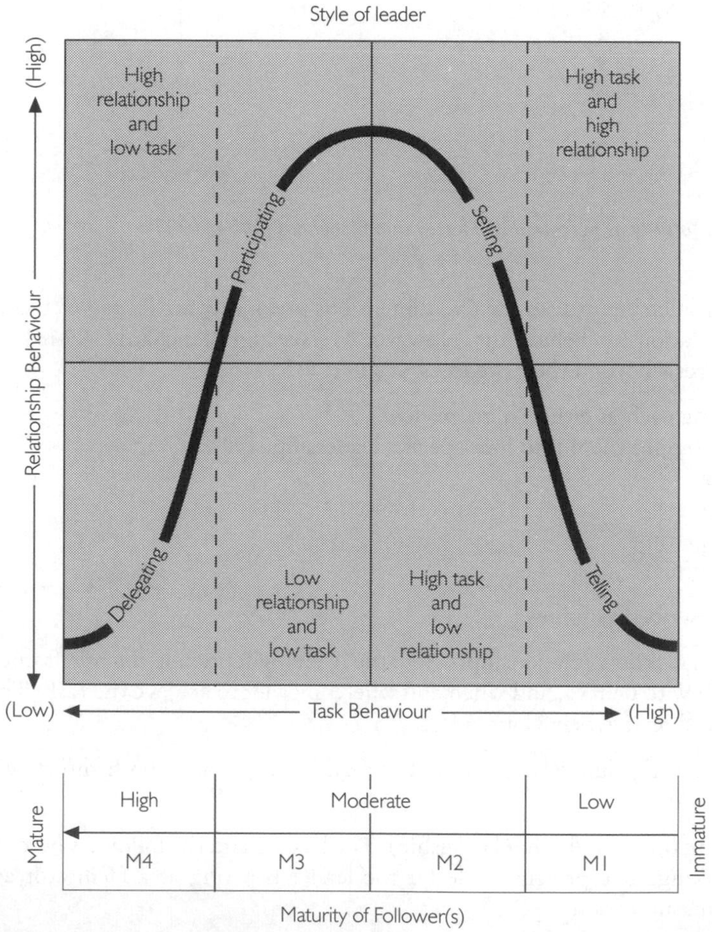

Figure 7.18 Situational leadership model, after Hersey and Blanchard (1988)

There are some key factors which are highlighted by reference to the above figure.

- As the followers increase in maturity, the leader decreases control over the activities of the group and the relationship behaviour as well.
- When at M1 the followers require clarity and as they move to M2, both high task and high relationship behaviour is needed from the leader.

- This high task behaviour will compensate for the followers' lack of skill.
- The high relationship behaviour is used in an attempt to get the followers to adopt what the leaders wants.
- When level M3 is reached there is an accompanying problem with motivation which needs to be made intrinsic through behaviours such as support, consultative, participative leadership styles.
- At the final stage, M4, the leader has become redundant because the followers are willing and able to adopt responsibility and accountability.

Table 7.15 below shows a strong link with Blake *et al.*'s (1964) Managerial Grid©: particularly in relation to the four extreme corners of the grid (refer to Figure 7.9).

Table 7.15 Comparison between Blake et al.*'s (1964) Managerial Grid© and Hersey and Blanchard (1974 and 1988) relating to leadership style*

Hersey and Blanchard	**Blake *et al.***
Telling	9,1
Selling	9,9
Participating	1,9
Delegating	1,1

It may well be argued, then, that situational leadership is the same as the Managerial Grid© with the exception of the replacement on the 9,9 ('one style for all occasions') with the recommendation that the 'right' style should align with the maturity of the followers. However, Hersey and Blanchard (1974, 1988) would challenge this latter view by arguing that the grid has its emphasis on the *concern* for both production and people which are at the relevant attitudinal dimension. In contrast, situational leadership emphasises task and is, therefore, relationship *behaviour*. It is the present author's opinion that this is a minute differentiation. What is important is that an understanding of situational leadership will be itself enhanced if consideration is also given to the ideas put forward within the Managerial Grid© of direct adaptation of the Managerial Grid© in relation to the four stages of follower maturity.

The situational leadership model has received little attention from researchers and very few other studies have tested its reliability and validity. Like a number of organisational ideas, the theory must be taken guardedly. What, at best, can be said in its favour is that current evidence does partially support the theory – especially for followers who have a low maturity.

Many of the issues involved in group leadership are summarised effectively in Nicholls (1985) where there is a challenge to Hersey and Blanchard's model (1974, 1988). Nicholls (1985) says that the latter paradigm goes against three logical concepts related to leadership:

- consistency
- continuity
- conformity.

Consistency. This is inconsistently dealt with by Hersey and Blanchard (1974, 1988) because it links the concern for task/relationships with ability/willingness.

Continuity. The development level continuum lacks this because it needs a willingness to appear, disappear and reappear as the development level increases.

Conformity. The work negates the role of conformity because it does not commence with a high tasks/high relationship style for a team which is simultaneously unwilling and lacking in skills.

Nicholls (1985) has propounded a model which corrects the above perceived errors in Hersey and Blanchard (1974, 1988) and, in doing this, a new model relating to situational leadership is put forward, as shown in Figure 7.19 below.

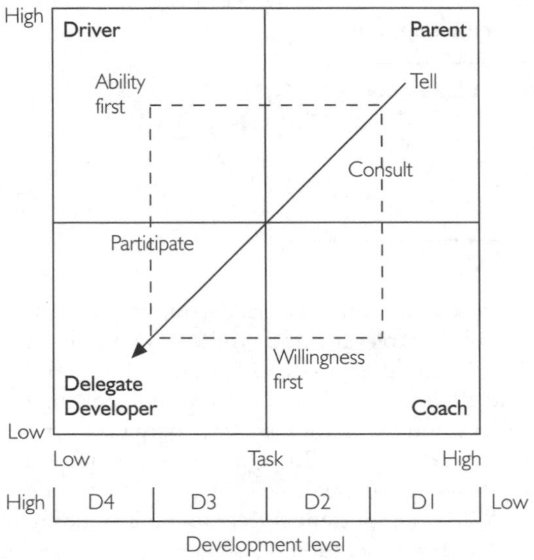

Figure 7.19 A model of situational leadership (Nicholls, 1985, p. 6)

Taking the model in Figure 7.19 above, some key points can be made:

1 For groups that comprise members who are both unskilled and unwilling and thus at a low development phase, the leader takes on the role of a *parent* who wishes to develop ability and social skills simultaneously. When both increase, the activity connected with the task and the relationship between members can be reduced in a symmetrical way. The result will then be a progression from 'telling' to 'consulting' to being in the role of a *developer* (bottom left-hand quadrant).

2 This developer role will then continue gently towards 'participation' and 'delegation' so that the ability and the willingness of members of the group are enhanced.

3 However, willingness and ability might not develop at the same pace – should willingness develop more quickly, then the leader needs to take the opportunity to be proactive as a *coach* who wishes to improve skills.

4 If, conversely, the skills develop more quickly than the willingness to do the task, then the leader will act as a *driver* and push the team towards its full potential to achieve the goal and to prevent unwillingness from causing a shortfall in performance.

However, like all models, Nicholls' model (1985) is an ideal and requires a smooth progression of the leader from the role of parent (high task/high relationship), following the usual progression tell-sell/consult-participative-delegate route, to the role of developer requiring a low task/low relationship style.

The key behaviour in this model is that of coach because it is usual that the skill (ability) and the willingness do not develop simultaneously and often are in conflict with each other. By coaching, the leader can help to develop the skills and use driving skills to create a happy and productive team.

Hersey and Blanchard (1988) may have pre-empted Nicholls (1985) because they comment in their work that one of the important things to remember is that when individuals are at the lower levels of readiness, the direction is being provided by the leader (Nicholls' (1985) 'driver'). At the higher levels where leader-direction is lessened the followers are becoming more responsible and accountable for their actions and so, according to Hersey and Blanchard (1988), they are now 'follower directed'. They go on to say that such a transition can be accompanied by a period of a feeling of loss where there is apprehension and insecurity within the team. As followers move from low levels of readiness to higher levels, the combinations of task and relationship behaviour appropriate to the situation begin to change and the team begins to overcome the grief at the loss of its driver!

Group dynamics across cultures

Just as individual behaviour will vary among cultures, so will interpersonal processes. One of the important areas where variation in culture is prevalent is in group dynamics. There are some key issues to be remembered:

- behaviour in organisational settings varies across cultures;
- culture is a major cause of behavioural variation;
- behaviour across cultures remains diverse where organisations themselves are becoming more similar – especially in design with flatter structures and the use of team work;
- the same manager will behave differently in different cultures;
- cultural diversity can be an important ingredient in achieving synergy.

Thus, cultures will differ in the importance that they place on group or team membership. There is continued research which focuses on how to deal with groups that are multi-cultural. Generally, a leader of a group which is culturally diverse can anticipate that:

- there will be a high probability of mistrust amongst group members;
- there will be considerable stereotyping;
- there will certainly be communication problems.

A leader of a group needs to ensure that a multi-cultural group will function smoothly – especially initially – and he or she will need therefore to spend additional time facilitating the group through the troughs as the group goes through the initial stages of the group-forming process discussed earlier. The leader should also understand that the group may well take longer to achieve its task despite having the advantage of new ideas and different viewpoints which will aid creativity and the quality of decision-making.

Working in teams and groups has become the norm in most organisations as they have dealt with the challenges of the revolution of flatter, delayered structuring. This is dealt with in the next chapter which considers the structure and design of organisations.

Questions for discussion

1 Do you (or would you want to) work within an autocratic, democratic, or *laissez faire* work environment? What are the advantages and disadvantages of each environment?

2 Is your Organisational Behaviour tutor someone who is high in concern for production or for people? What is his/her position on the Blake and Mouton (1991) Leadership Grid©?

3 How will you most likely make decisions based on your cognitive style and what might you overlook using your preferred approach?

References and further reading

Adair, J., 1975, *Action-Centred Leadership* (Cambridge: Cambridge University Press)

Allcorn, S., 'Understanding Groups at Work' in *Personnel*, Vol. 66, No 8, August 1989, pp. 28 – 36

Bales, R.F., 1950, *Interaction Process Analysis* (Reading, MA: Addison-Wesley)

Baron, R.A. and Greenberg, J., 1990, *Behaviour in Organisations: Understanding and Managing the Human Side of Work* (London: Allyn & Bacon)

Belbin, R.M., 1981, *Management Teams: Why They Succeed or Fail* (London: Butterworth-Heinemann)

Belbin, R.M., 1993, *Team Roles at Work* (London: Butterworth-Heinemann)

Benne, K.D. and Sheats, P., 1948, 'Functional Roles of Group Members' in *Journal of Social Issues*, Vol. 4, pp. 41-49

Blake, R.R., Mouton, J.S., Barnes, L.B. and Greiner, L.E., 'Breakthrough in Organization Development' in *Harvard Business Review*, November–December 1964, p. 136 (Boston: Harvard College Press)

Blake, R.R. and Mouton, J.S., 1985, *The Managerial Grid III* (Houston: Gulf Publishing Company)

Blake, R.R. and McCanse, A.A., 1991, *Leadership Dilemmas – Grid Solutions* (Houston: Gulf Publishing Company)

Daly, N., 'Staff consultation seen as business necessity' in *Personnel Today*, 19 June 1997, p. 15

Fiedler, F.E., 1964, *A Theory of Leader Effectiveness* (New York: McGraw-Hill)

Fiedler, F.E., 'Personality, Motivational Systems, and Behavior of High and Low LPC Persons'; Technical Report No 70-12, 1970, University of Washington, Seattle

Hackman, J.R., 'The Design of Work Teams' in J.W. Lorsch (ed.), 1987, *Handbook of Organizational Behaviour* (London: Prentice-Hall) pp. 315–342

Hatch, M.J., 1997, *Organization Theory: Modern Symbolic and Postmodern Perspectives* (Oxford: Oxford University Press)

Hersey, P. and Blanchard, K.H., 'So You Want to Know Your Leadership Style?' in *Training and Development Journal*, February 1974, pp. 1–15

Hersey, P. and Blanchard, K.H., 1988 (5th edn), *Management of Organizational Behavior: Utilizing Human Resources* (London: Prentice-Hall International)

House, R.J., 'Retrospective Comment' in L.E. Boone and D.D. Bowen, 1987 (2nd edn), *The Great Writings in Management and Organizational Behavior* (New York: Random House) pp. 354–364

Janis, I.L., 1982 (2nd edn), *Victims of Group Think: A Psychological Study of Foreign Policy Decisions and Fiascos* (Boston, MA: Houghton Mifflin)

Kretch, D., Crutchfield, R.S. and Ballachey, E.L., 1962, *The Individual in Society* (London: McGraw-Hill)

McGregor, D.M., 1960, *The Human Side of Enterprise* (New York: McGraw Hill)

Merrick, N., 'The Lions Share' in *People Management*, 12 June 1997, pp. 34–35, 37

Mullins, L., 1996 (4th edn), *Management and Organisational Behaviour* (London: Pitman)

Murnighan, J.K., 'Group Decision Making: What Strategies Should You Use?' in *Management Review*, February 1981, p. 61.

Nicholls, J.R., 1985 'A New Approach to Situational Leadership' in *Leadership and Organizational Development Journal*, Vol. 6, No 4

Pruitt, D.G., 1971, 'Choice-shifts in political decision-making' in *Journal of Personality and Social Psychology*, Vol. 20, pp. 339–360

Sharman, C., 'Looking for tomorrow's leaders' in *Management Today*, August 1997, p. 5

Shaw, M.E., 1976, *Group Dynamics* (Maidenhead: McGraw-Hill)

Tannenbaum, R. and Schmidt, W.H., 'How to Choose a Leadership Pattern' in *Harvard Business Review*, March–April 1958, p. 58

Tjosveld, D., 1991, *The Conflict-Positive Organization* (Reading, MA: Addison-Wesley)

Vroom, V.H. and Jago, A.G., 1988, *The New Leadership: Managing Participation in Organizations* (Englewood-Cliffs, NJ: Prentice-Hall)

Vroom, V.H. and Yetton, P.W., 1973, *Leadership and Decision-Making* (Pittsburg, PA: University of Pittsburg Press)

Ethical issues

Learning objectives

After studying this section you should be able to:

- appreciate the importance of ethical behaviour when making decisions;
- understand the role of ethical behaviour when working in groups and teams;
- identify the role of *groupthink* in the team decision-making model.

Introduction

As individuals develop ethical values, they are strongly influenced by the groups they associate with most closely and such *reference groups* have a profound effect on behaviour. There are two principal issues which relate to the role of an individual within a reference group. These are, firstly, *geographic location*, which can affect what is considered acceptable behaviour by different reference groups. For example, in the seaside town of Blackpool, a male entering a department store clad only in shorts and sports shoes is generally acceptable. Similar behaviour in Harrods, Knightsbridge, London, would be entirely out of place and such attire would result in the individual being asked to leave the store. By the same token, cities in the USA have ordinances forbidding the drinking of alcoholic beverages in spaces exposed to normal pedestrian traffic, such as shopping precincts; yet most European cities consider as proper and civilised the provision of outdoor facilities for customers who may wish to drink beer or wine at a table outside.

Secondly, the *type of work* undertaken by individuals influences what is considered appropriate behaviour. Chartered accountants, lawyers, scientists, physicians and university lecturers have different expectations of themselves and others than do general maintenance workers, machine operators, construction workers and fork-lift truck operators. What is right or wrong is established partly by the group with which each worker associates daily, and partly by the lessons learned from childhood and adult experiences.

Ethics and group decision-making

Ethical behaviour conforms to generally accepted norms, whereas unethical behaviour does not. Although some decisions made by managers have little or nothing to do with their own personal ethics, many other decisions are, in fact, influenced by the manager's own ethics. For example, decisions involving such disparate issues as hiring and firing employees, negotiating with customers and suppliers, setting wages and assigning tasks, and maintaining one's expense account, as can be seen in the case study below, are all subject to ethical influences.

CASE STUDY
The price of honesty

Hewlett-Packard has introduced a paperless expenses reporting system where employees enter their expenses through their computers onto an electronic form which they then electronically send to a financial services centre where reimbursements are paid electronically into the sender's bank account. This system has done away with the scrutinisation of hard-copy expenses sheets. Whilst such a system might appear to have given a corporate licence to swindle Hewlett-Packard, it appears that the system has helped the company to reduce the number of sites that handle general ledger accounting from 56 to two in the USA and from 25 to four in Europe. The company believes that this had produced savings of £645,000 a year, more than outweighing any abuse of the system by unscrupulous employees. A less tangible benefit is the goodwill that this trust in the honesty of employees engenders. The organisation is continuing to reduce its operating costs as a percentage of turnover from 40 per cent in 1988 to 25 per cent in 1995, so it would appear to be doing something right. But surely most employees are taking advantage of the lax expense reporting by making exaggerated claims?

Not so, the organisation reports. Senior management feels that people want to do the best for their company, so they are trusted and treated like adults and those who want to fiddle the organisation are in the minority. Perhaps the fact that Hewlett-Packard is an American-owned company has something to do with this. Like so many USA businesses, it seems to arouse fierce devotion from its employees rather than the cynicism that is often part of the European corporate psyche. The organisation does have one form of control, in that it keeps a record of the average living expenses in countries where employees travel and uses this as a measurement for expense claims. The management feels that the stricter the control the more people will find a way around it.

Adapted from A. Cohen, 'The price of honesty' in *Financial Times*, 2 September 1996, p. 16

As can be seen from the above case, whatever model of decision-making and control is adopted by individuals and groups, a key criterion is the ethical implications of the decision. The way people make their decisions will depend upon many influential factors such as individual differences and organisational control. Blanchard and Peale (1988) suggested that before making a decision, three things should be taken into account:

1 **ensuring that the decision is legal**, that is, making sure that the laws of the country and company policy are kept;

2 **ensuring that the decision is well-balanced**, that is, making sure that the decision is fair to all concerned and that it fosters a win-win relationship;

3 **considering how it makes the decision-maker feel** – ensure that the individual is proud of the decision and is happy to live with it.

CASE STUDY
Beech-Nut

Beech-Nut admitted that they had been selling millions of jars of 'phoney' apple juice that contained cheap concentrates and chemical additives. The organisation was running at a loss and managers were of the opinion that other companies were also selling fake apple juice. Beech-Nut were convinced that their fake juice was safe for consumers and that even if laboratory tests were carried out, they would not be able to come to the definite conclusion that it was different from real apple juice.

Adapted from R.R. Sims, 'Linking Groupthink to Unethical Behavior in Organizations', in *Journal of Business Ethics*, No 11, 1992, pp. 651–662

The above case shows that groups can make decisions that are unethical. Beech-Nut was perceived to be a reputable company and there was no evidence to prove the opposite. However, possibly because of groupthink, the organisation ignored caution and morality in favour of immediate profits, and by ignoring any dissent they suffered considerable damage to their reputation: a result of unethical practices.

It is possible to prevent unethical group decisions by avoiding groupthink. Groups can appoint a person whose role it is to constantly ask questions of the group related to what it is doing and who can also raise ethical issues for the group to consider. Another way is to place two groups together so that they can question the course of action being taken by the other group.

All decisions, whether made by an individual or by groups and teams, must be evaluated for their ethics. It is the responsibility of the organisation to reinforce ethical behaviour through praise and reward. All organisational members need to understand that effective and ethical decisions are not mutually exclusive.

In general, ethical dilemmas for managers may centre on direct personal gain, indirect personal gain, or simple personal preferences. Consider, for example, a top executive contemplating a decision about a potential takeover of another organisation. Her share option package may result in enormous personal financial gain if the decision goes one way, though the stakeholders may benefit more if the decision goes the other way. An indirect personal gain may result from a certain decision that does not directly add value to a manager's personal worth but does serve to enhance her career. Or the manager may face a choice for relocating a company section where one of the options is closer to her home.

Whenever groups make decisions they should carefully and deliberately consider the ethical content of those decisions. The goal is for the person making the decision to do so in the best interest of the organisation, as opposed to the best interests of the individual. The use of teams within which to discuss potential ethical dilemmas is helpful because others can often provide an objective view of a situation that may help to deter individuals from making unintentional unethical decisions.

From the cases it can be seen, therefore, that groups work, and group decisions reflect underlying ethical principles and rules be they individual or, as is more likely, based on membership of a group. Ethics deals with right or wrong in the actions and decisions of individuals and the organisations of which they are a part. Ethical issues are more common and complex than is generally recognised. According to Donaldson and Dumfee (1994) ethical issues do influence the decisions that employees make daily and some ethical issues involve factors that make the choice of 'right or wrong' muddy – thus many employees experience ethical dilemmas.

Trevino and Youngblood (1990) supported the view that ethical decision-making is extremely complex: thus there are no simple rules for coping with decisions that have an important ethical content. The best that can be done is to share ethical reasoning with others and that is encouraged by the use of high performance task teams. Organisations must structure the decision-making process in ways that consider the range and legitimacy of ethical pressures, for example working as a member of a diverse project team. According to Pettinger (1996) this also means: 'understanding where the greater good and the true interests of the organisation lie, and adopting realistic steps in the pursuit of this' (p. 390).

Questions for discussion

1 With reference to the case study 'The price of honesty', do you think that it is ethical for employees to carry out creative accounting regarding their expenses claims?

2 What principles and rules can be made about ethical decision-making from the 'Beech-Nut' case?

3 Is there a moral dilemma in expecting an individual to subordinate his or her individuality and autonomy to the will of the work group or team? Suppose you are a member of a work team that is ready to act in a way that you, personally, believe is unethical or immoral. What should you do? Will you be responsible for the actions of the entire team?

References and further reading

Blanchard, K. and Peale, N.V., 1988, *The Power of Ethical Management* (New York: Fawcett Crest)

Cohen, A., 'The price of honesty' in *Financial Times*, 2 September 1996, p. 16

Donaldson, T. and Dumfee, T.W., 'Toward a unified conception of business ethics: Integrative social contracts theory' in *Academy of Management Review*, 1994, No 19, pp. 252–284

Pettinger, R., 1996, *Introduction to Organisational Behaviour* (Basingstoke: Macmillan)

Sims, R.R., 'Linking Groupthink to Unethical Behavior in Organizations' in *Journal of Business Ethics*, 1992, No 11, pp. 651–662

Trevino, L.K. and Youngblood, S.A., 'Bad apples in bad barrels: A causal analysis of ethical decision-making behaviour' in *Journal of Applied Psychology*, 1990, No 75, pp. 378–385

Part 3: Understanding organisations

8 Organisational structure and design

Learning objectives

After studying this chapter you should be able to:

- discuss the link between organisational structure and design and individual behaviour in the workplace;
- define the organisational design processes of an organisation;
- explain the forces which reshape an organisation;
- analyse the role of power and responsibility in organisational design;
- describe how to select the most effective organisational design;
- discuss emerging organisational structures and designs.

Introduction

CASE STUDY
The Royal Dutch Shell Group

The old business hierarchies are a thing of the past. Or are they? In late September 1997 Shell announced yet another monster reorganisation – this time of its European oil operations. It said that twenty-eight general manager positions and up to seven layers of management were to be done away with. This is quite shocking. It is hard to believe the company had so many general managers and layers to begin with – let alone so many dispensable ones.

Shell is seen as one of the best managed companies Europe has. Moreover, it has traditionally led the field when it comes to reorganisation. So if the oil giant still has all these useless layers hidden away, how many do other companies have?

Adapted from L. Kellaway, *Financial Times*, 6 October 1997, p. 14

Organisational structure and design are key features in understanding how individuals behave in the workplace. Daft (1995) describes an organisational structure as being: 'the visible representation for a whole set of underlying activities and processes in an organisation' (p. 192).

Reporting on the work of Child (1984) he states that there are three key components in the definition of organisation structure:

1 Organization structure designates formal reporting relationships, including the number of levels in the hierarchy and the span of control of managers and supervisors.

2 Organization structure identifies the grouping together of individuals into departments and of departments into the total organization.

3 Organization structure includes the design of systems to ensure effective communication, co-ordination, and integration of effort across departments. (p. 192)

However, there is a distinction between organisational structure and organisational design. Daft (1995) defines organisational design as the 'administration and execution of the [organisation's] strategic plan' (p. 44).

Bedeian and Zamnuto (1991) support these views because they explicitly mean that organisations are:

- social entities
- goal directed
- specifically structured
- recognised as having a permeable boundary.

Social entities

Organisations are groups of people with needs and aspirations which the design of the organisation must take account of. These people and their roles are the foundation stones and building bricks of the organisation and they interact and cement together in order to achieve the objectives of the organisation as a whole. Current and projected trends in business management emphasise the importance and significance of human resource management along with its inherent practices of empowering individuals so that they can contribute more to achieving the organisation's goals.

Goal directed

An organisation exists for a purpose and it has a specific objective often defined in its vision or mission statement.

An example of a mission statement

The Roehampton Institute London (An Institute of the University of Surrey)

Roehampton Institute London is an open academic community committed to higher education through the promotion of effective learning, teaching, scholarship, and research.

It is a self-regulating college-based community built on the principles of toleration and respect for people and ideas, supported by the humanist and Christian principles of its four historic foundations.

It aims for academic excellence and seeks, through the encouragement of critical study and collaborative enquiry, to empower individuals of all ages and backgrounds to reach their full potential in a learner-centred environment.

It offers an extensive range of courses and programmes in the Arts, Education, Humanities, Sciences and Social Sciences.

It has a major vocational commitment to education, training and development for the caring professions, including teaching, health care, and therapeutic work.

It aims to be flexibly responsive to the personal and vocational academic requirements of individuals and groups, whether local, national, or international.

It pledges itself to continuous self-critical review of its standards and services in order to assure delivery of a learning experience of the highest quality for all who are able to benefit from it and who wish to have access to it.

Source: Roehampton Institute London, *Graduate and Postgraduate Prospectuses, 1998–1999*

More and more organisations are publishing their mission statement which is, according to Hannagan (1995), an attempt to 'encapsulate the purpose of their activity, as much as the direction they wish to take, in a single short statement' (p. 121).

As can be seen from the example from the Roehampton Institute London above, the mission statement addresses the key question 'What business are we in?', which is the basis of all mission statements: identifying the goals of the organisation.

Members of the workforce also have individual goals which, as we have seen in previous chapters, may be directed more towards satisfying their individual needs rather than the goals of the organisation. Organisational design is a key feature for allowing individuals to achieve their personal needs as well as the objectives of the organisation. If these two branches are not successfully married, then the organisation will cease to exist.

Activity systems which are deliberately structured

This means that the purpose of the organisation is to carry out work-related activities. This is designed within organisations in separate sub-divisions/sections/units, each with its own set of activities. Such a structure is deliberate and is used to co-ordinate work teams and sections. It is about controlling performance to ensure that it matches the goals and objectives of the organisation.

Permeable boundary

All organisations have an environment or boundaries within which they work and membership of which is very distinct. It is this boundary which determines who or what is 'inside' or 'outside' the organisation's environment. However, organisations are now finding that they cannot remain within their defined boundaries because in order to survive in a globalised arena they need to share information and technology. Examples here would be the use of virtual organisations and organisational networking, which are discussed later in this chapter. This is to the mutual advantage of all organisations because of the need to act quickly in order to compete. Organisations shape the lives of all organisational members and knowledgeable managers must shape their organisations in order for the business to survive in a society of competing organisations. This can be achieved through careful attention to the design of their organisation and the importance of the individuals who constitute it.

Organisational design, individuals and teams

The importance of motivation and how it can be harnessed through job design and the effective management of teams to achieve the goals of the organisation has been discussed in earlier chapters. Such effective management is particularly important in the modern, unstable, dynamic market environment which requires from all members of the workforce commitment, flexibility, and initiative. In order for this to come about it is necessary to both measure the input and output of the individual organisational member and control that individual – even if he or she is a member of a work team – to check that the goals are being met.

Careful attention to organisational design provides a framework within which individuals and groups can work effectively in order to meet collective goals. Such a framework also helps to influence and mould individuals and groups and, likewise, they will work within that design framework to influence the structure and its effectiveness in achieving the organisational goals. This is a dynamic process in which individuals amend and modify the existing formal structures of the organisation within which they work. How an individual's work is designed will determine the relationship between workers and this, in turn, may well affect the productivity, performance, and morale of that individual. It is therefore vital that managers are aware of the methods available in the organisation of work and how it can influence people's attitudes and behaviour.

Conversely, individuals and groups *are* the organisation's design and they make up the organisation's individual culture – its personality. In this respect, the culture of the organisation is more important than its formal design. Organisational culture is dealt with separately in the following chapter but in this chapter the concern is design issues which provide the shell within which an organisational culture grows and develops.

Organisational structure and design: key concepts

Organisations consist of many smaller units which are called *subsystems*.

Subsystems at your university

What subsystems are there in your university?

You will probably be able to identify your department, school, and faculty. What about the support services such as learning resources, registry, media resources? Where do they fit in as subsystems?

It is through the specific functions you have considered in the example above that organisations survive – without them they would die. In mature organisations such functions are inter-related and inter-connected and frequently overlap.

An example of function overlap

In a university most subsystems – be they a department, school or faculty – have networked computers to enable members to teach and to carry out their administrative duties. It is likely that technicians service this information processing function. In your university, what subsystem do these technicians belong to? The department? The school? The faculty?

It is likely that the technicians belong to a distinct department entitled Computer Services (or similar) – they are a distinct subsystem, yet they are their own system.

What subsystems actually do is participate in a *transformation process* – they turn inputs into outputs. This is shown in Figure 8.1 below.

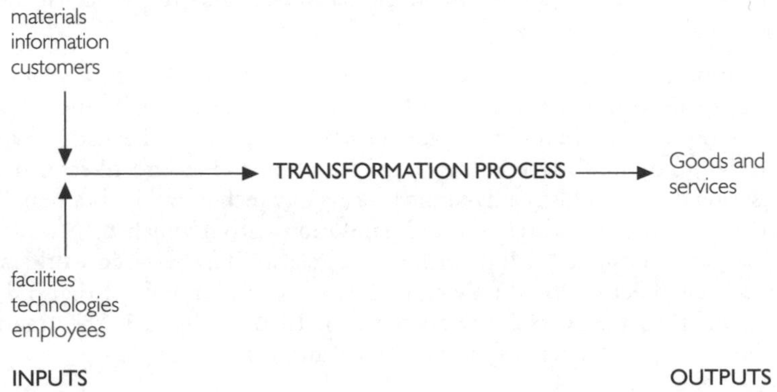

Figure 8.1 Organisations: the transformation process

Most systems which operate within an organisation have five essential functions:

- boundary spanning
- production
- maintenance
- adaption
- management

which are key to the transformation process as shown in Figure 8.2.

Boundary spanning

These are subsystems which are responsible for changes within the organisation's environment – they deal with the input and the output transactions. The inputs include the resources required, such as finance, workers, and materials. On the output side the boundary system creates the demand for the goods/services and markets the outputs. Departments within the boundaries (input and output) interact with the organisation's external environment. For example, at a university, boundary departments will include recruitment on the input side and career support services on the output side.

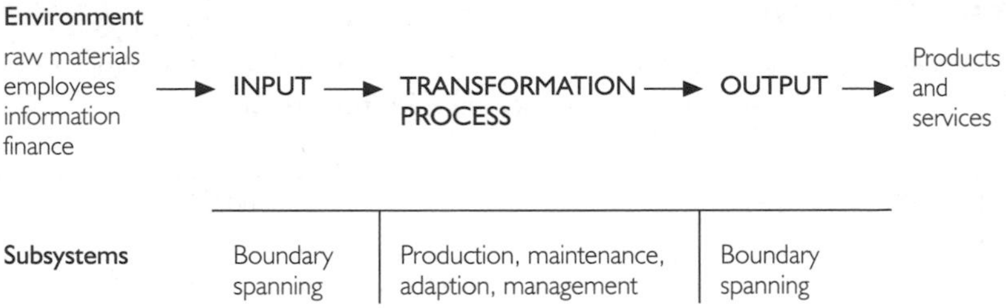

Figure 8.2 A system and its possible subsystems, after Daft (1996, p. 12)

Production

It is here that the principal transformation takes place. The production subsystem produces the product/service outputs of the organisation. For example, at university it includes the teachers and the classes, seminars, and tutorials which take place within the organisation.

Maintenance

This subsystem is responsible for the smooth running of the organisation, ensuring that the buildings are kept to a high standard and refurbished when necessary. It is also part of the maintenance function to attend to needs of the workers – their morale and physical comfort, for example. At university this would be the function performed by subsystems such as the dining rooms, human resource management department, and registry.

Adaption

This is a central subsystem because it is concerned with dealing with change: reactive and proactive. It is this subsystem which monitors the changing environment within which the organisation operates, keeping abreast of such things as technological developments and innovative features so that the organisation can deliver its outputs. At university it would be this subsystem which would monitor the requirements of central government and the demands of the validating bodies.This is often not a tangible subsystem because it operates within other subsystems.

Management

Unlike adaption, management is a distinct subsystem and is responsible for directing and co-ordinating all the other subsystems mentioned above. It is the hub of the subsystems within any organisation and provides the direction and control of the organisation's activities. It is also management which is responsible for developing the design of the organisation and directing the tasks within each of the other subsystems. At a university, the management subsystem might include the Vice Chancellor as chief executive officer, the Deans of Faculty, Heads of School, and Heads of Department as well as those managers in the supporting departments such as Human Resources, Registry, and Computer Services.

Stakeholder activity

As can be seen in Figure 8.3 below, the goals of the transformation process are seen differently by the differing stakeholders connected with the organisation.

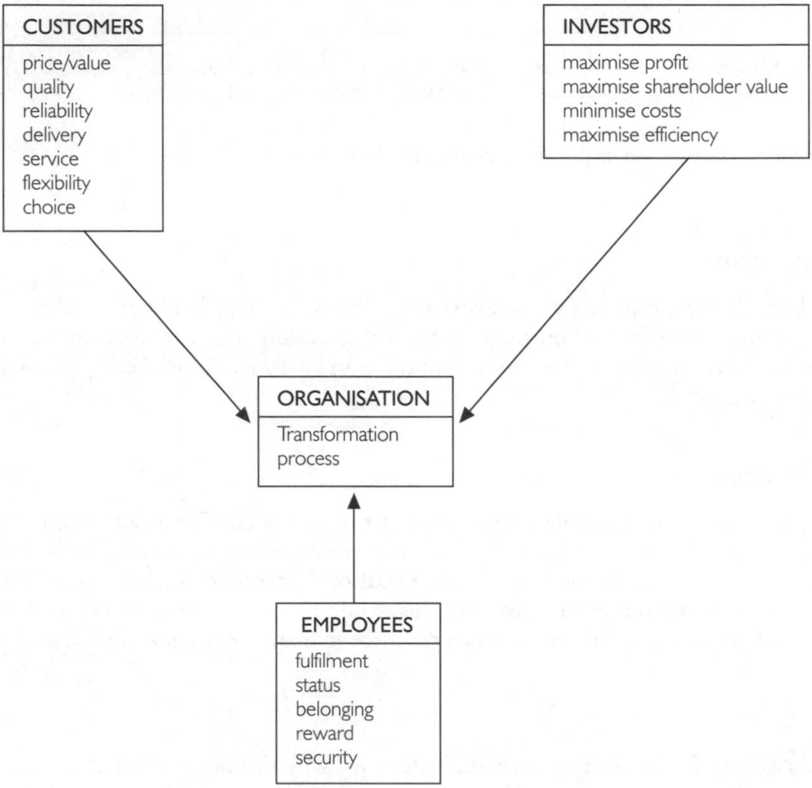

Figure 8.3 Organisations: competing goals

One approach to contemporary effectiveness is the *stakeholder approach* which integrates diverse organisational activities by focusing on the organisational stakeholders. A stakeholder is any individual or group which has a 'stake' in the performance of the organisation. In the stakeholder approach (also known as the constituency approach), the performance of the organisation can be measured by the relative satisfaction expressed by each of the stakeholders.

Stakeholders constitute diverse groups, making differing demands of the organisation. Therefore, the organisational design has to be such that it permits the continuing need to develop, modify, and discard organisational goals. The stakeholders as groups (customers, investors and/or employees) have the potential or real power to influence the organisation in its decisions. As can be seen in Figure 8.3 above, there are three key types of stakeholder: customers, investors, and employees – these are not mutually exclusive categories. For example, an employee could well be an investor in the organisation as well as a user of the final product/service. Figure 8.3 opposite shows three key component stakeholders; however, there are others who might hold an interest in the organisation, such as suppliers, national agencies, trades unions, and pressure groups. Each of these will have their own level of satisfaction and so the organisation has to survey each one to find out whether the organisation is actually achieving its goals. It is very difficult to satisfy the requirements of all the stakeholders all the time – some will be dissatisfied whilst others are satisfied.

It can be seen, therefore, that because the needs of each stakeholder are different, there is the suggestion that there are three key objectives in organisational design as can be seen in Figure 8.4 below.

- efficiency/productivity
- market forces
- motivation.

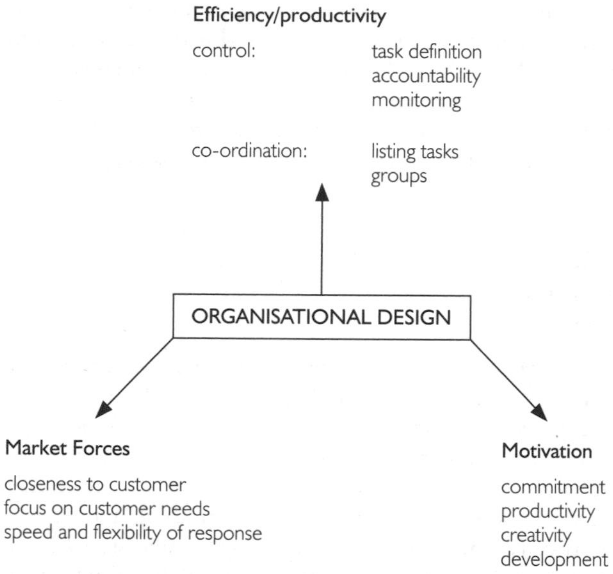

Figure 8.4 The key objectives for organisational design

Managers need to understand why the development of an effective organisational design is required in order to meet the above key objectives. Most researchers in the field comment on the role that structure has in relationship to good organisational performance. Drucker (1974) stated that even if the structure of an organisation is perceived as 'good' it did not necessarily mean that the organisation would be productive and meet its objectives. He believed that when the structure was 'poor' it meant that any sort of performance was impossible even if the managers and workforce were skilled and willing. It followed, therefore, that improving an organisational structure would result in an increase in the quality of performance. Child (1984) also underlined the potential impact of poor structure and design on an organisation by highlighting the impact of failing to meet the two key objectives – an effective structure and an effective design. He believed that there were a number of key variables which a weak organisation needed to attend to:

- low motivation
- delayed and inappropriate decision-making
- dysfunctional conflict
- uncoordination
- rising costs
- poor response to new opportunities and external change.

He believed that such weaknesses would be exacerbated by a poor organisational structure and design which would include a high level of bureaucracy.

Bureaucracy

This was a concept posited by Weber (1947), a sociologist who studied government organisations throughout Europe. He developed a framework of characteristics – mostly administrative – which, upon adoption, he believed would make organisations rational and efficient. As a sociologist, Weber's (1947) aim was to try to appreciate how organisations could be designed to play a more positive role in their larger environment. The structural model which he developed (bureaucracy) was, according to him, the most efficient way that organisations could achieve their objectives. It was characterised by:

- the division of labour
- clear hierarchy of authority
- formalised selection and recruitment procedures
- detailed rules and regulations
- impersonal relationships

and was to provide the backbone for the structure of most organisations of the time. It is only recently that organisations have begun to abandon such a bureaucratic structure because the world is rapidly changing and with global competition and unsettled environments, organisations have to deal with increasing complexity. Modern businesses also have increased numbers of professionals within their workforce, and since these people have been through a considerable length of time in formal training and experience, formalisation is not needed because such professional training regularises their standard of behaviour which itself acts as a substitute for bureaucracy. There has also been an increase in professional partnerships which comprise solely professionals, such as lawyers, dentists, doctors, and accountants. Organisations like these are on the increase with a resultant decrease in bureaucratic organisations.

The most beneficial organisation structure

Traditionally, there are thought to be three factors which influence which organisational structure might be the most beneficial:

- the organisational life cycle
- organisation-level technology
- environment.

The organisational life cycle

One way of considering organisational growth and change is provided by the concept of the *life cycle* which uses the analogy of a human being – it is born, grows older, and eventually dies. Like leadership style and systems of administration, the structure of an organisation follows a fairly predictable pattern through stages in the life cycle with such stages being sequential in nature and following a natural progression. Greiner (1972) took on the conventional wisdom that the larger the organisation was, the more likely its structure would be formalised. Quinn and Cameron (1983) agreed with Greiner (1972), stating also that organisations go through life cycles. Figure 8.5 below shows the organisational life-cycle according to these two works.

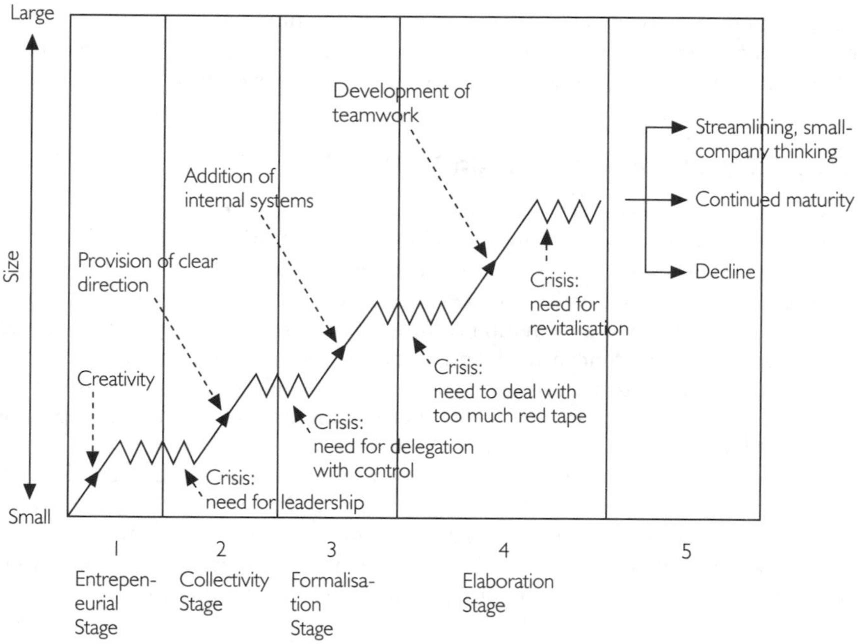

Figure 8.5 Organisational life cycle and its accompanying difficulties, after Quinn and Cameron (1983) and Greiner (1972)

It can be seen from Figure 8.5 that growth is not easy to achieve, because each time an organisation enters a new stage in its life cycle it enters a whole new arena with a new set of rules for how the organisation functions in relation to its internal and external environment.

Stage One – Entrepreneurial Stage

At this young phase the emphasis is on creating a product/service and marketing it, the founders acting as entrepreneurs and devoting all their energies to production and marketing: technical activities. The organisation is informal and non-bureaucratic and work hours are long and hard. Control is based on the owners' personal supervision and charisma and growth derives from the creation of a new productand/or service. Towards the end of this first phase comes a crisis of leadership which has to be resolved before phase two can be initiated.

Stage Two – Collectivity Stage

If such a leadership crisis is resolved, the emerging strong leadership will allow the organisation to develop clarity relating to objectives and direction. At this stage, departments are created with their accompanying hierarchy of authority, job assignments, and a beginning of division of labour. Employees still identify with the vision and mission of the original organisation and continue to work long hours with a view to helping the embryonic organisation to succeed. They have a sense of belonging and work collectively, communicating and controlling informally. As the organisation grows through direction this phase then culminates with a crisis of autonomy and moves into the third stage.

Stage Three – Formalisation Stage

This third stage involves the installation and use of rules and regulations, with set procedures and control systems being introduced. There begins to be control through delegation, with communication becoming less frequent and more formalised. The system takes on board more specialists to meets its needs, e.g. engineers, human resource management specialists, and information technology experts. At the apex of the organisation the top management concentrates on corporate strategy and planning, delegating day-to-day management to the middle managers (this could well be described as a typical bureaucracy). It is at this stage that product groups are set up in an attempt to improve the co-ordination of the organisation's activities while profit-related pay may be instituted in an attempt to ensure that managers work towards the organisational goals. When effective, growth is through delegation, with the new co-ordination systems and control systems enabling the organisation to continue growing. However, at the end of this phase there comes about a crisis of control as the organisation moves into the next phase: it passes from being a young organisation to being a mature one.

Stage Four – Elaboration Stage

The organisation is just moving from a crisis of red tape into a new environment of teamwork and collaboration – there is growth through co-ordination taking place. Bureaucracy reaches its limit of effectiveness during this stage and managers have gained experience in the effective confrontation of problems and interaction. Managers tend to work with the bureaucratic system without adding to it and they simplify the formal systems by replacing them with project teams and cell structures. This stage requires the move through the crisis of red tape and a move into the final stage which confronts a mature organisation.

Stage Five – Mature Stage

This is the development of growth through collaboration and requires bold leadership so that the organisation can face the growth cycle and move into a new era. It needs to go through revitalisation at this stage and thus meets yet another crisis.

As the organisation moves along each stage life becomes increasingly difficult for it. Most organisations do not make it through the first stage (entrepreneurial) and of those that do, approximately 85 per cent will fail to move on through the life cycle. As the survivors move onwards the transitions become even more difficult. For organisations who fail to resolve their end-of-stage real crises, there comes, at best, growth restriction or, at worst, demise – this could well be – according to Greiner (1972) – a 'crisis of overload'.

The principles of organisational design

There have been a number of writers who have attempted to establish the fundamental principles of organisational design, most of them concentrating on the wish for a commonly accepted set of rules which could be used in all circumstances. One of the leading writers in the classical management school, Urwick (1952), outlined ten basic principles of organisation which he felt could apply to all organisations – these are exemplified in Table 8.1 below.

Table 8.1 Ten principles of organisation, after Urwick (1952)

Defining organisational goals

Objectives
'Every organisation and every part of the organisation must be an expression of the purpose of the undertaking concerned, or it is meaningless and therefore redundant.'

Continuity
'Re-organisation is a continuous process: in every undertaking specific provision should be made for it.'

Specialisation
'The activities of every member of any organised group should be confined, as far as possible, to the performance of a single function.'

Defining individual tasks

Definition
'The content of each position, i.e. the duties involved, the authority and responsibility contemplated and the relationships with other positions, should be clearly defined in writing and published to all concerned.'

Co-ordination
'The purpose of organising *per se*, as distinguished from the purpose of the undertaking, is to facilitate co-ordination: unity of effort.'

Defining and linking groups

Balance
'It is essential that the various units of an organisation should be kept in balance.'

Controlling individuals and groups

Authority
'In every organised group the supreme authority must rest somewhere. There should be a clear line of authority to every individual in the group.'

Responsibility
'The responsibility of the superior for the acts of the subordinate is absolute.'

Correspondence
'In every position, the responsibility and the authority should correspond.'

Span of control
'No person should supervise more than five, or at the most, six direct subordinates whose work interlocks.'

Urwick's (1952) ideas concentrated on an attempt to provide a logical design and neglected to consider the relationships between the individuals within the organisation. Child (1984) developed this approach and outlined six dimensions related to the structure of organisations which needed to be considered by managers as shown in Table 8.2 below.

Table 8.2 Dimensions of organisational structure, after Childs (1984)

Defining and rewarding individual tasks

Tasks
How tasks are defined and allocated to individuals.

Motivation
How organisations motivate individuals through systems of appraisal and reward.

Defining and linking groups

Groups
How the various units within the organisation (subsystems) are defined and linked.

Communication
The systems for allowing individuals and teams to communicate in meeting organisational goals.

Controlling individuals and groups

Reporting relationships
Levels of authority and spans of control.

Delegation
Definition of individual responsibilities and systems for monitoring how responsibility is exercised.

Child's (1984) dimensions may be compared with the nine essential parameters to be considered in effective organisational design suggested by Mintzberg (1979) who divided these parameters into four main groups which are listed in Table 8.3 below.

Table 8.3 The parameters of organisational design, after Mintzberg (1979)

Task specialisation
How many tasks should a given role in the organisation have and to what level should each be specialised?

Task standardisation
To what extent should each task be standardised?

Task skills
What skills and knowledge are required for each role?

Unit grouping
On what basis should positions be sub-positioned and grouped?

Unit size
How large should each unit be and who should be accountable to whom?

Unit standardisation
To what extent should each unit be standardised?

Unit adjustment
What systems should be used to ensure standardisation among positions and units?

Delegation down
How much decision-making power and responsibility should be given to managers lower down the hierarchy?

Delegation across
How much decision-making power and responsibility should be devolved to the staff specialists and the workforce?

Mechanistic versus organic organisational designs

Organisations have to respond to their environmental and boundary changes and the accompanying uncertainty which a formal control structure imposes on employees. Burns and Stalker (1961) investigated this area by observing twenty industrial firms in England. They discovered that the organisation's external environment related strongly to the internal structure of management. For example, when the external environment was stable and the boundaries thus well ordered and defined, the organisation was identified as having a clear top-down hierarchy with set rules, regulations, and procedures – they were very formal, traditional and centralised, with decision-making centred at the apex. Burns and Stalker (1961) called such an organisation *mechanistic*.

Some decades later organisations are increasingly having to be proactive and cope with ever-changing environments and as a result they have to be more fluid in their organisational design using free-flowing and adaptive management techniques. The workforce have to be flexible and find their own answers to difficulties, working out for themselves what they have to do. In this *organic* organisation, the hierarchy of authority is not clear and decision-making is decentralised. Burns and Stalker (1961) noticed that a minority of organisations at the time were organic, and some were increasingly moving to that design from the more traditional mechanistic structures.

Burns and Stalker's (1961) work was comprehensive and dealt with a number of variables which affected the structure and design of an organisation. Table 8.4 identifies these.

Table 8.4 Two models of organisational design, after Burns and Stalker (1961)

Defining tasks	specialisation of tasks	multi-skilled workforce
	precisely defined and responsibilities	changing duties and responsibilities
	use of precisely-defined procedures/ instructions in completing tasks	emphasis on flexible problem-solving and creative skills in completing tasks
Linking individuals and groups	high degree of functional specialisation	emphasis on teamwork across functions
	culture of commitment to/ identification with particular department/function	culture of commitment to overall tasks or project
Distributing power	clear, centralised hierarchical structure	flat, decentralised structure
	precisely-defined levels of authority	loosely-defined levels of authority allowing decision-making to be devolved
	knowledge and power concentrated at top of organisation	knowledge and power distributed throughout the organisation
	emphasis on vertical interaction between superior and subordinate based on superior expertise and authority	emphasis on lateral communication between employees based on shared knowledge, authority and teamworking
	culture of obedience to organisation and superiors	culture of commitment to task and proactive contribution from all employees
Defining boundaries	relatively fixed organisational structure	fluid, adaptable organisational structure
	MECHANISTIC MODEL	**ORGANISATIONAL MODEL**

The individual identifying characteristics of each can be seen contrasted, as shown in Table 8.5 below.

Table 8.5 Mechanistic and organic organisational forms

Mechanistic	**Organic**
Tasks are broken down to specialised and separate parts.	Employees contribute to the common task of the subsystem.
Tasks are rigidly and clearly defined.	Tasks are refocused and redesigned by means of teamwork feedback.
There is a strict hierarchy of authority and control with many rules and regulations.	Less of a hierarchy of authority and control with few rules and regulations.
All knowledge and task control of tasks is concentrated at the apex of the organisation.	Knowledge and control of tasks can be found anywhere in the organisation.
The communication network is vertical.	Communication is horizontal and all-channel.

As can be seen from Table 8.4 and Table 8.5 above, as the environment changes and the boundaries become less rigid, an organisation will need to become more organic. This means a lessening in centralisation, with authority and control passing to the lower levels in the hierarchy thus intrinsically motivating all employees because they have moved from a task-oriented environment to one that is relation-oriented. Thus the organic structure encourages teamwork and an informal adoption of tasks and responsibilities. The final result is fluidity within the organisation which allows it to be proactive to change and meet the needs of its stakeholders.

The principal dimension which changes as the organisation adopts a more organic structure and design is that of power or co-ordination.

Organisation-level technology

Organisational level technologies are of two types:

- *Manufacturing firms*. This type includes the traditional manufacturing processes and the newer computer-based manufacturing systems.
- *Service firms*.

Manufacturing firms

The first and most influential study of manufacturing technology was that carried out in the mid 1950s by the industrial sociologist Joan Woodward (1958), who commenced her work with a field study of management principles used in one hundred firms in southeast Essex, England. The conventional management wisdom at that time was known as *the universal principles of management*. These were 'one best way' principles and prescriptors which effective organisations would adopt in any given situation. With the help of her research team, Woodward (1958) surveyed the organisations by interviewing managers, examining organisation records, and observed manufacturing systems. Her data included a comprehensive range of structural characteristics (including hierarchy of management), and also the dimensions of the management styles in operation – written versus verbal communication, use of rewards and punishments – as well as the manufacturing processes used in the production of the goods. Her team also collected data that reflected the commercial success of the individual organisation.

Woodward developed her own scale of measurement and then organised the firms according to the technical complexity of the manufacturing processes involved. This *technical complexity* represented the extent of mechanisation of the manufacturing processes and was summarised by Woodward into ten categories and then into three key classifications as shown in Table 8.6 below.

Table 8.6 Woodward's (1958) classification of 100 firms according to their systems of production

GROUP	CLASSIFICATION		COMPLEXITY
One Small batch and unit production	1	Production of single pieces to customer orders.	Low ↑
	2	Production of technically complex units one by one.	
	3	Fabrication of large equipment in stages.	
	4	Production of pieces in small batches.	
Two Large-batch and mass production	5	Production of components in large batches subsequently assembled diversely.	
	6	Production of large batches, assembly line type.	
	7	Mass production.	
	8	Continuous process production combined with the preparation of a product for sale by large-batch or mass production methods.	
Three Continuous process production.	9	Continuous process production of chemicals in batches.	
	10	Continuous flow production of liquids, gases, and solid shapes.	↓ High

Using this classification, Woodward's (1958) data appears to make sense – a few of her key findings are shown in Table 8.7 below.

Table 8.7 Relationship between technical complexity and structural characteristics, after Woodward (1965)

	TECHNOLOGY		
STRUCTURAL CHARACTERISTICS	**Unit Production**	**Mass Production**	**Continuous Process**
Number of management levels	3	4	6
Supervisor span of control	23	48	15
Direct/indirect labour ratio	9:1	4:1	1:1
Manager/total personnel ratio	Low	Medium	High
Workers' skill level	High	Low	High
Formalised procedures	Low	High	Low
Centralisation	Low	High	Low
Amount of verbal communication	High	Low	High
Amount of written communicatin	Low	High	Low
Overall structure	Organic	Mechanistic	Organic

Considerable information can be gleaned from Table 8.7 above:

- The number of management levels and the manager/total personnel ratio show definite increases as technical complexity increases from unit production to continuous production. This indicates that as technology becomes more complex the accompanying management intensity increases.
- Direct/indirect labour ratio decreases with technical complexity. This might be because complex machinery needs to be supported and maintained and this is carried out by indirect workers.
- Formalised procedures and centralisation score highly on mass production technology yet low for other technologies because of the standardised nature of the work task.
- Unit production and continuous process technologies need highly skilled and able workers to run the machines and systems; such workers need an accompanying high level verbal communication skill so that they can adapt to the changing technology.
- Since mass production is standardised and full of routine tasks, little verbal communication or skill is required from the workers.
- Overall, the management systems in both unit production and continuous processes technology are organic. They are more flexible and have fewer rules and less standardisation.
- Mass production is mechanistic, with standardised jobs and formalised procedures.

Woodward's (1958) work provided a key insight into technology and its role in organisational structure. As she said: 'Different technologies impose different kinds of demands on individuals and organisations, and those demands had to be met through an appropriate structure' (1965, p. vi).

Woodward (1958) also studied the success of the firms along other dimensions than technology, such as profitability, market share, stock price, and reputation in the environment. Whilst any measurement of effectiveness cannot be precise, she was able to rank the organisations on a scale of commercial success according to whether they displayed above average, average, or below average performance in their specific marketplace.

By comparing the structure–technology relationship against commercial success Woodward (1958) discovered that successful firms tended to be those that had structures and technologies which were complementary. She found that a large proportion of the firms investigated showed organisational characteristics which were near the average of their technology category – see Table 8.7 above. Below-average organisations tended to move away from the traditional structure usually associated with their technology type.

A second conclusion that Woodward (1958) came up with was that the structural characteristics could be clustered into either 'organic' or 'mechanistic': as researched also by Burns and Stalker (1961). That was, the successful small-batch and continuous process organisations had organic structures whereas the successful mass production organisations had mechanistic structures. As a result of their studies in a rayon factory, Burns and Stalker (1961) believed that neither mechanistic nor organic organisations were superior in design to each other; it depended upon the environment in which the individual organisation found itself, the product market and the technology of the manufacturing process being indicative of whether the organisation would be described as 'mechanistic' or 'organic'.

The validity of such research lies in the ability to successfully replicate findings. This was done of Woodward's (1958) work by Zwerman (1970). However, there have been fresh developments in the field of manufacturing technology with the introduction of robotics, numerically controlled machine tools and computerised software to assist in product design, engineering analysis, and the remote control of systems. By using *advanced manufacturing technology* (AMT) links can be made between manufacturing components that were previously isolated. AMT links robots, machines, product design, and engineering analysis by the co-ordination of one computer. Sometimes known as computer integrated manufacturing, the factory of the future, smart factories, or flexible manufacturing systems, AMT has revolutionised the workplace by enabling large factories to deliver a wide range of custom-designed products at low mass-production costs.

Service firms

The UK, like North America, has become a service-centred economy. New services, such as high-speed package deliveries, dog-walking, house cleaning, data base management, financial services, and entertainment, mean that service organisations are increasing more rapidly than manufacturing industries.

Another perspective on technology is that of production activities taking place within organisational departments. Departments often have the same characteristics as the service sector because they tend to provide services to other departments or project teams within the organisation. Such departments tend not to be in the functional core but are systems which provide others with support services such as human resource management, research and development, and finance. It is necessary to analyse the nature of such departmental technology and its relationship with departmental structure. The key work in this area was carried out by Perrow (1967) who concentrated on knowledge-based technology because he felt that Woodward's (1958) work in the 1950s concentrated on a manufacturing base. It was Perrow's view (1967) that technology needed to be operationalised in a more general way if the concept was to have any meaning across all organisations – not only those in the manufacturing sector. Perrow (1967) defined technology as: 'the action that an individual performs upon an object, with or without the aid of tools or mechanical devices, in order to make some change in that object' (p. 194).

He identified two dimensions of knowledge technology:

- task variability
- problem analysability.

Task variability is about the number of exceptions which workers encounter when carrying out their work. If the job is routine and monotonous there will be few task variabilities. An example of this would be a fish fryer in a fish and chip shop. At the other end of the continuum there are jobs which have considerable skill and task variety and in such jobs one would expect to find a high level of task variability. Such a job would be that of a chief executive officer or other executive manager. It can be seen, therefore, that task variability appraises work by evaluating it along a variety–routineness continuum.

Problem analysability assesses the type of search procedures followed to find successful methods for responding adequately to task exceptions. At one end of the continuum this could be well defined where an individual worker can utilise logic and analysis with reasoning in search of an effective solution.

For your consideration

Extreme version on the continuum

Imagine one of your student friends is a high 2.1 student and she has failed the examination in one of her courses. If this friend is a **well defined student** what would she then do?

You should have said that she would use logical analysis to find a solution to her problem. She would question whether she spent enough time studying for the examination and whether she studied the right topics. She would consider whether the examination questions were fair and compare her result with those of other students who took the same examination – how did they do? She would use logic to find the source of the problem and then rectify it.

For further consideration

The other end of the same continuum

Another friend has failed the same examination and he is also a 2.1 student and had expected to pass. However, this friend is an **ill defined student** – what would he have done in the same circumstances?

Such a student would have relied totally on his prior experience and upon his personal judgement and intuition to find a solution. If he carries out this strategy it would be more a case of accident than design and he might, by trial and error, be successful in the future.

It is possible to use these two dimensions to form a two-dimensional matrix, as shown in Figure 8.6 below, where the four cells represent four types of technology:

- routine
- engineering
- craft
- non-routine.

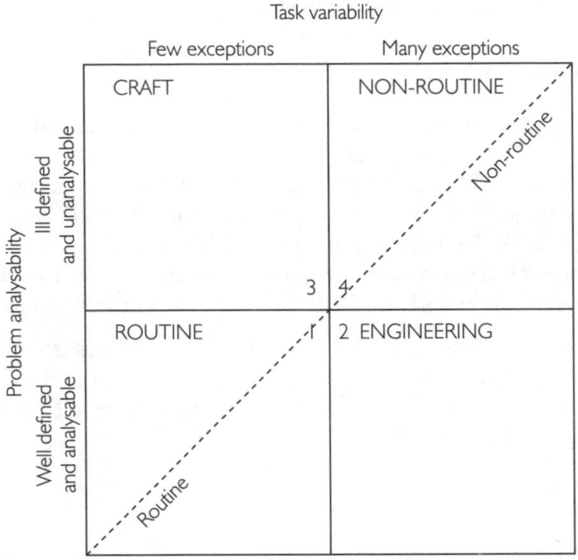

Figure 8.6 Technology classification, after Perrow (1967)

Routine technologies (box 1) have few exceptions and easy-to-analyse problems; for example, mass production processes used to make motor cars or to refine chemicals. A hamburger cook at McDonald's will also come into this category.

Engineering technologies (box 2) may have a number of exceptions, but all can be handled rationally and systematically. Examples here would be an accountant and a construction engineer.

Craft technologies (box 3) have a limited set of exceptions and deal with relatively difficult problems. Examples here would be a ballet dancer or a potter.

Non-routine technologies (box 4) have many exceptions with problems which are very difficult to analyse. The examples here would include the design of corporate strategy and research.

Perrow (1967) argued that if a problem could be studied systematically with the use of logical and rational analysis, boxes 1 or 2 would appear to be appropriate. For problems which can only be handled by intuition, guesswork, or personal judgement, the technology of boxes 3 or 4 would be appropriate. In circumstances where unusual or unfamiliar problems arise regularly, they would be represented in either boxes 2 or 4 and if they are familiar, then boxes 1 or 3 would be appropriate. According to Perrow (1967), task variability and problem analysability are positively correlated. That is, it would be difficult to find circumstances where tasks had very few exceptions and search was clearly unanalysable or where tasks had a great many exceptions and search was well defined and easily analysable. It follows, therefore, that the four technologies can be combined into a single routine–non-routine continuum: this is the dotted diagonal line in Figure 8.6 opposite.

Perrow (1967) believed that control and co-ordination methods should vary with the type of technology. When the technology is routine the organisation will be highly structured. It follows, then, that the non-routine technologies would require greater flexibility in their structure. Following on from this, Perrow (1967) went on to identify the principal facets of structure which could be modified to meet the available technology:

- the amount of *discretion* that can be exercised for completing the tasks;
- the *power* of groups to control the unit's goals and basic strategies;
- the extent of *interdependence* between these same groups;
- the extent to which these groups engage in *co-ordination* of their work using either feedback or the planning of others.

This implies that most routine technologies (box 1) can best be accomplished through standardised co-ordination and defined control. Such technologies would be aligned with organisational structures which are highly formalised and highly centralised. At the other end of the continuum, the non-routine technologies (box 4) demand flexibility and would therefore have a minimum degree of centralisation and formalisation. Craft technology (box 3) occupies the middle field and needs problems to be solved by those who have the greatest knowledge and experience, and through decentralisation. Engineering technology (box 2) has many exceptions with analysable search processes; it should have decisions centralised but should maintain flexibility through low formalisation. These predictions are shown in Table 8.8 below.

Table 8.8 Technology-structure predictions

		STRUCTURAL CHARACTERISTIC			
BOX	**TECHNOLOGY**	**FORMALISATION**	**CENTRALISATION**	**SPAN OF CONTROL**	**CO-ORDINATION AND CONTROL**
1	Routine	High	High	Wide	Planning and rigid rules
2	Engineering	Low	High	Moderate	Reports and meetings
3	Craft	Moderate	Low	Moderate-wide	Training and meetings
4	Non-routine	Low	Low	Moderate-narrow	Group norms and group meetings

Perrow (1967) did not empirically test his hypotheses relating to the two-by-two matrix of technologies and the predictions of what structural dimensions are most compatible with these technologies. However, subsequent work seems to give considerable support to his views. Organisations and subsystems with routine technologies do tend to have greater formalisation and centralisation than do those with non-routine technologies.

Organisational design and organisational environments

There have been a large number of studies carried out in the area of organisational environments and several have been highly influential in current organisational design. They are the work of: Burns and Stalker (1961), Emery and Trist (1965), Lawrence and Lorsch (1967).

Burns and Stalker (1961)

This work was carried out as a response to uncertainty about the amount of formal structure and control imposed on the workforce. Burns and Stalker (1961) studied twenty English and Scottish industrial organisations in an attempt to find out how their organisational structure and managerial practices might differ based on different environmental conditions. The researchers took the variables of rate of change in the organisations' scientific technology and their relevant product markets and compared them with the individual environmental conditions in which the organisations worked. Burns and Stalker (1961) found that the type of structure that existed in those firms working in a rapidly changing and dynamic environment was considerably different from that in organisations which had a stable environment. They found that *mechanistic structures* were those which had a high degree of centralisation, formalisation and complexity in that they carried out routine tasks using programmed behaviours and were very slow to respond to change in the environment. Conversely, *organic structures* were characterised by flexibility and adaptiveness, with communication being lateral rather than vertical. The emphasis was on loosely defined responsibilities and on the sharing of information.

Burns and Stalker (1961) believed that the most effective organisation was one which was adapted to the environment. Such organisations would utilise a mechanistic structure in times of stability but an organic one when the environment was turbulent. However, both researchers agreed that these two types of structure were at the far ends of the same continuum and no organisation could adopt the pure state of mechanistic or organic. They went on to say that no one structure was better than the other; it was the nature of the environment which dictated which structure was superior at the time.

Emery and Trist (1965)

Emery and Trist (1965) developed a more sophisticated model by identifying three kinds of environments that an organisation might confront and which would, consequently, affect the design of the organisation:

- placid-randomised environment
- placid-clustered environment
- turbulent-field environment

– each one being progressively more complex.

A *placid-randomised environment* is one that is relatively unchanging and thus poses the least threat to the organisation. This is a rare situation in the modern world.

A *placid-clustered environment* also has the feature that it changes slowly but any threats to the organisation are clustered rather than appearing at random. That is, the forces within the environment are linked to each other.

A *disturbed-reactive environment* is a very complex situation. This is where there are many competitors working towards similar ends and where a few organisations are influential enough to form a coalition in order to dominate. This organisation requires flexibility and adaptability in order to survive.

Emery and Trist (1965) did not make any attempt to suggest what type of organisational structure best matched each type of environment that they identified. However, it can be seen that one can match them with the mechanistic and organic structures identified by Burns and Stalker (1961) and that they agreed that only a flexible structure can respond promptly to changes.

Lawrence and Lorsch (1967)

The recognition that mechanistic and organic forms of organisations might co-exist within the same organisation was studied and developed further by Lawrence and Lorsch (1967). They chose ten firms in three distinct industries (plastics, food, and containers) in which to carry out their research. These categories were specifically chosen because they appeared to be the most diverse in nature.

Lawrence and Lorsch (1967) attempted to match the internal environments of each of the organisations with their respective external environments. They had the feeling that those firms which were more successful in the market would harbour a better match between external and internal environments than would the less successful ones. In measuring the external environment the researchers attempted to get to the bottom of the levels of uncertainty which included:

- the rate of change in the environment over time;
- the clarity of information that management held about the environment;
- the length of time it took for management to get feedback from the environment of actions taken by the organisation.

When investigating the internal environment of the organisation, Lawrence and Lorsch (1967) investigated two distinct dimensions:

- differentiation
- integration.

Differentiation is about the extent to which the factors below *differ* between the various parts of an organisation, and it was measured in a number of ways:

- by the degree to which departments exhibited a mechanistic or organic structure;
- managerial styles (whether formal or interpersonal);
- by how far department managers focused on the goals of their departments;
- by how far departments had a strategic, tactical or operational focus.

That is, it is: 'the degree to which the tasks and the work of individuals, groups and units are divided up within an organization' (p. 437).

For example, research departments tended to have a long-term strategic focus and because of the nature of their work (creative and experimental) they tended to have a more organic structure with an interpersonal management style. On the other hand, the production department had a more tactical and operational focus, being concerned with meeting due dates and controlling costs and maintaining quality. Such departments tended to be of a formal and mechanistic nature.

Lawrence and Lorsch (1967) used the term *integration* to describe the quality of collaboration between departments of an organisation. For example, your university may be divided into faculties, schools, departments, and divisions, but it is essential that the organisation ensures that all of these sections contribute to the objectives of the university as stated in their strategy – often through the mission statement – and the corporate strategy.

Lawrence and Lorsch (1967) also matched degrees of differentiation and integration against differing kinds of environment – from stable to dynamic. They found that, whilst in stable environments a high degree of integration was required to be successful, the most successful firms in more dynamic environments were those that combined a high degree of differentiation amongst departments, each retaining the focus and structure best suited to it, with a high degree of integration, allowing the departments to work together to achieve the overall goals of the business. They suggested that there were various ways in which integration might be achieved, with the central concern being customer focus. This can be done through the production of quality goods and services and responsiveness to the market through teamworking.

Organisational design and communication

Organisational design should permit effective communication among employees in all the subsystems because, without this, the organisation will not meet its goals. Figure 8.7 below illustrates how important it is that the structure and design of an organisation should fit the organisational goals. Therefore, the organisation has to be designed in such a way that it encourages information flow in both a vertical and horizontal manner as well as in relation to the organisation's environment – its boundaries.

Figure 8.7 An information-processing approach to organisational design, after Daft (1995, p. 193)

Linkage

Linkage is the extent of communication and co-ordination amongst the organisational subsystems and there are three considerations here:

- vertical
- horizontal
- boundary.

In order to co-ordinate the activities of the organisation among the various hierarchical levels it is necessary to have an effective system of communication (refer to Chapter 3 and Chapter 7 for a more detailed discussion on communication as it relates to learning and team working). The workforce at the foot of the hierarchy must know what the ultimate objectives are and those at the top need to be aware of what is being achieved at the lower end of the hierarchy. As was discussed at the beginning of this chapter, such achievements may also cross boundaries. Such activity is carried out through *vertical linkages* which Galbraith (1977) identified as:

- hierarchical referral
- rules and plans
- additional positions to hierarchy
- vertical information systems.

Hierarchical referral refers to the chain of command which is more apparent in traditional organisations with a steep hierarchy of command. For example, if an employee requires information in order to achieve a task, he can refer it to the next level up in the organisational hierarchy. If that person cannot provide the information, the request will go up the hierarchy until an answer is provided. The latter will then filter down the same process to the person who originally asked for the information. Such lines within an organisation act as communication channels (see Chapter 7).

Where tasks are repetitive and situations common, organisations institute *rules and plans* to cope with such eventualities. The rules are standardised information providers which allow the workforce to standardise their activities. A plan is also an information source, but it also provides detailed information – an example here would be a financial plan.

Organisations are extremely complex, thus reflecting the nature of the modern business world. As a consequence, there may be overloading on the managers, thus requiring their job specifications to be redesigned to allow a further input of staff to share the roles and responsibilities of that manager. This is *adding positions to the hierarchy* and is a feature of the traditional, top-down organisation. Assistants are added at the required points to help managers. This brings with it closer communication and control although it may be accompanied by additional costs.

By using *vertical information systems* an organisation can increase its vertical information capacity. This is the use of written documentation and computer-generated information which is distributed throughout the organisation. An example here is that of Bill Gates, Chairman of Microsoft, who communicates with all his managers through electronic communication systems each day.

As can be seen, there are a number of techniques which managers can use to bring about vertical linkage and all of these need to be considered when designing an organisation. Figure 8.8 below illustrates a ladder of mechanisms for vertical linkage and control within an organisation.

Additionally there are *horizontal information linkages* which refers to the amount of communication and co-ordination which is passed between the subsystems of the organisa-

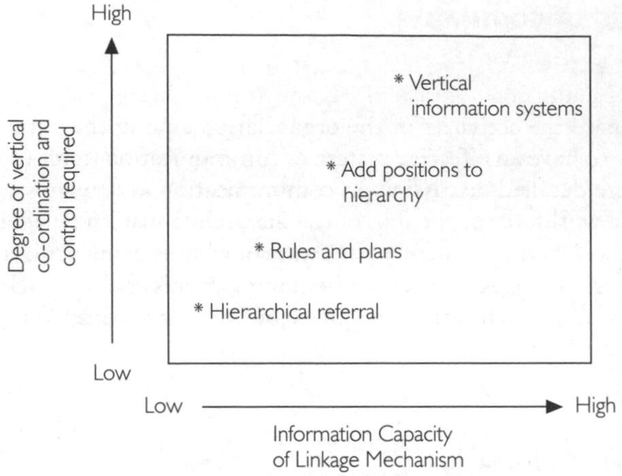

Figure 8.8 Ladder of mechanisms for vertical linkage and control, after Daft (1995, p. 195)

tion. With the use of effective horizontal communication comes harmony amongst the members of the organisation at all levels. Business today is full of change and uncertainty, so it is vital that horizontal communication is effective and flexible: it is about the exchange and sharing of information. There are a number of techniques which can be used to enhance horizontal information:

- through the written medium;
- accessibility to information processing at all levels;
- use of a person in each subsystem who liaises with other subsystems;
- use of a task force committee which has representatives from all the subsystems in it;
- full-time integrator whose sole task is that of co-ordinator between all subsystems;
- the use of work-based teams.

Both vertical and horizontal processes take place within the *boundaries* discussed earlier in this chapter. That is, they must relate to how the organisation relates to its stakeholders (see Chapter 3).

Distributing power in organisations

All organisations need to make decisions, so when organisations are designed attention must be paid to the issue of how an organisation should devolve the power and decision-making functions. There are a number of ways of analysing the distribution of power and responsibility within an organisation, four of which are:

- the scalar chain of command
- the span of control
- unity of command
- line, functional, and staff relationships.

The scalar chain of command

The early writers on organisation structure and design discussed earlier in this chapter tended to stress the hierarchical function – the chain of command. A scalar chain of command is such where the authority and responsibility are arranged hierarchically. It establishes the points at which a certain degree of power is defined and expressed, with staff at each point having comparable levels of authority within the hierarchy of command. Both flow in a clear, unbroken, vertical line from the apex to the base. The heart of the scalar chain is the need for clarity, so it is well defined as a continually clear line, as shown in Figure 8.9 below.

Chief Executive Officer
|
Directors
|
Managers
|
Deputy Managers
|
Supervisors
|
Supervisees

Figure 8.9 An example of a scalar chain in an organisation

Span of control

Span of control refers to the number of employees which one manager supervises. This, in turn, influences the shape and structure of the organisation. If the span of control is broad, there are few levels between the apex and the foot of the organisation. Conversely, with a narrow span of control there are more levels required for the same number of employees. In Figure 8.10 below can be seen two types of span of control.

(a) A narrow span of control (tall shape)

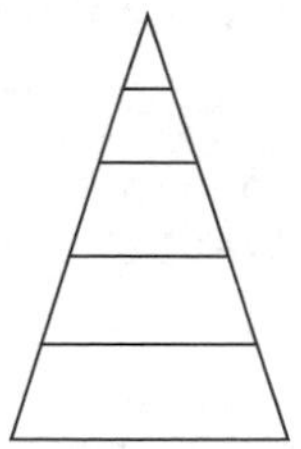

(b) A broad span of control (flat shape)

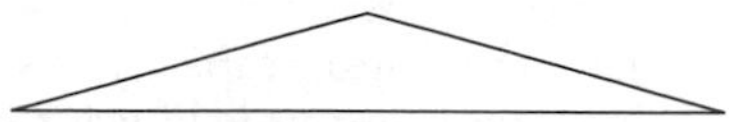

Figure 8.10 Span of control and the shape of the organisation

The scalar chain and span of control combine to make up the shape of an organisation as can be seen in Figure 8.11 below.

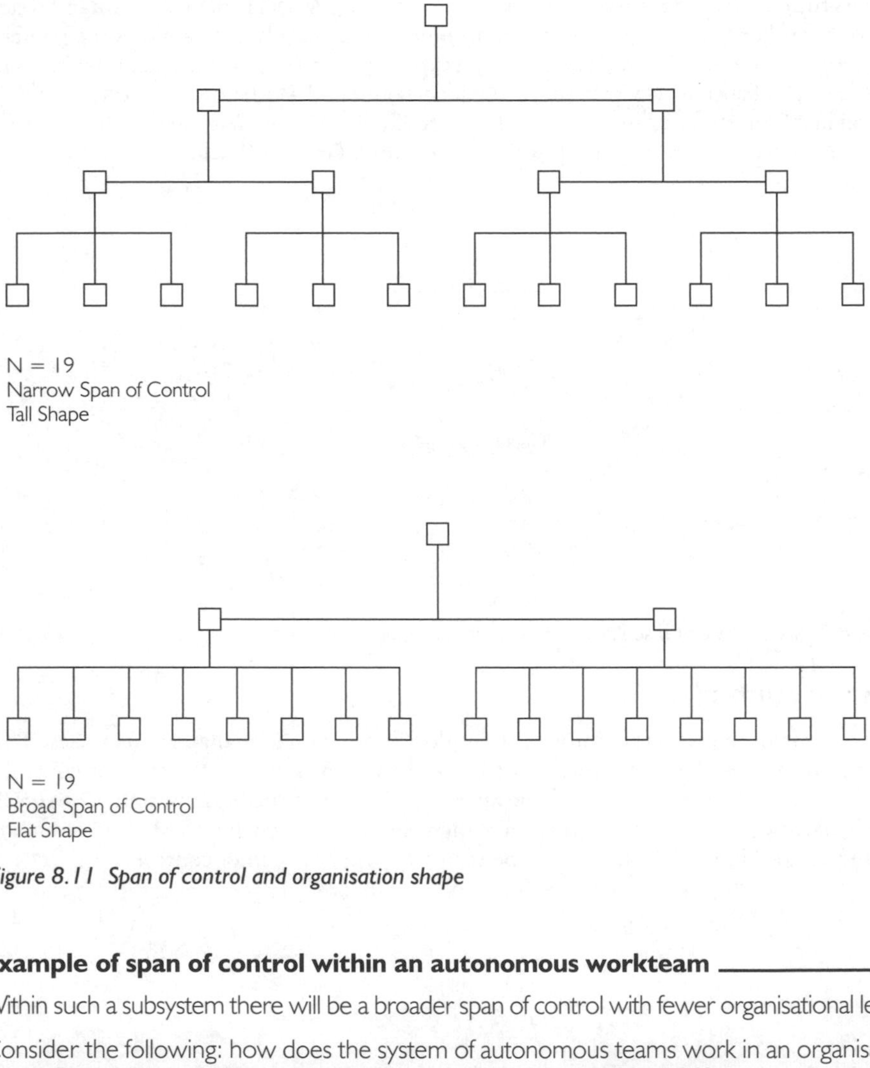

Figure 8.11 Span of control and organisation shape

Example of span of control within an autonomous workteam

Within such a subsystem there will be a broader span of control with fewer organisational levels.

Consider the following: how does the system of autonomous teams work in an organisation like McDonald's restaurants when teams are sized between 20 and 30?

The key issue here is the repetitiveness of simple tasks. At the higher level of the organisation, however, a manager will only be able to manage a team of 7–8 effectively.

As the example of Urwick (1952) indicates, most of the early scientific management writers suggested a ceiling of any span of control of between five and seven. After this point, it was felt that a manager would not have the time or capacity to support and direct any one subordinate effectively. The seminal writer in this field was Graicunas (1937), who used his mathematical background to produce a formula which could be used to calculate the span of control within a given organisational situation. He stated that if one calculated the total of direct and cross relationships, one could then give the limit for the number of subordinates who could be supervised effectively.

Key
n The number of subordinates.
R The number of inter-relationships.

$$R = n\left(\frac{2^n}{2} + n - 1\right)$$

Figure 8.12 Calculating the most effective span of control, after Graicunas (1937)

Try using Graicunas's (1937) formula

If Jane has five subordinates what will be the total number of inter-relationships that she will have?

Gary has six subordinates, so what will be his total number of inter-relationships?

You should have answered 100 and 222 respectively.

Most writers in this field suggest that it is better to avoid too broad or wide a span of control when attempting to analyse the best way to form work groups. Such ideas suggest that for effective group identity and interaction it is better to keep groups to a membership of five or six. As was seen in Chapter 6, if working teams become too large they break into a number of sub-teams which are likely to be informal in nature with their own leadership and, therefore, the manager and/or supervisor has lost control of the initial work team. Authority and cohesion will have thus become compromised with the result that the team and organisational goals are not likely to be achieved.

However, if the span of control is too narrow the managers/supervisors will experience reduced authority and control and will thus be unable to make effective decisions. It is also usual in such situations that the supervision becomes very restrictive which, in turn, results in demotivation for the team members and the manager/supervisor. Such a limited span of control could also allow for increased complexity within the scalar chain in that horizontal and vertical decision-making is complicated.

The view of the classical writers is still important in the current climate of restructuring of organisations to meet the demands of globalisation and diversity. In practice, the model of span of control used within an organisation will depend upon a number of key factors. In any discussion on the most appropriate organisational design, spans of control can vary widely and in some cases go beyond those suggested in the literature – yet such increased boundaries do not appear to compromise the effectiveness of organisations which use larger teams and groups. Therefore, an appropriate span of control will depend upon a number of factors, including:

- task complexity
- task predictability

- willingness, ability, intrinsic motivation of individuals to work independently
- physical location and geographical spread of subordinates to manager/supervisor
- available time for manager/supervisor to take responsibility for subordinates
- the manager's/supervisor's skills in managing differently sized teams
- the effectiveness of organisational control systems in the directing and monitoring of the performance of subordinates.

All the above points intimately concern the design of jobs (see Chapter 5) and the empowerment given to individuals.

Unity of command

The classical writers also concentrated on the unity of command – no one person should receive instructions from more than one superior. A complicated command structure results in a complexity which distracts from effective decision-making and the meeting of goals and objectives for both workteams and the organisation itself.

Modern organisations do not strictly adhere to these classical chains of command since they find that they have overlapping lines of both authority and responsibility which makes the process of management more difficult. If there is no defined unity of command, it is difficult to identify who is responsible for what and who directs whom. Also, the chain of command is not just a functional design, it is a key feature in the design of organisations as well – as has been brought about by the implementation of matrix structures discussed later in this chapter.

Line, functional, and staff relationships

The span of control is, therefore, the number of people who are subordinate to a single manager or supervisor and to whom they report and, as a consequence, the line, functional, and staff relationships are utilised. This means that – as can be seen from Figure 8.11 above – such relationships are a normal feature of departmental communication. When an issue is complex and non-routine the manager or supervisor has to increase his or her intervention in order to solve the problem. However, there are other times when the manager or supervisor has to become involved – usually when the workforce:

- is not willing to carry out the task;
- does not have the skills required to complete the task;
- is dealing with small complex tasks when interaction with managers and/or supervisors is essential.

A manager's level of authority is partly determined by his or her given span of control within the overall scalar chain. However, that position is determined by a number of other kinds of power relationships which are shown in Figure 8.13 below and comprise:

- line relationships
- functional relationships
- staff relationships.

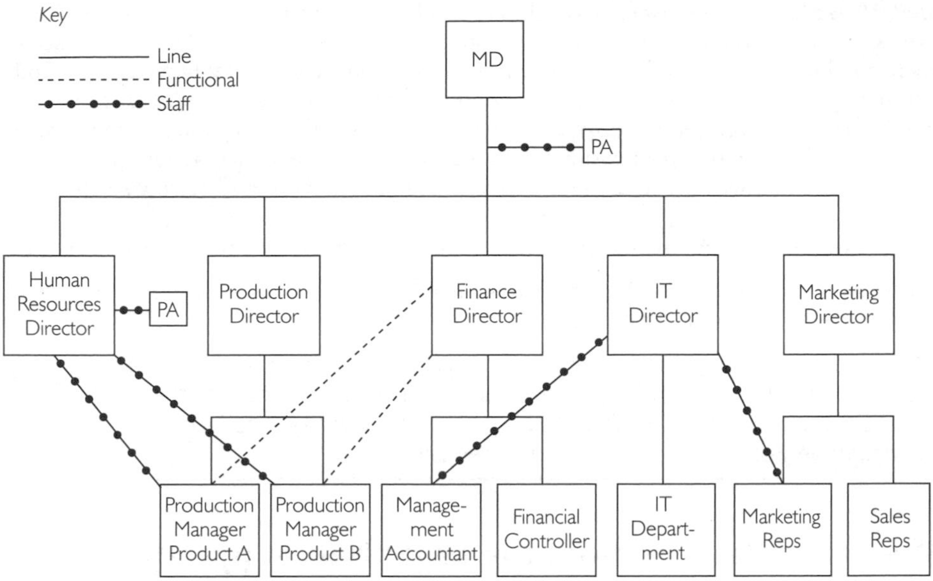

Figure 8.13 Line, functional, and staff relationships

Line relationships are those relationships between managers and their subordinates. They chart how authority over others flows down through the organisation's structure. In Figure 8.13 above a line relationship can be seen between the Managing Director and the other directors (for example, Production Director, IT Director, etc). These are the formal role and hierarchical relationships within the organisation.

Functional relationships are those between the different functions within the organisation where staff in one subsystem may have an element of authority over staff in another. In Figure 8.13, there is, for example, a functional relationship between the Finance Director and the Production Managers. In this case, the Production Managers need to liaise with the Finance Director in order to be funded – it is likely that the Finance Director will have a functional link with all subsystems! This is because the functional relationship can be subdivided into *task and element functions*. For example, whilst there is no direct line relationship between, say, the finance director and the individual production managers, the Finance Director (as the senior member of the management team responsible for finance issues concerning the whole organisation) may have the authority to vet any major capital expenditure by production managers or to question any significant variation of their budgets.

It is the director's senior position and scope of responsibility which gives the potential authority on matters relating to finance throughout the whole organisation. With this comes accountability and it is through other senior members of the organisation (the Managing Director, and fellow directors) that he agrees his framework of responsibility and accountability. Through such formal delegation of authority he is able to check budgets for others and vet capital expenditure requested by other systems within the organisation. However, when such procedures are not in place or are inadequate, there arise dysfunctional conflicts between the exercise of both line and functional authority.

Staff relationships are those where individuals provide a purely advisory or support service to others and where there is a limited element of authority or control. In Figure 8.13 above there will be a staff responsibility between the Information Technology Director and Product Managers because the former will be providing technical support for the production areas in relation to their computerised systems – his department will be providing them a service. In the same figure, a staff relationship can be found between the Managing Director and her Personal Assistant who provides the former with administrative and secretarial support.

What line, functional, and staff relationships are there at your university?

Think about how your own university is designed. Can you identify at least one example of each of line, functional, and staff relationships within it?

You will have an open-book here! An example of each would be: a line function between the Dean of Faculty to Heads of Schools; a functional link would be between the Secretary and the Deans; and a staff relationship between Media Services and the lecturers or between Computer Services and yourself as a computer user.

Vertical differentiation: the organisation pyramid

Vertical differentiation refers to the depth of the organisational structure. There is an increase in differentiation, and hence also in the complexity, as the number of hierarchical levels within the organisation increases. The more levels there are between the apex and the workers at the foot of the pyramid, the greater the possibility for ineffective communication and co-ordination of decision-making and control over the workers.

Depending on how they are applied, the interaction between types of authority relationships, such as the scalar chain and spans of control discussed above, produces a distinctive hierarchy within an organisation.

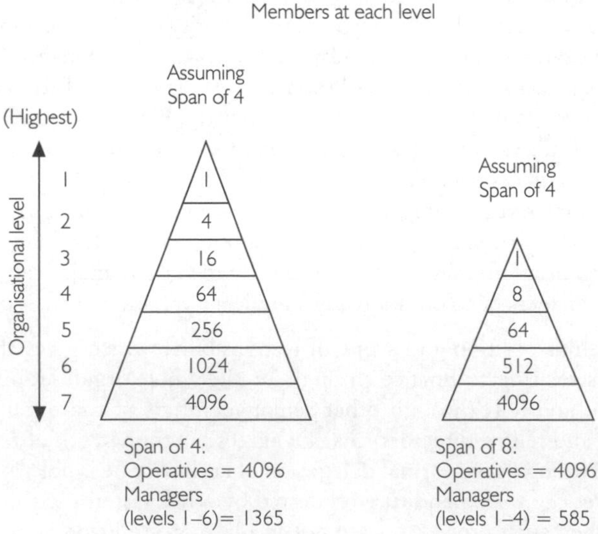

Figure 8.14 Organisational design and the spans of control, after Robbins (1991, p. 469)

However, vertical and horizontal differentiation should not be considered to be independent of one another. Vertical differentiation may well be the best way to respond to an increase in horizontal differentiation. For example, as specialisation increases it becomes essential that tasks are co-ordinated and controlled, and since high horizontal differentiation means that members will have a diverse background in willingness and skills it might well be hard for individual subsystems to see how their tasks fit into the greater whole. For example, an organisation specialising in the building of a new university campus will employ architects, surveyors, planners, masons, administrative workers, health and safety experts, lorry drivers, etc. However, someone has to co-ordinate all these workers to ensure that the campus is completed to tender. Therefore, there is a need for considerable co-ordination and this shows itself in the development of vertical differentiation.

Organisations which have the same number of workers do not necessarily have the same degree of vertical integration. Organisations can be tall with many levels of hierarchy or they can be flat, with few levels. The important factor which determines the height of the pyramid is the span of control which is in operation within the organisation – this can be seen in Figure 8.14.

An organisation which is mechanistic will tend to produce a tall pyramid whereas an organic organisation will have a flatter pyramid, as shown in Figure 8.10 on page 295.

Organising laterally

There is a dichotomy between mechanistic and organic structures because it is difficult to understand how far groups should be organised according to functional specialisation or to some other method of organisation. The issues of definition, linkage and control related to groups have been discussed in Chapter 6 and Chapter 7 where the role of groups and teams within organisations has been considered. However, it is necessary that consideration is given to how organisation design interacts with specific issues of the co-ordination of groups and teams.

Functional grouping

This is where the membership of a group depends upon the function of the group. Such groups are the most common and familiar and are found in mechanistic organisations where the management follows the principles of classical management. An example here would be where all members of the group carry out the same task, such as packaging goods.

Table 8.9 Advantages and disadvantages of functional groups

ADVANTAGES	DISADVANTAGES
Encourages specialisation	Difficult to link in transformation process
Increases expertise	Co-ordination overall is limited
Pools specialist skills	See minutiae rather than whole product/service
Effective division of labour	Pursue own interests
Defines task responsibility	Product rather than customer focused
	Integration with other subsystems
	Dysfunctional conflict with other systems
	Duplication of support functions
	Can be expensive to support

Locational grouping

This is a development of functional grouping because as an organisation grows and develops it becomes geographically dispersed. An example here would be a university which has a number of separate colleges which are on different geographical sites.

Product grouping

Another way of organising groups is by the product they create or the service they provide. This is yet another variant of functional grouping – even if it is more advanced. It has developed because of the necessity to increase a product range.

Market grouping

This is the organisation of groups according to the markets which are served by the organisation. For example, a university might group according to undergraduate and postgraduate courses.

Matrix grouping

This system of organisational design reflects the contingency approach – it is only useful in given situations, yet it is a common way of designing organisations. The matrix design attempts to combine two other organisation designs in an effort to gain the advantages of each: a functional grouping and a product grouping.

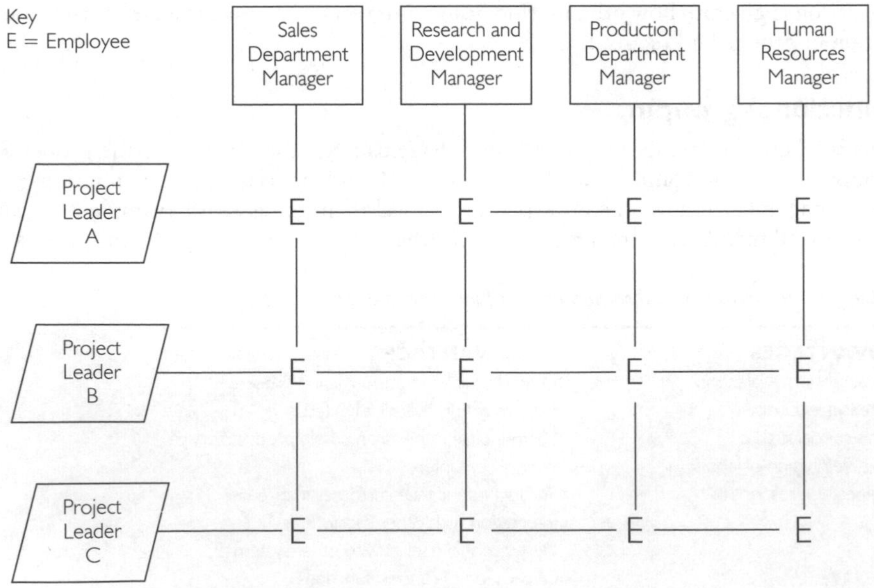

Figure 8.15 A matrix grouping

Figure 8.15 shows the most common form of matrix grouping where each department has a project leader, yet each employee is a member of a functional department *and* a project team. As a result, each member of the workforce has two supervisors: the head of department and the project leader.

Since the matrix grouping design is an amalgam of two other types of grouping (functional and product) it is best used as a grouping design when:

- the situation demands a dual focus on the issue, i.e. that environmental factors require that the organisation concentrate its efforts equally on:
  - responding to external factors
  - emphasising internal operations
- there is a high degree of information processing required;
- resources have to be shared.

The matrix grouping design is an attempt to define an organisation structure which:

- provides a flexible framework;
- utilises an environment where responses to external and internal pressures can be co-ordinated.

Advantages of matrix grouping

Apart from the two issues above (flexibility and improved co-ordination of activities) there are a number of other advantages attributed to a matrix grouping design.

- Individuals can be reassigned to different projects when their particular skills and information are required.
- A single leader can be assigned to a project rather than dividing it amongst several functional department heads.
- Communication is improved because members of the workforce can communicate on matters concerning the project with other members of the project team as well as with members of the functional department to which they belong.
- Problem-solving and decision-making are more creative because of the wider range of individuals who can be asked for their opinions.
- Co-ordination is by mutual agreement through frequent personal contacts and liaison systems.
- Specialists are not grouped together (as in functional grouping) but dispersed in market-oriented project teams.

Disadvantages of matrix grouping

Even though matrix grouping is a popular design and is used in a variety of organisations such as hospitals, banks, and manufacturing firms, it does bring with it some problems and disadvantages.

- Since individuals belong to two systems (functional and product) there might be role conflict amongst members of the workforce. For example, the Head of Human Resources might have been seconded to a project team which is working on the issue of the work environment: she is a functional head yet is a team player in the project team.
- There might be power struggles related who has authority over and within the project team.
- Inappropriate decision-making techniques might be used. Since it is a team, members of the project team might feel that group decision-making processes are always to be used, yet they might not always be appropriate.

- Individuals may belong to more than one project team and thus be confused about authority and accountability.

Bartlett and Ghosal (1990) believe that matrix structures may well have distinct advantages but they emphasise the fact that such structures become unmanageable given the following reasons:

- they often have to report to more than one person which could result in dysfunctional conflict and role/task confusion;
- because of the complexity of communication channels, there is the chance of message incongruence and overload;
- with the overlapping of responsibility comes the potential for the loss of accountability, thus disempowering the team.

Thus, project teams may well be expensive in the use of resources and therefore be an expensive feature of some organisations.

Team working and cell groups

In both Chapter 6 and Chapter 7 groups and teams are discussed in detail. In Chapter 6 a team was considered to be a task-oriented group which could be formally designated or which could informally evolve.

This is a definition which can be assigned to a *cell group*, which is usually found in the manufacturing industries. A cell group is a small team which makes entire products or provides an entire service from conception to after-sales service. When initiated in firms such as Toyota, Rank Xerox, and Hewlett-Packard, decision-making and task execution were initially under the direction of management. However, nowadays cell groups take total responsibility for all stages and are totally self-managed: they decide on all issues including recruitment and selection, firing of staff and the flow of the work – they are autonomous. However, as can be seen from the case study below, it is not always straightforward.

CASE STUDY

The Trouble with Teams: Togetherness has its Perils

Peter Cook, a British satirist who died on 9 January 1995, loved to poke fun at British private schools and their cult of team spirit. But if you listen to management theorists you would think that these schools had unwittingly stumbled upon the magic secret of business success. With teams all the rage, management theorists are earning fat fees by proffering advice on how to build teams and how to inculcate team spirit.

At first sight, the virtues of teamwork look obvious. Teams make workers happier by giving them the feeling they are shaping their own jobs. They increase efficiency by eliminating layers of managers, whose job was once to pass orders downwards. They also enable companies to draw on the skills and imagination of the whole workforce instead of relying on specialists to watch out for mistakes and to suggest improvements.

Having started with corporate giants such as Toyota, Motorola and General Electric, the fashion for teams has spread rapidly. A recent survey suggested that cell manufacturing (in which small groups of workers make entire products) is being experimented with at more than half of America's manufacturing plants; and teams are growing more powerful as well as more numerous. Their task was at first to execute decisions under the supervision of managers, not to make decisions. The current fashion, however, is for self-management.

Companies as different as Xerox (office equipment), Monsanto (chemicals) and Johnson & Johnson Sausage (foodstuffs) are allowing teams to decide on everything from hiring and firing to organising the flow of work. At New United Motor Manufacturing (a joint venture run in Fremont, California, by General Motors and Toyota), teams of workers elect their own leaders and invent ways of improving quality and efficiency.

Hewlett-Packard, a computer maker, has gone even further in mixing the specialisms represented in single teams. Its teams bring together engineers, technical writers, marketing managers, lawyers, purchasing professionals, and shop-floor workers. At Corning's, a ceramics plant in Erwin, New York, teams are fed business information so that they can understand how their plant is faring in the market. Informed workers, it is assumed, are less likely to make unreasonable wage demands. Still it would not surprise every inmate of a British private school to learn that teams are not always flawless ways to motivate and inspire people. Like many management fads, the one for teams is beginning to produce its trickle of disappointments. A T Kearney, a consultancy that continues to favour teams, found in a survey that nearly seven out of ten teams failed to produce the desired results.

A common error, says A T Kearney, is to create teams instead of taking more radical decisions. In many businesses it is still more effective to automate work than to reorganise the workforce. Years ago, Sweden's Volvo was praised for introducing self-governing teams in its car factories at Kalmar and Uddevalla in order to make the work more interesting. More interesting it duly became, but also so expensive that the company was forced to close the experimental plants and concentrate production at Gothenburg on a traditional assembly line.

Even when creating teams really is the appropriate solution to a firm's problem, managers often make a hash of running them. A typical mistake is the failure to set clear objectives. Another is to introduce teams without changing the firm's patterns of appraisal and reward from an individual to a collective system. That can send the workforce fatally mixed signals: employees are expected on the one hand to pull together, but on the other to compete for individual rewards.

Teamwork, moreover, costs money, the biggest additional expense being training. Not unreasonably, members of supposedly self-managing teams start wondering how to manage. This gives birth to an epidemic of woolly courses on conflict management and stress resolution. Meetings swallow time as empowered workers break off from the tedium of making things and chat endlessly instead about process improvement or production imperfections.

Although many such courses are superfluous, advocates of team-based production can see that the best teams are made up of people with broad enough skills to step easily into each other's shoes. Providing such cross-training, as the theorists call it, is arduous. In some of the more complicated team structures such as those in chemical plants it can take team members six to ten years to learn all the jobs they might be called upon to do.

However, the chief problem with teams is political. Almost invariably their creation undermines some existing distribution of power in a firm. Middle managers often see shop-floor teams as a threat to their authority, and perhaps to their livelihoods. Many workers see teams as a source of division and a goad to overwork. On at least two occasions, American unions have used the National Labour Relations Act of 1935 which makes it unlawful for an employer to dominate or interfere with the formation or administration of a labour organisation to foil attempts to introduce teamwork.

Besides, although the cheery vocabulary of teamwork makes excitable use of words such as empowerment, teams usually replace top-down managerial control with peer pressure, a force that is sometimes no less coercive. 'People try to meet the team's expectations' says one worker at New United Motors in Fremont, 'and under peer pressure they end up pushing themselves too hard.'

Some workers may prefer not being told what to do, shouldering the burden of decisions themselves. Those who welcome responsibility sometimes find it hard to discipline their wayward colleagues. And there is always the danger that teams will impose deadly uniformity and stifle the special qualities of individuals. As many a graduate of Britain's private schools will tell you, such places have made little use of the brainy wimp who hated rugby and spent a childhood shivering on the sidelines. That, in a way, was Peter Cook's point, and one that management theorists have been slow to notice.

Source: *The Economist*, 14 January 1995

Organisational design in a contemporary arena

There is a plethora of design theories and many organisational design alternatives facing managers today and there is no sign that this will abate. The array of choices can be confusing for any organisation which needs to manage itself within a design which is proactive and which meets the demands of a globalised and changing environment.

All that an organisation designer can do is to examine the existing company in a situational way and design a unique form of organisation which meets its needs. Many considerations need to be taken into account but the key ones are shown in Figure 8.16.

Downsizing

Downsizing is now common practice within organisations and has affected thousands of companies and millions of employees. According to Freeman and Cameron (1993) it has become so much a part of a modern organisation's revitalisation cycle that it is no longer

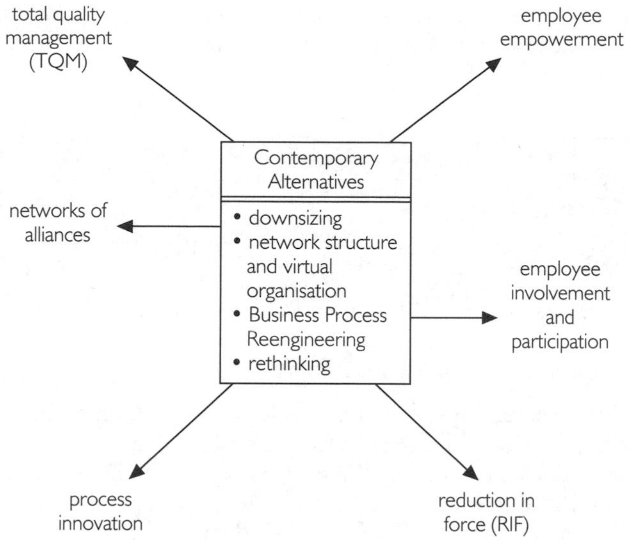

Figure 8.16 Contemporary organisational design issues

considered as being connected only to the decline and failure of an organisation but is a routine part of management. This trend of cutting staff throughout the organisation is aimed primarily at reducing the size of the corporate staff and middle management and to reduce costs: it is sometimes labelled 'downlayering' or 'rightsizing'.

Downsizing has brought with it mixed results which relate to the design of an organisation. There may be indiscriminate across-the-board cuts which leaves the organisation weak in certain key areas. However, positive results are that the organisation is in a position to initiate quicker decision-making processes because there are fewer layers of managers who have to consider the issues. Downsizing is not a new concept. Hall *et al.* (1967) posited that the relationship between size and structural complexity of organisations is not clear. They suggested that it is essential that the size of the organisation be examined in relation to the technology of the organisation.

Network structure and the virtual organisation

Modern organisations are attempting to offset the increased fragmentation of their structure in order to make a more coherent design which is often called a *network*. Hatch (1997) defines this as: '[an organisation] which replaces most, if not all, vertical communication and control relationships with lateral relationships' (p. 191).

In such organisations the formal ties which keep the various units of an organisation together are replaced by partnerships with other organisations. They tend to be identified with those organisations facing:

- rapid technological change
- shortened product lifecycles
- fragmented, specialised markets.

A network structure, therefore, utilises *outsourcing*, which means, according to Hatch (1997), that 'many of the activities of a once complex organization are moved outside the organization's boundary' (p. 191).

CASE STUDY
Outsourcing

It has been long accepted that the best way to deal with such tasks as catering or cleaning is to hand them to specialist firms.

But the notion that such critical functions as information technology, or business processes like accounting, administering pensions or answering customer enquiries, can be outsourced has only recently taken hold.

Firm indications on the size of the market are difficult to obtain because such a wide range of activities fit under the outsourcing umbrella. However, figures this year [1997] from the research company input [Vision 2010: Designing Tomorrow's Organisation, by the Economist Intelligence Unit] estimate the global market at £25.6 billion in 1996, rising to £66.9 billion by 2001.

Contracts for IT outsourcing in the UK reached £1.5 billion in 1996, up 15 per cent on 1995, according to the IT outsourcing firm ITnet. There were 133 contracts signed in the UK in 1996, with 91 agreed by companies outsourcing for the first time.

Adapted from the *Daily Telegraph*, 'Outsourcing', 28 May 1997, p. 2

When all the task activities of an organisation are outsourced, the result is a *virtual organisation*. Hatch (1997) gives the example of Benetton as a virtual organisation because it is made up of hundreds of small manufacturers making clothes and thousands of franchised sales outlets which rely on a central distribution channel which has a common information and control system. Another example would be The Body Shop.

Business Process Reengineering

Business Process Reengineering (BPR) has been discussed in Chapter 5. It is a concept which has an important relationship with the design of an organisation because re-engineering is the radical redesign of organisational processes to achieve major gains in cost, time, and the provision of services – normally with the aid of information technology. Conventional organisational design tends to encourage the organisation to take its current form and make incremental changes, whereas re-engineering is radical because it drives the organisation to renew its practices from scratch and redesign itself round its most important process. BPR is useful for those starting up an organisation because they can design the organisation as it should be for future success. However, existing organisations can also use BPR if they are willing to design for future success rather than from historical and traditional experience. The process starts from the outcomes – what the customer really wants – and then goes on to implementing a design strategy to meet that need. Once that strategy is established it is essential that there is strong leadership throughout the organisation so that a core team of people can design the organisation system which will achieve the required strategy. Re-engineering is not a tangible organisational form, it is a process – hence its name.

Rethinking

This is an ongoing popular view related to the design of organisations and involves managers looking at the organisation design in totally different ways which may entail abandoning the classic view of the organisation as a pyramid – however tall. Such structures have already been outlined in this chapter but they take a key role when considering contemporary design issues. Tomasko (1993) thought that such a traditional shape is inappropriate for current organisational design and that organisations often have too many levels of management arranged hierarchically so that efficiency and change are clumsy and unsure. One rethinking aspect is to consider designing the organisation as a dome rather than as a pyramid. Such a dome could be analogous to an open umbrella which covers and protects those underneath it but leaves them unshackled and able to do their work. Such a design would eliminate fixed internal units (the walls of a pyramid) to allow the workers to be flexible and able to interact with internal and external environmental forces. Such organisational design can be seen in Microsoft and the Royal Dutch-Shell Group, and is increasingly being seen in other organisations.

Contemporary organisational design

There are four dominant themes related to evolving design strategies:

- effects of information technology
- environmental change
- importance of human resources
- staying in contact with the customer.

Both *information technology* and *environmental change* are evolving so fast and so unpredictably that no organisation design will be stable over time. Changes in, for example, electronic information processing, transmission and retrieval are so vast and fast that effective use of *human resources*, the distribution of information, and the co-ordination of tasks need to be reviewed very frequently. Also, *initial and ongoing contact with the customer* is important in the design of organisations.

Such concepts appear to argue for a contingency organisation design approach but, as in other organisational constructs, 'there is no one best way'. In designing an organisation it is essential to consider a multiplicity of factors which have previously been discussed, including:

- sociotechnical systems
- structural imperatives
- corporate strategy
- changing information technology
- human resources
- the customer.

However, there are two key considerations which are all-important to the design of an organisation in the contemporary world:

- global forces
- the learning organisation.

Global forces

It is imperative that organisations constantly 'think global' if they hope to survive in the modern world. At one time or another all organisations will feel the impact of global competition because the world is a vast potential market. It is a matter of evolution rather than revolution because no one organisation can instantly 'become global' – it comes about through stages of development which are very similar to the life cycle explained earlier in this chapter.

As a consequence of globalised markets, organisations are having to be innovative and flexible in their structure and design since they have to extend their markets beyond the domestic to the multinational. This move means that the formerly domestic organisations are becoming more competitive and thus need to move away from the top-heavy, functionally operated structure towards the more horizontal structures where the focus is more on process than function and the organisation uses a flat hierarchy with empowered self-managed teams who make the decisions needed to satisfy the demands of the customer.

The first step towards this is *re-engineering* – the discarding of old systems and ideas to make ready for the new concepts of how work can be carried out in the current environment. This topic is discussed earlier in this chapter.

A second way to innovate is to introduce a *dynamic network structure* which employs the free market approach rather than the vertical hierarchy. In this design there are separate companies or individuals who are co-ordinated through a very small headquarters organisation. Such a design permits new workers to be added, or removed, as global circumstances demand.

However, an organisation needs to take into account how many opportunities it has for a globalised market because, if it is large, its products/services can be standardised to suit that market. It is important that a globalised organisation is in a position to compete on multiple-dimensions simultaneously through *heterarchy*, which is a development of horizontal organisation. In a heterarchy there are multiple centres with subsidiary managers who initiate strategy for the organisation, with co-ordination and control being achieved through the corporate culture and shared values.

The learning organisation

CASE STUDY
The Kalahari Bushmen

For hundreds of years, the Kalahari Bushmen were nomadic hunters and foragers in the harsh, unpredictable South African desert. They developed the skills to find water during drought, to live on reptiles and plants in the absence of game, and to fashion bows and arrows from their limited sources. They travelled in groups bound together by ties of kinship and friendship. Their mobility and few possessions enabled the Bushmen to switch easily to more successful groups, in this way capitalising on success wherever it was found over a wide geographical area. The flexible group system (known as the 'band system') was enhanced by values of equality, sharing, and gift giving. A hunter's kill would be used to feed neighbours, who would later reciprocate. Gift giving meant that useful artifacts and utensils were widely shared. Hunting camps had grass huts facing the centre of a circle where the cooking hearths were hubs of continuous discussion and social exchanges. The Bushmen of the Kalahari also bonded through a deep culture in their camps of shared mythology, stories and dances.

Then came along civilisation. In recent years, exposure to material wealth has fostered a transformation. The Kalahari Bushmen have now accumulated possessions, which hamper mobility, thus forcing a lifestyle shift from foraging to farming. A new community structure has evolved, with families living in separate, permanent huts. Entrances are located for privacy, and hearths have been moved inside. Survival skills have deteriorated, with bows and arrows produced only for curio shops. Without sharing and communication, a hierarchy of authority – the chief – is used to resolved disputes. Tension and dysfunctional conflict have increased, and the tribe's ability to handle drought and disaster today is non-existent. No longer are there shared stories and mythology that bind the tribespeople into a community.

Adapted from D.K. Hurst, 'Cautionary Tales from the Kalahari: How Hunters Become Herders and May Have Trouble Changing Back Again' in *Academy of Management Executive*, Vol. 3, No 5, 1991, pp. 74–86

The above case resembles a bureaucracy which provides a stable and safe environment thus leaving the Kalahari Bushmen unable to cope with sudden environmental changes. However, the entrepreneurial and learning organisation of today is based on a minimum of hierarchy, equality of rewards, shared culture, and a flowing, adaptable structure which is designed to seize opportunities and handle crises. Thus the hunter-forager society of the Kalahari Bushmen is a metaphor for the fluid learning organisation of today – an aspiration of all companies who survive today. It is through an understanding of the learning organisation that organisation designers can integrate the various techniques and methods discussed earlier in this chapter to become the learning organisation of today and the future.

Organisation design and corporate strategy

One of the most important tasks for leaders is to decide on the corporate strategy and objectives of their organisation and then to design an organisational form which is considered to be the best for meeting that strategy and goals. It is rather like a jigsaw puzzle – it is essential that all the pieces are present and that they will fit together into the right configuration which will provide and maintain the highest level of effectiveness. After having decided upon the corporate strategy, formulated the activities, and implemented them, the organisation has to be formed and designed. It is the design of the organisation which is the ultimate expression of the implementation of strategy.

Mintzberg (1979) suggested that every organisation comprises five sections, as shown in Figure 8.17.

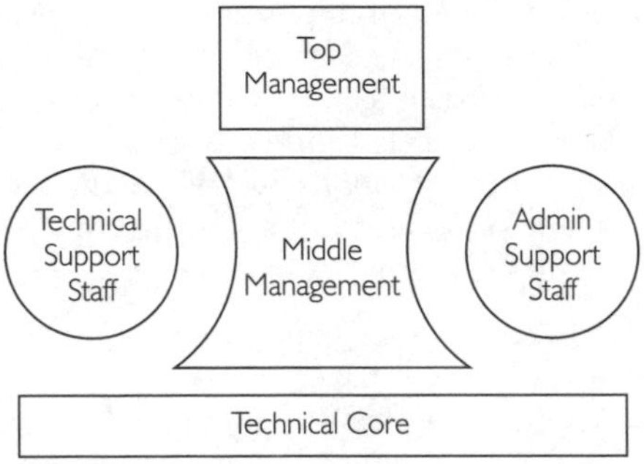

Figure 8.17 The five basic sections of an organisation, after Mintzberg (1979, pp. 103–116)

In this model senior management is at the apex with middle management at the intermediate level, and the technical core (engineers, analysts, researchers) includes the employees who carry out the basic work of the organisation. The administrative support staff provide the direct services (clerical, maintenance, post room). Each of the five sections may be variable in size and importance depending upon the environment, corporate strategy, and technology. Mintzberg's (1979) key point was that the top management can design an organisation to achieve harmony and fit amongst the key sections. An example here would be that a machine bureaucracy might be appropriate for a strategy of efficiency in an environment which is stable, whereas in a volatile environment the introduction of a machine bureaucracy would be an expensive error. It is up to the managers to design an appropriate structural configuration to fit the situation.

It is Mintzberg's (1991) later work which is of particular importance in the move towards a learning organisation. Here he proposes that an effective organisation must be a learning organisation which interplays seven forces. An organisation's design can be such that it fluctuates between these forces – as can be seen in Figure 8.18 opposite.

The first force is that of *direction* which incorporates the organisation's vision and mission and its goals and objectives which all identify the organisation's direction and purpose. The best example here would be an entrepreneurial organisation.

The second force is *efficiency* where there is a need to minimise the costs yet increase the benefits to all stakeholders. An example here would be the machine bureaucracy because of its focus on rationalisation, standardisation, and centralisation.

The third force, *proficiency*, means that the work tasks have to be carried out willingly and ably, such tasks requiring a high level of skill from the workforce. This would be prevalent in a professional bureaucracy where there are highly trained professionals who work together to achieve excellence and quality.

The fourth force, *innovation*, requires that the organisation develop new products/services so that it can adapt to a changing internal and external environment. An adhocracy organisation would succeed here because of its ability to deal with innovation and change.

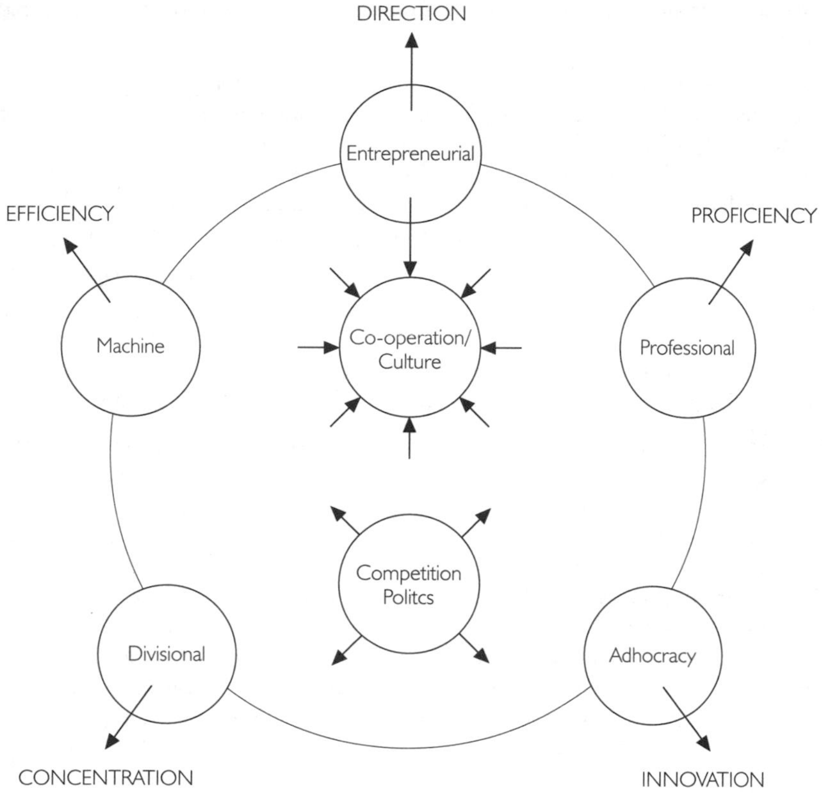

Figure 8.18 A system of forces and forms within organisations, after Mintzberg (1991)

The fifth force is that of *concentration*, which means that the organisation has to focus its efforts on specific markets. It would, therefore, have a divisional organisation with activities focused on specific products and markets.

Continuing to look at Figure 8.18 above, there are two additional forces: co-operation/culture and competition/politics. The former comes about because of the common culture values of the workforce in that it reflects the harmony and co-operation within a diverse workforce. However, competition can cause dysfunctional conflict, with departments and groups splitting in order to search for individual self-actualisation.

Mintzberg (1991) emphasises that the key issue is the need to have an organisational design which permits the balance of all seven forces. Individual organisations might stress a particular force depending upon the nature of their business, but there is increased pressure for effective co-operation and thus competition must be managed, and a co-operative model achieves greater success in most organisations.

No organisation can satisfy all its needs simultaneously; by understanding the forces and optimising them to achieve the corporate strategy and goals, an organisation can become effective through continual leadership which allows for constant reorganisation of the organisational design to fulfil strategy and meet the demands of the volatile global environment.

This chapter has attempted to show that corporate design is going through transformation from the traditional management school to full participation and empowerment of every employee. Accompanying this have been the new organisational forms such as modular organisations, virtual corporations, and horizontal organisations considered in this chapter. These forms have been brought about by two accelerating trends. Firstly, global competition and, secondly, the development of technology – both discussed in this chapter.

The key principle here is that managers must create organisational learning capability with an ability to learn and change faster than the competition – in some cases this may be the only way that an organisation can sustain a competitive advantage. Over the last few years there has been a considerable move towards the *learning organisation* which replaces any of the designs already discussed and which are summarised in Table 8.10 opposite.

Within the learning organisation all members are responsible for solving the problems thus allowing the organisation to continually experiment, improve, and increase its capability. It is in the key area of problem-solving that a learning organisation leads, in this way differing from the traditional organisation. It is not just in solving the problem that all employees within a learning organisation are involved but, significantly, in the identification of problems and in understanding the needs of the customer. By problem-solving, the employees are able to meet customer needs in unique ways. Thus a learning organisation can add value because it can define new needs and solve them before the problem actually arises. This is brought about by adding new ideas and through creative thinking and is not only applicable to just the service industries where ideas and information are of paramount importance.

In the manufacturing industries, ideas, information, and creativity will provide competitive advantage because products must change to meet new and challenging needs in the globalised and evolving technological environment. Examples here would be in the car industry where some manufacturers added built-in safety elements (air bags, side impact bars) to their cars. Another example is 3M (manufacturers of Sellotape) whose research and development department were looking into a new, strong self-adhesive, without success; yet after having put it aside, someone used it and devised, accidentally, Post-It stickers. A deliberate development would be in the case of The Body Shop, which anticipated the demand for natural cosmetics.

As Ulrich and Lake (1991) suggested, organisational learning capability is a critical source of competitive advantage. This view is shown in Figure 8.19 below.

It is not possible to define a learning organisation because it is an attitude and is best considered as an extension of concepts already considered in this book. However, it is typically associated with certain factors. In Figure 8.20 below can be seen how the learning organisation has moved beyond the traditional organisational hierarchy and horizontal organisation to the contribution of all the workforce to the strategic direction of their organisation. This contribution is made through teamwork and increased contact with the customer. Such an increase in employee responsibility has led to this learning organisation philosophy and is associated with an educated leadership, a strong and identifiable culture, widespread information sharing, and a shift from formal structures and systems to organic ones.

Table 8.10 Dimensions of five organisational types, after Mintzberg (1979, pp. 466–471)

DIMENSION	ENTREPRENEURIAL STRUCTURE	MACHINE BUREAUCRACY	PROFESSIONAL BUREAUCRACY	DIVISIONAL FORM FORM	ADHOCRACY
Strategy and innovation	Growth, survival	Defender; efficiency	Analyse; effectiveness, quality	Portfolio, profit	Prospector; innovation
Age and size goals	Young and small	Old and large	Varies	Old and very large	Young
Technology	Simple	Machines but not automated	Service	Divisible, like machine bureaucracy	Very sophisticated, often automated
Environment	Simple and dynamic	Simple and stable	Complex and stable	Relatively simple and stable; diversified markets	Complex and dynamic
Formalisation	Little	Much	Little	Within divisions	Little
Structure	Functional	Functional	Functional or product	Product, hybrid	Functional and product (matrix)
Co-ordination	Direct supervision	Vertical linkage	Horizontal linkage	Headquarters staff	Mutual adjustment
Control	Clan	Bureaucratic	Clan and bureaucratic	Market and bureaucratic	Clan
Culture	Developing	Weak	Strong	Sub-cultures	Strong
Technical support staff	None	Many	Few	Many at headquarters for performance control	Small and within project work
Administrative support staff	Small	Many	Many to support professionals	Split between headquarters and divisions	Many but within project work
Key part of organisation	Top management	Technical staff	Production core	Middle management	Support staff and technical core

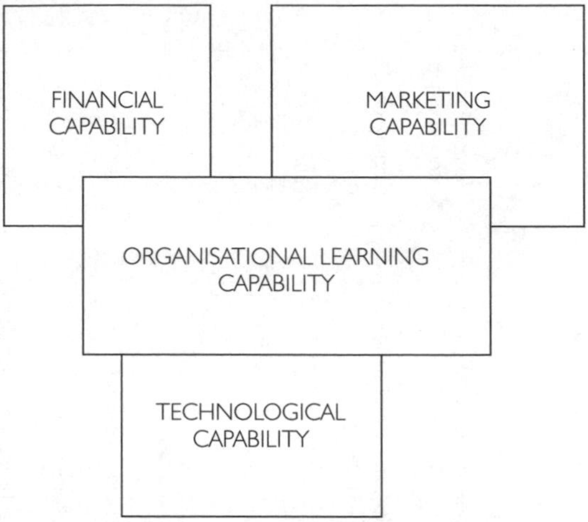

Figure 8.19 Organisational learning capability and competitive advantage, after Ulrich and Lake (1991, p. 77)

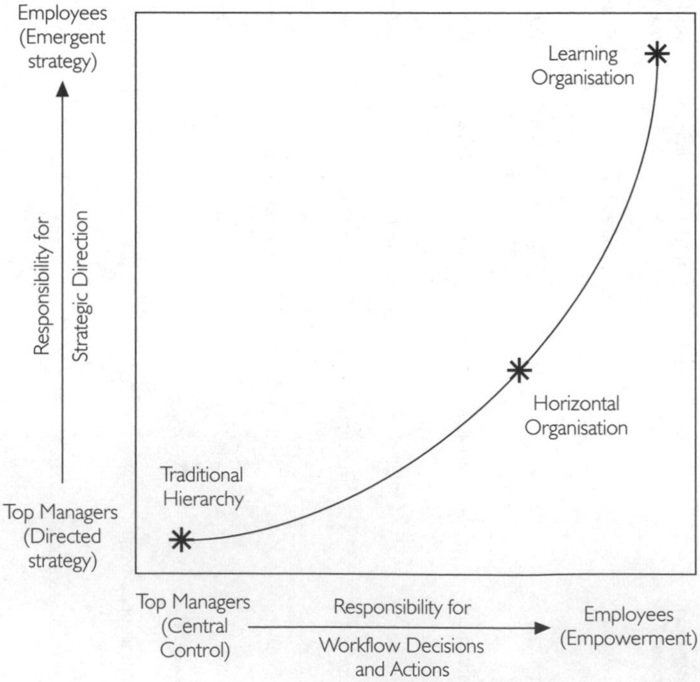

Figure 8.20 Evolution of a learning organisation adapted from Daft (1995, p. 492)

In 1995 ICL completed its cultural change to become a learning organisation and it continues to be so by ensuring that it does not become complacent. Mayo and Lank (1995) put forward a model which showed the organisation's learning organisation benchmark and this is shown in Figure 8.21 below.

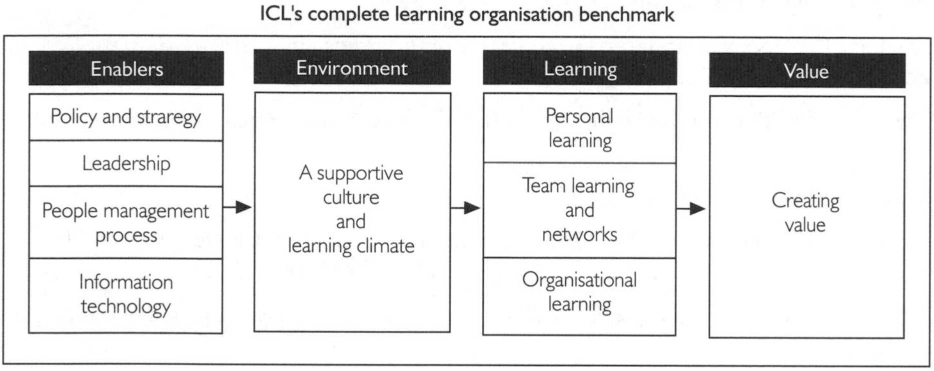

Figure 8.21 Mayo and Lank's Complete Learning Organisation Benchmark

From this chapter it can be seen that there has been a considerable shift from the traditional organisational design to that now commonly found in the globalised and technological market – the learning organisation. Such changes are revolutionary and are considered further in the next chapter which looks at the dynamics of organisations.

Questions for discussion

1. How would you characterise the university that you attend regarding basic structure and design features?
2. Discuss the nature of emerging organisational structures.
3. As an organisation changes its structure and design over time, how much commitment should it show to those who need to be retrained to adapt to the intended system? Is it acceptable for organisations to make such people redundant and bring in already trained staff in those areas where they are needed?

References and further reading

Bartlett, C.A., and Ghosal, S., 'Matrix Management: Not a Structure, a Frame of Mind', in *Harvard Business Review*, July/August 1990, pp. 138–145

Bedeian, H. and Zamnuto, R.F., 1991, *Organizations: Theory and Design* (Chicago: Dryden)

Buchanan, D. and Huczynski, A., 1997 (3rd edn), *Organizational behaviour: an introductory text* (London: Prentice-Hall)

Burns, T. and Stalker, G.M., 1961, *The Management of Innovation* (London: Tavistock)

Child, J., 1984 (2nd edn), *Organization: A Guide to Problems and Practice* (London: Harper & Row)

Daft, R.L., 1995 (5th edn), *Organization Theory & Design* (St Paul, MN: West Publishing)

Daily Telegraph, 'Outsourcing', 28 May 1997, p. 2

Drucker, P.F., 'New templates for today's organisations' in *Harvard Business Review*, January–February 1974, pp. 45–65

Economist, The, 'The Trouble with Teams: Togetherness has its Perils', 14 January 1995

Emery, F. and Trist, E.L., 'The Causal Texture of Organizational Environments' in *Human Relations*, February 1965, pp. 21–32

Freeman, S.J. and Cameron, K., 'Organizational Downsizing: A Convergence and Reorientation Framework' in *Organizational Science*, Vol. 4, 1993, pp. 10–29

Galbraith, J.R., 1977, *Organizational Design* (Reading, Mass: Addison-Wesley) pp. 81–127

Graicunas, A., 1937, 'Relationship in Organization' in *Papers on the Science of Administration* (Columbia: University of Columbia)

Greiner, L., 'Evolution and Revolution as Organizations Grow' in *Harvard Business Review*, Vol. 50, July–August 1972, pp. 37–46

Hall, R.H., Haas, J.E. and Johnson, N., 'Organizational Size, Complexity, and Formalization' in *American Sociological Review*, December 1967, pp. 903–912

Hannagan, T., 1995, *Management: Concepts and Practice* (London: Pitman)

Hatch, M.J., 1997, *Organization Theory: Modern Symbolic and Postmodern Perspectives* (Oxford: Oxford University Press)

Hurst, D.K., 'Cautionary Tales from the Kalahari: How Hunters Become Herders and May Have Trouble Changing Back Again' in *Academy of Management Executive*, Vol. 3, No 5, 1991, pp. 74–86

Kellaway, L, 'The Royal Dutch Shell Group', in *Financial Times*, 6 October 1997, p. 14

Lawrence, P. and Lorsch, J.W., 1967, *Organization and Environment: Managing Differentiation and Integration* (Boston: Harvard Business School, Division of Research)

Mayo, A. and Lank, E., 'Changing the soil spurs new growth' in *People Management*, 16 November 1995, pp. 26–28

Mintzberg, H., 1979, *The Structuring of Organisations* (London: Prentice-Hall International)

Mintzberg, H., 1991, *The Effective Organization: Forces and Forms*, Sloan Management Review Association, Winter 1991, pp. 54–67

Perrow, C., 'A Framework for the Comparative Analysis of Organizations' in *American Sociological Review*, April 1967, pp. 194–208

Quinn, R.E. and Cameron, K., 'Organizational Life Cycles and Shifting Criteria of Effectiveness: Some Preliminary Evidence' in *Management Science*, Vol. 29, 1983, pp. 35–51

Roehampton Institute London (An Institute of the University of Surrey), Graduate and Postgraduate Prospectuses, 1998–1999, inside cover

Robbins, S.P., 1991 (5th edn), *Organizational Behavior: Concepts, Controversies, and Applications* (London: Prentice-Hall International)

Thompson, D., 1967, *Organizations in Action* (New York: McGraw-Hill)

Tomasko, R., 1993, *Rethinking the Corporation* (New York: AMA-COM)

Ulrich, D. and Lake, D., 'Organizational Capability: Creating Competitive Advantage' in *Academy of Management Executive*, 1991, Vol. 5, No 1, pp. 77–92

Urwick, L., 1952, *Notes on the Theory of Organisation* (American Management Association)

Weber, M., 1947, *The Theory of Social and Economic Organizations* (translated by A.M. Henderson and T. Parsons) (New York: Free Press)

Woodward, J., 1958, *Management and Technology* (London: HMSO)

Woodward J., 1965, *Industrial Organisation: Theory and Practice* (Oxford: Oxford University Press)

Zwerman, W.L., 1970, *New Perspectives in Organizational Theory* (Westport, Conn: Greenwood)

9 Dynamics of organisations

Learning objectives

After studying this chapter you should be able to:

- understand the impact of organisational dynamics;
- appreciate the nature of organisational culture;
- be aware of some of the complexities involved in organisational culture;
- understand the different perspectives of organisational conflict;
- appreciate the intricacies of conflict management.

Introduction

CASE STUDY

John Brown Memorial Hospital

In the late 1980s the British government, alarmed at the ever increasing expenditure on the Health Service, introduced the Resource Management Initiative as a means whereby the control of expenditure within hospitals would devolve upon those who spent the money. In short, doctors and nurses were required to become involved in the effective management of budgets. This was a radical change within hospitals since it was traditional for medical staff to focus more upon patient treatment and care and less upon the management of the resources available for those purposes.

John Brown Memorial Hospital is an old, large, teaching hospital which has always been run along traditional lines. The pressure from the government to conform to the demands of the initiative means that it must now be restructured into a series of cost centres (called directorates), each of which is required to take responsibility for resources allocated to it. To assist in the management process each directorate would be headed by a director, normally a senior clinician. It was decided at an early stage that the number of directorates and their composition would be settled by participation from the organisation's membership. Once established, the internal arrangements of each directorate would be decided by the members of that directorate.

It was hoped that the involvement of those affected by the new arrangements would lessen the impact of the change and encourage ownership of the problem. In the event nothing could have been further from the truth.

The medical staff in particular expressed deep concern about the wisdom and efficacy of the proposed changes. There was dismay at the assault on established structures and procedures, and a fervent belief that the transfer of responsibility for expenditure would distract them from the exercise of their profession.

For example, it soon became clear that the members of some specialisms did not want to be part of any directorate in which certain other specialisms were represented. In other cases, early proposals for directorates posed real problems for many. Where should a neurologist specialising in children's ailments go? Should he join a directorate containing the bulk of his fellow professionals, or one set up to manage the children's hospital? Such considerations brought a clinician's twin loyalties to organisation and profession into sharp focus. Again, could professionals who were a minority group live easily in a directorate headed by a member of another profession? Would he understand their needs? Would he ensure they got a fair share of available resources?

A bigger problem for those likely to be appointed as directors concerned workload. To what extent would their duties as directors eat into the time they now devoted to clinical pursuits? It is clear that within the medical profession acceptance by fellow professionals depends upon a clinician's commitment to practice. If the task of director was to make substantial inroads into clinical practice then it would be difficult to find a respected clinician willing to take up the post.

In the end a forced change looked as if it would cause chaos, even though the people most affected had been asked to find a solution to the common problem.

The above case illustrates many of the problems to be found when there is a change to the existing dynamics of an organisation. The previous chapter investigated the role of organisational structure and design. Design is an important feature of organisational life since it provides the structure around which the enterprise's positions and activities are arranged. But it is only a starting point, for two reasons.

Firstly, *people* are required if an organisation is to be brought to life. They occupy the designated positions and carry out the required activities – but they are not automatons. As was seen in Chapter 4 people have minds of their own; they respond uniquely and in unexpected ways to organisational stimuli. Structure may dictate the *formal* arrangements of the organisation, but its members will move beyond the framework, generating tensions and creating conflicts.

Secondly, structure presents a static photograph of how an organisation looked (or was supposed to look) when it was designed. But as the case study above shows organisations are subject to change. At John Brown's Memorial Hospital the change initially concerned a restructuring exercise forced upon the organisation from outside. In the end the change eventually took place, but it was a painful process involving much more than a mere change in structure. While structure is a starting point, a necessary foundation, it does not adequately deal with the *dynamics* of organisations. It is this area that needs to be considered next.

This chapter examines three major influences on organisational dynamics:

- organisational culture
- intra-organisational conflict
- organisational change.

While there can be strong linkages between the above, each is a complex and interesting subject for study in its own right. Later in this chapter consideration will be given to the topics of conflict and culture, but it seems appropriate to begin with an examination of organisational change and the difficulties involved in its management.

Change and management

Change is a factor which some would regard as the most prevalent force throughout the twentieth century. This should not be taken to mean that the world has been static at any time. Far from it – the history of man is a history of continuous development.

However, it can be argued that this century has seen more change – *faster change* – than any other century in history. Consider the sequence of events depicted in Figure 9.1 below.

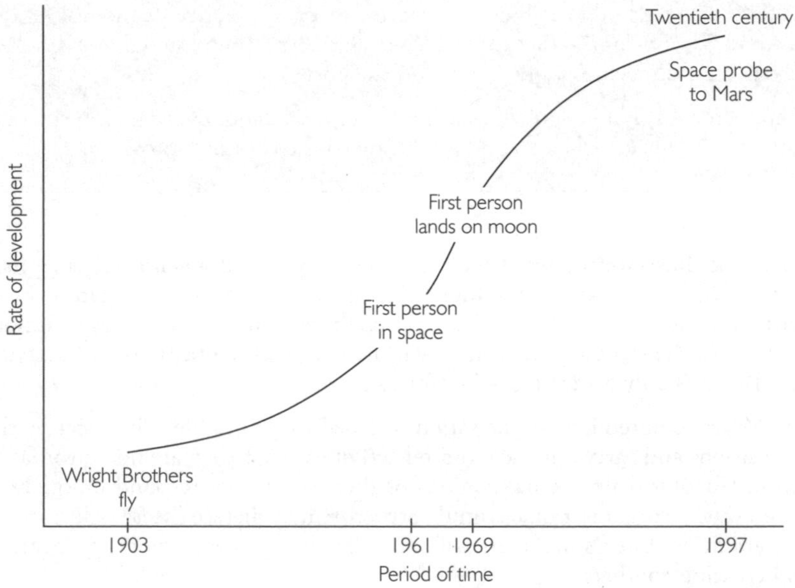

Figure 9.1 Developments in aeronautics in the twentieth century

After centuries of trying man eventually mastered the mysteries of flight in 1903 when Wilbur and Orville Wright flew a heavier-than-air machine in sustained flight for a distance of 852 feet. Just over half a century later that same technology (developed out of all recognition) allowed man to conquer space when, in 1961, Yuri Gagarin completed a single circumnavigation of the earth in just 108 minutes. Eight years after that, further developments permitted astronauts from the United States of America to fly to, and walk upon the surface of, the Moon. Since then there have been other moonwalks, space stations have been constructed, other countries have contributed to the exploration of space, and satellites have improved the state of telecommunications. In 1997 an unmanned space craft journeyed to Mars and placed a robot on its surface. That robot has already carried out more tasks than its human equivalents did on the Moon some thirty years earlier!

By any yardstick these are magnificent achievements which could not have been dreamt of by the Wright Brothers. More important for our purposes is the accelerated rate of development which occurred once the initial breakthrough had been made. While the example chosen plots the explosive growth in one branch of technology it takes only a moment's thought to relate this and other such developments to the way we live, work and organise ourselves to do business.

Try this

Consider the developments in aeronautics outlined above and relate them to your lifestyle.

Do you take holidays abroad?

Do you own a mobile phone?

How many television channels can you get on your receiver?

Consider how the development of this technology plays a part in your workplace, or your bank or university.

Can you think of other technologies which have changed dramatically the way we live?

Hint: Trace the development of computers since their commercial exploitation began in the mid-1950s.

Completion of the above exercise should raise awareness of the fact that change can have far-reaching effects on individuals and their workplace organisation. This creates many problems for management, and we will concentrate on the *management* of change. An examination of the types of change which can occur within organisations is therefore necessary, followed by an investigation into the different views on how much control the manager can exert on the management of change. There follows a consideration of a number of models which different commentators have devised to explain or facilitate the change process. The penultimate task is to focus on the human element and its action in, and reaction to, change and then, finally, to consider change from a postmodern perspective.

Types of change

Organisations need to be prepared to innovate and to change or they risk decline and death. Hatch (1997) points out that organisations will have to be built for change. Daft (1992) says that organisations must run fast to keep up with changes taking place around them; they must modify themselves not just from time to time, but all of the time.

All these writers point out the need – the continual need – for organisations to be mindful of change. The opening remarks in this section indicate how quickly change can take place, but it would be misleading to suggest that all change will occur so fast that it will demand constant and fundamental modification of all organisations.

Thus, the first category of change must relate to the extent to which changes affect the organisation. Daft (1992) distinguishes between those which have an *incremental* effect and those which have a *radical* effect. Incremental change is normally accomplished through the organisation's existing structure and processes and, in response to a dynamic environment, maintains the organisation's general equilibrium by a series of more or less continual relatively minor adjustments.

By contrast, radical change requires a new equilibrium to be established through transforming the whole organisation in one major upheaval. Most organisational change is incremental in nature, but radical change does occur – as, for example, with the very fundamental changes which have occurred in the British public sector over the last twenty years.

There is no easily defined end-point to change in that change is a continuous process within which the areas requiring consideration are always changing. Each one fits in with the four key areas that were believed by Kimberley and Quinn (1986) to be necessary to consider in any change process:

- strategic orientation
- political acceptance
- cultural change
- structural adjustment.

These are key features of a cyclical process, as shown in Figure 9.2 below.

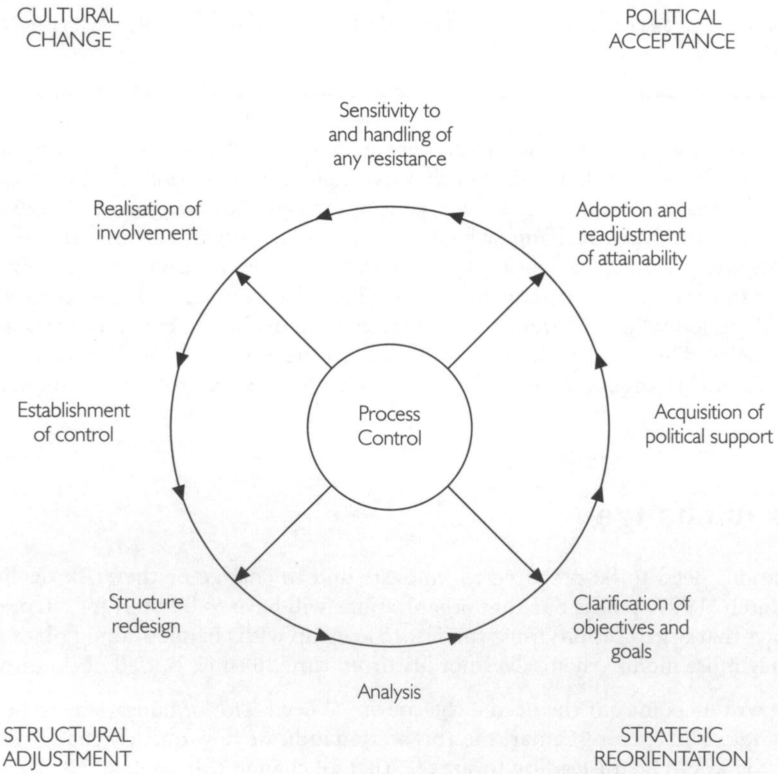

Figure 9.2 The cyclical and ongoing nature of change, after Kimberley and Quinn (1986)

Strategic reorientation

In the current competitive climate organisations need to ensure that they survive, and they thus have to remain aware of market changes and development. This requires a detailed analysis of the internal and external environment with an accompanying SWOT analysis. That is, to analyse the internal Strengths and Weaknesses as well as the Opportunities and Threats of the external environment.

Political acceptance

For change implementation to be successful, it is necessary for organisations to take on board the view of all stakeholders and to ensure they support any proposed changes.

Cultural change

Change is about moving on and in doing this the organisation itself will change and adopt a new personality – a different culture – which must absorb new ideas and practices.

Structural adjustment

In Chapter 5 the design and structure of organisations was discussed in detail, and Figure 9.2 above shows that the four key areas must be activated simultaneously.

The key elements of this model are:

- involvement
- direction
- control.

In times of change organisations will attempt to achieve a competitive edge on their rivals by planning how best to take advantage of changes in environmental conditions. *What* to change is important, and in most cases choice will focus on one or more of four different aspects of the organisation.

Technological change

Technological change is always a consideration, but, as with most terms in organisation theory, definitions abound. Child (1972) comments that the term 'technology' has been employed in almost as many different senses as there are writers on the subject. In the very narrow sense technology can be seen as the machinery employed to produce goods, but such a restrictive focus is likely to be misleading in today's world. Thus, Robbins's (1990) belief that it refers to the information, equipment, techniques and processes required to transform inputs into outputs makes more sense, since it encompasses all aspects of the term, including what is known as 'knowledge' technology, that is, the skills required within an organisation: this has been discussed in detail in Chapter 4.

The task of implementing changes in technology sounds deceptively simple, but can only be achieved after a number of broad-ranging decisions have been made. Few people would ignore very obvious considerations such as financial concerns and the availability of members with the necessary operational skills. Less obvious, but just as important, is consideration of issues such as the expected life and obsolescence of the technology and the timing of its adoption within the organisation.

Bateman and Zeithmahl (1993) assert that the adopters of new technologies fall into five groups:

- innovators
- early adopters
- early majority
- late majority
- laggards.

In their analysis they discuss the advantages and disadvantages, and the benefits and dangers associated with the actions of those in each category.

Structural change

Structural change (sometimes linked to system changes) relates to the administrative domain of the organisation. It involves matters concerned with management and includes changes to the organisation's structure, strategy, policies, co-ordinating mechanisms and reporting relationships. Mintzberg (1979, 1995), amongst others, has provided a range of configurations to choose from, but is adamant that choice of structure should not be determined by whim. Instead, it should be dictated by the organisation's fit with its environment. More on such issues follows. For the moment it is sufficient to acknowledge that, on occasion, it will be necessary to make changes to the structure of an organisation.

Change in organisational activities

This often occurs when organisations change their product or service outputs. Thus, Leavitt (1965) starts from the premise that organisations build things or design things or provide services, all with certain purposes in mind. These things answer the question 'What do organisations do?'. But organisations do many things at the same time. They make their products/services, build new facilities, search for new markets. They also engage in the counterpoint of all this by changing their products or services in response to market demand; by altering their premises in line with need; or by moving from one domain to another as opportunities present themselves. Since organisations live through time they find that tasks which were critical at one stage of development are less so when they develop further.

In the 1960s many organisations sought growth through the acquisition of other businesses. Frequently, those businesses were in areas not related to the organisation's core activity, and so the advantages associated with diversification were achieved. Thus, with each newly acquired business the tasks undertaken by the organisation would increase. However, the current trend among many concerns is to return to emphasis on the core activity – to concentrate on what they do best, or at least on what they prefer to do. To achieve this they engage in downsizing, or in restructuring, or even reverse previous make-or-buy decisions, and in doing so accomplish a change in organisational activity (tasks).

Try this

Trends in the television industry

When you are watching television tonight pay some attention to the credits which appear at the end of each programme.

Not so many years ago each programme would be attributed to the network on which it was shown (BBC or ITV) because these networks devoted much time, effort and available resources to programme making. The reasons for such behaviour can only be speculated upon. They may be *historical* (that's the way it began), for the purposes of *control* (the best way to control output is to make the output yourself), or even *personal* (producers of successful programmes might be accorded more power and status within the organisation).

Whatever the reason, programme making is on the decline. Nowadays, concentration is on other things: attracting viewers, selling advertising space, husbanding scarce resources. Making has been replaced by buying from a number of independent production companies who now supply the programmes transmitted.

Check it out tonight! Count the number of programmes made by those who specialise in programme production, compared to those which are made by the networks themselves.

People change refers to changes in the attitudes, skills, expectations, abilities and behaviour of the organisation's members, at all levels. What makes this the most difficult change of all to implement is people's capacity to act according to their own desires and motivations.

Interdependence of the elements

So far, only changes in technology, structure, tasks and people as if they occurred in isolation have been discussed. But as Leavitt (1965) pointed out, it is not possible to effect changes in one element and keep the others intact. The interactive nature of organisations means that a change made in one area is likely to affect the others as well and this is shown in Figure 9.3 below.

For example, the decision to change the tasks of an organisation by manufacturing a new product may require new technology to be introduced. This could lead to the hiring of

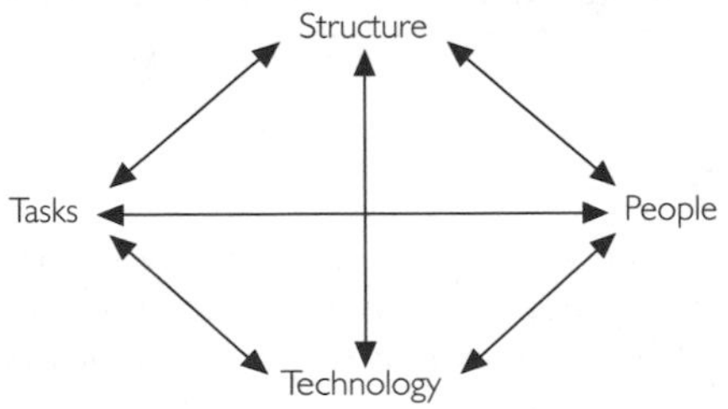

Figure 9.3 Interdependent organisational elements, after Leavitt (1965, p. 1145)

new personnel (or the retraining of existing staff) and a restructuring of the organisation. Change programmes that are designed to focus on only one of the four elements have little chance of success.

Change and managerial control

Changes in organisations may come from internal forces or from outside, and, while it would be wrong to generalise, Megginson *et al.* (1989) suggest that external change forces have a greater effect on organisations than internal stimuli.

This statement has a certain appeal and arguments in support fall into two categories. Firstly, it could be argued that as a general rule managers will seek to keep internal change initiatives to a minimum. In other words, there may be a certain reluctance on the part of management to introduce any more change than is necessary. Robbins and De Cenzo (1998) assert that if it was not for change the manager's job would be relatively easy, and since most people do not go out of their way to make life difficult for themselves it is unlikely that a policy of needless change will prevail. However, care must be taken here! It is not suggested that managers will fail to make changes when the need arises. Instead, the proposal is that the disruption and uncertainty which change brings to an organisation will ensure that managers will seek to control the introduction of change wherever possible.

Secondly, it can be argued that external pressures for change can be numerous and, more importantly, lie largely outside the control of the manager. It is widely acknowledged that organisations if they are to survive, depend upon, and must interact with, their external environment.

It is from the environment that organisations acquire raw materials, hire employees, raise capital, buy equipment. These inputs are then used to produce products or services which will be consumed by others in the environment. The extent to which the environment impacts upon the organisation also depends upon the actions of a host of other environmental actors including distributors, advertising agencies and even governments. In brief, an organisation's environment can be a complicated network of customers, suppliers, financial institutions, regulatory bodies and competitors – any or all of whom can bring change pressures to bear on the organisation.

But to what extent does the environment limit the actions of an organisation? To what extent are *changes* in the environment beyond the control of managers? The literature provides a variety of answers to these questions. There are a number of theories covering a spectrum of relationships.

Contingency theory

Briefly, contingency theory as it applies to organising states that the most effective way to organise is *contingent* upon some aspect(s) of the situation in which the organisation exists. These aspects have become known as contingency factors and are usually identified as:

- environmental instability
- technology
- organisational size
- strategy.

While there is some disagreement over which contingency factor most influences organisational structure, there is no doubt that the external environment is regarded universally as being of great importance.

For example, empirical work by Burns and Stalker (1961) showed that a stable environment required a mechanistic organisational structure while an organic structure would perform better in a changing innovatory environment. Similarly, Lawrence and Lorsch (1967) concluded that organisations performed better when the internal structural arrangements of an organisation matched the level of uncertainty in the environment.

More generally, Donaldson (1997) argues that under the tenets of contingency theory managers who wish to keep an organisation effective will adapt its structure to fit the contingency factors. This suggests that these external factors are to be regarded as an imperative, that is, the situation creates the circumstances and the manager merely responds. Further, it is argued that the manager has no real control over the nature of the response since he will have to adopt the structure required by the contingency factors in order to gain organisational effectiveness. In effect, under contingency theory the manager has little control of external factors.

Resource dependence

This theory, originally put forward by Pfeffer and Salancik (1978), is based on the assumption that organisations are controlled by their environments. Briefly, the theory examines an organisation's network to establish the power/dependence relationships that exist between the focal organisation and other actors in the network. Thus, an organisation's need for resources (raw materials, labour, capital, machinery and equipment, knowledge, outlets for its products or services) renders it dependent upon its environment from which these resources come.

Obviously, the greater the organisation's need for a particular resource the greater its dependence on that part of the environment which controls its supply. At first sight this might seem to be another theory which suggests that managers have little control. However, the theory recognises that managing dependencies can provide opportunities for the establishment of countervailing power. An organisation can balance the power of others by developing its own power. Thus, vulnerability to a single supplier of raw materials may sometimes be offset by establishing multiple sources of supply; dependency on customers (or suppliers) may be lessened by acquisition or merger strategies. In the same way the organisation's power base can be enhanced by achieving monopoly status in a niche market, cornering the market for a particular commodity or even developing patents or copyrights critical to the markets in which it operates.

In effect, while resource dependence theory acknowledges that the environment is a powerful constraint on organisational action it also believes that managers can use their creativity to reduce the effects of those constraints.

Strategic choice

The strategic choice thesis (Child, 1972) also advocates managerial ability by asserting that there is more scope for choice by management than contingency theory allows. Briefly, strategic choice theorists believe that this scope for choice arises because contingency factors should be regarded as *constraints* rather than *imperatives*, that is, as obstacles which impinge on the manager's decision-making rather than as mandates which direct it. When changes in the environment cause a disequilibrium between environment and structure the manager can still have considerable latitude for making choices. Two examples may make this clear.

First, when contingency pressures create a disequilibrium, fit can often be regained by adjusting the contingency. Thus, organisations can sometimes manipulate their environments by:

- using advertising to create demand for their products;
- engaging in mergers or joint ventures to limit the severity of competition;
- lobbying for changes in government regulation. In these cases management manipulate environmental forces to produce a situation more conducive to the organisation.

The previous example illustrates how managerial action might be employed to offset the effects of pressures from contingency factors. Conversely, management may elect to do nothing in the face of environmental changes. Thus, where an environment creates conditions which induce slack in the organisation it may persist with sub-optimal structures for long periods of time. Under strategic choice theory it is recognised that the term 'effectiveness' is open to interpretation, so rather than seek a structure which would result in *total* effectiveness, managers will often be content with one which provides a *satisfactory* outcome that is, they 'satisfice'.

The part which management plays in the choice of structure is underlined by the further argument that structural design (or change thereto) is not based on the objective characteristics of the environment. Instead, it is based on a perception and evaluation of the environment by organisational members. In other words, the structure chosen for the organisation will be influenced by the manager's perception regardless of the actual characteristics of the environment.

Strategic choice theory does not deny that there is a link between contingency factors and the structure of the organisation. The disagreement between contingency theory and strategic choice lies in the strength attributed to that link. As has been seen, contingency theory believes the link to be strong and deterministic in that contingency variables will determine the choice of structure. Strategic choice, on the other hand, acknowledges a loose coupling only. Thus, while there is some tendency for structure to be associated with contingency factors, *actual* structure depends upon managerial decision, which itself will be affected by managerial perceptions and evaluation. As Donaldson (1997) observes, strategic choice theorists bring the human actor back into organisation theory.

Institutional theory

This theory, originally associated with Selznick (1957) and developed by Powell and DiMaggio (1991), takes a more restrained view of the amount of creativity that will be shown by managers in controlling their environment. Once again, the theory recognises the demands which environments place upon organisations. However, this perspective argues that under conditions of high uncertainty organisations will imitate other organisations from the same institutional environment. An institutional environment is defined as including other similar organisations in the industry that deal with similar customers, suppliers and regulatory agencies.

The theory claims that managers in an organisation facing great uncertainty will assume that like organisations are facing similar uncertainty. As a result these managers will copy the structure and strategies of firms which appear to be successful. This mimicking has two effects. Firstly, it will tend to reduce uncertainty for the manager. Secondly, it will have a tendency to produce uniformity of operations within an industry.

Population ecology theory

The final theory which needs to be discussed is, like most of the others, concerned with the relationship between the environment and organisational structure. However, unlike the others, it does not focus on individual organisations, but upon groups or populations of organisations.

Population ecology theory argues that the environment selects certain types of organisation to survive and others to die, based on the fit between their structure and the characteristics of the environment. In effect, organisational forms either fit their environmental niche or they fail. The theory relies heavily on Darwin's (1809–1882) survival of the fittest principle, arguing that there is a natural selection process through which the environment selects some organisations to survive. Population ecology theorists believe that those which survive have resources and structural dimensions not possessed by those organisations which fail.

Central to the theory is the assumption that new organisations are always appearing in the population with the result that the population is always changing. This process of change is governed by three principles which occur sequentially:

- variation
- selection
- retention.

Variation occurs in the population through the establishment of new organisations and the adaptation of existing ones. These new or adapted organisations provide the range of choice for the environment to select from. It is believed that some variations will suit the environment and be retained; others will not be so fortunate and will either perish or move to an environment which is more supportive.

This theory provides little scope for management intervention and suggests that managers cannot completely control organisational outcomes. Much of what happens to organisations is the result of luck.

The theories: a summary

The theories discussed provide alternative views of the extent to which managers can influence change within their organisations. It should be remembered, however, that they are *theories* and suffer from various limitations which render each a less than perfect answer to questions of managerial control. They also give major emphasis to one relationship only – that between the organisation's structure and its environment. It is now necessary to consider change in a broader context by looking at some models which have been devised to explain the process of change.

Change models

Robbins (1990) makes the distinction between accidental change (that which 'just happens') and planned change (that which is consciously undertaken by an organisation in an attempt to remain current and viable). It is the latter type which interests organisational theorists since the act of planning for change provides them with an opportunity to construct models that explain how it may be accomplished. Robbins' (1990) own model is presented in Figure 9.4 below.

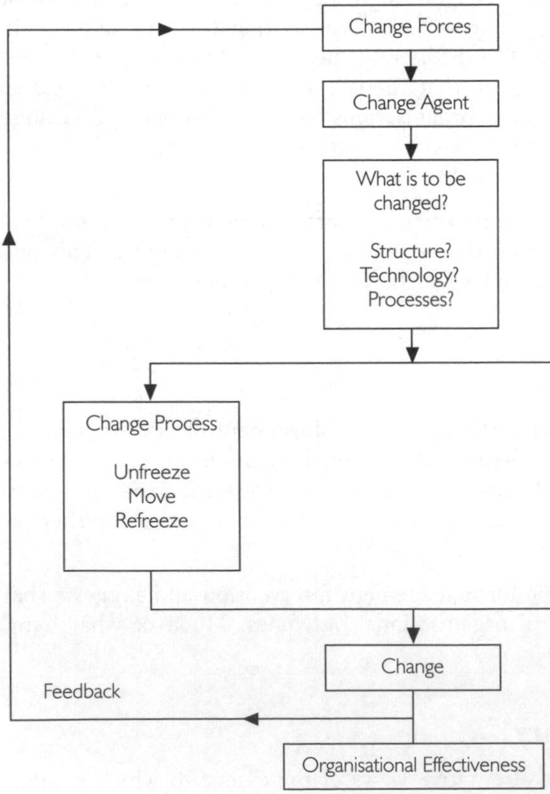

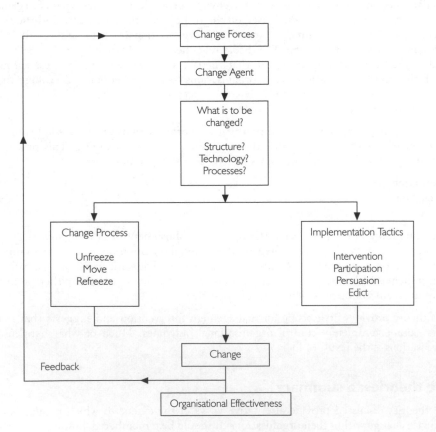

Figure 9.4 A model for managing organisational change, after Robbins (1990, p. 386)

In this model change is made necessary by the presence of certain forces. These are acted upon by a change agent who selects what is to be changed. Implementation is a two-stage process during which it is necessary to unfreeze the status quo, move the organisation to a new state and then refreeze it. This is achieved by one of four methods: the change agent may *intervene* (sell the change rationale to those affected), he may allow those affected to *participate* (delegate decision-making powers to them), he may attempt to *persuade* (often using those with expert knowledge to carry out the persuasion), or he may effect change by *edict* (simply announcing the changes that are to take place). Whichever method is used, the change is put in place and then tested to ensure that organisational effectiveness has increased. Notice also the feedback loop in recognition of the fact that the introduction of change into an organisation often necessitates other changes to be made.

At first sight, and looking solely at Figure 9.4, Robbins' (1990) model appears to conflict with some of the comments made above. For example, the model seems to suggest that it is possible to effect change by working on a single element (see the box 'What is to be changed?'). However, this is not the case, since the inclusion of the feedback loop is an acknowledgement of the 'knock-on' effect which occurs when change is introduced. It also appears as though people-change is ignored, but once again this is not the case – it is merely delayed until the implementation phase when minds need to be changed by using one of the four methods described above.

Robbins' (1990) model is a sophisticated and clearly thought out approach to organisational change which recognises the need for a change agent to take responsibility for the initiation and implementation of the process. The model also makes reference to organisational effectiveness, underlining the fact that change should not be undertaken for change's sake. Instead, change is introduced into an organisation for its improvement – to make it a 'better' organisation than it currently is. The acid test for any change initiative must clearly be the effect it has on the organisation's effectiveness.

In sharp contrast to the detail of Robbins' (1990) model is that constructed by Lewin (1951) who conceived change as a modification caused by two sets of opposing forces operating on an organisation. Specifically, at any moment in time an organisation can be seen as a body in equilibrium, held in that state by an equality between those forces that strive to maintain things as they are (the status quo) and those which are pushing for change (as shown in Figure 9.5 below). In this model the length of each arrow indicates the strength of each pressure on the process. Change is brought about by disturbing the equilibrium, that is by taking those steps which will lessen the pressures against change or strengthen the pressures in favour of change.

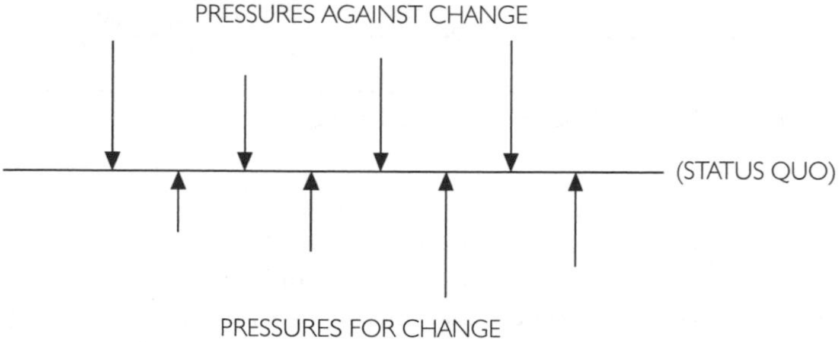

Figure 9.5 Lewin's (1951) model of organisational change

However, Lewin (1951) noticed that change often lasted only a short time before people and conditions reverted to their former state. It appeared that the introduction of change was not sufficient; to be effective the change process had to involve three related conditions experienced by individuals:

- *Unfreezing* – which entailed reducing or eradicating those behaviours striving to keep the organisation's behaviours in its present state. Once unfreezing has taken place the individual is ready to acquire new behaviour.
- *Changing* – shifting the behaviour to a new level. It means developing new behaviours which are commensurate with any structural and process changes which are introduced.
- *Refreezing* – this occurs when the new behaviour patterns are adopted as the accepted practice within the organisation. It is the successful completion of this stage which signals that the change is permanent.

It is interesting to note that Robbins' (1990) model includes this aspect of Lewin's (1951) work.

Lewin (1958) believed in force-field analysis because whenever the forces which favoured a change are greater than the resisting forces, the organisation will 'move' from one state to another. Through unfreezing within planned change, movement is brought about: rather like melting an ice cube, moving the resulting water about, and refreezing it into a ball or other shape. Lewin's (1951, 1958) model of organisational change is illustrated in Figure 9.6 below.

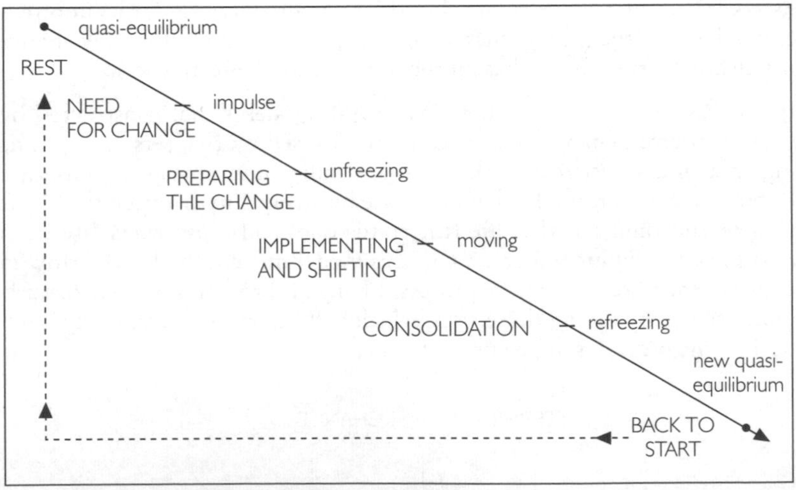

Figure 9.6 Lewin's (1951, 1958) model of organisational change

However, there are differences between the two models – in particular the centrality of the human element in the change process. While Robbins (1990) acknowledges the need to involve humans in the process, he does not include it directly in his 'things to be changed'. His primary focus is on the inanimate and administrative elements, and people involvement only comes into its own during the implementation stage of the model.

Lewin's (1951) model reverses these emphases. People, and their behaviours, are the capstones of the change process. It is their resistance to change which causes a change to fail, or be shortlived. It is people's behaviour that needs to be unfrozen at the earliest stage before the other steps in the model can be introduced. Megginson *et al.* (1989) confirm that effective change only takes place when organisation members modify their behaviours in the desired direction. However, the simplicity of the logic in Lewin's (1951) model cloaks the difficulties involved in behaviour modification.

There are a number of different ways of bringing about a change process as can be seen in Figure 9.7 below.

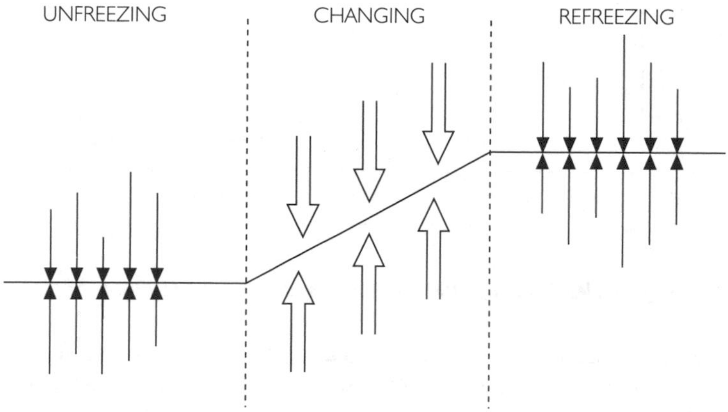

Figure 9.7 Phases in the process of change, after Keuning (1998, p. 352)

Psychological aspects of change

Clarke (1994) points out that resistance to change is a natural reaction. Most individuals derive great comfort from the status quo. No matter how boring the present situation is, how predictable or lacking in challenge it has become, there is still reassurance to be gained from the tedium. Individuals know what the organisation expects of them; they are *familiar* with present structures and systems, with ways of working and the people with whom they are expected to work. When change comes along it *threatens* and *frightens* us – it sends an individual on a journey into the unknown. It seeks to replace all that we know with a big scary uncertainty in which nothing will ever be the same again.

It is for all these reasons that people exhibit a reluctance to change, and when change occurs they frequently find it a painful experience. This can be likened to the changes that we are forced to face when we are in the midst of a personal crisis (a bereavement, for example). A person knows that they must let go of the past, but it is painful to do so. They know they must go through a period of adjustment, but that is also painful since it requires them to acknowledge that death has taken away for ever the person they loved. People tell them that 'life goes on', that they must make a new beginning, but at this point it is impossible to see how. Clarke (1994) has recognised the parallels between personal and organisational grief and has devised a model to explain the grief process and its diminution, as shown in Figure 9.8 below.

The pain levels are highest at the early stage when a person is faced with having to accept the end of the past. How long the pain will remain at those high levels will depend upon many factors – not least the individual's personal psyche. However, there is little doubt that having someone in support to ensure that time is made available to adjust, will play a large part in movement to the next stage. In the transition stage there will still be pain, but also a recognition that something has ended and that adjustment is required.

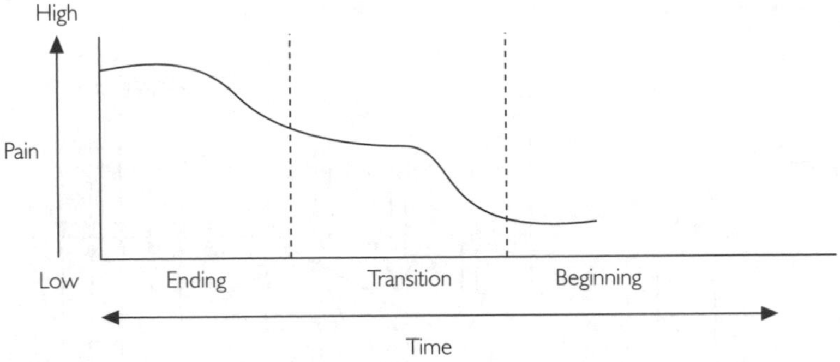

Figure 9.8 Mapping pain levels through the grief process, after Clarke (1994, p. 58)

Despite the evenness of the graph in Figure 9.8 above this will not occur in a smooth manner; sometimes a hopeful forward movement will be countered by regression. Even in the last stage – the beginning – pain will still be there. It would be unrealistic to expect organisational grief to disappear entirely. Indeed, the past may be eulogised, praised to a height which it never achieved when it was the present. All that can be hoped for is that the pain level will fall to a point where it can no longer militate against the effects of the change.

If a manager can identify where the resistance is located he or she may well be able to turn opponents into advocates. Keuning (1998) showed this in a model which is shown in Figure 9.9 below.

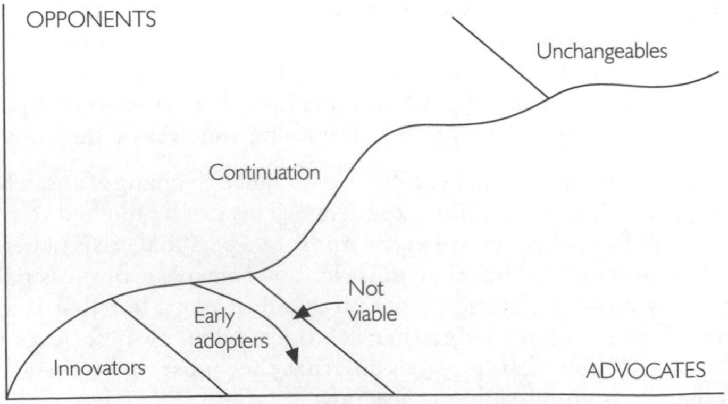

Figure 9.9 Overcoming resistance to change from opponents to advocates, after Keuning (1998, p. 353)

This model is based on the assumption that all members of the workforce affected by the change are in favour of the change, yet it does also consider that there will also be people who are unwilling to change or support a change. Keuning (1998) takes the view that resistance to change can be useful to the saneness of an individual in that it is 'one of the key mechanisms that protects the human being from chaos' (p. 353).

Robbins (1998) believed that there were five key sources of individual resistance to change:

- habit
- security
- economic factors
- fear of the unknown
- selective information processing.

But to make change happen requires the intervention of a skilled person capable of leading individuals through the change process. Buchanan and Boddy (1992) list a set of competences which change agents must possess if they are to carry out their task successfully. These they cluster around five broad headings as shown in Table 9.1 below.

Table 9.1 Change agent competences, after Buchanan (1992, pp. 92–93)

COMPETENCES	DESCRIPTION
Goal setting: Sensitivity to change Clarity in specifying Flexibility of response	The ability to set achievable goals to deal with externally generated changes.
Role specification: Team building abilities Networking skills Tolerance of ambiguity	The ability to merge stakeholders into a unit and to work comfortably in an uncertain environment.
Communication: Transmission Interpersonal skills Personal enthusiasm Stimulation (motivation and commitment)	The ability to effectively transmit the need for change zealously so that others may also be committed to the task.
Negotiation: Selling ideas to others Negotiation of resources	The ability to present a vision, to obtain resources and resolve conflict.
Managing up: Awareness Influencing skills Helicopter perspective	The ability to take politically broad view, to influence others and get them to coalesce.

These skills or competences were extracted from first-hand accounts of change projects given by the managers responsible for them, and have the ring of authenticity. While it would be wrong to suggest that change is all about people change, it is clear that the majority of competences outlined above focus on the people factor in the change equation. According to Buchanan and Boddy (1992), the change agents – in addition to any other skills they should possess – must be able to bring others along with them, infect them with their own enthusiasm, be able to visualise the broader picture and sell the need to work together for goals which are beyond those of the individual or his or her immediate group.

Change and postmodernism

The increasing rate of change has already been emphasised and has become the hallmark of the twentieth century. This text related the phenomenon to the development of technology and, from there, to change within organisations. However, theorists in organisation and management are not the only people to take note of this development. A number of commentators from a wide range of disciplines have noticed significant differences in the pace and nature of change as it relates to their particular specialism.

Crook *et al.* (1992) observe that radical social change is in progress which is shared widely. They use this observation to support the view that we are entering a genuinely new historical configuration, that is, that we are entering a new age. However, since the form that society will take is still not clear, we have little knowledge of how it will be structured, and as a result have just as few ideas about how it should be described. Since our present age is modernity, there is a logic which suggests that postmodern is as good a description as any – at least in the temporal sense!

But titles are of little importance. What is of significance is how this new age will affect the management of change. It is essential to begin by acknowledging that it is impossible to be precise at this stage; we are, after all, at the beginning of something which may take a long time to come to fruition. We must also remember that it is by no means certain that the new age will come to pass. The present trends are not irreversible.

Nevertheless, a great deal of attention has been paid to this speculative new age and the methods employed by its devotees. Postmodernists frequently begin their analysis of situations by the use of deconstruction: a process whereby the assumptions upon which arguments are based are identified and overturned. Once this happens the stage is set for the consideration of alternatives and/or multiple interpretations. These alternatives are limited only by man's ability to be creative.

Hassard (1993) has described postmodernism as the death of reason, thus suggesting that the rational, logical methodologies of the past are no longer appropriate. In effect, the thesis is that the nature of change cannot be adequately explained using the traditional tenets of a discipline. It requires new thinking and new approaches.

Handy (1989) writes of an age of *unreason* in which change is discontinuous (not part of an existing pattern) and requires discontinuous, upside-down thinking to deal with it – even if what emerges appears to be absurd at first sight.

Take, for example, the problem of control within organisations. Clegg (1990) identifies the bureaucratic form of organisation as being the major configuration in the twentieth century, its mechanistic form of operation permitting the enterprise to exercise tight control. But there is a price to be paid; the organisation is slow to change, rigid in structure and is highly centralised. It operates best in conditions of stability – the very conditions that this chapter has stated are ceasing to apply!

So what type of organisation is required for future conditions, should this trend continue? Obviously one which has the ability to operate flexibly (to cope with rapid change), yet provide necessary control. But flexibility and control are traditionally opposites; organisations *traditionally* are designed to achieve one or the other. Therefore, organisational theorists must concentrate on finding non-traditional, discontinuous solutions to the problems of the future.

A more detailed discussion of postmodernism is outside the scope of this book. It is one of those possibilities which lie just over the horizon of organisational theory and practice. It is necessary to turn attention to those behaviours associated with conflict within organisations.

Organisational conflict

It may be theoretically convenient to think of organisations as structures within which members co-operate with each other in pursuit of corporate objectives. This is often not the case.

Organisations are frequently structured in ways which are divisive, rather than collaborative. As was seen in the previous chapter, members are arranged in hierarchies where one level is distinguished from another in terms of power, control over their own destiny (and that of others), and reward. Departments are formed and tasked to undertake specific duties which may not be given equal recognition with others in the organisation. People are grouped according to their skills and abilities, and are rewarded in line with the value which others place on those skills – regardless of any estimate in the mind of the skill holder. These *structural* considerations (both vertical and horizontal) have the potential to disrupt the most carefully planned arrangements and to introduce conflict into a structure aimed at achieving harmony.

To this can be added a range of issues collectively known as *behavioural*. People enter the workplace to satisfy their own objectives and when these are in danger of being thwarted by the objectives of others there will be conflict. Members strongly identify with those who share a common mission or value and when the actions of others are seen as a threat to membership and/or the mission there will be conflict. As discussed in Chapter 2, individuals and groups frequently possess different perceptions of situations and events, will interpret the acts of others in line with their own perception and will show hostility when they see a gap between the behaviour exhibited and what they consider to be the desired behaviour.

These examples of structural and behavioural conflict reveal the opportunities for conflict to be found inside organisations. This section will examine the nature of conflict, discuss the very different views on the part it plays in the organisation and consider how the phenomenon may be managed.

The nature of conflict

The terms used in the section above give some indication of the nature of conflict. Conflict may be structural (caused or exacerbated by an organisation's structural arrangements for both its horizontal and vertical dimensions), or it may be behavioural (where the personalities of those involved provide the major impetus for the conflict). A further consideration – that of cognizance – was added by Brickman (1977) when he classified conflict as being either subjective (not real, but perceived to be so by the parties involved), or objective (actually existing although it may not be recognised by the parties). This idea of conflict needing to be felt *and* perceived can be seen in Pondy's (1969) model shown in Figure 9.10 below.

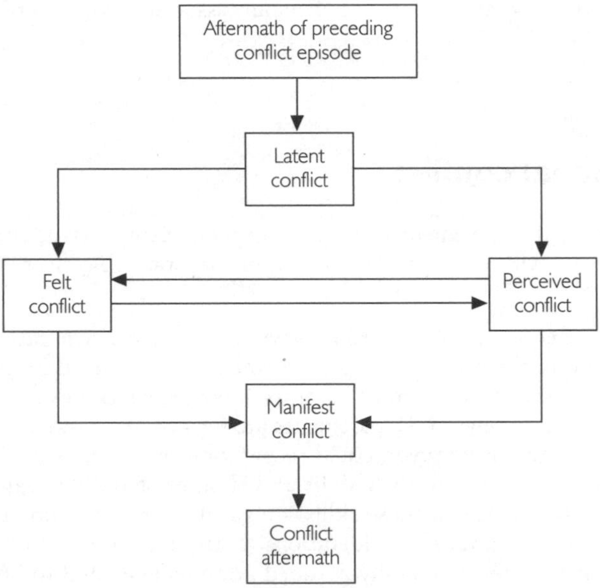

Figure 9.10 The dynamics of a conflict episode, after Pondy (1969, p. 306)

Pondy (1969) argues that conflict is best seen as a dynamic process where previous encounters between the parties have created an aftermath which affects the course of succeeding encounters. For the latent conflict to become manifest requires two things. First, it requires that there be a perception of conflict – the latent conflict must reach a level of awareness where at least one of the parties sees that a conflict situation exists. (This may not always happen since individuals tend to block out conflicts which are only mildly threatening.) Second, the conflict must be felt – one of the parties must personalise the conflict, that is, become tense, or anxious, or hostile as a result of the situation. When both feelings and perception are involved the conflict becomes manifest. Should the conflict not be resolved to the satisfaction of all participants an aftermath will remain to colour future relationships between the parties.

Previous references to 'structural/behavioural' or'subjective/objective' may create a wrong impression about the nature of conflict. These bi-polar 'either/or' classifications are seen by some to be too simplistic. Zhiyong Lan (1997) offers a four-type model which allows for different degrees of structure and for none as shown in Table 9.2 below.

Table 9.2 Types of conflict, after Zhiyong Lan (1997, p. 27)

CONFLICT TYPES	DESCRIPTION
Unstructured	Parties not bound by rules; impulsive and emotional choices.
Fully structured	Conflicts clearly defined; parties fully bound by rules, social norms and ethical standards.
Partially structured	Certain behaviours are constrained – others are left to free choice.
Revolutionary	Unstructured conflict on a massive scale; not bound by rules, culture or shared conceptual paradigms.

Fully structured conflicts usually have the means of their resolution embodied in the rule of law or in appropriate organisational policies. Thus, issues such as wage negotiations or budget allocations are recognised as conflictual circumstances, and the norms, rationale and decision processes for their resolution are defined in advance and initiated when the occasion demands.

Partially structured conflicts are those in which some aspects of the problem are amenable to resolution using laid down procedures – only those parts of the problem not covered by procedures necessitate some new form of conflict management. For example, most of the issues in an annual pay round will be covered by rules and procedures already agreed. Issues which fall outside these terms will require a new approach.

In contrast, unstructured conflicts are often due to impulses or non-rational behaviour. No 'rules of engagement' exist, or one or both parties believe that the situation is so unique that the existing rules cannot be applied. The intensity of such conflicts depends upon the number and strength of the factors involved, but it is recognised that such conflicts are extremely difficult to resolve. There are no guidelines to help the parties in the quest for a solution – indeed quite frequently the parties will not even share a common perception of the problem, much less a view of how it might be resolved.

Revolutionary conflict is an extreme case of unstructured conflict and can be said to be present when the situation is perceived to be vastly different from anything that has gone before.

Some indication of the nature of conflict may be gleaned from the definitions provided by authorities and commentators. Megginson *et al.* (1989) viewed conflict as any kind of opposition or antagonistic interaction between two or more parties, and believed it to lie along a continuum where at one extreme no conflict existed and at the other lay the act of destroying or defeating the opposing party. In between these two extremes lay all types of interpersonal, intragroup and intergroup conflicts. Such a broad definition encompasses the mildest of protests and the most wanton act of destruction; it also allows for individual and collective variations.

Robbins (1998) lends support to this view when he contends that conflict involves perceived incompatible differences resulting in some form of interference or opposition. This definition is also concerned with extremes moving from the subtle and quiet, to uncontrolled interference, to the obvious behaviours of labour withdrawal, riots and – ultimately – war.

In this book the perspective on conflict needs to be more specific. Thus, Thompson's (1960) assertion that conflict is any behaviour which an individual carries out in order to stop other members of the workforce achieving their objectives, gives the necessary focus and also makes reference to the interference and antagonism mentioned by other sources.

It also allows us to question the nature of conflict from another perspective, namely its effect on organisational affairs given that members expend energy in opposition to each other instead of working co-operatively towards the organisation's objectives.

Conflict and its effect on organisations

Traditionally, the term 'organizational conflict' carries a negative image. There are two reasons for this. Firstly, as Robbins (1998) points out, anti-conflict values permeate our society. From our early years we are inculcated with the value of getting along with others and avoiding conflicts. The home, school and church are three major influences on our lives that have reinforced this doctrine of conflict avoidance during our formative years. Little wonder then that the same attitude should remain with us in the world of work.

Secondly, Thompson's (1960) definition states that conflict is expressed in terms of antagonistic behaviour among members. This suggests an organisational malfunction since, as was stated earlier, it is usual to think of an organisation as a co-ordinated group of members working towards common goals. The outcome is therefore that conflict will hinder the co-ordination necessary to achieve the organisation's goals.

But such a negative connotation is only one of the perspectives propounded by modern theorists. Robbins (1998) identifies three such views prevailing at the present time:

- traditional view
- human relations view
- interactionist view.

The *traditional view* of conflict assumes that all conflict is bad and has a dysfunctional effect on an organisation's effectiveness. In line with the negative approach outlined above conflict is synonymous with violence and destruction and represents irrational behaviour. It is harmful to member relations and so renders the organisation less effective.

The *human relations view* argues that conflict is a natural occurrence within organisations. This perspective is in line with the remarks made at the beginning of this section: that the divisive nature of organisations makes conflict inevitable. The approach underlines the existence of conflict and acknowledges that it cannot be eliminated totally from organisations. Further, human relations theorists believe that in some cases its presence may even benefit the organisation.

The *interactionist view* of conflict advances the human relations view. While the latter group of theorists accept the existence of conflict, interactionists *encourage* it on the grounds that harmonious, peace-loving organisations are in danger of becoming non-responsive to the need for change and innovation. Eisenhardt *et al.* (1997) state this view succinctly when they observe that the absence of conflict is not harmony, it is apathy.

The management of conflict

The three approaches to conflict outlined above provide very different views of its effect on the organisation and, therefore, very different views on how it should be managed. Perhaps the most straightforward is the approach advocated by the traditionalists. In their eyes all conflict is counterproductive and the organisation should not allow conflict to arise. If it does, there is only one course of action – immediate steps must be taken to eradicate or resolve the conflict.

Although this approach is straightforward and in line with a traditional view on conflict, in today's world it is probably too simple. This view may be contrasted with that of the interactionist school who see a place for conflict within organisations. This is not to say that interactionists believe all conflicts to be good. Rather, some conflicts can be used to support the organisation's goals, and so are seen as 'functional'. Conversely, other conflicts prevent the organisation from achieving its goals; these are destructive forms and may be labelled 'dysfunctional'. Robbins (1998) points out that the demarcation between the two forms is not precise. No conflict incident can be tagged as acceptable or unacceptable under all conditions.

Functionality or dysfunctionality is often a matter of judgement and will depend upon all manner of conditions and circumstances. However, according to Hatch (1997), in each circumstance the level of conflict may be equated to the level of organisational performance, as shown by Hatch (1997) and given in Figure 9.11 below. The manager's response depends upon the conjunction of the two levels. Thus, too low a level of conflict will engender apathy within the organisation and will have an adverse effect on organisational performance. In this case the manager will take steps to *stimulate* the level of conflict. By the same token, too high a level of conflict will result in disruption and also have an adverse effect on organisational performance. The correct managerial strategy here will be to *reduce* the level of conflict (if that is possible), or to *resolve* it (if the force is totally destructive).

The implication of this theory is that there is a level of conflict which is appropriate for each organisation. The manager seeks to balance the level of conflict at that optimum which sustains a healthy and positive participation in the organisation's goals.

It should be noted that Robbins (1998) adds one caveat to this theory. While organisational performance, however defined, may be measured accurately there is no current instrument available capable of assessing whether a given conflict level is functional or dysfunctional. It appears, then, that whatever skills managers need to manage conflict they must add one more – the ability to judge when conflict levels in their organisation are optimal, too high or too low and will be encompassed in the culture of the organisation.

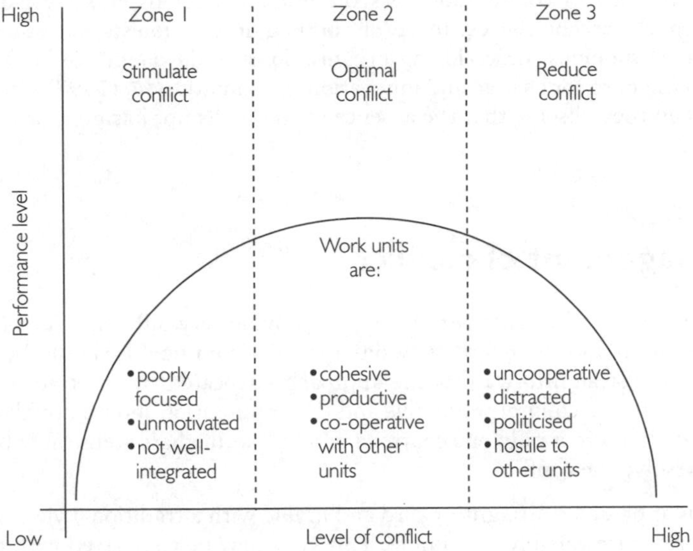

Figure 9.11 Conflict and organisational performance, after Hatch (1997, p. 305)

Organisational culture

If an examination is made of any two organisations in the same field of operation, it can be quickly noticed that there are a number of differences. If a woman walks from any Marks & Spencer's store into any branch of British Home Stores or Debenhams she will see that the shop assistants wear different uniforms, the merchandise is displayed differently, and the decor in each shop is quite distinctive. Such variations are very obvious and may be taken in at a single glance. Had she worked for one of these organisations and then went to work for another, many more differences would soon become apparent. In fact, the early days of the woman's new employment would be spent in adjusting to the disparate ways in which broadly similar tasks are done in her new job, and in learning the peculiarities and idiosyncrasies of the organisation.

These observations would appear to be rather fundamental to students of organisation theory. Everyone expects firms to be different. Indeed, it is these variations which distinguish one firm from another – the nature and content of such differences proclaiming the sort of firm it is to its members and clientele.

However, in recent times the study of these differences became the focus of attention for organisational theorists and commentators. The term 'organisational culture' was coined to describe the phenomenon.

Had this book been written about fifteen years ago organisational culture would have received no more than a passing reference. The burgeoning literature which now exists on this topic is testament to its place in mainstream organisational theory.

Yet it is not a concept which enjoys universal acceptance, either in terms of what it is or how it can be utilised within organisations. In this final section of the examination of organisational dynamics consideration is given to the value of studying organisational culture – to look at the:

- different ways of analysing the phenomenon
- problems of its management.

First, however, it is essential to review the history and definition of what is generally regarded as a difficult and complex concept.

Organisational culture: its history and meaning

The word 'culture' is derived from the idea of cultivation: that is the process of tilling and developing the land. In tracing its adoption as a *concept* by social anthropologists, Morgan (1997) notes that it refers to the pattern of development reflected in a society's system of knowledge, ideology, values, laws and day-to-day ritual. The concept was originally applied to observations of primitive societies, which suggested that different societies exhibit different levels and patterns of social development. Through time its application has been broadened to refer to societies generally.

There have been many attempts to explain how culture has come to be associated with organisations. Morgan (1997) proposes that the link between organisations and culture is metaphorical – by describing an organisation as a culture an attempt is being made to seek to understand one element of experience in terms of another. This view may be supported by Silverman's (1970) contention that organisations may be conceived of as mini-societies. Put simply, it could be argued that if societies possess cultures, then organisations as mini-societies can also have cultures.

An alternative explanation suggests that it was the growth of multinational companies in the 1960s that has brought culture to the fore. The spread of commercial operations from a *home* country to a variety of *host* countries was not without its problems. Home-based organisations hoping to replicate their ways of working in other localities found that this was not always possible. What worked at home did not always transfer successfully to a 'foreign' location. Those things which home nationals embraced as acceptable working practices would often prove not to be acceptable to organisation members living and working in host countries. Dissimilarities in national cultures provide an obvious explanation for these intra-organisational deviations. The work of Hofstede (1980) lends credibility to this theory. In a survey of work-related values among forty foreign subsidiaries of International Business Machines he provided evidence of differences in attitude expressed by managers in each country. Such attitudes were measured in terms of the four dimensions explained in Table 9.3 below, and the results, it was claimed, were in line with the attributes of each country's national culture. For example, masculinity refers to the clear separation of gender roles in focal societies. In highly masculine cultures men are expected to be assertive, with a high emphasis on work goals related to career advancement and earnings. In less masculine cultures there is greater emphasis on work goals related to interpersonal relationships, service and the physical environment. Hofstede (1980) found that women held fewer professional and technical jobs in highly masculine cultures like Japan, Austria and Venezuela than in the more feminine cultures of Sweden, Norway and the Netherlands.

Hofstede's (1980) work is very significant in terms of the development of corporate culture. Not only does it give emphasis to the cultural differences between countries (which is, of course, an anthropological approach), but it also emphasises the influence which national cultures have on the culture of organisations (an organisational perspective).

Table 9.3 Dimensions employed in the Hofstede Study (1980, p. 207)

Power distance
The extent to which members of a nation are willing to accept an unequal distribution of power, wealth and prestige.

Uncertainty avoidance
Refers to the degree to which members of a culture feel threatened by uncertainty, ambiguity and risk.

Individualism
The extent to which individuals are expected to act independently of other members of the society.

Masculinity
The extent to which the society expects there to be distinct gender roles. For example, in masculine culture men are expected to be more assertive, women more nurturing.

Nevertheless, despite Hofstede's (1980) work, which makes a landmark contribution to the development of the theory of organisational culture, it is important to note that the emphasis is on *societal* culture and its impact on organisations, not to any great extent on the cultural properties of the organisation itself.

Meek (1988) provided a variation of this theme when she maintained that the preoccupation with organisational culture is probably related to socio-economic factors in Western society. Briefly, most Western countries (it is claimed) have experienced a dramatic downturn in their economies which has helped to emphasise the structural inequalities inherent in these societies and has placed the structure of Western capitalism under severe pressure. However, once again the emphasis is on societal culture and its effect on organisations rather than the existence of an organisational culture *per se*.

Whether one accepts Meek's (1988) analysis or not, it provides a link with Ouchi's (1981) work in which productivity improvements in Japanese industry were contrasted with the decrease in productivity gains in the United States of America. Ouchi (1981) explained these differences in terms of variations in managerial practices, which themselves were related to Japanese culture. Ouchi (1981) recognised that it was impossible to re-create Japanese culture in the United States of America, but advocated that it was possible to take some of their better business practices and change the culture of USA corporations so that they benefited from them.

Ouchi's (1981) direct reference to *corporate* culture is by no means the first allusion to the existence of such a phenomenon. Jacques (1952) had referred to the *culture of the factory*, but it was Ouchi's (1981) work which caught the imagination of organisational commentators. In particular, note must be taken of Deal and Kennedy's (1982) seminal work on the examination of corporate cultures and Peters and Waterman's (1982) book – both of which achieved bestseller status worldwide. From that point on an ever growing number of writers on organisations have sought to show a nexus between their specialism and the new viewpoint. Over the last ten years the area of *organisational culture* has been the most fascinating area of research with attention drawn to aspects of organisational commitment, socialisation, and staff turnover.

Despite this widespread acceptance of the concept its transfer has not been without problems, not least in matters concerning its definition. Indeed, even in the world of social anthropology there are difficulties in this area. Cole (1988) believed that culture was at the centre of all writings concerning anthropology and yet there was no basis of agreement between the researchers other than what is meant by the term and none about what it *actually* is.

Evidence of this lack of clarity is provided by Kroeber and Kluckhohn (1952) who identified some 164 different definitions in existence at the time of their study. Despite this surfeit, writers on organisation theory have seen fit to add to the list – a small selection is overviewed below.

Bowen (1982) wrote in Deal and Kennedy (1982) that organisational culture was simply about the way things were done in the organisation.

Sathe (1983) concentrated on the importance of the understandings construed by members of the organisation which he thought went often unstated. He identified the organisation as a community which comprised individuals who had a lot in common.

Smircich (1983) took a different approach; he believed it to be symbolic and though it contained the same components as Gordon's (1991) he stressed the point that they all evolved.

Dennison (1984) did not argue about the components of organisational culture but stated that it was the core identify of an organisation.

Schein (1984) based his understanding of organisational culture on the basic assumption that a group has invented, discovered, or developed whilst coping with its need to integrate internally and adapt to the external environment. He related this to the way members needed to accept the problems of the organisation and thus internalise in relation to those problems.

Duncan (1989) agreed with previous writers but offered the view that such concepts were shared by all members of the organisation and the members were taught them as being the norm in the organisation they had just joined.

Gordon (1991) believed that it was composed of shared philosophies, ideologies, values, beliefs, assumptions, expectations, attitudes and norms.

As can be seen, the content and, indeed, the quality of these interpretations of organisational culture vary. Contrast Schein's (1984) very wordy description (which basically equates culture with a pattern of basic assumptions), with Smircich's (1983) defining list of attributes or Sathe's (1983) emphasis on understandings, or Bowen's (1982) simplistic and highly uninformative offering: the nature of the concept is no clearer. As has been noted above, at least anthropologists knew what the concept *was not*; there is nothing in the corporate literature on the subject to suggest that organisation theorists share even that certainty.

Two points are important here. First, it is dangerous to assume that any definition is free standing and complete, telling one all one needs to know about the concept. It is necessary to go to the source and check the context for which it was constructed. Second, definitions may not be concerned over-much with providing an exact meaning for the concept; instead they may have more to do with setting out the perspective from which it is viewed.

If it is accepted that culture is a concept with a variety of meanings, each of which may be derived from its author's perspective, then the way ahead becomes clearer.

The real value of Kroeber and Kluckhohn's (1952) work does not lie in the accumulation of 164 definitions, but in the authors' ability to bring order by classifying them into meaningful categories – see Table 9.4 below. By finding a suitable system of classification they have identified the various perspectives which have been employed in the study of culture – the *directions* in which anthropologists' research activities have taken them.

Table 9.4 Classification of definitions, after Kroeber and Kluckhohn (1952, p. viii)

Group A: Descriptive Broad definitions with emphasis on enumeration of content.		
Group B: Historical Emphasis on social heritage or tradition.		
Group C: Normative *Either* emphasis on rule or way *or* emphasis on ideals or values plus behaviour.		
Group D: Psychological	a	Emphasis on adjustment, on culture as a problem solving device.
	b	Emphasis on learning.
	c	Emphasis on habit.
	d	Purely psychological definitions.
Group E: Structural		Emphasis on the patterning of organisations of culture.
Group F: Genetic	a	Emphasis on culture as a product or artifact.
	b	Emphasis on ideas.
	c	Emphasis on symbols.
	d	Residual category definitions.
Group G: Incomplete Definitions		

In effect, what may have been seen as ambiguity, may be no more than a confused first glance at what can now be recognised as a multi-faceted concept. Culture may not, after all, be a concept with definitional problems, except for those problems which attend any concept which is rich in definition.

The constituents of organisational culture

Many of the interpretations provided earlier fall into Kroeber and Kluckhohn's (1952) Group A (descriptive) category, since they place an emphasis on the *enumeration of content*, and so give each author's opinion of the constituent parts of the concept. As we can see the inclusion of 'values' is a common theme, although from here the list is often widened to include 'norms, beliefs, customs' or 'symbols, myths, understandings'. It is this practice of providing a list of components which has most potential to do damage to the concept. Allaire and Firsirotu (1984) pointed out the presumption that the word 'culture' was really a short cue for those values, norms and beliefs that had been chosen as descriptors from the vast availability of definitions in literature on cultural anthropology.

Thus, while it is interesting to note the varied opinions of diverse authorities, their obvious disagreement makes this a flawed approach to the identification of the constituent parts of culture.

It is possible that more can be learnt from an examination of the various models which have been constructed by different authorities. Schein (1984) provides a framework which can be applied to organisational culture, but which could just as easily be applied in a societal setting – see Figure 9.12 below. This model is based on the belief that culture can be analysed at several different levels and that each level interacts with the next.

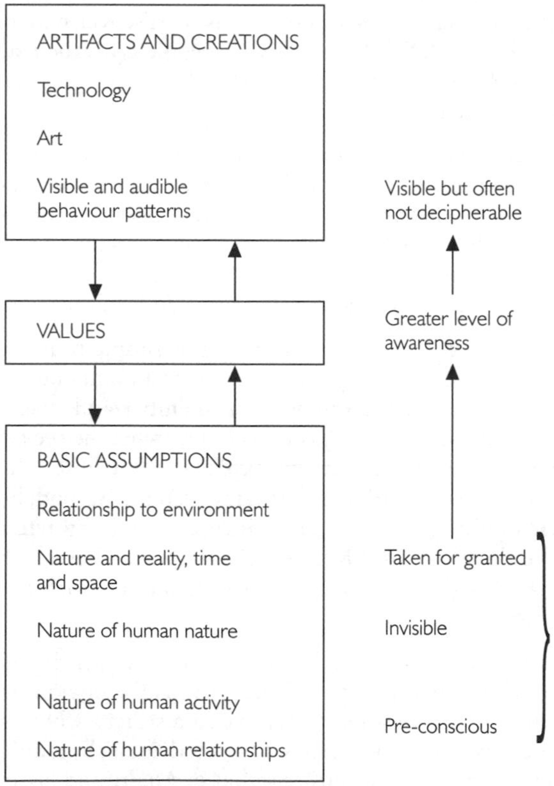

Figure 9.12 The levels of culture and their interaction, after Schein (1984, p. 4)

For example, it is claimed that the most visible aspects of a culture are its artifacts (those man-made parts of the organisation's internal environment which are most readily observed). Thus, an interested observer would be able to distinguish the unique way in which tasks are organised, the dress code of the members, the way people address each other, the stories which are employed to help new members in their orientation.

The difficulty here is that while data is easy to obtain it may be hard to interpret. It is simple to observe *how* an organisation constructs its internal environment – what patterns of behaviour are discernible among members – a more difficult task is to try to understand *why* members act as they do.

Any attempt to comprehend the behaviour of the organisation's members requires the researcher to work at Schein's (1984) second level – that of values. But values are not readily observable, and many different methods may be employed in an effort to identify them. Hatch (1997) provides details of a three-step model which may be used:

Step One data collection
Step Two data analysis
Step Three description.

Like Schein (1984), she suggests interviewing key members of the organisation to discover their ways of experiencing and interpreting their world – which is a constructivist view after the personal constructs theorist Kelly (1955). However, it is recognised that despite any best efforts, such values as individuals do discover may only be those which are manifest (easily discernible) or declared (what people *say* is the reason for their behaviour). The underlying reasons (the true reasons) for their behaviour may remain concealed or retained in the individual's unconscious.

To really understand a culture requires the researcher to delve into the underlying assumptions (level three). As can be seen from Figure 9.12 above, such assumptions are based in the individual's subconscious and are rarely discussed or even thought about. Schein (1984) believes that to achieve this level of understanding requires the co-operation of both an insider (who makes these unconscious assumptions) and an outsider (who helps in the uncovering process by asking the right kinds of questions).

It would be wrong to assume that this is a process as simple to put into practice as it is to put down on paper. Unfortunately, as Potter (1989) points out, there are two value systems at work here – that of the organisation member and that of the researcher or interviewer. In effect, the interviewer has two choices when he seeks to explain the data at his disposal. First, he may employ *etic* explanations (those which are cast in the observer's thought patterns, according to his value system). Second, he may utilise an *emic* explanation (which would seek to explain a culture entirely by reference to the participant's own beliefs and values). In this latter case the researcher is required to 'think like a native'. As one can imagine, this is the more difficult approach and is not without its dangers and its critics.

Schein's (1984) model acknowledges, albeit tacitly, the part which the larger society plays in the construction of an organisation's culture. It must be obvious that it would be virtually impossible for any organisation to survive in a society whose values were at odds with those of the organisation under review. One model which examines this relationship between societal and organisational culture is that of Allaire and Firsirotu (1984) – a simplified version of this model is shown in Figure 9.13.

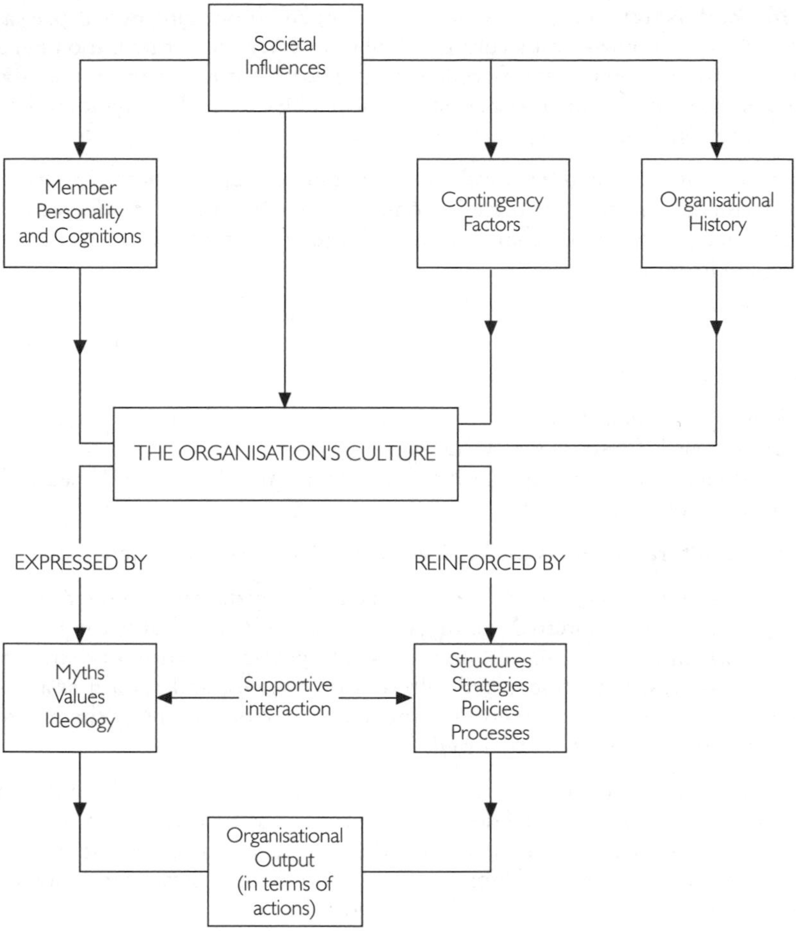

Figure 9.13 A framework for organisational culture, after Allaire and Firsirotu (1984, p. 214)

Basically, this model shows that an organisation's culture is derived from four main influences:

- Those from the ambient *society*, including the society's cultural, social, political and judicial systems. Since these factors will impinge upon everything within the society the diagram has been drawn to reflect this, as well as the direct impact on the organisation's culture.
- It is acknowledged that the individual *members* have a part to play in the construction of the culture. Each actor will have a set of values, assumptions and expectations, needs and motives which form their personality and the way in which they see things. In many cases, individuals will gravitate towards organisations with views and outlooks similar to their own, just as many organisations are careful to select workers who will fit in with the values of the organisation.

- Allaire and Firsirotu (1984) contend that an organisation's *history* will play a major role in the development of its culture. How (and when) the organisation began, the various transformations through which it has passed as it has evolved, the vision and values of the founder and other past leaders will all have left their mark on the organisation's personality.
- It is important to recognise the influence brought to bear by a host of *contingency factors* – factors upon which the organisation is dependent. The authors identify these as the technology, economics, competition and regulations that characterise the organisation and its industry.

As Figure 9.13 above shows, these four factors contribute to and sustain the organisation's culture. The cultural system itself finds expression in a variety of ways, most notably the organisation's:

- ideology (its system of beliefs)
- values (standards for social behaviour)
- myths (legends from the organisation's past which are glorified and used to bestow normality on present actions).

In effect, the cultural system is used to legitimise what the organisation does.

What the organisation does is embodied in and enabled by its structures, strategies, policies and processes (i.e. its internal workings). This network of formality can be examined to find the organisation's goals and objectives, the power and authority structure, the control mechanisms, recruitment and selection procedures, and reward systems. This 'sociostructural system' not only governs the day-to-day operations of the organisation but reinforces the cultural system as well.

This model suggests that the two sides of the organisation are mutually supportive, the cultural side informing the formal decisions and the sociostructural side progressing in a way which does not normally offend against the culture. The result is a series of organisational actions which satisfy the dictates of both, and, under normal circumstances, provide the organisation with stability and consistency.

The value of organisational culture as a concept

So far the discussion of organisational culture has focused on the complexities and confusions of the concept. It is therefore legitimate to ask whether it has any use in the practical world. Individuals may be aware that it is a borrowed concept, but not of the reason why it was borrowed. Is the world of organisations made richer or poorer by its adoption?

From the negative point of view it is possible to argue that the motives of the original, adopting theorists had much to do with self-interest. Hassard and Sharifi (1989) state that the concept of culture has become attractive because it offers a new panacea for corporate ills. It may be seen as a new approach to be used by management consultants, human resource specialists and organisational theorists in their attempts to solve their respective problems and to clarify their models and theories.

It is necessary to understand why the concept of culture has been so widely embraced. Child (1981) suggests that culture has been used as a residual explanator, to account for differences that the writer cannot otherwise explain. Traditional theories invariably depend upon (or are based upon) some rationale which demands a consistency of behaviour throughout the organisation. But few, if any, organisations can be seen to correspond perfectly to such theoretical models. They exhibit behaviours which are out of line with the selected paradigm; they act in ways which the theorist's model would regard as unpredictable. In short, organisations frequently conduct themselves in accordance with some internal logic which is unknown and incomprehensible to outsiders. The adoption of the culture concept has allowed the theorists to use this as an explanation for these behaviours. An example of idiosyncratic behaviour is provided in the case study given below.

CASE STUDY

The HP Way

Hewlett Packard are a Californian based organisation which has been engaged in the manufacture of computers since 1939. Over the years they have built up a distinctive way of working which is known as 'the HP way' and is applied not only within the USA, but at their other plants throughout the world.

The company believes in flexibility and in allowing workers to accept as much responsibility as they feel capable of accepting. The shop floor is open plan, even the general manager is in clear sight of everyone. The management style is entitled 'management by walking around' and a single status restaurant is provided where workers are encouraged to approach managers to join in discussions on any topic whether it is work related or not. Workers are free to leave their workplace and meet with colleagues. While coffee is provided all day, and anyone can break for coffee whenever they feel like it, a tone sounds at 1030. This signifies that all workers must now leave their locations and take part in a formal break.

Adapted from Channel 4, Forum TV presentation *A Gilded Cage*

The picture provided in the above example is of a highly flexible workplace in which organisation members have great control over their own actions. The reward system is based on a system of management by objectives and all workers are subject to a six-monthly review. What Hewlett Packard have managed to do is take a highly regimented management system and make it work in a very informal setting. Responsibility for productivity has been placed upon, and has been accepted by, the worker.

The 'idiosyncratic behaviour' can be found in the practice of a formal coffee break. The notion of workplace flexibility and coffee on tap militates against the need for such a break. It is explained within the company by recounting a piece of folklore concerning the behaviour of the founders in the early days when they operated out of the garage attached to one of their homes. 'Bill and Dave' would often be so engrossed in their work that they would work on through mealtimes, much to the annoyance of their wives and to the detriment of their health. To overcome this excessive concentration on work a bell was installed between kitchen and garage to ensure that meals and breaks would not be missed. Thus, the story implies that the same concern has prompted the perpetuation of the formal call to stop work, and should not be regarded as a form of control over workers' behaviour. But to relegate the concept of culture to a level where it is regarded as an explanatory device is to under-estimate its value within the organisation.

Robbins (1988) suggests that organisations by their very nature are conservative and seek to achieve internal stability. Most organisational designers facilitate the organisation's operation by creating separate departments, or distinct functions, or jobs which require discrete specialised skills. Such designs are constructed primarily in line with the organisation's needs *at that time* and are usually installed with permanence in mind. Stability is reinforced for the membership by the provision of further training, the establishment of appropriate procedures and the development of accepted norms of behaviour. A reward system bestows benefit on those who do their job well (that is, in accordance with the arrangements that have been specified).

At what point these actions stop being merely functional and take on the name of culture is not clear. In many cases they would appear to remain long after their original purpose has ceased to be and (just like Hewlett Packard's bell in the case study above) their continuation needs the support of stories about revered former members.

In effect, culture provides an organisation with stability and the means of preserving those parts of its history which are felt to be of value in the present.

Types of organisational culture

There have been a number of typologies of organisational culture, each of which provides some indication of the author's perspective on the subject. Here we will examine three such perspectives.

Deal and Kennedy (1982) investigated hundreds of organisations and suggested the existence of four common cultures – see Figure 9.14 below. These cultures are determined by two factors in the marketplace: the degree of risk which is associated with the activities of the organisation; and the speed at which the organisation and its members receive feedback on the effects of their decision-making.

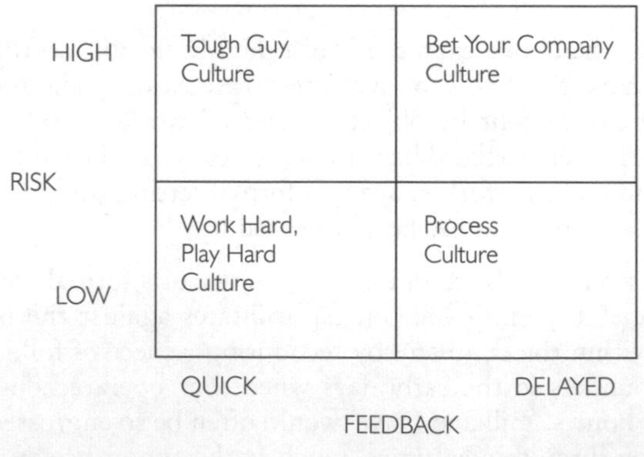

Figure 9.14 Typologies of corporate culture, after Deal and Kennedy (1982, pp. 104–108)

Using this approach the coincidence of High Risk and Quick Feedback produces a 'Tough Guy' culture where members, if they wish to succeed, must have a tough attitude and a concentration on short-term activities. Members, because of intense internal competition, do not co-operate with each other. The culture is weak and non-cohesive and employees burn out quickly.

In comparison, the difference between this and the 'Bet Your Company' culture lies in the fact that feedback from the marketplace is not so immediate. In this type of organisation the emphasis is still high risk, but there is a sense of deliberateness in their actions. Concentration is usually on large-scale projects where the extent and amount of the return on the investment may not be known for a period of years.

The 'Work Hard, Play Hard' culture entails low risk and quick feedback. Such organisations are customer oriented, and tend to concentrate on the present rather than the future. In many cases there will be an emphasis on quantity instead of quality. This type of organisation will try to combine fun (often with out-of-work activities for the staff) and action (highly dynamic).

The 'Process' culture is to be found in organisations where the risk is low and feedback from the marketplace is delayed. Here the primary focus is on the future, the organisation is structured hierarchically and decision-making starts at the strategic apex. Individuals respect authority and act co-operatively with others. The company makes extensive use of business meetings and as a result has a slow response time when problems arise.

While Deal and Kennedy's (1982) focus was on the marketplace – the external environment – Handy's (1985) approach sought to incorporate internal structure with a set of systems. He advocates four main types of culture as shown in Figure 9.15 on page 356.

It can be seen from these key approaches that organisational culture can serve two key functions:

- *Internal integration* – which provides the means through which members of the organisation can inter-relate.
- *External adaptation* – to assist the organisation to be proactive to change (which is normally thought to emanate from outside the organisation).

Egan's (1994) orientation is quite different; he asserts that organisational culture can be viewed from two internal perspectives – a top-down (management preferred) culture and a bottom-up (employee preferred) culture. In one sense this would seem to fly in face of the commonly held view that culture is something which is *shared* by members of the organisation. However, in another sense it could be argued that it would only be in exceptional circumstances that *all* members of an organisation fervently embraced *all* aspects of the culture.

Even in the field of social anthropology Kluckhohn and Strodtbeck (1961) argued that the *dominant* values of a culture tended to be over-stressed and the variant values largely ignored. In the world of organisational culture the extent to which the dominant values are embraced is known as 'cultural strength'. Schein (1984) stated that the strength of a culture can be defined in terms of (1) the homogeneity and stability of group membership, and (2) the length and intensity of shared experiences of the group.

Schein's (1994) use of the word 'group' prompts a reminder that an organisation comprises an indefinite number of groups (as discussed in Chapters 6 and 7). It is also necessary to consider the possibility that different employee perspectives, variations in dominant values and/or differences between groups may be such that within each culture there are a number of subcultures. Martin and Seihl (1985) support this view when they

CULTURE TYPE	DESCRIPTION	WHERE FOUND
Power (P[1])	Depicted as a spider's web, it illustrates a central power source with rays of influence spreading out from the central figure. 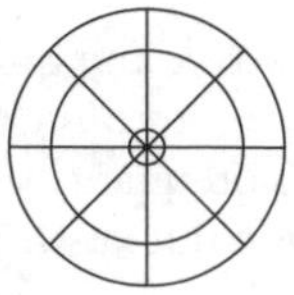	Trades unions. Small entrepreneurial organisations.
Role (R)	Depicted as a Greek temple with pediment (triangular, low-pitched gable) representing a small band of senior executives and a series of pillars. 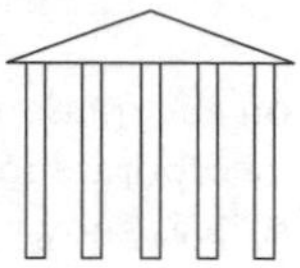	Bureaucracies.
TASK (T)	Shown as a net representing functional specialisms. 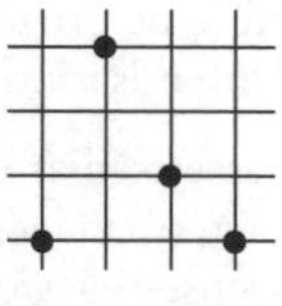	Matrix-type organisations. Project-teams where experts collaborate.
Person (P[2])	Represented as a cluster or galaxy in which individuals follow their own interests and share common resources. 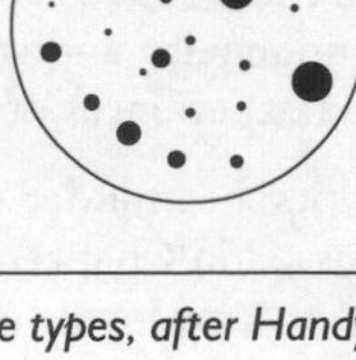	Barristers' chambers. Communes. Partnerships.

Figure 9.15 Typology of culture types, after Handy (1985, pp. 188–196)

propose that each culture is composed of various interlocking, nested and sometimes conflicting subcultures.

Brown (1995) confirms this when he states that most organisations of any size contain many subcultures. However, he focuses on the counter-cultural when he asserts that the beliefs, values and assumptions of these subcultures may compete with the dominant culture. Trice and Beyer (1993) attempt to reconcile these views by suggesting that organisations can have an overall culture (containing elements that are embraced by practically everyone) *and* a multiplicity of discrete subcultures which are held together, more or less strongly, by the overall culture.

Obviously, the strength of the culture and the existence of subcultures will have a part to play in the management of culture which we consider next.

Managing organisational culture

Hatch (1997) suggests that the question of whether or not cultures can be managed has provoked a long, and at times emotional, debate among organisation theorists. It should be noted that in most of the debate the word 'manage' is used as a synonym for 'change', so that much of the literature is focused on how to change an organisation's culture. It can be argued that this is a somewhat narrow view and Trice and Beyer (1993) acknowledge that the term can also be applied to the maintenance of existing cultures as well as the establishment of new ones.

Given that an organisation's culture is composed of relatively stable characteristics which tend to imply permanence, it may seem strange to suggest that cultures need to be maintained. However, there are good reasons why culture maintenance is required. This chapter is devoted to the notion of organisational dynamics and implicit in that is something that is repeated over and over again in this book, namely, that organisations change over time. These changes may occur as a result of external forces (i.e. when the environment alters and makes fresh demands upon the organisation), or internal forces (i.e. when the members employed in the organisation mature, or are exposed to new thoughts and experiences, or are succeeded by others with different values and perspectives). Such organisational changes may bring pressures to bear on the culture unless managers strive to keep the existing culture vital. Obviously, it is a foundation assumption within this argument that the guardians of the culture (top management) believe that the existing culture is worth preserving.

Nevertheless, the possibility of being able to change culture may be an attractive proposition. Not only would it place another tool in the manager's armoury for use when the occasion demands, but it would also provide managers with the ultimate form of control – control over behaviour by the manipulation of members' norms and values. While there are a number of counter-arguments about the feasibility, wisdom and even the ethics of attempting to change cultures, many commentators have provided frameworks and models for just that purpose.

Brown (1995), for example, presents a four-stage model based on earlier work by Silversweig and Allen (1976) as shown in Figure 9.16 below.

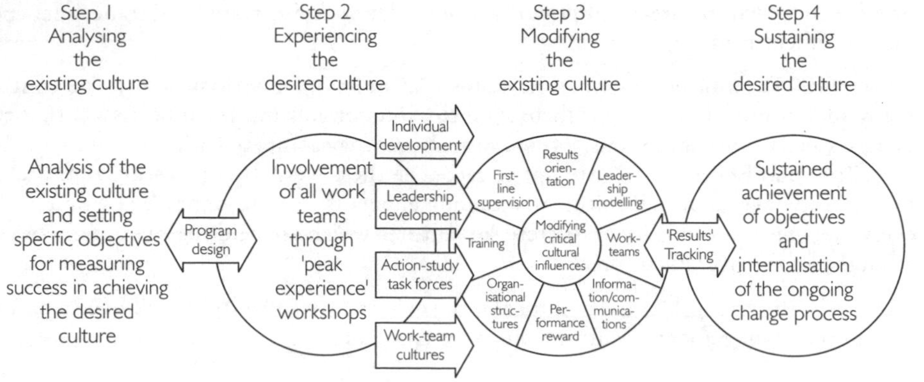

Figure 9.16 Normative systems model for organisational change, after Silversweig and Allen (1976, p. 150)

As can be seen, the model in Figure 9.16 above uses the existing culture as a base and expresses the desired culture in terms of a set of specific objectives which can be measured on a regular basis (Step 1). The model relies heavily on member involvement to identify the 'norm gap', to participate in construction of the desired culture (Step 2) and its implementation (Step 3), and to sustain it (Step 4).

The model can be criticised on two main grounds. First, it focuses on norms and is unconcerned with the deeper layers of culture (beliefs, values and assumptions); it is therefore quite simplistic. Second, the use of questionnaire surveys (to establish the existing and desired cultures) and workshops (as in Step 2) may be suspect. Questionnaire surveys may merely draw attention to issues thought to be important by the consultant. Workshops may be equally misleading, since it is not unknown for people in workshop situations to exhibit behaviour which they do not display in performance of their normal duties.

Despite these criticisms, the model has much to commend it. Indeed, the involvement of members in the culture change process provides a *prima facie* answer to one of the major ethical difficulties in this area – that managers will use their power to manipulate members' values to their own ends and desires.

Bate (1994) complains that many of the change models in use are not 'culture specific' but are simply borrowed and adapted from the current stock of change methods on offer. Further, there has been an absence of criteria through which the impact and effectiveness of culture change can be assessed. His model seeks to address these issues by identifying four common approaches to culture change (see Table 9.5) and a set of criteria as shown in Table 9.6.

None of these approaches is automatically right or wrong. They should be considered with regard to the design parameters to construct an approach to cultural change which is relevant and specific to their organisation.

As can be seen from Table 9.6, five criteria (or design parameters) identify a quality or characteristic which must be taken into account when designing a change programme. Each parameter relates to a particular aspect of the organisation.

Table 9.5 Common approaches to change, after Bate (1994, p. 168)

APPROACH	DESCRIPTION
Aggressive	Power coercive; Conflict-centred; Non-collaborative; Imposed; Unilateral; Decree approach
Conciliative	Group problem solving; Collaborative; Integrative; Joint approach
Corrosive	Political; Coalitional; Unplanned; Evolutionary; Informal approach

Table 9.6 Design parameters, after Bate (1994, pp. 204–205)

DESIGN PARAMETER	ASPECT OF ORGANISATION
Expressiveness The ability of an approach to express a new core idea	**The affective component** Feelings
Commonality The ability of an approach to create a unifying set of values	**The social component** Relationships
Penetration The ability of an approach to permeate different levels of the organisation	**The demographic component** Numbers involved
Adaptability The ability of an approach to adjust to changing circumstances	**The developmental component** Process
Durability The ability of an approach to create a culture that will be lasting	**The institutional component** Stature

Thus, each approach outlined in Table 9.5 can now be evaluated in terms of the parameters set out in Table 9.6 to establish where their strengths and weaknesses lie.

It is suggested that such an exercise would identify one approach which appears to have more strengths and fewer weaknesses than any other. Bate (1994) warns against the temptation to adopt this and to slot it into an organisation. This is too mechanical a solution to something as individual as culture change. In practical terms a culture change programme must be tailor-made to the organisation's own aims and requirements. A conciliative approach is not likely to achieve expressiveness; neither will adaptability be achieved through doctrine or aggression.

It is difficult to know where to stop when discussing culture and its management. As can be seen, it is a multi-faceted concept which is subject to many perceptions and managed – if it can be managed at all – through a variety of frameworks and models. It is an area which, in organisational theory terms, is relatively young and still developing. In years to come much of the current literature will seem inept and/or simplistic. It is certainly an area where problems (both theoretical and practical) remain to be solved. Perhaps Whittle *et al.* (1991) had the right idea when they likened culture change to a journey rather than a destination. The same metaphor could be said to apply to the concept itself.

CASE STUDY
Ajax Chemicals

Ajax Chemicals Ltd was founded in 1919 by William Snoddy after he was discharged from the army following the First World War. Snoddy had been an industrial chemist before the war, and, profoundly affected by the horrors of chemical warfare, he was determined to promote the use of chemicals for peaceful purposes. Over the years the company has grown from a five-man operation to its present size of 1,200 employees. Snoddy never married and was always dedicated to the welfare of his employees. He was a pioneer in the provision of free medical and dental care for employees and their immediate families. There is a non-contributory pension scheme for all employees with over three years service. The company is non-unionised.

'Old Bill', as he was affectionately known, was highly respected by all employees. The company had long since grown beyond the point where he could take personal charge of all activities, but he would often spend a day on the shop floor 'helping out' where he felt he was needed and offering advice to department heads. Bill regarded himself as a 'father figure' and since he grew up in an era where father knew best, the problems were obvious for those with management responsibilities.

When Snoddy died, he left the company in trust to his employees – one share per worker, regardless of position in the company. The trust (and the company) is governed by a board of trustees that includes company managers, key outsiders such as the company's lawyer and bank manager, and several non-managerial employee representatives. Dividends are paid out directly to employees from profit after making allowance for the various welfare benefits. Since the founder's death, output and turnover have been falling, causing a downturn in profits.

Company reports have always emphasised the company's loyalty to its workforce. When Snoddy was alive he claimed that he would always do what he could for employee welfare. Current events have caused many to think that a new approach to business is required.

The case above highlights the need for managers to analyse the internal strengths and weaknesses and the external opportunities and threats to the organisation for which they work. The case also shows the potential for dysfunctional conflict and the need for change. Such forces involved in organisational dynamics are many and complex and managers need to be aware of not only the significant aspects of change, conflict, and culture but also how they relate to their own management role.

Questions for discussion

1 Discuss what is meant by *organisational development* and suggest some reasons why it is undertaken by organisations.

2 Why is it necessary for a manager to understand the concept and implications of conflict within organisations?

3 How can managers assess the climate of their organisation and what actions can they take to change their organisation's culture?

References and further reading

Allaire, Y. and Firsirotu, M.E., 1984, 'Theories of Organizational Culture' in *Organization Studies*, Vol. 5/3, pp. 193–226

Bate, P., 1994, *Strategies for Cultural Change* (Oxford: Butterworth Heinemann)

Bateman, T.S. and Zeithmahl, C.F., 1993 (2nd edn), *Management: Function and Strategy* (Homewood: Irwin)

Brickman, J., 'A Conflict Resolution Approach to Public Administration' in L. Zhiyong, *Public Administration Review*, January/February 1997, Vol. 57, No 1, pp. 27–33

Brown, A., 1995, *Organisational Culture* (London: Pitman)

Buchanan, D. and Boddy, D., 1992, *The Expertise of the Change Agent* (Hemel Hempstead: Prentice Hall)

Burns, T. and Stalker, G.M., 1961, *The Management of Innovation* (London: Tavistock)

Channel 4, Forum TV presentation, *A Gilded Cage: The HP Way*

Child, J., 1972, 'Organization Structure and Strategies of Control: A Replication of the Aston Study' in *Administrative Science Quarterly*, Vol. 17, pp. 163–177

Child, J., 1981, 'Culture, Contingency and Capitalism in the Cross-National Study of Organizations' in B.M. Shaw and L.L. Cummings (eds), *Research in Organizational Behaviour*, Vol. 3 (JAI Press)

Clarke, E., 1994, *The Essence of Change* (Hemel Hempstead: Prentice Hall)

Clegg, S.R., 1990, *Modern Organisations* (London: Sage)

Cole, J.B. (ed), 1988, *Anthropology for the Eighties* (London: Free Press)

Crook, S., Pakulski, J. and Waters, M., 1992, *Postmodernization: Change in Advanced Society* (London: Sage)

Daft, R.L., 1992 (4th edn), *Organization Theory and Design* (St Paul: West Publishing)

Deal, T.E. and Kennedy, A.A., 1982, *Corporate Cultures: The Rites and Rituals of Corporate Life* (London: Addison-Wesley)

Dennison, D.R., 'Bringing Corporate Culture to the Bottom Line' in *Organizational Dynamics*, August 1984, pp. 5–22

Donaldson, L., 1997, *For Positivist Organization Theory* (London: Sage)

Duncan, W.J., 1989, 'Organizational Culture: Getting a Fix on an Elusive Concept' in *Academy of Management Executive*, No 3, pp. 229–236

Egan, G., 'The Shadow Side' in *Management Today*, September 1994, p. 37

Eisenhardt, K.M., Kahwajy, J.L. and Bourgeois, L.J., 'How Management Teams Can Have a Good Fight' in *Harvard Business Review*, July–August 1997, pp. 77–85

Gordon, G., 1991, 'Industry Determinants of Organizational Culture' in *Academy of Management Review*, No 16, pp. 396–415

Handy, C.B., 1985, *Understanding Organisations* (Harmondsworth: Penguin)

Handy, C.B., 1989, *The Age of Unreason* (Harmondsworth: Penguin)

Hassard, J., 1993, 'Postmodernism and Organizational Analysis: an Overview' in J. Hassard and M. Peters (eds), *Postmodernism and Organizations* (London: Sage)

Hassard, J. and Sharifi, S., 1989, 'Corporate Culture and Strategic Change' in *Journal of General Management*, Vol. 15, No 2, pp. 4–19

Hatch, M.J., 1997, *Organization Theory: Modern, Symbolic and Postmodern Perspectives* (Oxford: Oxford University Press)

Hofstede, G. (1980), *Culture's Consequences: International Differences in Work Related Values* (London: Sage)

Jacques, E., 1952, *The Changing Culture of a Factory* (London: Tavistock)

Kelly, G.A., 1953, *The Psychology of Personal Constructs*, Vols 1 and 2 (New York: Morton)

Keuning, D., 1998, *Management: A Contemporary Approach* (London: Pitman)

Kimberley, J.R. and Quinn, R.E., 1986, *New Futures: The Challenge of Managing Corporate Transitions* (London: Prentice-Hall)

Kluckhohn, F.R. and Strodtbeck F.L., 1961, *Variations in Value Orientations* (London: Row Peterson)

Kroeber, A.L. and Kluckhohn, C., 1952, *Culture: A Critical Review of Concepts and Definitions* (Boston: Harvard University Press)

Lawrence, P.R. and Lorsch, J.W., 1967, *Organization and Environment* (Boston: Harvard University, Division of Research, Graduate School of Business Administration)

Leavitt, H.J., 1965, 'Applied Organization Change in Industry: Structural, Technical and Human Approaches' in J.G. March (ed.), *Handbook of Organizations* (Chicago: Rand McNally)

Lewin, K., 1951, *Field Theory in Social Science* (New York: Harper & Row)

Lewin, K., 1958, 'Group Decisions and Social Change' in E.E. Maccoby, T.M. Newcomb and E.L. Hartley (eds), *Readings in Social Psychology* (New York: Rinehart Winston), pp. 197–221

Martin, J. and Seihl, C., 'Organizational Culture and Counterculture: An Uneasy Symbiosis' in *Organizational Dynamics*, Autumn 1985, pp. 52–64

Maund, L., 1994, 'The Role of Conflict in the Teaching and Learning of Undergraduates: A Case Study' (Unpublished PhD thesis, Guildford: University of Surrey)

Meek, L.V., 1988, 'Organizational Culture: Origins and Weaknesses' in *Organization Studies*, Vol. 9, No 4, pp. 453–473

Megginson, L.C., Mosley, D.C. and Petri, P.H., 1989 (3rd edn), *Management: Concepts and Applications* (New York: Harper & Row)

Mintzberg, J., 1979, *The Structuring of Organizations: A Synthesis of the Research* (Englewood Cliffs: Prentice Hall)

Mintzberg, J., 1995, *The Rise and Fall of Strategic Planning* (New York: Free Press)

Morgan, G., 1997 (4th edn), *Images of Organization* (London: Sage)

Ouchi, W.G., 1981, *Theory Z: How American Business Can Meet the Japanese Challenge* (London: Addison-Wesley)

Peters, T.J. and Waterman, R.H., 1982, *In Search of Excellence: Lessons from America's Best Run Companies* (New York: Harper & Row)

Pfeffer, J. and Salancik, G.R., 1978, *The External Control of Organizations: A Resource Dependence Perspective* (New York: Harper & Row)

Pondy, L.R., 'Organizational Conflict: Concepts and Models' in *Administrative Science Quarterly,* September 1969, p. 301

Potter, C.C., 1989, 'What is Culture: and Can It be Useful for Organisational Change Agents?' in *Leadership and Organization Development Journal*, Vol. 10, No 3

Powell, W.W. and DiMaggio, P.J. (eds), 1991, *The New Institutionalism in Organizational Analysis* (Chicago: University of Chicago Press)

Robbins, S.P., 1990, *Organization Theory: Structure, Design and Applications* (Englewood Cliffs: Prentice Hall)

Robbins, S.P. and DeCenzo, D.A., 1998 (2nd edn), *Fundamentals of Management: Essential Concepts and Applications* (Englewood Cliffs: Prentice Hall)

Sathe, V., 'Implications of Corporate Culture: A Manager's Guide to Action' in *Organization Dynamics*, Autumn 1983, pp. 5–19

Schein, E.H., 'Coming to a New Awareness of Organizational Culture' in *Sloan Management Review*, Winter 1984, pp. 3–16

Selznick, P., 1957, *Leadership in Administration* (New York: Harper & Row)

Silverman, D., 1970, *The Theory of Organizations* (London: Heinemann)

Silversweig, S. and Allen, R.F., 1976, 'Changing the Corporate Culture' in *Sloan Management Review*, Vol. 17, pp. 33–49

Smircich, L., 1983, 'Concepts of Culture and Organizational Analysis' in *Administrative Science Quarterly*, Vol. 28, No 3, pp. 339–358

Thompson, J.D., 'Organizational Management of Conflict' in *Administrative Science Quarterly*, March 1960, p. 389

Trice, J. and Beyer, J., 1993, *The Cultures of Work Organizations* (Englewood Cliffs: Prentice Hall)

Whittle, S., Smith, S., Tranfield, D. and Foster, M., 'Implementing Total Quality: Erecting Tents or Building Palaces' in P. Bate, 1991, *Strategies for Cultural Change* (Sheffield: Sheffield Business School, Change Management Research Unit)

Zhiyong, L., 1997, 'A Conflict Resolution Approach to Public Adminstration' in *Public Administration Review*, Vol. 57, No 1, pp. 27–33

10 The role of management

Learning objectives

After studying this chapter you should be able to:

- compare and contrast the managerial role in both a traditional and contemporary situation;
- discuss the relationship between management and organisational behaviour;
- analyse the development of management;
- describe the concepts of managerial ideology and the managerial prerogative;
- examine the place of decision-making in the managerial role;
- describe the role of management in a diverse workforce.

Introduction

CASE STUDY

Get the best out of staff

Being a manager used to involve getting people below you in the hierarchy to do what you wanted. Now, it seems, downwards is just one of *five* directions in which managers must operate.

According to Andrew Forrest (1997) a human resources director at the Industrial Society, 'five-way management' is in operation and consists of managing: upwards (your boss, shareholders, directors); across the organisation (teams, colleagues); outwards (suppliers, customers, regulators); downwards (employees, unions); and oneself.

The time-management trick is to ensure the right proportion of the day is spent on managing in each direction and, vitally, that two traps are avoided. These are, according to Forrest: spending most time on what you have always done; and spending most time on what you most enjoy, even if it is not the most important part of the job.

The technique of five-way management involves identifying the tasks employees need to perform, what they do best, and how they can work most effectively with their colleagues. Forrest says the traditional process of matching roles and people starts with the role and squeezes the person into it. He advocates a 'realistic and flexible approach' to role definition, believing that the organisation needs to have its objectives achieved, but that the days are past when that had to be by such tight definition of responsibilities that each person felt like a prisoner in a box. He believes that it is better to get into a negotiation with those whose roles are adjacent to your own, and adjust the boundaries so that everyone wins.

Adapted from D. Summers, 'Get the best out of staff' in *Financial Times*, 9 July 1997, p. 8

As the case study above shows, organisations work in a constantly changing environment with the requirement that they be proactive to change – or at the very least flexible enough to be quickly reactive. The traditional, mechanistic organisational design has been mostly superseded by the flatter, delayered, organic structure and new developments in technology have provided opportunities for the ambitious and motivated manager. The impact of these and other changes is heavy on both the workforce and their managers and, particularly, requires reshaping of jobs.

Organisations work in a dynamic, unstable and competitive market environment requiring quicker and more flexible decision-making processes. With this has come for the manager more responsibility, a wider brief, and an increased workload and its attendant problem of high stress. High technology and self-managed teams have been accompanied by access to increased levels and quantity of information. Thus there is more worker empowerment and emerging models of leadership. Less and less time is spent by managers on supervising the workforce and there has been an increase in their mentoring, coaching and co-ordinating roles. The underlying philosophy is that managers must now have a keen understanding of not only their own work, but also the work of others throughout the organisation.

This ongoing trend to delayer organisations and downsize the middle-management areas has added to the change in the role of organisations as highlighted above and has meant that such changes have threatened the role of the manager – they may well be becoming obsolete. However, if managers are aware of such changes they can capitalise on them and create their own opportunities – the role is one of evolution. Whilst no manager has the same environment as any other manager within the same organisation – or any other organisation – they have one thing in common: interaction with others. Nowadays most of a manager's time is spent in working with others and so the management process and the behaviour of individuals in organisations are integrated to a high degree.

The aim of this chapter is to consider the general field of management as it relates to the specific field of organisational behaviour discussed in the previous chapters. This is done by looking at managerial perspectives as they relate to organisational behaviour and then characterising the manager's task in terms of its functions, roles and required skills. Next comes the identification and discussion of some key managerial, organisational and competitive challenges and relating them to organisational behaviour concepts. Lastly, there is an investigation into how to manage organisational effectiveness in the context of organisational behaviour.

Managerial perspectives on organisational behaviour

Managerial titles

How many managerial titles can you come up with for management within your university?

You probably listed a number which included all or some of the following: Vice Chancellor, Rector, Head of Human Resources, Dean, Head of School, Head of Department, Faculty Officer, Registrar, Senior Academic Tutor ...

If you visited the offices of these people, they would probably have a corresponding name-plate and descriptor on their office/study doors.

Did you consider one called 'Organisational Behaviour Manager'?

If you have understood the concepts described in this book you would not have attributed such a role to a manager because organisational behaviour is not a function or area of responsibility but a perspective that all managers can use to perform their tasks more efficiently and effectively. It is through an understanding of these constructs that managers can better understand the people with whom they work. Most managers have subordinates, peers, and superiors and they need to manage work-related behaviours related to all of these – see Table 10.1 below for examples which are not mutually exclusive.

Table 10.1 Examples of managerial work-related concepts

ROLE	REQUIRED TO UNDERSTAND HOW TO
Subordinates	intrinsically motivate employees to increase their productivity design and redesign jobs as required turn dysfunctional conflict into functional conflict evaluate jobs help in goal setting assist in reward achievement.
Superiors	understand the principles of leadership appreciate aspects of power and politics make effective decisions appreciate importance of organisational culture
Colleagues	understand attitudinal processes appreciate individual differences interpret group dynamics appreciate importance of organisational culture appreciate aspects of power and politics
Outsiders	suppliers competitors clients officials – national and local pressure group representatives trades union officials understanding external environment appreciate international contexts
Self	understand personal needs and motives improve decision-making potential cope with stress continue with professional development

The role of management and an understanding of organisational behaviour are intertwined and neither is mutually exclusive. Organisational behaviour can provide the manager with some useful tools and concepts with which to manage effectively and efficiently within the organisation.

Management functions, roles and skills

Organisations decide upon their objectives and goals through their corporate strategy and such goals are often encompassed in the vision or mission statement which is usually on public display. In order to achieve these objectives, it is vital that the right people are in the right place at the right time, and all managers need to work together to achieve such goals. However, as the case study below indicates, this is not always true.

CASE STUDY

Whose side are you on?

Many managers appear to have forgotten a basic tenet of management – that results in process are not mutually exclusive but mutually supportive.

There appears to be an increasing absence of mutuality between senior and middle managers and it is readily apparent to those involved in management and organisational development in both the public and private sectors.

Traditionally, senior managers are concerned with setting the strategic direction and objectives for the organisation; middle managers with making it happen – resourcing and managing changes. The corollary is that senior managers are concerned with results and middle managers with how they are achieved.

The divide appears as middle levels complain that their seniors are solely concerned with short-term financial results and as seniors reply that the middle strata devote more effort to voicing problems than to finding solutions.

Certainly, at a senior level the reforms of the Conservative government have focused attention within the public sector upon financial results and it can be argued that their monetarist policies reinforced the long-held private sector view that UK investors chase short-term gains.

In both sectors the delayering of organisations has dramatically reduced the resources available to middle managers. The divide deepens as each accuses the other of pursuing their own personal rather than organisation ends. Middle accuse senior of being concerned with their own career advancement: senior accuse middle of directing their efforts to protecting their position. It also appears that each group fails to fully understand the issues faced by the other.

So is the divide unbridgeable? The basic tenet of management – that results and process are not mutually exclusive but mutually supportive – starts with the process by which strategic direction and objectives are set.

Involvement of middle managers in this process represents an opportunity for deep, mutual understanding between middle and senior levels in two key areas. Firstly, the relevance and importance of particular targets and secondly, that results achieved without commitment to organisational goals are indeed a pyrrhic victory – giving managers at all levels an ever steeper hill to climb in the future.

Organisations in all sectors operate in rapidly changing environments. Alienation of middle managers and frustration of senior levels are unnecessarily debilitating. Each strategic planning cycle is an opportunity to manage the changes required in a way that reinforces the organisation's ability to change more appropriately and more rapidly in the future. Sadly, this opportunity appears too often to be missed.

Adapted from M. Rawson, 'Whose side are you on?' in *Professional Manager*, November 1997, p. 3

It is through managers that organisations achieve their objectives for designing and carrying out their plans; and the role of a manager is a social process, with definitions of a manager's role interpreting this process – either implicitly or explicitly.

Parker Follett (1941) believed that the process of management was simply getting things done by other people. This traditional view still applies but its application is not now so simple. Drucker (1979) took a functional view, stating that:

> Management is tasks. Management is a discipline, but management is also people. Every achievement of management is the achievement of a manager. Every failure is a failure of a manager. (p. 14)

Brech (1975) took the social view and defined management as:

> A social process entailing responsibility for the effective and economical planning and regulation of the operations of an enterprise, in fulfilment of given purposes or tasks, such responsibility involving:
>
> (a) judgement and decision in determining plans and in using data to control performance and progress against plans;
> (b) the guidance, integration, motivation and supervision of the personnel composing the enterprise and carrying out its operations. (p. 19)

This theme was taken up by Drucker (1989) who believed that management was more an art than a science where there are no exact solutions and where the ultimate measure of effectiveness is that of the achievement of the organisational goals and a high business performance.

There is a school of thought which considers that management is a science; this idea is based on the view that if activities cannot be empiricised – that is, all knowledge derives from experience – then they are not worth doing. This was a view held in the early 1960s when it was felt that everything could be measured – particularly in the field of finance. With the continuing influence of technology has come a similar viewpoint but alongside this is the more important point that such figures and information must be accurate if the organisation is to meet its objectives and the needs of the customer. It is sometimes necessary for organisations to override the numerical evidence and take risks. An example here would be the development of the Sony Walkman, where the market research for this product strongly indicated that the product would not be a success. Whilst such an example does not detract from the value of market research, it does indicate that managers need to be able to take into account all factors when making their decisions. Others believe that management is not a discipline in itself but instead encompasses many factors – as has been indicated earlier – and is more of a descriptive label.

From the definitions available in writings, it seems that the commonest view is that management is about optimising all the resources (human, financial, and material) that are available to enable the organisation to achieve its objectives. Even so, the role of a manager can be conceptualised in a number of different ways which are generally built on the foundations of managerial functions, roles, and skills.

Thus, there is no one correct way for managers to behave or one right solution for each of the situations which they might come across – they need to be able to take the situational and contingency approaches.

Managerial functions

Management can be characterised according to the level of decision-making authority which a manager has within the organisation and the level of responsibility he or she has for others: the scalar chain. There are four key managerial functions within organisations which are shown in Figure 10.1 below.

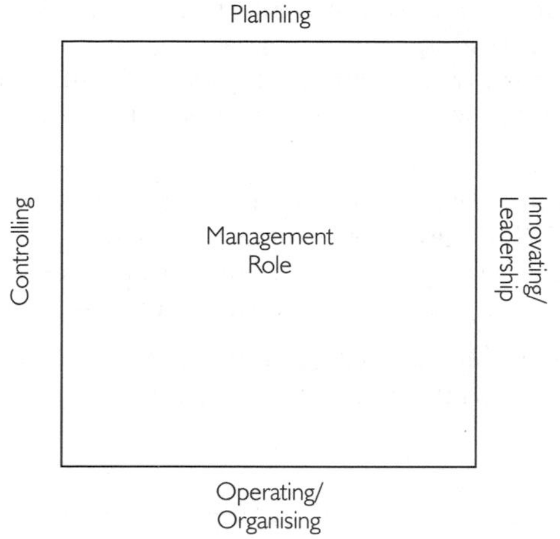

Figure 10.1 The management role

Planning is linked to corporate strategy because it is the process through which the organisation's desired future position is decided as well as how it might be achieved. This could involve a number of behaviours such as:

- investigating the external environment to see what the marketplace offers;
- agreeing on appropriate objectives;
- outlining strategies for achieving these objectives;
- developing appropriate strategies for achieving the agreed objectives.

Any manager carrying out planning activities must use a number of organisational behaviour concepts, such as perception and aspects of motivational theory and practice.

Organising is carried out through the process of:

- designing and redesigning jobs for the workforce;
- placing jobs into groups and sub-units;
- establishing patterns of control and authority between those jobs and sub-units.

The Gulf War can stand as an example of this process, where one General was responsible for organising all the factors unlike in previous wars, for example the Second World War, where each service controlled its own assets in the form of armaments, vehicles, and aircraft.

Through the organising (or operating) function the manager puts together the basic framework and structure of the organisation. For larger organisations, like British

Telecom, this can be a complicated and comprehensive exercise. Once again, this function requires the implementation of a number of the concepts of organisational behaviour.

Innovation (which some writers on the function of managers often label as *leadership*) is the finding and development of new ideas so that, for example, marketing goals can be achieved, benefits can be made from developing technology, and new processes and improvements can be incorporated into the organisation's workings. However, it is through leadership that the manager gets the members of the organisation to work together in order to achieve the organisational goals. For example, managers have to select and recruit staff and oversee training and development. From the organisational behaviour aspect, managers utilise views on motivation, leadership concepts, and team building.

Controlling is the function of monitoring and correcting the plans and activities of members of the organisation in order that the goals may be better achieved. This would require a manager to control such things as costs, inputs and staff. Organisational behavioural concepts would provide a manager with ideas for performance evaluations and reward systems, intrinsic motivation, and organisational authority and control.

The key functions of a manager are related to managing the resources of the organisation. Figure 10.2 below shows the link between the key managerial roles and the organisational resources.

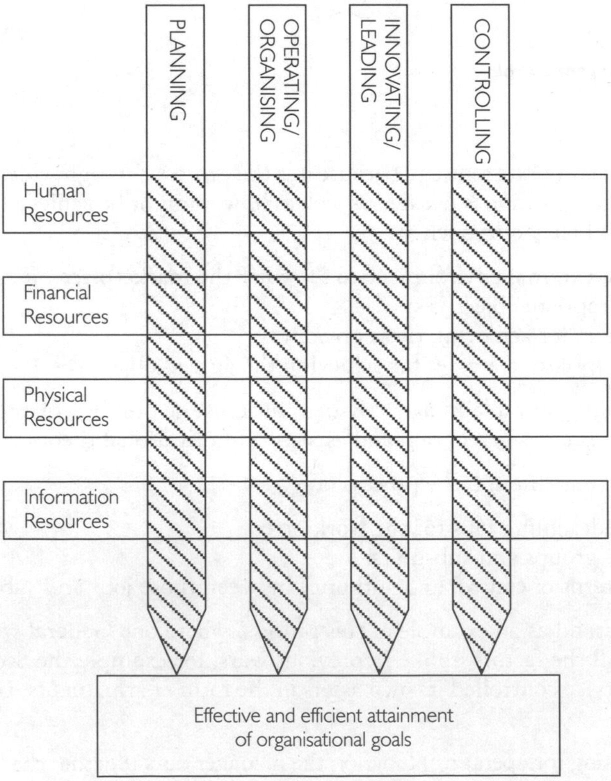

Figure 10.2 Basic managerial roles and their relationship with organisational resources

As can be seen from Figure 10.3 below, managers deal with a number of competing interests within the key areas of organisational aspects, individuals, and groups/teams – each of which draws from the organisational concepts which have been dealt with in this text.

Figure 10.3 Reconciling the competing interests of managers

Managerial roles

A role is a set of expected behaviour patterns attributed to someone occupying a given position in a social unit – such as an organisation. Managers play a number of different roles. Much of the knowledge related to managerial roles is based on the seminal work of Mintzberg (1975), who identified ten basic roles which he then clustered into three specific roles as listed in Table 10.2 below.

Table 10.2 Important managerial roles after Mintzberg (1975)

CATEGORY	ROLE	EXAMPLE
Interpersonal	Figurehead	Attend employee retirement ceremony
	Leader	Encourage workers to increase productivity
	Liaison	Co-ordinate activities of two committees
Informational	Monitor	Scan *People Management* for information about developments in human resource management
	Disseminator	Send out e-mails outlining new procedures
	Spokesperson	Hold press conference to announce new product
Decision-making	Entrepreneur	Develop an idea for a new customer service and convince others of its advantages
	Disturbance handler	Resolve dysfunctional conflict
	Resource allocator	Allocate financial resources to workteams
	Negotiator	Settle new terms of employment

Interpersonal roles (figurehead, leader, liaison) are those which are principally social because they are relational in nature – such managers have to communicate with people. They may well be *figureheads* for the organisation which means that they have to entertain important visitors and present performance awards or retirement gifts. In the role of *leader* they will recruit, select, train, develop, and intrinsically motivate employees. All these interpersonal roles are behavioural processes.

Informational roles (monitor, disseminator, spokesperson) involve aspects of information processing. Acting as *monitor* means seeking out information which might be of use to specific individuals or a team and when managers transmit this information they are acting as a *disseminator*. When speaking on behalf of the organisation, they are acting in the role of *spokesperson*. Again, the manager will draw upon organisational behaviour processes because information is about exchanges between people.

Decision-making roles (entrepreneur, disturbance-handler, resource allocator, negotiator) are equally important. As *entrepreneur* the manager initiates change by being innovative and implementing new strategies. In the role of *disturbance handler* the manager assists in the settlement of disputes between individuals or groups, and as *resource allocator* he or she decides how the resources of the organisation (see Figure 10.2 above) are to be distributed. Finally, as *negotiator* the manager represents the organisation in the external environment when, say, negotiating with customers, competitors, and pressure groups. As in the other two role categories outlined by Mintzberg (1975), this decision-making role calls for a number of behavioural processes.

Therefore, managerial roles can be placed into three key areas represented in Figure 10.4 below.

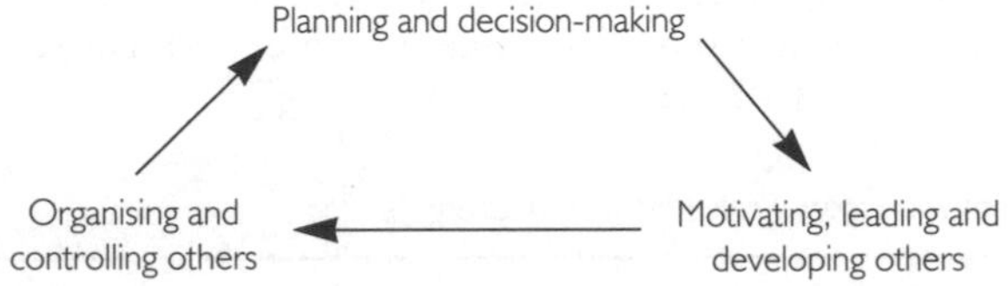

Figure 10.4 Key managerial roles

Managerial skills

Organisations are complex entities that are composed of diverse and often highly complex workforces operating in a globalised environment. Therefore, according to Katz (1987), successful managers of today must have effective technical, interpersonal, conceptual, and diagnostic skills.

Technical skills are the abilities that are required in order that the worker may attain the specific goals of the organisation. They are generally associated with the organisation as it goes through its transformational processes and examples are writing software, composing public announcements, and designing buildings.

Interpersonal skills include the manager's ability to communicate effectively with others along with the ability to understand the messages and also intrinsically motivate individuals and teams. As was discussed earlier, managers expend considerable time and energy on interpersonal relationships and it is therefore essential that they have the ability to get on with all kinds of people and at all levels.

Conceptual skill is the manager's ability to think. Managers should be able to take a holistic view and identify opportunities where others overlook them. The more acutely managers can think the more likely it is that they will see the opportunities that others miss. They will use conceptual skills to give their organisation a competitive advantage.

Diagnostic skills are employed by managers to enable them to understand the cause-and-effect relationships within the organisation so as to find the most effective solution to any problem. By using these optimal solutions, they may be able to reorientate the organisation's goals and become proactive.

Not every manager will have all the above skills and neither will managers have them in equal proportions. An effective manager will be aware of the four types of skills and will 'pick-and-mix' them as the situation requires – that is, will use the contingency approach. As shown in Figure 10.5 below, the mix tends to depend upon the manager's position in the organisation's hierarchy. First-line managers tend to depend significantly on their technical skills and less on their conceptual or diagnostic skills whilst managers at the apex exhibit the reverse – they employ diagnostic skills more and depend to a lesser degree on technical and interpersonal skills. Those managers in the middle of the hierarchy tend to utilise an even distribution of all four managerial skills. Whilst this figure shows the skills required at different organisational levels it is a fairly traditional model, and with the onset of delayering, downsizing and restructuring, the roles of middle managers and first-line managers are changing towards a requirement to be competent at all the organisational levels.

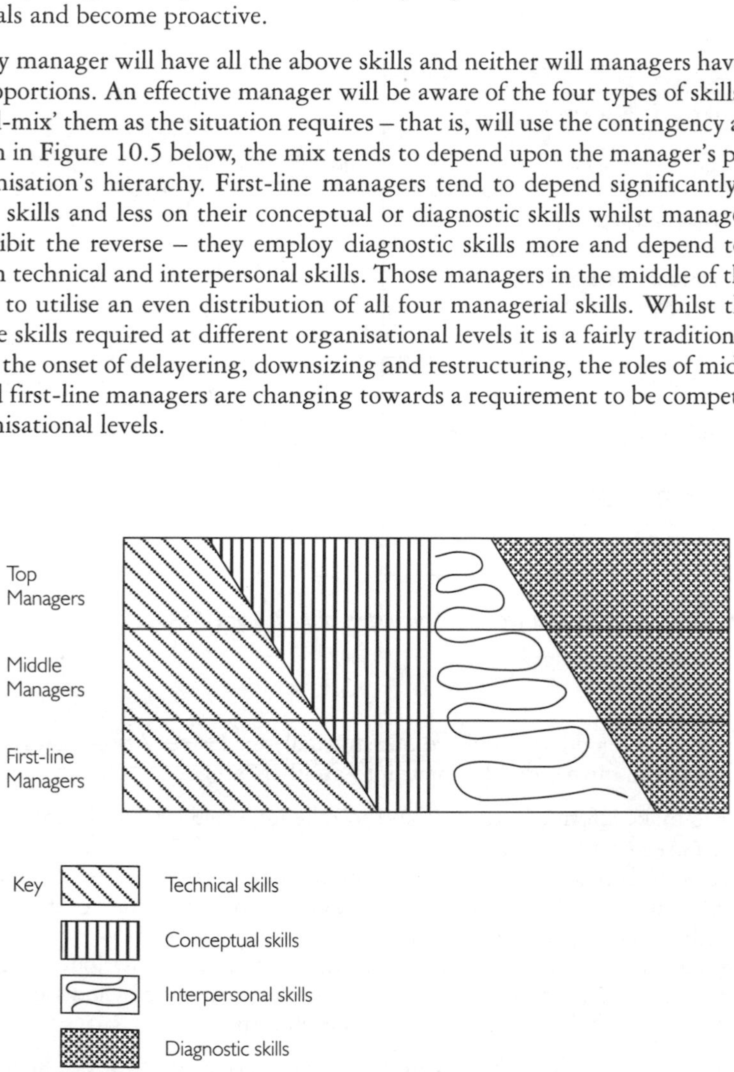

Figure 10.5 Managerial skills at different organisational levels

A key model which identifies the attributes needed by a successful manager has been put forward by Pedlar *et al.* (1994); it was based on their study which identified eleven qualities which are associated with successful managers in modern organisations and which are not apparent in unsuccessful managers. The researchers classified these eleven positive attributes into three areas as shown in Figure 10.6 below.

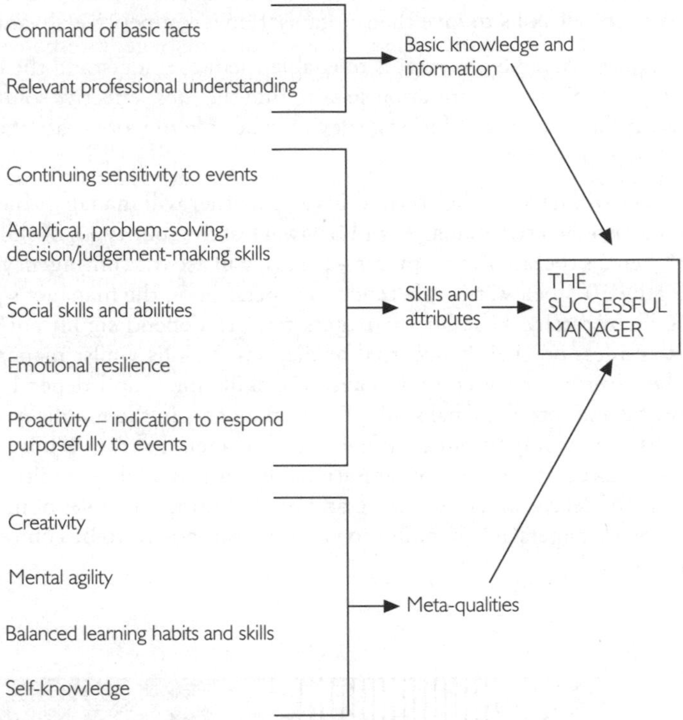

Figure 10.6 Eleven qualities of a successful manager, after Pedlar (1994, p. 24)

The qualities cross boundaries and are not mutually exclusive. Also, possession of one quality can result in further development into another category.

- In order to make informed decisions and to take informed action, the manager needs *basic knowledge and information*.
- The specific *skills and attributes* permit managers to be sensitive to the activities of stakeholders and directly affect both the behaviour and performance of themselves and others with whom they come into contact.
- It is through the *meta-qualities* that the manager fosters and redistributes the abilities, skills, and resources which are needed in specific circumstances by individuals and the organisation as a whole in order to meet their objectives.

Since the introduction of the Management Charter Initiative (MCI), 1988, there has been a move away from the more traditional roles and qualities of a manager towards the requirement for more sophisticated skills such as knowledge management and creativity. The MCI was drawn up as a result of investigation into the education, training and development of managers. There were two key inputs into the development of the MCI:

- **the Constable and McCormick Report of 1987** initiated by the British Institute of Management. This work investigated the development of British managers and concluded that many of them needed a broader professional training and education if their organisations were to be competitive. It was this report that brought continuous professional development to the fore, where the individual manager is responsible for continuing to maintain his or her professional knowledge and expertise.
- **the Handy Report of 1987**. Charles Handy led an international investigation in an attempt to find out if there was something special about what each nationality offered to the role of manager. His report highlighted the fact that expertise in functional and technical skills was insufficient in the modern business world and that managers must have considerable business knowledge with human and conceptual skills.

Also as a result of such investigations, managers have now moved into the competencies arena whereby they are assessed against national standards in key management functions and skills. Such competencies are broken down further into specific activities that managers need to undertake on a daily basis. This continuous professional development is formally and professionally recognised through such organisations as The Institute of Personnel and Development and the British Institute of Management.

Knowledge management

CASE STUDY

Knowledge management – how to make it work

Like people, companies use such a tiny proportion of their collective brainpower that any improvement has the potential to deliver disproportionate gains. No wonder chief executives are dazzled by the prospect.

But attempts to make systematic use of corporate knowledge assets are not a recent innovation. Motorola's company university and 3M's cross-divisional scientific networks are both successful home-grown learning and developing initiatives which predate the knowledge management craze. The best Total Quality Management programmes are systematic attempts to build company learning. In Japan, the detergents and cosmetics firm Kao has dedicated itself to becoming an industrial university, a factory for producing knowledge.

Research at the Santa Fe Institute and elsewhere is focusing on the creative learning process that takes place in what are coming to be thought of as 'communities of practice' where shared purpose is an important component of group learning. For instance, when a suspicious Rank Xerox tried to stop its repair technicians spending so much time gossiping in the office rather than being on the clients' premises, satisfactory repair rates plunged. What the company had not realised was that the technicians had been using their office time to postulate reasons to explain copier breakdowns undreamt of by the authors of the repair manuals.

But, how to get started? According to Chuck Lucier at Booz Allen & Hamilton, the starting point should be an urgent strategic priority, something which will benefit from and give leverage to the knowledge effort. For example, the aim might be to take an existing strength and build it into a strategic competitive advantage; to share learning around a group's subsidiaries by building a best-practices database; or to save costs with a corporate Yellow Pages.

Next, says Lucier, recognise that this is a change programme. Finally, build the infrastructure – nothing will happen without a knowledge engine. This means linking knowledge processes to business processes; including reward and recognition; designating a few people to manage the effort full time (the biggest single mistake that chief executives make is to refuse this investment); and, where necessary, apply IT.

Adapted from S. Caulkin, 'The Knowledge Within' in *Management Today*, August 1997, pp. 28–32

As the above case shows, effective knowledge management depends on harnessing expertise and more senior managers are taking on the responsibility for the intellectual capital of their organisations. However, Donkin (1997) reports that companies have not yet decided how best to manage knowledge workers – let alone how to meet the need for the emotionally intelligent employee.

The challenge to management

Managers are under ever-increasing stresses and strains in trying to meet their key objectives of attempting to maintain control over organisational processes through leadership, controlling, planning, and organising (see Figure 10.1 above). A key role is to deal with the tension between the status quo in the organisation and the requirement to proactively change in order to survive increased competition, work diversity, and increased global competition. Stability has disappeared and managers now have to work in an ever-changing environment – both internal and external. This has brought about a need for organisations to concentrate on their customers through a marketing culture. Even in large organisations managers need to be both specialists and generalists with the ability to utilise their skills on differing planes – see Figure 10.7.

Managerial ideology

During the first twenty-five years of the twentieth century professional management emerged; it adopted the concepts of organisational behaviour discussed in the text and thus developed as: '[a] social force, specialist occupational category and set of distinct working practices' (Thompson and McHugh, 1995, p. 103).

Such a view has developed today into what Bennett (1997) calls a 'managerial ideology' which, he says, '… describes the totality of the ideas, opinions and perspectives of those

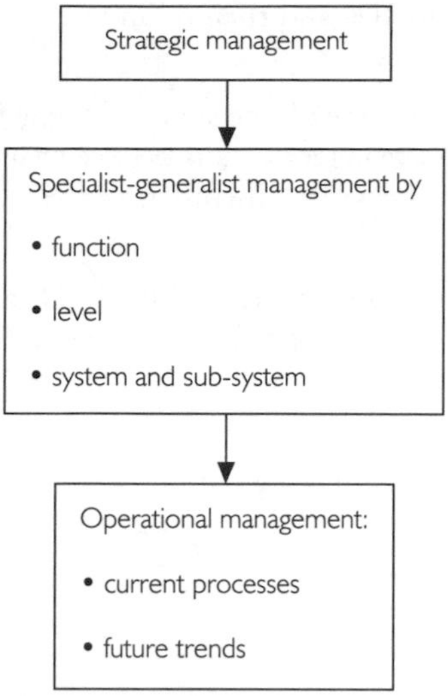

Figure 10.7 Levels of management related to the size of the organisation

who exercise formal authority in business situations and which seeks to explain and justify that authority' (p. 191).

However, Czarniawska-Joerges (1988) takes the view that ideology does not have a place in business, and states that ideology:

> ... is something that ought not to be found in business and administrative organizations, which are by definition non-ideological. Ideology's place is in political and religious organizations. Everywhere else it is a dangerous aberration and should be eliminated, in order to make room for science. (p. 9)

Whatever the viewpoint on ideology *per se* there is no doubt that recently the concept has become part of the portfolio of those who research into organisational theory and of those who adopt such ideas as managerial practices. This text has shown that there is no single right or wrong way to deal with the behaviour of individuals in organisations nor is there a universal view held by business managers because, as Bennett (1997) stated: '... ideology is heavily interconnected with general approaches to management and the latter vary from country to country and time to time' (p. 191).

There are four principal managerial ideologies:

- unitarism (and its contrast, *pluralism*)
- social Darwinism
- paternalism
- classical and human relations approaches.

Unitarism is derived from a school of political philosophy known as *utilitarianism*, whose doctrine is that the greatest happiness of the greatest number is the guiding principle of conduct, the criterion of what is right. Unitarism can be colloquially expressed as everyone 'being in the same boat' and individuals will quite naturally act as a team. Succinctly, it is the process of selling, say, an idea and then telling people to do it. Conversely, *pluralism* is the seeking of a compromise.

Social Darwinism relates to the principle of 'the survival of the fittest' and relies on *laissez faire* attitudes. In this instance, a manager would believe that the strong and able must be encouraged to survive whilst the weaker members of the workforce should be considered dispensable.

Paternalism could be said to be linked closely with pluralism because it is where the employer is assumed to have a moral responsibility for the welfare and happiness of each member of the workforce.

The *classical* and *human relations* approaches have been dealt with elsewhere in this text but the former would be where rules and regulations were used to manage a situation or make a decision and the latter would consider the organisational setting in which the situation occurs.

Consider this situation

You are one of four students who, as a team, have to produce a report for your course in Organisational Behaviour. Three of you have recognised that the fourth member is social loafing. How can this situation be viewed from various managerial ideological approaches?

The *unitarist* approach would be to view the social loafer as acting in an invidious manner and to consider the behaviour to be destructive to self, the rest of the team, and the organisation. A *pluralist* viewpoint would be to seek a compromise solution that satisfied all members of the team. This could well be in the form of a *paternalistic* approach where the rest of the team assumes a moral responsibility for the perceived social loafer. Another view might be that of *social Darwinism* when the team says that they have to get through and it's just tough luck on the social loafer – it's his or her own fault. The *classical management* approach would be to remind the social loafer that the team had agreed rules, regulations, and a clear division of responsibility and so there was no reason why the work should not have been done. Finally, a *human relations* approach would be to use the consideration that the behaviour might be because the loafer perceives a lack of need for the outcomes of the activity – an organisational consideration.

Managers' ideology will dictate how they influence everything around them and it will influence their opinions and their expectations of others. It is through their ideology that managers will filter information; for example, they might understate information which is actually vital to the welfare of others or they might simplify information on the assumption that others would not otherwise understand. According to Bennett (1997):

> Possession of a distinct ideology helps the individual to cope with:
>
> (a) uncertainty;
>
> (b) stress and other psychological demands at work; and
>
> (c) the strains that arise from ambiguities concerning the legitimacy of a manager's role. (p. 192)

These issues all relate to perceptual issues and to managers' roles concerning their right to manage others – their 'managerial prerogative'.

The managerial prerogative

Managers have control over the resources of the organisation and, additionally, the right to select and recruit staff – as well as dismiss them. As a consequence, it can be said that the management prerogative is an additional responsibility – it is a *moral* right. Such a moral right is based on a number of key assumptions which, according to Bennett (1997, p. 192) include:

- managers should focus their attention on pleasing the customer, not on trying to consistently please members of the workforce;
- information, training, skills and resources are in the hands of managers and so only they can make effective decisions;
- only management represents the organisation's interests and goals because only they own, or represent the owners of, the firm;
- managers are more objective than members of the workforce and therefore their decisions will benefit all members of the workforce;
- employee representatives lack the professionalism, training and basic education required to accurately assess the implications of important management decisions.

Collectively, this suggests that the members of the workforce are expected to trust the managers to make satisfactory decisions and to remain impartial and objective. The fact that they have the specialist skills and knowledge means, in itself, that managers know what is best for the organisation – such is the 'management prerogative'.

The development of women managers

CASE STUDY

Women who make a difference

Female entrepreneurs are more autocratic in their management style than men, operate with fewer levels of authority and use hardly any written rules, with most information stored in their head.

These are some of the early findings of a study by Syeda-Masooda Mukhtar, Fellow in Small and Medium Enterprise Management at Manchester Business School. 'I admit that I was taken aback myself', says Mukhtar, who had tended to subscribe to the stereotype of the consensual, collaborative female manager.

'These results are quite critical since there is a debate among policymakers about whether to treat female businesses differently.' She reckons her study is proof that there are indeed gender differences, which may in turn suggest the need for adjustments in the formulation of public policy, for instance, on skills training.

When quizzed about management styles, nearly 63 per cent of women said they practised no delegation of authority in running their businesses. Only 48 per cent of the men interviewed said that this was the case. These differences in management style held good across all sizes of companies surveyed, although differences were to be found among the few women running the (relatively) larger businesses.

Most of the women had no formal documented quality procedures, preferring informal techniques, such as memory power. The study claims to show that this does not make them worse managers; indeed they appear to pay just as much attention to matters such as budgetary control or setting strategy objectives.

The study suggests that if male and female entrepreneurs tend not to share attributes, they should perhaps not be judged by the same yardsticks. However, one of the things the research cannot gauge is which gender proves to be the more truthful when it comes to taking part in a survey.

Adapted from A. Mukhtar, 'Women who make a difference' in *Financial Times*, 18 February 1997, p. 13

Generally, women are significantly under-represented in UK management – even though Mukhtar (1997) in the case showed that: '... there was a dearth of data on the subject of women running their own businesses, even though their numbers had clearly increased' (p. 13).

Davidson (1991) stated that in 1989, 41 per cent of the UK labour force was made up of women and the proportion was expected to rise to approximately to 50 per cent by the onset of the millennium. However, only 11 per cent of general management in the UK are women. Davidson and Cooper (1992) further reported that the percentage of women represented at chief executive level was even lower – only 1 per cent reached the apex of organisational management.

Women are not only poorly represented in management positions but where they are to be found in management their role tends to be in what is commonly referred to as the 'softer' aspects of business – those which are traditionally considered to be within the 'female framework'. Examples here would be in human resource management, retailing, and customer services.

Inhibiting factors in the development of women managers

The seminal study in the UK in this area was commissioned by the Ashbridge Management College in 1980. This research emphasised a number of key factors which hindered women from becoming managers at the apex of an organisation. Table 10.3 highlights these.

The Ashbridge Management College (1980) report brought about a plethora of other studies in the field, the results of which tended to confirm the original findings. Key works reported were:

- Davidson (1984). This study offered a comprehensive list of factors which she suggested assisted in generating negative stress in women managers.
- Wentling (1992). This study reported that there were employers who refused to encourage the development of women managers and who strongly believed that

women lacked sufficient comprehension of political issues – in an organisational sense.

- Grondin (1990). This writer undertook a study on the issue of misperceptions about career opportunities which tended to keep women from progressing.
- Flanders (1994). This study highlighted a number of factors which kept women from senior management. Some of these were:
  - traditional work patterns
  - existing negative attitudes and prejudices
  - lack of positive role models
  - exclusion from the 'old boy network'.

Table 10.3 Key inhibitors to the development of women managers, after the Ashbridge Management Report (1980)

INHIBITOR	EXPLANATIVES
Career and personal factors	The career pathways to management were designed to suit men because they were based on traditional working patterns. For example, job mobility and commitment to full-time study in the early years of a career were designed to suit men. Many women were discriminated against in this design because it was necessary for them to take career breaks in order to raise a family. Women are still discriminated against in some selection and recruitment practices and also through the appraisal systems adopted within organisations. Examples here are when requests for specific qualifications are made but it was difficult for women to gain such qualifications in their early career years (e.g. career breaks inhibited this). Also, when women re-enter the workforce some organisations do not offer re-entry assistance and women usually have to start once again at the bottom of the career ladder.
Women's attitude and behaviour	Women exhibited a lack of confidence in their perceived ability with an accompanying belief that it was only the holding of formal qualifications that was required for career enhancement. They did not see that their skills were transferable to the workplace.
Attitudes of senior executives	Because of the paternal attitude of senior managers – men – women tended to be concentrated into jobs that men felt would be suitable for them. For example, personnel issues and contacts with customers.
Individual and organisational	There was a significant amount of prejudice against women as senior managers since men saw women as a threat to their positions and made assumptions that women were not as capable as men. Organisations with poor development systems were particularly concerned here in inhibiting the growth of women in management.

The development of women managers

In her work Davidson (1991) highlighted the fact that any organisation which did not take advantage of the availability of women in the labour force at management level was heading towards economic suicide. Apart from the economic issues, there were demographic reasons why women needed to be encouraged to develop their managerial skills to a high level – trends indicated that the availability of men for such roles was decreasing. Apart from the economic and demographic reasons for developing women managers there were other reasons for doing so. Fritchie and Pedler (1984) provided an extensive list of them and stated that there were potential benefits in having senior women managers. They included the participative nature of women and the caring styles they exhibited in the workplace.

Davidson (1991) went on to argue that the main step that organisations can take is to encourage all their managers, regardless of gender, to recognise the masculine/feminine strengths of all individuals and to build them into the management education and development programmes of the organisation. She also went on to say:

> ... when comparing male and female managers in terms of managerial efficiency and performance, numerous cross-cultural studies and reviews have concluded that there are far more similarities than differences. (p. 8)

Such a view has led to a cross-cultural perspective of management where managers are trained to recognise each other's differences – regardless of gender – and practise continuous self-development so that the organisation may more effectively reach its goals. Work in this field has been carried out by Fischer and Gleigm (1992) and Whitaker and Megginson (1992).

For the purpose of this discussion it is necessary to accept the principle that the tasks addressed by male and female managers are similar yet female managers face specific difficulties that are not faced by men. If this premise is accepted, then there is practical help available which will assist women to become integrated into the management career pathway. There are a number of ways in which women can be assisted; these are given in Table 10.4 below, although this list is not exhaustive.

Table 10.4 Practical ways of assisting women managers

- Integrating women's development into mainstream Human Resource Development
- Mentoring/providing role models
- Reviewing childcare provision
- Reviewing equal opportunities policies
- Auditing attitudes towards women
- Providing women-only training
- Encouraging women into management education
- Putting equality on the organisational agenda
- Reviewing selection/promotion/appraisal processes
- Promoting the network of women
- Assertiveness training
- Moving women out of the 'ghetto' into front-line positions
- Career planning strategies for women
- Training before promotion

Times have changed and women are now moving steadily into senior management levels. However, it is still necessary to consider factors which will enable them to gain equality and make up for the discrimination of past years. Some organisations are aware of this and do all they can to help women to compete on the same footing as their male colleagues. The key area of improvement has been in the area of networking and socialisation. Nowadays companies often employ some simple solutions for some difficulties; for example, bringing end-of-meeting refreshments into the conference room so that all managers can participate in the follow-up session – in the past the men used to decamp to the bar where women sometimes felt uncomfortable. Also hosting dinners in the conference centre can also assist in keeping all managers involved after the formal meeting. As the number of women in the workforce is increasing and more are gaining entry to the apex of the business, their different attitudes, backgrounds, and capabilities are becoming absorbed into the organisational culture.

Management and leadership

The term 'management' implies 'leadership', yet they are not the same – the success or failure of managers will depend upon their individual leadership qualities. The key focus here is on the ability of the manager to interact effectively with others. Proficiency in such skills will enable the manager to direct subordinates and guide and control their activities; and get them to accept direction and take initiative. It is through leadership that managers convince subordinates to follow rules and procedures as well as to accept changes. It is also through being a skilled leader that managers motivate others to develop their own ideas as well as to support those of their manager – there is no leadership without followership.

In order to act as a leader a manager requires appropriate authority to motivate subordinates, assign tasks, and enforce accountability from employees. Without leadership skills managers might well find that decisions and plans which are dependent upon the actions of others may never be implemented and that the organisation's objectives are not being met.

The leadership role and organisational design

As organisations flatten their structures, they face the challenge of finding new ways of leading and managing their employees: either as department leaders or leaders of small work teams – including self-directed teams. Problems occur when these subordinates are under-managed so that accountability is unclear, or decisions are forced through by those who speak loudest rather than on merit; problems also occur when subordinates are over-managed, so that employee responsibility and creativity are reduced. It is only through mastering the human touch that managers can enhance their ability to lead and thus, through self-knowledge, communicate better with other people in pursuit and attainment of organisational goals in times of difficulty and in times of growth.

Models of management

Most debates about management concern extreme positions; and models of management are linked closely to the manager's function as a leader – in particular, McGregor (1981) and his Theory X and Theory Y motivational approach, which was discussed in Chapter 4. This model is also used to look at the beliefs of managers. However, it is important that managers remember that such a model gives the extremes and that most managers fall somewhere between the two.

McGregor (1981) identified sets of beliefs as Theory X (basically negative) and Theory Y (basically positive) using X and Y to avoid value-laden labels. During his study McGregor observed the way that managers dealt with their subordinates and concluded that managers' views of the nature of human beings are based on a certain grouping of assumptions and that they tend to mould their behaviour towards subordinates according to these assumptions.

Assumptions held by managers under Theory X

- It is natural for employees to dislike work and they will do anything possible to avoid it.
- If the above principle is true, then subordinates need to be controlled and coerced into working and be threatened with punishment if they do not.
- Employees will always shirk responsibility and avoid the use of initiative, working only to orders from superiors.
- Subordinates have little ambition and are only interested in their security.

Assumptions held by managers under Theory Y

- Work is as much a part of life as rest and play.
- When committed to the organisation's objectives employees will exercise self-direction and self-control.
- Most employees seek responsibility.
- Subordinates show signs of innovation.

Consequences of Theory X and Theory Y

The consequences of Theory X have been the bane of businesses and organisations since it emerged into general management literature in the 1980s. When Theory X is adopted it can bring about a number of responses:

- The lower echelons of management are loath to make exceptions to the rules and regulations even when the alternative is just as effective.
  Example. A supervisor does not allow a subordinate access to the stock cupboard even though such access will result in a job being completed ahead of schedule.

- Rules are set up to attain certain objectives, yet the routine action supports the rules rather than an underlying principle.
  Example. The lunch break for office staff is from 1300 to 1400 even though a flexible lunch break period would mean that the department would always be manned.

- Individuals have no chance of self-actualising.
  Example. When tasks and their components are prescribed it leaves little opportunity for individuals to use their abilities to the full.

- When management is bureaucratic and ordered by rules and regulations, innovation is stifled and productivity is thereby decreased.
  Example. The concentration by individuals on rules and regulations means that they cannot make decisions concerning their own job performance.

If Theory Y is utilised the results might be:

- The lower levels of management concentrate on achievement of organisational objectives. Exceptions to the rule are supported when they increase productivity.
- When individuals work to routine this supports management objectives.

- When the subordinate is allowed to participate in decision-making this can increase motivation.
- Initiative and innovation increase productivity.

Hannagan (1995) developed a model (Figure 10.8) which showed the work of McGregor (1981).

MODERN		TRADITIONAL	
Theory Y	Participation Co-operation	Control Direction	Theory X
Work is natural	Communication Creativity	Orders Security	*Work is a necessity*

Figure 10.8 Management models based on Theory X and Theory Y, after Hannagan (1995, p. 40)

Management and decision-making

Decision-making is one of the most important – if not *the* most important – of all managerial activities. Decisions range from the most basic and routine to the sophisticated and out-of-the-usual. At whatever level, the results of decisions made by managers will affect members of the workforce: individually and collectively. Whether it is a high or low level decision, managers need to appreciate that they still need to make a choice which will result in the most appropriate course of action.

Decision-making is the process by which managers identify problems and make an attempt to resolve them. Managers have to make decisions all the time and the degree of difficulty will depend upon their position in the management hierarchy of the organisation and the level of responsibility which they have: it is about reaching conclusions to issues where there is a choice of action. It is important that managers make the correct decision because a poor decision can affect the flow of work and thus stifle the meeting of the organisation's objectives.

Managers who are identified as being competent are so because of their ability to make effective decisions. They may not always make the correct decision but they do know how to bring into play their knowledge of how people behave in organisations, they have an understanding of effective communication and, particularly, they are able to select appropriate decision-making strategies to increase the chance of success.

Models of decision-making

Managers think and reason before they act and because of this it is beneficial for managers, and others, to understand how the decision-making process works so that managers can explain and predict others' behaviour – the basis of organisational behaviour and the management of people within organisations. Since every decision requires interpretation and evaluation of information, data is received from a multiplicity of sources and it needs to be screened, processed, and interpreted – particularly in an organisational environment which increasingly uses technology and information processing systems. Managers will make their decisions either as individuals or as a member of a group (it is important to remember that individuals make decisions – even as a member of a group) and models of decision-making can help support the manager in effective decision-making: bringing a current problem state of affairs into line with a satisfactory state of affairs. Whether working individually or as a member of a group, the manager has to make an individual decision even if that decision might be affected by the decisions made by others within the group. Whatever the situation, the initial process is that of individual decision-making. There are a number of models of decision-making which may help the manager:

- observable and measurable
- optimising
- satisficing/bounded rationality
- implicit favourite.

Observable and measurable

Effective managers make their decisions as a result of experience through which they have observed and measured behaviours and the outcomes of previously made decisions. They do so in the same way as Kolb (1974) believes that individuals learn. As a result of studies he carried out in organisations, Kolb (1974) suggests that are four stages in influencing how people learn: the experience; observation and reflection; theorising and conceptualisation; testing and experimentation. To be effective the manager has corresponding needs made up of four different but complementary kinds of abilities, which Kolb (1974) illustrated as the model in Figure 10.9.

Decision-making is very much aligned to the model of learning propounded by Kolb (1974): it is a cyclical activity. Indeed, most management activities require the individual to use the model of learning. A basic model of decision-making requires observable and measurable behaviours and is best illustrated by a comparison with Kolb's (1974) model of learning – see Table 10.5.

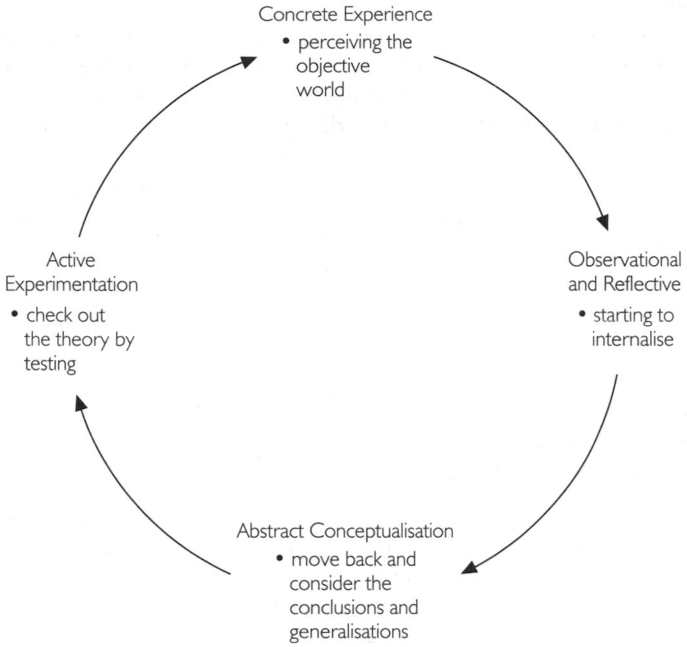

Figure 10.9 The learning cycle, after Kolb (1974)

Table 10.5 The process of decision-making as it relates to Kolb's (1974) model of learning

Kolb (1974)	**Observable and measurable decision-making model**
Concrete experience	Identifying problems
Observation and reflection	Generating alternatives and evaluating alternatives
Formation of abstract concepts and generalisations	Reaching decisions
Testing implications of concepts in new situations	Choosing implementation strategies

There are a number of models available to managers including:

- optimising model
- satisficing/bounded rationality model
- implicit favourite model
- management science approach
- Carnegie model
- incremental decision process model
- garbage can model
- contingency framework.

Optimising model

The optimising model is useful only when managers have to make a very simple decision which gives them very few alternative courses of action and which does not require the use of expensive resources such as time. It is limited in its application but it does give a basic foundation to the other, more complex, decision-making models. The optimising model provides a pattern of behaviour as the title indicates: it describes how individuals should behave in order to maximise a stated outcome. It requires managers to follow a number of graded stages, either explicitly or implicitly, when they make a decision and it can be seen how it relates to the process of learning and observing and measuring behaviour. Using this model the manager would:

- determine the need for the decision;
- identify the criteria against which the decision is to be made;
- rank the criteria;
- cultivate the alternatives;
- evaluate the alternatives;
- choose the best of the alternatives.

The optimising model is simple in that it does make some assumptions, not least of which is that of *rationality* because it assumes that the choices which will be made will be consistent and will provide added value. However, because managers are human beings it cannot be assumed that they will make rational decisions and the assumptions inherent in the concept of rationality (and hence the optimising model) need to be identified:

- **the goal of the decision is commonly accepted** and such a single, commonly accepted goal will not encourage dysfunctional conflict;
- **all the alternatives are known** and so there are no hidden difficulties which could affect the quality of the final decision;
- **all the alternatives are identifiable** so that they can be ranked;
- **all the alternatives are constant** and can therefore be stable over time;
- **the final decision will give added value** – the manager will choose the alternative which is ranked the highest and which will thus give the greatest benefit.

It can be seen that organisations, like life in general, do not offer situations where decisions are simple and thus the optimising model is limited in its usefulness. However, it does form the foundation of the more complex decision-making models available to a manager in today's complex organisations.

Satisficing/bounded rationality model

Since managers are more often faced with complex problems, their decisions will require them to reduce the problem to a level which can be understood and coped with. It is not possible for a human being to assimilate and understand all the information necessary for optimisation. In breaking down the component parts of a complex issue, the manager operates within the framework of *bounded rationality* and constructs simple models which contain the key features of the problem without engaging all the complexity of it. By doing so the manager can then act rationally within the limits of the now basic model. The notion of 'bounded rationality' was initially developed as a descriptor of reality rather than as a prescription for actions. The process that the manager will follow can be identified as:

- **identify the problem** by ascertaining what the need is for a decision;
- **simplify the problem** by using bounded rationality;

- **decide on the minimum standards required**, i.e. set the satisficing alternatives;
- **identify a framework of alternatives;**
- **compare the alternatives, in turn, against all the other alternatives** until all alternatives have been considered;
- **decide whether a satisficing alternative is present** – satisficing means that the manager will make a decision which is satisfactory rather than one which will result in a maximum level of performance;
- **if it is not present** search the alternatives for another alternative (and continue to do so until one is found);
- **select the satisficing choice**, i.e. the one that is the first 'good enough' choice.

Implicit favourite model

Like the satisficing model, the implicit favourite model is based on the idea that individuals solve problems by simplifying the process. However, the implicit favourite model differs in that the manager does not evaluate the alternatives until he has identified one of the alternatives as his 'favourite' choice. The procedure is as follows:

- **identify the problem** by ascertaining what the need is for a decision;
- **choose the implicit favourite** by selecting the alternative which is favoured;
- **identify the alternatives** to the favourite one chosen;
- **decide on the best choice;**
- **choose between the favourite and the best of the alternatives** selected above;
- **compare the choice** against the decision criteria that are biased towards the favourite;
- **select the implicit favourite.**

It is usual that the implicit favourite, even when compared against the alternative, is the final choice made by the manager. Consequently, it can be seen that the implicit favourite model is a competent and speedy decision-making model for the manager to use. However, it can also be noted that when a manager makes a decision it relies on rationality and so it is very important that the manager is seen to make decisions in a way which is perceived by others to be rational. In the implicit favourite model, the manager will develop a second-runner because it reassures him that he is seeking to be rational and reduces the subjectivity in that he has alternatives available.

Management science approach

This form of decision-making can be utilised when it is possible to analyse problems and when the variables involved can be easily identifiable and measured. This is usually carried out by means of mathematical models. Examples of use here would be for test marketing of a new product, drilling for oil or finding the right spot to build a new university campus.

Carnegie model

This decision-making model is based upon work done by researchers Cyert, March and Simon (1963), who were associated with the Carnegie-Mellon University. It is based on the assumption that building agreement through a managerial coalition is part of organisational decision-making. It takes time to discuss and bargain, so the search procedures in the making of decisions are usually simple and the chosen alternative satisfices rather than optimises problem solution. When the problem has been seen before, the organisation will rely on any previous procedures and rules in order to solve it. Daft (1995) summarises the Carnegie model as in Figure 10.10 below.

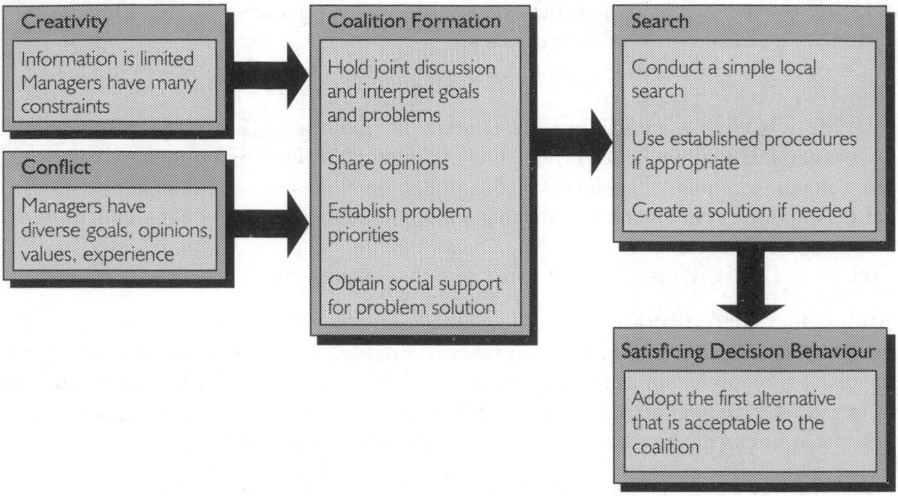

Figure 10.10 Choice processes in the Carnegie model, after Daft (1995, p. 374)

Incremental decision process model

Mintzberg (1976) identified twenty-five decisions made in organisations and proceeded to track the events associated with the decisions from start to finish. By doing so he identified each step in the decision sequence and it was, therefore, called the *incremental decision process model*. As a model of decision-making it concentrates on the sequence of activities from the identification of the problem to its potential solution. He discovered that the choices made by organisations are normally made in small stages rather than in one large decision. That is, organisations move through several decisions and may well hit problems on the way – called, by Mintzberg (1976), *decision interrupts*. This may result in the organisation having to return to the result of a previous decision and trying something new. Such decision loops, or cycles, offer a way by which organisations can learn which alternatives are likely to be more successful than others.

Garbage can model

When agreement cannot be reached the manager, as decision maker, is faced with uncertainty and ambiguity. In such circumstances the garbage can model can be used to best describe the organisational decision-making process as it occurs in organisations. It does not compare well with other models of decision-making since it concerns the pattern or flow of multiple decisions within organisations. The incremental and Carnegie models concentrate on how a single decision is made whilst the garbage can model helps the management to think of the organisation holistically and to consider the frequency of decisions being made by managers. As the name suggests, it is a random decision-making process and some organisations seem to have more than their fair share of this type of decision-making. Both Daft (1995) and Hatch (1997) use the university as an example of such an organisation, as did March (1958). He described universities as organisations which made decisions in a chaotic manner. Hatch (1997) defines this model as when:

> ... problems, solutions, participants, and choice opportunities are independent

> streams of events that flow into and through organisations, much like random selection of waste gets mixed together in a garbage can. (p. 278)

Since the process is random it means that there is an element of change and some choices may not solve the problem or, indeed, may make other problems.

Contingency framework
There are many models of decision-making because there are many situations in which the need for a decision appears – decision-making is situational and contingent upon the organisational setting.

Managers have a choice of models for decision-making and very few lack complexity which is why managers seek to find solutions which do not just optimise but satisfice, by considering their beliefs in the decision-making process. In this way managers can explain and predict the behaviour of themselves and others rather than appear to be making arbitrary and irrational decisions. However, as exemplified in the above models, most organisational decisions are not carried out in a logical or rational manner. Whilst decision-making models can help, most decisions are made in an atmosphere of chaos and are characterised by dysfunctional conflict, haste and errors. Because of such constraints, managers tend to make decisions based on intuition acting through a social process.

Managing management: frustration and stress

Some commentators believe that stress is a fashionable way of 'swinging the lead', others report that their research indicates that a certain amount of tension at work is healthy. However, too high a level of stress is negative and with it the objectives of the individuals and, therefore, the organisation will not be met. A key point related to stress in the workplace is that stress, like change, is self-perpetuating; so raising the awareness of frustration and stress could well result in negative stress for the manager. However, there is no doubt that workplace stress is a part of the life of a manager today; apart from having to cope with the intricacies of managing people in the workplace the manager has to operate in a complex environment which is being made ever more complicated by increased globalisation, work diversity, technological innovation and ethical factors. A consideration of frustration and stress, therefore, can help to link all the factors related to the behaviour of people as employees in the workplace. Stress can also be seen as an excess of perceived demands over an individual's ability to meet them. With this in mind, The Institute of Management Foundation (1997) recommends that individuals need to:

- recognise the symptoms of stress;
- search out the sources of the pressure;
- identify coping strategies.

This is because:

> Successive waves of downsizing, closures and reorganisations [have] put pressure on managers and employees alike. Additionally, technological changes to improve the speed of communications ... have created twenty-four hour accessibility. This is a potential recipe for disaster. The detrimental effects of poorly managed pressures can be measured in terms of the cost to organisations and society as a whole. It has been estimated that 40 million working days or £7 billion are lost annually due to stress.

> The cost to individuals is less easy to measure but it affects the quality of life and relationships and can be enormous. (p. 1)

Whilst managers, as others in the workplace, dream of reducing the strain of the complex working environment by rest and leisure activities, the reality is that they are not able to do so – the result is frustration and stress.

Frustration

When a manager is unable to achieve her objectives because something hinders, disturbs or thwarts her progress she will become frustrated. Such barriers could be situational or environmental, thus they are external to the manager and beyond her control. An example of this could be a computer software assisted presentation which 'crashes' during a session. They could also be internal such as the tendency to talk incessantly when she is unable to carry out an activity or deal with a difficult person. It is an individual condition which is based on individual perception and not on the external environment, as is often believed.

As was seen earlier when discussing aspects of motivation, needs are not always satisfied. As a result frustration, accompanied by tension, occurs. This is an increasing phenomenon as the complexity of the work environment and the demands made upon individuals within it result in more barriers being raised to frustrate personal ambition (the move to leaner and flatter organisations and its effect on promotion opportunities). Lack of knowledge and of continuous development opportunities (the technological revolution) also frustrates individuals. A young person who has career goals that require a university education but who lacks the intellectual aptitude for university work has overestimated her abilities. It applies also to a manager already on the career ladder in that she may be capable of carrying out the job specification but she has erected an individual barrier by undermining her own self-esteem. Individuals at work continually strive to achieve personal goals and are frequently frustrated by such internal factors as well as by external barriers erected by the organisation design and its environment. It should be remembered that the organisation is not composed of bricks and mortar, but people, and it is the actions of others that can frustrate the achievement of personal goals. For example, a manager who wants to ensure that a report gets to the CEO swiftly, could well be frustrated because the finance department has not provided the financial analysis required to accompany the report. Most on-the-job frustrations tend to result from dysfunctional conflict related to the dynamics of organisations and the restraints of organisational practices. As an organisation comprising human beings attempts to meet the needs of individual employees, there is a move from externalising to internalising individual needs.

In much the same way as conflict, frustration can be perceived as dysfunctional and it is in this state that individuals allow it to affect them. Managers need to appreciate that frustration can be functional and can be used to help them achieve personal and organisational objectives by means of:

- *Strengthening effort.* Sometimes frustration can act as a catalyst which stimulates the effect required to achieve the required objective. However, as was discussed in the chapter on motivation the goals must be achievable by a recognised procedure. If the latter is not provided, frustration could lead to the abandonment of the initial goal, which will be replaced by another which is seen to be achievable.

- *Evaluating other methods.* When a person is frustrated a common action is to choose a different method of achieving the desired objective. When tension is increased because a barrier (internal or external) cannot be eliminated, then the manager will find an alternative objective. For example, if the manager wants to achieve a high-quality report but the financial department does not provide the relevant information, he may well decide to do the research into the financial matters himself.
- *Trying another objective.* When frustrated a manager could choose a different objective which he knows he can achieve. Such a change in direction is very often attractive because he cannot remove the perceived barriers to his initial goal.

However, it is not always possible for a manager to eliminate the barriers which block the achievement of personal or organisational objectives. Whether these are real or not is irrelevant – they *are perceived as real to the individual.* In such a case the tension and frustration might well reach such a high level that the effects of it disrupt objective-directed activities. At this stage an individual usually becomes highly emotional and thus loses the ability to make rational decisions or deal positively with the situation. For example, when a manager has been working hard towards an attainable objective and finds that such work results in frustration, she may become emotional and actually cause physical and psychological damage to herself and others in the process. It is therefore vital that frustration is avoided, yet, as has been mentioned, a certain level of frustration and tension can act as a springboard to effective achievement of objectives. The level of frustration an individual can control is a matter of individual toleration, some people being able to tolerate high levels of frustration and others not so much. Some management tasks involve more pressure than others but all managers must be able to tolerate some frustration. Managers need to be able to recognise in themselves and in their colleagues and subordinates when a tolerance level has been exceeded and this is usually exhibited by the onset of aggressive behaviours and/or a withdrawal from the situation through stress behaviours and depression.

Stress management

Occupational health and organisational effectiveness are closely aligned and it is in the interest of the employer and employee that the workforce is in good health. The Institute of Personnel and Development (IPD) (1996) issued a keynote statement with a viewpoint, based on field research, which highlighted their belief that stress in the workplace has to be properly managed if it is to be controlled. They believe that:

- people work more effectively within a participative management style;
- people are better motivated when work satisfies economic, social and psychological needs;
- motivation improves if attention is paid to job design and work organisation. (p. 1)

In the same document the IPD addressed stress in a work setting, stating that it had become one of the principal health issues of the twentieth century. The point was made that stress was more common among manual workers than managers. With the flatter organisational structure has come increased pressure for the organisation to remain competitive in a globalised market. Change should make them more flexible and the combination of both places the workforce under considerable stress. The IPD (1996) acknowledges the fact that it is not always possible to prevent stress associated with job insecurity, but employers should be able to monitor and control the known causes of stress, which are:

- autocratic and erratic management
- ineffective communication processes
- overwork
- lack of autonomy over work practices.

The Health and Safety Executive recognises that occupational stress is within their remit and managers should appreciate this factor as well since guidance can be obtained from the Executive. In order to alleviate occupational stress a problem-solving approach needs to be adopted. Such an approach should take into account other key organisational concepts such as the culture of the organisation, individual circumstances and personality and the work itself.

There is a significant amount of literature available about occupational stress. However, it is vital that employers and managers – particularly those responsible for human resources development within the organisation – recognise that their responsibility stops with an appreciation of the relevant factors associated with stress and its management and that they are not qualified to intervene in cases of serious disorder or potential disorder. Such workers should be referred to the relevant practitioners through the organisation's occupational health system.

Recognising occupational stress

Arnold *et al.* (1997) define stress as: '... any force that pushes a psychological or physical factor beyond its range of stability, producing a strain within the individual' (p. 359).

It can be described as any experience which is unpleasant which either over- or under-stimulates an individual and which, in turn, has the potential to lead to ill-health. Additionally, individuals can feel threatened by knowing that stress constitutes a threat to them. Cummings and Cooper (1979) summarised a way of understanding stress in their schema shown in Figure 10.11.

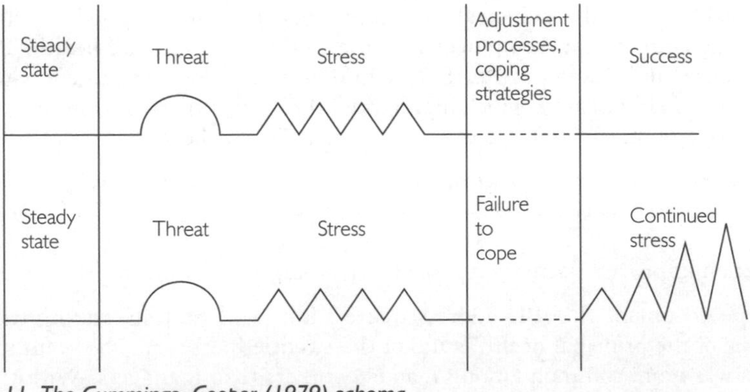

Figure 10.11 The Cummings–Cooper (1979) schema

Organisational effects of stress

Individuals exhibiting high stress within the workplace will affect the organisation and the achievement of organisational goals. There are four key areas where the consequences of high stress can be exhibited:

- *physical*: headaches, chronic indigestion, tiredness, ulcers, heart attacks;
- *psychological*: anxiety, chronic depression, aggression and bullying, low self-esteem;
- *behavioural*: eating disorders, abuse of drugs including nicotine and alcohol, emotional outbursts, sleeplessness;
- *organisational*: absenteeism, job-turnover, accidents, dysfunctional conflict, low productivity.

Occupational stress is a dynamic force which interacts with a number of key organisational issues. Arnold *et al.* (1997) identify five categories which are found to be causally responsible for work stress and common to all jobs:

- factors intrinsic to the job
- organisational role of the individual
- work relationships
- career development
- organisational structure and climate.

Arnold (1997) and his co-writers devised a model to explain the interaction of the above factors.

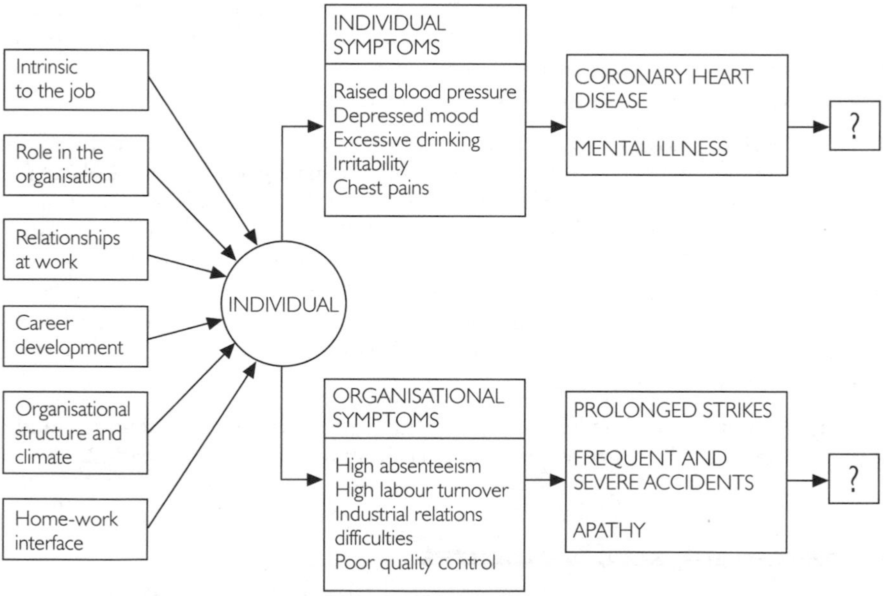

Figure 10.12 The dynamics of occupational stress, after Arnold et al. (1997)

Controlling stress

In order to control stress it is desirable for individuals to identify what is a bearable level of stress for them. Therefore, managers need to appreciate that they and their subordinates can each cope with differing levels of tension. As mentioned above, the control of stress should be placed in the hands of professionals. However, there are some basic strategies managers can use to control stress by controlling their individual behaviour. Such strategies include:

- avoidance of high-pressure situations;
- managing situations in such a way that tension and frustration is controlled;
- reacting to potential stress areas less intensely.

Managers should attempt to minimise stress in organisations and should understand that the effectiveness of any specific action will depend on the situational factors and the nature of the individuals involved. As mentioned above, a certain amount of tension and frustration can be positive yet managers can provide the foundations for aiding stress reduction by:

- aiding subordinates to recognise and analyse the sources of occupational stress;
- making informational material available to employees;
- providing professional counselling;
- offering stress-management training;
- listening to what employees say rather than superficially hearing them;
- avoiding telling the subordinate what to do.

Regardless of the tools available to managers, they should not try to practise psychotherapy or psychiatry unless they are qualified to do so. As in all organisational contexts, managers should only deal with areas in which they are competent, which are usually work-centred decision-making and problem-solving. Unfortunately, particularly in a large organisation, senior managers get so far removed from the front line that they have no idea of the impact of their decisions on their workforce.

Managers need to reassess their attitudes to work practices and understand the importance of organisational behaviour and how people are managed in the workplace. People need to perceive that they have a say over what they do and when they do it and that being told what to do all the time can be destructive. Positive stress programmes in the workplace can assist but senior management must be committed to them, no matter what level of staff they are eventually provided for. There are dire consequences for firms which choose not to reassess their negative attitudes towards workplace stress because it will show up in the form of lack of co-operation, less creativity, lower productivity, high turnover or employees not meeting their targets.

The way forward is to look at human relationships in the workplace and understand that employees are individuals and work more effectively in very different ways.

Management across cultures

The concept of organisational culture has been discussed in the previous chapter and variously throughout the text. This is because it is a key feature in organisations since the globalisation of business has brought about the impact of national cultures onto the domestic work scene. The UK, like most Western societies, is now multicultural and therefore within the workplace setting and outside it, individuals need to be able to cope with differing value systems and ways of behaving. All managers need to appreciate this factor – not just those who specifically work in a multinational setting.

Culture strongly influences the behaviour of managers – like others in society, they have to adopt the specific values, beliefs, traditions and standards of acceptable behaviour. Individuals tend to adhere to their own cultural heritage even when they are living and working outside their own country of origin. Second and subsequent generations of such individuals rapidly adapt to new cultures whereas their parents are often reluctant to change. Organisations mirror the outside society and thus managers also have to cope with such an issue.

The UK population comprises a number of different races and ethnicities, each of which creates its own sub-culture. As a result, there is a society full of bi-cultural (or even tri-cultural) individuals. Members of the African-British, Irish, Asian-British and other sub-cultures, for example, may adhere to beliefs, values and customs which are drawn from their racial, religious and ethnic backgrounds. Depending upon their degree of *acculturation* (the degree to which they identify with the dominant UK culture) some of these individuals operate in two cultures and adopt the behaviours suitable to the culture they are operating in. It is no different in an organisation where there is increasing workforce diversity in operation. *Ethnic identification* (the degree to which the individual identifies with the sub-culture) and acculturation have an inverse relationship. The higher the degree of ethnic identification, the lower the degree of acculturation and vice versa.

There are numerous factors which influence fundamental human behaviour. Managers must always remember that each member of the workforce is unique. That is, each one is different from their co-workers and, by the same token, each manager is different from their colleagues. However, there is a degree of difference because each difference is influenced by a number of complex interactions of forces, and each recognises similarities to others as well as differences. Table 10.6 summarises some of the major influences on human behaviour.

Table 10.6 Factors affecting individual behaviour

INFLUENCES	BEHAVIOUR
Physiological	General physical condition, age, gender and related factors. Also includes the central nervous system, blood composition, hormonal balance, absence or presence of diseases.
Learning	A change in behaviour due to experience which is encouraged by life-long exposure to all kinds of perceptions, rewards, punishments, environments and inter-relationships. Can also be as a result of training and development programmes.
Cognitive	This is individual thinking through which individuals decide to make changes throughout their lives. They will accept or reject information as well as evaluate what is presented to them in the form of rewards, expectations and values. Behaviour will depend upon each individual's locus of control.
Socio-biological	This is the nurture versus nature issue where what is learned (or not learned), what can or cannot be done, and the choices made by individuals are determined to a large extent by genetic characteristics. However, they can be adapted through an individual's environment.
Cultural	An individual's values and beliefs are very strong and depend upon the traditions of the society in which the individual is nurtured. Actions tend to be similar to those of each individual's group or society.

Since organisations are microcosms of society, a manager must be able, therefore, to manage a culturally diverse workforce. Jamieson and O'Mara (1991) believed that the key watchword for managing a culturally diverse workforce is the ability to be flexible. Through this flexibility and adaptability a manager can make any needed adjustments and individualise the treatment of the workforce rather than treat them collectively. They also suggested a model of diversity management which is based on accommodating differences and giving choices by adopting organisational policies, systems, and practices. Managers can thus adopt specific actions for managing diversity which include those specified in Table 10.7 below.

Table 10.7 Specific actions for managing diversity

SPECIFIC ACTION	DESCRIPTOR
Avoid stereotypical behaviour	Desist from making decisions and taking action which is based on stereotypes. Identify the preferences, rewards, and opportunities each individual owns and assign tasks accordingly.
Share information	Ensure that all members of the workforce have the same information concerning the organisational culture and other unwritten rules and regulations which they need in order to meet their objectives.
Provide necessary support systems	Individuals will succeed or fail depending upon the support given to them. Such systems as mentoring, coaching, training and development, can make a difference. Individuals need guidance in order to work effectively.
Examine processes	Constantly review organisational practices, culture, traditions, structure, design and other factors which could be significant to the employee's understanding of workforce diversity.

Managing for effectiveness

Management has its consequences for the organisation and its workforce – that is, management has outcomes and thus management can be seen as a transformation process. Figure 10.13 shows three basic levels of outcomes which will determine the effectiveness of any organisation at such levels:

- individual
- groups/teams
- organisation.

INDIVIDUAL LEVEL, OUTCOMES	GROUP/TEAM OUTCOMES	ORGANISATION LEVEL OUTCOMES
Productivity	Productvity	Productivity
Performance	Performance	Absenteeism
Absenteeism	Norms	Turnover
Turnover	Cohesiveness	Financial performance
Attitudes	Financial performance	
Workplace stress	Survival	
	Constituent satisfaction	

ORGANISATIONAL EFFECTIVENESS

Figure 10.13 Managing for effectiveness

Managers have to balance the above concepts optimally at all levels if they are to be effective in helping the workforce to meet the organisational objectives.

The future of management

But what of the future of management and its relationship to the management of people and organisations? Goffee and Hunt (1996) believe that although there are visions for the future, the hierarchical structures of organisations will persist since they are one of the most effective ways to manage resources, and that managers will be: '... employed to allocate resources and to create the conditions under which people are motivated to perform' (p. 4).

However, they do state that such hierarchical organisations will segment into flatter structures and thus the economies of scale argument will be increasingly balanced by the diseconomies of scale argument of the social scientists. This is better illustrated by saying that there are clear advantages in collecting more than 500 people in one location. Goffee and Hunt (1996) believe that there are, in this context, several changes in the selection, development, and reward of managers:

- feedback assessments will put a price on effectiveness in the management of relationships as opposed to just the management of outputs;
- career managers will be selected for their managerial competencies and not just for their technical expertise;
- there will be far greater recognition that some competencies are genetic and are not easy to develop;
- coaching managers will become a growth industry;
- effective managers will be highly prized.

CASE STUDY

Managers are a necessary part of business

Many contemporary efforts to rewrite the organisational landscape seem to devalue the role of the manager. But the fundamental requirement for management remains: to allocate scarce resources, and to manage people and tasks. The important debate hinges not on whether the function is necessary but on how it is to be fulfilled. There are differences here between countries and types of company.

Researchers suggest that effective managers need four skill sets: an ability to reduce chunks of information into simple frameworks; a capacity to develop people and build teams; presentational and communication abilities; and motivation. Even the best are not good at all of these and will acknowledge that they need the help of others. Yet successful managers differentiate themselves from the rest through (among other things) force of personality and competence in the job. In future the management of relationships is likely to become more important, career managers will be selected for their managerial competences not just their technical expertise, and coaching will become an even bigger growth business. The time available to deliver results is shrinking dramatically.

Source: R. Goffee and J.W. Hunt, 'The end of management? Classroom versus the boardroom' in *Financial Times*, Mastering Management, Part 20, 22 March 1996, p. 4

As the above case shows, Goffee and Hunt (1996) move towards relationship management, yet this is confused by an influx of new management ideas as reported in the case below.

> **CASE STUDY**
> **Instant coffee as management theory**
>
> For success in the £13-billion-a-year management-consultancy business, find a fad. In recent years total quality, culture change, core competencies, organisational flattening, benchmarking, outsourcing and downsizing have all been touted as the sole path to corporate salvation. For all the hype, fad-based management usually fails to deliver. Quality programmes are launched with great fanfare, then fade away. Cutting management layers often disrupts internal communications and many companies – among them Compaq and Harley-Davidson – have found outsourcing so hard to manage that some previously subcontracted production is now back in-house.
>
> Hilmer and Donaldson (1997) argue that every fad leads managers down one or more of several 'false trails'. These include believing that ready-made techniques can solve any problem: taking action, any action (the 'ready, fire, aim' stance of Tom Peters and Robert Waterman); flattening every structure in sight; and constructing corporate culture based on happy families, not hierarchies. Hilmer and Donaldson (1997) concede that these trails lead to some useful ideas. The snag, however, is that managers tend to take their usefulness on trust. This has spawned what the duo calls 'instant coffee' management: just open the jar and add water, no effort required. Worse, any manager who fails to follow the latest fad – regardless of its relevance – risks being thought unprofessional.
>
> According to Spitzer and Evans (1997), faddism should be replaced with what they – a mite faddishly – term the 'thinking organisation'. They state that thinking management is the approach of some of the most successful companies of recent decades, such as Sony, Hewlett-Packard and Johnson & Johnson. These firms, say Spitzer and Evans (1997), understand that there is no competitive advantage to be gained simply by adopting the same fad or strategy as your competitors. Instead, they have consistently outclassed the 'critical thinking skills' of their rivals in everything from product development to distribution and marketing – all with barely a fad in sight.
>
> It has to be asked: could fadless management be the next management fad?
>
> Adapted from *The Economist*, 'Instant coffee as management theory', 25 January 1997, p. 83

Whilst many management fads merely trivialise the business of managing, and a school of thought is that managers should go back to basics, others such as Clausen (1997) have a different view to the above case.

It can be seen that by its very nature, management requires an understanding and appreciation of human behaviour in organisations – organisational behaviour. By understanding all aspects of such behaviour a manager can better appreciate how all members of the workplace – superiors, fellow managers, and subordinates – can best achieve their objectives. The manager's job can be characterised according to functions, skills and roles, the basic functions being planning, organising, leading, and controlling through interpersonal roles such as informational and decision-making roles.

CASE STUDY FOLLOW UP
Fashion victims

Sir, It is true that companies often handle fads in a way that trivialises management. Some companies need the equivalent of anti-virus software to protect their way of doing business from mindless pursuit of the latest fashion. But if we set aside firms that over-adopt innovations (and, probably, also do a lot of other silly things), fads can be a positive force.

There are two points in time when a new management idea has positive potential for a company. One is when the idea first surfaces, before it becomes a fad. At this point, innovative companies can examine it in relation to their own needs without risk of being misled by hype. This is a time when instincts encourage prudent, rational consideration. On the other hand, there may not be much information or outside help available.

Another opportunity occurs after an idea becomes a fad. By this time it has accumulated experts, followers, and paraphernalia that connect with seemingly everything that counts in corporate life. Now the 'idea' is full of itself, and quite insensitive to whether or not – or how – it may fit a particular firm's situation. But with hype there is excitement and energy, the same as for fashion in the world at large. And there is a great deal of information and outside help available: articles, books, workshops, conferences, consulting presentations, and so on. During this period, companies and their managers can easily, cheaply and energetically explore new ideas.

If a company's people are reasonably grounded – if they share a sense of direction, know their priorities, and recognise their strengths and weaknesses – each fad that sweeps across the management landscape presents a modest opportunity to reassess and fine-tune the organisation. And every so often the opportunity may be truly significant, a chance to shape important, transfiguring changes. All it takes is perspective. Without that, success is unlikely anyway.

Source: L. Wallace Clausen, 'Fashion victims', letter to *The Economist*, 8 February 1997, p. 6

Managers of today are faced with a number of challenges including workforce diversity, the globalised market and developments in, and management of, technology. They increasingly take on the roles of investigating the most effective corporate strategy and matching the human resources to such a strategy. An appreciation of managing organisations and people is complex because each concept has its own individual complexities and nuances; suffice it to say that an organisation will only be as successful as its members – regardless of their role.

Questions for discussion

1 What is the biggest competitive challenge facing managers today and will that change within the next five years?

2 Which model of decision-making do you think is most often used in organisations today and why?

3 How can a manager encourage employees to strike a balance between their intellectual capabilities and their emotional knowledge?

References and further reading

Arnold, J., Cooper, C.L. and Robertson, I.T., 1997 (2nd edn), *Work Psychology: Understanding Human Behaviour in the Workplace* (London: Pitman Publishing)

Ashbridge Management College, 1980, *Employee Potential: Issues in the Development of Women* (London: Institute of Personnel (now Institute of Personnel and Management))

Bennett, R., 1997 (3rd edn), *Organisational Behaviour* (London: Pitman)

Brech, E.F.L., 1975 (3rd edn) *Principles and Practice of Management* (London: Longman)

Caulkin, S., 'The Knowledge Within' in *Management Today*, August 1997, pp. 28-32

Clausen, L. Wallace, 'Fashion victims', letter to *The Economist*, 8 February 1997, p. 6

Cummings, T. and Cooper, C.L., 1979, 'A cybernetic framework for the study of occupational stress' in *Human Relations*, Vol. 32, pp. 395–419

Cyert, R.M. and March, J.G., 1963, *A Behavioral Theory of the Firm* (Englewood Cliffs, NJ: Prentice-Hall)

Czarniawska-Joerges, B., 1988, *Ideological control in nonideologcal organizations* (New York: Praeger)

Daft, R.L., 1995, *Organization Theory and Design* (St Paul, MN: West Publishing)

Davidson, M., 1991, 'Women managers in Britain: issues for the 1990s' in *Women in Management Review*, Vol. 6, No 1, pp. 5–10

Davidson, M. and Cooper, C., 1992, *Shattering the Glass Ceiling: The Woman Manager* (London: Paul Chapman)

Donkin, R., 'Value and rewards of brainpower' in *Financial Times*, 11 June 1997, p. 14

Drucker, P.F., 1979, *Management* (London: Pan Books)

Drucker, P.F., 1989, *The Practice of Management* (London: Heinemann)

Economist, The, 'Instant coffee as management theory', 25 January 1997, p. 83

Employee Potential: Issues in the Development of Women (Wimbledon, London: The Institute of Personnel (now The Institute of Personnel and Development))

Fischer, M. and Gleigm, H., 1992, 'The gender gap in management' in *Industrial and*

Commercial Training, Vol. 24, No 4, pp. 5–11

Flanders, M., 1994, *Breakthrough: The Career Women's Guide to Shattering the Glass Ceiling* (London: Paul Chapman Publishing)

Fritchie, R. and Pedlar, M., 1984, 'Training men to work with women' in V. Hammond (ed.), *Practical Approaches to Women's Management Development* (Brussels, European Foundation for Management Development)

Goffee, R. and Hunt, J.W., 'The end of management? Classroom versus the boardroom' in *Financial Times*, Mastering Management, Part 20, 22 March 1996, p. 4

Grondin, D., 1990, 'Developing women in management programmes: two steps forward and one step back' in *Women in Management Review*, Vol. 5, No 3, pp. 15–19

Hannagan, T., 1995, *Management Concepts and Practices* (London: Pitman Publishing)

Hatch, M.J., 1997, *Organization Theory: Modern Symbolic and Postmodern Perspectives* (Oxford: Oxford University Press)

Hilmer, F. and Donaldson, L., 1997, *Management Redeemed: Debunking the Fads that Undermine our Corporations* (Free Press)

Institute of Management, The, 'Stress Management: Self-First' in *Checklist 034* undated, issued January 1997 (Institute of Management Foundation: Corby)

Institute of Personnel and Development, 'Occupational Health and Organisational Effectiveness', Key Facts, September 1996, published 19 December 1996

Jamieson, D. and O'Mara J., 1991, *Managing workforce 2000* (San Francisco: Jossey-Bass)

Katz, R.L., 'The Skills of an Effective Administrator' in *Harvard Business Review*, September–October 1987, pp. 90–102

Kolb, D.A., 1974, 'On Management and the Learning Process' in D.A. Kolb and J.M. McIntyre (eds), *Organisational Psychology: A Book of Readings* (Englewood Cliffs, NJ: Prentice Hall)

The Making of British Managers (The Constable and McCormick Report) 1987 (London: The British Institute of Management)

The Making of British Managers: A Report on Management Education, Training and Development in the United States, West Germany, France, Japan and the UK (The Handy Report) 1987 (London: National Development Office)

March, J.G. and Simon, H.A., 1958, *Organizations* (New York: Wiley)

McGregor, D., 1981 (2nd edn), *The Human Side of Enterprise* (New York: McGraw-Hill)

Mintzberg, H., 'Planning on the Left Side and Managing on the Right', in *Harvard Business Review* 1976, p. 54

Mintzberg, H., 'The Manager's Job: Folklore and Fact' in *Harvard Business Review*, July–August 1975, pp. 49–61

Mukhtar, A., 'Women who make a difference', *Financial Times*, 18 February 1997, p. 13

Parker Follett, M., 1941, *Collected Works* (New York: Harper & Brothers)

Pedlar, M., Burgoyne, J. and Boydell, T., 1994 (3rd edn), *A Manager's Guide to Self-Development* (Maidenhead: McGraw-Hill)

Rawson, M., 'Whose side are you on?' in *Professional Manager*, November 1997, p. 3

Spitzer, Q, and Evans, R., 1997, *Heads You Win: How the Best Companies Think* (London: Simon & Schuster)

Summers, D., 'Get the best out of staff' in *Financial Times*, 7 July 1997, p. 8

Thompson, P. and McHugh, D., 1995 (2nd edn), *Work Organisations: A Critical Introduction* (Basingstoke: Macmillan)

Wentling, R.M., 1992, 'Women in middle management: their career development and aspirations' in *Business Horizons*, Vol. 35, No 1, pp. 47–54

Whitaker, V. and Megginson, D., 1992, 'Women and men working together effectively' in *Training and Development UK*, Vol. 11, No 11, pp. 16–18

Ethical issues

Learning objectives

After studying this section you should be able to:

- appreciate the importance of ethical management behaviour;
- understand the role of social responsibility;
- identify the importance of ethical issues as they relate to globalisation.

Since ethical behaviour is acting in ways that are consistent with one's personal values and the commonly held values of the organisation and society, they therefore underlie ethical behaviour in all aspects of one's life. Personal adjustment at work has been a major concern of management analysis for a number of years and is an increasing ethical dilemma for both employer and employee. Recently, greater attention has been paid to the causes of destructive forms of frustration and stress in the work environment. A major concern has been the need for a better understanding of the reactions of people in the work environment.

Conflict, frustration and stress affect individuals differently. What may be highly stressful to one person may be a source of either satisfaction or indifference to others. Not only does the perception of conditions affect the ability to cope successfully with stress, but the degree of tolerance of stress helps determine specific types of reactions. Many higher level managers seem to enjoy high-stress situations and see them as challenges, while others at lower levels in the organisation view the same conditions as major threats.

Stress is an inevitable result of work and personal life. Distress is not an inevitable consequence of stressful events, however; in fact, well-managed stress can improve health and performance. Managers need to learn how to create healthy stress for employees in an ethical way in order that performance may be facilitated and so that there is well-being without distress. Managers can help employees by adjusting work loads, being sensitive to diversity amongst individuals concerning what is stressful, being sensitive to employees' personal life demands, and by avoiding ethical dilemmas.

Managers should be sensitive to early signs of distress at work, such as employee fatigue or changes in work habits, in order to avoid serious forms of distress. The serious forms of distress include violent behaviour, psychological depression, and cardiovascular problems. Distress is important to the organisation because of the costs associated with turnover and absenteeism, as well as poor quality production.

Managers should also be aware of gender, personality and behavioural differences when analysing stress in the workplace. Men and women have different vulnerabilities when it comes to distress. Men, for example, are at greater risk of fatal disorders, and women are more vulnerable to non-fatal disorders, such as depression. Personality hardiness and self-reliance are helpful in managing stressful events.

Managers can use the principles and methods of preventable stress management with an awareness of what is ethical in order to create healthier work environments. They can practise several forms of individual stress prevention to create healthier lifestyles for themselves, and they can encourage employees to do the same. Large organisations can create healthier work forces through the implementation of comprehensive health promotion programmes. Setting a good example may be one of the best ethical principles that a manager can follow in order to influence employees when it comes to preventative stress management.

Since ethical behaviour is about an individual's perception and understanding of what is right or wrong, good or bad, it is an ethical dilemma for managers when they come to demand consistently high levels of performance from their employees, and similarly high standards from their employers.

CASE STUDY

Keeping them happy

When the piranhas are fed in the London offices of Bloomberg, a financial news organisation, they get into such a feeding frenzy that they absentmindedly start taking lumps out of one another.

Some personnel managers might think this bloody spectacle is an odd approach to relieving executive stress. But tanks full of tropical fish are becoming an increasingly fashionable way for businesses to keep staff and customers happy. Some restaurants and dentists' waiting rooms have always had tanks, of course. But Nick Lloyd of Aquatic Design, a company specialising in exotic fish tanks, reports that sales to offices are also booming. He has recently installed a huge tank in Hutchison Telecom's London office.

Other customers of Mr Lloyd, such Michael Bloomberg, are persuaded of the tranquillising effects of watching puffers, guppies, wrasse, blennies and angel fish conducting their territorial disputes around a mock South Sea coral island. Mr Bloomberg has installed hundreds of fish tanks around his fast-growing world-wide news empire. 'Our main asset is our people', he explains. 'It's important to keep them happy.'

Tranquillity may not be the only effect of a fish tank. Perhaps it is no accident that the most profitable unit at Bloomberg's offices in London is sited right next to the piranha tank. 'Occasionally there is a corpse, which can be upsetting', admits Chris Peterson, head of Bloomberg's marketing department. But usually the piranhas swallow their prey whole.

A tropical-fish tank is cheap compared with a boardroom Picasso. The average cost, complete with cabinet and all the filters, is about £3,000. Maintenance is not a job for amateurs. Light, heat and water quality have to be strictly controlled to protect the fish from (you guessed it) stress. Fortnightly maintenance visits cost about £25 per tank. Food (except for piranhas) comes in bite-size frozen pellets of shrimp, cockles, krill and algae.

Compatibility is a problem. There are thousands of different species, some costing hundreds of pounds for a single fish, but not all of them get on with one another. Try putting a Cardinal in with a Batfish and you will have a terrible fight. 'Bullying is a difficulty', admits Mr Lloyd. 'Marine fish, if they are not compatible, will fight to the death.' They should feel at home in most offices.

Source: 'Keeping them happy' in *The Economist*, 25 November 1995, p. 32

According to Pettinger (1996): 'Organisations are bodies or entities created for a stated purpose' (p. 1). The effectiveness and success of an organisation are not determined solely by the abilities and motivations of employees and managers. Nor is the effectiveness measured solely by how well groups and teams work together – although both individual and group processes are crucial for organisational success. In order to give direction and order to the activities and interactions within organisations, objectives, structures, systems and processes are created and developed.

One of the key issues facing organisations is that of global competition, which is now on an unprecedented scale. Whilst the principal players in the world's economy are international or multinational organisations, smaller organisations are still affected because the emergence of these global organisations creates pressures on them to redesign and, in turn, internationalise their operations. There is a global market for most products, but in order to compete effectively in it, organisations must transform their design, structures, operations and cultures.

However, whilst people in some quarters – including the government – believe that British industry is heading for a global renaissance, Heller (1996) states that: 'the hard facts reveal a large gap between rhetoric and reality' (p. 24). In order to remain competitive organisations can no longer shrug off the ethical aspects of their business.

CASE STUDY
A moral stance

Executives in one of the UK's biggest construction companies, faced with opposition by anti-road protesters over a road building contract, were challenged by their human resource director recently to consider their moral stance on roads.

Some saw no reason to have any standpoint. The company was not responsible for road-building policy, and simply built roads to order. The director then asked them: would the company build gas chambers? No, it would not, they said.

The construction company had, in effect, drawn an ethical line in the sand, with gas chambers on one side and roads on the other. These lines are constantly shifting, according to John Drummond, managing director of Integrity Works, a UK-based-business ethics consultancy which has recently been working with Shell International, the oil company, on the revision of its business principles.

Shell's principles were first framed about 20 years ago and were intended to address, in particular, the issue of taking and offering bribes. The revised principles, published this year, include references to human rights. They come after criticism of Shell over its operations in Nigeria following the execution of Ken Saro-Wiwa, the Ogoni minority rights activist.

Such considerations have led to a growing interest in ethics among UK and European companies, partly driven by the stakeholder debate, partly by environmental concerns and partly because some companies believe that ethical values are central to good business.

Simon Zadek, research director of the New Economics Foundation, a UK-based non-profit-making organisation that researches and advises on ethical and social issues affecting business, estimates that between 7 and 15 per cent of FTSE companies are experimenting with or examining the idea of social audits so that they can ensure their business practices are fully aligned with their principles or ethical codes.

The Body Shop and the Co-operative Bank have helped pioneer ethical and social audits in the UK, while Ben & Jerry's, the premium ice cream manufacturer, and Johnson & Johnson, the pharmaceuticals company, are held up as examples of ethical companies in the US. But the ethical movement is spreading into other big companies. British Telecommunications recently embarked on a full-scale social audit and Grand Metropolitan is also piloting the idea.

Many ethical programmes in the US have been developed to meet Federal sentencing guidelines laid down in 1991. If companies follow the guidelines they may find themselves in a better position legally if they are charged with malpractice or corruption offences. The guidelines cover establishing corporate codes of ethics, the carrying out of ethical audits and the duty of senior executives to take responsibility for ethics.

Daiwa Bank, which scored poorly under the guidelines rating system, was fined $340m (£227m) and forced to give up its operations in the US when it admitted two years ago to having concealed losses by one of its traders from the US regulator.

The risk of such penalties has led to a growth of consultancies in the US advising on ethical issues. There have been moves to establish similar reviews in the UK. Sheena Carmichael, director of Ethos, a UK-based consultancy, has conducted ethical audits in a number of National Health Service Trusts which have highlighted, among other issues, the prevalence of prescription fraud.

Managers have been slow to address ethical issues, she says:'They must become aware that there are ethical aspects to almost every decision they make.'

Some consultants have cbosen to make distinctions between ethical and social audits. Ms Carmichael regards the ethical audit as more an internal management information tool, while the social audit is an external-facing exercise designed to enable an organisation to account for its actions.

Mr Zadek points out that social audits must take account of constantly changing mores and be sensitive to cultural differences in different countries. 'Five years ago Nike wouldn't have considered children in Bangladesh to be significant stakeholders in their business. Today they are, because consumers in the UK and the US decided that their welfare was important', he says.

The European social audit model, he says, involves the use of various measures to look at areas such as staff turnover, and reviews of management systems backed by external verification. Many of these measures, he says, already exist in companies but have not previously been united under the social audit umbrella.

Guy Dehn, director of Public Concern at Work, a UK charity which gives advice to corporate whistleblowers, suggests that companies have a financial incentive to pursue ethical codes. But he also argues that companies should think more deeply about their potential moral role in society. 'People are working in their companies for most of their waking hours, so business has enormous power to influence their ethical values and this should not be ignored.'

Source: R. Donkin, 'A moral stance' in *Financial Times*, 8 September 1997, p. 16

Globalisation will help in understanding the needs of current constituents, as well as of future clients. Learning about various cultures enables organisational members to understand that other companies' missions and objectives are not vastly different from their own, and that they need not surrender their company loyalty to interact and negotiate with others – nor need they compromise their ethical principles.

CASE STUDY

The protection of reputation becomes a core concern

The days when companies could do as they pleased, fly in the face of public opinion, turn a deaf ear to the cries of staff, routinely give 'no comment' to the press and speak to the City only via their profit margins are long over. High-profile public relations débâcles as varied as British Airways (Dirty Tricks), McDonald's (McLibel) and Shell (Brent Spar) clearly illustrate that, in the 90s, corporate reputation has become more important and more vulnerable than ever before.

Source: 'The protection of reputation becomes a core concern' in *Management Today*, October 1997

Organisations increasingly have to focus on challenges such as workforce diversity, technological change, ethical behaviour, and global competition. Global challenges increasingly require employers and employees to consider cultural differences and to regard appreciation of the culture as vital for organisational survival. Cultural diversity encompasses all forms of differences amongst individuals, including age, gender, race, sexual orientation and ability. Technological changes reshape jobs and the workforce, management is challenging, and ethical issues are compounding the complexity.

Questions for discussion

1 It is a belief that managers are suffering from the results of:
   (a) unreasonable deadlines;
   (b) working excessive hours and at weekends;
   (c) implementing redundancies;

(d) coping with intimidation;
(e) office politics.

Is it ethical to expect managers to work under such conditions? Should they be informed of the risks?

2 In the case entitled 'Keeping them happy' it is said that 'Bullying is a difficulty'. Is any sort of bullying in the workplace ethically acceptable?

3 Suppose that an organisation prescribes certain healthy behaviours for all employees, such as regular exercise during the working day and the practice of relaxation. Is it ethical for an organisation to influence these employee behaviours, or does this infringe on their individual rights?

References and further reading

Donkin, R., 'A moral stance' in *Financial Times*, 8 September 1997, p. 16

Economist, The, 'Keeping them happy', 25 November 1995, p. 32

Heller, R., 'Drunk on misguided optimism' in *Management Today*, August 1996, p. 24

Management Today, 'The protection of reputation becomes a core concern', October 1997, p. 14

Pettinger, R., 1996, *Introduction to Organisational Behaviour* (Basingstoke: Macmillan)

Glossary

Achievement-oriented leadership
A leadership style where the leader sets challenging objectives and expects the very best from all subordinates at all times.

Action-centred leadership
Where a leader recognises that there are certain traits, qualities, capabilities, and attitudes required of a leader within the interconnecting functions of task, team, and individual.

Adaptability
The capacity to adjust to changing circumstances.

Adaption
A central subsystem which is concerned with dealing with change: reactive and proactive. It monitors the changing environment in which the organisation operates, keeping abreast of technological developments and innovative features so that the organisation can deliver its outputs.

Additive tasks
Types of group tasks where the co-ordinated efforts of individual members of the group are added together to form the group's product.

Adjourning/dying
When a group has completed its task, it will no longer have an objective and so the members will go their separate ways and the group 'dies'.

Advanced Manufacturing Technology (AMT)
Technology which includes a wide range of equipment which adds to the manufacturing process.

All-channel
A communication network where all the members of the network are free to communicate with one another.

Anthropology
The study of human societies and customs.

Applied research
Research which attempts to solve particular problems or answer a specific question or questions.

Artifacts/object language
The communication that results from the display of material things such as clothes, furniture, methods of transport, and architectural arrangements.

Attribution theory
A theory that explains how individuals pinpoint the causes of the behaviour of themselves and others.

Authoritarian
A person who favours obedience to authority and differences in power and status in hierarchical systems.

Authority
The right or power to enforce obedience.

Autocratic leadership
A style of leadership in which the leader dictates decisions to subordinates using strong, directive, controlling techniques.

Barriers to effective communication
Factors which can impair effective communication.

Basic research
Research which is aimed at adding new knowledge to an existing body of knowledge.

Behaviour
The manifestation of motives which are learned needs which induce individuals to pursue particular goals because they are socially valued.

Benchmarking
The process whereby an organisation attempts to find out how a competitor does things better than it does and then measures itself against these findings.

Boundary spanning
Subsystems which are responsible for changes in the organisation's environment – they deal with the input and output transactions.

Bounded rationality
A theory which suggests that there are limits on how rational a decision-maker can actually be.

Brainstorming
A creative technique for eliciting ideas which could then be used to make an effective decision.

Bureaucracy
A structure where routine activities are carried out through specialisation, formal rules and regulations; and where functional tasks are organised into functional departments with narrow spans of control and a centralised authority, and decisions are made in line with the hierarchical chain of command.

Business Process Re-engineering (BPR)
A label given to the redesign of an organisation; it may include breaking away from outdated rules and assumptions that underlie how tasks should be performed. A key principle is the elimination or prevention of barriers which could themselves create a distance between employees and their customers.

Career
A pattern of work-related activities and experiences that span the working life of an individual.

Case study
The development of detailed, thorough knowledge about a single 'case', or a small number of related 'cases'.

Causality
When changes in the independent variable are assumed to cause changes in the dependent variable.

Cell
A model of office design where individuals have a high level of autonomy and low interaction.

Cell groups
A small team which makes entire products or provides an entire service from conception to after-sales service.

Centralisation
The degree to which decisions are made at the top of the hierarchy of an organisation.

Chain
A communication network where each individual can communicate with the person above and/or the person below.

Change
The process by which changes occur within an organisation.

Change agent
An individual or group who undertakes the task of introducing and managing a change within an organisation.

Charismatic leadership
A leadership style where the individual relies upon personal abilities and talents in order to have a profound effect on followers.

Chronemics
The use of time in non-verbal communication.

Circle
A communication network where each individual can communicate with the people on both sides but not with anyone else.

Classical conditioning
The modification of an individual's behaviour so that a conditioned stimulus is matched with an unconditioned stimulus.

Closed system
An organisational system which is not dependent on its environment because it is enclosed and totally autonomous.

Club
A model of office design where jobs require high autonomy and high interaction.

Coercive power
Power that is based on an agent's ability to force another person to do something.

Cognition
Individual thinking through which individuals decide to make changes in their lives.

Cognitive dissonance
An incompatibility or tension in an individual which results from experiencing dysfunctional conflict between attitudes and behaviour.

Cognitive evaluation theory
A theory which predicts that the bestowal of extrinsic rewards upon behaviour which has previously been intrinsically rewarded generally brings about a reduction in the overall level of motivation.

Cognitive moral development
The process of moving through stages of maturity in terms of making ethical decisions.

Cognitive process
The assumption that individuals are conscious and active in how they learn, using past experiences as a basis for current behaviour.

Cognitive resource theory
A theory which proposes that a leader will obtain team effectiveness by personally making decisions related to performance (strategic planning and decision-making) and communicating them to the team using directive behaviour.

Cognitive style
The preference which an individual has when gathering data and/or evaluating alternatives.

Cohesiveness
The strength of individuals' desire to become a member of a group and their commitment to the group.

Collectivism
A cultural orientation in which individuals belong to tightly knit social frameworks, and depend strongly on large extended families or class.

Commonality
The capacity of an approach to create a unifying set of values.

Communication
The transference and understanding of a shared meaning.

Communication apprehension
Undue tension and anxiety about any or all forms of communication.

Communication barriers
Factors such as physical separation, status difference, gender differences, cultural diversity, and language and meaning which may impair effective communication.

Communication fidelity
The degree of correspondence between the message intended by the sender and the message understood by the receiver.

Communication networks
The channels through which information passes.

Communicator
The individual who originates a message.

Compensatory tasks
When the product of the group's efforts is the average of all the individual contributions and encapsulates the benefits of differing points of view and compromise.

Complexity
The extent to which the job design approach is likely to require changes in multiple factors, involvement of individuals with diverse skills at various organisational levels, and high levels of decision-making skills for successful implementation.

Conceptual skill
The ability of an individual to think abstractly and to take a holistic view in the identification of opportunities to give the organisation a competitive advantage.

Conflict
Dysfunctional conflict is present in any situation where incompatible goals, attitudes, beliefs or behaviours lead to disagreement between individuals or cause opposition.

Consensus
A collective opinion, a majority view, a general agreement or compromise.

Consideration
The extent to which a leader is likely to have job relationships characterised by mutual respect for subordinates' ideas, and regard for their feelings.

Consistency
Behaviour of an individual which conforms to previous or expected patterns.

Constructive alternativism
The attempt by an individual to construct his own version of his world when it is constantly changing and he cannot grasp or comprehend it.

Contingency theory
A theory concerning the most effective way to establish power/dependence relationships that exist between the focal organisation and other actors in the network.

Contingency theory (related to organising)
The most effective way to organise is *contingent* upon some aspect(s) of the situation in which the organisation exists.

Contingency theory of motivation
This theory was predicated on the idea that different ways of motivating people are required for different individuals and circumstances: it was situational and environmental.

Controlling
The function of monitoring and correcting the plans and activities of members of an organisation in order that goals may be better achieved.

Correlation co-efficient
The indication of the strength of a relationship between two or more variables.

Cost
The price of production or supply which correlates the expense of materials and labour to prices and wages with the additional apportionment of overhead expenses.

Cultural environment
The norms, values, attitudes and goals of a group.

Culture
The distinctive ways in which different human populations or societies organise their lives.

Culture strength
Can be defined in terms of (1) the homogeneity and stability of group membership, and (2) the length and intensity of shared experiences of the group.

Data
Facts which have not been interpreted or analysed.

Decision-making
Choices made from two or more alternatives.

Decoding
The process by which the receiver of a message interprets the symbols contained in the message and determines what such symbols refer to.

Delphi Technique (DT)
A technique for gathering the judgements of experts for assistance in the making of decisions.

Democratic leadership
A style of leadership where the leader shares decision-making with subordinates. The leader collaborates, reciprocates and interacts with followers in the workplace.

Den
A model of office design where employees have low autonomy and high interaction.

Dependency
The type of relationship which individual B has when individual A possesses something that B wants.

Dependent variable
A response that is affected by an independent variable.

Diagnostic skills
Skills which an individual uses to identify and understand the cause-and-effect relationships within the organisation in an attempt to find the most effective solution to a problem.

Differentiation
The cognitive and emotional differences between managers within an organisation as they relate to the functional departments and formal structure of the organisation.

Directive leadership
A style of leadership where the leader liaises with followers and lets them know what is expected of them, timetables their work and gives specific help for task accomplishment.

Disposition
The characteristics of an individual's personality which include emotions, cognitions, attitudes, values and the tendency for an individual to respond to different situations in a similar way.

Distinctiveness
An informational cue indicating the degree to which an individual behaves in the same way in a variety of situations.

Distributive justice
Related to an individual's belief that he/she has actually received a fair reward or anticipates that he/she will receive a fair reward.

Disturbed-reactive environment
A complex environment where many competitors work towards similar ends and where few organisations are influential enough to form a coalition in order to dominate.

Dogmatism
The tendency to assert or impose personal opinions and to disregard the views and beliefs of others. Intolerance of and lack of openness to other opinions.

Downsizing (downlayering, rightsizing)
The reduction in staff numbers throughout an organisation.

Durability
The ability of an approach to create a culture that will be lasting.

Dysfunctional conflict
An unhealthy, destructive disagreement between two or more people.

Electronic Information Processing
The linking of everyone by computer to encourage the flow of ideas from the margin.

Electronic conferencing
Meetings where individual members interact by using computers and video.

Emergent behaviour
Behaviour which comes about as a result of interpersonal communication between group members and the interplay of their emotions and sentiments.

Empowerment
Related to the organisational arrangements that allow employees more autonomy, discretion and unsupervised decision-making responsibility. Encompasses the principle of participation and is relevant to all aspects of an individual's existence.

Enacted role
The behaviour which the individual actually engages in.

Enacted values
Values which reflect the actual behaviour of individuals.

Encoding
The process by which a sender's ideas are turned into symbols that constitute the message – putting into words.

Environment
The institutions or forces outside an organisation that have the potential to affect the organisation's performance.

Equity theory
A justice theory which asserts that members of any workforce wish to be treated fairly and have a desire to perceive equity in relation to others and avoid inequity with them.

Ergonomics
The study of the physical environment and particularly in relation to equipment design: the analysis and design of work equipment to fit human physical and cognitive capabilities.

ERG theory
There are three groups of core needs: Existence, Relatedness, Growth.

Espoused values
What members of an organisation say that they value.

Ethical behaviour
Behaving in a way that corresponds with one's ethical beliefs and in line with the beliefs commonly held by the organisation and society in general.

Ethical dilemma
A situation forcing an individual to choose between two equally undesirable alternatives which conflict with the individual's view of what is 'right' or 'wrong', with the result that the decision made may be ethically unacceptable.

Ethics
A code of moral principles or values which a person holds for making judgements about is right or wrong.

Evaluation apprehension
A fear of being evaluated or judged by another person.

Expectancy
The perceived probability of performing sufficiently well to achieve the outcome required, and, thus, the reward – the belief of individuals that the more effort they put in, the higher their level of performance will be.

Expert power
The power that exists when an individual has information or knowledge that another individual does not have but wants and needs. Similar to referent power and one individual can have both.

Expert systems
Computer-based applications which use a computer representation of the expertise attributed to humans in a specialised field of knowledge in order to solve problems.

Explicit knowledge
Those things an individual can write down and record.

Expressiveness
The ability of an approach to express a new core idea.

External system
The formal system which evolved because of the existing beliefs about how organisations should be managed.

Extinction
An alternative to punishment, being any behaviour which is used in an attempt to weaken a behaviour in others by attaching some sort of consequences (positive or negative) to it.

Extrinsic rewards
Tangible outcomes for effort which usually derive from the organisation itself and then act on individuals within the workplace.

Extrovert
An individual who exhibits behaviour which indicates that he or she is energised by interaction with other people; an outgoing or sociable person.

Feedback
Information received back by an individual as a result of carrying out a task, concerning the effectiveness of his or her work performance.

Feedback loop
The pathway that permits two-way feedback.

Feeling
A preference for making decisions in a personal, value-oriented way.

Field experiment
Research which takes place in the outside environment where the researcher makes an attempt to control the variables and manipulates others in order to gauge the effects of the manipulated variables on the outcome variables.

Field survey
The reliance on a questionnaire distributed to a sample of people selected from a wider population.

First impression error
The tendency to formulate long-lasting opinions about another individual based on initial perceptions which are usually inaccurate.

Followership
The process of being guided and directed by a leader in the workplace.

Formal group
Designated group which has been defined by the organisation's structure and has thus been purposefully created and stipulated to help accomplish the organisation's collective purpose.

Formal leadership
Most work groups have a formal leader who is identified by his or her role title.

Formal status
Prestige associated with a position, as distinct from the person who may occupy that position.

Forming
The first key stage in the way a group develops.

Frustration
A possible reactive outcome when an individual's motivational driving force is blocked before the desired goal is achieved by the individual.

Fully structured conflict
Conflicts which are clearly defined and where the parties concerned are fully bound by rules, social norms, and ethical standards.

Functional conflict
Where disagreement between two or more people is healthy and constructive.

Functional grouping
Where the membership of the group depends upon the function of the group.

Functional relationships
Relationships between the different functions within the organisation where staff in one subsystem may have an element of authority over staff in another.

Fundamental attribution error
The tendency to make attributions to internal causes when focusing on someone else's behaviour.

Garbage can model of decision-making
When problems, solutions, participants, and choice opportunities are independent streams of events

that flow into and through organisations; the model can be likened to random waste getting mixed up together in a garbage can.

Generalisability
The degree to which the results of research are applicable to groups of individuals other than those who participated in the study.

Glass ceiling
An invisible barrier that keeps women from rising above a certain level within an organisation.

Goal setting
The process of deciding on the required objectives of an organisation which will ultimately guide and direct the behaviour of individuals in the organisation.

Group
Any number of people who (1) interact with one another; (2) are psychologically aware of one another; and (3) perceive themselves to be in a group.

Group cohesion
What keeps a group together – it cannot be seen.

Group maintenance roles
Activities which are centred on any behaviour which helps to build a group attitude or which aids in the maintenance of the group's norms.

Group processes
The order of interaction between members of a group including the verbal and non-verbal interactions of all members of the group.

Groupthink
The psychological drive for consensus at any cost that suppresses dissent and appraisal of alternatives in cohesive decision-making groups.

Growth factors
Factors within a job which, when present, have a positive function in motivating individuals.

Halo effect
A kind of implicit personality theory, in which one positive (or negative) trait is used to infer other positive (or negative) traits.

Hawthorne Studies
Research carried out in the 1920s and 1930s which suggested that there was an informal organisation within a formal one.

Hedonism
A doctrine or belief in which pleasure is seen as the highest good. In general usage, it is the indulgence in sensual pleasures and a hedonist is a person who opts for comfort and pleasure and avoids anything that brings with it pain or discomfort.

Heredity
The factors that were determined at a person's conception – the genetic constitution of an individual.

Heterarchy
A development of horizontal organisation where there are multiple centres with subsidiary managers who initiate strategy for the organisation as a whole, co-ordination and control being achieved through corporate culture and shared values.

Heuristic
A way to make a decision through trial and error.

Hierarchical referral
The chain of command which is more apparent in traditional organisations with a steep hierarchy of command.

Hive
A model of office design where workers have a low level of autonomy and low interaction.

Holistic learner
Individuals who want to see the 'whole picture' and how their present learning fits into the organisation goals as a whole in order to understand what the purpose of their learning is.

Human relations approach
A view on motivation that suggested that favourable attitudes in employees result in motivation to work even harder.

Humanistic theory of personality
An approach which emphasised individual growth and improvement and which represents a school of thought which dismisses scientific attempts to study human beings; it sees such attempts as inappropriate.

Hygiene factors
Factors within a job which, when adequate, placate workers, e.g. organisational policy, salary, work environment, yet, when absent or inadequate, make individuals dissatisfied.

Hypothesis
A testable proposition about the relationship between two or more events or concepts.

Identity crisis
A phase stemming from a feeling of lack of self-worth in which an individual feels the need to establish an identity within an organisation or society.

Idiographic
Identifying the unique personality characteristics of individuals.

Impression management
The process by which individuals try to control the impressions others have of them.

Incremental change
Maintains the organisation's general equilibrium by a series of more or less continual relatively minor adjustments.

Independent variable
The presumed cause of some change.

Individual differences
The way in which factors such as personality, skills, abilities, perception and values differ from one person to another.

Individualism
The extent to which individuals are expected to act independently of other members of society.

Individual roles
Roles which aid the individuals within a group to meet their personal needs.

Inequity
A perception by a person that more is being given by that person than is being received, or less is being given than is being received.

Inertia
This is when an individual begins to play a role within the group but does so passively and reacts only to others' ideas and suggestions; that is, when that person does not act proactively, then inertia is in operation.

Informal group
Unofficial groups which form within an organisation.

Informal leader
An individual whose influence within a group develops over a period of time and is based on that individual's unique ability to help the group achieve its goals.

Initiating structure
The extent to which a leader is likely to define and structure their own role and the role of subordinates in the search for goal attainment.

Innovation
The finding and development of new ideas. Labelled by some writers as *leadership*.

Inputs
Related to motivation, this is what individuals bring with them, such as: education, past experience, knowledge, loyalty, and effort.

Institutional environment
Includes other similar organisations in the industry who deal with similar customers, suppliers and regulatory agencies.

Institutional theory
A theory which recognises the demands which environments place upon organisations; it argues that under conditions of high uncertainty organisations will imitate other organisations from the same institutional environment.

Instrumentality
The calculation of the number and degree of rewards resulting from achieving an outcome.

Integrity/honesty tests
Tests which are designed to predict whether or not a member of the workforce is likely to engage in behaviour which will lead to dishonesty on the job or be counter-productive to the interests of the organisation for which he or she works.

Interaction Process Analysis (IPA)
A tool for describing and analysing the interactions of group members.

Internal system
The informal system that groups utilise: the norms and values of a group.

Interpersonal skills
The ability of a person to communicate with others along with the ability to understand and interpret messages correctly and intrinsically motivate self and others.

Intrinsic rewards
These are intangible and derive from the experience of work itself for each individual: a sense of challenge and achievement, recognition, and responsibility.

Introvert
An individual who directs their thoughts or mind inwards; someone whose behaviour indicates they are energised by internal factors rather than external ones.

Intuition
A fast, positive force in decision-making which is utilised at a level below consciousness and which involves learned patterns of information.

Isolation
Either physical or psychological. Physical isolation results in psychological deprivation.

Job
A group of stated work and task activities that a member of the workforce engages in.

Job Characteristics Model (JCM)
A model which allows for the understanding of person–job fit through the interaction of core job dimensions with critical psychological states within an individual.

Job design
The way that tasks are combined to form complete jobs in the workplace.

Job Diagnostic Survey (JDS)
A survey tool designed to measure the elements of skill variety, task identity, task significance, autonomy, and feedback in the Job Characteristics Model.

Job enlargement (horizontal job loading)
Involves giving the worker more tasks which other workers might have performed.

Job enrichment
Designing or redesigning jobs by incorporating motivational factors into them.

Job redesign
Focuses on how existing jobs can be changed.

Job rotation
The moving of individual workers from one task to another in an effort to minimise boredom and monotony or to give new employees a holistic view of the organisation's activities.

Job satisfaction
A pleasurable or non-pleasurable result of work-related appraisal or job experiences.

Judging
The making of decisions through the use of closure and completion.

Justice theories of motivation
These theories concentrate on the cognitive process because an individual will make a decision as to whether the effort is worth it.

Kinesics
The study of body movements, including posture.

Laboratory experiment
An experiment which takes place in an artificial environment where the researcher has control over the variables being investigated.

Laissez-faire
A style of management or leadership in which the leader fails to accept the responsibilities of role/position or abstains from interfering.

Leader
An advocate for bringing about change and for new approaches to problem solving.

Leadership
The process of guiding and directing the behaviour of followers within the workplace.

Learning
A process of change in behaviour through experience and which is encouraged by life-long exposure to all kinds of perceptions, rewards, punishments, environments and inter-relationships. Can also be as a result of training and development programmes.

Learning curve
Shows the relationship between behaviour, action, and experience during each learning experience.

Learning cycle
A cyclical appreciation of learning strategies with learners moving round the cycle and utilising one or more of the learning styles.

Learning organisation
An attitude which is considered to be relevant to any organisation which has developed the continuous capacity to adapt to the environment and to change and which supports the self-development of members of the workforce towards this end.

Least-preferred co-worker (LPC)
The person a leader has least preferred to work with over his or her career.

Least-preferred Co-worker Questionnaire (LPCQ)
A questionnaire that is used to measure whether an individual is task or relationship oriented.

Legitimate power
Power that is based on position and mutual agreement and is similar to authority.

Line relationships
Relationships between managers and subordinates.

Linkage
The extent of communication and co-ordination amongst an organisation's subsystems.

Locational grouping
A development of functional grouping when an organisation grows and develops and becomes, for example, geographically dispersed.

Locus of control
The extent to which an individual believes that his or her behaviour has a direct impact on the consequences of that behaviour.

Machiavellianism
An attribute of personality where an individual behaves in a way which is aimed at gaining power and controlling the behaviour of others.

Maintenance
A subsystem which is responsible for the smooth running of the organisation; e.g. a system to ensure that the buildings are kept to a high standard and refurbished when necessary. It is also part of the maintenance function to attend to the needs of the workers – their morale and physical comfort.

Management
A distinct subsystem which is responsible for directing and co-ordinating all the other subsystems of an organisation.

Management by objectives (MBO)
A goal-setting programme which is based on the interaction and negotiation between employees and their managers.

Management prerogative
A moral right based on the implicit understanding between managers and workforce members that managers are trusted to make satisfactory decisions and to remain impartial and objective. The fact that they have the specialist skills and knowledge means, in itself, that managers know what is best for the organisation.

Management science approach to decision-making
An approach used when it is possible to analyse problems and when the variables involved can be easily identified and measured.

Managerial Grid©
A nine-by-nine matrix outlining eighty-one different leadership styles.

Managerial ideology
The totality of ideas, opinions and perspectives which seeks to explain and justify the authority of those who exercise formal authority in business situations.

Managerial role
The ability to plan, organise, co-ordinate and control activities in the pursuit of effective performance.

Market grouping
Organisation of groups according to the markets served by the organisation.

Masculinity
The extent to which a society expects there to be distinct gender roles.

Matrix grouping
A common system of organisational design which reflects the contingency approach – it is only useful in given situations.

Matrix structure
A strong form of horizontal linkage in which both the product and functional structures are simultaneously implemented.

Meaninglessness
The inability to recognise the contribution which individuals make to the total work output.

Mechanistic
A system of organisation which is characterised by bureaucratic systems encompassing roles, regulations, a clear hierarchical pattern of authority and centralised decision-making.

Method study
Part of work study which allows managers to systematically record and critically examine tasks as they are currently being carried out and propose easier and more effective methods related to a reduction in cost.

Mission statement
A short written statement by an organisation which encapsulates the purpose of its activity, as much as the direction it wishes to take.

Moral maturity
The level of an individual's cognitive moral development.

Motivation
The driving force which makes an individual act to meet a need which will result in either fulfilment or frustration.

Motivation factor
A work condition which is related to the need for individual psychological growth.

Motivational content approaches
Approaches to motivational theory which place the emphasis on *what* motivates.

Motivational process approaches
Approaches to motivational theory which emphasise the *actual process* (or method) of motivation.

Motives
The channels through which an individual thinks a need can best be satisfied; they thus reflect the specific behavioural choices enacted by that individual.

Mourning
When a group has been disbanded, some individuals might mourn its passing because there is no longer a place for them to satisfy their needs.

Multiple leaders
A group has at any one time a number of goals which could mean that the leadership role will change

depending on the nature of the task/s to achieve the goals.

Myers-Briggs Type Indicator (MBTI)
A personality test that taps four characteristics and classifies people into one of sixteen personality types.

Need
Anything individuals perceive they want and is usually something they must have in order to survive; therefore it is usually physiological in nature: water, food. It is a stimulus for satisfaction.

Need for achievement
An easily perceived manifestation that is related to the individual's desire for competition, excellence, goals which challenge, persistence and overcoming of difficulties.

Need for affiliation
An easily perceived manifestation that is related to the individual's need to establish and maintain warm and intimate relationships with others.

Need for power
An easily perceived manifestation that is related to the individual's need to make an impact on others and to influence them.

Need hierarchy
A theory which states that behaviour is determined by a progression of physical, social, and psychological needs.

Negative affect
Where an individual emphasises the negative aspects of self, others, and the environment.

Network structure
A structure where an organisation replaces most, if not all, vertical communication and control relationships with lateral relationships.

Nominal Group Technique (NGT)
A group decision-making technique where individual members meet face to face to share their ideas and judgements in a systematic but independent fashion.

Nomothetic
Identifying personality factors applying to people in general.

Non-verbal communication
The inclusion of all elements that do not involve words or language, such as: proxemics, kinesics, facial and eye contact, paralanguage, chronemics, and object language.

Norming
The third stage in the way a group develops.

Norms
Rules and sets of behaviour that are expected and accepted by all members of a group or team.

Object language
Sometimes known as *artifacts,* this refers to the communication that results from the display of material things such as clothes, furniture, methods of transport, and architectural arrangements.

Office technology
Concentrates on storage, retrieval, presentation, and the manipulation of information.

Open-book management
This form of management gives employees all the information that an owner gets if owners want employees to act as though they were owners and had the best interests of the organisation at heart.

Open system
An organisational system which, in order to survive, must interact with the environment.

Operant conditioning
A type of conditioning which occurs when behaviour is modified through the use of positive or negative consequences following specific behaviours.

Organic
A system of organisation which has free-flowing systems with adaptive processes, unclear authority hierarchy and where decision-making is decentralised.

Organisational behaviour
An area of study which investigates the impact that individuals, groups and structure within an organisation have on meeting the organisation's goals.

Organisational behaviour modification
The use of operant conditioning theory to get members of the workforce to behave in a required way.

Organisational commitment
The orientation of an individual to the organisation's goals measured in terms of loyalty, attitude and involvement.

Organisational conflict
Any situation within an organisation where incompatible goals, attitudes, beliefs, values, emotions or behaviours lead to any form of disagreement or opposition among two or more individuals or groups. Such conflict is dysfunctional but can be turned into functional conflict.

Organisational culture
A pattern of basic assumptions held by members of the workforce which are considered to be valid and reliable and which are taught to newcomers to the organisation through artifacts, stories, myths, legends and rites.

Organisational design
The process of constructing and adjusting an organisation's structure to achieve its goals; it provides the structure around which the enterprise's positions and activities are arranged.

Organisational environment
The elements which exist outside the framework of an organisation and which have the potential to affect all aspects of the organisation's activities.

Organisational life cycle
A concept which considers organisational growth and change using the analogy of a human being – it is born, grows older and eventually dies.

Organisational structure
The linking of functional departments and tasks within an organisation.

Organisations
Social arrangements which are designed for the controlled performance of collective goals.

Organising (operating)
The function by which the manager puts together the basic framework and structure of the organisation.

Outcomes
Related to motivation, this is what an individual receives in exchange for inputs. Examples of outcomes are salary, social recognition and intrinsic rewards.

Outsourcing
Where many of the activities of a once complex organisation are moved outside the organisation's boundary.

Paralanguage
Variations in speech, such as pitch, loudness, tempo, tone, duration, laughing and crying.

Partially structured conflict
Conflict where certain behaviours are constrained and where others are left to free choice.

Participation
Brought about by giving individual workers a voice in making decisions about their own work.

Participative leadership
A leadership style where the key dimension is consultation when the leader asks followers for their opinion and acts upon it.

Participative management
The process of giving individuals a say in decisions relating to their work.

Paternalism
An attitude where the employer is assumed to have a moral responsibility for the welfare and happiness of the workforce.

Penetration
The ability of an approach to permeate different levels of the organisation.

People change
Changes in the attitudes, skills, expectations, abilities and behaviours of the organisation's members, at all levels.

Perceived role
When an individual believes that he or she has to behave in an expected way.

Perception
The process by which individuals interpret sensory impressions, so that they can assign meaning to the environment.

Performance related pay
Employees' pay that depends partly upon their performance.

Performing
The fourth stage in the way a group develops.

Permeable boundary
An environment or boundary within which members of the workforce work where membership of such a framework is very indistinct.

Personality
A stable set of characteristics and tendencies that determine how commonalities and differences in the psychological behaviour (thoughts, feelings, and actions) of people have a continuity in time and that may not be easily understood as the sole result of the social and biological pressures of the moment.

Phenomenological
A type of approach to research which tries to understand individuals in the light of their experience and their perception of their own world rather than through the eyes and perception of others.

Physical environment
Terrain, climate, and design of the workplace within which an individual or group functions.

Placid-clustered environment
An environment which has the feature that it changes slowly but any threats to the organisation are clustered rather than appearing at random.

Placid-randomised environment
An environment that is relatively unchanging.

Planned change
The change consciously undertaken by an organisation in an attempt to remain current and viable.

Planning
The process through which the organisation's desired future position is decided as well as how it might be achieved – linked to corporate strategy.

Polarisation
The tendency for group members to shift their views on a given issue to ones that are more extreme in the same direction as the views they held previously.

Political-economic approach
The belief that an individual was motivated by self-interest for economic gain in order to buy the necessities of life.

Pooled interdependence
This happens when an employee can carry out a job without communicating to any extent with others in the organisation.

Population ecology theory
A theory which argues that the environment selects certain types of organisation to survive and others to die based on the fit between their structure and the characteristics of the environment.

Positive affect
Where an individual emphasises the positive aspects of self, others, and the environment.

Power
The ability to influence the behaviour of another individual.

Power distance
The extent to which members of a nation are willing to accept an unequal distribution of power, wealth and prestige.

Powerlessness
The inability to influence any aspect of working conditions including the amount of work, the quality, speed, and direction.

Procedural justice
The extent to which the procedures for the allocation of rewards used within an organisation are fair.

Product grouping
Organising groups by the products created or the service provided by the organisation.

Production
A subsystem which produces the product/service outputs of the organisation.

Productivity
A performance measure used in conjunction with others, such as the cost of the transformation process, quality of product/process, and delivery to customers.

Professional management
A social force, specialist occupational category and set of distinct working practices.

Projection (also known as assumed similarity)
The attributing of one's own characteristics to other individuals.

Proxemics
The study of an individual's perception and use of space, including territorial space.

Psychodynamic theory
A personality theory that emphasises the unconscious determinants of behaviour.

Psychological contract
An unwritten agreement which sets out what a member of the workforce wants from his or her employer and vice versa.

Psychometric tests (occupational testing, psychological testing)
Sophisticated tests to measure an individual's capacities in a variety of areas such as intelligence and ability.

Punishment
The attempt to eliminate undesired behaviours in an individual by either bestowing negative consequences for that behaviour or by withholding the positive consequences (the rewards).

Pygmalion effect
Popularised term for the self-fulfilling prophecy.

Quality circles
An organisational system which attempts to empower individuals by allowing them to meet periodically to discuss any concerns that they have and to assess solutions to meet the problem.

Quality of working life (QOWL)
The degree to which people are able to satisfy their important personal needs through their work.

Radical change
Requires a new equilibrium to be established by transforming the whole organisation in one major upheaval.

Reciprocal interdependence
Occurs when outputs from one individual (or team) become the inputs for others and vice versa.

Reference groups
Groups by which individuals are strongly influenced and with which they associate most closely.

Referent power
Elusive power which is based on charisma – interpersonal attraction. An individual has power over another because the latter identifies with the former or wants to model themself on him or her.

Reflective listening
The skill of listening which results in the recipient of a communication fully understanding the contents of the message.

Reinforcement
The attempt to induce required behaviour in others by the use of positive rewards or by withholding negative consequences.

Reliability
The extent to which a measure is consistent over a period of time.

Required behaviour
Behaviour expected from individuals by the management in order for the task to be successfully completed.

Research design
The set of procedures used to test predicted relationships among phenomena being investigated.

Resource dependence
A theory based on the assumption that organisations are controlled by their environments.

Rethinking
An ongoing view related to the design of organisations whereby managers look at the organisation design in radical ways which may involve abandoning the classic view of the organisation as a pyramid.

Reward power
Power based on the individual's ability to control the rewards that another individual wants.

Revolutionary conflict
Unstructured conflict on a massive scale which is not bound by rules, culture or shared concepts.

Risk propensity
The degree to which an individual is prepared to make changes and take risky decisions.

Risky shift
A shift in direction made by a group if they think that a riskier course of action should be taken.

Role
A set of expected behaviour patterns attributed to someone occupying a given position in a social unit – such as an organisation.

Role ambiguity
Occurs when an individual is uncertain as to the exact nature of a particular role.

Role conflict
Arises when the demands of, or messages about, roles are essentially clear but contradict one another to some extent.

Role demands
Functions which relate to the role or part an individual plays in the organisation or work group.

Role incompatibility
Occurs when the role of the incumbent contains incompatible elements.

Role overload
The result of an individual not being able to cope with several roles simultaneously.

Role underload
Occurs when an organisation does not utilise the individual's skills in a way that he or she could manage.

Satisfice
In the context of making a decision, to choose the alternative which is satisfactory/good enough, because the time and cost involved in further decision-making are excessive.

Scalar chain of command
A chain of command where authority and responsibility are arranged hierarchically.

Scientific management
A classical approach to management where the underlying belief was that decision-making (particularly when related to organisational decisions and job design) should be based upon rational scientific procedures.

Selective perception
The ability (often unconscious) to select and concentrate on certain sensory data whilst screening out other data.

Self-efficacy
An individual's beliefs and expectations about his or her ability to accomplish a specific task or job in an effective way.

Self-fulfilling prophecy
Any situation in which the expectations of an individual about others can affect any interaction with them in such a way that the expectations of the perceiver are fulfilled.

Self-serving bias
The tendency to attribute one's successes to internal causes and one's failures to external causes.

Sensing
A preference for collecting information through the use of all the senses.

Sequential interdependence
What happens when one worker has to complete certain tasks before another worker can perform his or her specific tasks.

Serialistic learner
A person who tends to focus narrowly on the particular task or topic and who needs to learn step by step, concentrating first on the details and on the connected logic, and progressively building up skills and developing understanding.

SMART system
A system used by some organisations to communicate their approach to effective goal attainment. An acronym which stands for: **S**pecific, **M**easurable, **A**ttainable, **R**ealistic, **T**ime-bound.

Socio-biological
The nurture versus nature issue where the choices made by individuals are determined to a large extent by genetic characteristics although they can be influenced by an individual's environment.

Social comparison
A view that suggests that group members may want to make a positive impression on their fellow group members, and do so by strongly endorsing predominant cultural values.

Social Darwinism
Refers to the principle of 'the survival of the fittest' and relies on *laissez faire* attitudes.

Social learning theory
The belief that learning happens because individuals observe the behaviour of others and model themselves upon them.

Social loafing
A phenomenon where individuals do not put as much effort into working in a group as they would if they were working alone.

Social perception
The process of interpreting information about other individuals.

Social responsibility
The obligation that an individual member has to his employers to behave in an ethical manner.

Sociometry
A measuring technique which can show patterns (sociograms) of human relationships between members of a group.

Sociotechnical systems approach
An approach that combines the needs of individuals with the needs of technical efficiency.

Solo leader
The opposite of a team leader, being a type of leader who can be identified by certain behaviour characteristics including ruling absolutely without limits, taking risks with other people, taking a directive approach, identifying stated tasks and objectives, using coercive power to make people comply, and considering themself as a role model.

Span of control
The number of employees which one manager supervises.

Stakeholder
Anyone who has a legitimate interest in the activities of an organisation.

Stakeholder approach (constituency approach)
The performance of the organisation can be measured by the relative satisfaction expressed by each of the stakeholders.

Staff relationships
Relationships where individuals provide a purely advisory or support service to others and where there is a limited element of authority or control.

Status
The prestige ranking of an individual within a group.

Stereotyping
Judging another individual on the basis on one's perception of the group to which that individual belongs.

Storming
The second stage in the way a group develops.

Stress
Any force that pushes a psychological or physical factor beyond its range of stability, producing a strain within the individual.

Structural changes
Involves matters concerned with management and includes changes to the organisation's structure, strategy, policies, co-ordinating mechanisms and reporting relationships.

Structure
The formal reporting relationships, groupings, and systems of an organisation.

Supportive leadership
A leadership style where the leader shows concern for his or her followers and is always supportive.

Synergy
A positive force that occurs when group members stimulate new solutions to problems through the process of mutual influence and encouragement within a group.

Tacit knowledge
What resides in an individual's head.

Task interdependence
The degree to which decision-making and co-operation between two or more workers is needed for them to perform their jobs effectively.

Task uncertainty
Relates to the amount of knowledge that a worker has about how to perform the task when the time comes for it to be carried out.

Task variability
The number of exceptions to the work norm which a worker encounters when carrying out his or her work.

Team
A task-oriented work group which can be formally designated or which can informally evolve.

Team leader
The opposite to a solo leader being a leader who exhibits characteristics such as sharing the leadership role, limiting his or her role deliberately, expressing vision and mission, respecting other people's skills and talents, and delegating tasks and responsibilities.

Technical skills
The abilities which are required so that a worker can attain the specific goals of an organisation.

Technocentric
Making technology and engineering central to decisions related to job design.

Technological environment
The level of knowledge which a group collectively has.

Technological interdependence
The level of the inter-relatedness of an organisation's technological elements.

Technology
Refers to the information, equipment, techniques and processes required to transform inputs into outputs.

Technophiles
Individuals who are convinced that all new technology must be an asset to management.

Technosceptics
Individuals who identify any number of organisational problems each time a new technology is introduced into the workplace.

Telecommuting
Transmitting work from a home computer to the office by the use of a modem.

Theory
A description, usually founded on research, which explains how the characteristics or variables of an organisation are causally related.

Theory X
A group of assumptions about how to motivate individuals who are motivated by lower-order needs. Based on the belief that individuals dislike work, are lazy and avoid responsibility and that they have to be coerced into performing.

Theory Y
A group of assumptions about how to motivate individuals who are motivated by higher-order needs. Based on the belief that individuals enjoy work, are creative, seek responsibility and are self-directed.

Thinking
A preference for making decisions in a logical and objective way.

Trait theory
A theory of personality which states that in order to understand individuals, it is first necessary to break down behaviour into patterns which can be observed.

Uncertainty avoidance
The degree to which members of a culture feel threatened by uncertainty, ambiguity and risk.

Unitarism
A managerial ideology which is derived from a political philosophy known as utilitarianism, whose doctrine is that the greatest happiness of the greatest number is the criterion of what is right.

Unity of command
Where one person receives instructions from not more than one superior.

Unstructured conflict
Conflict where the parties concerned are not bound by rules and thus make impulsive and emotional choices.

Valence
Anticipated reward from an outcome – the value or importance that an individual gives to a reward.

Validity
The extent to which completed research actually measures what it sets out to measure.

Variable
Any general characteristic that can be measured and that changes either in amplitude, intensity, or both.

Vertical differentiation
The depth of the organisation's structure.

Virtual office
An ordinary office complemented by fairly everyday equipment like mobile phones and laptop computers which mean that office workers do not need to be in the office itself to get on with their job.

Virtual organisation
When all the task activities of an organisation are outsourced.

Virtual teams
When team members communicate through video conferencing, electronic mail (e-mail), and shared software programmes.

Want
A non-essential item that an individual feels he or she must have: e.g. television set.

Wheel network
A communication network where information flows between the person at the end of each spoke (subordinate) and the person in the middle (manager).

Work
Mental or physical activity that has productive results.

Work-flow uncertainty
The amount of knowledge that a worker has concerning when the inputs are due to be received and when they will require processing.

Work measurement
Techniques which are specifically designed with a view to a trained operative carrying out a specific task at a defined level of performance and quality.

Worker flexibility
Involves organisations enhancing their effectiveness by training workers to perform a variety of tasks.

Work study
The application of techniques to investigate method study and work measurement.

Workforce diversity
The heterogeneity of the workforce within organisations with the inclusion of different groups such as those related to gender, age, disabilities, sexual orientation, values, and education.

Index